circulating copy

BUSINESS/SCIENCE/TECHNOLOGY DIVISION
CHICAGO PUBLIC LIBRARY
400 SOUTH STATE STREET
CHICAGO, IL 60605

QH
541.15
.R45
R55
1996

M.B HWLCSC

As the human impact on the earth leads to ever mo
degradation, the restoration of dwindling populations of numerous plant and
animal species is becoming ever more important. In this unique volume, the
political, biological and experimental procedures affecting the restoration of
populations of both plants and animals are examined using case studies to
illustrate basic points. Conceptual issues concerning the organization and management of restoration efforts and plans for the restoration of a wide variety of
species including the Pitcher's thistle and woodland caribou are outlined. The
success and progress of implemented plans for other species such as the
Lakeside daisy and black-footed ferret are then evaluated, and the book ends
with a broad overview, suggesting future opportunities and problems. The
book will interest especially students and practitioners of restoration ecology.

CHICAGO PUBLIC LIBRARY

FORM 19

RESTORATION OF ENDANGERED SPECIES

RESTORATION OF ENDANGERED SPECIES

Conceptual Issues, Planning, and Implementation

Edited by
MARLIN L. BOWLES AND
CHRISTOPHER J. WHELAN
The Morton Arboretum, Lisle, Illinois

CAMBRIDGE
UNIVERSITY PRESS

Published by the Press Syndicate of the University of Cambridge
The Pitt Building, Trumpington Street, Cambridge CB2 1RP
40 West 20th Street, New York, NY 10011-4211, USA
10 Stamford Road, Oakleigh, Melbourne 3166, Australia

© Cambridge University Press 1994

First published 1994
First paperback edition 1996

Printed in Great Britain at the University Press, Cambridge

A catalogue record for this book is available from the British Library

Library of Congress cataloguing in publication data

Restoration of endangered species : conceptual issues, planning,
and implementation / edited by Marlin L. Bowles and Christopher J. Whelan.
p. cm.
Papers from a Symposium on Recovery and Restoration of Endangered Plants and Animals
organized for the Second Annual Conference of the Society for Ecological Restoration
held in Chicago, Ill., 1990.
Includes index.
ISBN 0-521-41863-1 (hc)
1. Restoration ecology–Congresses. 2. Endangered species – Congresses. 3. Nature conservation
– Congresses. I. Bowles, Marlin L. II. Whelan, Christopher J. III. Society for Ecological
Restoration. Conference (2nd : 1990 : Chicago, Ill.) IV. Symposium on the Recovery and
Restoration of Endangered Plants and Animals (1990: Chicago, Ill.)
QH541.15.R45R55 1994
333.95'153–dc20 93-43593 CIP

ISBN 0 521 41863 1 hardback
ISBN 0 521 57422 6 paperback

TAG

BUSINESS/SCIENCE/TECHNOLOGY DIVISION
CHICAGO PUBLIC LIBRARY
400 SOUTH STATE STREET
CHICAGO, IL 60605 R0129235128

Contents

List of contributors		*page* ix
Foreword		xi
Acknowledgments		xiii
I	**Conceptual issues in restoration ecology**	**1**
1	Organizational and managerial guidelines for endangered species restoration programs and recovery teams *Tim W. Clark, John R. Cragun*	9
2	Genetic considerations for plant population restoration and conservation *Charles B. Fenster, Michelle R. Dudash*	34
3	Managing genetic diversity in captive populations of animals *Robert C. Lacy*	63
4	The relationship of rarity to plant reproductive biology *Stephen G. Weller*	90
5	Experimental evidence for insect impact on populations of short-lived, perennial plants, and its application in restoration ecology *Svaťa M. Louda*	118
II	**Restoration planning**	**139**
6	Impacts of biological invasions on the management and recovery of rare plants in Haleakala National Park, Maui, Hawaii *Lloyd L. Loope, Arthur C. Medeiros*	143
7	Disturbance-dependent persistence of rare plants: anthropogenic impacts and restoration implications *Noel B. Pavlovic*	159
8	A metapopulation approach to Pitcher's thistle (*Cirsium pitcheri*) recovery in southern Lake Michigan dunes *A. Kathryn McEachern, Marlin L. Bowles, Noel B. Pavlovic*	194
9	Restoration of woodland caribou to the Lake Superior region *Peter J. P. Gogan, Jean Fitts Cochrane*	219

vii

III   Implemented restorations   **243**

10   The swift fox reintroduction program in Canada from 1983 to
     1992   *Ludwig N. Carbyn, Harry J. Armbruster, Charles Mamo*   247
11   Restoration of the endangered black-footed ferret: a twenty-year
     overview   *Tim W. Clark*   272
12   Development and implementation of a recovery program for
     the federally threatened Lakeside daisy (*Hymenoxys*
     acaulis var. *glabra*)   *Marcella M. DeMauro*   298
13   Demographic monitoring and the recovery of endangered
     plant populations   *Bruce M. Pavlik*   322

IV   Synthesis and future directions: biology, politics and reality   **351**

14   Restoration ecology: living with the Prime Directive
     Joel S. Brown   355
Taxonomic Index   381
Subject Index   387

Contributors

Harry J. Armbruster
Canadian Wildlife Service, Room 210, 4999-98th Avenue, Edmonton, Alberta, Canada T6B 2X3

Marlin L. Bowles
The Morton Arboretum, Lisle, Illinois 60532, USA

Joel S. Brown
Department of Biological Sciences, University of Illinois, 845 W. Taylor St., Chicago, Illinois 60607, USA

Ludwig N. Carbyn
Canadian Wildlife Service, Room 210, 4999-98th Avenue, Edmonton, Alberta, Canada T6B 2X3

Tim W. Clark
Northern Rockies Conservation Cooperative, Jackson, Wyoming, 83001 USA, and School of Forestry and Environmental Studies, Yale University, New Haven, Connecticut 06511, USA

Jean Fitts Cochrane
US Fish and Wildlife Service, Ecological Services and Endangered Species, 605 West 4th Avenue, Room G-62, Anchorage, Alaska 99501, USA

John R. Cragun
College of Business, Department of Management and Human Resources, Utah State University, Logan, Utah 84322, USA

Marcella M. DeMauro
Forest Preserve District of Will County, 22606 S. Cherry Hill Rd, Joliet, Illinois 60433, USA

Michelle R. Dudash
Department of Botany, The University of Maryland, College Park, Maryland 20742, USA

Charles B. Fenster
Department of Botany, The University of Maryland, College Park, Maryland 20742, USA

Peter J. P. Gogan
Greater Yellowstone Field Station, National Ecological Research Center, National Biological Survey, P. O. Box 168, Yellowstone National Park, Wyoming 82190, USA

Robert C. Lacy
Department of Conservation Biology, Chicago Zoological Park, Brookfield, Illinois 50513, USA

Lloyd L. Loope
National Park Service, Haleakala National Park, Box 369, Makawao, Hawaii 96768, USA

Svaťa M. Louda
School of Biological Sciences, University of Nebraska, Lincoln, Nebraska 68588, USA

Charles Mamo
University of Calgary, Faculty of Environmental Design, 2500 University Drive NW, Calgary, Alberta, Canada T2N 1N4

A. Kathryn McEachern
National Biological Survey, Channel Islands Field Station, 1901 Spinnaker Dr., Ventura, California 93001, USA

Arthur C. Medeiros
National Park Service, Haleakala National Park, Box 369, Makawao, Hawaii 96768, USA

Bruce M. Pavlik
Department of Biology, Mills College, Oakland, California 94613, USA

Noel B. Pavlovic
National Biological Survey, Porter, Indiana 46304, USA and Department of Biological Sciences, 845 W. Taylor St., University of Illinois, Chicago, Illinois 60607, USA

Stephen G. Weller
Department of Ecology and Evolutionary Biology, University of California, Irvine, California 92717, USA

Foreword

Restoration ecology is a rapidly growing and intellectually exciting field devoted to the challenging, if not unattainable, task of fixing damaged ecosystems or reestablishing components of ecosystems. The field's vitality is reflected in the founding of the Society for Ecological Restoration in 1987, and more recently, with the launching of its new journal, *Restoration Ecology*. Ecological restoration is not, however, without its frustrations. Mistakes could be devastating, leading ultimately to the extinction of a species. Unfortunately, restoration ecology is likely to become increasingly difficult in the future, as more species and the ecosystems in which they live are threatened. Despite the relative youth of the field of restoration ecology, an appraisal of its present state can benefit practitioners and students alike. We view this book as an attempt to examine a broad range of issues involved in the process of species restoration. The issues range from the political to the biological, from the theoretical to the practical, from planning and managing restoration efforts to monitoring restored populations.

Most of the authors contributing to this book first presented their work at a Symposium on the Recovery and Restoration of Endangered Plants and Animals organized for the Second Annual Conference of the Society for Ecological Restoration, held in Chicago, Illinois in 1990. We organized the symposium to provide a forum for government representatives, conservationists, and biologists to share ideas, recent findings, techniques, and future concerns.

Our primary goal for this book is to move beyond issues of simply conserving and managing existing natural systems or individual species, and to examine further the political, biological, and experimental procedures affecting restoration of extirpated or reduced populations. A secondary goal of the book is to consider restoration problems and examples of both plants and animals. These two major groups of organisms obviously differ in many profound ways

xi

biologically.   Do the differences demand different restoration strategies?
Should this be of concern to agencies regulating restoration policies? On the
other hand, animals share many basic biological characteristics with plants.
Do these shared traits indicate common strategies for restoration of both animals and plants?   Although final answers to these questions may not yet be
available, this book forges new ground in addressing them.

   Another important and sometimes contentious issue that arises when both
planning and implementing restorations is that organisms do not recognize
political boundaries.   Yet federal, state, and local governmental agencies do.
Often, regulations regarding restoration differ between adjacent states, and this
can complicate (at the least) restoration efforts. How are restoration ecologists
to deal with such political problems? Should we be considering standardizing
regulations throughout the country? Regardless, some of the examples in this
book demonstrate that cooperation can occur between levels of government,
among states, and even between countries when planning and implementing
restorations.

   The book is divided into four major sections: Conceptual issues in restoration ecology; Restoration planning; Implemented restorations; and Synthesis
and future directions. We believe it will become clear that restoration ecology
provides opportunities for testing ecological theories as well as serving conservation needs, and we hope this book will be useful to both students and practitioners.

Acknowledgments

We thank the participants of the 1990 Society for Ecological Restoration conference and symposium, including the speakers, the audience, and the sponsors. Initial symposium planning benefitted from the help of Marcy DeMauro and Noel Pavlovic. We are pleased to thank the Department of Conservation Biology of the Brookfield Zoo, and Dr George Rabb, its Director, for fostering support for the symposium. Academic Press kindly allowed us to reproduce previously published figures. The Emily Rodgers Davis Endowment to the Morton Arboretum, the Illinois Department of Energy and Natural Resources, and the United States Fish and Wildlife Service provided financial support for the Symposium on Restoration of Endangered Animals and Plants. We received further publishing support from Chevron USA, Inc., and the Monsanto Chemical Corporation. Many colleagues, too numerous to name, helped with stimulating reviews of the contributions. Our special thanks go to Copy Editor Robyn Flakne, whose excellent help greatly improved the manuscripts, and Jenny McBride, who helped with proofing and constructing the index. C.J. Whelan thanks Anna for patience and help with final-proofing manuscripts. Finally, we thank Dr Alan Crowden and the staff of Cambridge University Press for their enthusiasm, encouragement, and generous help.

I

Conceptual issues in restoration ecology

Conservation biology has been described as a mission-oriented science aimed at preserving biological diversity (Soulé 1986, Temple *et al.* 1988, Gibbons 1992). Thus, conservation biology may be simply envisioned as maintenance or preservation, much like keeping an automobile well-lubed, with proper tire inflation, clean filters, adequate antifreeze, etc. Restoration ecology, an important and growing discipline within the field of conservation biology, aims to reestablish or rehabilitate damaged or lost plant and animal populations or species assemblages native to the area of interest (Jordan, Gilpin & Aber 1987). Returning to the metaphor of the automobile, this is more like going to a junkyard, purchasing the component parts, and reassembling a working automobile. Restoration ecology, like much of conservation biology, often relies on fundamental autecological knowledge of the target species (Soberón 1992), but restoration ecology also provides unique opportunities for testing basic ecological theories (Jordan *et al.* 1987). Thus, restoration ecology can also be viewed as a truly powerful research technique, for surely, restoration of a viable population or species assemblage demonstrates ecological understanding as nothing else can.

Restoration ecology straddles an interface between the economic and political demands of human society, and the biological requirements of the species or communities targeted for restoration. Hence, conceptual issues important to restoration ecology range from the sociopolitical, including organization and management of restoration efforts, to the biological, such as population viability analysis, conservation genetics, metapopulation biology, landscape ecology, etc. As Brown (Chapter 14) points out, restorationists cannot ignore the fact that society will suffer missed economic opportunities when land is dedicated for restoration, as opposed to, say, a shopping mall or a housing subdivision. This issue is complex and divisive, and as world population continues to grow, it is likely to become increasingly so. On the other hand, these competing demands of society and nature may foster the evolution of a land ethic, as envisioned by Aldo Leopold, in which land use is examined 'in terms of what is ethically and esthetically right, as well as what is economically expedient' (Leopold 1947, in Meine 1988).

Population viability analysis (PVA) is a powerful tool that predicts the probability of persistence of a species (or population) over a specified amount of time with a specified probability (e.g. 95% probability of surviving for 100 years), given various management or restoration strategies (e.g. Shaffer 1981, 1990, Murphy, Freas & Weiss 1990, Menges 1990, Ginzburg, Ferson & Akçakaya 1990). PVA is a form of risk assessment that can account for factors such as effective population size, the relative importance of genetic drift versus natural selection, loss of heterozygosity, likelihood of fixation of mutant alleles, and various stochastic events, such as environmental (e.g. weather) or demographic (e.g. variation in birth rates) effects or catastrophes (e.g. Goodman 1987, Quinn & Hastings 1987). Although the technique is still in the developmental phase (Shaffer 1990), its utility in formulating and evaluating possible restoration strategies for many species cannot be questioned (e.g. Chapters 9 and 11). For some species with particular life history characteristics, such as plants with clonal growth, PVA may be less effective, and other, non-integrated methods of trend analysis may be more appropriate (Chapter 13).

For many reasons, including financial, logistic, bureaucratic, and biological, restorations are often attempted with small populations at several sites. Thus, the process of restoration, at least initially, is often destined to result in a system of subdivided populations. As this volume demonstrates, restorationists have recognized the applicability of the theories of metapopulation biology (e.g. Gilpin & Hanski 1991) to these situations. A metapopulation, stated simply, consists of more-or-less loosely coupled, interacting populations, in which the probability of extinction may be locally high, but uncorrelated among populations. Metapopulation dynamics include local population extinction, local population establishment or reestablishment, and some movement or linkage among the various local populations. Metapopulation management, that is, managing the linkage among restored populations can, for instance, decrease local population extinction probabilities, or help maintain genetic variability, thereby substituting for altered or damaged ecosystem processes. Furthermore, captive breeding facilities for both animals and plants maintain essentially fragmented populations that may require application of metapopulation theory (or theoretical precursors to it; see Chapter 3). Hence, both in captive propagation and in restoration, metapopulation theory may receive practical application, which in turn is likely to lead to rapid, further development of the theory.

As with newly restored populations, a frequent consequence of a declining population is a subdivided population structure, necessitating surviving in a fragmented landscape. Fragmented landscapes influence movement and dispersal of organisms, rates of gene flow, and invasion by exotic competitors, among many other factors. A fast-growing interest in 'landscape ecology' (e.g. Forman & Godron 1986) is now addressing these and other issues from the landscape perspective. Restoration ecology should lead to a blending of advances derived from landscape ecology and metapopulation biology, along with other aspects of conservation biology. For instance, the landscape perspective views boundaries between different landscape types as 'semipermeable membranes', affecting flow of individuals between them. Similarly, conservation biologists recognize the dispersal value of habitat 'corridors' for desirable species, as well as their potential dangers, such as allowing the spread of fire, disease, or exotic species (Simberloff *et al*. 1992). Thus, the interspersion of landscape types, together with the location of habitat corridors, can affect the likelihood of migration between restored populations, directly influencing the degree of coupling of restored, local populations (a metapopulation). This in turn, can influence the need or the extent of continued management intervention as opposed to reliance on naturally occurring processes.

Reintroductions often involve translocating genotypes across geographic ranges. Some have criticized this practice, arguing that organisms tend to be highly locally adapted, and that such movements introduce 'incorrect' genotypes where they do not belong. This is an intriguing and controversial problem in which the need to maximize genetic diversity is balanced against maintenance of coadapted gene complexes (Avise 1992, Ellstrand 1992), and will probably vary tremendously from species to species (Hamrick 1992), regardless of animal or plant. From the theoretical perspective, such factors as rates of gene flow among subpopulations, effective population size, mutation rates, and type of breeding system or social structure, may all be important. From the empirical perspective, field experimentation could do much to resolve controversies and lead to practical and useful guiding procedures.

Successfully restored populations or communities will likely be limited to legally protected preserves, national and state parks and forests, or natural areas owned by private conservation organizations such as the National Audubon Society, the Nature Conservancy, and the World Wide Fund for Nature (WWF). Meanwhile, remaining unprotected large blocks of natural areas are constantly shrinking from ever expanding human populations, business interests, recreational impacts, and government mismanagement. Hence, restoration ecology and the disciplines it embraces are likely to assume increased importance, not only with restored populations, but also with extant populations living in an increasingly fragmented world. Restoration ecologists, therefore, are in the perhaps unenviable position of having to most quickly field-test the practical implications of metapopulation theory, preserve design and linkage, and a host of other issues.

The five chapters in this section present an overview of a broad range of conceptual issues involving restoration ecology. These include theories concerning organizational management, genetic population structure, maintenance of genetic variation in captive populations, breeding systems, trophic interactions, and surrogate species.

In Chapter 1, Clark & Cragun draw from the literature of organizational management, arguing that endangered species restoration relies on more than the biology of the organism, and that knowledge of organizations as well as management skills will lead to better functioning within recovery teams and increased restoration success. They distinguish between task forces, directed at short-term problems, and project teams, directed at long-term problems. They go on to describe organizing, planning, leading, and controlling programs in a way useful to a wide range of recovery efforts. Finally, they present two strategies to help the organizational management of endangered species recovery teams. The first helps team members to identify organizational problems, develop alternate strategies, and to evaluate and implement action plans. The second allows assessment of the utility of a program's 'culture' to the recovery task. They argue persuasively that, by adding organization and management skills to their working skills, biologists will greatly enhance the difficult work of endangered species recovery.

In Chapter 2, Fenster & Dudash discuss genetic considerations for plant population restorations, focusing on rare taxa that are often restricted to small population size. Small populations may have been subject to past population bottlenecks, and genetic manipulation may be required to recover declining populations or to restore or maintain evolutionary potential. They consider the genetic basis of inbreeding depression, suggesting that it is possible to purge an inbred population of deleterious alleles by selective breeding if overdominance is not the cause of inbreeding depression. If traits are polygenic, however, they warn that response to selection will not be rapid. Fenster & Dudash then examine the consequences of mixing distant gene pools and outbreeding depression, stressing the need for experimental studies on the outcomes of crossing genetically different populations. Although such mixing may result in the disruption of coadapted gene complexes, heterosis or appearance of adaptive novel genotypes may outweigh such problems. They next propose that detection of isozyme and chloroplast DNA variation within a species using a phylogenetic approach combined with crossing programs can provide a method to identify genetic variation important to endangered species preservation and restoration.

As Lacy points out in Chapter 3, maintenance of genetic variation and evolutionary potential are not concerns for rare or isolated plant populations alone. Lacy discusses the theory, rationale, and breeding strategies for minimizing loss of genetic variability in captive populations. He shows how captive propagation of animals in zoos or other facilities can lead to loss of genetic variation through random drift, genetic adaptation through selection to the captive environment, and thus, inadequate genetic variation for reintroduction to a restored environment. Zoo biologists, Lacy indicates, have devised techniques for analyzing such problems and minimizing their impact. In this chapter he discusses the initial founder population, numbers of founder progeny that will minimize loss of genetic variation, and strategies for pairing mates, as well as movements of animals between subpopulations at different breeding facilities. As Weller (Chapter 4) points out, many of these recommendations are as applicable to certain plant species as they are to animals.

Weller (Chapter 4) reviews relationships between plant reproductive biology and types of plant rarity, and the effect of plant breeding system on genetic diversity and restoration of rare plant populations. Plant breeding systems usually have not contributed in themselves to plant rarity. Rather, many systems may have developed in relation to ecological and physiological adaptations, or as family characteristics. Nonetheless, plant breeding systems can have profound effects on genetic variation. Weller notes that rarity is more often associated with human-caused disturbances, ranging from outright loss of habitat to introduction of exotic species. In some cases, species adapted to widespread distribution patterns or large populations may suffer reduced reproduction in fragmented populations. Consequently, breeding systems, along with other life history characteristics, are fundamentally important in *ex situ* propagation and restoration efforts. For example, breeding systems are critical to the restoration of many declining Hawaiian plants, such as the self-incompatible, monocarpic silverswords (Loope & Medeiros, Chapter 6), and breeding system was the key to recovery of a Lakeside daisy population (DeMauro, Chapter 12). Weller concludes with protocols for determining the breeding systems in rare species, and warns of the potential for genetic change in long-term propagation efforts.

Louda, in Chapter 5, discusses two issues of tremendous importance. She first demonstrates the potential role of interactions among trophic levels in restoration success. Second, she suggests using common, non-endangered 'surrogate' species to examine important restoration issues experimentally when it is not possible to use the targeted endangered species. As Louda has clearly shown, plant damage from herbivores, in particular insect herbivores, is often ubiquitous and chronic. Herbivory can lead to population limitation, reduction of individual fitness, and exacerbation of competitive effects from nearby plants. These effects of herbivores can potentially constrain restoration success, if not prevent it outright. Unfortunately, the elegant experiments used to reach these conclusions are often simply not possible to conduct with species targeted for restoration. Consequently, Louda advocates the use of 'win–win' experiments with endangered species, based on initial work with surrogates. For instance, based on her experiments in limiting insect impacts on the surrogate Platte thistle, Louda predicts a positive trophic response in the closely related, ecologically similar, threatened Pitcher's thistle. Her suggestion of use of surrogate species echoes a similar one by Fenster & Dudash (Chapter 2), and obviously could have immense utility, provided time is available to do the preliminary work in the first place.

Literature cited

Avise, J. C. (1992) Molecular population structure and the biogeographic history of a regional fauna: a case history with lessons for conservation biology. *Oikos*, **63**, 62–76.

Ellstrand, N. C. (1992) Gene flow by pollen: implications for plant conservation genetics. *Oikos*, **63**, 77–86.

Forman, R. T. T. & Godron, M. (1986) *Landscape Ecology*. New York: John Wiley & Sons.

Gibbons, A. (1992) Conservation biology in the fast lane. *Science*, **255**, 20–22.

Gilpin, M. E. & Hanski, I. (1991) *Metapopulation Dynamics: Empirical and Theoretical Investigations*. London: Academic Press.

Ginzburg, L. R., Ferson, S. & Akçakaya, H. R. (1990) Reconstructibility of density dependence and the conservative assessment of extinction risks. *Conservation Biology*, **4**, 63–70.

Goodman, D. (1987) How do any species persist? Lessons for conservation biology. *Conservation Biology*, **1**, 59–62.

Hamrick, J. L. (1992) Patterns and levels of gene flow in plant populations. Abstract. *Experimental and Molecular Approaches to Plant Biosystematics. V. International Symposium, June 11-15, 1992*. St Louis: International Organization of Plant Biosystematists.

Jordan, W. R. III, Gilpin, M. E. & Aber, J. D. (1987) *Restoration Ecology. A Synthetic Approach to Ecological Research*. Cambridge University Press.

Leopold, A. (1947) The ecological conscience. *Bulletin of the Garden Club of America*. September, 45-53.

Meine, C. (1988) *Aldo Leopold. His Life and Work*. Madison: University of Wisconsin Press.

Menges, E. S. (1990) Population viability analysis for an endangered plant. *Conservation Biology*, **4**, 52–62.

Murphy, D. D., Freas, K. E. & Weiss, S. B. (1990) An environment-metapopulation approach to population viability analysis for a threatened invertebrate. *Conservation Biology*, **4**, 41–51.

Quinn, J. F. & Hastings, A. (1987) Extinction in subdivided habitats. *Conservation Biology*, **1**, 198–209.

Shaffer, M. L. (1981) Minimum population sizes for species conservation. *BioScience*, **31**, 131–4.

Shaffer, M. L. (1990) Population viability analysis. *Conservation Biology*, **4**, 39–40.

Simberloff, D., Farr, J. A., Cox, J. & Mehlman, D. W. (1992) Movement corridors: conservation bargains or poor investments? *Conservation Biology*, **6**, 493–504.

Soberón M. J. (1992) Island biogeography and conservation practice. *Conservation Biology*, **6**, 161.

Soulé, M. E. (1986) *Conservation Biology: The Science of Scarcity and Diversity.* Sunderland, Massachusetts: Sinauer Associates.

Temple, S. A., Bolen, E. G., Soulé, M. E., Brussard, P. F., Salwasser, H. & Teer, J. G. (1988) What's so new about Conservation Biology? In *Transactions of the 53rd North American Wildlife and Natural Resources Conference*, ed. McCabe, R. E., pp. 609–12. Washington, D.C.: Wildlife Management Institute.

1

Organizational and managerial guidelines for endangered species restoration programs and recovery teams

TIM W. CLARK AND JOHN R. CRAGUN

Introduction

Endangered species recovery is always difficult, and biologists need to use the best tools, skills, and experience available. While the use of appropriate biological tools is essential for successful recovery, other factors are also indispensable. These include problem analysis and problem-solving strategies, organizational design, work group effectiveness, effectiveness of interpersonal relationships, and clarity and specificity of goals and objectives. Inadequacy in any of these factors may result in inefficiency and ineffectiveness of the recovery job; ultimately, the species may not be recovered! Professional biologists and managers readily recognize the biological dimensions of recovery work, but largely overlook or depreciate the value of organizational factors. Because of the urgency and the sense of finality inherent in recovery efforts, professionals would do well to attend to such factors.

In this chapter, we introduce some organization and management concepts and recommendations that can help the work of conservationists. Specifically, we 1) provide some background on *organization designs* and *management processes* that are useful in species recovery; 2) examine the endangered species *task environment* in organizational terms; 3) identify the *task force/project team* model as the most appropriate for recovery work; 4) describe the four *functions of management*—organizing, planning, leading, and controlling—in these teams; 5) examine *task-oriented teams* versus power-, role-, or people-oriented teams; 6) introduce a procedure to analyze problems and develop action plans; and 7) offer, in an appendix, a method for developing *action plans*. A test for workers to evaluate whether their program's *culture* is appropriate for the recovery task is available from the authors.

We offer only an introduction to the complex organization and management dimension of species recovery. More comprehensive treatments of these

9

themes are given by Argyris & Schon (1978); Etheredge & Short (1983); Clark (1989); Westrum (1986); Clark & Westrum (1989); and Clark, Crete & Cada (1989). To provide access to the literature, a wide variety of organization and management studies are cited. We use several terms, including teams, programs, and organizations or agencies, in this chapter. The team is the small group of people formally or informally designated to devise recovery plans, carry out field work, or otherwise work to restore species. The program, with its formal and informal elements, includes the overall restoration effort, of which the team may be only one part. The organization, called an agency when it is a government organization, is the parent institution to which the program and the team may belong. Most restoration efforts involve many organizations and agencies, several programs, and a variety of teams. Some elements are relatively permanent (e.g. US Fish and Wildlife Service), and others are temporary (e.g. certain kinds of teams).

The organizational dimension of species recovery

The wildlife and conservation literature is full of references to how important *organizational arrangements* are to species recovery efforts (e.g. Clark 1984a,b; Jackson 1986; Snyder 1986). Understanding your organization and knowing how to make it work for species recovery can make the difference between a program that succeeds and one that fails. Organizational arrangements include *formal* and *informal structures* and *management* processes. Galbraith (1977) found that organizational designs and operating styles can be major factors that limit how effectively and efficiently individuals relate formally and informally within and between organizations, and how well they can solve problems (i.e. 'organizational bottleneck'). Clarke & McCool (1985, p. 2) noted that 'whether natural resource programs succeed or fail in their objectives is largely dependent upon the nature of the organization mandated to carry out' the work. That this is true for endangered, threatened, and rare species, too, is documented by Wydoski's (1977) work on the management of endangered Colorado fishes, Jackson's (1986) work on the red-cockaded woodpecker (*Picoides borealis*), Ream's (1986) work on the northern Rocky Mountain wolf (*Canis lupus*), Snyder's (1986) review of the California condor (*Gymnogyps californianus*) recovery efforts, and Carr's (1986) review of the black-footed ferret (*Mustela nigripes*) program.

Furthermore, the importance of organizational and managerial dimensions of species recovery is reported from a wide range of circumstances. For example, Stanley-Price (1989, p. 25) noted that 'a re-introduction project must consider biological factors without neglecting socio-economic, political, logistic and administrative aspects'. Menkhorst, Loyn & Brown (1990, p. 244) observed, 'Of major importance in ensuring cooperation was the establishment in 1983 of a coordinating committee, the Orange-bellied Parrot Recovery Team'. Casey, Clark & Seebeck (1990, p. 285) concluded:

Failure to collaborate, in fact, may consign endangered species programs to a low-profile, slow-moving, unfocused condition. On the other hand, large coalitions may have difficulty reaching a consensus, their decision-making may be cumbersome, slow and incremental. They may get side-tracked by political considerations rather than staying task-oriented. Often, leadership and roles are not clear, and conflict may become unmanageable.

Culbert & Blair (1989, p. 3) observed, 'Political factors can weigh heavily in the selection process because [recovery] team members are chosen by the regional director of the FWS'. And finally, Campbell (1980:267) concluded, 'laws and bureaucratic procedures can complicate efforts'. It is abundantly clear that organizational and managerial dimensions are of paramount importance to recovery programs and teams. Unfortunately, none of the above references, and few of the references we found, described the organization and management dimensions in any critical depth or detail.

One exception was Clark & Harvey's (1991) account of the black-footed ferret program, which examined organization and management pathologies using organizational theory, design, and management literature. The account briefly introduced five program implementation problems, all connected to weaknesses in the organization and management of the restoration effort. The first problem was organizing and managing the complexity inherent in the participating organizations, programs, and teams. Most of the complexity was ignored, and a bureaucratic arrangement was heavily stamped over the participants and their working relationships. The second problem was 'goal displacement', in which control goals became so important to high-level bureaucratic officials that they displaced task goals (saving the species). This led to conflict, procedural differences, a breakdown in communication, and a host of other problems. The third problem was organizational structure: an inappropriate design was used to coordinate the coalition of participants. Organizational structure has profound effects on the allocation of tasks and resources, the distribution of information, and the overall effectiveness of the program and team. The bureaucratic design was unable to coherently relate participants. The fourth problem was 'intelligence failure', in which high-quality, accurate, and reliable data (intelligence) were simply dismissed by top-level officials when the data ran counter to their preferred policy. The final problem was that critical management action was delayed because it was needed at a time that did not correspond to the slow planning and decision-making of the officials.

These are only five organization and management problems that can plague a recovery program and team. If they become pathological, the program and team can fail.

Romesburg (1981) suggested that wildlife professionals need to understand and apply *science* as an explicit process, a philosophy, and an epistemology to increase the knowledge base for wildlife management. Our investigations of the organizational dimension of conservation work, and our experience in several recovery programs, have led us to conclude that an explicit understanding of how organizations are made up and work is also basic to conservation. By studying the activities and structure of recovery teams, we can learn which activities and structures best support the biological work of species recovery.

Conservation biologists may argue that each project is unique, that each species is unique, and that nothing from the organization and management literature, with its analytical case histories and theory, can be of practical use to them. Organizational designers, sociologists, and policy analysts would strongly disagree. Extensive research on many different kinds of organizations has revealed common problems, patterns, and concerns (Hrebiniak 1978). For example, Galbraith (1977) estimated that only 25–50% of the variance in designs and behavior of organizations is due to their unique attributes. If this is true, then 50–75% of organizational behavior, patterns, and problems are common to all or most organizations, including those concerned with species recovery.

People are surrounded by organizations all their lives. Organizations are so pervasive and influential that they are taken for granted. This led Jelinek, Litterer & Miles (1981, p. 4) to observe, 'People who live their entire lives in organizations and are surrounded by them have only the vaguest knowledge of their workings–or underlying logics'. Despite their chronic and obvious problems, embarrassingly little attention is paid to designing and managing organizations and decision-making processes. Problems have been expressed within species restoration organizations by workers ranging from top administrators to field technicians; by outsiders affected by the organization's activities and policies; and by the public, the press, and others (e.g. Weinberg 1986). Yaffee (1982) described many of these problems in his classic study of the implementation of the Endangered Species Act, including slow decision-making; incompetence being rewarded while aggressive, effective action is penalized; overly rigid bureaucratic controls; long hierarchies of authority; and importantly, scientific and bureaucratic conservatism. These problems are probably more prevalent than is currently recognized in recovery efforts (see Tobin 1990, Kohm 1991).

Organizational designers stress that inappropriate organizational arrangements and poor decision making cause faulty information flows and inappropriate action. Also, if an organization is sufficiently mismatched to the task at hand, it may not meet its goals. In endangered species work, this means that if we bring the wrong type of organizational arrangements (i.e. rigid bureaucratic management) to a task—even if we use the correct biological tools—we may not be able to recover the species. Yaffee (1982, p. 9) recognized this and stressed the urgency of determining the type of organizations that can best facilitate the recovery of endangered species, noting, 'While policies are written in words on paper, they exist only in the form of individuals, organizations, and agencies that implement them and the nature of the information, resources, authority, and incentives that flow between these actors'.

Those concerned with endangered species conservation can make the job harder than it should be. They may unconsciously create impediments or barriers as a direct consequence of how they organize themselves and how they structure their thinking, beginning with how they identify problems, how they define solutions, and especially how they design and implement jobs and working relationships (Dery 1984). Biologists need to learn how different organizational designs and management modes can either facilitate or hinder their work. Only then can they insist on designs and systems of management that are tailored to conservation work. The next few sections examine the work of species recovery: the *task environment* in which the work must be carried out, the *organizational designs* that are needed, and the utility of *task forces* and *project teams* in doing the work.

Task environments and information processing models

The work of addressing organizational designs and other issues resembles the work of an architect planning a house. The architect starts with an understanding of the building site, its character and shape, and then considers the requirements of the occupants, costs, building codes, and other relevant factors. These considerations are like the task environment facing an endangered species program (Fig. 1.1). The *task environment* is all those forces and factors—technical, organizational, and policy—that affect the work of species recovery. In designing an organization, assessing the task environment appropriately is the first step. The second step is to understand what kind of organization would best meet all the conditions of the task environment. It can then be decided whether the organization's current design and work program are compatible with the existing parent organization or agency structures and cultures. The third step is to consider alternatives and tradeoffs, and make appropriate design changes to correct limitations and perceived pitfalls (Lorsch 1977). Managers

Fig. 1.1. An organization must be designed and managed to match the work required of it. The two major variables are the task environment and the organization. The work, and all the forces and factors influencing the work, make up the task environment. It must be continuously assayed and understood correctly for there to be a match with the organization. The organization must be organized and managed appropriately to carry out the work. Closed feedback loops are necessary for realistic definition of the evolving work and for constantly improved organizational performance.

who are not informed about the most useful organization design tools or how to apply them have to rely on tradition and intuition rather than solid management and organization rationale.

Task environments can be characterized by their degree of certainty. Uncertainty is the difference between what conservationists know when they start a recovery effort and what they must eventually know to be successful. For example, conservationists may not be able to determine a species' limiting factors in time to prevent extinction. Uncertainty leads to unpredictability, problematic conditions, and dangerous situations (National Academy of Sciences 1986). Compared with most wildlife conservation challenges, recovery tasks are generally uncertain. The recovery program must understand the degree and type of uncertainty and organize and manage itself in response. The National Academy of Sciences (1986) listed five sources of uncertainty in ecological systems; all five are present in recovery programs.

First, the relationships between the endangered species and its biological and physical environment are often complex. Relationships may be indirect, nonlinear, and have thresholds that may be difficult to learn about. *Second*, predictable natural variability will be present. *Third*, unpredictable variability will exist in the organisms' behavior; thus, population responses can never be predicted precisely. *Fourth*, errors of estimation and measurement will be unavoidable and can be large. The small numbers of organisms will mean small sample sizes; thus, demanding statistical significance for decison making may be unwise or even catastrophic. And *fifth*, there will be a lack of knowl-edge about the species and details of the environment. Recovery may be impossible without information that may not now exist.

Collectively, these five characteristics of ecological systems and many endangered species' ecology represent types of uncertainty that can create a complex, diverse, unstable, and difficult recovery *task environment* (Hrebiniak 1978).

Comparable uncertainty exists at the organizational level. Organizational designers offer information processing models for programs confronted by much uncertainty (e.g. Tushman & Nadler 1978). The recovery program's structure should be quite different from that of a program that carries out routine tasks with little uncertainty, low stakes, and well-established standard operating procedures. It should have the capacity to get and process information matched to the demands of the uncertain task environment. Also, because different pro-gram structures have different information processing capabilities, the most useful structure for a given endangered species should be chosen and managed carefully. To the extent that a program's information processing requirements change over time, the task of program design and management is continuous. These uncertainties are further complicated by differences between people, such as motivation, commitment, personality, communication skills, tolerance for ambiguity, capacity to handle stress, and need for recognition.

Task forces and project teams

Task forces and *project teams* are the most appropriate models for endangered species recovery (see Larson & LaFasto 1989, Varney 1989). Task forces tackle temporary problems (e.g. deciding whether or not to capture the last few individuals of an endangered species), and project teams address problems that need long-term, continuous coordination (e.g. multiple-year efforts to restore species). Both types of team should be coordinated by direct horizontal contact among team members, with little coordination from upper hierarchical levels (Daft 1983). Such teams are useful because in the unpredictable endangered species recovery task, problems arise that do not respond to the traditional rules, roles, and regulations of bureaucratic management (Galbraith 1977). Team flexibility is essential to respond quickly to changing tasks and demands. The amount of administrative control over the team will vary from case to case, but administrators who are committed to the task should provide the lati-tude necessary for professionals to do the work.

The team should be goal- and action-oriented, focusing on getting the job completed successfully (Harrison 1972, 1975) and willing to accept the uncertainty and risk inherent in endangered species recovery. Individual team members must be good learners, perceptive, energetic, willing to work without close supervision or extensive rules and regulations, and professional in demeanor (Clark 1986a). Members should have appropriate formal training in areas related to the recovery process (e.g. population or habitat ecology, genetics, modeling), experience in other endangered species projects, high standards of performance, and problem-solving skills. Team membership should be based on the individual's contribution to the recovery task, not on the political representation he or she can provide.

Considerable emphasis must be given to quality information flow and continuous evaluations. Team members should all be 'reflective practitioners' as described by Schon (1983), continuously evaluating their own and others' actions. Critical evaluations focusing on team accomplishments provide the basis for continual improvements.

The Montana Black-Footed Ferret Working Group, as it was made up and functioned between 1984 and 1987, embodied many of the organization and management characteristics described here. It was composed of people from government agencies with legal mandates to recover the ferret, and non-governmental people who had extensive first-hand experience with ferrets. The mid-level managers and biologists were strongly oriented toward ferret recovery over political representation of the perspectives of their employing organizations. The Working Group met three to four times per year, and the members democratically decided upcoming tasks and volunteered to do them. Between meetings, ongoing work was passed around and extensive phone calls and correspondence kept the work progressing. In this way, interest, knowledge, responsibility, and accountability were matched. The Working Group performed well in searching for new ferret populations, finding transplant sites, educating the public, and developing needed planning and policy documents.

Granted, the task environment of the Ferret Working Group during this period was somewhat simpler than that of many ongoing endangered species recovery programs (e.g. that for the California condor). For example, interest groups that might oppose ferrets and protection of their essential habitat, prairie dog colonies, had not raised conflicting voices. As the program moves toward ferret reintroduction, different agencies will have different management responsibilities, which will likely lead to conflict and politicization of the effort. The early structure and functioning of the Working Group—established *prior* to the onset of these anticipated problems—could, if carried over, ameliorate them. The team's original strengths were its task-orientation and flexibility, which, if they can be maintained, can aid current and future efforts. In recognition of the Montana Working Group's accomplishments, and because of the importance of organizational variables in species recovery programs, one of six major goals written into the Black-Footed Ferret Recovery Plan reads, 'Establish organizational arrangements to accomplish tasks and increase communication' (Forrest & Biggins 1987, p. 69).

Managerial processes

Organization and management concepts have wide application in problem-solving situations, whether they involve recovering species or conducting other complex tasks (Mintzberg 1971; Brickloe & Coughlin 1977; Peters & Waterman 1982; Kanter 1983; Boone & Kurtz 1984; Steers, Ungson & Mowday 1985). *Management* is the use of people and other resources to accomplish objectives (Boone & Kurtz 1984). Four management processes essential to all recovery programs are organizing, planning, leading, and controlling (Boone & Kurtz 1984). *Organizing* is the process of arranging people and physical resources to carry out plans and accomplish organizational objectives. *Planning* is the process by which objectives are set, the future assessed, and courses of action developed to accomplish objectives. *Leading* is the act of motivating or causing people to perform certain tasks to achieve specified objectives. *Controlling* is the process by which it is determined whether organizational objectives are being achieved and whether actual operations are consistent with plans.

We cannot specify in detail organizational and management directives for any single one of the several hundred endangered species programs in the United States or elsewhere, but this overview of terminology, theory, and perspectives will have practical value as program participants apply the concepts to their own efforts. The prescriptions outlined here are based on recommendations by experts coping with high-uncertainty problems such as endangered species recovery, numerous discussions with participants in such efforts, and our own experience over the past 18 years. Becoming aware of these issues will make program and team members more sensitive to, and more forthright in addressing, potential impediments. Because the work of species recovery is carried out by small teams—planning teams, field teams, evaluation teams, and decision-making teams—the following descriptions focus on the structure and dynamics of teams.

Organizing teams

The team should construct a map of tasks, responsibilities, and reporting relationships, and provide a mechanism for linking and coordinating organizational elements into a coherent whole (Daft 1983). The team can also define the personal characteristics and skills required of each team member.

How the team is organized and how it relates to the parent agency or organization are important considerations. Overall, the team should have little formalization and few hierarchical levels, rules, and regulations (Daft 1983). There should be minimal centralization of decision-making and other managerial functions. For example, referring problems upward within bureaucratic hierarchies may destroy team cohesion. It will also frequently result in critical time lags if decisions by top management are delayed too long, if lines of communication become too long, if too many people are involved, or if the relevancy of the issue becomes distorted. Ideally, the recovery team should have both major decision-making discretion and immediate and direct access to higher levels of administration. Multiple hierarchical levels within a team should generally be avoided, because they reduce the team's responsiveness. A single competent and responsive team leader should be sufficient. All other team members should be equally empowered, and distinguished only in terms of the specific skills they bring to the recovery process. Coordination and control should come about through frequent group meetings and professional norms.

The team should emphasize successful completion of the task and good working relationships among the members. To the extent that team members need to work together on subsequent projects, it is essential that they have a base of cooperation and trust (Lubmann 1979, Barber 1983). If the team is together for only a short time, personal needs become less important, as long as members are compatible enough to complete the task.

Teams should be structurally and politically insulated from the outside, so that, for example, one organization's ephemeral public relations concerns do not impair the team's effectiveness, or so that administrators with little sensitivity to the problems or solutions of the recovery effort do not undermine or override the team's activities. At the same time, the team should have open scientific and technical discourse with outsiders.

In all organizations and in all teams, there is both a *formal* and an *informal structure*. The formal structure is represented by the formal organizational chart and reflects the hierarchy of control and formal channels of interactions (Schon 1971). If formal organizational arrangements are ill-matched to the recovery job, team members may develop informal arrangements, which reflect how things best work rather than how they are officially designed to work (Schon 1971). The informal structure that emerges can often best respond to changing circumstances through informal friendships and acquaintanceships. Ideally, the formal organization will permit the informal organization to function to meet the recovery task.

Members of recovery teams can harness the informal structure as it emerges (Farris 1971). *First*, acknowledge the emerging of the informal structure and encourage teamwork. The common task and goals should be clarified. Meetings should allow individuals to practice acting as a team. Meetings should be true give-and-take problem-solving discussions, not merely information exchanges or 'negotiations.' The more informal the meeting, the better. *Second*, allow the team to select its own leader. Knowing and accepting the task to be accomplished, team members will generally identify a person with whom they feel they can work and whom they can help to meet goals. The major function of a team leader is to create an environment that will release the technical contributions each individual offers. A team leader needs to be a credible professional, but need not be more technically proficient than every other member of the team. The team leader should be able to stimulate and recognize creative ideas, foster the development of ideas, give constructive feedback, and knock down the roadblocks to accomplishing the task. *Third*, informal organization can be enhanced if the team leader helps team members exchange technical information and participate in exchanges. The team leader should seek scientific ideas from outside the team as well as from within. The team leader cannot be 'all things to all people,' but he or she must be skilled at allowing talent in the team to perform well.

Planning in teams

Planning requires continual reevaluation, analysis, and adjustment of activities toward the defined goals (Boone & Kurtz 1984). It also requires a timetable. Successful planning is based on a deep look within the organization, a broad look around and outside the organization, and a long look ahead. Ian E. Wilson (cited in Boone & Kurtz 1984, p. 99) observed, 'No amount of sophistication is going to allay the fact that all your knowledge is about the past and all your decisions are about the future'.

Plans need to be responsive to changes suggested by field operations. Extensive preplanning, or rigid overplanning, should be avoided. A three-step planning process suggested by Boone & Kurtz (1984) involves 1) setting organizational objectives or determining desired ends; 2) articulating planning premises or assumptions about the constantly changing task environment; and 3) developing methods to control the operation of the plan, including continual analysis and evaluation.

Establishing a plan involves decision-making, which is the process of identifying options and selecting courses of action to perform given tasks. Plans are a type of decision, made in advance, about what to do and how to do it.

Planning decisions are complexly interrelated; decision-makers must understand the system of decisions being made. Planning decisions collectively focus teams on objectives to be met in the future (Boone & Kurtz 1984).

A decision analysis approach has been described by Behn & Vaupel (1982) and has been applied in endangered species recovery planning by Maguire (1986a,b). It has proven useful in unpredictable technical and sociopolitical environments, simultaneously maximizing species survival and minimizing financial costs (Maguire 1986a). For example, Maguire *et al.* (1988) used it to select a recovery strategy for black-footed ferrets in Montana and later to examine whether the remaining wild ferrets should be taken into captivity (Maguire 1989). More recently, Maguire (1991) used decision analysis in the form of a decision tree to illustrate the range of choices professional conservation biologists have in their careers. All team members should know about this technique.

The steps involved in decision analysis are 1) define objectives for management and criteria to measure progress, 2) specify alternative management actions, 3) list random events that can affect management actions, 4) describe the outcomes of each action and event combination and evaluate according to the criteria, 5) estimate the probability of each event occurring, 6) calculate the expected outcomes and identify the action with the best expectation of success according to the criteria, 7) resolve any conflicting criteria via tradeoff analysis, and 8) document the analysis. The problem may be outlined in a decision tree, which 'lays out in schematic form the decision alternatives, the uncertain events, the possible outcomes of such events, and the consequences of each outcome, all in the order that the decision maker will face them' (Behn & Vaupel 1982, p. 28).

The program evaluation and review technique (PERT) is another promising planning tool in endangered species recovery (Richardson *et al.* 1986). PERT, developed in the 1950s along with the standard agenda technique (Goodall 1985), is useful for working out the details of a complex plan of action (Bormann 1975). PERT involves identifying all 'events and activities which must take place to carry out a decision, and then drawing up a sequential diagram of those activities, using an hour-by-hour, day-by-day, week-by-week plan' (Goodall 1985, p. 236). For each activity, all resources (personnel, information, finances, and material) required to achieve the task are also identified. Statistical procedures can be used in PERT planning.

Leading teams

Several studies have demonstrated that team leadership should be task-oriented (Fiedler 1967). Task-oriented groups expect their leader to influence the group toward accomplishing the task. If the leader is also concerned with maintaining healthy working relationships within the group, much of the dissent that can destroy group effectiveness can be avoided (House & Mitchell 1974).

Teams are sometimes composed of highly trained professionals. The team members expect to use their skills, and they can usually see how their skills can be applied to the task. It is important that their views be recognized, and that they be involved in decision-making and planning. If this occurs, the leader will be viewed as supportive and approachable, and the members' commitment to the task and work group will be strengthened.

Team leaders should possess the ability to rigorously separate scientific facts and inferences from judgments reflecting policy and politics (Harville 1985). No single characteristic is more important for team effectiveness. A team leader may have two possibly incompatible roles as a project leader and as an employee of one of the primary agencies involved in the recovery program. To satisfy both roles, the leader must avoid letting his or her employer's views or other political considerations dominate the project leader role.

The team leader should be not only a team builder, but also a skilled conflict manager. Differences of perception and interests coupled with emotionalism can grow to levels that render the team unproductive. However, some conflict in team activities is inevitable, and when a group is experiencing moderate conflict, team performance may be enhanced (Brown 1983). The leader must strive to keep all conflict within a productive range. The basic question is whether individual, team, program, or organizational differences in values and perceptions (e.g. conflicts between federal and state governments) begin to create emotions to the point that interaction becomes strained or counterproductive. Brown (1983) identified a number of intervention options designed to manage conflict productively (e.g. use intermediaries or representatives), and these should be part of any team leader's repertoire. Team leaders should be evaluated on the overall performance of the team, not only on their individual performance or on the basis of their employing agency's incentives.

Controlling teams

Team control is necessary to maintain working relationships and to ensure that performance standards are met. The control function will largely be self-imposed by the members, assuming a commitment to the task, an environment that provides feedback on team performance, a fair evaluation system, and appropriate recognition and rewards for performance.

While generally it might be assumed that all team members have an equal commitment to the recovery assignment, this might not be true. Personal, task, or situational factors may cause the commitment and energy level to vary from person to person, and this unevenness may cause some internal conflicts. It is not sufficient, especially with professional persons, to assume that the members will easily and uniformly agree with the direction given by higher levels of administration, but controlling and influencing the performance of the team will be easier if all individuals endorse the norms of the group and the objectives of the task. To accomplish this, all team members should be part of defining the problem, designing appropriate strategies, and agreeing upon the standards on which performance will be judged. Once the team has been a part of the overall planning decision process, it becomes much easier to discuss levels of performance, compare them with the standards previously agreed upon, provide appropriate recognition for those tasks done well, and establish the subsequent tasks.

There should be regular feedback on individual and team performance, and it is essential that rewards and recognition be made contingent upon successful task completion. A clear but flexible relationship between goals, team performance, evaluation, and rewards is necessary for control. Rewarding a group or an individual for non-performance gives mixed signals about what is valued in an organization.

As the number of team members increases, so does the challenge to keep things coordinated. With larger numbers, it becomes much easier for things to 'slip by', and team members find it easier to avoid responsibility by 'passing the buck'. Also, it becomes easier for subgroups or cliques to form, which may be detrimental to the task if they have goals that are incompatible with those of the team.

Understanding the culture of your organization, program, or team

The central determinant of the character of every organization, program, or team is a *culture* (sometimes called ideology or system of thought). The culture is a set of values and cognitive perspectives that are largely shared by members. The culture of an organization conveys the feeling or pervasive way of life that dominates its programs and teams (Harrison 1972). Some people become highly socialized to these cultures, whereas other people are less well socialized. Harrison (1972, p. 119) notes, 'An organization's culture affects the behavior of its people, its ability to effectively meet their needs and demands, and the way it copes with the external environment'. Much of the conflict between and within organizations is the result of cultural differences between organizations or subunits within the same organization (e.g. ideological value differences common to state rights vs. federalism issues in wildlife and land management) (Clark 1986a). Individuals enter organizations because they share the values and views of the organization. If they do not, they must become socialized to them if they are to remain on the job. People who are very highly socialized to the culture are often considered 'company men', especially if the culture is power- or role-oriented. An organization's culture directly affects how well a program or a team can solve problems. The concept of culture and its controlling influence on performance has been described by Roy (1977), Deal & Kennedy (1982), and many others.

Harrison (1972, p. 120) described six functions of a culture: 1) it provides the values and goals towards which the effort is to be directed and by which the organization evaluates its success and worth; 2) it prescribes relationships between individuals and the overall effort, acting as a form of social contract that shapes what is expected from people; 3) it guides how behavior should be controlled and identifies which controls are legitimate; 4) it depicts the characteristics and qualities that members are to value or vilify, thus setting the reward or punishment systems; 5) it tells members how to treat one another and people in other organizations (competitively or collaboratively, honestly or dishonestly, closely or distantly); 6) it establishes guidelines and methods for dealing with the external environment, including people in other organizations, either hostilely or benignly.

The previous descriptions of species recovery task forces and project teams in the context of their managerial functions—organizing, planning, leading, and controlling—are all characteristic of task-oriented cultures. Not all teams, programs, or organizations, however, are task-oriented. There are also power, role, and people orientations (Harrison 1972). A power culture tries to dominate its environment and vanquish all opposition. It is characterized by interpersonal conflicts because of constant competition for advancement and advantage. A role culture is bureaucratic, with extensive rules, roles, and regulations, and concern for legitimacy, hierarchy, status, and symbols of rank. Goal displacement, in which the goals of controlling the program or team and other participants displace the goals of getting the job done, is common. Rules and role conformity are overemphasized, creative and innovative behavior is discouraged, and ritualistic responses to problems are all that is permitted. Role cultures match well with stable, predictable task environments. A person culture is rare. It emphasizes the personal goals and needs of its members. A task culture rewards the accomplishments of the pre-eminent goal (e.g. recovering the species). Interpersonal interactions are structured and managed around the overriding goal. Task cultures are supported by flexible structures and an open, supportive problem-solving climate. A questionnaire about organizational, program, or team cultures that can be self-administered to learn about your own organization's culture is available from the authors on request.

If the culture is well matched to the work to be done, it will aid job completion; if it is not, it will hinder the work. An endangered species recovery effort's culture should be predominantly task-oriented. If, instead, the culture is power- or role-oriented, it would be poorly suited to the complex recovery task. The importance of the culture's effect on the quality of work is often unrecognized or unappreciated (Peters & Waterman 1982); this is especially true in governmental agencies.

In recovery work supported by a task culture, recovering the species is the highest goal (Harrison 1972). The key is that the program or team's structure, functions, and activities are all evaluated in terms of their contribution to species recovery. Little or nothing is permitted to get in the way of accomplishing recovery. For example, if rigid authority or the outmoded roles of traditional bureaucracies impede the recovery task, they are eliminated or changed. If individuals lack the technical knowledge or skill to perform the task, they are helped to get it or they are replaced. If social considerations (e.g. bureaucratic politics) or personal needs (e.g. status) threaten to upset effective problem-solving, they are suppressed.

In task cultures, members have no ideological commitment to authority and order *per se*. Authority is considered legitimate if it is based on knowledge and competence and is used to meet the recovery task, otherwise authority is considered illegitimate. Traditional rules, roles, and regulations can constrain the creativity and innovative problem-solving necessary to address highly uncertain tasks, and organizations should try to remove these constraints. The structure of task-oriented efforts is shaped and changed to meet the changing requirements of the task to be accomplished. There is a strong emphasis on rapid, flexible responses to what the task environment demands. Collaboration is sought if it will advance the recovery task goal. There is little 'advantage seeking' relative to other groups or organizations.

Analyzing organizational problems and developing action plans

Endangered species recovery requires a framework for analyzing organizational problems and for implementing change based on a wide range of technical, group, and organizational issues. The disciplined intervention suggested by Table 1.1 and the Appendix to Chapter 1 is appropriate for various problems. For example, a recovery team may recognize that their day-to-day effectiveness is hampered by a perceived lack of freedom to confront one another on relevant issues. Having agreed that they need to talk more openly, each team member waits for someone else to begin. After considerable frustration, they may ask, 'Why can't we change the way we work together?'

Table 1.1. *Outline for analyzing problems and developing action plans.*
See Appendix I for full explanation.

1.	Problem identification
	a) identify problem
	b) translate problem to objectives
	c) understand problem
	d) assess your control over problem
	e) restate objectives
	f) identify 'facilitating' and 'hindering' forces
	g) evaluate
2.	Development of alternative strategies
	a) analyze the above
	b) select strategy
3.	Develop action plan
	a) identify specific tasks
	b) identify persons responsible
	c) establish timelines
	d) discuss plan
4.	Implement and evaluate action plans
	a) develop criteria to evaluate
	b) discuss plan with supervisor
	c) implement
	d) evaluate

In this example, there may be many reasons to change in the direction of more openness. *First*, team members must perform effectively for their own sakes and for the good of the team and their employing organizations. *Second*, they are functionally interdependent, because each member may possess a unique skill and all must work together to accomplish the goal. *Third*, there may be work-related problems that hinder the team's effectiveness (responsibility without authority and unclear job definitions are common problems). *Fourth*, there may be interpersonal tension because teams are made up of representatives of different organizations, each with a distinct culture (thus, competition or passive or active conflict may ensue). Changes, even if their necessity is well recognized, are not always easily made. Often the causes of the problems are hidden in the sociology of the team and require a thorough description and diagnosis. Many of the barriers to effective team behavior may be embedded in the policy context of the members' work or in the incompatible cultural values and structures of the agencies or organizations involved (Clark & Kellert 1988). For some problems, professional organizational consultants may be required. Other problems, both organizational and technical, can be effectively addressed directly by the team, following the systematic process of problem solving and action planning outlined in Table 1.1 and detailed in the Appendix. The system is self-explanatory and could be used by teams, agencies, and organizations experiencing technical, organizational, or other problems.

Conclusions

There is continuing evidence of poor performance in endangered species efforts in the USA (e.g. Yaffee 1982, Tobin 1990, Kohm 1991). Traditionally, workers have attributed the problems to bureaucratic foibles ('that's just the way the system works'), to colleagues they consider uncommitted, uninformed, or unintelligent, or to poor data or lack of data. But many of these problems can be traced to the poor design and mismanagement of organizations, programs, and teams. Once biologists understand this, they will be able to apply the terms, concepts, and descriptions in this paper and the literature cited to identify, analyze, and begin to rectify the problems in their own efforts. Performance can be measured by its *effectiveness* in achieving the ultimate goals, its *efficiency* in the use of time, money, labor, and other resources, and the *equality* it affords the workers and people affected by the effort. The job of restoring species and their habitats is difficult enough without being hampered by poorly designed and mismanaged programs or teams, especially when researchers in the field of organizational design and behavior have already provided valuable paradigms and techniques that are directly applicable to conservation efforts. Detailed case studies, as called for by Clark (1986b), of a range of recovery programs could serve as the basis for improved performance in the future.

Acknowledgments

Denise Casey of the Northern Rockies Conservation Cooperative, Bruce Marcot of the US Forest Service, Marlin Bowles, Robyn Flakne, and Chris Whelan of the Morton Arboretum, and two anonymous individuals reviewed the manuscript. Their very useful comments significantly improved it. We sincerely thank them for their time and perspectives. Marcia Casey typed earlier versions of the paper. Support for much of the background work for this paper came from the World Wildlife Fund-US, The Eppley Foundation for Research, Wildlife Preservation Trust International, Nu Lambda Trust, and US Fish and Wildlife Service Section 6 endangered species monies to Montana Department of Fish, Wildlife, and Parks. Numerous discussions with colleagues in endangered species work nationally and internationally were invaluable. Our appreciation goes to John Weaver, US Forest Service; Ron Crete, Wayne Brewster, and Chris Servheen, US Fish and Wildlife Service; John Cada, Dennis Flath, and Arnold Dood, Montana Department of Fish, Wildlife and Parks; Garry Brewer, Stephen Kellert, Bill Burch, and John Wargo,

Yale University; Chuck Carr, Wildlife Conservation International; Buff Bohlen, World Wildlife Fund-US; Jon Jensen and Bill Konstant, Wildlife Preservation Trust International; and Paul Buller, Utah State University.

Literature cited

Argyris, D. & Schon, D. (1978) *Organizational Learning: a Theory of Action Perspective*. Reading: Addison-Wesley.

Barber, B. (1983) *The Logic and Limits of Trust*. New Brunswick: Rutgers University Press.

Behn, R. D. & Vaupel, J.W. (1982) *Quick Analysis for Busy Decision Makers*. New York: Basic Books.

Boone, L. E. & Kurtz, D. L. (1984) *Principles of Management*. New York: Random House.

Bormann, E. G. (1975) *Discussion and Group Methods: Theory and Practice*, 2nd edn. New York: Harper and Row.

Brickloe, W. D. & Coughlin, M. T. (1977) *Managing Organizations*. Encino: Glencoe Press.

Brown, L. D. (1983) *Managing Conflict at Organizational Interfaces*. Reading: Addison-Wesley.

Campbell, S. (1980) Is reintroduction a realistic goal? In *Conservation Biology; an Evolutionary-Ecological Perspective*, ed. Soulé M. E. & Wilcox, B. A., pp. 263–9. Sunderland, Massachusetts: Sinauer.

Carr, A. (1986) Introduction: the black-footed ferret. *Great Basin Naturalist Memoirs*, **8**, 1–7.

Casey, D., Clark, T. W. & Seebeck, J. H. (1990) Conclusions. In *Management and Conservation of Small Populations*, ed. Clark, T. W. & Seebeck, J. H., pp. 283–8. Chicago: Chicago Zoological Society.

Clark, T. W. (1984a) Strategies in endangered species conservation: a research view of the ongoing black-footed ferret conservation studies. In *Symposium on Issues in Technology and Management of Impacted Western Wildlife, Steamboat Springs, Colorado, November, 1982*, ed. Comer, R. D., Merino, J. M., Monarch, J. W., Pustmueller, C., Stallmaster, M., Stocker, R., Todd, J. & Right, W., pp. 145–154. Boulder, Colorado: Montana Bureau of Land Management.

Clark, T. W. (1984b) Biological, sociological, and organizational challenges to endangered species conservation: the black-footed ferret case. *Human Dimensions of Wildlife Newsletter*, **3**, 10–15.

Clark, T. W. (1986a) Professional excellence in wildlife and natural resource organizations. *Renewable Resources Journal*, **4**, (Summer), 8–13.

Clark, T. W. (1986b) Case studies in wildlife policy education. *Renewable Resources Journal*, **4** (Fall), 11–17.

Clark, T. W. (1989) *Conservation Biology of the Black-footed Ferret, Mustela nigripes*. Wildlife Preservation Trust Special Scientific Report No. 3.

Clark, T. W., Crete, R. & Cada, J. (1989) Designing and managing successful endangered species recovery programs. *Environment Management*, **13**, 159–70.

Clark, T. W. & Harvey, A. H. (1991) Implementing recovery policy: Learning as we go? In *Balancing on the Brink of Extinction: The Endangered Species Act and Lessons for the Future*, ed. Kohm, K. A., pp. 147–63. Washington, D.C.: Island Press.

Clark, T. W. & Kellert, S. R. (1988) Towards a policy paradigm of the wildlife sciences. *Renewable Resources Journal*, **6**, 7–16.

28 *T. W. Clark and J. R. Cragun*

Clark, T. W. & Westrum, R. (1989) High performance teams in wildlife conservation: a species reintroduction and recovery example. *Environmental Management*, **13**, 663–370.

Clarke, J. N. & McCool, D. (1985) *Staking Out the Terrain: Power Differentials Among Natural Resource Management Agencies*. Albany: State University of New York Press.

Culbert, R. & Blair, R. (1989) Recovery planning and endangered species. *Endangered Species Update*, **8**, 64–65.

Daft, R. L. (1983) *Organization Theory and Design*. St. Paul: West Publishing.

Deal, T. E., & Kennedy, A. A. (1982) *Corporate Cultures: the Rites and Rituals of Corporate Life*. Reading: Addison-Wesley.

Dery, D. (1984) *Problem Definition in Policy Analysis*. Lawrence: University of Kansas Press.

Etheredge, L., & Short, J. (1983) Thinking about government learning. *Journal of Management Studies*, **20**, 42–58.

Farris, G. (1971) Organizing your informal organization. *Innovation*, **16**, 19–29.

Fiedler, F. E. (1967) *A Theory of Leadership Effectiveness*. New York: McGraw-Hill.

Forrest, S. C. & Biggins, D. E. (1987) *Black-footed ferret recovery plan draft. Summer 1987*. Denver: U.S. Fish and Wildlife Service, Region 6.

Galbraith, J. R. (1977). *Organizational design*. Reading: Addison-Wesley.

Goodall, H. L. Jr. (1985) *Small Group Communication in Organizations*. Dubuque: Brown Publishing.

Harrison, R. (1972) *Understanding your organization's character. Harvard Business Review*, May-June, 119–28.

Harrison, R. (1975) Diagnosing organizational ideology. In *Handbook for group Facilitators*, ed. Pfeiffer, J. W. & Jones, J. E., pp. 169–76. San Diego: University Associates.

Harville, J. P. (1985) Expanding horizons for fisheries management. *Fisheries*, **10**, 14–19.

Hebden, J. E. (1986) Adopting an organization's culture: the socialization of graduate trainees. *Organizational Dynamics*, Summer, 54–72.

House, R. J. & Mitchell, T. R. (1974) Path-goal theory of leadership. *Journal of Contemporary Business*, **4**, 81–97.

Hrebiniak, L. G. (1978) *Complex Organizations*. New York: West Publishing.

Jackson, J. A. (1986) Biopolitics, management of federal lands, and the conservation of the red-cockaded woodpecker. *American Birds*, Winter, 162–8.

Jelinek, J., Litterer, J. A. & Miles, R. E. eds. (1981) *Organizations by Design: Theory and Practice*. Plano: Business Publishing, Inc.

Kanter, R. (1983) *The Change Masters*. New York: Simon and Schuster.

Kohm, K. A. ed. (1991) *Balancing on the Brink of Extinction—the Endangered Species Act and Lessons for the Future*. Washington, D.C.: Island Press.

Larson, C. E. & LaFasto, F. M. J. (1989) *Teamwork: What Must Go Right/What Can Go Wrong*. Newbury Park: Sage Publication.

Lorsch, J. W. (1977) Organizational designs: a situational perspective. *Organizational Dynamics*, Autumn, 2–14.

Lubmann, J. (1979) *Trust and power*. New York: John Wiley and Sons.

Maguire, L. A. (1986a) Using decision analysis to manage endangered species populations. *Journal of Environmental Management*, **22**, 345–360.

Maguire, L. A. (1986b) *An Analysis of Augmentation Strategies for Grizzly Populations*. Report to U.S. Forest Service, 25 March, 1986. Regional Office. Missoula: U.S. Forest Service.

Maguire, L. A. (1989) Managing black-footed ferret populations under uncertainty: capture and release decisions. In *Conservation Biology and the Black-Footed*

Ferret, ed. Seal, U. S., Thorne, E. T., Bogan, M. A. & Anderson, S. H., pp. 286–92. New Haven: Yale University Press.

Maguire, L. A. (1991) Risk analysis for conservation biologists. *Conservation Biology*, **5**, 123–4.

Maguire, L. A., Clark, T. W., Crete, R., Cada, J., Groves, G., Shaffer, M. L. & Seal, U. S. (1988) Black-footed ferret recovery in Montana: a decision analysis. *Wildlife Society Bulletin*, **16**, 111–20.

Menkhorst, P. W., Loyn, R. H. & Brown, P. B. (1990) Management of the orange-bellied parrot. In *Management and Conservation of Small Populations*, ed. Clark, T. W. & Seebeck, J. H., pp. 239–252. Chicago: Chicago Zoological Society.

Mintzberg, H. (1971) Managerial work: analysis from observation. *Management Sciences*, **18**, B97–B110.

National Academy of Sciences. (1986) *Ecological knowledge and environmental problem-solving: concepts and case studies*. Washington, D.C.: National Academy Press.

Peters, T. J. & R. H. Waterman, Jr. (1982) *In Search of Excellence: Lessons from America's Best-run Corporations*. New York: Warner.

Ream, R. R. (1986) The political environment for management of a wilderness species. In *National Wilderness Research Conference*, ed. R. C. Lucas, Vol. 1, pp. 176–9. Ogden, Utah: *Intermountain* Research Station.

Richardson, L., Clark, T. W., Forrest, S. C. & Campbell, T. M. III. (1986) Black-footed ferret recovery: a discussion of some options and considerations. *Great Basin Naturalist Memoirs*, **8**, 169–184.

Romesburg, H. C. (1981) Wildlife science: gaining reliable knowledge. *Journal of Wildlife Management*, **45**, 293–313.

Roy, R. H. (1977) *The Cultures of Management*. Baltimore: Johns Hopkins University Press.

Schon, D. A. (1971) *Beyond the Stable State*. New York: W. W. Norton.

Schon, D. A. (1983) *The Reflective Practitioner*. New York: Basic Books.

Snyder, N. F. R. (1986) California condor recovery program. In *Raptor Conservation in the Next 50 Years*, ed. Senner, S. E., White, C. M., & Parrish, J. R., Raptor Research Report No. 5, pp. 56–61. Hasting: Raptor Research Foundation.

Stanley-Price, M. R. (1989) *Animal Re-introductions: the Arabian Oryx in Oman*. New York: Cambridge University Press.

Steers, R. M., Ungson, G. R. & Mowday, R. T. (1985) *Managing Effective Organizations*. Boston: Kent Publishing.

Tobin, R. J. (1990) *The Expendable Future: U.S. Politics and the Protection of Biological Diversity*. Durham: Duke University Press.

Tushman, M. L. & Nadler, D. A. (1978) Information processing as an integrating concept in organizational design. *Academic Management Review*, **3**, 613–624.

Varney, G. H. (1989) *Building Productive Teams: An Action Guide and Resource Book*. San Francisco: Jossey-bass Publishers.

Weinberg, D. (1986) Decline and fall of the black-footed ferret. *Natural History Magazine*, **95**, 62–69.

Westrum, R. (1986) Management strategies and information failure. In *Information systems; failure analysis*, ed. Wise, J. & Debons, A., pp. 109–28. New York: Springer-Verlag.

Wydoski, R. S. (1977) Realistic management of endangered species—an overview. *Proceedings of the Annual Conference of the Western Association of Game and Fish Commissions*, **57**, 273–286.

Yaffee, S. L. (1982) *Prohibitive Policy: Implementing the Endangered Species Act*. Cambridge, Massachusetts: MIT Press.

Appendix to Chapter 1

Analyzing problems and developing action plans for endangered species recovery

A procedure useful in analyzing a problem and developing an action plan for endangered species is outlined. Our 14-step procedure includes example work sheets to be filled out by you and your team. It can be applied to solving organizational as well as technical problems. It is self-explanatory.

Steps to follow in analyzing a problem and developing an action plan

Problem identification

STEP 1.   Identify a problem you feel is important to the success of your organization over which you exercise some control.

STEP 2.   Translate the problem identified into an 'objective' statement and write that objective on the *Problem Solving Worksheet.*
Remember: to increase the probability of success, objectives must be:

> *specific*: having a special application or reference; specified; explicit, particular, precise, or definite
> *realistic*: concerned with what is real or practical; representing things as they really are
> *attainable*: that which can be reached, achieved, or accomplished by continued effort
> *measurable*: that which can be measured, which is the process of ascertaining extent, dimensions, quantity, etc.
> *acceptable*: pleasing to the receiver, agreeable, welcome; worthy of being accepted, i.e. received with approval or favor

STEP 3.   Understand the problem(s) by answering the following:

> 1. I understand the problem *specifically* to be . . .
> 2. Examples of the problem that I have observed or experienced are . . .
> 3. The people (at all levels) directly involved in the problem are . . .
> The ways in which each one influences the operation of my unit are . . .
> 4. Those circumstances or conditions in the environment which contribute to the problem are . . .

STEP 4.   Assess the degree to which you can control or influence the problem and what the probabilities of success are.

STEP 5.   Restate your objective if necessary.

STEP 6.   Enter on your page 1 of the *Problem Solving Worksheet* those 'facilitating forces' which you could use to help move toward reaching your objective. Enter also those 'hindering forces' which stand in your way of reaching your objective.

STEP 7.   Evaluate each of these entries (from STEP 6) in terms of how important they are. Identify those which are most important.

Development of alternative strategies

STEP 8. Analyze your entries on page 1 and list on page 2 various strategies you could implement to reach your objective. Your strategies should consider both increasing the facilitating forces and *decreasing the hindering forces.*

STEP 9. Select the one best strategy or *combination of strategies* which help meet your objective.

Development of your action plan

STEP 10. Enter on page 3 of the *Problem Solving Worksheet* the specific tasks to be accomplished, who will do each task, and a date by which it should be completed. Also indicate in the section titled 'Planning Notes' any details related to the various tasks, such as other people involved, arrangements to be made, etc.

Implementation and evaluation of action plan

STEP 11. Specify those criteria that can be used to determine how effective you are in meeting your objective.

STEP 12. Discuss with your supervisor your action plan and specifically consider how he/she could assist you in meeting the various tasks

STEP 13. Implement your plan, conduct an ongoing evaluation, and adjust as necessary.

STEP 14. Evaluate the success of your efforts.

NOTE: The *Problem Solving Worksheets* are basically an outline. It is very likely that you will have more than one page on each section.

WORKSHEET PAGE 1

Problem Solving

Objective
To: _____
_____
_____

Facilitating forces	Hindering forces

++++++

WORKSHEET PAGE 2

Strategies for Improvement

Objective :   To _____

_____

_____

++++++

WORKSHEET PAGE 3

Planning Details

Objective :   To: _____

_____

_____

TASK TO BE ACCOMPLISHED	WHO WILL DO IT	WHEN WILL IT START	WHEN WILL IT BE DONE	PLANNING NOTES: (Who else is involved, what resources are required, etc.)

+++++

WORKSHEET PAGE 4

Action Plan Assessment Form

Statement of Objective

_____

_____

_____

Criterion	Meets Criterion Yes No	If not, suggestions for improvement
1. The plan logically leads to goal achievement.		
2. Action steps are clear.		
3. Action steps are complete.		
4. Actions are within the control & influence of the participant.		
5. Time frames are real.		
6. Plan is feasible: it makes sense, can be done.		
7. Plan deals with concrete actions that can be monitored.		
8. Plan has work-group commitment and support.		
9. The responsibilities of people involved are clearly outlined.		
10. Roadblocks have been identified & can be overcome.		
11. Results can be measured & it will be known when task has been accomplished.		

2

Genetic considerations for plant population restoration and conservation

CHARLES B. FENSTER AND
MICHELE R. DUDASH

Introduction

Successful restoration policy involves three basic criteria. First, sufficient habitat must be protected for the continued persistence of a species (Gilpin & Soulé 1986). Second, demographic information must be collected to determine which life history stages are most critical to survival, reproduction, and long-term population vigor (Marcot & Holthausen 1987, Lande 1988). Third, once these fundamental criteria for population survival are met, genetic variation can be considered as an issue in restoration and conservation policy. Overall, we believe that genetic issues may be more pertinent to population restoration than to population conservation. In attempting to conserve taxa, one is initially interested in saving numbers of individuals regardless of their relatedness. Given that natural areas managers will have the opportunity to reintroduce populations that have been extirpated in nature, it seems reasonable that any genetic manipulations that may help restore a population's vigor *in situ* for the short or long term may be beneficial.

Rare and endangered taxa often exist as a few relatively small populations (Holsinger & Gottlieb 1989) subject to population bottlenecks. Thus, genetic drift and mating among relatives contributes to the loss of genetic variation and reduction in the population's overall vigor through inbreeding depression (Lacy 1987, Polans & Allard 1989). A short-term conservation goal should be to ensure that the vigor of a population is maintained or restored in the face of inbreeding by appropriate manipulation of the remaining genetic variation (Ledig 1986). Little is known of the consequences of mixing distant gene pools in natural populations in order to increase genetic variation (Templeton 1986). A long-term goal of any conservation or restoration policy must be to preserve the evolutionary potential of a species by maintaining its genetic variation either by partitioning genetic variation among individuals within a population or by partitioning genetic variation between populations (Riggs 1990). In the past few decades there has been an explosion of techniques to document genetic variation at the molecular level (Cohn 1990). There is a need to synthesize information gathered from molecular studies with patterns of morphological variation to determine the role of molecular markers as indicators of important subsets of genetic variation.

In contrast to animals, many plant species are asexual, and upwards of 20% of all plant species are primarily selfing; the rest exhibit varying degrees of outcrossing (Fryxell 1957, Jain 1976). This great range in mating systems may dictate alternative restoration strategies.

The primary objective of this chapter is to outline experiments to address genetic issues in plant population restoration and conservation using common species as *model systems*. This approach allows us to test the consequences of genetic manipulation to restore or maintain population vigor, as well as to determine appropriate techniques for identifying important subsets of genetic variation. General principles learned from common species may be applied to the restoration and conservation of endangered taxa. This chapter focuses on methods to restore a population's vigor following extreme inbreeding by determining 1) the genetic basis of inbreeding depression in natural populations, 2) whether it is possible to purge a population of inbreeding depression with a selected breeding program, 3) the consequences of mixing distant gene pools (i.e. outbreeding depression), and 4) whether the genetic variation of our remaining source populations influences their potential colonizing ability. In addition, methods are described to identify important subsets of genetic variation using phylogenetic approaches based on molecular data. We propose to complement the molecular phylogenetic approach with quantitative genetic techniques to assess whether different lineages within a species have different evolutionary potentials. The relevance of mating system is addressed for each of the issues raised above.

Genetic manipulation to restore population vigor

Inbreeding depression

Inbreeding depression occurs when selfing or mating between relatives results in a general decline in the vigor of the resulting progeny. Deterioration of the gene pool through inbreeding has been documented in both crops (e.g. Neal 1935, Wright 1977) and natural populations (e.g. Schemske 1983, Schoen 1983, Ritland & Ganders 1987, Dudash 1990, Fenster 1991b). Detection of inbreeding depression is often dependent upon the environment in which it is examined (Dudash 1990). Progeny of *Sabatia angularis* grown in benign (i.e. greenhouse and garden) environments exhibited less inbreeding depression

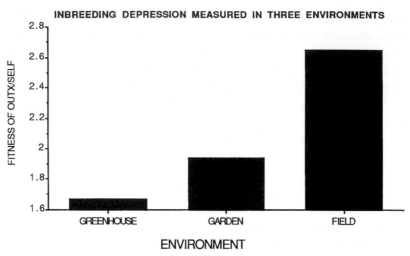

Fig. 2.1. Relative fitness of outcrossed progeny to selfed progeny of *Sabatia angularis* grown in the greenhouse, garden, and field (from Dudash 1990).

than progeny grown in the natural field habitat (Fig. 2.1; Dudash 1990). Thus, studies contrasting performance of inbred and outbred progeny in the greenhouse (e.g. Schemske 1983, Waller 1984, Mitchell-Olds & Waller 1985, Sakai, Karoly & Weller 1989) are probably conservative estimates of the effects of inbreeding depression. Many studies of progeny performance (i.e. fitness) have not been conducted throughout the entire life cycle of plants. A more robust estimate of progeny performance can be attained if it is assessed at as many points in the life cycle as possible. Although annual plants can be followed throughout their entire life cycle (i.e. seed to seed), many endangered species have longer lifespans, and thus cannot be studied at this level of completeness. Genetic manipulations of populations of long-lived organisms will require decisions about how to quantify and measure the resulting progeny's fitness. Ritland (1990) has developed a method to estimate inbreeding depression from electrophoretic data alone that may be helpful in assessing inbreeding depression for long-lived organisms. Although inbreeding depression is a generally accepted phenomenon in crops (Simmonds 1981, Hallauer & Miranda 1985), there are still only a few published studies that clearly document its importance in natural plant populations measured *in situ* (e.g. Schoen 1983, Kohn 1988, Dudash 1990, Fenster 1991b). These studies document only the short-term (one generation) consequences of extreme inbreeding. As we discuss below, the genetic basis of inbreeding depression, i.e. the role of dominance vs. overdominance in heterosis and epistasis in inbreeding depression, will determine the long-term consequences of inbreeding.

Note that limited gene flow resulting in population structure will cause an eventual loss of heterozygosity and increase in inbreeding (Crow & Kimura 1970). Most plant populations have considerable population subdivision (Levin 1981, Loveless & Hamrick 1984). Thus, even if random mating occurs within the limits of realized gene flow, there will be considerable mating among relatives. Consequently, it may be common for progeny from random mating within populations to incur a cost of inbreeding depression compared with longer-distance crosses (Fenster 1991b).

Genetic basis of inbreeding depression

Two models of the genetic basis of inbreeding depression are reviewed by Charlesworth & Charlesworth (1987). Inbreeding depression is due to 1) the expression of recessive or partly recessive deleterious alleles expressed in the homozygous state (partial dominance model), or 2) heterozygote superiority in which the heterozygote is more fit than either homozygote (overdominance model). These two mechanisms are not mutually exclusive, and they may occur at the level of a single locus or many loci, complicating the empirical determination of the underlying genetic mechanisms of inbreeding depression (Moll, Lindsey & Robinson 1964). Several studies using crop species have suggested that the expression of recessive deleterious alleles explains the observed inbreeding depression better than does overdominance (Comstock & Robinson 1948, Robinson, Comstock & Harvey 1949, Gardner 1962, Moll *et al.* 1964). As we demonstrate below, determining the genetic basis of inbreeding depression in natural populations facilitates the success of a program designed to rid a population of inbreeding depression.

One approach to determining the genetic basis of inbreeding depression has recently been summarized by Bulmer (1985). First, inbred lines must be generated from as many families within a population as possible, because the family attrition rate may be high (80–95%) following enforced inbreeding (Frankel & Soulé 1981). Plant breeders commonly refer to inbred lines as those having undergone five generations of selfing (Simmonds 1981). This breeding program would result in a 32-fold reduction of heterozygosity. Once inbred lines are generated, a diallel crossing program is used to generate F1, F2, and backcross progeny that eventually are grown together to assess the consequences of the crossing program and calculate the degree of dominance expressed. This approach cannot account for epistasis and linkage, which must be assessed independently (see Bulmer 1985).

Selective purging of inbreeding depression

The genetic basis of inbreeding depression has broad implications for restoration policy. If dominance is responsible for inbreeding depression, then the genetic load can be purged through a controlled breeding program. However, if overdominance is the cause, a breeding program will not as readily rid a population of inbreeding depression. In either case, if the traits responsible for the expression of inbreeding depression are polygenic, they will not respond to artificial selection as rapidly as will traits controlled by a few genes (Lande & Schemske 1985).

Thorough studies of non-crop species are needed to determine whether enforced inbreeding can reduce inbreeding depression by selecting for vigorous inbred lines in plants. Templeton & Read (1984) were able to reduce the inbreeding depression of a captive population of Speke's gazelle using a controlled inbreeding program. However, they have not yet tried to reintroduce Speke's gazelle from this program into the wild. Testing the relative vigor of inbred lines selected for high fitness under natural conditions should be easier for plants than for animals, and may become a paradigm for both animal and plant population restorations.

To assess the possibility of purging a population of inbreeding depression, the performance of inbred lines of plants selected for high vigor could be compared with that of progeny from open-pollinated seed in native and novel habitats. In a glasshouse experiment on a highly outcrossing population of tristylous *Eichhornia paniculata*, Barrett & Charlesworth (1991) demonstrated that enforced selfing purged the population of deleterious recessive alleles. No additional decline in fitness resulted from five generations of selfing compared with one generation of selfing. Additionally, when inbred lines were crossed, they resulted in progeny of superior fitness compared with the original outbred parental population. Thus, during the five generations of selfing there appears to have been selection against different homozygous alleles among the inbred families, resulting in greater heterozygosity among the intercrossed lines compared with the base population. Their empirical and theoretical results are in agreement with a partial dominance- based model of inbreeding depression.

Populations exposed to bottlenecks frequently experience a reduction in the mean of quantitative characters due to inbreeding depression (Bryant, McCommas & Combs 1986; Polans & Allard 1989). It might be expected that populations exposed to frequent bottlenecks would be purged of inbreeding depression due to mating with close relatives (Lande & Schemske 1985). Brewer *et al.* (1990) found that peripheral populations of *Peromyscus* mice had lower genetic diversity than central populations, suggesting that they had been exposed to bottlenecks. However, no correlation was observed between genetic diversity in mice populations and the degree of inbreeding depression, suggesting a role for overdominance in the observed heterosis of this obligatory outcrossing species. In contrast, as discussed below, there is frequently a correlation between the degree of selfing and inbreeding depression, with selfers generally experiencing far less heterosis than outcrossers when individuals are outcrossed.

Mating system and inbreeding depression

Inbreeding depression is expected to be greater in outcrossing than in selfing populations, because there is a greater opportunity to purge deleterious alleles (Wright 1977, Falconer 1981). Recent theoretical considerations of mating system evolution (Charlesworth & Charlesworth 1979, 1987, 1990, Holsinger 1988, Charlesworth, Morgan & Charlesworth 1990) have made clear predictions regarding changes in inbreeding depression with changes in selfing rates, but the expectations differ depending on the genetic basis of inbreeding depression. If heterosis is dominance-based, deleterious recessive alleles are expected to be absent in selfers. In contrast, selfers may exhibit heterosis if there is heterozygote advantage due to overdominance.

Inbreeding depression has been examined in primarily selfing species, but either the magnitude is much less (Wright 1977 and references therein, Svensson 1988, Griffing 1989, Holtsford & Ellstrand 1990) than that of primarily outcrossing species, or inbreeding depression is not detected (Levin 1989) compared with outcrossing species. These empirical and theoretical results suggest that the maintenance of high levels of heterozygosity and avoidance of inbreeding depression may not be important issues in selfing species. However, because much of the observation of inbreeding depression in selfers has been confined to crop species, there is a need to examine the role of contrasting mating system on levels of inbreeding depression in natural populations of congeners.

Outbreeding depression

Outbreeding depression occurs when the mating of individuals from distant source populations results in progeny having reduced vigor. This phenomenon can be observed in the F1, F2, backcross, or later generations of crosses between gene pools. The consequences of backcrosses are especially relevant when F1s are introduced into areas where the parental gene pool is still extant, as in the case of the restoration of Mead's milkweed (M. Bowles, personal communication). The consequences of mixing distant gene pools will depend on both the mode of gene action and the selective agents responsible for adaptive differentiation. Thus, it is important to have an understanding of the genetic basis and selective agents of outbreeding depression. In addition, we need to know at what spatial scale crosses between gene pools result in outbreeding depression, and the magnitude of hybrid breakdown.

Causes of outbreeding depression

The genetic basis of outbreeding depression may be associated with two modes of gene action. First, outbreeding depression may be a consequence of alleles selected for their individual effect, and the hybrid offspring are adapted to neither parental environment. An example may be the observation that when hybrids between species are formed, they commonly occur in habitats intermediate to those of the two parents, but cannot survive in either parental environment (Stebbins 1977). Another mechanism for outbreeding depression is the breakup of coadapted gene complexes (*sensu* Wright 1969), resulting from epistatic interaction in fitness of alleles across loci, or genes selected for their joint effects on fitness (Falconer 1981). This is most likely observed in the F2 generation, because additional opportunities for recombination occur during meiosis of the F1, and there is loss of heterozygosity in the F2 compared with the F1 (Falconer 1981, Lynch 1991). Both types of gene action may contribute to outbreeding depression, but to date we have little empirical evidence indicating the genetic basis of outbreeding depression. However, whether outbreeding depression is the consequence of the breakdown of epistatic or coadapted gene complexes has important implications for restoration following the mixing of gene pools. If genes have been selected for their additive effect, it is much more likely that heterosis following long-distance crosses will balance or outweigh any outbreeding depression. If populations are locally adapted through the evolution of coadapted gene complexes, then progeny vigor following the mixing of gene pools may be greatly suppressed.

Templeton (1986) reviews two major selective agents that may result in the expression of outbreeding depression when gene pools are mixed. First, hybrid offspring may have lower fitness when the parental populations have differentiated to local environmental selection pressures, resulting in ecotypic differentiation (Gregor 1930, 1938; Turreson 1922). Note that the role of epistasis in the formation of coadapted gene complexes associated with ecotypic differentiation is largely untested. Under the combined influence of drift and selection, different populations may have different genetic solutions to the same selective pressures (Cohan 1984). Although populations may appear to be phenotypically similar, crosses among them may lead to a breakdown of coadapted gene complexes if there are epistatic interactions on fitness. Second, coadapted gene complexes may confer intrinsic adaptation, where genes adapt primarily to the genetic environment defined by other genes, as in cases in which populations of the same species may exhibit different chromosomal races (Templeton, Sing & Brokaw 1976; Cicmanec & Campbell 1977) or in which modifiers appear to have evolved to ameliorate the genetic load specific to a population (reviewed in Dobzhansky 1970). Coadapted gene complexes may include both cytoplasmic (maternally inherited) and nuclear genes. Cytoplasmically inherited genes are known to have large effects on plant traits (Grant 1975, Roach & Wulff 1987). Important interactions between nuclear and cytoplasmic genes have been documented, e.g. male sterility (Meagher 1988) where nuclear genes act on particular cytoplasmic sterility genes to restore pollen production (reviewed in Frank 1989). Crosses between species and subspecies often result in an increasing role for maternal inheritance compared with crosses between more related taxa (Wright 1968). Presumably, these examples demonstrate that many traits are an expression of coadapted nuclear and non-nuclear genomes.

Scale for detection of outbreeding depression

Although there is often a genetic basis for striking morphological differences among plant populations, there are often no postzygotic reproductive isolating mechanisms associated with these differences (see Clausen & Heisey 1958). Therefore, plants that are genetically and phenotypically distinct may be crossed to produce viable F1 progeny. Outbreeding depression has historically been associated with crossing events of very long distances at the level of populations, races, or subspecies (e.g. Kruckenberg 1957, Dobzhansky 1970, Sobrevila 1988).

The experiments with maize by Moll *et al.* (1965) demonstrated a classic case in which heterosis does not increase uniformly with genetic divergence. Moll *et al.* *a priori* postulated a relative rank of divergence among different maize cultivars based on probable ancestry, geographical separation, and adaptation to different environments. Crosses were performed between cultivars from four regions of North America (southeast USA, midwest USA, Puerto Rico, and Mexico). They observed an outcrossing depression in progeny performance in traits correlated with fecundity, while still detecting heterosis among all of the long-distance crosses (see Fig. 2.2 for details). It may be insufficient to examine the fitness of F1 progeny resulting from crosses between genetically divergent or geographically separated populations. Outbreeding depression due to placing genes with epistatic effects on fitness in different genetic backgrounds may occur to a greater extent in the F2 progeny (Fig. 2.2), because recombination in the F1 would lead to a greater breakdown of coadapted gene complexes. By contrasting F1 and F2 fitness, Moll *et al.* (1965) were able to examine the role of coadapted gene complexes in the success of cultivars in their native environments. In the absence of epistasis, the F2 is expected to decline in fitness or yield to half the difference between the F1 and average of the two parents (midparents, or MP), or $F2 = (F1 + MP)/2$ (Wright 1968, Falconer 1981). This is because the heterozygosity of the F2 is

F2 vs. F1 PROGENY PERFORMANCE
in Maize

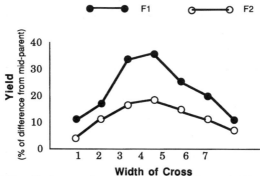

Fig. 2.2. The relationship between heterosis and width of cross in F1 (filled circles) and F2 (open circles) progeny of maize. The heterosis is expressed as the percentage of difference from the midparent. Width 1 = crosses within a region, width 2 = southeast × midwest, width 3 = southeast × Puerto Rico, width 4 = midwest × Puerto Rico, width 5 = southeast × Mexico, width 6 = midwest × Mexico, and width 7 = Puerto Rico × Mexico (from Moll *et al.* 1965).

expected to be half that of the F1, and thus the F2 would have half the expression of heterosis. Note that with F3 and later generations, heterozygosity should be maintained at half the level of the F1 if there is random mating. Deviations of the F2 from (F1 + MP)/2 will be due to additive × additive and dominant × dominant epistasis (Lynch 1991). Because the F2 were nearly intermediate between the F1 and midparents in yield, there is little evidence for a role of epistasis for fitness or coadaptation for the ecotypic differentiation observed among the maize cultivars. At all crossing distances except the lowest, the F2 were slightly higher in fitness than (F1 + MP)/2, suggesting that less-related varieties of maize harbored loci that acted favorably in combination. This is contrary to the expectation that local populations consist of coadapted gene complexes (Lynch 1991). Instead, the observed optimum in yield for the F1 and F2 at intermediate crossing distances suggest that a balance between heterosis and non-epistatic hybrid breakdown has been reached. Non-epistatic hybrid breakdown refers to the phenomenon in which alleles are selected for their individual additive effects and hybrid offspring are adapted to neither parental environment. It is important to emphasize that only by creating F2 or backcrosses can one partition the effects of dominance vs. epistatic interactions. Tight linkage among epistatically interacting loci will minimize F2 breakdown. However, a comparison of the increased amount of epistatic breakdown observed in the F3 vs. the F2 will allow a more precise estimate of the formation of coadapted gene combinations. Also note in the maize example that even with a decrease in heterosis at all widths of crosses, all of the F2 progeny were still experiencing a degree of heterosis compared with their mid-parents. *Thus, even if we have no other choice but to mix distant gene pools, heterosis may outweigh any deleterious consequences of breaking up co-adapted gene complexes.*

Unfortunately, the experimental evidence of scale-dependent heterosis and outbreeding depression carried through to the F2 generation is largely confined to organisms (such as maize) that have been the objects of artificial selection acting on additive genes. It is much more time-efficient to artificially select on genes with additive effects. Crosses between divergent lines, cultivars, or populations would not be expected to exhibit a breakdown of coadapted gene complexes if selection was not acting on interacting genes. We are more likely to observe the breakdown of coadapted gene complexes in crosses among natural populations, in which selection has had the opportunity to act on both the additive and interactive effects of genes. A greater proportional decrease in F2 progeny vigor than expected based on inbreeding depression alone was observed in laboratory populations of some *Drosophila* species (Brnic 1954, Wallace & Vetukhiv 1955). Burton (1987, 1990) observed F2 hybrid breakdown in the laboratory following crosses between populations of the marine copepod *Tigriopus californicus*, and demonstrated that hybrid breakdown is also scale-dependent. Fenster (1991b) did not detect any evidence of outbreeding depression in *Chamaecrista fasciculata* after comparing the performance of progeny generated from parental crossing distances ranging from 1 to 1000 m. There was a decelerating gain in F1 progeny fitness as the distance between the gene pools increased (Fig. 2.3A). Fenster (1988) also calculated genetic similarity among parents and found that genetic similarity was inversely related to progeny performance throughout the parental crossing distance range (Fig. 2.3B). The plateau of genetic similarity with distance corresponds to the observation that gene flow in *C. fasciculata* is limited (Fenster 1991a). In contrast, Waser & Price (1989 and earlier references cited therein) have demonstrated outbreeding depression in *Ipomopsis aggregata* on a local scale in the F1 generation. In their work, the progeny of parents separated by 10 m had a higher probability of surviving than did the progeny of parents separated by 1 and 100 m. Determining the relationship between progeny fitness and genetic similarity is important in devising management strategies for other species. For example, progeny vigor may increase up to some degree of genetic distance, reach a plateau, and then decline, as observed by Moll *et al.* (1965). If baseline studies are performed, some predictions of the consequences of crossing genetically differentiated populations can be made.

C. B. Fenster and M.R. Dudash

A: Effect of Interparent Distance on Progeny Fitness

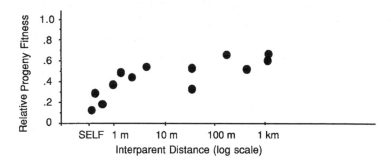

B: Relationship Between Interplant Distance and Genetic Similarity

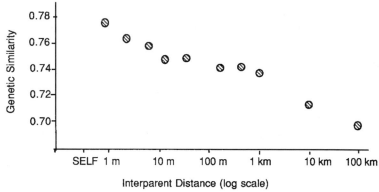

Interparent Distance (log scale)

Fig. 2.3. Relative progeny fitness (A) and genetic similarity (B) for *Chamaecrista fasciculata* calculated from isozyme analyses comparing progeny generated from a range of interparent distances, from self-pollination to interparent distances of 1 m to 100 km (from Fenster 1988, 1991).

Mating system and outbreeding depression

The amount of recombination determines the extent to which linkage disequilibrium can be formed between loci with fitness interactions (Lewontin & Kojima 1960, Lewontin 1974, Clegg 1984, Hastings 1985). With greater linkage, epistasis for fitness does not have to be as high as it does with lower linkage for the formation of epistatic gene complexes. Since inbreeding effectively reduces the level of recombination in a population (Bodmer & Parsons 1962), we expect outbreeding depression to be greatest for species with high selfing rates.

Some of the clearest evidence for epistatic selection has been documented in selfing organisms. Populations of highly selfing *Avena barbata* are monomorphic for alternative alleles at seven loci in xeric and mesic environments on a broad (Clegg, Allard & Kahler 1972) and local scale (Hamrick & Allard 1972, Allard *et al.* 1972). Quantitative characters were also differentiated between the two ecotypes (Hamrick & Allard 1972, 1973), suggesting that the two alternative gene complexes include loci on all chromosomes. Similar results have been observed by Nevo and colleagues (Nevo *et al.* 1981, 1983, 1986) for wild populations of the selfing *Hordeum spontaneum*, recognized as the progenitor of cultivated barley. In addition, composite crosses of selfing barley (from strains collected worldwide) formed adaptive four-locus interactions through time (Clegg *et al.* 1972, Weir, Allard & Kahler 1972, Allard 1975). The results of these experiments suggest that epistatic gene complexes can be formed rapidly when recombination is limited or the approach to linkage equilibrium is decreased by selfing. Thus, in contrast to the case of inbreeding depression, selfers may experience a greater degree of outbreeding depression for any given crossing distance. Little empirical work has been directed towards documenting the role of mating system in outbreeding depression. Ideally, outbreeding depression could be compared between pairs of congeners with contrasting mating systems.

Measuring outbreeding depression

To determine the consequences of mixing distant gene pools, it is necessary to cross individuals within a population and individuals from pairs of populations of increasing geographic and genetic distance. F1 progeny should have the highest heterozygosity if inbreeding is occurring within parental source populations. F2s would be generated by random crosses between the F1s to minimize inbreeding for each cross type. The performance of the progeny would be measured by growing the progeny from the crossing array in each parental source location and in novel environments. If there is adaptation of the source populations to local environmental conditions, or intrinsic adaptation, then F2 progeny may exhibit hybrid breakdown independent of heterosis observed in the F1 generation. However, novel genotypes may arise in the F2 generation that might confer equal or higher fitness gains than those of the parental source populations.

Observation of the relationship between inbreeding and vigor may allow us to examine the role of selection to modify the genetic load specific to populations. The deleterious consequences of continued inbreeding can result from three types of interaction among homozygous loci (Crow & Kimura 1970), which are described in Fig. 2.4. Loci can act either additively (linear decline of fitness with inbreeding), with reinforcing epistasis (the homozygosity of loci reduces fitness greater than the sum of their individual effects), or with diminishing epistasis (the homozygosity of loci reduces fitness less than the sum of

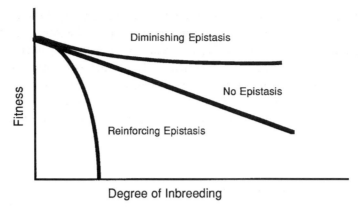

Fig. 2.4. Decline in fitness with inbreeding under no epistasis, diminishing epistasis, and reinforcing epistasis (from Crow & Kimura 1970).

their individual effects). These measures of epistasis include both dominant × dominant and additive × dominant interactions (Lynch 1991). Whether modifiers have evolved to ameliorate the genetic load has important implications for population restoration. Long-distance crosses may break up the ameliorating effects of modifiers, so that inbreeding results in a much greater loss of vigor (reinforcing epistasis) compared with inbreeding in intact populations (diminishing epistasis or linear decline).

The experimental evidence is limited, but the accumulation of non-lethal mutations in *Drosophila* stocks over time results in an accelerated decline in vigor (Mukai 1969). Deviations from linearity of fitness with degree of inbreeding were also observed in poultry (Sheridan 1980), mice and guinea pigs (Kinghorn 1982, 1987) and maize (Schnell & Becker 1986) (see also examples cited in Geiger 1988). Earlier work with maize demonstrated that yield declined linearly with degree of inbreeding (Neal 1935). Differences in the outcome of the maize experiments may have resulted from different lines tested in different environments. *Crosses between coadapted peaks may break down the modifying influence of the genetic background. Therefore, inbred lines derived from crossing widely separated parents may have a greater degree of reinforcing epistasis compared with lines derived from within natural levels of gene flow. The contributions of dominant × dominant and additive × dominant interactions to epistasis for fitness need to be quantified.*

Most examples of epistatic interactions have been restricted to quantifying non-additive interactions among nuclear loci. Like that of mitochondria, the chloroplast genome is cytoplasmically inherited and has been documented to have important interactions with the nuclear genome. Frequently, pollen and seed have different dispersal distances; e.g. Fenster (1991a), suggesting that spatial patterns of genetic variation should differ for nuclear (pollen- and seed-dispersed) and cytoplasmic (seed-dispersed) genes. Nuclear–cytoplasmic interactions may evolve on a different spatial scale than strictly nuclear inter-actions. We can examine scale-dependent nuclear–cytoplasmic interactions by comparing the relative fitness of backcross progeny that have their cytoplasmic and nuclear genome from either similar or different gene pools. Thus, the role of nuclear–cytoplasmic interactions in scale-dependent epistasis for fitness can be quantified.

A cautionary note

Hybridization, resulting in secondary contact between races or populations that have long been isolated from one another, may be quite common in the evolution-ary history of species (Anderson 1949, Stebbins 1950, Mayr 1970, Wright 1977). The exchange of genes from distant populations may occur through rare long-distance gene dispersal or, more likely, through a series of range expansions and contractions throughout the evolutionary history of a species. Gene flow between populations that differ greatly in their genetic composition may have con-sequences similar to hybridization at higher levels; e.g., introgression, breakup of character correlations, and change in the mode of inheritance of traits. Artificial mixing of distant gene pools may parallel the dynamics of gene flow during the evolutionary history of a species. Breakup of coadapted gene complexes may lead to genetic systems that confer even higher adaptation to the environment. In any event, the composition of gene pools may be part of a dynamic process of isola-tion and mixing. *Thus, preservation of the genetic integrity of a species may be an ideal with no natural basis; therefore, it should not be used,* a priori, *as an ob-stacle to the mixing of gene pools.* Nevertheless, we should not take irreversible steps in our fragile existing populations. The artificial mixing of distant gene pools should be tested during species reintroductions in which we have limited options, or tested in model systems using common species.

Genetic diversity of source populations

Genetic diversity in the source gene pool may influence the colonizing ability and prolonged persistence of a population (Polans & Allard 1989, Barrett & Kohn 1991). In outcrossing species, the mean fitness of a population may correspond to levels of genetic diversity. Thus, an alternative to mixing distant gene sources to restore population heterozygosity would be to choose only populations with high levels of genetic diversity for restoration programs.

Quattro & Vrijenhoek (1989) observed that natural populations of Topminnows containing high genetic isozyme diversity had a greater probability of survival and experienced earlier fecundity than natural populations with no detectable electrophoretic variation. Note that in selfing species isozyme diversity is often low or absent (Fenster & Ritland 1993). However, selfers may have equivalent levels of within-population quantitative genetic variation (Hillel, Feldman & Simchen 1973, Clay & Levin 1989, D. E. Carr & C. B. Fenster, unpublished data). Thus, choosing those populations of selfers that have higher than average levels of quantitative genetic variation for restoration programs may result in a lower probability of extinction.

Maintenance of the evolutionary potential of a species

Because a successful conservation policy must include the maintenance of the evolutionary potential of a species by preserving genetic diversity (e.g. Frankel & Soulé 1981, Allendorf & Leary 1986), important subsets of genetic variation within a species must be identified and preserved. Molecular markers, such as isozyme or DNA variation, may be *relatively* quick and affordable methods of identifying important subsets of genetic variation. The morphological diversity most closely associated with a species' ability to maintain its range, however, may be partitioned differently from molecular markers (Brown *et al.* 1978, Lewontin 1984). A distinction should be made between present morphological diversity among populations and the evolutionary potential of populations. Populations that are phenotypically differentiated from one another may be interchangeable if one can evolve into the other given the appropriate selective regime. However, as will be discussed below, populations with different amounts of genetic variation and patterns of covariation are not interchangeable; one cannot evolve into the other even with identical selection pressures. If different populations of a species have different sets of evolutionary constraints associated with different patterns of genetic variance and covariance, we should aim to preserve the evolutionary potential by sampling among populations. If we do not conserve the full evolutionary potential of species, we may irreversibly reduce their range.

Recent developments in molecular genetics, combined with more traditional quantitative genetic techniques, greatly increase our ability to detect different levels of genetic variation within a species. This section describes a synthetic approach that allows detection of levels of genetic variation important to the preservation and restoration of rare and endangered species. The experiments discussed involve detection of isozyme and chloroplast DNA variation within common native species, using a phylogenetic approach combined with extensive crossing programs. Results from these experiments may be used to formulate conservation and restoration policy for rare and endangered taxa.

Evolutionary lineage

Extant species represent successful evolutionary experiments. One of the roles of conservation biologists is to ensure that this unbroken genetic ancestry is preserved. Genetic differentiation at the species level is only one point in a continuum of genetic divergence beginning within the population and extending across a species. Methods are needed to detect ancestral relationships that represent subsets of genetic variation important to maintaining the evolutionary potential of a species.

One method of partitioning genetic diversity within a species is to determine independent evolutionary lineages (Avise *et al.* 1987, Templeton 1989) (Fig. 2.5). Because a lineage represents an unbroken genetic heritage, it may be the most appropriate level for conserving genetic diversity. A species is composed of many lineages, each with a unique history of selection pressures and genetic bottlenecks. The number of lineages uncovered within a species will depend largely on the methods used to detect them. For example, given a complete genetic history of a species, we could discriminate among lineages within a population using pedigree analysis. It is likely, however, that genetic variation important to conservation issues resides at or above the population level. Methods are needed to detect lineages at the level of groups of populations. The mating system will also determine the number of lineages within a species. Plants with limited recombination, such as selfers and apomicts, will exhibit a

Species Consist of Lineages

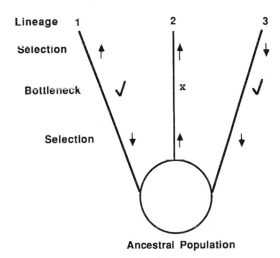

Fig. 2.5. Genetic variation can be partitioned into various lineages (different lines in the figure) that have different histories of selection (direction of selection given by arrows) and drift (presence or absence noted by check or x).

greater number of unique lineages for nuclear, biparentally inherited genes than species with higher rates of recombination. Because lineages in selfers and apomicts do not represent the free recombination found in outcrossers, the evolutionary time scale that they represent will be much smaller than it will be in outcrossers. Thus, restoration policy aimed at conserving evolutionary lineages must take into account the mating system of the target species.

Detection of evolutionary lineages

Taxonomies based on morphological data alone may not be adequate to identify subsets of genetic variation within a species (Avise 1989a). Recent surveys have demonstrated that mitochondrial DNA (mt-DNA) variation often exists within animal species (Avise & Nelson 1989). Since mt-DNA is maternally inherited, each of these maternal lineages represents its own history of past selection and genetic drift (Avise 1989b). Application of lineage analysis using mt-DNA variation to conservation biology is exemplified by the case of the dusky seaside sparrow, *Ammodramus maritimus nigrescens.* Avise (1989a) demonstrated that the endangered dusky seaside sparrow was part of a lineage that included seaside sparrows from the Atlantic coast. Conservation efforts aimed at preserving the gene pool of the dusky seaside sparrow had been directed towards crossing the endangered taxon with a different lineage from the Gulf coast. In this case, traditional taxonomies were unable to detect the important divergence of seaside sparrows between Atlantic and Gulf coastal populations, but the divergence was detected by molecular techniques.

Plant mt-DNA is too conservative in its primary sequence, and evolves too rapidly in terms of its size, to be useful for detection of major genetic differences within species (Palmer 1987, Sederoff 1987). However, restriction fragment length polymorphisms in maternally transmitted chloroplast DNA (cp-DNA) evolve slowly enough to provide resolution of genetic variation from above the population level to the species level for some species (Palmer 1987). Thus, analysis of cp-DNA variation may reveal independent and anciently derived maternal lineages within a plant species consisting of groups of populations. There have been few studies attempting to document cp-DNA variation within a plant species. When it has been studied, different lineages have often been identified (Clegg, Brown & Whitfield 1984a, Banks & Birky 1985, Soltis, Soltis & Ness 1989, Fenster & Ritland 1992, but see Clegg, Rawson & Thomas 1984b, Clegg 1987).

Fig. 2.6 shows a within-species phylogeny using cp-DNA of *Mimulus guttatus* (Fenster & Ritland 1992). Although the number of cp-DNA mutations detected is limited, they do allow us to make some inferences about the detection of different lineages. For example, it appears that populations 7 and 8 are derived from an ancestral population with a genotype similar to that of population 6, and that pop-

cp-DNA Phylogeny of <u>Mimulus guttatus</u>

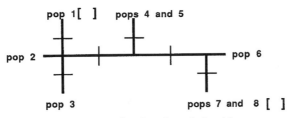

Fig. 2.6. An unrooted Wagner tree showing the relationships among populations of *Mimulus guttatus* using cp-DNA variation. Each hash mark represents a different cp-DNA mutation. For example, population 1 has diverged from populations 7 and 8 by 4 mutations. Brackets represent genetic variance–covariance matrices (from Fenster & Ritland 1992).

ulations 6, 7, and 8 are more closely related to one another than they are to population 1. The lineages detected by cp-DNA variation may identify populations with different evolutionary potentials, since each lineage represents a different history of selection and drift. Maintenance of the full evolutionary potential may depend on the preservation of the genetic diversity from each of these lineages.

Isozyme analysis is a common approach for partitioning genetic variation within a species. Isozyme variation can be used to group populations based on their genetic similarity. This is often done using dendrograms constructed from Nei's genetic distances (Nei 1972). Thus, subsets of populations that represent the range of isozyme diversity within a species can be identified. The advantages of using cp-DNA variation over isozymes are that cp-DNA is maternally inherited with limited recombination, and that it represents a gene lineage. Synapomorphies, or shared derived characters used to infer ancestral relationships, are more apparent with cp-DNA than with isozymes. Thus, it is easier to resolve intraspecific phylogenetic patterns and detect lineages using cp-DNA (Moritz & Hillis 1990). Nevertheless, there are a number of approaches for using continuous data (e.g. isozyme frequencies) in the construction of phylogenies (Felsenstein 1981, 1985a,b, Rogers 1986, Swofford & Berlocher 1987). For some taxa, cp-DNA may be too conservative to determine gene lineages (Clegg 1987). In such cases, isozyme variation may be relied upon to estimate genetic relationships among populations. In addition, because so many studies using isozyme variation have been conducted, there is fairly good agreement on taxonomic affinities based on genetic distances. Local races of species generally have genetic distances of approximately 0 to 0.05, while subspecies have genetic distances of 0.02 to 0.20 (Nei 1976). In addition, in species that are highly selfing, clonal, or apomictic, isozyme variation may be in linkage disequilibrium with important ecological variation (Allard *et al.* 1972, Hamrick &

Allard 1972, Nevo *et al.* 1986). Isozyme variation may thus be an indicator of important ecological variation in species with limited recombination.

Role of evolutionary lineages in conservation biology

Grouping populations on the basis of their cp-DNA or isozyme affinities is only the first step in determining major subsets of genetic variation. We need to know whether the subsets of genetic variation identified by cp-DNA or isozyme affinities are actually groups with different evolutionary potentials. Ideally, lineages that have unique evolutionary and ecological roles would be identified. Fortunately, animal and plant breeders have used quantitative genetic techniques with great success to predict responses to artificial selection (Falconer 1981). These same methods can be used to predict the ability of populations to respond to natural selection, thus providing a gauge of the evolutionary potential of a population.

First, consider single trait selection. The response to selection (R), or the change in the mean of a trait in a population from z to z^* , is proportional to the amount of genetic variation for that trait (Var_G) and the selection differential (S) (Falconer 1981):

$$R=\overline{z^*}\text{-}\overline{z} \propto Var_G S \qquad\qquad \text{Eq. 2.1}$$

For outcrossing populations, only the additive component of genetic variation (loci segregating alleles with additive effects) will respond to selection acting on individuals. Note that for apomicts, clonal species, and selfers, the response to selection will also depend on non-additive genetic effects, such as dominance or epistasis.

However, traits do not evolve independently. For example, there is often genetic variation for yield components in crops, but different yield components are often negatively correlated with one another (Adams 1967). Thus, breeders can select for greater seed number, but often at the cost of lower protein content per seed (Simmonds 1981). We can model multitrait selection by expanding Eq. 2.1 above to the multivariate equivalent:

$$
\begin{vmatrix} \overline{z}_1^* \\ \overline{z}_2^* \\ . \\ . \\ . \end{vmatrix}
-
\begin{vmatrix} \overline{z}_1 \\ \overline{z}_2 \\ . \\ . \\ . \end{vmatrix}
\propto
\begin{bmatrix} Var_G & & \\ & \cdot\ Cov_G & \\ & & \cdot \end{bmatrix}
\begin{vmatrix} S_1 \\ S_2 \\ . \\ . \\ . \end{vmatrix}
\qquad\qquad \text{Eq. 2.2}
$$

Thus, the change in mean of suites of characters represented by the two vectors on the left side of the equation will depend not only on the genetic variance and selection on a particular trait, but also on how these traits genetically covary (Lande & Arnold 1983). In other words, a character can evolve in response to both direct selection on a trait and indirect selection on genetically correlated traits.

The following scenario might help to clarify the importance and consequences of two populations sharing similar vs. dissimilar genetic variance–covariance matrices. Imagine two populations that have genetically differentiated from one another owing to locally divergent selection pressures. Perhaps one population is adapted to a coastal climate and the other to alpine conditions, such as observed by Clausen & Heisey (1958) in their classic studies of ecotypic differentiation along the altitudinal transect from Stanford to Timberline in California. If the two populations have identical genetic variance–covariance matrices, then, given time and similar selection pressures, the coastal population may evolve the same suite of characters that confer adaptation to the alpine environment as the alpine population and vice versa. However, if the two populations differ in their genetic variance-covariance matrices, then selection for adaptation to the alpine environment on the genotypes from the coastal population will not result in the same suite of characters. The latter scenario has two implications. First, if we preserve only one population, we will have lost a unique subset of genetic variation that defines the species. Second, we may irreversibly reduce the potential range of the species if there is no genetic variation in either population allowing for the potential to evolve adaptations to either environment.

Both theoretical and empirical studies suggest that genetic variances and covariances may be altered by either strong selection (Crow & Kimura 1970, Sheridan & Barker 1974, Falconer 1981, Istock 1983, Lofsvold 1986, Billington, Mortimer & McNeilly 1988) or drift due to founder events and inbreeding in small populations (Lande 1976, Avery & Hill 1977). Among-population variation in the genetic covariance structure implies that populations will respond differently to the same selection pressures and that each population represents an important lineage with its own potential to evolve. Consequently, it is essential to determine if the genetic variance–covariance matrix is stable across populations. Since cp-DNA lineages represent ancient divergence events within a species, it seems likely that if populations have evolved different variance–covariance matrices, these differences would occur at the level of cp-DNA lineages. Similarly, populations with greater genetic distance between them should share fewer historical processes, and should be good starting points in determining the stability of the genetic variance–covariance matrix.

There are a number of techniques for determining the genetic variance–covariance matrix using quantitative genetics, which involve the analysis of families or parent–offspring regressions (Falconer 1981). These methods are often time-consuming and impossible to accomplish for organisms with long lifespans. However, there is some empirical evidence that the phenotypic variance–covariance matrix is similar to the genetic variance–covariance matrix (Cheverud 1988, but see Willis, Coyne & Kirkpatrick 1991). This means that traits of individuals in natural populations can be measured in the field and used to estimate a population's evolutionary potential. Perhaps of greater promise is the technique derived by Ritland (1989) to estimate genetic variances and covariances for a population by using genetic markers (such as isozymes or DNA variation) to infer genetic relatedness among individuals. Once the relationships among individuals are known, one can estimate how quantitative genetic variation is partitioned among or within families, or even among full and half-sibs. These methods have added power because measurements of genetic parameters are made in the most appropriate environments, i.e. natural populations. These methods suggest that estimation of a population's evolutionary potential may be accomplished without conducting crosses.

There are at least two approaches to determining the stability of the genetic variance–covariance matrix. Returning to the within-species phylogeny of eight populations of *Mimulus guttatus* (Fig. 2.6), it might be asked to what extent the genetic architecture differs among the different lineages. To answer would require testing whether different evolutionary lineages have different genetic variance–covariance matrices and hence different evolutionary potentials. For example, does the genetic variance–covariance matrix of population 1 differ from the matrix of population 8? Knowledge of evolutionary lineages may allow determination of the consequences of mixing gene pools from within vs. between lineages. Perhaps the consequences of crosses between populations 7 and 8 would be very different from those of crosses between 1 and 7 or 1 and 8.

Another approach is to try to disrupt the genetic variance–covariance matrix. Different selection intensities to disrupt character correlations could be tested to determine the stability of the matrix in natural populations. For example, different lines could be exposed to different levels, in terms of magnitude and sign, of two-trait selection for several generations. Once the lines have diverged, the genetic correlations could be tested for any differences among the lines. In addition, the effect of bottlenecks on the stability of the matrix could be tested by taking replicate populations through a series of population reductions and comparing the genetic variances and covariances before and after the bottlenecks.

Summary

We do not propose that all of the experiments described here are necessary for the formulation of restoration policy for every species. However, we do contend that baseline data collected from a number of *model systems* would provide insight for the formulation of restoration policy. Although the use of common species is advocated, studies using rare species would also allow resource managers to make educated decisions (as in the case of Lakeside daisy; see DeMauro, Chapter 12 of this volume). The consequences of manipulating genetic variation to restore or increase the vigor of a small population must be determined. In addition, markers that delineate genetic diversity important to the maintenance of a species' evolutionary potential are needed. Chloroplast DNA and isozyme variation may serve as markers of significant evolutionary events (i.e. selection, gene flow, and drift) that might alter the evolutionary potentials of populations. It is important to note that often there is no opportunity for defining significant lineages within species. Most rare species occur in fewer than 10 populations, and the vast majority of threatened species occur in fewer than 20 populations (Holsinger & Gottlieb 1989). However, we certainly have a greater opportunity to save species before they become endangered. Identification of important lineages may be a necessary part of the blueprint for the survival of species that are now widespread, but could soon become fragmented and endangered. In the absence of such information, resource managers must rely on their knowledge of the demography and ecology of the species. The preservation of ecotypes or populations representing the extremes of the range of the species should be paramount. This is the necessary approach to making critical decisions regarding the restoration of populations and the conservation of genetic diversity until more baseline data are collected.

Acknowledgments

The authors thank Marlin Bowles, Kent Holsinger, Robert Lacy, and Stephen Weller for comments on an earlier version of the manuscript.

Literature cited

Adams, M. W. (1967) Basis of yield component compensation in crop plants with special reference to the field bean *Phaseolus vulgaris*. *Crop Science*, **7**, 505–10.

Allard, R. W. (1975) The mating system and microevolution. *Proceedings XIIIth International Congress of Genetics, Part II Genetics*, **79**, Supplement, 115–26.

Allard, R. W., Babbel, G. R., Clegg, M. T. & Kahler, A. L. (1972) Evidence for coadaptation in *Avena barbata. Proceedings of the National Academy of Sciences*, **69**, 3043–48.

Allendorf, F. W. & Leary, R. F. (1986) Heterozygosity and fitness in natural populations of animals. In *Conservation Biology: The Science of Scarcity and Diversity*, ed. M. E. Soulé. pp. 57–76. Sunderland: Sinauer Associates.

Anderson, E. (1949) *Introgressive Hybridization*. New York: John Wiley and Sons.

Avery, P. J. & Hill, W. G. (1977) Variability in genetic parameters among small populations. *Genetical Research*, **29**, 193–213.

Avise, J. C. (1989a) A role for molecular genetics in the recognition and conservation of endangered species. *Trends in Ecology and Evolution*, **4**, 279–281.

Avise, J. C. (1989b) Gene trees and organismal histories: a phylogenetic approach to population biology. *Evolution*, **43**, 1192–208.

Avise, J. C., Arnold, J., Bal, R. M., Bermingham, E., Lamb, T., Neigel, J. E., Reeb, C. A. & Saunders, N. C. (1987) Intraspecific phylogeography: The mitochondrial DNA bridge between population genetics and systematics. *Annual Review of Ecology and Systematics*, **18**, 489–522.

Avise, J. C. & Nelson, W. S. (1989) Molecular genetic relationships of the extinct dusky seaside sparrow. *Science*, **243**, 646–648.

Banks, J. A. & Birky, C. W. Jr. (1985) Chloroplast DNA diversity is low in a wild plant, *Lupinus texensis. Proceedings of the National Academy of Sciences*, **82**, 6950–6954.

Barrett, S. C. H. & Charlesworth, D. (1991) Effects of a change in the level of inbreeding on the genetic load. *Nature*, **352**, 522–524.

Barrett, S. C. H. & Kohn, J. R. (1991) Genetic and evolutionary consequences of small population size in plants: implications for conservation. In *Genetics and Conservation of Rare Plants*, ed. Falk, D. A. & Holsinger, R. E., pp. 3-30. Oxford University Press.

Billington, H. L., Mortimer, A. M. & McNeilly, T. (1988) Divergence and genetic structure in adjacent grass populations. I. Quantitative Genetics. *Evolution*, **42**, 1267–1279.

Bodmer, W. F. & Parsons, P. A. (1962) Linkage and recombination in evolution. *Advances in Genetics*, **11**, 1–100.

Brewer, B. A., Lacy, R. C., Foster, M. L. & Alaks, G. (1990) Inbreeding depression in insular and central populations of *Peromyscus* mice. *Journal of Heredity*, **81**, 257–266.

Brown, A. H. D., Nevo, E., Zohary, D. & Dagan, O. (1978) Genetic variation in natural populations of wild barley (*Hordeum spontaneum*). *Genetics*, **49**, 97–108.

Brnic, D. (1954) Heterosis and the integration of the genotype in geographic populations of *Drosophila pseudoobscura. Genetics*, **39**, 77–88.

Bryant , E. H., McCommas, S. A. & Combs, L. M. (1986) The effect of an experimental bottleneck upon quantitative genetic variation in the housefly. *Genetics*, **114**, 1191–211.

Bulmer, M. G. (1985) *The Mathematical Theory of Quantitative Genetics*. Oxford: Clarendon Press.

Burton, R. S. (1987) Differentiation and integration of the genome in populations of the marine copepod *Tigriopus californicus. Evolution*, **41**, 504–13.

Burton, R. S. (1990) Hybrid breakdown in developmental time in the copepod *Tigriopus californicus. Evolution*, **44**, 1814–22.

Charlesworth, D. & Charlesworth, B. (1979) The evolutionary genetics of sexual systems on flowering plants. *Proceedings of the Royal Society of London*, B 205, 513–30.

Charlesworth, D. & Charlesworth, B. (1987) Inbreeding depression and its evolutionary consequences. *Annual Review of Ecology and Systematics*, **18**, 237–68.

Charlesworth, D. & Charlesworth, B. (1990) Inbreeding depression with heterozygote advantage and its effect on selection for modifiers changing the outcrossing rate. *Evolution*, **44**, 870–88.

Charlesworth, D., Morgan, M. T. & Charlesworth, B. (1990) Inbreeding depression, genetic load, and the evolution of outcrossing rates in a multilocus system with no linkage. *Evolution*, **44**, 1469–89.

Cheverud, J. M. (1988) A comparison of genetic and phenotypic correlations. *Evolution*, **42**, 958–68.

Cicmanec, J. C. & Campbell, A. K. (1977) Breeding the owl monkey (*Aotus trivirgatus*) in a laboratory environment. *Laboratory Animal Sciences*, **27**, 517.

Clausen, J. & Heisey, W. (1958) Experimental studies on the nature of species. IV. Genetic structure of ecological races. *Carnegia Institute of Washington Publications*, **615**, 1–312.

Clay, K. & Levin, D. A. (1989) Quantitative variation in *Phlox*: comparison of selfing and outcrossing species. *American Journal of Botany*, **76**, 577–88.

Clegg, M. T. (1984) Dynamics of multilocus genetic systems. In *Oxford Surveys in Evolutionary Biology, 1*, ed. Dawkins, R. & Ridley, M., pp.160–83. Oxford University Press.

Clegg, M. T. (1987) Preface, plant molecular evolution. *American Naturalist*, **130**, 51–5.

Clegg, M. T., Allard, R. W. & Kahler, A. L. (1972) Is the gene the unit of selection? Evidence from two experimental populations. *Proceedings of the National Academy of Sciences*, **69**, 2474–78.

Clegg, M. T., Brown, A. H. D. & Whitfield, P. R. (1984a) Chloroplast DNA diversity in wild and cultivated barley: Implications for genetic conservation. *Genetical Research*, **43**, 339–43.

Clegg, M. T., Rawson, J. R. Y. & Thomas, K. (1984b) Chloroplast DNA variation in pearl millet and related species. *Genetics*, **106**, 449–61.

Cohan, F. M. (1984) Can uniform selection retard random genetic divergence between isolated conspecific populations? *Evolution*, **38**, 495–504.

Cohn, J. P. (1990) Genetics for wildlife conservation. *BioScience*, **40**, 167–71.

Comstock, R. E. & Robinson, H. F. (1948) The components of genetic variation in populations of biparental progenies and their use in estimating the average degree of dominance. *Biometrics*, **4**, 254–66.

Crow, J. F. & Kimura, M. (1970) *An Introduction to Population Genetics*. New York: Harper and Row.

Dobzhansky, T. (1970) *Genetics of the Evolutionary Process*. New York: Columbia University Press.

Dudash, M. R. (1990) Relative fitness of selfed and outcrossed progeny in a self–compatible, protandrous species, *Sabatia angularis* L. (Gentianaceae): A comparison in three environments. *Evolution*, **44**, 1129–39.

Falconer, D. S. (1981) *Introduction to Quantitative Genetics*. New York: Longman.

Felsenstein, J. (1981) Evolutionary trees from gene frequencies and quantitative characters: Finding maximum likelihood estimates. *Evolution*, **35**, 1229–42.

Felsenstein, J. (1985a) Confidence limits on phylogenies. An approach using the bootstrap. *Evolution*, **39**, 783–91.

Felsenstein, J. (1985b) Phylogenies from gene frequencies: A statistical problem. *Systematic Zoology*, **34**, 300–11.

Fenster, C. B. (1988) Gene flow and population differentiation in *Chamaecrista fasciculata* (Leguminosae). Ph.D. dissertation, Chicago: University of Chicago.

Fenster, C. B. (1991a) Gene flow in *Chamaecrista fasciculata* (Leguminosae) I. Gene dispersal. *Evolution*, **45**, 398–409.

Fenster, C. B. (1991b) Gene flow in *Chamaecrista fasciculata* II. Gene establishment. *Evolution*, **45**, 410–22.

Fenster, C. B. & Ritland, K. (1992) Chloroplast DNA and isozyme diversity in two *Mimulus* species (Scrophulariaceae) with contrasting mating systems. *American Journal of Botany*, **79**, 1440–7.

Frank, S. A. (1989) The evolutionary dynamics of cytoplasmic male sterility. *American Naturalist*, **133**, 345–76.

Frankel, O. H. & Soulé, M. E. (1981) *Conservation and Evolution*. Cambridge University Press.

Fryxell, P. A. (1957) Mode of reproduction of higher plants. *Botanical Review*, **23**, 135–233.

Gardner, C. O. (1962) Estimates of genetic parameters in cross-fertilizing plants and their implications in plant breeding. In *Statistical Genetics and Plant Breeding*. ed. Hanson, W. D. & Robinson, H. F., pp. 225-52. National Academy of Sciences National Research Council Publication 982. Washington, D.C.

Geiger, H. H. (1988) Epistasis and heterosis. In *Proceedings of the Second International Conference on Quantitative Genetics*, ed. Weir, B. S., Eisen, E. J., Goodman, M. M. & Namkoong, G., pp. 395-9. Sunderland: Sinauer Associates.

Gilpin, M. E. & Soulé, M. E. (1986) Minimum viable populations: processes of species extinction. In *Conservation Biology: The Science of Scarcity and Diversity,* ed. Soule, M., pp. 19–34. Sunderland: Sinauer Associates.

Grant, V. (1975) *Genetics of Flowering Plants*. New York: Columbia University Press.

Gregor, J. W. (1930) Experiments on the genetics of wild populations. I. *Plantago maritima. Journal of Genetics*, **22**, 15–25.

Gregor, J. W. (1938) Experimental taxonomy 2. Initial population differentiation in *Plantago maritima* in Britain. *New Phytologist*, **37**, 15–49.

Griffing, B. (1989) Genetic analysis of plant mixtures. *Genetics*, **122**, 943–56.

Hallauer, A. R. & Miranda, J. B., Fo. (1985) *Quantitative Genetics in Maize Breeding*. Ames: Iowa State University Press.

Hamrick, J. L. & Allard, R. W. (1972) Microgeographical variation in allozyme frequencies in *Avena barbata*. *Proceedings of the National Academy of Sciences*, **69**, 2100–4.

Hamrick, J. L. & Allard, R. W. (1973) Correlations between quantitative characters and allozyme genotypes in *Avena barbata*. *Evolution*, **29**, 438–42.

Hastings, A. (1985) Multilocus population genetics with weak epistasis. I. Equilibrium properties of two-locus two allele models. *Genetics*, **109**, 799–812.

Hillel, J., Feldman, M. W. & Simchen, G. (1973) Mating systems and population structure in two closely related species of the wheat group I. Variation between and within populations. *Heredity*, **30**, 141–67.

Holsinger, K.E. (1988) Inbreeding depression doesn't matter: The genetic basis of mating system evolution. *Evolution*, **42**, 1235–44.

Holsinger, K. E. & Gottlieb, L. D. (1989) The conservation of rare and endangered plants. *Trends in Ecology and Evolution*, **4**, 193–4.

Holtsford, T.P. & Ellstrand, N.C. (1990) Inbreeding effects in *Clarkia embloriensis* (Onagraceae) populations with different outcrossing rates. *Evolution*, **44**, 2031–46.

Istock, C. A. (1983) The extent and consequences of heritable variation for fitness characters. In *Population Biology Retrospective and Prospect*, ed. King, C. E. & Dawson, P. S., pp. 61–9. New York: Columbia University Press.

Jain, S. K. (1976) The evolution of inbreeding in plants. *Annual Review of Ecology and Systematics*, **7**, 469–95.

Kinghorn, B. (1982) Genetic effects in crossbreeding. III. Epistatic loss in crossbred mice *Zeitschrift für Tierzuchtung und Zuchtungsbiologie*, **100**, 209–22.

Kinghorn, B. (1987) The nature of two-locus epistatic interactions in animals: evidence from Sewall Wright's guinea pig data. *Theoretical and Applied Genetics*, **73**, 595–604.

Kohn, J. R. (1988) Why be female? *Nature*, **355**, 431–33.

Kruckenberg, A. R. (1957) Variation in fertility of hybrids between isolated populations of the serpentine species *Steptanthus glandulosus*. *Evolution*, **11**, 185–211.

Lacy, R. C. (1987) Loss of genetic diversity from managed populations: Interacting effects of drift, mutation, immigration, selection and population subdivision. *Conservation Biology*, **1**, 143–58.

Lande, R. (1976) The maintenance of genetic variability by mutation in polygenic characters with linked loci. *Genetical Research*, **26**, 221–35.

Lande, R. (1988) Genetics, and demography in biological conservation. *Science*, **241**, 1455–60.

Lande, R. & Arnold, S. J. (1983) The measurement of selection on correlated characters *Evolution*, **37**, 1210–26.

Lande, R. & Schemske, D. W. (1985) The evolution of self-fertilization and inbreeding depression in plants. I. Genetic models. *Evolution*, **39**, 24–40.

Ledig, F. T. (1986) Heterozygosity, heterosis, and fitness in outbreeding plants. In *Conservation Biology, The Science of Scarcity and Diversity,* ed. Soulé, M. E., pp. 77–104. Sunderland: Sinauer Associates.

Levin, D. A. (1981) Dispersal versus gene flow in plants. *Annals of the Missouri Botanical Garden*, **68**, 233–53.

Levin, D. A. (1989) Inbreeding depression in self-fertilizing *Phlox*. *Evolution*, **43**, 1417–23.

Lewontin, R. C. (1974) *Genetic Basis of Evolutionary Change*. New York: Columbia University Press.

Lewontin, R. C. (1984) Detecting population differences in quantitative characters as opposed to gene frequencies. *American Naturalist*, **123**, 115–24.

Lewontin, R. C. & Kojima, K. (1960) The evolutionary dynamics of complex polymorphisms. *Evolution*, **14**, 458–76.

Lofsvold, D. (1986) Quantitative genetics of morphological differentiation in *Peromyscus*. I. Tests of homogeneity of genetic covariance structure among species and subspecies. *Evolution*, **40**, 559–73.

Loveless, M. D. & Hamrick, J. L. (1984) Ecological determinants of genetic structure in plant populations. *Annual Review of Ecology and Systematics*, **15**, 65–95.

Lynch, M. (1991) The genetic interpretation of inbreeding depression and outbreeding depression. *Evolution*, **45**, 622–9.

Marcot, B. G. & Holthausen, R. (1987) Analyzing population viability of the spotted owl in the Pacific Northwest. *Transactions of the North American Wildlife Nature Reserves Conference*, **53**, 333–47.

Mayr, E. (1970) *Populations, Species and Evolution*. Cambridge: Harvard University Press.

Meagher, T. R. (1988) Sex determination in plants. In *Plant Reproductive Ecology, Patterns and Strategies*, ed. Lovett Doust, J. & Lovett Doust, L., pp. 125–38. New York: Oxford University Press.

Mitchell-Olds, T. & Waller, D. M. (1985) Relative performance of selfed and outcrossed progeny in *Impatiens capensis*. *Evolution*, **39**, 533–44.

Moll, R. H., Lindsey, M. F. & Robinson, H. F. (1964) Estimates of genetic variances and level of dominance in maize. *Genetics*, **49**, 411–23.

Moll, R. H., Lonnquist, J. H., Velez Fortuno, J. & Johnson, E. C. (1965) The relationship of heterosis and genetic divergence in maize. *Genetics*, **52**, 139–44.

Moritz, C. & Hillis, D. M. (1990) Molecular Systematics: context and controversy. In *Molecular Systematics,* ed. Hillis, D. M. & Moritz, C., pp. 1–10. Sunderland: Sinauer Associates.

Mukai, T. S. (1969) The genetic structure of natural populations of *Drosophila melanogaster.* VII. Synergistic interaction of spontaneous mutant polygenes controlling viability. *Genetics*, **61**, 749–61.

Neal, N. P. (1935) The decrease in yielding capacity in advanced generations of hybrid corn. *Journal of the American Society of Agronomy*, **27**, 666–70.

Nei, M. (1972) Genetic distance between populations. *American Naturalist*, **106**, 283–92.

Nei, M. (1976) Mathematical models of speciation and genetic distance. In *Population Genetics and Ecology*, ed. Karlin, S. & Nevo, E., pp. 723–65. New York: Academic Press.

Nevo, E., Brown, A. H. D., Zohary, D., Storch, N. & Beiles, A. (1981) Microgeographic edaphic differentiation in allozyme polymorphisms of wild barley (*Hordeum spontaneum*, Poaceae). *Plant Systematics and Evolution*, **138**, 287–92.

Nevo, E., Beiles, A., Storch, N., Doll, H. & Andersen, B. (1983) Microgeographic edaphic differentiation in hordein polymorphisms of wild barley. *Theoretical and Applied Genetics*, **64**, 123–32.

Nevo, E., Avigdor, B, Kaplin, D., Goldenberg, E. N., Olsvig-Whittaker, L. & Navea, Z. (1986) Natural selection of allozyme polymorphisms: A microsite test revealing ecological genetic differentiation in wild barley. *Evolution*, **40**, 13–20.

Palmer, J. D. (1987) Chloroplast DNA evolution and biosystematic uses of chloroplast DNA variation. *American Naturalist*, **130**, Supplement, S6–29.

Polans, N. O. & Allard, R. W. (1989) An experimental evaluation of the recovery potential of rye grass populations from genetic stress resulting from restriction of population size. *Evolution*, **43**, 1320–4.

Quattro, J. M. & Vrijenhoek, R. C. (1989) Fitness differences among remnant populations of the endangered Sonoran Topminnow. *Science*, 245, 976–8.

Riggs, L. A. (1990) Conserving genetic resources on-site in forest ecosystems. *Forest Ecology and Management*, **35**, 45–68.

Ritland, K. R. (1989) Gene identity and the genetic demography of plant populations. In *Population Genetics, Plant Breeding and Gene Conservation*, ed. Brown, A. H. D., Clegg, M. T., Kahler, A., & Weir, B. S., pp. 181–99. Sunderland: Sinauer Associates.

Ritland, K. R. (1990) Inferences about inbreeding depression based on changes of the inbreeding coefficient. *Evolution*, **44**, 1230–41.

Ritland, K. & Ganders, F. R. (1987) Crossability in *Mimulus guttatus* in relation to components of gene fixation. *Evolution*, **41**, 772–86.

Roach, D. A. & Wulff, R. D. (1987) Maternal effects in plants. *Annual Review of Ecology and Systematics*, **18**, 209–36.

Robinson, H. F., Comstock, R. E. & Harvey, P. H. (1949) Estimates of heritability and the degree of dominance in corn. *Agronomy Journal*, **41**, 353–9.

Rogers, J. S. (1986) Deriving phylogenetic trees from allele frequencies: a comparison of nine genetic distances. *Systematic Zoology*, **35**, 297–310.

Sakai, A. K., Karoly, K. & Weller, S. G. (1989) Inbreeding depression in *Schiedea globosa* and *S. salicaria* (Carophyllaceae), subdioecious and gynodioecious Hawaiian species. *American Journal of Botany*, **76**, 437–44.

Schemske, D. W. (1983) Breeding system and habitat effects on fitness components in three neotropical *Costus* (Zingiberaceae). *Evolution*, **37**, 523–39.

Schnell, F. W. & Becker, H. C. (1986) Yield and yield stability in a balanced system of wildly differing populations structures in *Zea mays* L. *Plant Breeding*, **97**, 30–8.

Schoen, D. J. (1983) Relative fitnesses of selfed and outcrossed progeny in *Gilia achilleifolia* (Polemoniaceae). *Evolution*, **37**, 292–301.

Sederoff, R. R. (1987) Molecular mechanisms of mitochondrial genome evolution in higher plants. *American Naturalist*, **130**, Supplement, S30–45.

Sheridan, A. K. (1980) A new explanation for egg production heterosis in crosses between White Leghorns and Australorps. *British Poultry Science*, **21**, 85–8.

Sheridan, A. K. & Barker, J. S. F. (1974) Two-trait selection and the genetic correlation. II. Changes in the genetic correlation during two-trait selection. *Australian Journal of Biological Sciences*, **27**, 89–101.

Simmonds, N. W. (1981) *Principles of Crop Improvement*. London: Longman Press.

Sobrevila, C. (1988) Effects of distance between pollen donor and pollen recipient on fitness components of *Espeletia schultzii*. *American Journal of Botany*, **75**, 701–24.

Soltis, D. E., Soltis, P. S. & Ness, B. D. (1989) Chloroplast-DNA variation and multiple origins of autoploidy in *Heuchera micrantha* (Saxifragaceae). *Evolution*, **43**, 650–6.

Stebbins, G. L. (1950) *Variation and Evolution in Plants*. New York: Columbia University Press.

Stebbins, G. L. (1977) *Processes of Organic Evolution*. 3rd edn. Englewood Cliffs, New Jersey: Prentice-Hall.

Svensson, L. (1988) Inbreeding, crossing and variation in stamen number in *Scleranthus annuus* (Caryophyllaceae), a selfing annual. *Evolutionary Trends in Plants*, **2**, 31–7.

Swofford, D. L. & Berlocher, S. H. (1987) Inferring evolutionary trees from gene frequency data under the principle of maximum parsimony. *Systematic Zoology*, **36**, 293–325.

Templeton, A. R. (1986) Coadaptation and outbreeding depression. In *Conservation Biology, The Science of Scarcity and Diversity,* ed. Soulé, M. E., pp. 105–16. Sunderland: Sinauer Associates.

Templeton, A. R. (1989) The meaning of species and speciation: a genetic perspective. In *Speciation and its Consequences*, ed. Otte, D. & Endler, J. A., pp. 3–27. Sunderland: Sinauer Associates.

Templeton, A. R. & Read, B. (1984) Factors eliminating inbreeding depression in a captive herd of Speke's gazelle (*Gazella spekei*). *Zoo Biology*, **3**, 177–99.

Templeton, A. R., Sing, C. F. & Brokaw, B. (1976) The unit of selection in *Drosophila mescatorum*. I. The interaction of selection and meiosis in parthenogenetic strains. *Genetics*, **82**, 349–76.

Turreson, G. (1922) The species and the variety as ecological units. *Hereditas*, **3**, 100–13.

Wallace, B. & Vetukhiv, M. (1955) Adaptive organization of the gene pools of *Drosophila* populations. *Cold Spring Harbor Symposium on Quantitative Biology,* **20**, 303–9.

Waller, D. M. (1984) Differences in fitness between seedlings derived from cleistogamous and chasmogamous flowers in *Impatiens capensis*. *Evolution*, **38**, 427–40.

Waser, N. M. & Price, M. V. (1989) Optimal outcrossing in *Ipomopsis aggregata*: Seed set and offspring fitness. *Evolution*, **43**, 1097–109.

Weir, B. S., Allard, R. W. & Kahler, A. L. (1972) Analysis of complex polymorphisms in a Barley population. *Genetics*, **72**, 505–23.

Willis, J. H., Coyne, J. A. & Kirkpatrick, M. (1991) Can one predict the evolution of quantitative characters without genetics? *Evolution*, **45**, 441–43.

Wright, S. (1968) *Evolution and the Genetics of Populations*. Volume I. *Genetic Biometric Foundations*. Chicago: The University of Chicago Press.

Wright, S. (1969) *Evolution and the Genetics of Populations*. Volume 2. *The Theory of Gene Frequencies*. Chicago: The University of Chicago Press.

Wright, S. (1977) *Evolution and Genetics of Populations*. Volume 3. *Experimental Results and Evolutionary Deductions*. Chicago: The University of Chicago Press.

3

Managing genetic diversity in captive populations of animals

ROBERT C. LACY

Introduction

The best opportunity for endangered species recovery exists when there are still populations throughout the original range, even if the populations are small and widely separated. As long as organisms persist in natural, though perhaps highly degraded or modified, habitats, recovery can be achieved by habitat improvement, reduction in causes of mortality, and other management actions that allow existing populations to expand. The second best opportunity for endangered species recovery exists when the species has been eliminated over portions of its range, but still survives in healthy populations in other portions of its range. In such cases, organisms can be translocated to vacant habitats, after the original causes of decline and local extinction have been ameliorated.

Often, however, action for endangered species recovery is delayed beyond the point when *in situ* management or even translocation among natural areas is possible. Remnant wild populations, if they exist at all, may not be self-sustaining, and it may be impossible to reverse their decline before the projected date of extinction. For example, black-footed ferrets (*Mustela nigripes*) were thought to be extinct until a single population of about 30–50 adults was discovered near Meeteetse, Wyoming, in 1981 (see Clark 1989, and Chapter 11). That population crashed in 1985 and 1986, when a plague epidemic decimated the prairie dog colony that was the primary food base for the ferrets, and then an epidemic of distemper decimated the ferrets themselves. Analyses of the rate of loss of ferrets indicated that the species would soon be extinct unless animals could be rescued from the Meeteetse area (Seal *et al.* 1989).

Similarly, the Florida panther (*Felis concolor coryi*), the last remaining subspecies of puma in the eastern United States, exists only as a fragmented population of 30–50 cats in southern Florida. Extensive field research by state and federal wildlife agencies has demonstrated that mortality is not compensated

63

fully by births. The Florida panthers are subject to a number of risks, including road kills, poisoning by mercury acquired from a contaminated environment through the food chain, poor or no reproduction by some animals perhaps partly due to inadequate prey, and severe inbreeding. Although ameliorating actions are being taken, the population continues to decline and habitat continues to be converted to agricultural uses. Analysis has shown that the population has little chance of persisting in its present habitat, and the wild population cannot provide the surplus animals needed to establish a translocated population elsewhere (Seal & Lacy 1989).

In these two cases, and tragically in others (e.g. California condors and red wolves), the last chance for recovery lies in the capture of some or all of the remnant population, propagation of that captive population, and release back into natural habitats. In some cases (e.g. beach mice [*Peromyscus polionotus trissyllepsis*], Holler *et al.* 1989; Bali myna [*Leucospar rothschildi*]; Arabian oryx [*Oryx leucoryx*], Stanley-Price 1989; and *Partula* snails, IUCN 1987), captive populations were established before the wild populations entered terminal decline, and captive propagation for eventual reintroduction requires no further removal of animals from the wild.

Captive propagation and reintroduction is not the ideal means of achieving recovery of endangered species. Compared with maintenance of adequate natural habitats, captive propagation is an inefficient use of scarce resources for conservation because it is extremely expensive (Conway 1986). Moreover, the prognosis for reintroduction is often poor. While in captivity, stocks undergo genetic, behavioral, and physiological changes, and released animals may not be capable of readapting to natural environments. Golden lion tamarins (*Leontopithecus rosalia rosalia*) released in Brazil initially had little ability to locomote quickly through the rain forest, were confused by novel foods, and were unwary of predators. Fortunately, preconditioning, training, and some harsh experience in the Brazilian forest have resulted in the integration of released tamarins into natural populations (Kleiman *et al.* 1986). Siberian ferrets (*Mustela eversmanni*) were given trial releases as surrogates for closely related black-footed ferrets, and all were rapidly lost to predators in spite of prior aversive conditioning (Biggins *et al.* 1990).

The changes that can doom future recovery often occur before captive propagation begins. It is likely that Florida panthers are already so inbred, with little or no opportunity for outbreeding in the tiny population, that a pure strain of Florida panther (as opposed to a hybrid crossed with other subspecies) could never have adequate fecundity to thrive in the wild. All male Florida panthers are cryptorchid (having just one or no descended testicle) and have extremely poor sperm quality and quantity (Seal & Lacy 1989, Miller *et al.* 1990), evidence that inbreeding, as a consequence of population decline, might doom recovery efforts. Interestingly, recent genetic evidence suggests that some of the 'Florida panthers' are hybrids that resulted from a release of a different subspecies into the Everglades National Park (O'Brien *et al.* 1990); perhaps that infusion of genetic variation has helped the population to persist as long as it has.

Regardless of the serious problems that can impede captive propagation schemes for conservation, at times these intensive and drastic efforts are the only rational hope for recovery, and they can be successful. Captive populations are safeguarded from many sources of natural mortality (e.g. predation, severe weather, many diseases and parasites, food shortages), thereby allowing rapid population growth. The same nurturing and protection that results in behavioral, physiological, and some genetic changes in captivity can also produce the large numbers of animals needed for successful reestablishment of natural populations.

In this chapter, I will focus on management techniques for minimizing the genetic changes that can occur through generations of captive breeding and could make eventual restoration into the wild more difficult or impossible. Parallel considerations about behavior, reproduction, nutrition, and other aspects of biology are equally necessary for a successful program to breed animals for restoration.

Genetic consequences of captive propagation

Genetic changes that occur in a captive population fall into two general classes, both of which can be problematic for restoration. First, selection will eliminate alleles that are maladaptive in the captive environment, and second, random genetic drift will cause the cumulative loss of both adaptive and maladaptive alleles. Both selection and drift are sampling processes; one is biased sampling, one is random. The fundamental problem in maintaining genetic variation in a captive population is that each generation is a sample of the previous generation. Through generations of captive propagation, we invariably alter the gene pool of the population that we hope to restore to its native environment.

Selection for adaptations to captivity can be strong. A common cause of mortality of captive antelopes is the trauma that occurs when a startled animal runs into a fence. Antelopes respond to sudden noises by turning away from the noise, running a distance, and then stopping and turning to identify the cause of the noise. Such behavior is adaptive on the plains, where predation by large felids and canids is common. In a zoo, where sudden noises and movements by visitors are common, a startled antelope can break its neck on a fence.

A deaf antelope, or one that ignores sudden movements and noises, is much better adapted to life in a zoo than would be an alert antelope. The benevolence of the captive environment itself has deleterious consequences, because it can disrupt adaptations that evolved over millennia in less benign natural habitats. The genetic changes that facilitate breeding success in captivity are likely to inhibit success if and when the population is returned to the wild.

Genetic drift, random fluctuations in allele frequencies, can rapidly change the genetic composition of small, captive populations. Rare alleles that might confer important adaptations in some natural environments are likely to be lost by genetic drift in small populations (Nei, Maruyama & Chakraborty 1975, Allendorf 1986, Maruyama & Fuerst 1985, Fuerst & Maruyama 1986). The converse can also occur, with deleterious alleles increasing to high frequency by chance. A translocation of the Y chromosome onto an autosome has been found in one of the six male golden-headed lion tamarins (*Leontopithecus rosalia chrysomelas*) imported to the USA that have living descendants (M. Foster, personal communication). That male was prolific, siring 10 of the 52 viable births (as of late 1989) of that endangered taxon in the country (Mace & Mallinson 1989). The translocation may have been passed on to all of the offspring, as all were male. Thus, this genetic abnormality, which was likely present at low frequency in the ancestral wild population, is now present in a substantial proportion of the captive population, and the population sex ratio is skewed towards males.

To preserve genetically those animals which we hope someday to restore to the wild, captive management must minimize both adaptive and non-adaptive genetic changes. Primarily during the past decade, biologists have been developing techniques and strategies for keeping evolution in captivity to a minimum (e.g. Denniston 1977, Flesness 1977, Foose 1983, Ralls & Ballou 1983, Foose *et al.* 1986, Frankham *et al.* 1986, Fuerst & Maruyama 1986, MacCluer *et al.* 1986, Mace 1986, Thompson 1986, Lacy 1987, 1988a, Foose & Ballou 1988, Geyer & Thompson 1988, Lacy 1989, Geyer, Thompson & Ryder 1989, Thomas 1990, Ballou & Foose 1994). Although proposed techniques and prescriptions cover a range of considerations, there is some consensus on what constitutes good and bad management.

Franklin (1980) suggested that for endangered species management, whether in captivity or in the wild, a short-term minimum effective population size should be kept above 50 to avoid the immediate deleterious effects of inbreeding. For long-term management, he suggested keeping the effective population size above 500, to allow new mutations to restore heterozygosity and additive genetic variance as rapidly as it is lost by random drift. The concept of the effective size of a population was originally introduced by Wright

(1931) as the number of individuals at which, if there were completely random union of gametes, the population would lose heterozygosity at the rate observed under actual mating conditions. Loss of heterozygosity is just one consequence of genetic drift, and the concept of effective size has also been expanded to mean the number of individuals at which a genetically ideal population (one with random union of gametes) would drift at the rate of the observed population; the rate of genetic drift could then be measured as the sampling variance of gene frequencies from parental to offspring generations (the 'variance effective number'), instead of the rate of change of heterozygosity or inbreeding (the 'inbreeding effective number'). In a population of constant size, the various concepts of effective size will be the same, but in a population that is changing in size, the manifestations of genetic drift (increasing inbreeding coefficient, loss of heterozygosity, variance in allele frequencies) can occur at somewhat different times, and the various measures of effective size can have different values (Wright 1969, Crow & Kimura 1970). Both the inbreeding and the variance effective size will be depressed relative to the census number if there is an unequal sex ratio, non-random production of offspring, or fluctuations in numbers across generations. Because the effective population size will usually be much smaller than the mean census size, Franklin's 50/500 rule must generally be multiplied severalfold to obtain the minimum population for management (Lande & Barrowclough 1987).

In the management of captive populations for eventual release into the wild, the goal is not so much to maintain a balance between genetic losses and new mutation during the course of evolutionary change, but rather to minimize all evolutionary change, whether due to random drift or to selection of adaptations to captivity (Lacy 1987). Thus, genetic management of captive populations has generally focused on retention of initial genetic variation, more than on long-term balance between evolutionary forces. Soulé *et al.* (1986) proposed a goal for captive breeding of the retention of at least 90% of the genetic variation in the source (wild) population for 200 years. The duration was chosen in the hope that the human population trend and values toward wildlife and wilderness would change within the next two centuries. This proposal has been widely adopted by Species Survival Plans of the American Association of Zoological Parks and Aquariums, although often with a shorter time frame, reflecting more optimistic visions for the restoration of some species and for the availability of cryogenic methods for preserving gene diversity.

The concept of 'genetic variation' encompasses several levels of variation (e.g. genetically determined variation in morphology or behavior, variation in chromosomal structure, or molecular variation in genes or in their direct products, proteins) and several often related measures at each level (e.g. additive, dominance, and epistatic variation in metric traits, polymorphism, allelic diversity, and heterozygosity of genes). The phenotype of an organism determines its properties and fitness, and selection acts on phenotypes; thus quantitative genetic variation in phenotypes would seem to be the level of variation of most interest to genetic management for conservation. Yet the underlying bases for quantitative variation are complex, diverse, and difficult to uncover (Falconer 1981). In contrast with the science of animal breeding, which relies heavily on quantitative genetic methodologies, relatively little attention has been paid to quantitative genetic variation in the design of management plans for conservation (but see Lande, 1994). Most attention has focused on theoretical models, empirical measures, and prescriptions related to the management of the underlying molecular genetic variation. In that respect, variation can be partitioned into two fundamental classes: the presence of multiple genetic variants within a population (polymorphism of loci, or numbers of alleles per locus); and the mean or expected diversity per individual, which depends upon both the presence of variants and the frequencies, especially the evenness, of those variants in the population (measured as heterozygosity, inbreeding, or effective number of alleles).

Heterozygosity can refer to two related concepts, one measuring diversity within individuals, the other measuring populational diversity. The proportion of loci for which the average individual is heterozygous is commonly termed 'observed heterozygosity'. The probability that two homologous genes randomly drawn from a population are distinct alleles is termed the 'expected heterozygosity' or 'gene diversity' (Nei 1973), and is the mean heterozygosity that would exist if the population were in Hardy–Weinberg equilibrium. Over relatively short time scales, the fitness of individuals in a population is often related to observed heterozygosity (Mitton & Grant 1984, Allendorf & Leary 1986), and the rate at which a population responds to selection is proportional to additive genetic variance (Fisher 1958) and related to expected heterozygosity. The 90% guideline suggested by Soulé *et al.* (1986) referred to expected heterozygosity, and most management programs have used expected heterozygosity as the index of genetic variability. The possibility for a population to adapt at all, however, depends ultimately on the presence of sufficient variants (Robertson 1960, James 1971), so allelic diversity may be critical to long-term persistence (Selander 1983).

Phases of captive propagation

Demographically, the history of a captive population can be divided into three phases. Initially, the stock is founded with wild-caught animals; next, the population grows from these founders to the maximum size that can be supported with the resources allocated to the taxon, and finally, the population is maintained at this captive equivalent of an ecological carrying capacity (Lacy 1989). Animals to be reintroduced to the wild can be produced after the captive carrying capacity has been reached. These three phases of captive propagation present somewhat different genetic problems and opportunities; thus, they also require different management strategies.

If a goal for maintaining variation, such as the 90% for 200 years goal, is chosen, then the number of animals needed to achieve this goal is determined by the compounded genetic losses that occur in the three phases (Soulé *et al.* 1986). To a minor extent, a lack of management possibilities or lack of success at one phase can be compensated for by more aggressive management during another phase. However, severe genetic losses during earlier phases, particularly losses of alleles, are irreversible in later phases, and may make the conservation objectives unattainable.

Founder phase

At the founding of a captive population, the goal is to acquire as good a representation of the wild population as possible. Ideally, the gene pool of the captive population would match that of the ancestral wild population, with the same alleles, at the same frequencies, and in the same linkage combinations. Often, as with California condors, Florida panthers, and black-footed ferrets, the wild population will have declined to very few animals and therefore will already have lost considerable genetic variation (Lacy & Clark 1989). For this reason, and because founder stock cannot be obtained without damaging a very small remnant wild population, the International Union for Conservation of Nature and Natural Resources–The World Conservation Union recommended that programs of captive propagation for conservation should begin when a taxon still numbers in the thousands in the wild (IUCN 1988). Animals chosen as founders should be as close as possible to a random genetic sample of the wild population. Often, however, founders are taken from a narrow part of range, with a strong likelihood that the founders include close relatives, and the captive population can at best contain genetic variation representative of one local, and perhaps locally adapted, subpopulation. A random sampling of the genetic diversity present in a wild population may not be as simple as randomly sampling individuals from across a species' range. Detailed knowledge of the structure of genetic variation in the wild would be needed to determine a collection scheme that would adequately sample that genetic variation.

Even if the founder genes are randomly drawn from the species' gene pool,

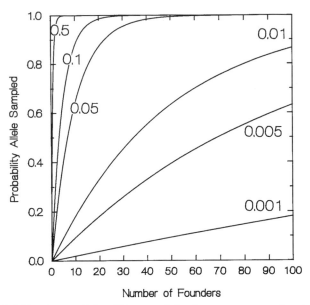

Fig 3.1. Probability that an allele will be sampled at least once among founders drawn at random, for alleles of various frequencies (0.001, 0005, 0.01, 0.05, 0.1, and 0.5) in the wild (source) population.

obtaining founders is still a sampling process that will omit some of the genetic variation present in the wild. The probability that a particular allele will be included among the founders is determined by the frequency of the allele in the population (p), and is equal to

$$\Pr[\text{allele sampled}] = 1-(1-p)^{2N} \qquad \text{Eq. 3.1}$$

in which N is the number of founders. As shown in Fig. 3.1, very large numbers of founders may be required to give even a 50% probability that a rare allele would be sampled. Although some authors have recommended that many founders be used (e.g. Fuerst & Maruyama 1986), the difficulty of sampling the wild population adequately to acquire rare alleles in a captive stock has led to little practical consideration being given to this aspect of genetic management. Although few capture efforts have been designed to acquire high allelic diversity in the founders, strategies for retaining whatever variants are present in the founders are being explored (Thompson 1986, Geyer & Thompson 1988, Geyer et al. 1989, Thomas 1990).

   The mean (expected) heterozygosity in a founder stock is easily derived from sampling theory:

$$H_f = H_w * [1-1/(2N)] \qquad \text{Eq. 3.2}$$

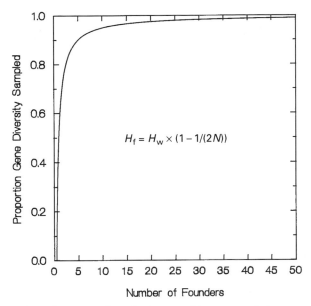

Fig 3.2. Proportion of the gene diversity (expected heterozygosity) present in the wild population (H_w) sampled in founders (H_f) drawn at random.

in which H_f and H_w are the mean heterozygosities in, respectively, the N founders and the wild population from which the founders were randomly sampled (Crow & Kimura 1970). To obtain most of the heterozygosity present in the wild population, only modest numbers of founders are needed (Fig. 3.2). Several authors have recommended obtaining at least 20 unrelated (randomly sampled) founders, yielding 97.5% of the expected heterozygosity of the wild population, because little additional heterozygosity is obtained with additional founders (Soulé *et al.* 1986, Foose *et al.* 1986). It might be necessary to capture more than 20 animals, however, to assure that at least 20 survive to reproduce in captivity. Unfortunately, in contrast to the IUCN recommendation regarding captive propagation for conservation, wildlife agencies have at times waited until there were fewer than 20 remaining animals to begin capture of founders. At that point, a lack of genetic variation may both impede recovery of the wild population and prevent the establishment of a captive population able to provide genetically diverse animals for reintroduction.

For ease of analysis, the founders of a captive stock are usually defined as those animals at the top of the pedigree, with no known genealogical interrelationships. Wild-caught animals that do not breed are not founders, because they do not contribute to the pedigree of the captive population. If some animals at the start of population management are known to be related, the founders are considered to be the ancestors, unrelated to all other founders, from which the stock descended.

Often, designed management of a captive population for conservation begins a number of generations after the capture of the founder stock. In this case, the founders of the managed population are captive-born, rather than wild-caught, and they share close pedigree relationships, rather than being a random sample of the wild population. If the pedigree from the wild-caught ancestors to the initial managed population is known, the amount of heterozygosity lost during the generations in captivity prior to genetic management can be calculated. The mean kinship among all pairs of animals within a population is, by definition, the mean proportion of the genes that are identical by descent (Ballou 1991, Ballou & Lacy 1994). Thus, it is proportional to the loss of expected heterozygosity or gene diversity. The loss of heterozygosity in a population can also be determined from stochastic simulation of the transmission of alleles through a pedigree ('gene drop' simulations; MacCluer et al. 1986, Princée 1988). Two unique alleles at a hypothetical locus are assigned to each animal at the top of the pedigree (so that the initial observed heterozygosity is 100%), and the Mendelian transmission of alleles through the pedigree is simulated numerous times. The mean heterozygosity of the simulated descendant populations gives an estimate of the proportional heterozygosity remaining across the genome.

Given the heterozygosity retained (determined either by calculation of mean kinship or by stochastic simulation), it is simple to solve Eq. 3.2 for N, determining the number of wild-caught founders that would be needed to provide the amount of genetic variation estimated to be in the present, descendant population. This measure of genetic variation of a population has been termed the 'founder genome equivalent' (Lacy 1988a, 1989). If all wild-caught animals are prolific and breed equally, the descendant population will be genetically unchanged from the wild-caught founders, and the number of founder genome equivalents will equal the number of founders. If some founders have only a few descendants, some of their alleles will be lost from the captive population and the number of founder genome equivalents will be less. When captive propagation programs are started, 20 founder genome equivalents (97.5% of wild heterozygosity) are commonly sought (Lacy 1988a, 1989).

The genetic diversity of a captive population is usually calculated relative to the genetic diversity that existed in the wild population at the time of capture of the ancestral founders. (The genetic diversity of the wild population can be estimated from the diversity in the founders by solving Eq. 3.2 for H_w.) If the wild population is very small, its genetic diversity may decline even more rapidly than that of the captive population. Thus, a captive population, while it may have less genetic variation than did its wild ancestors, may have more variation than does the current wild population.

Growth phase

Each generation of captive breeding also involves an incomplete sampling of genes. To minimize the probability that founder alleles are lost in subsequent generations, as many progeny as possible should be produced from each founder. With a limited population size, minimal loss of founder alleles will be achieved if all founders contribute an equal number of progeny. For any given founder allele, the probability that it is lost in the first generation is given by $(0.5)^n$, in which n is the number of progeny from that founder. Thus, seven progeny provide greater than 99% assurance that a founder allele is retained, and authors have recommended obtaining seven progeny per founder (e.g. Ballou & Foose 1994). If genetic loci all independently assorted during meiosis, probabilities of allelic loss would be independent, and the combined probability that no alleles from a founder would be lost would be the product of all individual allele probabilities. With an estimated 100 000 genetic loci per vertebrate genome, about 17 progeny per founder would be needed to provide a 50% chance that *all* genes from that founder were retained. Because of linkage among loci, however, fewer progeny are needed to assure retention of all founder alleles. Given the typical size of and amount of recombination in a vertebrate genome, 12 offspring are sufficient to provide 99% probability that all alleles of a founder are transmitted to at least one offspring (Thompson 1994).

If the entire captive space for the population is available from the start of the program, it is optimal to expand the captive population to fill that capacity in one generation, with an equal number of progeny per founder. Slower growth will increase the probability that founder alleles will be lost, because the number of progeny sampled is less initially, and the number of animals possessing each founder allele and therefore capable of transmitting it to the next generation will be less each generation until the carrying capacity is reached.

Heterozygosity will decline with genetic drift, as allelic variants are lost and as remaining alleles become unequal in frequency. The expected rate of loss of gene diversity (expected heterozygosity) is independent of the initial number and frequencies of alleles, as long as there exists some gene diversity. Eq. 3.2 defines the expected losses of heterozygosity at each generation, if H_t is replaced by the heterozygosity in the offspring generation, H_w is replaced by the heterozygosity of the parental generation, and N is replaced by the inbreeding effective number of animals in the parental generation. As with allelic variation, it is easiest to assume that each founder is heterozygous, with two unique alleles at a hypothetical locus. Genotype frequencies in a founder population of all heterozygotes are not in accord with Hardy–Weinberg expectations. With a finite number of founders, N_f, the expected heterozygosity in those founders, $H_f = 1 - 1/(2N_f)$, is less than the 100% observed heterozygosity assumed for the founders. Estimates of expected heterozygosity in subsequent generations give the proportional gene diversity relative to the wild stock from which the founders were sampled. Strategies described above for optimizing retention of allelic variation will also maximize the retention of expected heterozygosity (Foose & Ballou 1988).

Although the ideal strategy is clear, in practice founders will not all produce exactly the desired number of progeny. If some founders breed poorly, a conflict arises between the goals of maximizing population growth and equalizing progeny per founder. Genetically, continuing to breed prolific founders to fill the spaces left by the poor breeders will lead to better allelic retention (because the probability of each founder's alleles being retained is maximized within the constraint of the number of progeny that can be produced by that founder), but can also lead to more rapid future decreases in heterozygosity (because the offspring generation can become predominantly the descendants of a few founders). Genetic losses in all future generations are strongly dependent upon the population size, however, so the advantages of rapid population growth during the early generations of captive breeding will usually more than offset the disadvantages of unequal production by founders. Moreover, if growth is rapid enough to minimize allelic loss, unequal frequencies of founder alleles can often be corrected in later generations, after the population has reached the planned size (see below).

The strategy of maximal reproduction in early generations of captive propagation is inconsistent with, and I believe should always take precedence over, several other possible management goals. Population managers often desire to cull animals that appear to have genetic defects. Even in those rare cases where such a strategy is defensible (see below), there is no advantage to be gained by culling during the growth phase. Selective removal of animals should occur only when that removal provides space for more genetically valuable animals that would otherwise be excluded. By delaying selective culling, recombination of genes in an increasing number of animals will lessen the impact on other alleles, by reducing the linkage of desirable alleles to the offending allele.

The ultimate goal of captive breeding for conservation is often the restoration of wild populations. As further genetic deterioration of the captive population occurs with each generation in captivity, there can be an understandable desire to begin releases as soon as possible. Release of animals while the captive population is still in the growth phase, however, is counterproductive in the long term. Demographically, the target number of animals for release will be produced fastest if all animals are invested back into reproduction until the maximum manageable number of breeders is achieved. Genetically, the best representation can be released if all animals are kept in the captive breeding pool until captive capacity is reached. Earlier releases accelerate genetic losses in the stock that must sustain future releases.

Capacity phase

After the population reaches the ultimate capacity of the managed resources, or any time that resources are temporarily limiting further population expansion, imbalances in the representation of founder alleles in the population can be rectified. Although alleles that were totally lost from the population cannot be recovered except by acquisition of more founders or by mutation, disparities in founder allele frequencies due either to random drift or to selection can be partly reversed. To do so, priority for breeding is given to animals that are most likely to have genes that are unique or rare in the population. Heterozygosity will be maximized if those animals with the lowest overlap of genes are bred.

The coefficient of consanguinity or kinship is defined as the probability that two homologous genes, drawn at random from two individuals, will be identical by descent (Malécot 1969, Crow & Kimura 1970). The mean kinship of an animal to each of the animals of the living population is the mean proportion of genes shared by descent from common ancestors in the known pedigree. Thus, mean kinship provides an inverse measure of genetic value (Ballou 1991, Ballou & Lacy 1994). Moreover, because the inbreeding coefficient is equal to the kinship between the parents (Crow & Kimura 1970), the overall mean kinship of the population (the mean of all pairwise kinship values, including the kinship of each animal to itself) is the mean inbreeding coefficient expected if the population were to breed randomly for one generation and is also the proportional loss of heterozygosity to that point in time.

Various strategies for maximizing retention of genetic variation have been used in endangered species breeding programs, including random mating, avoidance of close inbreeding, circular mating schemes designed for maximal avoidance of inbreeding (Flesness 1977), equalization of family sizes (thereby maximizing the effective population size), equalization of founder contributions (which might require adjustment of family sizes in a current generation to compensate for unequal family sizes in previous generations), giving breeding priority to animals with the highest probability of carrying unique alleles, and giving breeding priority to animals with the lowest mean kinship. Ballou (1991) and Ballou & Lacy (1994) compared strategies for assigning genetic value to breeding animals, and assessed how well each retains heterozygosity and allelic variation. They concluded that no strategy tested outperforms a prioritization based on mean kinship. However, closely comparable results could sometimes be obtained by selecting breeders with the highest probability of carrying unique alleles or by using a circular mating scheme designed for maximal avoidance of inbreeding. Regular systems of breeding can be effective in preserving genetic variation, but their use is contingent upon reliable production of progeny by each pair. This can be achieved only by producing a surplus of animals to provide back-up and then culling those not subsequently needed for breeding.

A simple and common approach to genetic management is to pick matings that avoid immediate inbreeding. Avoidance of inbreeding will often preserve genetic variation well, but it is difficult to determine what combination of matings in a complex pedigree will yield the lowest overall inbreeding. Moreover, minimizing inbreeding in the proximate generation can force greater inbreeding in future generations than would otherwise be necessary. For example, zero inbreeding in the next generation could be achieved by mating all females to a newly acquired male founder. This, however, would force all matings of the next generation to be between half- or full-siblings. Correspondingly, strategies for the long-term maximal avoidance of inbreeding often result in greater than random inbreeding for the first few generations.

Regardless of the technique used to assign matings, very close inbreeding (e.g. half-sib matings or closer) should be avoided because of the high probability of inviable or infertile offspring. Frankel & Soulé (1981) recommended keeping the per generation increase in inbreeding below 1% (their 'basic rule of conservation genetics'), which would proscribe matings between second-cousin or closer relatives. Often, however, a limited number of founders and limited resources for maintaining large stocks precludes such a conservative strategy. If there are reasonable prospects for restoration of wild populations within a few generations, the goal of keeping cumulative inbreeding below 10% (Soulé *et al.* 1986) should be adequate.

Because the goal is to minimize losses of the founder stock's genetic variation, one approach to selecting matings is to give priority to those animals that descend from founders with the lowest representation in the descendant population (e.g. Foose 1983, Templeton & Read 1983). Descendants are combinations of the genes from several founders, however, and no completely satisfactory method has been developed for summarizing the multiple contributions to an individual's genome into a single measure of founder value. The search for such a statistic has been largely abandoned, because mean kinship provides a genetic ranking that allows for optimal retention of heterozygosity

(Ballou 1991, Ballou & Lacy 1994). Ranking genetic value based on an average value of contributing founders could at best only equal the usefulness of mean kinship.

Usually, maximizing retention of heterozygosity will optimally or nearly optimally retain allelic diversity (Ballou & Lacy 1994). This is not always the case, however, because animals that have unique or rare alleles can also have very common alleles at other loci or at the homologous genes. Mating such animals may reduce heterozygosity because they share genes with much of the population, yet not breeding them may result in the loss of rare alleles. It is possible to manage for retention of rare alleles, either by using simulation methods to determine the proportion of genes in each individual that are unique or very rare in a population (MacCluer *et al.* 1986), or by using exact methods of analysis to determine the probability of unique genes (Thompson 1986, Geyer & Thompson 1988, Geyer *et al.* 1989, Thomas 1990).

The conflict between preserving allelic diversity and preserving heterozygosity can be avoided. Genetically valuable males should be paired with genetically valuable females, so that descendant animals will not contain combinations of rare and common founder alleles. If rare alleles were to be carried only by animals that also contain very common alleles, it would be impossible to increase the numbers of the rare alleles without simultaneously making the common alleles even more common. Perhaps the best overall strategy for retention of both heterozygosity and allelic diversity is to mate animals with the lowest mean kinship, giving somewhat higher priority to any animals with an unusually high probability of having many rare or unique alleles, and avoiding pairings among very close relatives. In practice, reconciling conflicts among genetic goals is usually easier than reconciling conflicts with social compatibility of animals, and with logistics such as getting desired pairs to the same facility for mating.

The above guidelines for genetic management have several corollaries that may be counterintuitive. As mentioned above, it is advisable to pair genetically valuable males with equally valuable females. This simultaneously optimizes heterozygosity and allelic diversity, and it facilitates genetic management in future generations. If animals of equal value are paired, then valuable genes from both sides of the progeny's pedigree can be preferentially propagated. Animals whose parents are of lesser value can be given less priority, simultaneously decreasing genes from both parents. Mere avoidance of inbreeding will often result in animals of little genetic value, related to much of the population, being mated to genetically valuable animals with few relatives. A better strategy is to mate valuable animals to other valuable animals, breed their (valuable) progeny preferentially until they are no longer rare, and then cross them to the lines that had been relatively common. This approach may require moderate inbreeding of common lines for a few generations until the initially rarer lines can be brought up to proportional representation, but will reduce inbreeding in future generations.

Mating of animals with the lowest mean kinship will automatically favor continued breeding by a parental generation over replacement of aging breeders by the offspring generation. Offspring are genetic subsets of their parents, and they can never have lower mean kinship to the population than do both parents. (An offspring's kinship to each animal other than its parents is equal to the mean of the kinships of the parents to that other animal, and an offspring is related by at least one-half to each parent, while the parents may not be related to each other.) Replacing animals as breeders only when they die or are physiologically unable to reproduce has several additional genetic advantages. Genetic drift occurs at the transition of generations, and alleles can be lost from a breeding population only when breeders are retired. The perfect genetic management would be to immortalize the original wild-caught animals (Ballou 1984).

Additional options in genetic management

Selection

Animal breeding was developed for and has traditionally focused on improvement of domesticated livestock, so it is not surprising that recommendations for the genetic 'improvement' of captive populations of wildlife by artificial selection have occasionally been made. For example, the cooperative management program for the Asian wild horse (*Equus przewalskii*) in European zoos is considering the selective elimination of horses that show coat color variations believed to have been derived from hybridization with a domestic horse (Zimmermann 1989a,b). Less-deliberate selection against phenotypes that are perceived to be deleterious and genetically based indubitably occurs with considerable frequency. Given that the goal of most wildlife breeding programs is to retain the genetic characteristics of the founder stocks with as little change as possible during generations in captivity, any proposal to artificially select against genes within the stock must be viewed with caution and perhaps skepticism. It would require extreme hubris to think that we could design programs of artificial selection on individual traits or loci that would be effective at preventing genetic change across the genome. Alteration of the gene pool to preserve phenotypes in a captive environment would not likely preserve phenotypes when a population is restored to its natural habitat. One of the primary advantages of breeding programs that focus on pedigree analysis, rather than assessment of phenotype, is that the strategy will minimize both natural selection (likely favoring different traits than those selected in the wild) and deliberate or unintentional artificial selection (almost certainly favoring different traits than those selected in the wild).

Several possible advantages of artificial selection for conservation can be envisioned (Frankham *et al.* 1986). First, as in the case of the Asian wild horse, an attempt might be made to reverse genetic changes (in this case, introgression from another species) that occurred during captive propagation. Until 1988, the North American breeding program for the Asian wild horse recommended not breeding stallions with some documented domestic horse ancestry (Ryder & Wedermeyer 1982). That policy has now been reversed, because analyses showed that about 30% of the non-domesticated founder alleles would be lost from the population if the strategy were continued, as some founder genes were present only in descendants of a domestic mare (Geyer *et al.* 1989). The North American management plan now calls for maintenance of two Asian wild horse gene pools: one without known representation from domestic horses, and one with both domestic horse genes and also a greater diversity of Asian wild horse genes.

Artificial selection against a single gene (e.g. a color variant) that is presumed to have descended from domestic horses, as is prescribed in the European management plan, might be little better than a random cull, and could be much worse. After generations of recombination and independent assortment of genes, Asian wild horses with one visible 'domestic' gene may not have many more genes from domestic ancestors than would Asian wild horses chosen at random. Because color would likely be a genetic marker shared by Asian wild horses of recent common ancestry, removal of those horses could eliminate entire families from the breeding program. Artificial selection strategies focus on management of phenotypes determined by a few loci, with the attendant cost of less than optimal management of the rest of the genome. Pedigree analysis allows optimization of genetic variation across the genome, recognizing that genotypes at some loci will, by chance, drift further from the original or otherwise desired frequencies than would be the case if those loci had been the focus of management.

A second possible justification for artificial selection is to remove traits that impede captive breeding, thereby preventing extinction of the captive population (Frankham *et al.* 1986). A similar suggestion is that wildlife managers should work to eliminate genes that are thought to be deleterious both in captivity and in the wild. I argue that such practices would rarely result in benefits that outweigh the genetic damage. Given that little is known regarding the determinants of fitness, and especially regarding the constancy of fitness rankings among alleles across a range of environments, it is unlikely that population managers could identify genetic traits that were consistently deleterious. Even if a trait is decidedly harmful, there is little to be gained by artificial selection. Alleles that cause mortality, infertility, or serious handicap would be eliminated by natural selection, although the efficacy of that selection could be weakened if managers re-paired animals (thereby protecting the recessive alleles from exposure as homozygotes) when the deleterious effects were seen in their offspring. Although the selective elimination of heterozygous carriers of deleterious recessive alleles can speed the elimination of such alleles from a population, that strategy also carries a cost. Twice as many genetic deaths occur when alleles are purged via the removal of heterozygotes than via the removal of homozygotes.

The program for breeding Speke's gazelle (*Gazella spekei*) devised by Templeton & Read (1983, 1984) is often interpreted (e.g. Frankham *et al.* 1986, Simberloff 1988) as a plan to reduce the genetic load of a remnant population by deliberately breeding very close relatives and then selecting for animals showing no deleterious effects. This interpretation is not entirely correct. The program primarily acknowledged and monitored inevitable inbreeding, allowing natural selection to remove recessive deleterious alleles. Although the program did not maximally avoid inbreeding in the proximate generation, it did avoid close inbreeding, and it did maximize the diversity of founder genes in each animal in order to *minimize* inbreeding in later generations.

A third possible justification for artificial selection is to attempt to increase the populational variability by selecting animals found empirically to have greater variation or distinctive alleles. Hughes (1991) suggested that captive breeding programs could focus almost entirely on preserving diversity at the MHC locus. Hedrick *et al.* (1986) recommend against using variation in allozymes to select animals for breeding, because measures of allozyme variation at a few tens of loci are likely to correlate only poorly with overall genome variation and with fitness. Hughes' suggestion has been criticized on similar grounds by Gilpin & Wills (1991), Miller & Hedrick (1991) and Vrijenhoek & Leberg (1991). Mendelian genetics follows simple probabilistic rules and a mean across tens of thousands of loci will closely match the statistical expectation, so estimates of variation (e.g. mean kinship, inbreeding coefficients) derived from theory will be more accurate than assessments based on molecular data. Molecular data can provide paternity or maternity determination (Lacy *et al.* 1988), and this is a prerequisite to using pedigree analysis for optimal genetic management of previously incomplete pedigrees (Lacy *et al.* 1994). Molecular data can also identify genealogical relationships among founders and can define the boundaries of natural populations from which founders were drawn (Avise & Nelson 1989, Wayne & Jenkins 1991). Thus, empirical data on molecular or phenotypic variation can provide measures of the amount and distribution of genetic variation that we wish to preserve (Lacy 1988b), and can provide a means of monitoring the performance of genetic management (Wayne *et al.* 1986), but do not provide efficient means of selecting the best matings during the course of a breeding program.

Even when universally undesirable genes have been identified, genetic damage can be done by artificial selection programs. All organisms have a combination of adaptive and at least temporarily maladaptive genes. Selection cannot remove some alleles from the population without incidentally removing others. This is especially so in the small populations characteristic of conservation programs, because genetic drift can cause considerable linkage disequilibrium. A common, unwitting, and especially damaging artificial selection can occur when population managers focus efforts on good breeders. If proven breeders have succeeded owing to chance or to non-genetic qualities, then retaining them as the primary breeders amplifies the impact of genetic drift with deliberate selection, and consequently severely constricts the breeding population. If proven breeders are genetically well-adapted to the captive environment, then such a practice amplifies the effects of natural selection with very strong artificial selection for production of a domesticated, zoo-adapted population.

Propagation programs can minimize unintended selection by managing pedigrees for maximal retention of genetic variation and by spreading the captive population over a number of captive habitats. Dispersing the population will diversify natural selection, avoiding strong selection for genes adaptive in specific captive conditions. (Ironically, the trend toward shared management protocols and husbandry practices, well-intended to improve the quality of care for animals in captivity and the success of breeding programs, may create common conditions for inadvertent selection.) If a large fraction of the original variation can be preserved through generations of captivity, natural selection can proceed with truly adaptive evolution after a population has been restored to a natural habitat.

Population subdivision

Most natural populations are not contiguous and panmictic, but instead are composed of a number of smaller units that are connected by occasional migration. Such a metapopulation structure can be used as a management tool in captive breeding. Dispersing a captive population over diverse environments can avoid variation-depleting directional selection and foster variation-preserving diversifying selection. Dispersal also protects the population from epidemic disease and other management catastrophes. Population subdivision can also minimize some of the effects of genetic drift. While each smaller population will lose genetic diversity to drift, and perhaps selection, at a faster rate than would a single, large, panmictic population, isolated or partly isolated smaller populations will tend to diverge genetically, losing different genetic variants. The metapopulation (the smaller populations taken together) will therefore retain greater gene diversity (expected heterozygosity) and greater allelic diversity than would a panmictic population (Chesser, Smith & Brisbin Jr. 1980; Lacy 1987).

Deliberate fragmentation of a population has several potentially serious drawbacks that must be evaluated before and during the implementation of such a strategy. Animals within each isolated population will become more inbred because of the smaller choice of mates and greater genetic drift. If populations are so small that inbreeding reduces individual fitness, the goals of the breeding program could be compromised. If inbreeding depression were not so severe as to jeopardize the populations, however, a heterogeneous population reconstituted later by mixing animals from the isolated small populations would be expected to have greater genetic variation and perhaps higher individual fitness than would have been the case if it had not been temporarily divided. Moreover, moderate episodic inbreeding can remove some of the genetic load of deleterious recessive alleles that contributes to inbreeding depression (Templeton & Read 1983, 1984).

The ability of a metapopulation to retain greater genetic variation than a panmictic population strongly depends on the persistence of each component population. If one of these goes extinct, genetic variants unique to it will also be lost. The variation-preserving property of a metapopulation results primarily from the independent maintenance of population size of each component unit, acting in the same way as a breeding strategy that assures that each lineage within a population maintains proportional representation in the gene pool.

Population subdivision will cause genes to be exposed to selection in a different and more homogeneous genetic background. To the extent that gene fitness is determined by epistatic interactions, selection could favor different genes in a homogeneous background than it would in a more heterogeneous background. It is impossible to know if such altered selection would accelerate or slow the loss of genetic diversity.

Some of the risks of population subdivision can be countered by occasional migration among the component populations. Migration of approximately one animal between populations per generation will prevent excessive inbreeding within populations (within the limitations imposed by the metapopulation size), but at a cost of reduced effectiveness of the subdivided population structure in retaining variation overall (Varvio, Chakraborty & Nei 1986; Lacy 1987). If 5–10 animals per generation migrate, genetic divergence among component populations is largely prevented (Allendorf 1983, Lacy 1987), and the metapopulation is therefore equivalent to a panmictic population. Movement of enough animals (several per generation per population) to provide the demographic stability necessary to prevent population extinctions would likely eliminate the genetic effects (good and bad) of population division. Perhaps the wisest approach to managing population structure is to mimic the degree of isolation typical of natural populations of the species before human-induced decimation and fragmentation.

Restoration of a wild population from captive stock

Although the ultimate conservation goal of captive breeding is often to supplement or restore populations in the wild, little attention has been devoted to determining how to choose animals from a captive population for release (but see Haig, Ballou & Derrickson 1990). Given the uncertain fate of released animals and of restored populations, it would be wise to protect the investment made in securing a genetically diverse captive stock by releasing only those animals that are surplus to the genetic needs of continued captive propagation. This means that animals released, at least initially, would be those descending from the most prolific lineages in captivity. Over time, the genetic composition of the restored population can be diversified by the release of descendants from other lineages.

Summary

Captive populations of wildlife can provide the large numbers of animals needed for successful reintroduction into more natural habitats. Genetic changes occurring during generations of captivity can, however, make the captive-bred stock unsuitable for release. Altered natural selection can adapt a population to captivity and random genetic drift in small populations can deplete the genetic variation necessary for readaptation to a natural or restored environment.

Zoo biologists have developed techniques for analyzing and then managing the genetic diversity of captive populations, with the overall goal of minimizing both random and selective changes. Although techniques are still evolving, a number of guidelines for more effective management have emerged. To give the opportunity for long-term viability, a captive population should be initiated with at least 20 founders (wild-caught animals that reproduce in captivity). This founder stock should be expanded rapidly to the capacity of the captive habitat. If possible, 7–12 progeny should be produced from each founder, thereby reducing the probability of loss of any allele present in the founders to less than 1%. The captive capacity should be large enough to assure that no more than about 10% of the original gene diversity is lost during the intended duration of the captive population. After the population reaches the predetermined capacity, or during the growth phase if resources temporarily limit the number of breeding pairs, priority should be given to breeding those animals with the lowest mean kinship to the living, captive-born population. To further protect rare alleles from loss, additional emphasis should be placed on obtaining progeny from any animals with a substantial portion of their genomes unconnected by descent to any other animals within the captive stock. Genetically valuable animals, those with lowest mean kinship, should be mated to other genetically valuable animals, thereby preventing irreversible linkages of rare and common lineages. If both parents of an animal are alive, the progeny cannot be as valuable genetically as are the parents (because the progeny contains a subset of the genes in the two parents); producing further siblings is preferable to producing grand-offspring. Thus, rather than retiring pairs with many progeny from breeding, some of their offspring could be declared surplus and the original breeders should be kept in the breeding pool for the duration of their reproductive lifespans. Intentional and, to the extent possible, even unintentional artificial selection against alleles perceived as deleterious should be avoided when the goal of captive breeding is to provide a stock for possible restoration to natural environments. It would be virtually impossible to know which alleles would be favored in a future environment, and it is difficult to purge the population of some alleles without causing incidental damage to the diversity of the rest of the genome. The captive population should be spread over a number of facilities, diversifying the captive environment to the extent compatible with species needs and geographically isolating populations to reduce the probability of catastrophic loss of the entire metapopulation. Animals should be moved between populations when necessary to prevent close inbreeding; this will be approximately one or a few migrants per generation.

The above management rules will minimize genetic drift, minimize inbreeding, and minimize genetic response to selection for adaptations particular to the captive environment. Release of captive-born animals into the wild should occur only after the captive population has reached its planned capacity. The released animals should be those not needed to assure the continued maintenance of the captive population, as long as it is to be used as the source population for further restoration efforts.

Acknowledgments

Effective strategies for managing genetic diversity in captive populations have evolved rapidly because of the concerted and collaborative efforts of many people (see references). I am particularly indebted to Jon Ballou (National Zoological Park, Smithsonian Institution) and Tom Foose of the Captive Breeding Specialist Group (Species Survival Commission, IUCN) for their constant challenging of inadequate methods, and for the insights they have offered toward finding better answers. I thank also three reviewers who provided valuable critiques of this paper.

Literature cited

Allendorf, F. W. (1983) Isolation, gene flow, and genetic differentiation among populations. In *Genetics and Conservation: A Reference for Managing Wild Animal and Plant Populations*, ed. Schonewald-Cox, C. M., Chambers, S. M., MacBryde, B. & Thomas, W. L., pp. 51–65. Menlo Park: Benjamin/Cummings.

Allendorf, F. W. (1986) Genetic drift and the loss of alleles versus heterozygosity. *Zoo Biology*, **5**, 181–90.

Allendorf, F. W. & Leary, R. F. (1986) Heterozygosity and fitness in natural populations of animals. In *Conservation Biology: The Science of Scarcity and Diversity*, ed. Soulé, M. E., pp. 57–76. Sunderland: Sinauer Associates.

Avise, J. C. & Nelson, W. S. (1989) Molecular genetic relationships of the extinct dusky seaside sparrow. *Science*, **243**, 646–8.

Ballou, J. (1984) Strategies for maintaining genetic diversity in captive populations through reproductive technology. *Zoo Biology*, **3**, 311–24.

Ballou, J. D. (1991) Management of genetic variation in captive populations. In *The Unity of Evolutionary Biology, Proceedings IV International Congress on Systematics and Evolutionary Biology*, ed. Dudley, E. C., pp. 602–10. Portland, Oregon: Dioscorides Press.

Ballou, J. D. & Foose, T. J. (1994) Demographic and genetic management of captive populations. In *Wild Mammals in Captivity*, ed. Kleiman, D. G., Lumpkin, S., Allen, M., Harris, H. & Thompson, K. Chicago, Illinois: University of Chicago Press. (In press.)

Ballou, J. D,. and Lacy, R. C. (1994) Identifying genetically important individuals for management of genetic diversity in pedigreed populations. In *Population Management for Survival and Recovery*, ed. Ballou, J. D., Foose, T. J. & Gilpin, M. Columbia University Press. (In press.)

Biggins, D. E., Hanebury, L. R., Miller, B. J. & Powell, J. A. (1990) Release of Siberian polecats (*Mustela eversmanni*) on a prairie dog colony. Abstracts, 70th Annual Meeting of the American Society of Mammalogists, Frostburg, Maryland, 19–23 June 1990.

Chesser, R. K., Smith, M. H. & Brisbin, I. L. Jr. (1980) Management and maintenance of genetic variability in endangered species. *International Zoo Yearbook*, **20**, 146–54.

Clark, T. W. (1989) *Conservation biology of the Black-Footed Ferret*. Philadelphia: Wildlife Preservation Trust International.

Conway, W. G. (1986) The practical difficulties and financial implications of endangered species breeding programmes. *International Zoo Yearbook*, **24/25**, 210–19.

Crow, J. F. & Kimura, M. (1970) *An Introduction to Population Genetics Theory.* New York: Harper and Row.

Denniston, C. (1977) Small population size and genetic diversity: Implications for endangered species. In *Endangered Birds. Management Techniques for Preserving Threatened Species*, ed. Temple, S. A., pp. 281–9. Madison: University of Wisconsin Press.

Falconer, D. S. (1981) *Introduction to Quantitative Genetics*, 2nd edn. New York: Longman.

Fisher, R. A. (1958) *The Genetical Theory of Natural Selection*, 2nd edn. New York: Dover.

Flesness, N. (1977) Gene pool conservation and computer analysis. *International Zoo Yearbook*, **17**, 77–81.

Foose, T. J. (1983) The relevance of captive populations to the conservation of biotic diversity. In *Genetics and Conservation: A Reference for Managing Wild Animal and Plant Populations*, ed. Schonewald-Cox, C. M., Chambers, S. M., MacBryde, B. & Thomas, W. L., pp. 374–401. Menlo Park: Benjamin/Cummings.

Foose, T. J. & Ballou, J. D. (1988) Population management: theory and practice. *International Zoo Yearbook*, **27**, 26–41.

Foose, T. J., Lande, R., Flesness, N. R., Rabb, G. & Read, B. (1986) Propagation plans. *Zoo Biology,* **5**, 139–46.

Frankel, O. H. & Soulé, M. E. (1981) *Conservation and Evolution.* Cambridge University Press.

Frankham, R., Hemmer, H., Ryder, O. A., Cothran, E. G. Soulé, M. E., Murray, N. D. & Snyder, M. (1986) Selection in captive populations. *Zoo Biology*, **5**, 127–38.

Franklin, I. R. (1980) Evolutionary change in small populations. In *Conservation Biology: An Evolutionary-Ecological Perspective*, ed. Soulé, M. E. & Wilcox, B., pp. 135–49. Sunderland: Sinauer Associates.

Fuerst, P. A. & Maruyama, T. (1986) Considerations on the conservation of alleles and of genic heterozygosity in small managed populations. *Zoo Biology*, **5**, 171–9.

Geyer, C. J. & Thompson, E. A. (1988) Gene survival in the Asian wild horse (*Equus przewalskii*): I. Dependence of gene survival in the Calgary Breeding Group pedigree. *Zoo Biology*, **7**, 313–27.

Geyer, C. J., Thompson, E. A. & Ryder, O. A. (1989) Gene survival in the Asian wild horse (*Equus przewalskii*): II. Gene survival in the whole population, in subgroups, and through history. *Zoo Biology*, **8**, 313–29.

Gilpin, M. & Wills, C. (1991) MHC and captive breeding: A rebuttal. *Conservation Biology*, **5**, 554–55.

Haig, S. M., Ballou, J. D. & Derrickson, S. R. (1990) Management options for preserving genetic diversity: Reintroduction of Guam rails to the wild. *Conservation Biology*, **4**, 290–300.

Hedrick, P. W., Brussard, P. F., Allendorf, F. W., Beardmore, J. A. & Orzack, S. (1986) Protein variation, fitness, and captive propagation. *Zoo Biology*, **5**, 91–9.

Holler, N. R., Mason, D. W., Dawson, R. M., Simons, T. & Wooten, M. C. (1989) Reestablishment of the Perdido Key Beach Mouse (*Peromyscus polionotus trissyllepsis*) on Gulf Islands National Seashore. *Conservation Biology*, **3**, 397–404.

Hughes, A. L. (1991) MHC polymorphism and the design of captive breeding programs. *Conservation Biology,* **5**, 249–51.

International Union for Conservation of Nature and Natural Resources (IUCN). (1987) Snails race to extinction. *IUCN Bulletin*, **18**,(7–9), 3.

International Union for Conservation of Nature and Natural Resources (IUCN). (1988) *The IUCN Policy Statement on Captive Breeding*. Gland: International Union for Conservation of Nature.

James, J. W. (1971) The founder effect and response to artificial selection. *Genetical Research*, **12**, 249–66.

Kleiman, D. G., Beck, B. B., Dietz, J. M., Dietz, L. A., Ballou, J. D. & Coimbra–Filho, A. F. (1986) Conservation program for the golden lion tamarin: Captive research and management, ecological studies, educational strategies, and reintroduction. In *Primates: The Road to Self-Sustaining Populations*, ed. Benirschke, K., pp. 959–79. New York: Springer-Verlag.

Lacy, R. C. (1987) Loss of genetic diversity from managed populations: Interacting effects of drift, mutation, immigration, selection, and population subdivision. *Conservation Biology*, **1**, 143–58.

Lacy, R. C. (1988a) Genetic variability in captive stocks: Assessing past loss, present status, and future outlook. *AAZPA 1988 Annual Proceedings*, pp. 113–21.

Lacy, R. C. (1988b) A report on population genetics in conservation. *Conservation Biology*, **2**, 245–7.

Lacy, R. C. (1989) Analysis of founder representation in pedigrees: Founder equivalents and founder genome equivalents. *Zoo Biology*, **8**, 111–24.

Lacy, R. C., Ballou, J. D., Princée, F., Starfield, A. & Thompson, E. (1994) Pedigree analysis. In *Population Management for Survival and Recovery*, ed. Ballou, J. D., Foose, T. & Gilpin, M., New York: Columbia University Press. (In press.)

Lacy, R. C. & Clark, T. W. (1989) Genetic variability in black-footed ferret populations: Past, present, and future. In *Conservation Biology and the Black-Footed Ferret*, ed. Seal, U. S., Thorne, E. T., Bogan, M. A. & Anderson, S. H., pp. 83–103. New Haven: Yale University Press.

Lacy, R. C., Foster, M. L. & the Primate Department Staff. (1988) Determination of pedigrees and taxa of primates by protein electrophoresis. *International Zoo Yearbook*, **27**, 159–68.

Lande, R. (1994) Streamlining the millennium ark: Breeding strategies based on the dynamics of genetic variance in quantitative traits. In *Population Management for Survival and Recovery*, ed. Ballou, J. D., Foose, T. & Gilpin, M. New York: Columbia University Press. (In press.)

Lande, R. & Barrowclough, G. F. (1987) Effective population size, genetic variation, and their use in population management. In *Viable Populations for Conservation*, ed. Soulé, M. E., pp. 87–123. Cambridge University Press.

MacCluer, J. W., VandeBerg, J. L., Read, B. & Ryder, O. A. (1986) Pedigree analysis by computer simulation. *Zoo Biology*, **5**, 147–60.

Mace, G. M. (1986) Genetic management of small populations. *International Zoo Yearbook*, **24/25**, 167–74.

Mace, G. M. & Mallinson, J. J. C. (1989) 1989 *International Studbook Golden-Headed Lion Tamarin (Leontopithecus chrysomelas)*. Jersey: Jersey Wildlife Preservation Trust.

Malécot, G. (1969) *The Mathematics of Heredity*. English translation by D. M. Yermanos. San Francisco: W. H. Freeman.

Maruyama, T. & Fuerst, P. A. (1985) Population bottlenecks and non-equilibrium models in population genetics. II. Number of alleles in a small population that was formed by a recent bottleneck. *Genetics,* **111**, 675–89.

Miller, A. M., Roelke, M. E., Goodrowe, K. L., Howard, J. G. & Woldt, D. E. (1990)

Oocyte recovery, maturation and fertilization in vitro in the puma (*Felis concolor*). *Journal of Reproduction and Fertility*, **88**, 249–58.

Miller, P. S. & Hedrick, P. W. (1991) MHC polymorphism and the design of captive breeding programs: Simple solutions are not the answer. *Conservation Biology*, **5**, 556–8.

Mitton, J. B. & Grant, M. C. (1984) Associations among protein heterozygosity, growth rate, and developmental homeostasis. *Annual Review of Ecology and Systematics*, **15**, 479–99.

Nei, M. (1973) Analysis of gene diversity in subdivided populations. *Proceedings of the National Academy of Sciences*, **70**, 3321–23.

Nei, M., Maruyama, T. & Chakraborty, R. (1975) The bottleneck effect and genetic variability in populations. *Evolution*, **29**, 1–10.

O'Brien, S. J., Roelke, M. E., Yuhki, N., Richards, K.W., Johnson, W. E., Franklin, W. L., Anderson, A. E., Bass, O. L. Jr, Belden, R. C. & Martenson, J. S. (1990) Genetic introgression within the Florida panther *Felis concolor coryi*. *National Geographic Research*, **6**, 485–94.

Princée, F. P. G. (1988) Genetic variation in the zoo population of the red panda subspecies *Ailurus fulgens fulgens*. *Zoo Biology*, **7**, 219–31.

Ralls, K. & Ballou, J. (1983) Extinction: lessons from zoos. In *Genetics and Conservation: A Reference for Managing Wild Animal and Plant Populations*, ed. Schonewald-Cox, C. M., Chambers, S. M., MacBryde, B. & Thomas, W. L., pp. 164–84. Menlo Park: Benjamin/Cummings.

Robertson, A. (1960) A theory of limits in artificial selection. *Proceedings of the Royal Society of London*, **B153**, 234–49.

Ryder, O. A. & Wedermeyer, E. A. (1982) A cooperative breeding programme for the Mongolian wild horse *Equus przewalskii* in the United States. *Biological Conservation*, **22**, 259–71.

Seal, U. S. & Lacy, R. C. (1989) Florida panther population viability analysis. *Report to the U.S. Fish and Wildlife Service*. Apple Valley: Captive Breeding Specialist Group, SSC, IUCN.

Seal, U. S., Thorne, M. A., Bogan, E. T. & Anderson, S. H. eds. (1989) *Conservation Biology and the Black-Footed Ferret*. New Haven: Yale University Press.

Selander, R. K. (1983) Evolutionary consequences of inbreeding. In *Genetics and Conservation: A Reference for Managing Wild Animal and Plant Populations*, ed. Schonewald-Cox, C. M., Chambers, S. M., MacBryde, B. & Thomas, W. L., pp. 201–15. Menlo Park: Benjamin/Cummings.

Simberloff, D. (1988) The contribution of population and community biology to conservation science. *Annual Review of Ecology and Systematics*, **19**, 473–511.

Soulé, M., Gilpin, M., Conway, W. & Foose, T. (1986) The millennium ark: How long a voyage, how many staterooms, how many passengers? *Zoo Biology*, **5**, 101–13.

Stanley-Price, M. R. (1989) *Animal reintroductions. The Arabian oryx in Oman.* Cambridge University Press.

Templeton, A. R. & Read, B. (1983) The elimination of inbreeding depression in a captive herd of Speke's gazelle. In *Genetics and Conservation: A Reference for Managing Wild Animal and Plant Populations*, ed. Schonewald-Cox, C. M., Chambers, S. M., MacBryde, B. & Thomas, W. L., pp. 241–61. Menlo Park: Benjamin/Cummings.

Templeton, A. R. & Read, B. (1984) Factors eliminating inbreeding depression in a captive herd of Speke's gazelle. *Zoo Biology*, **3**, 177–99.

Thomas, A. (1990) A comparison of an exact and a simulation method for calculating gene extinction probabilities in pedigrees. *Zoo Biology*, **9**, 259–74.

Thompson, E. A. (1986) Ancestry of alleles and extinction of genes in populations with defined pedigrees. *Zoo Biology*, **5**, 161–70.

Thompson, E. A. (1994) Genetic importance and genomic descent. In *Population Management for Survival and Recovery*, ed. Ballou, J. D., Foose, T. J. & Gilpin, M. New York: Columbia University Press. (In press.)

Varvio, S.-L., Chakraborty, R. & Nei, M. (1986) Genetic variation in subdivided populations and conservation genetics. *Heredity*, **57**, 189–98.

Vrijenhoek, R. C. & Leberg, P. L. (1991) Let's not throw out the baby with the bathwater: a comment on management for MHC diversity in captive populations. *Conservation Biology*, **5**, 252–4.

Wayne, R. K., Forman, L., Newman, A. K., Simonson, J. M. & O'Brien, S. J. (1986) Genetic monitors of zoo populations: morphological and electrophoretic assays. *Zoo Biology*, **5**, 215–32.

Wayne, R. K. & Jenkins, S. M. (1991) Mitochondrial DNA analysis implying extensive hybridization of the endangered red wolf *Canis rufus*. *Nature*, **351**, 565–8.

Wright, S. (1931) Evolution in Mendelian populations. *Genetics*, **16**, 97–159.

Wright, S. (1969) *Evolution and the Genetics of Populations*. Volume 2. *The Theory of Gene Frequencies*. Chicago: University of Chicago Press.

Zimmermann, W. (1989a) The Przewalski horse EEP as an example on the organisation and progress of an European breeding programme. *6th EEP Conference, Ouwehands Zoo, Rhenen 21–24 May 1989*, pp. 23–4.

Zimmermann, W. (1989b) Jahresbericht EEP Przewalskipferd. *6th EEP Conference, Ouwehands Zoo, Rhenen, 21–24 May 1989*, pp. 131–2.

4

The relationship of rarity to plant reproductive biology

STEPHEN G. WELLER

Introduction

Although many aspects of rarity have been studied, the relationship of plant reproductive biology and rarity is poorly understood. In this chapter, I will address this relationship, which is relevant to recent efforts to conserve rare plant species *ex situ* and to reintroduce rare species to habitats within their former ranges.

Reproductive systems in flowering plants are extraordinarily diverse. Unlike the majority of terrestrial animal species, which have separate female and male sexes, most flowering plants are hermaphroditic, producing male and female gametes in the same flower or in separate flowers on the same plant. Despite the potential for self-fertilization, diverse mechanisms have evolved that promote outcrossing, presumably to avoid the loss of fitness that often results from self-fertilization. Some of these mechanisms are spatial or temporal separation of pollen and stigmas; self-incompatibility, which prevents self-fertilization and matings among individuals possessing the same incompatibility type; and dioecy, or the separation of sexual function on different individuals (Table 4.1).

Outcrossing plant species depend on animals, wind, or water as pollen vectors. The degree of specialization of the pollen vector and the nature of the morphological and physiological adaptations of the plant species determine how effectively pollen is transferred among individuals of the same species. Some plant species have evolved adaptations for pollination by a very limited array of pollinators, although such specialization may be uncommon.

Many characteristics of plant reproductive systems may be associated with rarity. For example, in species with gametophytic self-incompatibility (Table 4.1), as many as 45 S alleles have been detected (Emerson 1939, 1940); in species with sporophytic self-incompatibility, fewer S alleles occur (Karron, Marshall & Oliveras 1990). As populations drop to very small numbers, genetic drift may overwhelm the tendency for frequency-dependent selection to maintain self-incompatibility alleles (Wright 1939). Eventually only a few incompatibility types would be found; pollinations between cross-incompatible individuals would fail to produce seed. Among species possessing heteromorphic self-incompatibility, only two or three incompatibility types, each associated with a characteristic floral morphology, occur in populations. Thus, reductions in population size might have very severe effects on seed production.

Self-incompatibility is often associated with low seed production (Charlesworth 1989) even when compatible pollen is available and incompatible pollen does not prevent compatible pollen from germinating and growing. Such species may have limited capacity for initiating or maintaining populations. Clonal propagation could exacerbate low seed production in self-incompatible populations, because pollen transfer among flowers within the clone would fail to produce seed. A population that might appear large and genetically diverse could in fact consist of relatively few genetically distinct individuals with limited cross-compatibility.

In small populations of dioecious species, the occurrence of staminate (male) and pistillate (female) individuals could depress sexual reproduction as a result of lowered effective population size. The apparent reduced ability of self-incompatible and dioecious species to engage in long-distance colonization (Baker 1955, 1967) indicates that these species are more likely to go extinct than self-compatible species, which can initiate a new population from a single propagule.

Because some plant species depend on animals to transfer their pollen, they could be vulnerable to extinction if their pollen vectors are themselves rare or endangered. As specialized pollinators go extinct, introduced species may substitute for them. Whether or not these introduced pollinators are as effective is usually not known. Less effective pollen transfer could increase the rate of inbreeding and lead to offspring showing reduced fitness.

The distinction between natural rarity and anthropogenic rarity

To understand the relationship of plant breeding systems to rarity, species that have always been rare must be distinguished from those that are now rare because of loss of habitat, collection, elimination of natural pollinators, and other changes induced by humans. Naturally rare species may be restricted by features of their breeding systems. Species that are rare because of human activities may have declined simply through loss of habitat. Features of their breeding system, however, may make certain species especially vulnerable to

Table 4.1. *A synopsis of reproductive systems in flowering plants emphasizing features important in ex situ propagation and restoration*

Distribution of sex phenotypes in population	Presence of self-compatibility (SC) versus self-incompatibility (SI)	Morphological and temporal features affecting outcrossing in hermaphroditic species	Mating system	Mode of pollination	Considerations for *ex situ* propagation & restoration
Monomorphic (all individuals in population have female and male function)	Individuals in population self-compatible, level of self-fertilization variable	Cleistogamy (closed flowers) leads to self-fertilization Autogamy promotes high levels of selfing, may be obligate or facultative Spatial separation of anthers and stigmas (herkogamy) may promote outcrossing & minimize pollen/stigma interference Temporal separation of anthers and stigmas (dichogamy) may promote outcrossing and minimize pollen/stigma interference	Virtually complete selfing in autogamous & cleistogamous species to high levels of outcrossing, depending on the degree of herkogamy and/or dichogamy	No biotic agents required for autogamous and cleistogamous species, vectors essential in other cases	For autogamous species, sampling of many populations may be necessary to ensure an adequate representation of genetic variability in ex situ populations. For outcrossing species, more variability is likely within populations.
	SI present, control gametophytic (incompatibility reaction controlled by haploid genotype of pollen grain)	Spatial separation of anthers and stigmas (herkogamy) may mini-mize pollen/stigma interference Temporal separation of anthers and stigmas (dichogamy) may minimize pollen/stigma interference	High level of outcrossing in large populations, although inbreeding may occur. Reduction in the number of SI alleles may lead to failure of sexual reproduction	Agents required, may be biotic or abiotic	Reciprocal full-sib matings possible among progeny from a single individual, leading to high levels of inbreeding. Large numbers of SI alleles usually present in populations, loss of alleles could lead to reproductive failure.

	Breeding system	Pollen vector	Mating system	Implications for conservation
	SI present, control sporophytic (incompatibility reaction of pollen grain determined by the genotype of plant producing pollen grain)	High level of outcrossing in large populations, consanguineous matings lead to inbreeding in small populations	Required, may be biotic or abiotic	Not all combinations of full-sib matings lead to seed production, reducing potential level of inbreeding in artificial breeding programs. In fragmented populations loss of SI alleles may lead to reproductive failure.
	Heteromorphic SI present, two or three reproductive morphs occur in population	Highly outcrossing, consanguineous matings lead to inbreeding in small populations	Required, biotic in all observed cases	In *ex situ* populations, all reproductive morphs must be maintained. Morphological differences among morphs can be used to identify SI alleles.
Dimorphic (unisexual individuals found in populations)	SI absent	High level of outcrossing; in small populations, consanguineous matings may lead to inbreeding.	Biotic or abiotic vectors essential for pollen transfer, dicliny is usually associated with wind pollination or pollination by non-specialized pollen vectors	Number of individuals required in *ex situ* breeding programs will be doubled compared with hermaphroditic species, males and females should be equally represented

this or to other human activities. For example, a vital pollinator could be lost well before the habitat of the plant species is eliminated, but the destruction of pollinator populations has as significant an impact as habitat destruction. Regardless of the cause of rarity, information on breeding systems is essential for *ex situ* conservation and reintroduction programs.

The relationship of breeding systems and rarity to genetic variability

The widespread application of starch gel electrophoresis has provided a general overview of the effects of plant breeding systems on genetic variability, as measured by the isozymes commonly assayed in electrophoretic studies. Comprehensive surveys by Hamrick and his associates (e.g. Hamrick & Godt 1990) have shown that selfing plant species have a lower percentage of polymorphic loci (41.8%) than outcrossing animal-pollinated (50.1%) and wind-pollinated (66.1%) species (Table 4.2). The number of alleles per locus, as well as H_{es}, a measure of genetic diversity, are also lower in selfing species. When populations of selfing species are contrasted to populations of outcrossing species, the differences are still more striking (Hamrick & Godt 1990). Genetic variation is distributed *among* populations of selfers; for outcrossers, most genetic variation occurs *within* populations. The G statistic, which ranges from 0 to 1, quantifies these differences; high values of G_{ST} indicate little genetic diversity within populations, but considerable diversity among populations. For selfers, G_{ST} was 0.510, compared with 0.197 and 0.099 for outcrossing animal- and wind-pollinated species, respectively (Table 4.2).

Thus, there is no doubt that breeding systems have profound effects on genetic variation in plant species. Are these effects important to the persistence of plant species? Stebbins (1957) argued that in largely outcrossing genera, highly selfing species are for the most part derived, and essentially evolutionary deadends. Darwin (1900), and many others in recent years, have observed that selfing is usually deleterious for species. Persistent selfing, however, perhaps as a result of environmental factors, is expected to purge a population of deleterious alleles (Lande & Schemske 1985), perhaps resulting in vigorous populations of selfers. There are many widespread, highly successful selfing species, indicating that selfing does not absolutely constrain success, as measured by persistence in ecological time. Furthermore, recent theoretical work has demonstrated that intermediate selfing rates may be stable under some conditions (Uyenoyama 1986, Charlesworth & Charlesworth 1987, Charlesworth, Morgan & Charlesworth 1990).

Selection may adjust selfing rates upward or downward, but the timeframe

Table 4.2. *Average measures of allozyme variation for species classified by breeding systems and geographic range*

Standard errors in parentheses. H_{es} is a measure of genetic variability. G_{ST} describes the proportion of variation occurring among populations of a species. Different superscripts within columns indicate significant differences at the 5% level (separate statistical tests were used for breeding systems and geographic range comparisons, respectively). Values for N are total sample sizes, and those in parentheses indicate sample sizes of taxa used to calculate G_{ST} values. See Hamrick & Godt (1990) for more details.

Factor	N	% Polymorphic loci	H_{es}	G_{ST}
Breeding systems				
Selfing	123 (78)	41.8 (2.9)[A]	0.124 (0.011)[A]	0.510 (0.035)[A]
Mixed mating, animal pollinated	64 (60)	40.0 (3.5)[A]	0.120 (0.015)[A]	0.216 (0.024)[B]
Outcrossing, animal pollinated	172 (124)	50.1 (2.0)[A]	0.167 (0.010)[A]	0.197 (0.017)[B]
Outcrossing, wind pollinated	105 (134)	66.1 (2.7)[B]	0.162 (0.009)[A]	0.099 (0.012)[C]
Geographic range				
Widespread	105 (87)	58.9 (3.1)[A]	0.202 (0.015)[A]	0.210 (0.025)[A]
Endemic	81 (52)	40.0 (3.2)[B]	0.096 (0.010)[B]	0.248 (0.037)[A]

Source: Hamrick & Godt (1990).

for such evolutionary events is uncertain. In artificial breeding programs using various species, deleterious alleles have been reduced in frequency after relatively few generations of selfing (Wright 1977), but whether or not a species could survive in the wild if forced into selfing, perhaps because it has lost a specialized pollinator, is unclear.

Plant species with restricted ranges have reduced allozyme variation relative to species with broader geographic ranges (Hamrick & Godt 1990). The percent polymorphic loci, number of alleles per locus, and genetic diversity are significantly lower for endemic than widespread species (40.0% vs. 58.9% polymorphic loci, 1.80 vs. 2.29 alleles per locus, and 0.096 vs. 0.202 H_{es}, or genetic diversity; see Table 4.2). Very similar patterns hold for variation at the population level (Hamrick & Godt 1990). G_{ST} among populations is higher for endemic than widespread species, although differences were not significant (Table 4.2).

Electrophoretic studies, which now encompass a large number of species possessing varying attributes, provide convincing evidence that breeding system and geographic range significantly affect genetic diversity. Electrophoretic studies, unfortunately, may be misleading; little is known of the relationship between electrophoretic variation and quantitative variation, and the enzymes surveyed represent a very small subset of those found in plants. Moreover, current electrophoretic studies provide little help in assessing the relationship of breeding systems to rarity, because it is unknown whether breeding systems are significantly associated with geographic range. Are restricted endemics (*sensu* Rabinowitz 1981) more likely to have selfing breeding systems than species with broad geographic ranges? Such an association could indicate a cause-and-effect relationship, although if the relationship were very tight, it would be difficult to determine whether selfing leads to endemism or the reverse. To assess cause and effect, any detected associations would have to be compared against breeding system patterns in widespread species, ideally by using phylogenetic approaches.

Have breeding systems influenced rarity?

Despite longstanding interest in rare plants (Kruckeberg & Rabinowitz 1985), only a few empirical studies (e.g. Harper 1979, Karron 1987a,b; Connor 1988, Karron *et al.* 1988, Karron 1989) have explicitly addressed the relationship between rarity and breeding systems. A number of studies, however, have recorded information relevant to this question. In the following sections, those studies of breeding systems that include any information on whether the species is widespread or a restricted endemic are surveyed. Cases in which rarity is anthropogenically caused are noted. The species included are categorized according to whether there was no obvious relationship of the breeding system to rarity, or whether they had a breeding system attribute likely to be associated with rarity. Within each of these categories, species are grouped according to basic breeding system characteristics including self-compatibility, homomorphic self-incompatibility, heteromorphic self-incompatibility, and dioecy (see Table 4.1). Species for which there have been no tests of self-incompatibility are grouped with self-compatible species. Where possible, widespread and rare congeners were compared in the hope of more readily identifying factors contributing to rarity.

Examples in which no relationship between breeding system and rarity could be detected

In most case studies it has been difficult to show that breeding systems caused rarity. It is important to recognize, however, that it is often impossible to pinpoint any particular cause for rarity. The failure to establish a relationship between breeding system and rarity may simply mean that a critical aspect of the breeding system was not studied.

Self-compatibility

Cantino (1985) studied *Synandra hispidula* (Labiatae) to determine whether its rarity could be attributed to its breeding system. Despite its showy flowers, *S. hispidula* has some capacity for autogamous seed production (46% seed set for flowers screened from pollinators, compared with 80% seed set for hand self-pollination and open-pollinated flowers). Cantino (1985) concluded that rarity could not be attributed to poor pollination. A longer-term study would be useful to determine the degree to which levels of pollination vary over time.

Mehrhoff (1983) compared the reproductive biology of two *Isotria* (Orchidaceae) species. Both are widely distributed, but they differ greatly in rarity. The rare species, *I. medeoloides*, is known from approximately 20 populations encompassing about 500 individuals (Mehrhoff 1983). In contrast, *I. verticillata* is very common near the center of its range; genetically distinct individuals may produce several hundred ramets apiece. The reproductive biology of the two species is different; clonal *I. verticillata* is self-compatible but depends on insects for pollination, while non-clonal *I. medeoloides* is autogamous. Mehrhoff, however, concluded that seed germination and seedling establishment were more critical to the rarity of *I. medeoloides* than its reproductive biology, presumably because the species is non-clonal.

Dierenger (1982) concluded that the rare self-compatible *Orchis spectabilis* (Orchidaceae) receives few visits from pollinators, but nevertheless produces enough seeds 'to replace existing populations'. No demographic studies were carried out to support this claim. Fruit production following self-pollination was very low (1 fruit per 25 pollinations), indicating that outcrossing is important for this species, although the number of controlled outcrosses was too low ($n = 1$) to rule out difficulties in the pollination process as the cause of low fruit production. Open pollination resulted in 0–11% fruit production, depending on the year and population (Dierenger 1982).

Bender (1985) could not attribute the rarity of *Cypripedium candidum* (Orchidaceae) to its breeding system, and suggested that loss of specialized habitat was a more important explanation. *Cypripedium candidum* reportedly has reduced seed set following self- or sib-pollination (Klier, Leoschke & Wendel 1991; Bender [1985] and M. Bowles [personal communication] have obtained apparently viable seed after self-pollinating the plants). This species produces large clones, and habitat loss is likely to result in population fragments that each have only one or a few genotypes (Klier *et al.* 1991). Under such conditions, consanguineous mating should become more common, and perhaps less seed will be produced.

Loveless & Hamrick (1988) compared widespread *Cirsium canescens* with the restricted Great Lakes endemic *Cirsium pitcheri*. Both species are self-compatible. *Cirsium pitcheri* has a mixed mating system with outcrossing rates ranging from 35 to 88%. *Cirsium pitcheri* is essentially a genetically depauperate version of *C. canescens*, probably because of historical events associated with the origin of *C. pitcheri* after the last glaciation (Loveless & Hamrick, 1988). No features of the breeding system or other aspects of the life history were identified as contributing to the reduced genetic variation in *C. pitcheri*.

Vokou, Petanidou & Bellos (1990) showed that *Jankaea heldreichii* (Gesneriaceae) depends on pollinators for seed production, but a large proportion (68.2%) of open-pollinated flowers set fruit even though relatively few pollinator visits were observed. No tests were made for self-incompatibility. The authors concluded that in this species, specific ecological requirements may be most important in limiting distribution (Vokou *et al.* 1990).

Five species of self-compatible *Mabrya* (Scrophulariaceae), all restricted endemics of North American deserts, were analyzed genetically by Elisens & Crawford (1988). The species were electrophoretically distinct and morphologically divergent. All had adaptations for outcrossing, including showy flowers with spatial and temporal separation of anthers and stigmas. One showed little capacity for self-pollination and was largely outcrossing; the other four had mixed mating systems. Despite this difference in mating systems, all five have similarly restricted distributions, and there is little reason to believe that reproductive biology has differentially influenced their distribution. All species of *Mabrya* have very restricted habitat preferences, which may be the predominant factor leading to rarity (Elisens & Crawford 1988).

Connor (1988) studied 15 rare New Zealand grasses. All of these species were hermaphroditic except for a dioecious *Poa* species; females of this species appeared to set seed apomictically. One hermaphroditic species, *Rytidosperma tenue*, produced no seed, but the cause of sterility was unknown. The effect of breeding system on the rarity of these grasses was minimal.

Homomorphic self-incompatibility

Pedicularis furbishiae (Scrophulariaceae) possesses homomorphic self-incompatibility (Macior 1978), but has high seed set before predation (Menges, Waller & Gawler 1986), indicating that the number of self-incompatibility alleles is high enough not to interfere with seed production. *Pedicularis furbishiae* has no detectable genetic variation at 22 inferred loci, perhaps because of recurrent genetic bottlenecks (Waller, O'Malley & Gawler 1987). This species is restricted to north-facing banks of the St. John River, where occasional ice scouring of the bank opens new sites for colonization (Menges 1990). It seems likely that the extreme habitat specialization of this species has contributed more to its rarity than have features of its breeding system, although its lack of genetic variability cannot be eliminated as a potential factor in its rarity.

Karron (1987a) found little evidence that homomorphic self-incompatibility was related to rarity in a study comparing widespread and rare species in eleven genera. There was no consistent relationship between self-incompatibility and geographic distribution among these genera; self-incompatibility occurred in both rare and widespread species.

A more detailed study of two widespread and two restricted species of *Astragalus* (Karron *et al.* 1988) showed that one of the restricted species, *A. osterhouti*, had reduced genetic variability, as expected according to theory, but the other restricted species, *A. linifolius*, had genetic variability comparable to that of one of the widespread species. Consistent with this observation, substantial inbreeding depression was noted at the seedling stage (Karron 1989). Both of the rare *Astragalus* species in this study had higher levels of self-compatibility than self-incompatible *A. pectinatus*, their closest relative. In this case, self-compatibility may be a consequence of rarity, and may assure reproduction in small populations where pollinators may be scarce (J. D. Karron, personal communication).

More extensive analyses of outcrossing rates would be useful for understanding the relationship of self-incompatibility to levels of inbreeding. To understand the relationship of levels of genetic variability to geographic distribution, it might be essential to understand the history of genetic bottlenecks in the population, as emphasized by Karron *et al.* (1988).

In another study comparing widespread and restricted taxa, Fritz-Sheridan (1988) examined *Erythronium grandiflorum* var. *grandiflorum*, a common taxon, and *E. grandiflorum* var. *candidum*, a relatively rare taxon. Both varieties are self-incompatible, and various bee species are responsible for pollen transfer. There was no indication that pollinators visited either variety preferentially, nor was there evidence for pollinator limitation, or any other explanation for the rarity of *E. grandiflorum* var. *candidum* (Fritz-Sheridan 1988).

Denton (1979) compared levels of self-compatibility in rare and widely dispersed taxa of *Sedum* section *Gormania* (Crassulaceae). The four taxa with restricted distributions have the highest degree of self-compatibility in the genus, and occur at the lowest elevations, where early drying limits the duration of active growth. Most of the widespread species have moderate levels of self-compatibility; one has strong self-incompatibility. All *Sedum* species produce showy flowers that require pollinators for seed production (Denton 1979); whether loss of self-incompatibility lowers the outcrossing rate is unknown. After selfing, however, the restricted *Sedum* species have high seed production; self-compatibility may have been selected in them because it permits more rapid seed production, before moisture becomes limiting in their lower, drier habitat. Another possible explanation for the high seed production of the restricted *Sedum* species is lowered inbreeding depression. Even outcrosses in such populations are likely to be between genetically similar individuals, and may have led to a reduction in the level of inbreeding depression. In any case, the differences in level of self-compatibility among restricted vs. widespread *Sedum* taxa provide no obvious clues for the basis of rarity unless, as Denton (1979) suggests, retention of moderate to strong self-incompatibility has facilitated range expansion among some *Sedum* taxa.

In closely related species of *Oenothera*, there is again no obvious relationship between breeding systems and rarity. The range of self-incompatible *O. grandis* is relatively restricted compared with that of the closely related autogamous *O. laciniata*, a species that occurs throughout the eastern United States (Dietrich & Wagner 1988). In contrast, Wagner, Stockhouse & Klein (1985) found that two self-compatible species with restricted ranges (*O. brandegeei* and *O. cavernae*) were closely related to a subspecies of the widespread, self-incompatible *O. caespitosa*. The distribution pattern of *O. brandegeei* and *O. cavernae* is very similar to that of the very restricted *Stephanomeria malheurensis*, a self-compatible species derived from widespread, self-incompatible *S. exigua* subsp. *coronaria* (Brauner & Gottlieb 1987).

Factors likely to influence the range of self-incompatible and self-compatible congeners are the time of origin of a derived self-compatible race, and the propensity toward weediness of the self-compatible entity. Without such information, the relationship between self-incompatibility and rarity is difficult to predict.

Self-incompatibility and self-compatibility occur in *Dendroseris* (Asteraceae), a genus endemic to the Juan Fernandez Islands (Crawford & Stuessy 1987). *Dendroseris litoralis*, a self-compatible species, is found almost exclusively in cultivation. In contrast, *D. micrantha*, a self-incompatible species, is found in several natural populations. No other species in this genus have been tested for the presence or absence of self-incompatibility, however, and detecting a relationship between self-incompatibility and rarity may be very difficult for island species, which are especially subject to anthropogenic influences.

Gynodioecy, subdioecy, and dioecy

Species of *Schiedea* and *Alsinidendron* (Caryophyllaceae: Alsinoideae), a monophyletic assemblage of 28 species restricted to Hawai'i, have highly variable breeding systems ranging from dioecy to cleistogamy (Weller *et al.* 1990). Two gynodioecious species are federally endangered, but some of the common species also have diclinous breeding systems. Hermaphrodites occur in wet to mesic forests for the most part, and populations are usually, though not always, less dense than those of diclinous species. Facultative or obligate autogamy is found in the three species of *Alsinidendron* that have been studied; all three are very rare. All of these populations consist of a few individuals; the largest population of any of the species has only fourteen individuals (S. G. Weller & A. K. Sakai, personal observation). In the greenhouse, two species with more extreme autogamy are somewhat weedy, in part because seeds are produced readily without pollinators. In the field, autogamous seed production provides no apparent advantage in the face of relentless habitat loss (J. Obata, personal communication).

In *Schiedea* and *Alsinidendron* there is little evidence that shifts in breeding systems have influenced rarity. One problem in interpreting these patterns is that rarity may be a very recent phenomenon for many plant groups in the Hawaiian Islands, where extinction rates have climbed dramatically in recent years. Because the flora has been disturbed wholesale, any patterns in species distributions related to breeding systems may have been obscured.

When the rarity of diclinous versus hermaphroditic species is compared for all endemic and indigenous species in the Hawaiian flora, the likelihood of extinction appears higher for hermaphroditic species (G=4.60, df=1; P<0.05; A. K. Sakai, W. L. Wagner, D. L. Ferguson and D. R. Herbst, personal communication). This is somewhat counterintuitive, given that hermaphroditic species may benefit from assured fertility. Diclinous species in the Hawaiian flora often have small, apparently unspecialized flowers (A. K. Sakai *et al.*, personal communication); this may have given them an advantage relative to hermaphroditic species, which may require more specialized pollinators. A likely alternative explanation is that the endemic species of lobelioids, which are uniformly hermaphroditic, have had a disproportionately high number of extinctions (W. L. Wagner, personal communication). Again, the recent and rapid destruction of the Hawaiian flora and fauna may mean that apparent relationships are artifacts, and actual relationships are obscured.

Examples in which reproductive systems may influence rarity

In a number of species, reproductive systems do appear to be associated with restricted distributions. In the following discussion, the role of homomorphic and heteromorphic self-incompatibility in determining rarity will be discussed first. Then, cases in which the loss of specialized pollinators may have led to rarity will be discussed.

Homomorphic self-incompatibility

Homomorphic self-incompatibility is extremely widespread in the flowering plants (Charlesworth 1985) and, as previously discussed, cannot always be demonstrated to contribute to rarity. In species possessing homomorphic self-incompatibility, alleles occurring at the *S* locus may be very numerous (e.g. Campbell & Lawrence 1981), but if *S* alleles specify similar incompatibility phenotypes in pollen and stigmas or styles, matings are prevented. When a population becomes very small, drift should reduce the number of *S* alleles it contains. If the population is extremely reduced, species with this incompatibility system could fail to reproduce. An accurate knowledge of the size of a population is essential for predicting the numbers of incompatibility alleles it will contain. For example, the number of incompatibility alleles for *Oenothera organensis* appeared far too large given the apparently small population (Emerson 1939, 1940), but subsequent studies demonstrated that the population was far greater than was initially estimated (Levin, Ritter & Ellstrand 1979).

Aster furcatus (Asteraceae) is a self-incompatible species in which declining population size has led to reduced numbers of incompatibility alleles in populations (Les, Reinartz & Esselman 1991), despite the counteracting force of frequency-dependent selection. Sexual reproduction in this Midwestern aster is further complicated by clonal growth, which may result in reduced seed production if pollen is transferred among members of the same clone.

Although *A. furcatus* is self-incompatible, electrophoresis detected very little genetic variability within populations (Les *et al.* 1991), perhaps indicating that reductions in population sizes have resulted in lowered genetic variation. Alternatively, small populations may have been established through a single colonization, persisting afterward through clonal growth. Les *et al.* (1991) argue that reduced electrophoretic variation provides no indication of the allelic diversity at the self-incompatibility locus. Thus, conservation recommendations based only on electrophoretic diversity could be disastrous for self-incompatible species.

A dramatic loss of self-incompatibility alleles has occurred in *Hymenoxys acaulis* var. *glabra*, a species reduced in Illinois to three individuals possessing the same self-incompatibility type (DeMauro, Chapter 12 of this volume). Achenes were obtained from the Illinois plants only after they were mated to individuals from Ohio, which possessed different *S* alleles. The reintroduction of this species has depended on creating F1 hybrids between the Illinois and Ohio plants, thus maximizing the number of incompatibility alleles in the reconstructed population. Similarly, new *S* alleles introduced to populations of *Aster furcatus* lacking variability at the *S* locus could rejuvenate the populations (Les *et al.* 1991). The benefit of this approach must be weighed against the disadvantage of increasing genetic homogeneity among populations.

Clonal reproduction and chromosomal rearrangements leading to sterility may explain the unusual reproductive biology of *Erythronium propullans* (Liliaceae), a self-incompatible species found only in two Minnesota counties (Banks 1980) that produces almost no seed under natural conditions. Artificial crosses among widely separated individuals also failed to yield seed, although interspecific crosses with sympatric *E. albidum* did produce a few seeds (Banks 1980). Electrophoretic studies (Pleasants & Wendel 1989) show that *E. propullans* is genetically diverse within and among populations, providing no support for Banks' hypothesis that *E. propullans* may represent a single self-incompatible clone. Based on electrophoretic results, biogeographic information, and morphological similarities, *E. propullans* probably originated from *E. albidum*. Its sterility may result from chromosomal rearrangements during the speciation process (Pleasants & Wendel 1989), and its persistence presumably results from clonal growth.

Thien, White & Yatsu (1983) described the interaction between clonal growth and self-incompatibility in *Illicium floridanum* (Illiciaceae). The species has extensive clonal growth, and pollinator flights of the diverse insects that visit *I. floridanum* are short relative to the size of clones possessing the same incompatibility alleles; thus seed production is low (Thien *et al.* 1983). Seed production is greater following interpopulation crosses, indicating that within populations some inbreeding depression may be expressed, due to biparental inbreeding. Thien *et al.* (1983) suggest that self-incompatibility combined with the short flight distances of the predominant pollinators may explain the rarity of related angiosperms.

Heteromorphic self-incompatibility

The distribution of heteromorphic self-incompatibility in a number of genera indicates that restricted endemism may be influenced by reproductive biology. In heterostylous reproductive systems, two (distyly) or three (tristyly) reproductive morphs are found in populations. Reproductive morphs are self-sterile, but cross-compatible with different reproductive morphs. Numerous evolutionary modifications of heterostyly are known, including the evolution of self-compatibility and often homostyly (Ganders 1979; Barrett, Morgan & Husband 1989), and the evolution of distyly from tristyly (Ornduff 1972, Weller 1976). Because the morphology of the reproductive morphs is distinctive, biogeographic patterns associated with breeding system modifications are often discernible.

In a number of genera, breeding systems thought to be ancestral are found in species with limited distributions. For example, *Primula tschuktschorum* (Primulaceae) is a distylous species restricted to the Bering Strait area; *P. eximia* is a more widely distributed homostylous species presumed to have been derived from the distylous species (Kelso 1987). The homostylous derivative is self-compatible, and probably self-fertilizes extensively because of the physical proximity of the anthers and stigmas. Kelso (1987) suggests that reduced pollinator availability resulted in selection for homostyly in the distylous ancestor of *P. eximia*, and attributes the rarity of *P. tschuktschorum* in part to its requirement for insect pollination. Further studies of pollen loads and fruit and seed production in these species would be of interest. Based on the figure of *P. eximia*, this species appears to be a long homostyle, presumably derived from the ancestral distylous form by recombination within the heterostyly supergene. Long homostyles are expected to prevail in populations, because their pollen is more likely to participate in outcrossing than the pollen of short homostyles, which is produced in anthers near the base of the corolla (Crosby 1949).

Rarity is also associated with distyly in *Amsinckia* (Boraginaceae). Distylous species are found in central California; homostylous, apparently derived species have a much wider distribution (Ray & Chisaki 1957, Ganders 1975a). The reproductive systems of all four distylous species have been studied in detail: *A. douglasiana*, *A. vernicosa* var. *furcata*, and *A. grandiflora* have remnant cryptic self-incompatibility (Weller & Ornduff 1977, 1989; Ganders 1976; Casper, Sayigh & Lee 1988), while distylous races of *A. spectabilis* are completely self-compatible (Ray & Chisaki 1957, Ganders 1975b). Whether or not distyly and remnant self-incompatibility are the cause of rarity in *Amsinckia* is difficult to ascertain, because the distylous species appear in several cases to be restricted to unusual soil types (F. R. Ganders, personal communication). Several distylous species have reduced nutlet production relative to derived homostylous species, even when large quantities of compatible pollen are applied to the stigmas (Casper *et al.* 1988, Weller & Ornduff 1977).

Despite a few striking exceptions, such as *Lythrum salicaria*, tristyly is often associated with rarity or restricted endemism. In *Oxalis* section *Corniculatae*, tristylous species have more restricted distributions than derived distylous and homostylous species (Ornduff 1972). No tristylous species in section *Corniculatae* retain full trimorphic incompatibility relationships; in *O. sukdorfii* modified self-incompatibility is found in the long- and short-styled forms (Ornduff 1964). The remaining tristylous species in section *Corniculatae* appear to be completely self-compatible (Mulcahy 1964, Ornduff 1972), as are related distylous species (Ornduff 1972). Many semi- and quasi-homostylous species in section *Corniculatae* are widespread weeds (Ornduff 1972); their spread has probably been aided by their autogamous reproductive systems.

The distribution of tristylous and distylous breeding systems has been studied among the North American species of *Oxalis* section *Ionoxalis* (Denton 1973, Weller & Denton 1976). Tristylous species are for the most part restricted endemics in southern Mexico. Distylous species, thought to be derived from tristylous ancestors, have higher ploidal levels and range farther north. Distylous species retain strong self-incompatibility, and the reason for their wider distribution, compared with their tristylous relatives, is unclear. Several distylous species have very extensive clonal growth (Denton 1973), which may account for the greater geographic ranges of these species. In section *Ionoxalis*, the evidence for a relationship between tristyly and rarity may be circumstantial, because the trend from tristyly to distyly may parallel changes toward polyploidy and clonal spread.

In *Eichhornia* (Pontederiaceae), tristylous populations also have narrower distributions than derived dimorphic and monomorphic populations (Barrett *et al.* 1989). For *E. crassipes*, emphasis on clonal growth in adventive areas may be responsible for loss of style form diversity. In *E. paniculata*, an annual or short-lived perennial dependent on seed for reproduction, stochastic events associated with colonization, automatic selection of selfing alleles, and fertility assurance in the absence of pollinators may explain why the species is dimorphic or monomorphic throughout much of its range (Glover & Barrett 1986). As in the case of *Oxalis* section *Ionoxalis*, the rarity of tristylous populations in *Eichhornia* may be in part an artifact of the ease with which tristyly is modified as other changes occur, and of the widespread nature of the derived populations.

Pollinator rarity

Many plant species are obligately pollinated by specific animals; if their pollinators are lost or reduced in number, the plants could become rare. Specifically, many potential pollinators of the Hawaiian flora have been documented as extinct or declining in numbers, leading to the suspicion that rarity among

Hawaiian plant species may result from the lack of appropriate pollinators.

This possibility was examined for *Clermontia arborescens* (Lobeliaceae; Lammers, Weller & Sakai 1987), a species thought to depend for pollination on the i'iwi (*Vestiaria coccinea*), a Hawaiian honeycreeper (Spieth 1966, Berger 1981). During the study, no i'iwi were observed visiting *C. arborescens*; a single native bird, the amakihi (*Loxops virens*) made one visit (Lammers *et al.* 1987). The majority of visits were made by an introduced bird species, the Japanese White-eye (*Zosterops japonica*), which is apparently ubiquitous throughout the Hawaiian Islands. Whether the Japanese White-eye serves as a pollinator, however, is unknown; *C. arborescens* was producing fruit in the study area, but some species of *Clermontia* are autogamous and do not require pollinators for fruit production (Cory 1984). Clearly, if introduced bird species can serve as effective pollinators, the loss of native bird species that has occurred in many areas of Hawaii may not have predictable effects on ornithophilous plant species.

The degree of outcrossing effected by introduced versus native pollinators requires further investigation. When *Platanthera praeclara*, the western prairie fringed orchid of North America, is visited by introduced *Manduca* sp. (Sphingidae) hawkmoths, pollination is decreased. These hawkmoths have long tongues and their eyes do not contact the pollinaria, a requirement for pollen transfer. They thus act as nectar thieves, and their visits may decrease the attractiveness of the orchid to the shorter-tongued hawkmoth species that serve as pollinators (Sheviak & Bowles 1986).

Stenogyne kanehoana (Lamiaceae), an endemic mint of the Hawaiian Island of O'ahu, is at present restricted to a single population of two or three individuals (Herbst 1991). This species is large-flowered, and probably was pollinated by a honeycreeper now extinct on O'ahu. It has not produced fruit in recent years, which may reflect the loss of native pollinators. The continued existence of this species apparently depends on the persistence of the remaining adult plants, as there is no indication of any type of reproduction. In the short term, the massive encroachment of alien plant species is a greater threat to the persistence of *S. kanehoana* than failure to produce seed.

The elimination of specialized pollinators is a very serious problem for self-incompatible monocarpic species. The monocarpic Hawaiian silversword, *Argyroxiphium sandwicense*, is self-incompatible (Carr, Powell & Kyhos 1986) and depends on native bees for pollination. It is projected that as introduced ants eliminate colonies of native bees, silverswords will produce less seed (Loope & Medeiros, Chapter 6 of this volume).

In determining how the loss of a specialized pollinator will affect a plant species, it is important to consider the potential occurrence of substitute pollinators, the lifespan of the plant species, and whether or not it is self-incompatible. In most cases, it seems unlikely that highly specialized plant–pollinator interactions will be the cause of rarity; however, reduced visitation by *any* pollinators may contribute to rarity in some taxa.

For example, Karron (1987b) demonstrated that the restricted endemic *Astragalus linifolius* is visited by many of the same insect species that visit its widespread congener, *A. lonchocarpus*. The number of pollinator visits to the rare species, however, was far lower, which contributed to its lower fruit production. Karron (1987b) suggested that competition for pollinators may explain the lower visitation to *A. linifolius* although no obvious differences in floral biology or phenology between the species were noted.

Hopper, Campbell & Moran (1982) noted that an isolated tree of the rare *Eucalyptus caesia* produced virtually no fruit, probably owing to the absence of honeyeaters, the primary pollinators of this species. In other populations, there was no evidence of the reduced fruit production that might result from limited honeyeater activity.

Menges (1991) demonstrated that for hummingbird-pollinated *Silene regia* (Caryophyllaceae), a prairie species severely reduced in numbers by population fragmentation, the percentage of germination was greater for seeds collected from plants in larger populations, and suggests that one explanation could be that the smaller populations received fewer pollinator visits, which might lead to a higher proportion of geitonogamous pollinations. Seeds resulting from these pollinations would be affected by inbreeding depression, possibly causing the reduced germination characteristic of the small populations.

Pellmyr (1985) compared the breeding systems of *Actaea rubra* and *A. pachypoda*, and found that in Finland, where *A. rubra* is rare, it lacks adaptations with which North American populations of both species attract pollinators. He attributed the rarity of Finnish populations of *A. rubra* to low visitation rates by pollinators.

Conclusions and suggestions for evaluating breeding systems of rare plant species

There is little compelling evidence that plant breeding systems or pollination biology have had a pervasive effect in determining rarity. In 48 of the 84 cases examined here, no obvious relationship between plant breeding systems and rarity could be detected (Table 4.3). In the remaining 36 cases, rarity may be associated with breeding systems, but heterostylous species, which accounted for 22 of the 36 cases, probably inflate this figure. Heterostyly may be associated with rarity directly, but it may also be associated with other factors that

Table 4.3. *Synopsis of relationship of breeding systems to rarity*

Characterization of breeding system	Species for which there is no obvious relationship between rarity and breeding systems	Species where breeding systems may affect rarity	Feature of breeding system potentially influencing rarity	Is rarity anthropogenically induced?	Reference
Monomorphic self-compatibility	Alsinidendron (Caryophyllaceae) 3 spp.			Yes	Weller & Sakai (1990, unpublished)
	Cirsium pitcheri (Asteraceae)			Yes	Loveless & Hamrick, 1988
	Cypripedium candidum (Orchidaceae)			Yes	Bender, 1985; Klier et al., 1991
	Dendroseris litoralis (Asteraceae)			Yes	Crawford & Stuessy, 1987
	Isotria medeoloides (Orchidaceae)			No	Mehrhoff, 1983
	Jankaea heldreichii (Gesneriaceae)			Yes	Voukou et al., 1990
	Mabrya (Scrophulariaceae) 5 spp.			No	Elisens & Crawford, 1988
	Oenothera brandegeei (Onagraceae)			No	Wagner et al., 1985
	Oenothera cavernae (Onagraceae)			No	Wagner et al., 1985
	Orchis spectabilis (Orchidaceae)			No	Dierenger, 1982
	Poaceae - 13 New Zealand ssp.			No	Connor, 1988
	Schiedea (Caryophyllaceae) 5 spp.			Yes	Weller & Sakai (1990, unpublished)
	Sedum section Gormania (Crassulaceae) 4 spp.			No	Denton, 1979
	Stephanomeria malheureusis (Asteraceae)			No	Brauner & Gottlieb, 1987
	Synandra hispidula (Lamiaceae)			No	Cantino, 1985
		Actaea rubra (Ranunculaceae)	Low pollinator visitation	No	Pellmyr, 1985
		Clermontia arborescens (Campanulaceae)	Loss of pollinators	Yes	Lammers et al., 1987
		Platanthera praeclara (Orchidaceae)	Nectar thievery by introduced moth	Yes	Sheviak & Bowles, 1986
		Rytidosperma tenue (Poaceae)	Seed sterile, cause unknown	No	Connor, 1988

Category	Species (Family)			Reference
Monomorphic, homomorphic self-incompatibility	*Silene regia* (Caryophyllaceae)	Reduced pollinator visitation	Yes	Menges, 1991
	Stenogyne kanehoana (Lamiaceae)	Pollinator loss	Yes	Herbst, 1991
	Astragalus osterhouti (Fabaceae)		No	Karron, 1989; Karron et al., 1988
	Dendroseris micrantha (Asteraceae)		No	Crawford & Stuessy, 1987
	Erythronium grandiflorum (Liliaceae; var. *grandiflorum*)		No	Fritz-Sheridan, 1988
	Oenothera grandis (Onagraceae)		No	Dietrich & Wagner, 1988
	Pedicularis furbishiae (Scrophulariaceae)		No	Menges, *et al.*, 1986; Macior, 1978
	Argyroxiphium sandwicense (Asteraceae)	Potential loss of pollinators	Yes	Carr *et al.*, 1986
	Aster furcatus (Asteraceae)	Loss of SI* alleles	Yes	Les *et al.*, 1990
	Astragalus linifolius (Fabaceae)	Reduced pollinator visitation	Yes?	Karron, 1987b
	Erythronium propullans (Liliaceae)	Sterility resulting from chromosomal rearrangements	No	Banks, 1980; Pleasants & Wendel, 1989
	Hymenoxys acaulis var. *glabra* (Asteraceae)	Loss of SI alleles	Yes	DeMauro, this volume
	Illicium floridanum (Illiciaceae)	Extensive clonal growth in combination with SI	No	Thien *et al.*, 1983
Monomorphic, presence/absence of self-incompatibility unknown	*Eucalyptus caesia* (Myrtaceae)	Pollinator loss	Yes	Hopper *et al.*, 1982

Table 4.3. (*cont.*)

Characterization of breeding system	Species for which there is no obvious relationship between rarity and breeding systems	Species where breeding systems may affect rarity	Feature of breeding system potentially influencing rarity	Is rarity anthro-pogenically induced?	Reference
Heteromorphic self-compatibility (occasional cryptic self-incompatibility or self-compatibility)		*Amsinckia* (Boraginaceae) 4 spp.	Distyly, specialized soil preferences?	Yes	Ray and Chisaki, 1957; Ganders, 1975a, 1975b, 1979; Casper *et al.*, 1988
		Eichhornia (Pontederiaceae) 2 spp.	Tristyly	No	Barrett *et al.*, 1989; Glover & Barrett, 1986
		Oxalis section *Corniculatae* (Oxalidaceae) 2 spp.	Tristyly	No	Ornduff, 1964; Ornduff, 1972
		Oxalis section *Ionoxalis* (Oxalidaceae) 13 taxa	Tristyly	No	Denton, 1973; Weller & Denton, 1976
		Primula tschuktschorum (Primulaceae)	Distyly	No	Kelso, 1987
Dimorphic	(Poaceae) 1 sp. *Schiedea* (Caryophyllaceae) 3 spp.			No Yes	Connor, 1988 Weller & Sakai (unpublished)

*SI = Self-incompatibility

have a more direct influence on distribution. Aside from heterostyly, plant rarity was most likely to be associated with pollinator rarity or a nectar thief (8 cases), or loss of *S* alleles (3 cases, Table 4.3). Although among the species examined pollinator rarity was as likely to affect self-compatible as self-incompatible species (Table 4.3), the effects of pollinator rarity are likely to be exacerbated by self-incompatibility. As expected, anthropogenically induced rarity was common among species that had lost pollinators or self-incompatibility alleles.

Cases in which breeding systems appear to have influenced rarity provide guidelines for future research. Species with heteromorphic self-incompatibility may be especially sensitive to human disturbance if they occur in naturally small populations. Homomorphic self-incompatibility, especially in species with extensive clonal growth, may become important in rarity as populations are fragmented, with each fragment possessing only a few genetically distinct individuals. As the disruption of natural communities continues, the loss or decline of pollinators may adversely affect reproduction in both self-compatible and self-incompatible plant species before the physical destruction of the plant species themselves becomes important.

Wholesale destruction of natural areas may have contributed far more to rarity than have plant breeding systems or pollination biology, but failure to understand the details of plant reproductive biology could spell disaster for the management of remnant populations, *ex situ* maintenance, and reintroduction into natural or restored habitats of rare plants. For example, the strategies for maintaining a cleistogamous species in cultivation would be far different from those used to maintain habitually outcrossing species that could experience strong inbreeding depression. The reintroduction of a wind-pollinated herb that depends on proximity to other plants for pollination would be considerably different from the reintroduction of a plant species that depends on specialized pollinators capable of flying over relatively long distances. Without a thorough knowledge of reproductive and pollination biology, we are unlikely to prevent the loss of many plant species now bordering on extinction.

Applying the analysis of breeding systems to the conservation of rare species

The following protocol is suggested for the analysis of breeding systems of rare species as applied to *ex situ* conservation programs. First, the distribution of sex among individuals should be investigated. If a species is dioecious, more individuals must be maintained in cultivation than if it were hermaphroditic, and breeding programs similar to those described for animals by Lacy

(Chapter 3 of this volume) can be used for *ex situ* propagation. If a species is hermaphroditic, it must be tested for the presence and type of self-incompatibility. With gametophytic self-incompatibility, reciprocal full-sib crosses are compatible. With sporophytic self-incompatibility, however, reciprocal crosses often fail. These differences offer advantages and disadvantages in *ex situ* breeding programs. With gametophytic self-incompatibility more crosses produce seeds, but the level of inbreeding could be greater. With sporophytic self-incompatibility, there are fewer incompatibility alleles relative to gametophytic self-incompatibility, suggesting that considerable care must be exercised when sampling species with sporophytic systems to avoid an overly small sample of self-incompatibility alleles in a captive population.

Both self-incompatible and self-compatible species are subject to inbreeding, and care must be taken in captive breeding programs to maintain the maximum possible level of outcrossing (see Lacy, Chapter 3 of this volume). Self-compatible, highly selfing species present special problems because genetic variability is distributed among, rather than within, populations. Sampling a number of wild populations would be essential for maximizing genetic variation for captive breeding. Care in maximizing outcrossing or the level of genetic variability, however, does not avoid the more subtle effects of selection in greenhouses or botanical gardens. Novel phenotypes exposed in these environments may be favored by selection, creating populations of species better adapted to cultivation than to survival in the wild (Weis 1992). The perennial, often clonal nature of many plants in part offsets the complications of inadvertent selection of inappropriate genotypes. For example, it was possible to maintain self-sterile genotypes of *Hymenoxys acaulis* var. *glabra* for a number of years because this species propagates clonally (DeMauro, Chapter 12 of this volume). In many cases it may be possible to reintroduce the same genotypes removed from the natural environment. Reintroduction should nevertheless occur as soon as feasible, because selection in the greenhouse or botanical garden is ultimately unavoidable, and plants in cultivation are likely to acquire diseases or pests that could compromise attempts to reestablish populations.

The dependence of most plant species on pollinators introduces another level of complexity for captive breeding programs. Reintroducing a species critically dependent on an extinct pollinator will be of little use. Even when introduced pollinators substitute for extinct pollinators, the effect on gene flow and selection must be understood. The detailed population studies essential to acquire this information may not be feasible, especially when the natural environment has been extensively disrupted. Plant species that reproduce autogamously or have wind or water pollination will introduce different concerns. Establishing the appropriate population density for reintroduction will be essential for species with abiotic pollination because pollen transfer is distance-dependent. Tailoring reintroduction plans to different modes of reproduction found among species may be time-consuming, but it is essential to prevent reproductive failure under natural conditions.

Reintroduction schemes will be of little value unless the reproductive systems of reintroduced species are monitored in detail. Because the effort will be substantial, the most satisfactory compromise may be detailed monitoring of a subsample of species reintroduced into natural environments. The difficulties associated with *ex situ* propagation and restoration of rare species underscore the advantage of protecting natural environments before species become rare.

Acknowledgments

I thank Ann K. Sakai, Warren L. Wagner, Diane L. Ferguson, and Derral R. Herbst for permission to cite unpublished data. I am grateful to Marlin Bowles, Marcella DeMauro, Michele Dudash, Charles Fenster, Jeff Karron, and Ann Sakai for manuscript review.

Literature cited

Baker, H. G. (1955) Self-compatibility and establishment after 'long-distance' dispersal. *Evolution*, **9**, 347–9.

Baker, H. G. (1967) Support for Baker's Law - As a rule. *Evolution*, **21**, 853–6.

Banks, J. A. (1980) The reproductive biology of *Erythronium propullans* Gray and sympatric populations of *E. albidum* Nutt. (Liliaceae). *Bulletin of the Torrey Botanical Club*, **107**, 181–8.

Barrett, S. C. H., Morgan, M. T. & Husband, B. C. (1989) The dissolution of a complex genetic polymorphism: the evolution of self-fertilization in tristylous *Eichhornia paniculata* (Pontederiaceae). *Evolution*, **43**, 1398–416.

Bender, J. D. (1985) The reproductive biology of *Cypripedium candidum* Muhl. ex Willd. (Orchidaceae). *Ohio Journal of Science*, **85**, 12.

Berger, A. J. (1981) *Hawaiian Birdlife*, 2nd edn. Honolulu: University of Hawaii Press.

Brauner, S. & Gottlieb, L. D. (1987) A self-compatible plant of *Stephanomeria exigua* subsp. *coronaria* (Asteraceae) and its relevance to the origin of its self-pollinating derivative *S. malheurensis*. *Systematic Botany*, **12**, 299–304.

Campbell, J. M. & Lawrence, M. J. (1981) The population genetics of the self-incompatibility polymorphism in *Papaver rhoeas*. II. The number and frequency of *S*-alleles in a natural population (R106). *Heredity*, **46**, 81–90.

Cantino, P. D. (1985) Facultative autogamy of *Synandra hispidula* (Labiatae). *Castanea*, **50**, 105–11.

Carr, G. D., Powell, E. A. & Kyhos, D. W. (1986) Self-incompatibility in the Hawaiian Madiinae (Compositae): An exception to Baker's rule. *Evolution*, **40**, 430–4.

Casper, B. B., Sayigh, L. S. & Lee, S. S. (1988) Demonstration of cryptic incompatibility in distylous *Amsinckia douglasiana*. *Evolution*, **42**, 248–53.

Charlesworth, D. (1985) Distribution of dioecy and self-incompatibility in angiosperms. In *Evolution: Essays in Honour of John Maynard Smith*, ed. Greenwood, P. J. & Slatkin, M., pp. 237–68. Cambridge University Press.

Charlesworth, D. (1989) Evolution of low female fertility in plants: pollen limitation, resource allocation and genetic load. *Trends in Ecology and Evolution*, **4**, 289–92.

Charlesworth, D. & Charlesworth, B. (1987) Inbreeding depression and its evolutionary consequences. *Annual Review of Ecology and Systematics*, **18**, 237–68.

Charlesworth, D., Morgan, M. T. & Charlesworth, B. (1990) Inbreeding depression, genetic load, and the evolution of outcrossing rates in a multilocus system with no linkage. *Evolution*, **44**, 1469–89.

Connor, H. E. (1988) Breeding systems in New Zealand grasses X. Species at risk for conservation. *New Zealand Journal of Botany*, **26**, 163–7.

Cory, C. (1984) Pollination biology of two species of Hawaiian Lobeliaceae (*Clermontia kakeana* and *Cyanea angustifolia*) and their presumed coevolved relationship with native honeycreepers (Drepanidae). M. A. thesis, Fullerton: California State University.

Crawford, D. J. & Stuessy, T. F. (1987) Allozyme divergence and the evolution of *Dendroseris* (Compositae: Lactuceae) on the Juan Fernandez Islands. *Systematic Botany*, **12**, 435–43.

Crosby, J. L. (1949) Selection of an unfavourable gene-complex. *Evolution*, **3**, 212–30.

Darwin, C. (1900) *The Effects of Cross and Self Fertilisation in the Vegetable Kingdom,* 2nd edn. London: John Murray.

Denton, M. F. (1973) A monograph of *Oxalis*, section *Ionoxalis* (Oxalidaceae) in North America. *Publications of the Museum, Michigan State University, Biological Series*, **4**, 455–615.

Denton, M. F. (1979) Cytological and reproductive differences in *Sedum* section *Gormania* (Crassulaceae). *Brittonia*, **31**, 197–211.

Dierenger, G. (1982) The pollination ecology of *Orchis spectabilis* L. (Orchidaceae). *Ohio Journal of Science*, **82**, 218–25.

Dietrich, W. & Wagner, W. L. (1988) Systematics of *Oenothera* section *Oenothera* subsection *Nutantigemma. Systematic Botany Monographs*, **24**, 1–91.

Elisens, W. J. & Crawford, D. J. (1988) Genetic variation and differentiation in the genus *Mabrya* (Scrophulariaceae-Antirrhineae): Systematic and evolutionary inferences. *American Journal of Botany*, **75**, 85–96.

Emerson, S. (1939) A preliminary survey of the *Oenothera organensis* population. *Genetics*, **24**, 538–52.

Emerson, S. (1940) Growth of incompatible pollen tubes in *Oenothera organensis. Botanical Gazette*, **101**, 890–911.

Fritz-Sheridan, J. K. (1988) Reproductive biology of *Erythronium grandiflorum* and *candidum* (Liliaceae). *American Journal of Botany*, **75**, 1–14.

Ganders, F. R. (1975a) Heterostyly, homostyly, and fecundity in *Amsinckia spectabilis* (Boraginaceae). *Madroño*, **23**, 56–62.

Ganders, F. R. (1975b) Mating patterns in self-compatible distylous populations of *Amsinckia* (Boraginaceae). *Canadian Journal of Botany*, **53**, 773–9.

Ganders, F. R. (1976) Pollen flow in distylous populations of *Amsinckia* (Boraginaceae). *Canadian Journal of Botany*, **54**, 2530–535.

Ganders, F. R. (1979) The biology of heterostyly. *New Zealand Journal of Botany*, **17**, 607–35.

Glover, D. E. & Barrett, S. C. H. (1986) Variation in the mating system of *Eichhornia paniculata* (Spreng.) Solms. (Pontederiaceae). *Evolution*, **40**, 1122–31.

Hamrick, J. L. & Godt, M. J. W. (1990) Allozyme diversity in plant species. In *Plant Population Genetics, Breeding, and Genetic Resources*, ed. Brown, A. H. D., Clegg, M. T., Kahler, A. L. & Weir, B. S., pp. 43–63. Sunderland: Sinauer Associates.

Harper, K. T. (1979) Some reproductive and life history characteristics of rare plants and implications of management. *Great Basin Naturalist Memoirs*, **3**, 129–37.

Herbst, D. R. (1991) Endangered and threatened wildlife and plants; proposed endangered status for a plant, *Stenogyne kanehoana* (no common name). *Federal Register*, **56**, 2493–6.

Hopper, S. D., Campbell, N. A. & Moran, G. F. (1982) *Eucalyptus caesia*, a rare mallee of granite rocks from south-western Australia. In *Species at Risk Research in Australia*, ed. Groves, R. H. & Ride, W. D. L., pp. 46–61. Canberra: Australian Academy of Science.

Karron, J. D. (1987a) A comparison of levels of genetic polymorphism and self-compatibility in geographically restricted and widespread plant congeners. *Evolutionary Ecology*, **1**, 47–58.

Karron, J. D. (1987b) The pollination ecology of co-occurring geographically restricted and widespread species of *Astragalus* (Fabaceae). *Biological Conservation*, **39**, 179–93.

Karron, J. D. (1989) Breeding systems and levels of inbreeding depression in geographically restricted and widespread species of *Astragalus* (Fabaceae). *American Journal of Botany*, **76**, 331–40.

Karron, J. D., Linhart, C. A., Chaulk, Y. B. & Robertson, C. A. (1988) Genetic structure of populations of geographically restricted and widespread species of *Astragalus*. *American Journal of Botany*, **75**, 1114–9.

Karron, J. D., Marshall, D. L. & Oliveras, D. M. (1990) Numbers of sporophytic self-incompatibility alleles in populations of wild radish. *Theoretical and Applied Genetics*, **79**, 457–60.

Kelso, S. (1987) *Primula tschuktschorum* and *Primula eximia* (Primulaceae: section *Crystallophlomis*): A distylous species and its homostylous derivative from the Bering Strait Region, Alaska. *Brittonia*, **39**, 63–72.

Klier, K., Leoschke, M. J. & Wendel, J. F. (1991) Hybridization and introgression in white and yellow ladyslipper orchid (*Cypripedium candidum* and *C. pubescens*). *Journal of Heredity*, **82**, 305–18.

Kruckeberg, A. R. & Rabinowitz, D. (1985) Biological aspects of endemism. *Annual Review of Ecology and Systematics*, **16**, 447–79.

Lammers, T. G., Weller, S. G. & Sakai, A. K. (1987) Japanese White-eye, an introduced passerine, visits the flowers of *Clermontia arborescens*, an endemic Hawaiian Lobelioid. *Pacific Science*, **41**, 74–7.

Lande, R. & Schemske, D. W. (1985) The evolution of self-fertilization and inbreeding depression in plants. I. Genetic models. *Evolution*, **39**, 24–40.

Les, D. H., Reinartz, J. A. & Esselman, E. J. (1991) Genetic consequences of rarity in *Aster furcatus* (Asteraceae), a threatened, self-incompatible plant. *Evolution*, **45**, 1641–50.

Levin, D. A., Ritter, K. & Ellstrand, N. C. (1979) Protein polymorphism in the narrow endemic *Oenothera organensis*. *Evolution*, **33**, 534–42.

Loveless, M. D. & Hamrick, J. L. (1988) Genetic organization and evolutionary history in two North American species of *Cirsium*. *Evolution*, **42**, 254–65.

Macior, L. W. (1978) The pollination ecology and endemic adaptation of *Pedicularis furbishiae* S. Wats. *Bulletin of the Torrey Botanical Club*, **105**, 268–77.

Mehrhoff, L. A. (1983) Pollination in the genus *Isotria* (Orchidaceae). *American Journal of Botany*, **70**, 1444–53.

Menges, E. S. (1990) Population viability analysis for an endangered plant. *Conservation Biology*, **4**, 52–62.

Menges, E. S. (1991) Seed germination percentage increases with population size in a fragmented prairie species. *Conservation Biology*, **5**, 158–64.

Menges, E. S., Waller, D. M. & Gawler, S. C. (1986) Seed set and seed predation in *Pedicularis furbishiae* S. Wats, a rare endemic of the St. John River, Maine. *American Journal of Botany*, **73**, 1168–77.

Mulcahy, D. (1964) The reproductive biology of *Oxalis priceae. American Journal of Botany*, **51**, 1045–50.

Ornduff, R. (1964) The breeding system of *Oxalis suksdorfii. American Journal of Botany*, **51**, 307–14.

Ornduff, R. (1972) The breakdown of trimorphic incompatibility in *Oxalis* section *Corniculatae. Evolution*, **26**, 52–65.

Pellmyr, O. (1985) The pollination biology of *Actaea pachypoda* and *A. rubra* (including *A. erythrocarpa*) in northern Michigan and Finland. *Bulletin of the Torrey Botanical Club*, **112**, 265–73.

Pleasants, J. M. & Wendel, J. F. (1989) Genetic diversity in a clonal narrow endemic, *Erythronium propullans*, and its widespread progenitor, *Erythronium albidum. American Journal of Botany*, **76**, 1136–51.

Rabinowitz, D. (1981) Seven forms of rarity. In *The Biological Aspects of Rare Plant Conservation*, ed. Synge, H., pp. 205–17. New York: John Wiley & Sons.

Ray, P. M. & Chisaki, H. F. (1957) Studies on *Amsinckia*. I. A synopsis of the genus, with a study of heterostyly in it. *American Journal of Botany*, **44**, 529–36.

Sheviak, C. J. & Bowles, M. L. (1986) The prairie fringed orchids: a pollinator–isolated species pair. *Rhodora*, **88**, 267–90.

Spieth, H. T. (1966) Hawaiian honeycreeper, *Vestiaria coccinea* (Forster), feeding on lobeliad flowers, *Clermontia arborescens* (Mann) Hillebr. *American Naturalist*, **100**, 470–3.

Stebbins, G. L. (1957) Self fertilization and population variability in the higher plants. *American Naturalist*, **91**, 337–54.

Thien, L. B., White, D. A. & Yatsu, L. Y. (1983) The reproductive biology of a relict - *Illicium floridanum* Ellis. *American Journal of Botany*, **70**, 719–27.

Uyenoyama, M. K. (1986) Inbreeding and the cost of meiosis: The evolution of selfing in populations practicing biparental inbreeding. *Evolution*, **40**, 388–404.

Vokou, D., Petanidou, T. & Bellos, D. (1990) Pollination ecology and reproductive potential of *Jankaea heldreichii* (Gesneriaceae); a Tertiary relict on Mt Olympus, Greece. *Biological Conservation*, **52**, 125–33.

Wagner, W. L., Stockhouse, R. E. & Klein, W. M. (1985) The systematics and evolution of the *Oenothera caespitosa* species complex (Onagraceae). *Annals of the Missouri Botanical Garden*, **69**, 1–103.

Waller, D. M., O'Malley, D. M. & Gawler, S. C. (1987) Genetic variation in the extreme endemic *Pedicularis furbishiae* (Scrophulariaceae). *Conservation Biology*, **1**, 335–40.

Weis, A. E. (1992) Plant variation and the evolution of phenotypic plasticity in herbivore performance. In *Ecology and Evolution of Host Plant Resistance*, ed. Fritz, R. F. & Simms, E. L., pp. 140–171. Chicago: University of Chicago Press.

Weller, S. G. (1976) Breeding system polymorphism in a heterostylous species. *Evolution*, **30**, 442–54.

Weller, S. G. & Denton, M. F. (1976) Cytogeographic evidence for the evolution of distyly from tristyly in the North American species of *Oxalis* section *Ionoxalis. American Journal of Botany*, **63**, 120–5.

Weller, S. G. & Ornduff, R. (1977) Cryptic self-incompatibility in *Amsinckia grandiflora*. *Evolution*, **31**, 47–51.

Weller, S. G. & Ornduff, R. (1989) Incompatibility in *Amsinckia grandiflora* (Boraginaceae): Distribution of callose plugs and pollen tubes following inter- and intramorph crosses. *American Journal of Botany*, **76**, 277–82.

Weller, S. G., Sakai, A. K., Wagner, W. L. & Herbst, D. R. (1990) Evolution of dioecy in *Schiedea* (Caryophyllaceae: Alsinoideae) in the Hawaiian Islands: Biogeographical and ecological factors. *Systematic Botany*, **15**, 266–76.

Wright, S. (1939) The distribution of self-sterility alleles in populations. *Genetics*, **24**, 538–52.

Wright, S. (1977) *Evolution and the Genetics of Populations*. Volume 3. *Experimental Results and Evolutionary Deductions*. Chicago: The University of Chicago Press.

5

Experimental evidence for insect impact on populations of short-lived, perennial plants, and its application in restoration ecology

SVAŤA M. LOUDA

Introduction

Successful management of vegetation and the restoration of threatened or endangered plant populations clearly depend on the unambiguous identification of the factors that determine and limit plant abundance and distribution (e.g. Harper 1977, Jordan, Gilpin & Aber 1987). Physical conditions, plant physiological responses, and plant competitive interactions are often important (e.g. Harper 1977, Chabot & Mooney 1985, Pickett & White 1985, Grace & Tilman 1990), and these factors are usually evaluated. However, trophic interactions, such as those involving plant consumption by insects and pathogens, may also be critical in the growth, reproduction, and population dynamics of native plants (e.g. Harper 1969, Whittaker 1979, Rausher & Feeny 1980, Dirzo 1984, Howe & Westley 1988, Burdon 1987, Hendrix 1988, Burdon, Jarosz & Kirby 1989, Louda 1989), but are seldom evaluated in plans for the management or restoration of threatened plant species.

In this chapter, after presenting some background on insect herbivory in plant dynamics, I review several key results from two field experiments that excluded flower- and seed-feeding insects from native plants. I then use these results to: challenge the view that insect damage can be assumed to be irrelevant to plant success, suggest patterns of significant insect damage to seeds of native plants, and make two recommendations involving assessment of insect herbivory to improve the management and restoration of rare and threatened plant species. The evidence suggests that evaluation of insect herbivory is generally warranted. Insect herbivory can be a critical, limiting factor, particularly in determining the abundance and distribution of relatively short-lived, herbaceous, perennial plants. This appears especially true where both insect damage and regeneration failure are observed in declining populations of a rare or threatened plant.

Insect herbivory in plant performance

Analysis of plant growth, reproduction, density, and distribution has tradition-ally emphasized plant response to variation in physical conditions and resource availability (e.g. Curtis 1959, Weaver 1954, 1965, Harper 1977, Newman 1982, Tilman 1982, 1988). Attempts to understand the consequences of dam-age by small invertebrate herbivores for individual plants and for populations of plants have accelerated only in the past 20 years or so (Harper 1969, Janzen 1971, Whittaker 1979, Hodkinson & Hughes 1982, Crawley 1983, Dirzo 1984, Hendrix 1988, Louda 1989, Louda, Keeler & Holt 1990a). These attempts have created some controversy, and two opposing schools of thought have emerged.

One school argues that chronic damage by coevolved, adapted insects is sel-dom a significant factor in plant success (e.g. Owen 1980, Crawley 1989a,b), except possibly under outbreak conditions (Barbosa & Schultz 1987). Several observations are used to support this interpretation. For example, it has been observed that the 'world is green' (Hairston, Smith & Slobodkin 1960; Slobodkin, Smith & Hairston 1967), that chronic insect damage to the foliage of adults of the dominant plant species averages only 5–10% of net productiv-ity (e.g. Odum 1959, Hairston *et al.* 1960), and that there is little evidence of competition among phytophagous insects for food resources (Strong, Lawton & Southwood 1984). Furthermore, most plants have some capacity to compen-sate for tissue damage or removal (Hendrix 1979, 1984, McNaughton 1983, 1986, Maschinski & Whitham 1989). Also, plant-feeding insects have ene-mies, which may help reduce herbivore impact (Lawton & McNeill 1979, Strong *et al.* 1984). Finally, seed supply often seems to exceed the numbers required for recruitment, at least at the level of replacement (Harper 1977, Crawley 1990).

The other school, however, points out that such observational evidence is incomplete and inconclusive. For example, to insects the world may actually be colored 'brown and fibrous' or 'chemically noxious' (Ehrlich & Birch 1967, Feeny 1976). Also, chronic insect damage to foliage can be high, even on adults of dominant forest trees (Morrow & LaMarche 1978; Lowman 1984a,b; Fox & Morrow 1983, 1986; Morrow & Fox 1989), and insect damage and its effects are often much heavier on young individuals, especially seeds (see Janzen 1971, Fenner 1985). Also, in spite of some interesting exceptions, pos-sibly including grasses (Belsky 1986, 1987), complete compensation for loss of tissue and seeds to insects generally falls short of complete recovery. Furthermore, the success of plant regrowth and compensation depends directly on the availability of time and resources for regrowth (Cottam, Whittaker &

Malloch 1986, Karban & Courtney 1987, Maschinski & Whitham 1989, Polley & Detling 1989, Louda *et al.* 1990a). Thus, the impact of chronic insect consumption is difficult to discern without experiment.

The accumulating experimental evidence on insect herbivory suggests that the interactions are complex, subtle, and often more important in plant dynamics than suspected (Harper 1969, Whittaker 1979, Dirzo 1984, Marquis 1984, Stamp 1984, Crawley 1985, 1987, Hendrix 1988, Louda 1988, 1989, Louda *et al.* 1990a). Experimental exclusions of insects provide strong evidence with which to estimate the actual effect of insect feeding on plant performance.

The exclusion tests available show that chronic insect herbivory can have a highly significant negative effect on plant survival, growth, flowering, seed set, or successional success (Cantlon 1969; Rockwood 1974; Morrow & LaMarche 1978; Waloff & Richards 1977; Parker & Root 1981; Brown 1982; Louda 1982a,b, 1984, 1989; Hendrix 1984; Kinsman & Platt 1984; Parker 1985; Parker & Salzman 1985; Hendrix, Brown & Gange 1989; Louda, Potvin & Collinge 1990b). Exclusion of insects also illustrates that they can alter plant competitive ability (Windle & Franz 1979; Bentley & Whittaker 1979; Bentley, Whittaker & Malloch 1980; Fowler & Rausher 1985; Cottam *et al.* 1986; Louda *et al.* 1990a).

Insect herbivory that affects the production, maturation, or dispersal of seeds may be especially critical in determining the success of plant reproduction (e.g. Janzen 1971, Fenner 1985, Hendrix 1988, Louda 1989). Reliance on recruitment from seed varies among plant species (Grubb 1977), and contrary to usual expectation, the number of seeds produced may not exceed the number that allows for persistence. Experiments show that inflorescence-feeding insects limited seedling establishment and density for two composite shrubs (Louda 1982a,b, 1983) and for a native thistle (Louda *et al.* 1990b). These tests were done *in situ*, and thus combine desirable aspects of observational data with experimental evidence. If their results are generalizable, they suggest that the population consequences of insect consumption may be generally underestimated, especially for large-seeded, short-lived perennials with a colonizing life history strategy (Louda 1989).

The consequences of insect seed-consumption for seed production or for seedling recruitment cannot be evaluated using estimates of damage levels to seeds. Observational measures of damage generally underestimate the role of insects in reducing viable seed (Anderson 1988). Furthermore, since other factors may restrict seedling establishment even from abundant seed (Harper 1977, Crawley 1990), the seed-to-seedling linkage must be evaluated experimentally (Louda 1982a,b, 1983, 1989). The two main types of experiment that provide data on the role of seed limitation in seedling recruitment and plant density are artificial seed augmentation and consumer exclusions, both during seed development and after seed dispersal.

Artificial seed augmentation, which involves dispersing seeds by hand into marked quadrats (Harper 1977), is the classical test of the tightness of the seed-to-seedling linkage (see Darwin 1859; Foster 1964 in Harper 1977; Putwain, Machin & Harper 1968; Platt 1975; Werner 1977; Harper 1977; Gross & Werner 1982; Gross 1984; Crawley 1990). Seed augmentation generally results in significant increases in the recruitment of seedlings by large-seeded, nondominant herbaceous perennial plants, especially in open vegetation or disturbance patches.

Consumer exclusion allows a more direct measure of predator effects on the seed-to-seedling linkage. The *in situ* exclusion of consumers is more realistic, and allows assignment of causality, because it examines more natural seed release patterns, seed densities, and timing of seed release, while allowing other processes that influence the linkage to proceed as usual. Thus, such tests measure the direct impact of seed consumers, such as flower- and seed-feeding insects, on seedling densities. If seed-feeding insects significantly affect seedling numbers, then their exclusion should result in increased seedling densities around the parent plant. Few experiments testing this prediction have yet been published (see Fenner 1985, Howe & Westley 1988, Hendrix 1988, Louda 1989).

The results of two series of experimental studies of insect influence on the seed-to-seedling linkage suggest that where plant regeneration and population persistence depend directly on successful seed input, insect seed predation can be the most significant process limiting regeneration of the population. For many threatened plant species that depend on current seed supply for regeneration, seed predation can become a severe hazard as populations decline. Therefore, more attention should be paid to phytophagous insects in the management, restoration, and eventual delisting of threatened plant species.

Case 1: Goldenbushes, mid-successional shrubs in chaparral

Experimental studies of two native goldenbushes, which replace each other along the environmental gradient from coast to mountains in southern California (Fig. 5.1), demonstrate that insects feeding on flowers and developing seed can have significant demographic and distributional effects on the seedling recruitment and population dynamics of their host plant species (Louda 1978, 1982a,b,c, 1983, 1988). The species that predominates near the coast is coastal goldenbush, *Isocoma veneta* Nutt. (Nesom 1989), until recently considered to be *Haplopappus venetus* ssp. *vernonioides* (Nutt.) Hall (Hall 1928, Munz 1974).

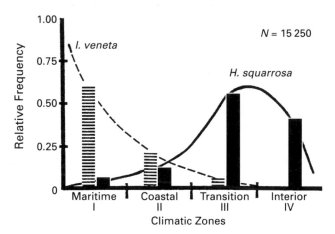

Fig. 5.1. Observed frequency of occurrence and replacement of *Isocoma* (*Haplopappus*) *veneta* (broken line and bars) at the coast by *Harzardia* (*Haplopappus*) *squarrosa* spp. *grindelioides* (solid line and bars) in the inland portion of the gradient from ocean to foothills of the coastal mountains in San Diego County, southern California, USA (adapted with permission from Louda 1989). Predispersal seed predation limits viable seed and seedling establishment at all sites for both species (Louda 1982a,b, 1983). Interestingly, the replacement of the two species along the gradient is best explained by differential predation pressure along the gradient: much higher seed losses for *H. squarrosa* caused by inflorescence-feeding insects near the coast (Louda 1982b) plus significantly more intense seedling losses for *I. veneta* caused by vertebrate herbivores inland (Louda 1983).

The species that predominates near the mountains is scaly goldenbush, *Hazardia squarrosa* (H. & A.) Green var. *grindelioides* (D.C.) Clark, comb. nov. (Clark 1977), which had been called *Haplopappus squarrosus* var. *grindelioides* (DC.) Keck (Hall 1928, Munz 1974). These species are quite similar in stature, general appearance, phenology and insect herbivore guilds.

Three results are important here. First, insects feeding on the developing inflorescences limited both the number of viable seeds and the number of seedlings recruited by both species at all study sites (Louda 1982a,b, 1983). Second, the distribution of the inland species, scaly goldenbush, was compressed and displaced away from the coast by more intense predispersal seed predation coastally (Louda 1982b). Third, the distribution of coastal goldenbush was also compressed, but it was displaced toward the coast by the combination of intense seed reduction by insects all along the gradient and by higher consumption of seedlings by vertebrate herbivores in the inland portion of an environmental gradient (Louda 1983). In summary, inflorescence-feeding insects limited the abundance of seedlings of both species of goldenbush all along the gradient, and damage by these insects was the primary factor in significantly altering the distribution of scaly goldenbush on the gradient (Louda 1978, 1982a, b, 1988).

Case 2: Platte thistle, a fugitive species in grassland

Grasslands worldwide are generally characterized by the mosaic of a few dominant grasses, interspersed with a surprising diversity of herbaceous perennial forbs (Weaver 1954, 1965, Risser *et al.* 1981). Many characteristic grassland forbs appear to depend on seed recruitment into disturbances for both local and metapopulation persistence (e.g. Platt 1975, Platt & Weis 1977, 1985, Goldberg & Werner 1983, Louda *et al.* 1990b). Many of the forbs of the once–extensive grasslands of the northcentral Great Plains, USA, also have diverse guilds of phytophagous insects (S. M. Louda, personal observation). To better understand such forb-insect interactions, the Platte thistle (*Cirsium canescens* Nutt.; Fig. 5.2A), a short-lived forb of Sandhills prairie, was studied, and the effects of predispersal flower- and seed-feeding by insects, postdispersal seed predation by vertebrates, and grass interference with seedling survival and growth on its population dynamics were tested (Louda *et al.* 1990b, Louda & Potvin 1994).

Sandhills prairie covers most of central Nebraska, USA (19300 sq. mi.), and forms the largest grass-stabilized continental dune system in the western

A   B

Fig. 5.2. Platte thistle, *Cirsium canescens.* (A) upper part of plant with inflorescence, illustrating leaf characters and flowerheads in five stages of development (from bottom: one in small bud, one in large bud, one in partial flower, two in full flower, and terminal one in maturing seed stage) (B) Dissection of a maturing seed stage flowerhead illustrating typical damage and pupae of the tephritid flies that feed on developing flowers and seed, and two or three viable, undamaged seeds at outside edge of head and outside the head.

hemisphere (Bleed & Flowerday 1989). The vegetation of the Sandhills is a special type of 'mixed' grassland (Weaver 1954, 1965), dominated by a distinctive combination of short, mid, and tall prairie grasses and forbs (Keeler, Harrison & Vescio 1980, Kaul 1989). Because the soils are fine sands and the annual rainfall is relatively low, soil moisture deficit stress occurs with some frequency, especially in the heavily vegetated interdune areas (Barnes & Harrison 1982, Barnes & Heinisch 1984).

Platte thistle is broadly, but sparsely, distributed throughout the Sandhills. Its microhabitats include the large disturbances called blowouts or smaller openings among clones of prairie grasses. Platte thistle is closely related to the federal–threatened Pitcher's thistle (*Cirsium pitcheri* [Torrey ex. Eaton] Torrey & Gray), which is endemic to the grassland dunes around Lakes Michigan, Superior, and Huron (Johnson & Iltis 1963, Keddy & Keddy 1984, Loveless 1984, Harrison 1988, Loveless & Hamrick 1988, McEachern, Magnuson & Pavlovic 1989, McEachern *et al.* Chapter 8 of this volume). Based on electrophoretic evidence, Loveless & Hamrick (1988) make a case for Platte thistle as the putative progenitor for Pitcher's thistle. They suggest that populations moved from the Sandhills into similar sand habitats to the northeast after the last glacial retreat, and differentiated relatively recently.

Platte thistle has a perennial, monocarpic life history, and reproduces only from seed. Plants grow as rosettes for two to four years, and then bolt, flower, and die. Insects do some damage to the foliage (W. O. Lamp, personal observation; S. M. Louda, personal observation), but much more striking damage to the developing inflorescences (Fig. 5.2B). Early instars feed on the floral tubes, later instars consume ovules, and both burrow into the receptacle disk; levels of damage to inflorescences average between 35 and 75% of the florets initiated (1977–1979, 1984–1991) (Lamp & McCarty 1979, 1981, 1982, Louda *et al.* 1990b). The insects that cause this damage are two species of picture-winged flies (Tephritidae: *Orellia occidentalis* (Snow), *Paracantha culta* (Wiedmann)), and a moth (*Homeosoma stypticellum* Grote: Pyralidae) related to the sunflower moth (Lamp & McCarty 1979, 1982).

At least three types of biological interaction could potentially influence the population dynamics of fugitive species, such as thistles. First, damage by insects to flowers and developing seeds can limit the success of plant reproduction and subsequent recruitment (Louda 1978, 1982a,b, 1983, Lamp & McCarty 1981, 1982). Second, postdispersal seed consumption by birds and rodents can also limit recruitment from seed, as found for several European species of thistle (de Jong & Klinkhamer 1988a,b, Klinkhamer, de Jong & van der Meijden 1988). Third, such species may be limited more by competition with established grasses than by absolute seed availability (Platt, Hill & Clark

1974, Platt 1975, Harper 1977, Platt & Weis 1977, 1985, Goldberg & Werner 1983, Crawley 1990). Consequently, three concurrent experiments were run to evaluate the influence of these three biotic interactions on the abundance and distribution of Platte thistle. The experiments were done from 1984 to 1990 at Arapaho Prairie, a Nature Conservancy preserve of Sandhills grassland in east–central Nebraska (Louda *et al.* 1990b, Louda & Potvin 1994).

In the first experiment, insecticide (Isotox, Chevron Chemical) was used to reduce the damage caused by insects to the developing flower heads in 1984 and 1985. There were three treatments: localized (flowerhead only) hand application of small amounts (50–100 ml) of insecticide-in-water, water-only, or nothing. The treatments were applied biweekly during the critical oviposition period of the flowerhead insects (May to mid-June, 1984 and 1985; 4 applications per year). The treatments at each location were switched between the two years to control for the effect of microclimatic variation among areas on treatment outcome. Both the development of viable seed within seedheads and the establishment of successful seedlings within grids around the experimental plants in the subsequent year were recorded, and seedlings were marked and followed to maturation. There was no evidence of plant toxicity or pollination reduction with insecticide application (Louda *et al.* 1990b, Louda & Potvin 1994). No significant differences were found in treatment effects between years, and the data are here combined to summarize the outcome.

The plants in all three treatments initiated a similar number of flowers (Fig. 5.3A). Insecticide application reduced insect damage to developing flowers and seeds by over 75%, leading to a significantly greater number of viable seeds (Fig. 5.3B). Thus, flowerhead insects significantly decreased the number of viable seeds that were matured and released by Platte thistle. The reduction in damage by insects and the concommittant increase in viable seed in the insecticide-treated plants led to a four- to six-fold increase in the new seedlings that established, thus increasing the seedling plant population density dramatically (Fig. 5.3C). This increase in seeds and then in seedlings subsequently led to a highly significant increase in the number of adult flowering plants in the next generation, four years later (1988 and 1989; Fig. 5.3D). The experiment thus clearly demonstrates the vital influence that flower- and seed-feeding insects have on seed supply, on seedling recruitment, and eventually on adult plant density of Platte thistle within its characteristic habitat.

Damage to developing flowers and seeds had a greater effect than did postdispersal predation on seeds by vertebrates. In the vertebrate exclosure experiment, 30 seeds, 15 buried and 15 scattered on the soil surface, were placed within a 30×30-cm plot. This seed density (333 m^{-2}) is within the range of potential seed density in the vicinity of an adult plant. Each of the 10 replicates

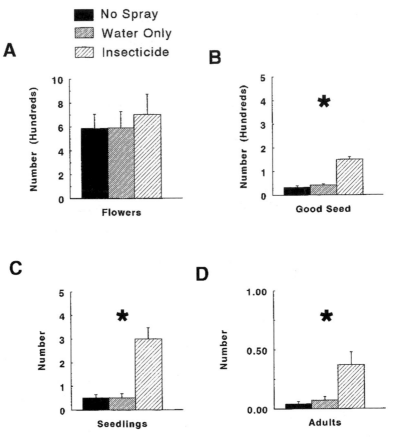

Fig. 5. 3. Summary of the results of the insecticide exclusion of inflorescence-feeding insects from developing flowerheads, 1984–1990, according to insecticide spray, water-only spray, and no spray treatments (see text): (A) number of flowers initiated; (B) number of viable, undamaged (good) seeds for release; (C) average number of seedlings established by each plant; and (D) number of flowering adults that were eventually produced per parent plant (adapted from Louda *et al.* 1990b, Louda & Potvin 1994).

contained three such plots, with either a complete enclosure cage of 1.25 cm (0.5 in.) hardware cloth, a comparable cage that was open on two sides and the top, or no cage. Five replicates were placed within grass vegetation, and five were placed in open areas near a large blowout in September 1984. Seedling emergence, growth, and survival were monitored over the next two years. The results under these experimental conditions show that overall germination rates were low, and that postdispersal seed predation had a small, but significant, effect on seedling recruitment in the open habitat associated with blowouts (Fig. 5.4).

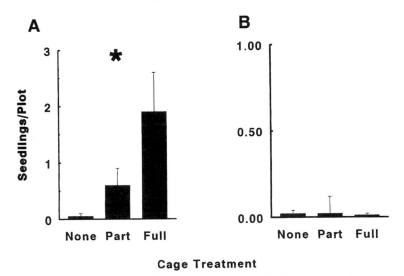

Cage Treatment

Fig. 5.4. Average number of seedlings surviving per plot in the cage exclusion of post-dispersal vertebrate seed predators, 1985–88, according to total, partial, and no caging (see text): (A) in disturbed blowout areas; and (B) in stabilized grassland vegetation adjacent to the blowout areas (adapted from Louda *et al.* 1990b).

Finally, the effects of competition from established grasses on the survival and growth of new seedlings were tested in a transplant experiment. In each of five sets of six seedlings, three seedlings were planted into an open area within a clone of *Panicum virgatum* and three seedlings, in a comparable spatial array, were planted into the open area between grass clones (Louda *et al.* 1990b). Grass competition greatly decreased seedling survival and growth over the subsequent two years (Fig. 5.5).

Analysis of the three experiments together allows an initial prediction of the relative contribution of the three types of biotic interaction to the dynamics of Platte thistle (*Cirsium canescens*) under natural conditions in Sandhills prairie. The insecticide exclusion experiment showed that flower and seed consumption by insects caused a highly significant reduction in both the number of seedlings established and the flowering plants that eventually resulted. Predispersal damage to flowerheads was responsible for a reduction in individual plant fitness, which led to population limitation. Plant competition and spatial or habitat variation amplified the influence of such interactions on plant demography (Louda *et al.* 1990b). Because these effects occurred with ambient levels of postdispersal seed consumers, because they occurred in grassland as well as in blowouts, because such factors as germination and seedling survivorship were comparable among treatments, and because the levels of insect

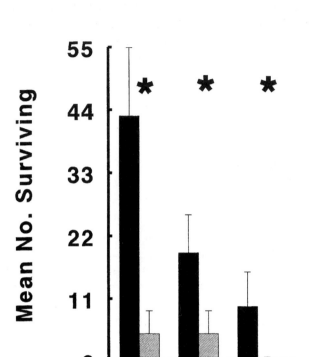

Fig. 5.5. Survival of Platte thistle seedlings transplanted into the open areas between grass clones versus into the open areas within grass clones (see Louda *et al.* 1990b).

damage were near average (Louda & Potvin 1994), insect destruction of flowers and developing seed can be considered the most important limiting factor in the recruitment and local abundance of Platte thistle. Moreover, the effects of the biotic interactions were cumulative. Postdispersal seed predation and seedling competition with established grasses augmented the effects of the major decrease in seed caused by the damage inflicted by flower- and seed-feeding insects.

Implications for restoration ecology

From the studies of goldenbushes and Platte thistle, it is clear that flower- and seed-feeding insects can have a highly significant effect on plant recruitment, abundance, distribution, and persistence. On the basis of these studies, a general methodological recommendation can be made for managing and rebuilding populations of threatened plant species. The recommendation also leads to a specific suggestion for the restoration of declining populations of the threatened Pitcher's thistle (*Cirsium pitcheri*), using experimental results with its nearest relative, Platte thistle (*Cirsium canescens*).

General methodology

The studies to date suggest that a mixed strategy of observational and experimental studies should become standard. Traditional observational studies of the natural history of threatened plant species need to be continued. However, actual tests of the factors that are thought to be important in controlling population dynamics and limiting density and distribution are also critical (see also Pavlik, Chapter 13 of this volume). To do this while minimizing any potential negative impacts on the threatened or endangered species, a comparative approach can be taken. After essential aspects of the ecological similarity are established observationally, a more common, but closely related and ecologically similar, species could be used for the experimental studies. Critical results should then be validated with comparable, but smaller-scale, tests on the protected species. The results would provide a strong conceptual and empirical basis for restoration management.

Positive tests, such as excluding predators suspected of being significant, hold particular promise and merit serious use. Such tests are 'win–win' experiments. The potential for damage to the threatened or endangered species should be low, and the potential for positive effect should be high. The synthesized results of the comparative observations and experiments could then be used to guide management to augment the growth and densities of appropriate populations of the threatened or endangered plant under natural circumstances.

In summary, augmentation and restoration strategies would have a stronger and more scientific basis if the traditional, observational study of a threatened or endangered plant's dynamics and interactions were matched with experimental determination of the relative importance of the factors suspected to be controlling its population demography. Emphasis should be placed on designing 'win–win' experiments and possible strategies of restoration management. Initially, experiments should be restricted to an ecologically similar, closely related, but non-threatened species, if available. Significant experimental results should then be retested in small-scale validation experiments on the threatened species. This process should enhance the effectiveness of restoration, and it should increase the probability of sustainable results after intervention.

A combined observational and experimental approach is also an efficient information-generating design, and can maximize our capacity to detect the really critical processes in the dynamics of rare plant species. Such an approach could be applied without jeopardizing the populations of threatened or endangered plants, and it avoids reliance on inherently tenuous extrapolations of causality from observational data alone. Specifically, experimental information on critical processes in the dynamics of a closely related, ecologically analogous species should provide objective, mechanistically based, specific recommendations for potential manipulations that have a high probability of increasing recruitment and persistence in populations of threatened or endangered plants.

Prediction for Pitcher's thistle

The parallels between the federal threatened Pitcher's thistle (*Cirsium pitcheri*) and its closest known relative, Platte thistle (*C. canescens*), are striking. These include: open sand habitat, early-season-growth phenology, monocarpic life history, comparable or identical flowerhead insects, relatively high levels of observed seed damage, and dependence upon current seed for recruitment (Lamp & McCarty 1979, 1981, 1982; Keddy & Keddy 1984; Loveless 1984; Loveless & Hamrick 1988; McEachern *et al.* 1989; Louda *et al.* 1990b; McEachern *et al.*, Chapter 8 of this volume).

Both species of thistle often have problems producing large numbers of viable seeds; good seeds of both are often difficult to find. The data substantiating this observation for Platte thistle are extensive and consistent among years and studies (e.g. Lamp & McCarty 1979, 1981, 1982; Louda *et al.* 1990b). Furthermore, it is clear that, for Platte thistle, insect damage to flowers and seeds is a major factor in its low levels of viable seed and low population recruitment and density (Fig. 5.3; Louda *et al.* 1990b). Pitcher's thistle also has low levels of seed viability, and good seed is usually scarce (Loveless 1984; Loveless & Hamrick 1988; McEachern *et al.* 1989; M. Bowles, personal communication). Insects and major insect damage in the inflorescences of Pitcher's thistle are often reported (Keddy & Keddy 1984, Loveless 1984, Loveless & Hamrick 1988). The levels of damage observed appear similar to those documented for Platte thistle.

The similarities between these species suggest that the experimental outcomes for the more common, non-threatened Platte thistle should form a reasonable model for biological predictions for the management of Pitcher's thistle. The most obvious prediction is that Pitcher's thistle's production of viable seed and establishment of seedlings could be increased significantly by restricting the damage caused by its flower- and seed-feeding insects. Increased seedling establishment and subsequently higher population densities within the protected dune habitat should stem the declines in populations of Pitcher's thistle that have recently been documented (McEachern *et al.* 1989, Chapter 8 of this volume) especially at Indiana Dunes National Lakeshore. Because extinction probabilities tend to be inversely related to population densities (Gilpin & Soulé 1986), this intervention, if successful, should increase the probability that self-perpetuating populations can be established in good to excellent protected habitat. Although factors such as rabbit herbivory, trampling, and competition from grasses might interfere with their success, protecting the plants from insect herbivory should at least increase the likelihood of seedling establishment, the base on which other mortality factors operate.

Both the available evidence and the theory of predator–prey interactions support this suggestion. However, the factors affecting Platte thistle in the continental dune system may not have the same relative effect on Pitcher's thistle in the Great Lakes dune system. Thus, a small-scale experimental validation of the effect of insect herbivory on Pitcher's thistles' seedling establishment and plant dynamics is being done (S. M. Louda & A. K. McEachern, unpublished data). As previously discussed, an insect-exclusion experiment is a positive ('win–win') manipulation. It is unlikely that the thistles will be harmed, and there is a high, logically predicated possibility that seed supply, seedling establishment, and plant density of Pitcher's thistle will be enhanced. If larger, and possibly more, populations of Pitcher's thistle result, sustainable population levels might be reached, obviating the need for further intervention.

Conclusions

Recent analyses of the influence of insects on the reproduction and establishment of native plants in several ecosystems suggest that more attention should be paid to insect impact in the management and restoration of threatened plant species. The experimental results presented in this chapter challenge the view that insect damage does not influence the success of native plants and they suggest patterns of interaction effects. The experimental results can be used to make recommendations for the management of threatened or endangered plant species, as illustrated for Pitcher's thistle. As demonstrated, preliminary experiments useful in determining the management of a threatened or endangered species can be carried out on an ecologically similar, non-threatened, close relative, and confirmed in small-scale experiments on the threatened or endangered species itself.

In two species of goldenbush, seedling recruitment by both species was limited by insect feeding on flowers and seeds at all sites along the environmental gradient. The distribution of scaly goldenbush was compressed, with insects essentially excluding it from the coastal area by more intense predispersal seed predation there. Inland, the distribution of coastal goldenbush seedlings was reduced significantly by the combination of intense predispersal seed predation augmented by more intense vertebrate herbivory on seedlings. In the Platte thistle, insect feeding on flowers was responsible for significant reduction of individual plant fitness, population limitation, amplification of the effects of plant competition, and spatial variation in the influence of such interactions on plant demography. Together, these findings show that insect pests can limit recruitment, abundance, and distribution of short-lived herbaceous perennial plants within their usual environment.

The ecological similarity of a threatened native thistle, Pitcher's thistle (*Cirsium pitcheri*), to Platte thistle (*C. canescens*), its putative progenitor, is strong. Such similarities and the experimental results from the more common Platte thistle suggest a scientific approach to the management and stabilization of threatened plants within protected habitats. Based on the results of a series of experiments with Platte thistle, I propose three predictions for the restoration and enhancement of Pitcher's thistle. First, insecticide exclusion of flower- and seed-feeding insects should increase the maturation and release of of viable seed by Pitcher's thistle, as it did for Platte thistle (Fig. 5.2B). Second, the successful production of increased numbers of viable seed by Pitcher's thistle should improve its seedling establishment success, as it did for Platte thistle (Fig. 5.2C). And third, higher seedling recruitment should lead to increased densities of flowering adults in the next generation, as it did for Platte thistle (Fig. 5.2D), at least in open habitats.

In general, I suggest that the management and enhancement of threatened plant species will be improved by comparative experimental analyses of ecologically similar, but more common, plant species. This approach depends on insights gained through parallel observation and experimental analysis of a more common species that is ecologically analogous to the threatened species. Such insights should lead to improved management and predictions for the enhancement and restoration of populations of the threatened species. Information on potentially critical biotic interactions for more common ecological analogs can clearly contribute to our understanding and to our capacity to manage and restore populations of threatened or endangered plant species with consistent and chronic damage by insect pests.

Literature cited

Anderson, A. N. (1988) Insect seed predators may cause far greater losses than they appear to. *Oikos*, **52**: 337–40.

Barbosa, P. & Schultz, J. C. eds. (1987) *Insect Outbreaks*. Orlando: Academic Press.

Barnes, P. W. & Harrison, A. T. (1982) Species distribution and community organization in a Nebraska Sand Hills prairie as influenced by plant/soil water relationships. *Oecologia*, **52**, 192–201.

Barnes, P. W. & Heinisch, S. P. (1984) Vegetation patterns in relation to topography and edaphic variation in Nebraska Sand Hills prairie. *Prairie Naturalist*, **16**, 145–58.

Belsky, A. J. (1986) Does herbivory benefit plants? *American Naturalist*, **127**, 870–92.

Belsky, A. J. (1987) The effects of grazing: confounding of ecosystem, community, and organism scales. *American Naturalist*, **129**, 777–83.

Bentley, S. & Whittaker, J. B. (1979) Effects of grazing by a chrysomelid beetle, *Gastrophysa viridula*, on competition between *Rumex obtusifolius* and *Rumex crispus*. *Journal of Ecology*, **67**, 79–90.

Bentley, S., Whittaker, J. B. & Malloch, A. J. C. (1980) Field experiments on the effects of grazing by a chrysomelid beetle (*Gastrophysa viridula*) on seed production and quality in *Rumex obtusifolius* and *Rumex crispus*. *Journal of Ecology*, **68**, 671–74.

Bleed, A. & Flowerday, C. eds. (1989) *An Atlas of the Sand Hills*. Lincoln: University of Nebraska.

Brown, V. K. (1982) The phytophagous insect community and its impact on early successional habitats. In *Proceedings of the 5th International Symposium on Insect–Plant Relationships*, ed. Visser, J. H. & Minks, A. K., pp. 205–13. Wageningen: PUDOC.

Burdon, J. J. (1987) *Diseases and Plant Population Biology*. Cambridge University Press.

Burdon, J. J., Jarosz, A. M. & Kirby, G. C. (1989) Pattern and patchiness in plant–pathogen interactions – causes and consequences. *Annual Review of Ecology and Systematics*, **20**, 119–36.

Cantlon, J. E. (1969) The stability of natural populations and their sensitivity to technology. *Brookhaven Symposium in Biology,* **22**, 197–205.

Chabot, B. F. & Mooney, H. A. eds. (1985) *Physiological Ecology of North American Plant Communities*. New York: Chapman and Hall.

Clark, W. D. (1977) *Chemosystematics of the Genus* Hazardia *(Compositae: Astereae)*. Ph.D. dissertation, Austin: University of Texas.

Cottam, D. A., Whittaker, J. B. & Malloch, A. J. C. (1986) The effects of chrysomelid beetle grazing and plant competition on the growth of *Rumex obtusifolius*. *Oecologia*, **70**, 452–56.

Crawley, M. J. (1983) *Herbivory: The Dynamics of Animal–Plant Interactions*. Berkeley: University of California Press.

Crawley, M. J. (1985) Reduction of oak fecundity by low density herbivore populations. *Nature*, **314**, 163–64.

Crawley, M. J. (1987) The effects of insect herbivores on the growth and reproductive performance of English oak. In *Insects – Plants. Proceedings of the 6th International Symposium on Insect–Plant Relationships,* ed. Labeyrie, V., Fabres, G. & Lachaise, D., pp. 307–11. Dordrecht: Dr W. Junk.

Crawley, M. J. (1989a) Insect herbivores and plant population dynamics. *Annual Review of Entomology*, **34**, 531–64.

Crawley, M. J. (1989b) The relative importance of vertebrate and invertebrate herbivores in plant population dynamics. In *Insect–Plant Interactions,* ed. Bernays, E. A., pp. 45–71. Boca Raton: C.R.C. Press.

Crawley, M. J. (1990) The population dynamics of plants. *Philosophical Transactions of the Royal Society, London* (B), **330**, 125–40.

Curtis, J. T. (1959) *The Vegetation of Wisconsin.* Madison: University of Wisconsin Press.

Darwin, C. R. (1859) *On the Origin of Species by Means of Natural Selection.* London: J. Murray (Dover Edition).

de Jong, T. J. & Klinkhamer, P. G. L. (1988a) Population ecology of the biennials *Cirsium vulgare* and *Cynoglossum officinale* in a coastal sand dune area. *Journal of Ecology,* **76**, 366–82.

de Jong, T. J. & Klinkhamer, P. G. L. (1988b) Seedling establishment of the biennials *Cirsium vulgare* and *Cynoglossum officinale* in a coastal sand-dune area: The importance of water for differential survival and growth. *Journal of Ecology,* **76**, 393–402.

Dirzo, R. (1984) Herbivory, a phytocentric overview. In *Perspectives on Plant Population Ecology,* ed. Dirzo, R. and Sarukhan, J., pp. 141–65. Sunderland: Sinauer Associates.

Ehrlich, P. R. & Birch, L. C. (1967) The 'balance of nature' and 'population control'. *American Naturalist,* **101**, 97–107.

Feeny, P. (1976) Plant apparency and chemical defense. *Recent Advances in Phytochemistry,* **10**, 1–40.

Fenner, M. (1985) *Seed Ecology.* London: Chapman and Hall.

Foster, J. (1964) Studies on the Population Dynamics of the Daisy, *Bellis perennis.* Ph.D. thesis, Bangor: University of Wales.

Fowler, N. L. & Rausher, M. D. (1985) Joint effects of competitors and herbivores on growth and reproduction in *Aristolochia reticulata. Ecology,* **66**, 1580–87.

Fox, L. R. & Morrow, P. A. (1983) Estimates of damage by insect grazing on *Eucalyptus* trees. *Australian Journal of Ecology,* **8**, 139–47.

Fox, L. R. & Morrow, P. A. (1986) On comparing herbivore damage in Australian and north temperate systems. *Australian Journal of Ecology,* **11**, 387–93.

Gilpin, M. E. & Soulé, M. E. (1986) Minimum viable population sizes: processes of species extinction. In *Conservation Biology. The Science of Scarcity and Diversity,* ed. Soulé, M. E., pp. 19–34. Sunderland: Sinauer Associates.

Goldberg, D. E. & Werner, P. A. (1983) The effects of size of opening in vegetation and litter cover on seedling establishment of goldenrods (*Solidago* spp.). *Oecologia,* **60**, 149–55.

Grace, J. B. & Tilman, D., ed. (1990) *Perspectives on Plant Competition.* New York: Academic Press.

Gross, K. L. (1984) Effects of seed size and growth form on seedling establishment of six monocarpic perennial plants. *Journal of Ecology,* **72**, 369–87.

Gross, K. L. & Werner, P. A. (1982) Colonizing abilities of 'biennial' plant species in relation to ground cover: Implications for their distribution in a successional sere. *Ecology,* **63**, 921–31.

Grubb, P. J. (1977) The maintenance of species richness in plant communities: the importance of the regeneration niche. *Biological Reviews,* **52**, 247–70.

Hairston, N. G., Smith, F. E. & Slobodkin, L. B. (1960) Community structure, population control, and competition. *American Naturalist,* **94**, 421–25.

Hall, H. M. (1928) *The Genus Haplopappus.* Publication 389. Washington, D.C.: Carnegie Institute.

Harper, J. L. (1969) The role of predation in vegetational diversity. *Brookhaven Symposium on Biology,* **22**, 48–62.

Harper, J. L. (1977) *The Population Biology of Plants*. New York: Academic Press.

Harrison, W. F. (1988) Endangered and threatened wildlife and plants: Determination of threatened status for *Cirsium Pitcheri*. *Federal Register*, **53**, 27137–41.

Hendrix, S. D. (1979) Compensatory reproduction in a biennial herb following insect defloration. *Oecologia*, **42**, 107–18.

Hendrix, S. D. (1984) Reactions of *Heracleum lanatum* to floral herbivory by *Depressaria pastinacella*. *Ecology*, **65**, 191–7.

Hendrix, S. D. (1988) Herbivory and its impact on plant reproduction. In *Plant Reproductive Ecology,* ed. Lovett Doust, J. & Lovett Doust, L., pp. 246–63. Oxford University Press.

Hendrix, S. D., Brown, V. K. & Gange, A. C. (1989) Effects of insect herbivory on early plant succession. Comparison of an English site and an American site. *Biological Journal of the Linnean Society*, **35**, 205–216.

Hodkinson, I. D. & Hughes, M. K. (1982) *Insect Herbivory*. London: Chapman and Hall.

Howe, H. F. & Westley, L. C. (1988) *Ecological Relationships of Plants and Animals*. New York: Oxford University Press.

Janzen, D. H. (1971) Seed predation by animals. *Annual Review of Ecology and Systematics*, **2**, 465–92.

Johnson, M. F. & Iltis, H. H. (1963) Preliminary reports on the flora of Wisconsin. No. 48: Compositae I – Composite Family. *Transactions of the Wisconsin Academy of Arts and Sciences*, **52**, 255–342.

Jordan, W. R., Gilpin, M. E. & Aber, J. D. eds. (1987) *Restoration Ecology: A Synthetic Approach to Ecological Research.* Cambridge University Press.

Karban, R. (1987) Environmental conditions affecting the strength of induced resistance against mites in cotton. *Oecologia*, **73**, 414–19.

Karban, R. & Courtney, S. (1987) Intraspecific host plant choice: lack of consequences for *Streptanthus tortuosus* (Cruciferae) and *Euchloe hyantis* (Lepidoptera: Pieridae). *Oikos*, **48**, 243–8.

Kaul, R. B. (1989) *Plants*. In *An Atlas of the Sand Hills*, ed. Bleed, A. & Flowerday, C. pp. 127–42. Lincoln: University of Nebraska – Lincoln.

Keddy, C. J. & Keddy, P. A. (1984) Reproductive biology and habitat of *Cirsium pitcheri*. *The Michigan Botanist*, **23**, 57–67.

Keeler, K. H., Harrison, A. T. & Vescio, L. (1980) The flora and Sand Hills prairie communities of Arapaho Prairie Arthur County, Nebraska. *Prairie Naturalist*, **12**, 65–78.

Kinsman, S. & Platt, W. J. (1984) The impact of a herbivore upon *Mirabilis hirsuta*, a fugitive prairie plant. *Oecologia*, **65**, 2–6.

Klinkhamer, P. G. L., de Jong, T. J. & van der Meijden, E. (1988) Production, dispersal and predation of seeds in the biennial *Cirsium vulgare*. *Journal of Ecology*, **76**, 403–14.

Lamp, W. O. & McCarty, M. K. (1979) A preliminary study of seed predators of Platte thistle. *Transactions of the Nebraska Academy of Sciences*, **7**, 71–4.

Lamp, W. O. & McCarty, M. K. (1981) Biology and ecology of Platte thistle (*Cirsium canescens*). *Weed Science*, **29**, 686–92.

Lamp, W. O. & McCarty, M. K. (1982) Predispersal seed predation of a native thistle, *Cirsium canescens*. *Environmental Entomology*, **11**, 847–51.

Lawton, J. H. & McNeill, S. (1979) Between the devil and the deep blue sea: On the problem of being a herbivore. In *Population Dynamics*, ed. Anderson, R. M., Turner, B. D. & Taylor, L. R., pp. 223–44. Oxford: Blackwell Scientific Publications.

Louda, S. M. (1978) A Test of Predispersal Seed Predation in the Population

Dynamics of *Haplopappus* (Asteraceae) Ph.D. thesis, Riverside: University of California.

Louda, S. M. (1982a) Limitation of the recruitment of the shrub *Haplopappus squarrosus* (Asteraceae) by flower– and seed–feeding insects. *Journal of Ecology*, **70**, 43–53.

Louda, S. M. (1982b) Distribution ecology: Variation in plant recruitment over a gradient in relation to insect seed predation. *Ecological Monographs*, **52**, 25–41.

Louda, S. M. (1982c) Inflorescence spiders: a cost/benefit analysis for the host plant *Haplopappus venetus* Blake (Asteraceae) *Oecologia*, **55**: 185–91.

Louda, S. M. (1983) Seed predation and seedling mortality in the recruitment of a shrub, *Haplopappus venetus* (Asteraceae), along a climatic gradient. *Ecology*, **64**, 511–21.

Louda, S. M. (1984) Herbivore effect on stature, fruiting and leaf dynamics of a native crucifer. *Ecology*, **64**, 511–21.

Louda, S. M. (1988) Insect pests and plant stress as considerations for revegetation of disturbed ecosystems. In *Rehabilitating Ecosystems*, ed. Cairns, J., pp. 51–67. Boca Raton: CRC Press.

Louda, S. M. (1989) Predation in the dynamics of seed regeneration. In *Ecology of Soil Seed Banks*, ed. Leck, M. A., Parker, V. T. & Simpson, R. L., pp. 25–51. New York: Academic Press.

Louda, S. M., Keeler, K. H. & Holt, R. D. (1990a) Herbivore influences on plant performance and competitive interactions. In *Perspectives on Plant Competition*, ed. Grace, J. B. & Tilman, D., pp. New York: Academic Press.

Louda, S. M. & Potvin, M. A. (1994) Inflorescence-feeding insects reduce seed, alter cohort demography and reduce lifetime fitness of a native thistle (*Cirsium causcens*). *Ecology* (in press).

Louda, S. M., Potvin, M. A. & Collinge, S. K. (1990b) Predispersal seed predation, postdispersal seed predation and competition in the recruitment of seedlings of a native thistle in sandhills prairie. *American Midland Naturalist*, **124**, 105–13.

Loveless, M. D. (1984) Population Biology and Genetic Organization in *Cirsium pitcheri*, an Endemic Thistle. Ph.D. thesis. Lawrence: University of Kansas.

Loveless, M. D. & Hamrick, J. L. (1988) Genetic organization and evolutionary history in two North American species of *Cirsium*. *Evolution*, **42**, 254–65.

Lowman, M. D. (1984a) An assessment of techniques for measuring herbivory: Is rainforest defoliation more intense than we thought? *Biotropica*, **16**, 264–68.

Lowman, M. D. (1984b) Spatial and temporal variability in herbivory of Australian rain forest canopies. *Australian Journal of Ecology*, **10**, 7–14.

Marquis, R. J. (1984) Leaf herbivores decrease fitness of a tropical plant. *Science*, **226**, 537–9.

Maschinski, J. & Whitham, T. G. (1989) The continuum of plant responses to herbivory: the influence of plant association, nutrient availability, and timing. *American Naturalist*, **134**, 1–19.

McEachern, K., Magnuson, J. A. & Pavlovic, N. B. (1989) *Preliminary results of a study to monitor Cirsium pitcheri in Great Lakes National Lakeshores*. Science Division, Indiana Dunes National Lakeshore. Washington, D.C.: United States National Park Service.

McNaughton, S. J. (1983) Compensatory plant growth as a response to herbivory. *Oikos*, **40**, 329–36.

McNaughton, S. J. (1986) On plants and herbivores. *American Naturalist*, **128**, 765–70.

Morrow, P. A. & Fox, L. R. (1989) Estimates of pre–settlement insect damage in Australian and North American forests. *Ecology*, **70**, 1055–60.

Morrow, P. A. & LaMarche, V. C. (1978) Tree ring evidence for chronic insect suppression of productivity in subalpine *Eucalyptus*. *Science*, **201**, 1244–46.

Munz, P. A. (1974) *A Flora of Southern California*. Berkeley: University of California Press.

Nesom, G. L. (1989) New combinations in *Ericameria* (Compositae:Asteraceae). *Phytologia*, **67**: 104–16.

Newman, E. I. ed. (1982) *The Plant Community as a Working Mechanism*. Oxford: Blackwell Scientific Publications.

Odum, E. P. (1959) *Fundamentals of Ecology*. Philadelphia: W. B. Saunders Company.

Owen, D. F. (1980) How plants may benefit from the animals that eat them. *Oikos*, **35**, 230–5.

Parker, M. A. (1985) Size–dependent herbivore attack and the demography of an arid grassland shrub. *Ecology*, **66**, 850–60.

Parker, M. A. & Root, R. B. (1981) Insect herbivores limit habitat distribution of a native composite, *Machaeranthera canescens*. *Ecology*, **62**, 1390–2.

Parker, M. A. & Salzman, A. G. (1985) Herbivore exclosure and competitor removal: Effects on juvenile survivorship and growth in the shrub, *Gutierrezia microcephala*. *Journal of Ecology*, **73**, 903–13.

Pickett, S. T. A. & White, P. S. (1985) *The Ecology of Natural Disturbance and Patch Dynamics*. New York: Academic Press.

Platt, W. J. (1975) The colonization and formation of equilibrium plant species associations on badger disturbances in a tall–grass prairie. *Ecological Monographs*, **45**, 285–305.

Platt, W. J., Hill, G. R. & Clark, S. (1974) Seed production in a prairie legume (*Astragalus canadensis* L.): interactions between pollination, predispersal seed predation and plant density. *Oecologia*, **17**, 55–63.

Platt, W. J. & Weis, I. M. (1977) Resource partitioning and competition within a guild of fugitive prairie plants. *American Naturalist*, **111**, 479–513.

Platt, W. J. & Weis, I. M. (1985) An experimental study of competition among fugitive prairie plants. *Ecology*, **66**, 708–20.

Polley, H. W. & Detling, J. K. (1989) Defoliation, nitrogen, and competition: Effects on plant growth and nitrogen nutrition. *Ecology*, **70**, 721–7.

Putwain, P. D., Machin, D. & Harper, J. L. (1968) Studies in the dynamics of plant populations. II. Components and regulation of a natural population of *Rumex acetosella* L. *Journal of Ecology*, **56**, 421–31.

Rausher, M. D. & Feeny, P. P. (1980) Herbivory, plant density, and plant reproductive success: the effect of *Battus philenor* on *Aristolochia reticulata*. *Ecology*, **61**, 905–17.

Risser, P. G., Birney, E. C., Blocker, H. D., May, S. W., Parton, W. J. & Wiens, J. A. (1981) *The True Prairie Ecosystem*. Stroudsburg: Dowden, Hutchinson and Ross.

Rockwood, L. L. (1974) Seasonal changes in the susceptibility of *Crescentia alata* leaves to the flea beetle *Oedionychus* sp. *Ecology*, **55**, 142–48.

Slobodkin, L. B., Smith, F. E. & Hairston, N. G. (1967) Regulation in terrestrial ecosystems, and the implied balance of nature. *American Naturalist*, **101**, 109–24.

Stamp, N. E. (1984) Effect of defoliation by checkerspot caterpillars (*Euphydryas phaeton*) and sawfly larvae (*Macrophya nigra* and *Tenthredo grandis*) on their host plants (*Chelone* spp.) *Oecologia*, **63d**, 275–80.

Strong, D. R., Lawton, J. H. & Southwood, R., Sir (1984) *Insects on Plants: Community Patterns and Mechanisms*. Cambridge, Massachusetts: Harvard University Press.

Tilman, D. (1982) *Resource Competition and Community Structure*. Princeton: Princeton University Press.

Tilman, D. (1988) *Plant Strategies and the Dynamics and Structure of Plant Communities*. Princeton: Princeton University Press.

Waloff, N. & Richards, O. W. (1977). The effect of insect fauna on growth, mortality and natality of broom, *Sarothamnus scoparius*. *Journal of Applied Ecology*, **14**, 787–9.

Weaver, J. E. (1954) *North American Prairie*. Lincoln: Johnson Publishing Co.

Weaver, J. E. (1965) *The Native Vegetation of Nebraska*. Lincoln: University of Nebraska Press.

Werner, P. A. (1977) Colonization success of a 'biennial' plant species: experimental field studies of species cohabitation and replacement. *Ecology*, **58**, 840–9.

Whittaker, J. B. (1979) Invertebrate grazing, competition and plant dynamics. In *Population Dynamics*, Symposia of the British Ecological Society, ed. Anderson, R. M., Turner, B. D. & Taylor, L. R., pp. 207–22. Oxford: Blackwell Scientific.

Windle, P. N. & Franz, E. H. (1979) The effects of insect parasitism on plant competition: greenbugs and barley. *Ecology*, **60**, 521–9.

II

Restoration planning

The four chapters in this section focus on restoration planning for species that have unknown recovery potential. This requires setting goals scaled to the needs of the restoration (Allen & Hoekstra 1987), which can range from species-specific autecological requirements, to organization of species assemblages, to landscape-level processes. In addition, means are needed to determine the efficacy of management protocols in meeting the restoration goals. We see contrasts and similarities in planning the recoveries of elements of an extremely decimated Hawaiian flora, two disturbance-adapted plant species, and the woodland caribou. Each of the target species declined because of a broad range of human-caused impacts, including competition from exotic species, disease, disruption of community processes, exploitation, grazing, and predation. The restorationists are challenged not only with reducing ongoing impacts, but also with recovery of small and often non-reproductive populations.

Loope & Medeiros (Chapter 6) address a cascading series of plant recovery problems caused by exotic species in Haleakala National Park. Almost total loss of lower elevation ecosystems has occurred owing to overgrazing by introduced goats and pigs, and invasions continue of fire-adapted, exotic plants and alien insects that threaten native pollinators. When grazing was eliminated to allow recovery of some plant communities, at least two rare Hawaiian plant species, *Mariscus hillebrandii* and *Bidens micrantha*, subsequently increased. Recovery for other species, however, is more complex. *Plantago pachyphylla* has not responded to reduced grazing, while *Sisyrinchium* has declined owing to competition from an exotic grass. Reduced populations, breeding systems, and potential pollinator losses place further restraints on recovery of other species. *Schiedea haleakalensis*, which has a poorly understood breeding system, may be reproductively limited by its small population size. Self-incompatibility and a requirement for insect pollination limit reproduction in the

139

monocarpic Hawaiian silversword genus *Argyroxiphium*. *A. sandwicense* has recovered from overcollection and grazing but now is threatened by loss of its pollinator to predation by the recent invasion of the Argentine ant. Reproduction may be entirely lost in *A. virescens*, which has declined to a single individual. Although tissue culture may eventually produce additional plants, their self-incompatibility barrier must be broken for reproduction to occur.

The next two chapters address the importance of disturbance processes to rare plant species recovery. Pavlovic (Chapter 7) emphasizes the need to understand the disturbance adaptations of plants targeted for recovery and identifies the importance of concordance or discordance of life-history stage characteristics of plants with the scale of natural and anthropogenic disturbance regimes. As a model, Pavlovic conducts an experimental analysis of disturbance adaptations of fame flower, a rare savanna species that occupies a continuum of habitat disturbance ranging from natural to anthropogenic. He then classifies disturbance-adapted rare plants into three categories, according to their responses to alteration of natural disturbance regimes. Species adapted to dynamic disturbance regimes, such as the furbish lousewort and heart-leaved plantain, often decline with alteration of natural disturbance processes, and require recovery of landscape-scale processes. Species in a second group that includes many perennials, such as some terrestrial orchids, appear to have intermediate spatial scale requirements and can persist under natural conditions but can also colonize artificial disturbances that simulate natural regeneration niches. The third group includes annual species that have apparently lost their natural habitat or disturbance regimes and are therefore restricted to artificial disturbance regimes. This includes annuals with persistent seed banks and perennial species with vegetative propagation. Recovery of species belonging to these groups will require different approaches and an understanding of life histories and spatial scale requirements; they represent serious challenges to the restoration ecologist.

McEachern, Bowles & Pavlovic (Chapter 8) illustrate the complexities of recovering an early-successional, disturbance-adapted species by planning the restoration of Pitcher's thistle, a Great Lakes shoreline endemic. This species maintains metapopulation dynamics by colonizing a shifting landscape of active blowouts and foredunes, where populations persist through mid-successional stages. The authors analyze the landscape-scale disturbance processes upon which this thistle is dependent and demonstrate how recreational use and development have caused its decline and local extirpation by altering natural disturbance processes. By comparing plant communities with and without extant thistle populations, they identify potential habitat for this species in

Illinois and plan its restoration there. At the Indiana Dunes, they analyze a metapopulation in decline due to fragmentation, artificial disturbance, and various biological processes, and recommend procedures to rehabilitate declining populations and to restore metapopulation dynamics.

Gogan & Cochrane (Chapter 9) conclude that management of populations of woodland caribou restored to the Lake Superior region of the United States, like the Pitcher's thistle, would require management at the metapopulation scale. For this species, recovery problems include relatively low reproductive rates, special habitat requirements of calves to escape predation by gray wolves and black bear, avoidance of habitat of alternate wolf prey such as moose, and avoidance of meningeal brain-worm, transmitted by white tailed deer. Gogan & Cochrane evaluate four potential restoration sites, considering size, habitat characteristics, presence of potential predators, competitors and disease, along with results of previous caribou translocations in or around Lake Superior. In addition, they use population viability analysis to evaluate various restoration scenarios. Of the four sites, Isle Royale, Michigan, is essentially predator- and disease-free, but population viability analysis suggests that it is too small to support a viable caribou population without continued translocation. Further complications at Isle Royale include a declining wolf population and an increasing moose population. As virtually no woodland caribou populations are extant in the United States, any restoration attempt will require animals translocated from Canada. The authors describe a plethora of agency regulations, permits, and demands that must be met for caribou translocation. The formation of a private corporation that lacks bureaucratic regulations, with members representing private interests, along with state, provincial, and federal organizations, has been critical in coordinating recovery efforts.

The four chapters in this section illustrate a number of similar ecological characteristics of the target organisms, but a range of recovery goals, from individual species to landscape-scale processes. Competition and/or predation by species introduced by humans, or species that have expanded owing to human alteration of the environment, pose threats for endemic Hawaiian plants and woodland caribou. Yet while community recovery is the primary goal for restoration of Hawaiian plants, recovery is at the species level for the caribou. Disease and predation are critical factors for both woodland caribou and Pitcher's thistle. Restoration planning calls for avoidance of wolf predation and meningeal brainworm for caribou, while pre- and postdispersal seed predation will likely affect thistle restoration. McEachern, Bowles & Pavlovic suggest that metapopulation restoration is an ecological requirement for Pitcher's thistle persistence. Similarly, Gogan & Cochrane predict that woodland caribou can be restored only in small habitats isolated from their major, contiguous range, and hence, will also require metapopulation management (e.g. as a core–satellite metapopulation). Pavlovic demonstrates the importance of disturbance regimes for species and illustrates the value of experimentation in understanding their requirements. Such approaches have also been integral for planning the restoration of the disturbance-adapted Pitcher's thistle. Finally, organization and management of the restoration plans for both woodland caribou and Pitcher's thistle require coordination and cooperation of various governmental agencies. For woodland caribou, restoration planning has involved a private organization (North Central Caribou Corporation), and agencies of two federal governments, along with various state and provincial agencies. Avoidance of potential conflict between state and federal agency objectives is critical in the recovery of Pitcher's thistle.

Literature cited

Allen, T. F. H. & Hoekstra, T. W. (1987) Problems of scaling in restoration ecology: a practical application. In *Restoration Ecology. A Synthetic Approach to Ecological Research*, ed. Jordan, W. R. III, Gilpin, M. E. & Aber, J. D., pp. 289-99. Cambridge University Press.

6

Impacts of biological invasions on the management and recovery of rare plants in Haleakala National Park, Maui, Hawaiian Islands

LLOYD L. LOOPE AND ARTHUR C. MEDEIROS

Introduction

Biological invasions assisted by humans are impoverishing biological diversity worldwide (MacDonald *et al.* 1989, Diamond 1989). Such invasions are particularly devestating to the biota of oceanic islands such as Hawaii (Williamson 1981, Brockie *et al.* 1988, Hawaii Department of Land and Natural Resources *et al.* 1991). Ecosystems of the Hawaiian Islands are much more vulnerable to biological invasions than are continental ecosystems, because the organisms in them have evolved in isolation from many of the forces that have shaped continental organisms, including foraging and trampling by herbivorous mammals, predation by ants and mammals, virulent diseases, and fires (Loope & Mueller–Dombois 1989). Lowland ecosystems of the Hawaiian Islands were substantially modified by Polynesians prior to western contact (Kirch 1982); after Cook's 'discovery' of the islands in 1778, the rate of modification accelerated and extended to higher elevations (Cuddihy & Stone 1990).

Ecosystems of low and middle elevations of the Hawaiian Islands have been drastically altered. Biological diversity has eroded more rapidly in Hawaii than in any other state. Though only 19 Hawaiian plant species have been federally designated as Endangered (US Fish and Wildlife Service 1990), it is estimated that of 1094 Hawaiian native taxa of flowering plants, 10% are extinct, 12% endangered, 4% vulnerable, and 12% rare (Wagner, Herbst & Sohmer 1990). Many Hawaiian botanists consider these figures conservative. Several conservation groups filed suit against the US Fish and Wildlife Service for listing few of the eligible Hawaiian species, and the Service agreed to propose 186 more species for listing by late 1992 (Anonymous 1990). The commitment of several state and federal agencies to the conservation of Hawaiian biological diversity has increased substantially during the past decade and, through interagency cooperation, the potential exists for substantial successes (e.g. Hawaii State Department of Land and Natural Resources *et al.* 1991). An integrated effort combining land protection, management against exotic species, protection of listed species, both *ex situ* and *in situ* species recovery, and community restoration will be most successful in meeting this commitment.

Haleakala National Park: An Overview

Haleakala National Park is located on Maui, the second largest island (1864 km^2) in the Hawaiian archipelago. Maui is situated on two large shield volcanoes, and the National Park is on the larger and younger of the two (Fig. 6.1). The park consists of an 11 400 ha irregular wedge-shaped area that surrounds Haleakala volcano, extending from sea level up to the 3056-m volcano summit. Haleakala National Park was established as part of Hawaii National Park in 1916, and as a separate National Park in 1961. It preserves the outstanding biological, geological, and scenic resources of Haleakala volcano, Kipahulu Valley, and adjacent coastal lands for visitor enjoyment and scientific study. A

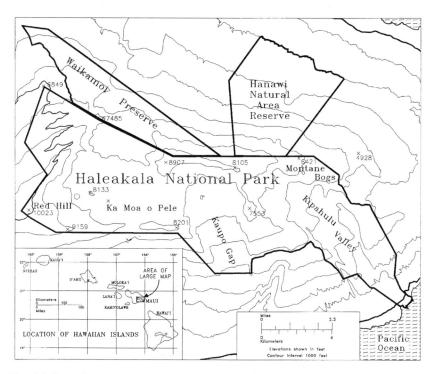

Fig. 6.1. Location, geography, and topographic relief of Haleakala National Park and adjacent natural areas on Maui, Hawaiian Islands.

large portion of the Park's rain forest is set aside as a Scientific Reserve and closed to the public. With adjacent conservation lands to the north, including Waikamoi Preserve (managed by The Nature Conservancy), Hanawi State Natural Area Reserve, and other state lands, the contiguous near-pristine area comprises over 20 000 ha.

Haleakala volcano is less than one million years old and has erupted as recently as about 200 years ago. It has a highly dissected topography, relatively well-developed soils, and a wide range of climatic conditions. Mean annual rainfall ranges from 100 cm to 1000 cm; most occurs on the windward slope, leaving a cinder desert within the rain shadow of the crater. This wide array of ecological factors supports a rich variety of forest, shrub, and alpine plant communities along elevational and moisture gradients. Relatively intact examples of these ecosystems remain, especially in extreme habitats such as at high elevations, on sparsely weathered volcanic substrates, on soils with aluminum toxicity, in caves, in montane bogs, and along coastal strand (Loope & Mueller-Dombois 1989).

About 95% of the park area (that above 600 m) is dominated by native species. This biota is rich by the standards of most isolated oceanic islands, consisting of 246 species of flowering plants, 104 ferns, 173 mosses and liverworts, 15 birds, one mammal, four fish, 23 known molluscs, and over 1000 known arthropod species. Over 90% of these species are endemic to the Hawaiian Islands, and many are endemic to Maui (Table 6.1). Some species of plants and invertebrates have their last refuge in the Park. Many invertebrates are likely to be undescribed local endemics. For example, during May–June 1991, 43 previously undescribed carabid beetle taxa were collected from East Maui (J. Liebherr, personal communication). Alien species are predominant below 600 m, and the alien biota of the entire park area includes 303 flowering plant species, 19 gymnosperms, 12 ferns, 9 mammals, 17 birds, 5 amphibians, 3 reptiles, 9 molluscs, and about 400 arthropods.

In spite of Haleakala's role as part of one of the most viable conservation units in the State of Hawaii, six of the Park's native bird species are federally endangered, and many invertebrate and plant species are sufficiently rare and threatened to merit listing. Seven plant taxa formerly native to the Park are known to be extinct, and 15 others have been extirpated from the Park in this century (Table 6.2). Active management has begun to reverse the chronic decline of the Park's resources.

Invasions and their effects on Haleakala National Park

Foraging and trampling by ungulates, especially feral goats (*Capra hircus*) and pigs (*Sus scrofa*), are widely recognized by scientists and managers in Hawaii

Table 6.1. *Endemic vascular plant species within*
Haleakala National Park restricted to Maui

Nomenclature of flowering plants follows Wagner *et al.*
(1990).

Species restricted to East Maui:

Argyroxiphium virescens	Asteraceae
Artemisia mauiensis	Asteraceae
Calamagrostis expansa	Poaceae
Clermontia samuelii	Lobeliaceae
Clermontia tuberculata	Lobeliaceae
Cyanea aculeatiflora	Lobeliaceae
Cyanea pohaku	Lobeliaceae
Cyanea aff. *glabra*	Lobeliaceae
Cyanea horrida	Lobeliaceae
Cyanea longissima	Lobeliaceae
Cyrtandra hashimotoi	Gesneriaceae
Dryopteris sp.	Aspidiaceae
Dubautia dolosa	Asteraceae
Dubautia menziesii	Asteraceae
Dubautia platyphylla	Asteraceae
Dubautia reticulata	Asteraceae
Geranium arboreum	Geraniaceae
Geranium hanaense	Geraniaceae
Geranium multiflorum	Geraniaceae
Labordia venosa	Loganiaceae
Lobelia grayana	Lobeliaceae
Pelea balloui	Rutaceae
Pelea ovalis	Rutaceae
Peperomia kipahuluensis	Piperaceae
Pipturus forbesii	Urticaceae
Polystichum sp.	Aspidiaceae
Pritchardia arecina	Arecaceae
Santalum haleakalae	Santalaceae
Schiedea haleakalensis	Caryophyllaceae
Schiedea implexa	Caryophyllaceae
Silene cryptopetala	Caryophyllaceae
Silene degeneri	Caryophyllaceae
Stenogyne haliakalae	Lamiaceae
Stenogyne rotundifolia	Lamiaceae
Wikstroemia monticola	Thymelaeaceae

Species restricted to East and West Maui:

Argyroxiphium grayanum	Asteraceae
Cyanea kunthiana	Lobeliaceae
Lobelia hillebrandii	Lobeliaceae
Phyllostegia bracteata	Lamiaceae
Pelea orbicularis	Rutaceae

Table 6.2. *Vascular plant taxa formerly occurring in Haleakala National Park that are now either extinct or extirpated from the park, with dates of last records*

Extinct

Tetramolopium lepidotum subsp. *arbusculum* (1841)	Asteraceae
Silene cryptopetala (1870s)	Caryophyllaceae
Cyanea pohaku (1910)	Lobeliaceae
Schiedea implexa (1910)	Caryophyllaceae
Cyanea longissima (1927)	Lobeliaceae
Silene degeneri (1927)	Caryophyllaceae
Stenogyne haliakalae (1937)	Lamiaceae

Extirpated

Huperzia haliakalae (1841)	Lycopodiaceae
Phyllostegia bracteata (1918)	Lamiaceae
Asplenium kaulfussii (1919)	Aspleniaceae
Clermontia lindseyana (1919)	Lobeliaceae
Clermontia peleana (1919)	Lobeliaceae
Lindsaea repens var. *macraeana* (1919)	Lindsaeaceae
Platanthera holochila (1919)	Orchidaceae
Solanum incompletum (1919)	Solanaceae
Vandenboschia draytoniana (1919)	Hymenophyllaceae
Panicum tenuifolium (1937)	Poaceae
Ranunculus hawaiensis (1945)	Ranunculaceae
Ranunculus mauiensis (1945)	Ranunculaceae
Argyroxiphium virescens (1959)	Asteraceae
Asplenium leucostegioides (1976)	Aspleniaceae
Gardenia remyi (1980)	Rubiaceae

as the most destructive forces in Hawaiian ecosystems. These animals have reduced or eliminated populations of native plants, facilitated alien plant dispersal and establishment, and hastened soil erosion (Stone & Loope 1987).

Other alien animals pose serious but more subtle threats to Haleakala ecosystems. Alien birds disperse alien seed, act as disease vectors, and compete with native birds (Scott *et al.* 1986). Alien rats (*Rattus* spp.) and mice (*Mus domesticus*) can damage native species (Stone & Loope 1987), and the predacious snails *Euglandina rosea* and *Oxychilus alliarius* are impacting native snails (Howarth & Medeiros 1989). Alien insects such as the predacious Argentine ant (*Iridomyrmex humilis*) and western yellowjacket (*Vespula pensylvanica*), the European earwig (*Forficula auricularia*), and a wasp (Encyrtidae: *Capidosoma bakeri*) that parasitizes native noctuid moths, threaten not only endemic invertebrate taxa, but entire ecosystems through impoverishment of pollinators and thus, perhaps, reduced seed set and fecundity of endemic plant species (Cole *et al.* 1992; Gambino, Medeiros & Loope 1987, 1990; Beardsley 1990).

Invasive plant species that are spreading in the Park and threaten to replace native vegetation include molasses grass (*Melinis minutiflora*), strawberry guava (*Psidium cattleianum*), blackberry (*Rubus argutus*), Australian tree fern (*Cyathea cooperi*), kahili ginger (*Hedychium gardnerianum*), gorse (*Ulex europaeus*), three pine (*Pinus*) species, and blue gum (*Eucalyptus globulus*) (Loope, Nagata & Medeiros, 1992). The invasive Pampas grass *(Cortaderia jubata)* was recently established on East Maui and first observed in the Park in 1989. Other alien plant species present on Maui that threaten to invade and seriously impact Park vegetation include clidemia (*Clidemia hirta*), miconia (*Miconia calvescens*), banana poka (*Passiflora mollissima*), and fountain grass (*Pennisetum setaceum*).

Despite state and federal efforts to control the introduction and spread of alien plants and animals (The Nature Conservancy of Hawaii & Natural Resources Defense Council 1992), they appear to be the greatest long-term threat to the integrity of Haleakala's ecosystems. Although only a small fraction of alien introductions are likely to significantly affect native species, cumulative impacts may have a profound effect on long-term conservation. Haleakala National Park is increasing efforts to eliminate new alien species before they become so extensively established that mechanical and chemical controls are ineffective (Loope *et al.* 1992, Loope & Medeiros 1991).

Active management of biological invasions

Efforts to combat alien species at the landscape scale have had positive effects in Haleakala National Park. Park resource managers used fencing to essentially eliminate a population of about 2000 goats from the Park, including Haleakala Crater in 1986 and 1987, ending nearly 200 years of severe ecological damage. The release from heavy browsing has allowed the diversity and cover of native vegetation to increase through resprouting and reproduction from seed. Koa (*Acacia koa*), a tree of mesic to wet forests, is regenerating abundantly in eastern Kaupo Gap. The native shrubs mamani (*Sophora chrysophylla*), pukiawe (*Styphelia tameiameiae*), aalii (*Dodonaea viscosa*), ulei (*Osteomeles anthyllidifolia*), and ohelo (*Vaccinium reticulatum*) are becoming widely established, and in some areas are replacing the alien grasses that persisted under goat browsing.

Following the removal of the goats, however, some alien plants have also increased, and continue to threaten native ecosystems. For example, aggressive invasion by the fire-adapted molassesgrass (*Melinis minutiflora*) increases fuel loads in formerly barren mid-elevation habitats (Hughes, Vitousek & Tunison 1991). As a result, wildfires are now a serious threat to fire-sensitive native vegetation in Kaupo Gap. Early stages of molasses grass invasion are being retarded with herbicides, allowing greater, earlier native species recovery.

Table 6.3. *Federal listing status of plant taxa used as subjects of case histories*

Categories based on US Fish and Wildlife Service (1990, 1991): T = proposed federal threatened, E = proposed federal endangered, X = believed extinct, * = not proposed for listing, but rare in Haleakala National Park.

Taxon	Category
Argyroxiphium sandwicense subsp. *macrocephalum*	T
Mariscus hillebrandii	*
Bidens micrantha subsp. *kalealaha*	E
Schiedea haleakalensis	E
Plantago pachyphylla	*
Sisyrinchium acre	*
Argyroxiphium virescens	X

Feral pigs were effectively controlled by snaring in rain forests of the upper Kipahulu Valley in 1987 and 1988, but follow-up efforts are essential (Anderson & Stone 1993). The potential for recovery has been demonstrated in 10-year exclosures, where understory vegetation, especially ferns, small herbs, and bryophytes, has increased (A.C. Medeiros, unpublished data and personal observation). As recovery progresses, watershed conditions should improve because increased vegetation cover should buffer against rapid runoff and erosion and the consequent siltation of streams. Pigs are also being removed from non-forested units of the Park, and fencing now protects some montane bog and grassland habitats for rare species and communities.

Rare plant species and restoration case studies

The control of goats, pigs, and alien plants at Haleakala National Park constitutes a landscape scale program of ecological restoration. Many rare plant taxa are being monitored to detect individual species responses to management, and to provide guidance for the restoration of some extirpated plants. The following case studies illustrate findings for seven plant species (Table 6.3), several of which are proposed as endangered or threatened by the US Fish and Wildlife Service.

Mariscus hillebrandii (Cyperaceae)

The endemic sedge *Mariscus hillebrandii* has increased dramatically since the Park has been protected from goats. It is present, but uncommon, in `a`a lava fields at lower elevations in Maui, but within the Park it was collected—and noted as very rare—only in 1919 and 1937. It began to reappear within the Park in 1979, first in a fenced exclosure in western Kaupo Gap, and later along molasses grass monitoring transects (A. C. Medeiros & L. L. Loope, personal observation). *M. hillebrandii* has now been discovered to be widely scattered throughout a 100 ha area in western Kaupo Gap. We attribute this sudden appearance over a broad distribution to germination from soil seed banks.

Bidens micrantha subsp. kalealaha (Asteraceae)

The 19 Hawaiian *Bidens* species exhibit more morphological diversity than does the rest of the genus on five continents (Ganders & Nagata 1984). *Bidens micrantha* subsp. *kalealaha* is an erect shrub up to 1.5 m tall, with dissected leaves and yellow flower heads. This proposed federal endangered species probably was once widespread on East Maui and Lanai, but it has been reduced by feral goats to about 2000 individuals in four populations on inaccessible cliff faces on leeward East Maui (US Fish and Wildlife Service 1991). The Park population is found on the inner walls of Haleakala Crater at 1800–2320 m elevation.

In October 1990, three years after feral goats were eliminated from Haleakala Crater, seven juveniles and a larger flowering *Bidens micrantha* subsp. *kalealaha* appeared on talus slopes and along stream-courses at the base of the steep walls of western Kaupo Gap at 1800–1900 m. These plants were apparently the offspring of plants growing on the cliff faces above. This was the first time that this species has been found away from its now-typical cliff habitat. There appears to be ample habitat for a further increase of this species now that feral goat browsing has been eliminated.

Schiedea haleakalensis (Carophyllaceae)

Schiedea haleakalensis is a shrub 30 to 60 cm tall with narrow, almost needle–like leaves and clusters of small flowers that have reddish to green sepals and mature to woody capsules. Like *Bidens micrantha* subsp. *kalealaha*, *S. haleakalensis* has been confined to cliff habitat by goat browsing and is proposed as federal endangered. Only two populations, with a total of 100–200 individuals, exist, both within Haleakala Crater (US Fish and Wildlife Service 1991).

Schiedea haleakalensis is diclinous (S. Weller, personal communication) and possibly gynodioecious (A. C. Medeiros, personal observation), which would require mixed sexes within populations for successful cross-pollination and seed set. Although we have observed small flies and moths visiting flowers at both populations, natural reproduction has not occurred and may be limited

Table 6.4. *Frequencies of selected rare native plant species at study sites undergoing chronic damage by feral pigs in* Carex- *and* Oreobolus-*dominated montane bog communities*

Data based on presence in 1 m² plots (Medeiros *et al.* 1991).

	Carex communities		*Oreobolus* commmunities	
	1982	1988	1982	1988
Plantago pachyphylla	0.24	0.10	0.80	0.47
Argyroxiphium grayanum	0.43	0.31	0.07	0.04
Trisetum glomeratum	0.03	0.02	0.35	0.15
Carex thunbergii	0.29	0.19	—	—
Selaginella deflexa	—	—	0.30	0.08
Geranium hanaense	0.04	0.05	0.03	0.01
Viola maviense	—	—	0.06	0.03

by the plant's breeding system. However, fertile seeds were obtained from plants in 1991, and nine plants were greenhouse-propagated (S. Weller, personal communication). Thus, we are planning propagation of greenhouse and garden populations that can be used as sources of propagules for reintroduction.

Plantago pachyphylla (Plantaginaceae)

Plantago pachyphylla formerly occurred at medium to high frequencies in sedge-dominated (*Carex* spp. or *Oreobolus furcatus*) montane bogs at 1650–1905 m. *Plantago pachyphylla* and other bog vegetation declined precipitously between 1982 and 1988 as a result of feral pig digging and subsequent alien plant invasion (Medeiros, Loope & Gagne 1991). Although the pigs have been removed, the bog species have not recovered (Table 6.4), possibly because of the persistence of alien plants.

In one studied bog, *P. pachyphylla* has not recovered after pig removal even without competition from alien plants (Loope *et al.* 1991). Its frequency had declined from 60% in 1973 to 5% in 1981, when the bog was fenced. By 1984, the other native vegetation had regained its original cover, but even after six additional years of protection, *P. pachyphylla* had not increased significantly (Loope *et al.* 1991). Reproductive and demographic studies of this species are clearly needed to determine why community restoration management has not helped it to recover.

Sisyrinchium acre (Iridaceae)

Sisyrinchium acre is a small, yellow-flowered iris endemic to high-elevation (2000–2500 m) shrubland on Maui and Hawaii. In an opportunistic experiment, this species was found to be an excellent colonizer, but poor at competing with alien grasses. Several months after an eight-year-old tree fall of alien pines was removed, over 100 *S. acre* seedlings (which are easily identifiable by their distinctive glaucous foliage and morphology) appeared from a soil seed bank. This allowed their fates and the fates of other plants appearing from seed to be compared between a managed plot, from which alien plants were periodically removed, and an unmanaged plot.

In the managed plot, bare ground accounted for 90% of the cover. Half of the remaining cover of native plants was from *S. acre*, which increased from 76 to 376 individuals in one year. In the unmanaged plot, 49 *S. acre* plants increased to only 56 in one year, while alien grass and forb cover increased to 90% and overtopped the *S. acre* individuals. *Holcus lanatus*, the primary invading grass, may be allelopathic (Watt 1978). The more common native species that also appeared in the tree fall area included the sedges *Carex wahuensis* and *C. macloviana*, the rush *Luzula hawaiiensis*, and the herb *Gnaphalium sandwicensium* subsp. *hawaiiense*. The shrubs *Vaccinium reticulatum*, *Sophora chrysophylla*, and *Coprosma montana* resprouted from old stumps.

Argyroxiphium sandwicense subsp. *macrocephalum* (Asteraceae)

Argyroxiphium sandwicense subsp. *macrocephalum*, the Haleakala silversword or ahinahina, is one of 28 species in the endemic *Madiinae* complex, which is derived from a western North American ancestor that underwent spectacular adaptive radiation in the diverse Hawaiian environment (Carr 1985, 1987; Baldwin, Kyhos & Dvorak 1990). The molecular and physiological diversity of this group give it the potential to elucidate evolutionary processes and mechanisms (Carr 1987, Baldwin *et al.* 1990, Robichaux *et al.* 1990).

A. sandwicense subsp. *macrocephalum* is endemic to 1000 ha at 2100–3000 m in the crater and outer slopes of Haleakala volcano. It is considered rare because of its highly restricted distribution (Rabinowitz, Cairns & Dillon 1986), and has a current population of about 50 000 individuals (Loope & Crivellone 1986). This monocarpic, self-incompatible plant produces a flower stalk 1–2 m tall with 100–500 maroon–purple flower heads; it can flower in as little as three years in cultivation, but normally requires several decades in natural habitat (Kobayashi 1973, 1991).

By the 1920s, this species was nearly extinct because of browsing by goats and cattle and collection by tourists. Often a living silversword was pulled up and brought back from a trip up Haleakala to prove that the party had reached the very

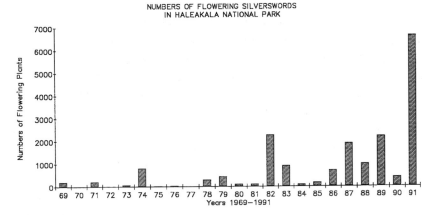

Fig. 6.2. Numbers of flowering silversword (*Argyroxiphium sandwicense* subsp. *macrocephalum*) in Haleakala National Park, 1969–91 (source: Kobayashi 1973, Loope & Crivellone 1986, unpublished data)

summit. Haleakala silverswords have thrived under protection, increasing from 1470 plants in 1935 to 6528 plants in 1991 (Kobayashi 1991) on the Ka Moa o Pele cinder cone. Although flowering is variable, annual numbers of flowering plants have increased from the hundreds in the 1970s to the thousands by the late 1980s, with more than 6000 in 1991 (Fig. 6.2). In permanent plots, plant numbers have been stable or slightly increasing during the past decade, but with annual fluctuations in the recruitment and survival of juvenile plants (Loope & Crivellone 1986; Fig. 6.3). For the first few years after establishment, seedlings are very susceptible to the impact of heavy rains and the accompanying sheet erosion.

To reproduce, *A. sandwicense* subsp. *macrocephalum* relies on cross-pollination by insects, and it is vulnerable if pollinators are lost. Because the Hawaiian Islands lack endemic ants, native insects are not adapted to ant predation, and the recent invasion and spread of the predacious Argentine ant (*Iridomyrmex humilis*) may seriously threaten silverswords. Although it is presently found in only a small portion of upper-elevation habitats and has not expanded its range in recent years, the Argentine ant has the potential to spread throughout much of the Haleakala Crater and western slope ecosystem (Cole *et al.* 1992), where it could eliminate pollinators and curtail silversword reproduction. The Argentine ant's spread is being monitored, and control strategies are being developed.

Argyroxiphium virescens (Compositae)

Like other *Madiinae*, *Argyroxiphium virescens* is monocarpic and self-incompatible, and thus highly vulnerable to extinction from shrinking populations and loss of pollinators. This species is endemic to East Maui, and was abundant in

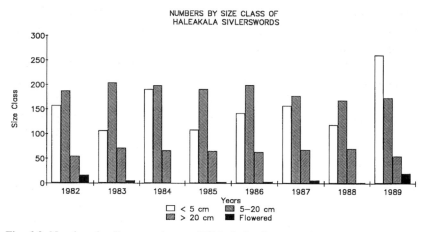

Fig. 6.3. Numbers by diameter classes of Haleakala silversword (*Argyroxiphium sand-wicense* subsp. *macrocephalum*), 1982–89. Data summarized from eleven 5 m × 20 m permanent plots in Haleakala Crater.

Haleakala National Park in the early 1900s. By the 1940s, it was near extinction from cattle, goat, and pig grazing. The last known individual flowered and died in the park in 1959; however, two plants resembling this species were discovered in 1973, and one of these has been used in an eleventh-hour recovery attempt.

The two juvenile plants resembling *Argyroxiphium virescens* were discovered in Hanawi State Natural Area Reserve, adjacent to Haleakala National Park's northern boundary (B.H. Gagne, personal communication). The larger plant was already protected from grazing because it grew on a steep cliff; in 1982, the smaller plant was protected in an exclosure. In 1989, the larger plant flowered and was identified as either *A. virescens* or an *A. virescens* × *A. sandwicense* hybrid (G.D. Carr, personal communication). As expected, none of the 200 seeds from this individual were viable, although numerous potential pollinators had visited the flower spike (A.C. Medeiros, personal observation). Thus, only one known possible *A. virescens* remains.

In late 1990, a plan was developed in cooperation with the Center for Plant Conservation to save *Argyroxiphium virescens*. This species is a good candidate for recovery because of the existence of natural habitat for reintroduction to the wild, the interest of state, federal, and private agencies in reintroduction, the availability of propagation facilities at Haleakala National Park headquarters, the potential for conservation of a silversword relative, and the challenge of recovering a near-extinct, self-incompatible species.

The *Argyroxiphium virescens* recovery plan objectives and accomplishments include:

1) A systematic search of potential habitat for additional individuals. Ground and helicopter surveys of potential *A. virescens* habitat in 1990 and 1991 failed to locate additional plants.

2) Experimental tissue culture of the surviving individual (as well as any new individuals that might be found), which offers the potential to propagate large numbers of plants from vegetative material (Ferguson & Pavlik 1990). Undifferentiated cells (callus) and shoots, but not roots, have been produced from leaf mesophyll at Mills College in early 1991 (Ferguson & Pavlik 1991).

3) Through chloroplast or nuclear DNA analysis, which has been conducted on the *Madiinae* (Baldwin *et al.* 1990), determine the taxonomic status of the surviving individual or individuals by comparison with living material of *A. sandwicense* subsp. *macrocephalum* and *A. grayanum* and, if possible, with dried herbarium specimens of *A. virescens*. Living tissue has been sent to the University of Arizona for analysis.

4) Attempt germination of *A. virescens* seeds from herbarium specimens. Approximately 200 *A. virescens* seeds from the B.P. Bishop Museum herbarium have been sent to the University of Arizona (L. Mehrhoff, personal communication). In general, seeds of the *Madiinae* are not known for longevity, and results are as yet unknown.

The single known living plant that could be *Argyroxiphium virescens* was double-rameted, and one of the ramets flowered in 1991. Although seeds were collected, they appear to be nonviable. Although efforts to reproduce this individual *in vitro* are encouraging, self-incompatibility is likely to prevent the production of viable seed from clones. Sporophytic self-incompatibility in the Compositae may be overcome to some extent by techniques such as bud pollination, use of microspores that have not yet received incompatibility proteins, use of foreign 'mentor' pollen to induce growth of normally incompatible pollen, or fertilization *in vitro* of excised ovaries (de Nettancourt 1977). Thus, it may be possible to promote seed production from flowering plants derived from tissue culture of the remaining plant. This, however, may ultimately be insufficient for recovery if only a single reproductive genotype occurs within a cloned population. Despite concerted efforts thus far, the survival of *A. virescens* is anything but assured.

Conclusions

Population depletion from past grazing and the continuing impacts of biological invasions present formidable challenges to the recovery of rare plants in Haleakala National Park. Faced with landscape-wide damage and limited staffing, Hawaiian resource managers have concentrated on ecosystem-level management; the management of individual Hawaiian species is in its infancy. With increasing conservation efforts, Hawaii will become a proving ground for integrated ecosystem and species restoration. Program strategies include sustained mechanical and chemical control of alien species, research and monitoring, public education, and enlisting the support of local and state government agencies. With continued active management, the prognosis for preservation of the remaining ecosystem components of Haleakala seems favorable.

Alien invertebrates pose complex problems requiring research and continual surveillance. Prospects for controlling many alien invertebrate species are not promising. A better understanding of the biological interrelationships between native and alien species may be crucial in the success of management and long–term conservation of native ecosystems.

The incipient recovery of *Mariscus hillebrandii* and *Bidens micrantha* suggests that the removal of feral ungulates and restoration of habitats have been effective. However, the lack of reproduction in *Schiedea haleakalensis* and *Plantago pachyphylla* shows that the removal of feral ungulates does not guarantee recovery of rare plant species. The recovery of *Sisyrinchium acre* may depend on its being protected from competition with aggressive alien plants. *Argyroxiphium sandwicense* subsp. *macrocephalum*, a spectacular species that has become a symbol of Haleakala National Park, has recovered dramatically over the past 50 years because it has been protected from grazing and collection, but it is vulnerable if alien insects impact its pollinators. *Argyroxiphium virescens* illustrates the potential and the pitfalls of working to save plant species on the verge of extinction. Long-term success in preserving all species will require cooperative efforts, often involving sophisticated propagation techniques as well as habitat protection.

Literature cited

Anderson, S. J. & Stone, C. P. (1993) Snaring to control feral pigs (*Sus scrofa*) in a remote Hawaiian rain forest. *Biological Conservation*, **63**, 195–202.
Anonymous. (1990) Sierra Club Legal Defense Fund, Inc. lawsuit and settlement agreement. *Hawaiian Botanical Society Newsletter*, **29**, 7–20.
Baldwin, B. G., Kyhos, D. W. & Dvorak, J. (1990) Chloroplast DNA evolution and adaptive radiation in the Hawaiian silversword alliance (Asteraceae – Madiinae). *Annals of the Missouri Botanical Garden*, **77**, 96–109.
Beardsley, J. W. (1990) Notes and exhibitions. *Proceedings of the Hawaiian Entomological Society*, **30**, 10–11.
Brockie, R. E., Loope, L. L., Usher, M. B. & Hamann, O. (1988) Biological invasions of island nature reserves. *Biological Conservation*, **44**, 9–36.
Carr, G. D. (1985) Monograph of the Hawaiian Madiinae (Asteraceae): Argyroxiphium, Dubautia, and Wilkesia. *Allertonia*, **4**, 1–123.
Carr, G. D. (1987) Beggars ticks and tarweeds: masters of adaptive radiation. *Trends in Ecology and Evolution*, **2**, 192–5.

Carr, G. D., Powell, E. A. & Kyhos, D. W. (1986) Self-compatibility in the Hawaiian Madiinae (Compositae): an exception to Baker's rule. *Evolution,* **40,** 430–434.

Cole, F. R., Medeiros, A. C., Loope, L. L. & Zuelhke, W. W. (1992) Effects of the Argentine ant on arthropod fauna of Hawaiian high–elevation shrubland. *Ecology,* **73,** 1313–22.

Cuddihy, L. W. & Stone, C. P. (1990) *Alteration of Native Hawaiian Vegetation: effects of humans, their activities and introductions.* Cooperative National Park Resources Study Unit, Department of Botany. Honolulu: University of Hawaii Press.

Diamond, J. (1989) Overview of recent extinctions. In *Conservation for the twenty-first century,* ed. Western, D. and Pearl, M. C., pp. 37–41. Oxford University Press.

Ferguson, N. J. & Pavlik, B. M. (1990) Endangered Contra Costa wallflower propagated by tissue culture (California). *Restoration and Management Notes,* **8,** 50–1.

Ferguson, N. J. & Pavlik, B. M. (1991) *Micropropagation of Argyroxiphium virescens (Haleakala greensword) for conservation and reintroduction. I. Explant sterilization and callus initiation.* Department of Biology. Oakland: Mills College.

Gambino, P., Medeiros, A. C. & Loope, L. L. (1987) Introduced *Paravespula pensylvanica* (Saussure) yellowjackets prey on Maui's endemic arthropod fauna. *Journal of Tropical Ecology,* **3,** 169–70.

Gambino, P., Medeiros, A. C. & Loope, L. L. (1990) Invasion and colonization of upper elevations on East Maui (Hawaii, U.S.A.) by the Western Yellowjacket *Vespula pensylvanica* (Hymenoptera: Vespidae). *Annals of the Entomological Society of America,* **83,** 1088–95.

Ganders, F. L. & Nagata, K. M. (1984) The role of hybridization in the evolution of Bidens on the Hawaiian Islands, In *Plant Biosystematics,* cd. W. F. Grant, pp. 179–194. Toronto: Academic Press Canada.

Hawaii Department of Land and Natural Resources, U.S. Fish and Wildlife Service, & The Nature Conservancy of Hawaii. (1991) *Hawaii's Extinction Crisis: a Call to Action.* Honolulu: The Nature Conservancy of Hawaii.

Howarth, F. C. & Medeiros, A. C. (1989) Non-native invertebrates. In *Conservation Biology in Hawaii,* ed. C. P. Stone and D. B. Stone, pp. 82–87. Cooperative National Park Resources Studies Unit, Department of Botany. Honolulu: University of Hawaii.

Hughes, R. F., Vitousek, P. M. & Tunison, J. T. (1991) Effects of invasion by fire-enhancing C4 grasses on native shrubs in Hawaii Volcanoes National Park. *Ecology,* **72,** 743–7.

Kirch, P. V. (1982) The impacts of prehistoric Polynesians on Hawaiian ecosystems. *Pacific Science,* **36,** 1–14.

Kobayashi, H. K. (1973) Ecology of the Silversword, Haleakala Crater, Hawaii. Ph.D. dissertation, Honolulu: University of Hawaii.

Kobayashi, H. K. (1991) *Status of the Haleakala silversword, Argyroxiphium sandwicense DC. ssp. macrocephalum (Gray) Meyrat at Ka-Moa-o-Pele cinder cone and Kalahaku overlook, Haleakala National Park.* Hawaii Natural History Association Technical Report. Maui: Haleakala National Park.

Loope, L. L. (1991) Miconia calvescens: an ornamental plant threatens native forests on Maui and Hawaii. *Hawaii Landscape Industry News,* **5,** 18–19.

Loope, L. L. (1992) Preventing establishment of new alien species in Haleakala National Park and on the island of Maui, Hawaii. *The George Wright Forum,* **9,** 20–31.

Loope, L. L. & Crivellone, C. F. (1986) *Status of the Haleakala Silversword: Past and Present.* Cooperative National Park Resources Study Unit, Department of Botany Technical Report 58. Honolulu: University of Hawaii.

Loope, L. L. & Mueller-Dombois, D. (1989) Characteristics of invaded islands, with special reference to Hawaii. In *Biological Invasions: a Global Perspective*, ed. Drake, J., Castri, F. di, Groves, R., Kruger, F., Mooney, H., Rejmanek, M., Williamson, M., pp. 257–80. Chinchester: John Wiley & Sons.

Loope, L. L. & Medeiros, A. C. (1991) Andean Pampas grass (*Cortaderia jubata*), an invasive species on Maui. *Hawaii Landscape Industry News*, **5**, 20–1.

Loope, L. L., Medeiros, A. C. & Gagne, B. H. (1991) *Studies in the montane bogs of Haleakala National Park. Recovery of vegetation of a montane bog following protection from feral pig rooting.* Cooperative National Park Resources Study Unit, Department of Botany Technical Report 77. Honolulu: University of Hawaii.

Loope, L. L., Medeiros, A. C., Minyard, W., Jessel, S. & Evanson, W. (1992) Strategies to prevent establishment of feral rabbits on Maui, Hawaii. *Pacific Science*, **46**, 402–3.

Loope, L. L., Nagata, R. J. & Medeiros, A. C. (1992) Alien plants in Haleakala National Park. In *Alien Plant Invasions in Native Ecosystems of Hawaii: Management and Research*, ed. Stone, C. P., Smith, C. W., and Tunison, J. T. Cooperative National Park Resources Study Unit, Department of Botany Technical Report. Honolulu: University of Hawaii Press.

MacDonald, I. A. W., Loope, L. L., Hamann, O. & Usher, M. B. (1989) Wildlife conservation and the invasion of nature reserves by introduced species: a global perspective. In *Biological Invasions: a Global Perspective*, ed. Drake, J., di Castri, F., Groves, R., Kruger, F., Mooney, H., Rejmanek, M., Williamson, M., pp. 215–115. Chichester: John Wiley & Sons.

Medeiros, A. C., Loope, L. L. & Gagné, B. H. (1991) *Studies in the montane bogs of Haleakala National Park. Degradation of vegetation in two montane bogs: 1982–1988.* Cooperative National Park Resources Study Unit, Department of Botany Technical Report 78. Honolulu: University of Hawaii.

Nettancourt, N de. (1977) *Incompatibility in angiosperms. Monograph on Theoretical and Applied Genetics*. Berlin: Springer-Verlag.

Rabinowitz, D., Cairns, S. & Dillon, T. (1986) Seven forms of rarity and their frequency in the flora of the British Isles. In *Conservation Biology: the Science of Scarcity and Diversity*, ed. Soulé, M., pp. 182–204. Sunderland: Sinauer Associates.

Robichaux, R. H., Carr, G. D., Liebmann, M. & Pearcy, R. W. (1990) Adaptive radiation of the Hawaiian silversword alliance (Compositae: Madiinae): ecological, morphological, and physiological diversity. *Annals of the Missouri Botanical Garden,* **77**, 64–72.

Scott, J. M., Mountainspring, S., Ramsey, F. L. & Kepler, C. B. (1986) *Forest Bird Communities of the Hawaiian Islands: Their Dynamics, Ecology and Conservation.* Studies in Avian Biology, No. 9. Los Angeles: Cooper Ornithological Society.

Stone, C. P. & Loope, L. L. (1987) Reducing negative effects of introduced animals on native biota in Hawaii: what is being done, what needs doing, and the role of national parks. *Environmental Conservation*, **14**, 245–54.

U.S. Fish and Wildlife Service. (1990) Endangered and threatened wildlife and plants: review of plant taxa for listing as endangered or threatened species. *Federal Register,* **55**, 6184–229.

U.S. Fish and Wildlife Service (1991) Fifteen Hawaiian plants proposed in May for Endangered Species Act protection. *Endangered Species Technical Bulletin*, **16**, 1, 5–7.

Wagner, W. L., Herbst, D. R. & Sohmer, S. H. (1990) *Manual of the Flowering Plants of Hawaii.* Honolulu: Bernice P. Bishop Museum and University of Hawaii Press.

Watt, T. A. (1978) The biology of *Holcus lanatus* L. (Yorkshire fog) and its significance in grassland. *Herbage Abstracts*, **48**, 195–204.

Williamson, M. (1981) *Island Populations*. Oxford University Press.

7

Disturbance-dependent persistence of rare plants: anthropogenic impacts and restoration implications

NOEL B. PAVLOVIC

Introduction

Plants have evolved in heterogeneous environments under a variety of abiotic and biotic disturbances that vary in gradients of frequency, intensity, extent, and predictability across and within communities (White 1979, Pickett & White 1985). As a result, most plant species are adapted to disturbance at some scale for their regeneration (Platt 1975, 1976, Grubb 1977, Huntly & Inouye 1988, Klinkhamer & De Jong 1988), and persist in space and time through differential sensitivity of life stages, seed dispersal mechanisms, seed dormancy strategies, or modes of vegetative growth (Brown & Venable 1986, Silvertown 1987, Caswell 1990).

For rare plants with specialized adaptations to natural disturbance regimes, variation in the scale of disturbance can be critical in determining their population viability (Menges 1991a) and restoration needs. The effects of disturbance on these plants can be viewed according to their realized niche spaces, which are maintained by the natural disturbance regimes. Novel disturbances that mimic natural disturbance regimes may expand or replace realized niche space, allowing the species to persist or even increase in population size. In contrast, novel disturbances that do not mimic natural disturbances could eliminate realized niche space, thus threatening the viability of the plant species in question. Thus, many species have been extirpated or reduced in abundance (Hodgson 1991, Schoener 1987), while others (e.g. ragweed) have experienced new or expanded ecological and evolutionary opportunities (Marks 1983).

Humans can impact the niche space of disturbance-adapted rare plants directly or indirectly (Rykiel 1985, Grime 1979, Pickett & White 1985, Petraitis, Latham & Niesenbaum 1989, Bowles *et al.* 1992). Direct disturbances influence survivorship of individuals. Indirect disturbances affect resource levels or other conditions that then influence individual survivorship (Hobbs & Huenneke 1992) and often involve complex changes in community

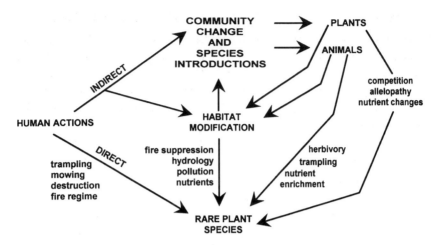

Fig. 7.1. Direct and indirect pathways by which human actions can affect disturbance-dependent rare plants. Feedback between community change and habitat modification can produce cascading effects that ultimately influence rare plant populations.

structure and composition (Fig. 7.1). For example, exotic species whose invasion is facilitated by disturbance may alter competitive relationships (Denslow 1985, Hobbs & Huenneke 1992) or produce novel disturbance regimes (Hughes, Vitousek & Tunison 1991, Stone & Scott 1985, Howarth 1985, Smith 1985, MacDonald *et al.* 1991) that negatively impact rare plants (Hamann 1979, Loope & Medeiros, Chapter 6 of this volume). Disturbance-adapted plants can also be impacted by biotically or abiotically driven community changes that alter disturbance regimes, such as the interactive effects of succession and disturbance on shifting vegetation patterns of dune systems (Olson 1958).

In this chapter, I examine how natural and anthropogenic disturbances affect disturbance-dependent rare plants and explore the implications for conservation and restoration of these species. In this context, I first review my research on the ecology and life history of fame flower (*Talinum rugospermum*), a rare perennial herb that occupies both natural and anthropogenic disturbance patches. I then examine rare plant life history in relation to three disturbance response categories: 1) species limited to natural disturbance regimes, 2) species that occur under both natural and human disturbance regimes, and 3) species confined to anthropogenic disturbance regimes. In doing so, I develop the concept of concordance versus discordance between scale of the disturbance regime and species life history and demonstrate its relevance to rare plant restoration.

Disturbance effects on habitats and populations of fame flower

Fame flower (*Talinum rugospermum*) is an iteroparous succulent herb that depends on abiotic or biotic disturbance to persist. Under natural conditions, fame flower is an interstitial species that occupies bare soil patches created by fire, drought, sand deposition, and biotic disturbances (Plumb 1979). It occupies sand savanna and sand prairie in the midwestern US, although it is occasionally found in prairie developed on sandstone or basalt bedrock (Fernald 1950, Glenn-Lewin & Ver Hoef 1988, Cochrane 1993). Fame flower seeds require light for germination (Baskin & Baskin 1988). As a result, increased tree canopy and leaf litter cover caused by fire suppression limit fame flower, but plants often colonize and persist in anthropogenic disturbance patches. For example, 70% of the 13 Indiana fame flower populations occur along trails or roadsides adjacent to closed sand savanna. Therefore, it appears that the natural disturbance patches occupied by fame flower can be mimicked by human disturbance. To test this hypothesis and to characterize the disturbance regimes to which fame flower is adapted, I examined ecological and demographic characteristics of fame flower populations in natural and anthropogenic habitats along an apparent patch disturbance gradient. At Tolleston Dunes, Indiana Dunes National Lakeshore, these conditions included anthropogenically modified habitats, savanna, and prairie. Portions of this gradient were represented at Jasper-Pulaski and Willow Slough Fish and Wildlife Areas in Indiana, St. Croix National Scenic Riverway of Wisconsin and Minnesota, and two sites in southeast Minnesota.

Habitat characteristics

Composition and structure of plant communities occupied by fame flower were classified by TWINSPAN (Gauch & Whittaker 1981) using frequencies of species by dm^2 and bare ground cover from within meter squared plots. Anthropogenic disturbances, which increase bare ground patch size, occurred at two levels: light disturbances flattened vegetation and compacted soil, while heavy disturbances (from off-road vehicles) excavated soil and uprooted fame flowers. Once the classification was produced, frequencies were summed by the following life form groups to examine structural habitat characteristics: upright forbs, prostrate forbs, graminoids, and trees and shrubs.

TWINSPAN classified four habitats within which fame flower grows: savanna, prairie, anthropogenically disturbed vegetation (both light and heavy), and successional vegetation recovering from former episodic human disturbance. Savanna and prairie were both grass-dominated but differed by canopy cover of black oak (*Quercus velutina*) and presence of goat's rue

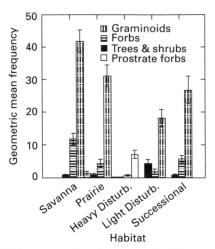

Fig. 7.2. Mean (± S.E.) frequency of species summed by life form in different fame flower habitats. Comparisons among life form characteristics (geometric mean frequency (± S.E.)) of fame flower habitats.

(*Tephrosia virginiana*) in savanna. In habitats characterized by human distur-bance, forb frequency was reduced, thereby allowing dominance by grasses (e.g. *Panicum implicatum*) and sedges (e.g. *Carex pensylvanica* and *Cyperus filiculmis*), but at reduced frequencies relative to prairie and savanna (Fig. 7.2). Light anthropogenic disturbance allowed high frequencies of black oak seedlings, while heavy disturbance resulted in lower frequencies of oak seedlings and graminoids (Fig. 7.2). Successional habitats were structurally similar to prairie in terms of plant life form, but had high frequencies of weedy native species, including lovegrass (*Eragrostis spectabilis*), wormwood (*Artemisia caudata*), and carpet weed (*Mollugo verticillata*), moderate frequen-cies of crabgrass (*Digitaria sanguinalis*) at one site, and intermediate frequen-cies of *Carex pensylvanica*. Thus human disturbance degrades the natural community by producing large areas of bare ground, eliminating forbs, increas-ing the frequency of weedy native species, and fostering exotic invasion.

Effects of human disturbance on soils

Principal components analysis (PCA) was used to analyze relationships among 12 soil variables across the habitats occupied by fame flower, and to compare the effects of natural versus anthropogenic patch disturbances on fame flower. The extreme end points of the gradient, blowout and black oak woods, where fame flower rarely grows, were also sampled to show the full variation in soil

Table 7.1. *Principal components of soil substrates colonized by fame flower*

Factor loadings are given in columns and largest values are in bold. The range of values for each variable is shown in the last column. See Fig. 7.3 for soil graph by habitat.

Soil variable	PC-1	PC-2	PC-3	RANGE
% variation explained	45	32	10	
PC axis 1				
CEC[1] (meq/100 g)	**0.986**	0.110	0.044	0.4 – 6.9
Ca (ppm)	**0.943**	0.306	0.021	50 – 1000
OM[1] (%)	**0.926**	–0.152	–0.079	0.4 – 5.6
Kjeldahl N (%)	**0.915**	–0.306	0.020	0.001 – .209
Mg (ppm)	**0.914**	0.331	0.102	5 – 120
PC axis 2				
Hydrogen ion (%)	0.086	**-0.972**	–0.122	0 – 52
pH	–0.050	**0.969**	0.137	5.0 – 7.6
Ca (%)	0.103	**0.918**	–0.107	37 – 76
PC axis 3				
Phosphorous (ppm)	-0.071	0.082	**0.794**	6 – 91

[1] CEC = cation exchange capacity, OM = organic matter

chemistry. PCA revealed a soils gradient corresponding to the disturbance gradient (Fig. 7.3). Organic matter and associated soil characteristics (CEC, Ca, Kjeldahl N, and Mg) were the strongest factors among habitats; pH and associated soil characteristics (Ca and H+) were the strongest secondary factors, and phosphorous the strongest tertiary factor (Table 7.1). Across the gradient, organic matter ranged from less than 1% in blowouts to 6% in savanna and black oak woods ($F_{4,31}$ = 63.7, $P < 0.001$). Undisturbed savanna soils, where fame flower rarely grows, had high levels of organic matter and nutrients, while natural interstitial disturbance patches, where fame flower often grows, had intermediate soil characteristics (Fig. 7.3). In comparison, anthropogenic disturbance patches occupied by fame flower had intermediate soil conditions similar to the interstitial patches.

Spatial patterns: density in relation to habitat, patch size and disturbance from fire

To determine how disturbance affected fame flower abundance in different habitats classified by TWINSPAN, seedling, juvenile, and adult densities were measured in relation to bare ground cover from meter squared plots. Temporal

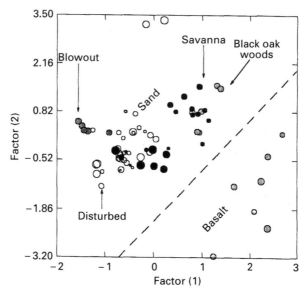

Fig. 7.3. Principal components analysis ordination of soil chemistry by habitat. First axis (Factor 1) is primarily increasing organic matter and cation exchange capacity; second axis (Factor 2) is increasing pH, and third axis (shown by symbol size) is increasing phosphorous. Soils of anthropogenic disturbances (open circles) are analogous to those in natural patch disturbances in savanna patches (filled circles). Blowout, black oak woods, and basalt prairie (all shown as hatched) represent extremes on the PCA axes.

changes in *Talinum* dispersion were examined by calculating variance to mean ratios of density in the various habitats from the years 1985 to 1991. To assess the role of patch size in seedling establishment, bare ground cover was correlated with fame flower density. Finally, to determine the effect of fire in creating disturbance patches in fame flower habitat, fame flower seedling, juvenile, and adult densities were quantified before and after a late winter (1989–90) head fire in savanna vegetation at Willow Slough.

Fame flower showed high sensitivities to different levels and types of disturbance (Fig. 7.4). It was most abundant either under light human disturbance or in savanna, and was least abundant under either heavy anthropogenic disturbance or in prairie; abundance in successional habitat was intermediate ($F_{4,102}$ = 6.624, $P < 0.0001$). This demonstrates that light anthropogenic disturbance patches are similar to favorable conditions for fame flower under natural habitat conditions. However, light anthropogenic disturbance and wildfire aggregated the structure of fame flower populations (Fig. 7.5) compared with those in savannas. In contrast, heavily disturbed populations were consistently more randomly distributed because of frequent mortality and chronically low densities. Heavy human disturbance creates large patches of bare ground where,

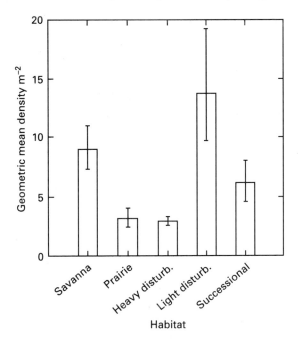

Fig. 7.4. Effects of habitat on fame flower density (± S.E.) based on TWINSPAN classification of species composition and bare ground ($F_{4,102} = 6.624$, $P<0.000 1$). Data were taken from three sites in Indiana, two in Minnesota, and three in Wisconsin.

once disturbance has been relaxed, fame flower may achieve locally high densities comparable to post-fire natural populations. Despite temporal fluctuations in population structure within and among habitats, fame flower has the largest variation in patch densities under a light human disturbance regime.

Seedling and total fame flower density were weakly and positively correlated with bare ground patch size in savanna and lightly disturbed habitat (Fig. 7.6). Fire had no effect on live vegetation cover, but increased bare ground by reducing litter cover (Fig. 7.7). As expected, more than four times as many fame flower seedlings appeared in the 1990 growing season following fire than in 1989 and 1991. During this same interval adult density remained constant. Few of the 1990 cohort survived to 1991, but those that did increased the juvenile size class (Fig. 7.7). Thus, disturbance area and fire interact in creating regeneration niches for fame flower.

For fame flower, the importance of disturbance regime to plant persistence lies in the relation between the spatial and temporal scale and intensity of disturbance, and the plant's population size and timing of life history stages. A life-cycle model (e.g. Bowles 1983, Brown & Venable 1991) can be used to interpret this relationship and its effects on other disturbance-dependent

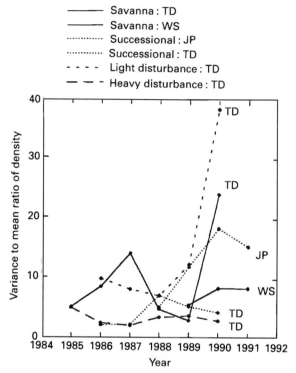

Fig. 7.5. Temporal changes in variance to mean ratio of fame flower density by Indiana habitats (JP=Jasper–Pulaski, TD=Tolleston Dunes, and WS=Willow Slough). Habitats are based on TWINSPAN classification (see Fig. 7.4).

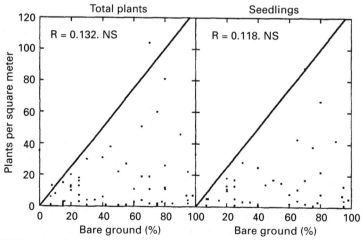

Fig. 7.6. Relationship between bare ground cover and total fame flower and seedling density. Data are combined from savanna and lightly disturbed plots. Pearson product moment correlation coefficients (R) do not differ significantly from zero.

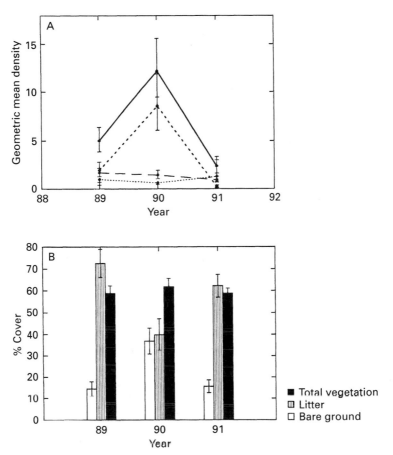

Fig. 7.7. Effects of a dormant season (April 1990) fire on fame flower population (A) and habitat structure (B) in a natural savanna. Points on lines represent mean ±S.E. of seedlings (short dash), juveniles (dotted), adults (long dash), and totals (solid lines).

species (Fig. 7.8). In this model, life history stages interact with disturbance regimes either temporally, such as seed longevity and dormancy, age to maturity, and adult life span and dormancy, or spatially, including pollen and seed dispersal, and clonal spread (Fig. 7.8). Discordant disturbances disrupt the life cycle, whereas concordant disturbances are those to which plants are adapted, or are less disruptive.

Interstitial fame flower habitats are maintained primarily by dormant season fires (Fig. 7.8A). Light human disturbance may mimic the spatial or temporal scales of natural disturbance and be concordant with the species' life history (Fig. 7.8). However, more severe disruptions may produce a temporal and spa-

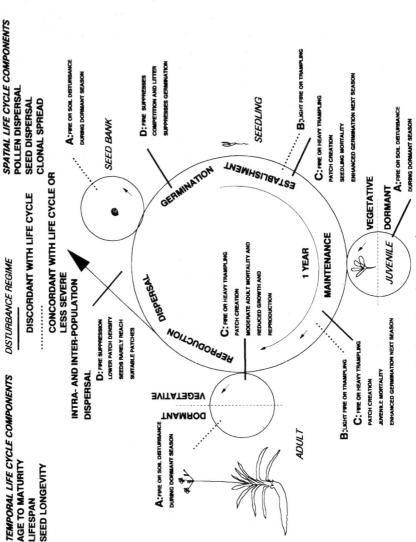

For figure legend see opposite page.

tial shift in fame flower distribution and abundance, and heavy or frequent human disturbance in the growing season may be discordant with fame flower's life history by preventing plants from reaching maturity or by damaging and killing adults (Fig. 7.8C). If intense human disturbance that creates large bare sand patches is followed by a reduced intensity or frequency of disturbance, fame flower may recover to achieve large, continuous populations. Because fame flower lacks a large persistent seed bank, it relies on small-scale disturbance patch mosaics, local seed dispersal, and adult tolerance of disturbance for persistence. Interpatch dispersal is enhanced for larger fame flowers in which the horizontal inflorescence peduncle extends more than a decimeter into adjacent patches (N.B. Pavlovic, personal observation) Fire suppression (Fig. 7.8D) increases the areas between disturbance patches, effectively isolating populations and increasing their extinction probability because interpatch dispersal is no longer possible. After extreme fire protection and fuel buildup, severe natural fires may destroy populations or leave surviving plants too far from the burn centers to allow recolonization.

Anthropogenic impacts on the persistence of disturbance-dependent rare plants

I next examine 12 other disturbance-dependent rare plants (Table 7.2) and their life history interactions with altered disturbance regimes. These species are classified into three response categories: 1) species that persist only under natural disturbance regimes in natural habitats and decline under human impact, 2) species that occur under both natural and anthropogenic disturbance regimes and habitats, and 3) species that no longer occur in natural habitats, but persist in anthropogenically disturbed habitats.

Species that persist only in natural habitats

There are a few known examples of rare disturbance-dependent species that have not yet been found to persist in human derived habitats. Four such species

Fig. 7.8. Effects of disturbances (dormant season fire (A), light fires or trampling (B), intense fire or heavy trampling (C), and fire suppression (D)) on fame flower life cycle. The life cycle is composed of stage transitions and cycles within stages (seed bank, juvenile and adults). Disturbances that are discordant with the life cycle are illustrated by solid lines that intersect the life cycle. These may prevent the recruitment of new individuals into the population. Disturbances that impact life history stages, but do not disrupt the cycle are represented by dotted lines. Since disturbances may affect many life stages of the species those designating the same event are labeled with the same letter (e.g. A). Life cycle model *sensu* Brown & Venable (1991).

Table 7.2. *Characteristics of disturbance-dependent rare plant species that are found in only native habitats, only anthropogenic habitats, or both (see text for references)*

Species	Life-history	Genetic diversity	Population characteristics	Disturbance type and scale
Species limited to native communities				
Pedicularis furbishiae	iteroparous perennial no seed bank	low	metapopulation	natural stochastic ice-scour of river banks large scale relative to local population
Plantago cordata	iteroparous perennial no seed bank	high	metapopulation	natural stochastic erosion of stream gravel bars large scale relative to local population
Cirsium pitcheri	monocarpic perennial no seed bank	low	metapopulation	natural stochastic dune processes large scale relative to local population
Howellia aquatilis	annual no seed bank	low	metapopulation	seasonal pond water level fluctuations large scale relative to local population
Species found in native and anthropogenic habitats				
Platanthera leucophaea	iteroparous perennial no seed bank	high	fragmented populations	natural biotic or pyric, or anthropogenic patch disturbances small to large scale relative to local population
Thelymitra epipactoides	iteroparous perennial no seed bank	?	fragmented populations	natural biotic or pyric, or anthropogenic patch disturbance small scale relative to local population
Dicerandra futescens	iteroparous perennial seed bank	?	fragmented populations	natural pyric or biotic, or anthropogenic patch disturbance small scale relative to local population
Talinum rugospermum	iteroparous perennial limited seed bank	?	fragmented populations	natural pyric or biotic, or anthropogenic patch disturbance small scale relative to local population
Species currently confined to anthropogenic habitats				
Amsinckia grandiflora	annual seed bank	low	highly isolated populations	natural biotic or pyric patch(?) disturbances natural scale unknown
Trifolium stoloniferum	stoloniferous perennial seed bank(?)	low	highly isolated population remnants	natural biotic disturbance, anthropogenic mowing natural scale unknown
Lesquerella lescurii	winter annual seed bank	?	localized populations	natural flooding, anthropogenic plowing small scale relative to local population
Lesquerella stonensis	winter annual seed bank	?	localized populations	natural flooding, anthropogenic plowing small scale relative to local population

are the federal endangered Furbish's lousewort (*Pedicularis furbishiae*), the heart-leaved plantain (*Plantago cordata*), the federal threatened Pitcher's thistle (*Cirsium pitcheri*), and the aquatic *Howellia aquatilis*. These species occur in habitats that experience large-scale, dynamic, and often stochastic disturbances. Most have low genetic diversity, persist as groups of dynamically interacting populations, i.e. metapopulations, and lack persistent seed banks. Thus they are susceptible to anthropogenic impacts, which may rarely replicate the landscape-scale disturbance regimes to which they are adapted.

Furbish's lousewort (*Pedicularis furbishiae*) is a genetically depauperate (Waller, O'Malley & Gawler 1988) hemiparasitic herb endemic to the St. John's River in Maine (Macior 1980). It grows primarily in an ephemeral shrub transition zone between the riverbank cobble zone and boreal forest, which is created and destroyed by ice scouring or sometimes eliminated by successional change.

Since Furbish's lousewort lacks a persistent seed bank, new habitats can be colonized only by dispersal from extant populations occurring elsewhere. Following colonization of newly created habitat, seed production for population growth or further colonization is possible only after a three-year period after which plants are mature (Menges 1990). The Furbish's lousewort is adapted to a particular range in frequency and dispersion of ice scour patches, and alteration of this regime will affect the longevity and colonization rate of populations. The Furbish's lousewort metapopulation appears to be declining; its annual population extirpation rate (2.6%) exceeded the establishment rate (1.3%) from 1980 to 1991 (Menges & Gawler 1993). Menges (1990) speculated that catastrophic runoff as a result of logging produced greater variance and severity in river flooding, thus eliminating potential habitat in time and space. Furbish's lousewort's low genetic variability may also prevent adaptation to novel habitats resulting from an altered disturbance regime.

The heart-leaved plantain (*Plantago cordata*) is a genetically diverse (Mymudes & Les 1993) semi-aquatic herb that has declined throughout the eastern United States. It colonizes silt-free gravel bars of forest streams, where it persists until its habitat is lost through succession or recurring disturbance (Meagher, Antonovics & Primack 1978, Bowles & Apfelbaum 1989). This species apparently lacks a seed bank and may occur as metapopulations. Bowles & Apfelbaum (1989) found that conversion of upland vegetation to agriculture increased the magnitude of stochastic storm flooding events, causing erosion, siltation, and loss of plantain populations. They hypothesized that naturally forested watersheds provided a buffering effect by reducing environ-

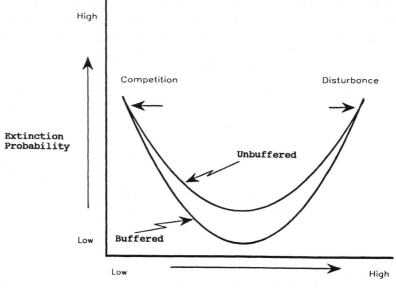

Fig. 7.9. Conceptual relationship between species extinction probability and disturbance regime in buffered and unbuffered habitats as applied to heart-leaved plantain
(Bowles & Apfelbaum 1989). Extinction is lowest under moderate disturbance in
buffered watersheds. Plant succession and competition or more frequent or intense
disturbance increase extinction probability. Populations in unbuffered watersheds
(i.e. unimpeded drainage and extreme erodibility) have a greater probability of going
extinct under all conditions.

mental variance, thereby allowing maintenance of plantain populations under
intermediate disturbance regimes (Fig. 7.9).

Pitcher's thistle (*Cirsium pitcheri*) is a monocarpic perennial herb with low
genetic diversity (Loveless & Hamrick 1988). It is endemic to the western
Great Lakes shoreline dunes where metapopulations occupy dynamic complexes composed of foredunes, blowouts, and vegetated dunes (McEachern *et
al.*, Chapter 8 of this volume). Natural shoreline processes and stochastic storm
events create and destroy the early-successional habitats on which Pitcher's
thistle depends. This thistle has declined in the southern part of its range owing
to human-altered shoreline processes, recreational impact, various biotic
processes including herbivory and seed predation, and perhaps by stress from
greater drought frequency (Pavlovic *et al.* 1993).

Howellia aquatilis is an annual herb of the Pacific northwest that is
restricted to ephemeral ponds having coarse-textured organic substrates
(Lesica 1992). It lacks a persistent seed bank (and genetic diversity) and thus
depends on dispersal to occupy ponds (Lesica *et al.* 1988, Lesica 1992).

Howellia can flower and set seed only when submerged in water. Seeds can germinate only in late summer drawdown conditions. Since annual precipitation determines pond depth, suitable habitats are spatially dynamic in time, and the species may persist only in clusters of ponds as metapopulations. In addition, each life history stage during the growing season occurs in successively lower pond water levels (Lesica *et al.* 1988). Human disturbance that alters the hydrological regime, such as modifying water chemistry or increasing siltation rates, will negatively impact this species.

Rare species that are confined to natural habitats may not have experienced anthropogenic disturbance, or they are adapted to natural disturbance regimes that are apparently easily disrupted or rarely replicated by human disturbance. For example, species such as *Pedicularis furbishiae* and *Plantago cordata* have generation times that are closely tied to the frequency of their natural disturbance regimes and occur in habitats that experience landscape scale disturbances where whole populations are often destroyed as disturbance intensity exceeds a threshold in severity. Since they lack a persistent seed bank and clonal propagation, dispersal to other suitable patches is critical for their persistence, and human impacts may alter disturbance patch density, disrupt dispersal to suitable patches, or destroy individuals before reproduction can occur. Current rates and intensities of disturbance require a positive ratio between population establishment and extinction.

Species found in both anthropogenic and natural disturbance regimes

Almost 60 rare species that occupy both natural and anthropogenic habitats, like fame flower, have been identified world-wide. Although these species appear to be independent of plant families or natural communities (Table 7.3), seventy-five percent of them are perennial. Twenty-two percent occur in late-successional communities, where they likely occupy disturbance gaps. Here I consider eight rare species for which both natural and anthropogenic disturbance regimes have been identified: the Australian metallic sun orchid (*Thelymitra epipactoides*), the US federal threatened eastern prairie fringed orchid (*Platanthera leucophaea*), the Florida endemic scrub balm (*Dicerandra frutescens*), and five others in less detail.

Although often characteristic of canopy gaps in late-successional communities, terrestrial orchids are well known for colonization of anthropogenic disturbance patches (Sheviak 1974, Case 1991). For example, the Australian metallic sun orchid (*Thelymitra epipactoides*) requires patch disturbances caused by echidna digging, fire, and death or herbivory of dominant vegetation for population regeneration (Calder, Cropper, & Tonkinson 1989). When

Table 7.3. *Rare plants that are reported from both natural and anthropogenic habitats, or are known to be favored by human disturbance*

Plants are listed by family and then alphabetically by genus.

Family species	Natural habitats	Anthropogenic habitats	Life cycle	Country	Source
SELAGINELLACEAE					
Selaginella rupestris	sand prairie	abandoned trails & roads	Perennial	USA	5
CYPERACEAE					
Scirpus hallii	sedge meadow	sand mine (wet)	Annual	USA	5
JUNCACEAE					
Juncus scirpoides	sedge meadow	sand mine (wet), abandoned trails & roads	Perennial	USA	5
LILIACEAE					
Calochortus albus	grassland	roadcuts and trails	Perennial	USA	12
Calochortus longebarbatus	grassland	roadsides	Perennial	USA	15
Dichelostemma ida-maia	open woods	roadsides	Perennial	USA	10
Fritillaria pluriflora	grassland	roadsides	Perennial	USA	15
Fritillaria roderickii	grassland	roadsides	Perennial	USA	15
IRIDACEAE					
Iris tenuis	moist woods	clearcuts, power line ROWs	Perennial	USA	10
Sisyrinchium angustifolium	prairie	former homesite or power line ROWs	Perennial	USA	5
Sisyrinchium dichotomum	open upland woods	highway rights of way	Perennial	USA	25
ORCHIDACEAE					
Isotria medeoloides	mesic deciduous woodlands	old logging roads, old fields, secondary growth	Perennial	USA	17
Orchis militaris	chalk grassland	chalk mine, roadside verge	Perennial	UK	11

Species	Habitat (natural)	Habitat (disturbed)	Life form	Country	Ref.
Platanthera leucophaea	prairie	pastures, successional fields	Perennial	USA	4
Platanthera peramoena	mesic woods	wetlands with forest succession	Perennial	USA	23
Spiranthes lucida	forested fen	homesite	Perennial	USA	5
Thelymitra epipactoides	heathland	roadsides, firelanes, ditches	Perennial	Australia	7
POACEAE					
Aristida tuberculosa	dry sand prairie	sand mine (dry)	Annual	USA	5
Avena maroccana	meadows?	fields, roadsides	Perennial	Morocco	16
Milium effusum	mesic woods	trail edges	Perennial	USA	5
Poa alsodes	mesic woods	trail edges	Perennial	USA	5
Poa marcida	hemlock forest	skid roads	Perennial	USA	21
RESTIONACEAE					
Alexgeorgea subterranea	sand heath	roadsides	Perennial	Australia	8
ASTERACEAE					
Boltonia decurrens	wet meadows	ditches & old fields	Perennial	USA	19,22
Centaurea lainzii	mountains	roadside	Perennial	Spain	14
Cirsium peckii	rocky canyon rims	roadsides	Perennial	USA	10
Helianthus schweinitzii	upland woods, clearings	roadsides, power line ROW's	Perennial	USA	27
BRASSICACEAE					
Draba incana	limestone grassland	mine spoil	Annual	UK	6
Lesquerella aurea	open rocky slope	roadsides	Annual	USA	20
Lesquerella filiformis	limestone glades	roadside outcrops	Annual	USA	19
Lesquerella gooddingii	open ponderosa pine forest	roadsides	Annual,Biennial	USA	20
Lesquerella lescurii	forested floodplains	agricultural fields	Annual	USA	1
Lesquerella stonensis	forested floodplains	agricultural fields	Annual	USA	1
CISTACEAE					
Helianthemum bicknellii	?	grassy bald	Perennial	USA	
Helianthemum dumosum	open sandy woods	rurways, golf courses, cemeteries	Perennial	USA	9

Table 7.3. (*cont.*)

Family species	Natural habitats	Anthropogenic habitats	Life cycle	Country	Source
Hudsonia tomentosa	sand prairie	sand mine (dry)	Perennial	USA	5
CAMPANULACEAE					
Campanula aparinoides	?	drainage ditch	Perennial	USA	23
CARYOPHYLLACEAE					
Silene regia	prairie	roadside	Perennial	USA	18
ERICACEAE					
Arctostaphylos densiflora	grassland	roadside	Perennial	USA	28
Rhododendron bakeri	?	grassy bald	Perennial	USA	23
EUPHORBIACEAE					
Euphorbia telephioides	wet savanna, seepage bogs	powerline ROWs	Perennial	USA	26
FABACEAE					
Astragalus altus	Douglas fir forest	roadsides	Perennial	USA	20
Astragalus kentrophytus	bluffs and dunes	roadsides	Perennial	USA	20
Astragalus tyghensis	sagebush and bunchgrass	roadsides	Perennial	USA	10
Dalea scariosa	sandy clay bluffs	roadsides	Perennial	USA	20
Lupinus duranii	pumice flats	roadsides	Annual	USA	15
Lupinus milo-bakeri	?	roadsides and orchard	Annual	USA	15
Lupinus monoensis	pumice flats	roadsides	Annual	USA	15
Lupinus spectabilis	serpentine outcrops	roadsides	Annual	USA	15
LEITNERIACEAE					
Leitneria floridana	swamps	roadsides	Perennial	USA	19

Family / Species	Natural habitat	Disturbed habitat	Life form	Country	Ref.
MALVACEAE					
Sidalcea campestris	grasslands	roadsides, fences, ditches	Perennial	USA	10
PAPAVERACEAE					
Argemone pleiacantha ssp. pinnatisecta	rock canyon slopes and bottoms	roadsides	Perennial	USA	20
POLYGONACEAE					
Polygonella articulata	sand prairie	sand mine (dry)	Perennial	USA	5
PORTULACACEAE					
Talinum rugospermum	prairie, savanna	abandoned trails and roads	Perennial	USA	5
PROTEACEAE					
Orothamnus zeyheri	montane seeps	fire lanes, footpaths	Perennial	S Africa	3
RANUNCULACEAE					
Ranunculus ophioglossifolius	fen	human trails	Annual	UK	13
Thalictrum cooleyi	savanna	roadsides, clearcuts,	Perennial	USA	24
SCROPHULARIACEAE					
Agalinis acuta	sandy plains and oak scrub	roadsides	Annual	USA	9
STACKHOUSIACEAE					
Stackhousia tryonii	grasslands	fencelines and power lines	Perennial	Australia	2

1 Baskin & Baskin 1990, Baskin et. al. 1992
2 Batianoff et al. 1990
3 Boucher 1981
4 Bowles 1983, 1994
5 Bowles et al., 1990
6 Bradshaw & Doody 1978
7 Calder et al., 1989
8 Carlquist 1976
9 Crow 1982
10 Eastman 1990
11 Farrell 1985
12 Fiedler 1987
13 Frost 1981
14 Gomez-Campo & Malato-Beliz 1985
15 Martz 1987
16 Mathez et al. 1985
17 Mehrhoff 1989
18 Menges 1988
19 Morgan 1984
20 New Mexico Native Plant Protection Advisory Committee 1984
21 Palmer et al., 1987
22 Schwegman & Nyboer 1985
23 White 1984
24 Wilczynski 1989
25 US Fish and Wildlife Service 1991a
26 US Fish and Wildlife Service 1991c
27 US Fish and Wildlife Service 1991d
28 York 1987

anthropogenic disturbances mimic natural disturbance processes, this orchid colonizes tracks, drainage channels, fire breaks, and bare ground patches in sandy
heaths and heathy woodlands, and often grows on bare ground with other ruderal
native species (Calder *et al.* 1989). Similarly, highest plot densities for the eastern prairie fringed orchid (*Platanthera leucophaea*) occur in anthropogenically
disturbed grasslands, which were thought to be analogous to natural regeneration
patches but on a larger scale (Bowles 1983). Under more dynamic anthropogenic
disturbance regimes, such as in wildlife management areas, this orchid may persist as metapopulations in which populations colonize early- to mid-successional
habitat and decline with advancing succession (Bowles 1994).

The Florida endemic scrub balm (*Dicerandra frutescens*), a short-lived
perennial herb, occurs with increasing density along a disturbance gradient
from mature sand pine scrub through recently burned oak-hickory scrub to
abandoned fire lanes (Menges 1991b, 1992). Fire in scrub habitats, which kills
vegetative scrub balm, produces the open interstitial patches that allow regeneration from seed banks. Fire rarely occurs in fire lanes because of low vegetative cover; therefore the fire lanes are suitable regeneration niches because of
the human disturbance that created them. In addition, scrub balm has greater
seedling recruitment, survival, and growth in oak–hickory scrub and fire lanes
compared with pine scrub. Although the proportion of flowers that set fruit is
highest in oak scrub, flowers and fruit per branch and seeds per fruit are highest
in fire lanes. Thus different habitats along a disturbance gradient not only support different plant densities, but also have different effects on individual plant
size and reproduction, and thus on population demography.

The responses of *Dicerandra frutescens* to natural and anthropogenic disturbances are comparable to those of rare plants of dry sand savannas in the central US. For example, the annuals *Polygonella articulata* and *Aristida
tuberculosa* and the perennial *Hudsonia tomentosa* colonize large-scale sand
mining disturbances that are analogs of smaller scale fire and wind-maintained
openings (Bowles *et al.* 1990). In a more complex situation, the sedges *Scirpus
hallii* and *Juncus scirpoides* appear in abandoned sand mines where exposed
water table fluctuations apparently simulate natural drawdowns (Bowles *et al.*
1990). Such coastal plain species persist naturally in the midwestern US by
reappearing from seed banks after reduction of competitive dominants by lake
level fluctuations (Wisheu & Keddy 1989). When species' natural regeneration niches occur across a gradient of patch sizes, such as with the scrub balm
Dicerandra frutescens, the likelihood of occurrence of a similar-sized anthropogenic patch is increased.

In general, these species appear adapted to a gradient of small- to large-
patch disturbance sizes that can be mimicked at some scale, frequency, and/or

intensity by anthropogenic disturbances. Other rare plants that occur under both natural and anthropogenic disturbance regimes appear to follow a similar pattern, with adaptation to regeneration in small-scale patch disturbances that can be ecologically mimicked by anthropogenic disturbance, but often at a variety of spatial scales. Thus, the terrestrial orchids *Platanthera leucophaea* and *Thelymitra epipactoides* may colonize anthropogenic disturbances that mimic their natural disturbance regimes.

Species currently confined to anthropogenic habitats

Under extreme human impacts, some disturbance-dependent species have become almost entirely confined to anthropogenic habitats (Martz 1987). For example, in England, *Lythrum hyssopifolia* occurs only in depressions in annually plowed agricultural fields (Preston & Whitehouse 1986), and in the United States, many California plants are found entirely in anthropogenic habitats (Heady 1987). I review four species in this category: the federal endangered large-flowered fiddleneck (*Amsinckia grandiflora*) and running buffalo clover (*Trifolium stoloniferum*), and the mustards *Lesquerella lescurii* and *L. stonensis*. These species have lost either their natural habitats or their natural disturbance regimes and have persisted only in anthropogenically disturbed or derived habitats.

Amsinckia grandiflora is an orange-flowered heterostylous (Weller & Ornduff 1977) annual herb that likely has a long-term seed bank (Pavlik, Nickrent & Howald 1993). The plant is known from three declining populations in California grasslands that have been severely altered by fire suppression, grazing, and exotic species invasion (Heady 1987, McClintock 1987, Pavlik *et al.* 1993). To determine a disturbance regime necessary for *Amsinckia grandiflora* recovery, Pavlik (Chapter 13 of this volume) applied clipping, burning, and herbicide treatments in grazing exclosures, and found that reduction of annual grass competition by fire favored its short-term persistence.

Running buffalo clover (*Trifolium stoloniferum*), a stoloniferous perennial herb, was thought to be extinct (Brooks 1983) until rediscovered in West Virginia (Bartgis 1985, McDonald, Butterworth & Stihler 1992), Kentucky (Campbell *et al.* 1988), Ohio (Cusick 1989) and Indiana (Homoya, Aldrich & Jacquart 1989). This clover was formerly dependent on disturbance from bison and elk (Campbell *et al.* 1988). It now occurs in well-drained alluvial forest or successional plant communities in which it is favored by mowing, trampling, grazing, or natural disturbances that remove herbaceous competition (Homoya *et al.* 1989). Modern populations are small compared with historic descriptions (Cusick 1989, Campbell *et al.* 1988), and their decline appears to be primarily due to the alteration of disturbance regime and secondarily due to loss of habitat. Low allozyme genetic variation within populations (Hickey, Vincent & Guttman 1991) may be contributing to, or a result of, its decline.

The mustards *Lesquerella lescurii* and *L. stonensis* are endemic to small areas of Kentucky and adjacent Tennessee in the United States, where they persist under anthropogenic disturbance regimes because of their obligate winter-annual life cycles (Baskin & Baskin 1990, Baskin, Baskin & Chester 1993). Both species formerly occurred in floodplain forests where stream erosion created early-successional disturbance patches, while *L. lescurii* also occurs in rocky glades. Natural floodplain forest habitat no longer exists for these species, and they are essentially restricted to extensive areas of agricultural fields established within their former range. Although spring plowing and stochastic stream flooding destroy individual plants, the populations survive as persistent seed banks. This seed bank is supplemented in years of above-normal rainfall, when plowing is delayed until after plants have matured.

These rare plants have lost either their natural habitats (e.g. *Lesquerella lescurii* and *L. stonensis*) and/or their natural disturbance regimes (e.g. *Trifolium stoloniferum* and *Amsinckia grandiflora*) and have persisted when anthropogenic disturbances mimic natural disturbance regimes and habitats. These conditions may be sub- or supra-optimal for species survival, and their persistence may depend upon vegetative spread (*T. stoloniferum*) or seed banks (*L. lescurii*, *L. stonensis* and *A. grandiflora*) allowing survival under a broad range of disturbance regimes at a scale that is fostered by human activities. For example, in buffalo clover and large-flowered fiddleneck, original natural grazing or fire disturbances have been replaced by human disturbance or pasturing that differ in scale or intensity, and the species are in decline. On the other hand, seed banks enhance the persistence of *Lesquerella* species as long as human disturbance creates extensive regeneration patches. When these criteria are met, anthropogenic disturbances may promote relatively high population densities, but extreme disturbance levels disrupt community structure and may cause population decline, as in fame flower. Such species probably are dependent on microsite variation within populations and thus are able to persist as isolated populations (Menges 1991a) rather than metapopulations.

Discussion

Concordance and discordance of anthropogenic disturbance regimes

Focusing on the direct and indirect disturbance pathways (Fig. 7.1) by which human activities impact endangered plants can assist in identifying the ultimate causes for their decline and possible means for mitigating the impacts. Such an approach, however, may not necessarily reveal the relationships among life history, population dynamics, and scale of disturbance that are so important in restoring and protecting endangered plants. Rare, successional plants are dependent on relative rates of disturbance and succession. Natural or anthropogenic shifts in these two processes can thus lead to concordance or discordance between plant stage-specific life histories and the scale of disturbance. Hence, when considering anthropogenic disturbance, it is important to identify to what extent humans affect the scale of these processes. Interaction between the scale of human disturbance and the species' life history produces the three species distribution types discussed previously.

Discordance between anthropogenic disturbance regimes and plant life history results from spatial, temporal, and/or intensity scales of disturbance that differ from those of natural disturbance to which plants are adapted. Temporal discordance of anthropogenic disturbance occurs either by damping (e.g. *Howellia*) or amplifying (e.g. *Pedicularis*) the disturbance frequency or intensity such that plants are unable to reach maturity, produce seed, or establish. The most important life history traits for persistence in such regimes are the time to reach maturity and resistance stages such as seed banks that are dispersed in time. Spatial discordance of anthropogenic disturbance occurs by increasing interpopulation or interpatch distance such that populations (e.g. *Pedicularis*) or subpopulations (e.g. *Talinum*) become so isolated that dispersal to suitable patches is impossible. This is especially true for species that lack persistent seed banks and persist as metapopulations (Table 7.2). Human disturbances fragment habitats in patterns that rarely conform to the natural disturbance scales under which metapopulation species evolved. Human effects often cause species decline because they effectively isolate or eliminate local populations, or promote dispersal to unsuitable habitats (Lande 1987), thus increasing rates of population extirpation compared to colonization. Lower or higher intensity of disturbance can cause the disappearance of patches or catastrophic destruction of populations (e.g. *Plantago*). In other examples, intense growing-season trampling by humans has caused declines in the sentry milk-vetch (*Astragalus cremnophylax* var. *cremnophylax*) (US Fish & Wildlife Service 1991b), sea rocket (*Cakile edentula*) (Pavlovic & Bowles 1994), and Missouri bladderpod (*Lesquerella filiformis*) (Thomas & Willson 1992).

In many cases it is clear that the spatial, temporal, and/or intensity aspects of disturbance interact. Such interaction is well-illustrated with fire-dependent species such as fame flower. At one extreme, fire suppression can lead to development of a thick litter layer that may shade and eliminate the species. Moreover, conflagrations of heavy fuel loads may be so large and so hot that they destroy the remaining population. In addition, surviving populations may be too remote to recolonize the burn areas. At the other extreme, natural or prescribed fires may be so frequent that there is little fuel build-up, and thus there may be no real hot spots to eliminate competitors that hinder establishment and growth. Similarily, a spatial and temporal contrast occurs between confined domestic grazers that cause repeated local disturbances and nomadic bison that produced many scales of disturbance extent and intensity. These differences between the scales of cattle and bison grazing and trampling may account for the decline of running buffalo clover populations.

Concordance between human disturbance and plant life history results from mimicking the scale of natural disturbance regimes. Rare plants that are currently confined to anthropogenic disturbance regimes (Tables 7.2 and 7.3) are either annuals with persistent seed banks and poor dispersal or perennials having vegetative propagation. Annuals can be successful with limited seed bank replenishment, even with small disturbance patches, as long as appropriate regeneration conditions occur within the life span of seed bank populations. Species found in both natural and anthropogenic disturbance regimes may have intermediate requirements for the spatial scale and longevity of disturbances (Table 7.2). Since many of these species are perennials (Table 7.3), they may colonize large-scale human disturbances after disturbance is relaxed. Thus the intensity and frequency of anthropogenic disturbance is sufficient to favor the species, but at a larger spatial scale, producing a seemingly greater abundance of individuals. In this case, anthropogenic disturbance regimes mimic only two aspects (intensity and frequency) of the natural disturbance regime.

Restoration of disturbance processes and disturbance regimes

The concept of concordance between disturbance scale and life cycle is central to *in situ* restoration of rare plants, because it focuses attention on the important relationship among scale of disturbance and species abundance, distribution, and persistence. Restoration of disturbance processes for rare plants should include identification of the type of abiotic or biotic disturbance regime to which the target species is adapted (e.g. flooding for *Lesquerella stonensis* versus bison trampling and wallowing for *Trifolium stoloniferum*), the appropriate disturbance frequency (e.g. 3 years to maturity for *Pedicularis furbishiae*), the necessary patch disturbance spatial scale (*e.g.* microsite for *Talinum rugospermum* and landscape for *Pedicularis furbishiae* and *Howellia aquatilis*), appropriate population structure for persistence (local population versus metapopulation), and disturbance intensity. Recovery of a declining rare species may require reintroduction or management of the natural disturbance regime, elimination of a damaging anthropogenic disturbance regime, or introduction of a novel disturbance regime. Removal of exotic species and restoration of natural disturbance regimes have caused 'extirpated' species to reappear (Cunningham & Milthorpe 1981, Loope & Scowcraft 1985) or promoted rare plant survival and/or reproduction (Cunningham & Milthorpe 1981, Loope & Scowcroft 1985, Willoughby 1987, Elkington 1981).

Concordant anthropogenic disturbance may postpone species extinction by providing refugia for disturbance-dependent plants, but also presents management dilemmas when the species' former natural habitat is destroyed and unknown (e.g. White 1984, Bowles *et al.* 1990). Management to maintain single-species populations is attractive because it is easy to quantify management goals and identify disturbances that promote large population size, but there are serious pitfalls (Dunn 1987, Freas & Murphy 1988). For example, large population size is a good hedge against genetic and demographic stochasticity (Goodman 1987), but it does not protect against environmental stochasticity except when it ensures occupation of a diversity of microsites (Stacey & Taber 1992). Use of human disturbance to maximize population size of a single species can alter community composition, causing loss of native species and potential invasion of exotic species (Hobbs & Huenneke 1992), alter viability by changing population genetic structure (DeMauro, Chapter 12 of this volume), alter a species' evolutionary course by creating a novel selective environment (Denslow 1985, Sousa 1984, Barrett 1983, Warwick 1990, Brown & Pavlovic 1992), and increase density-dependent disease or predation. Agricultural disturbance has been a boon for *Lesquerella lescurii* and *L. stonensis* but may provide different selective and evolutionary effects compared with natural flooding events. Thus, boosting of a rare species' local density to high levels comparable to those found in anthropogenic habitats may be an inappropriate restoration goal.

Spatial scales of disturbance patches and patch mosaics are critical restoration parameters for dispersal-dependent plant species that occur as metapopulations or as spatially fragmented populations that require localized patch disturbances for persistence (Menges 1991a). Manipulating reserve design to lower environmental variance is one way to prevent extinction of local populations, metapopulations and even species (Goodman 1987). For metapopulation-dependent species, restoration of within-population disturbance regimes may be insufficient, and protection or reintroduction of landscape level disturbance processes in both occupied and unoccupied habitats may be needed (Pavlovic *et al.* 1993, McEachern *et al.*, Chapter 8 of this volume, Pickett & Thompson 1978). Restoration of a regional landscape disturbance regime will be difficult in a mosaic of land-uses and ownerships, e.g. watershed protection of stream hydrology for the heart-leaved plantain (Bowles & Apfelbaum 1989) or Furbish's lousewort (Menges & Gawler 1993), but may be impossible if the original biotic disturbance agent was migratory or has a home range larger than reserve size.

When introduction of disturbance-dependent species is required, appropriate disturbance regimes and habitats must be identified or determined experimentally. Bowles *et. al.* (1993) approached this problem for *Cirsium pitcheri* by comparing the community structure and disturbance regimes of potential restoration sites against existing populations, and then planned for restoration at the metapopulation level (McEachern *et al.*, Chapter 8 of this volume). With *Amsinckia grandiflora*, which had no extant viable populations in a natural community, Pavlik (Chapter 13 of this volume) examined macroclimate, soil, exposure, community associates and degree of disturbance to select an introduction site and then used experimental treatments to determine the appropriate disturbance regime. The analyses used in these studies, like those for fame flower, should be a prerequisite for any species restoration and introduction. For species confined to anthropogenic habitats, a variety of paleoecological, historical, and ecological approaches (Marks 1983, Gehlbach & Polley 1982) can help identify former native habitats. Static and experimental demographic (Menges 1986, Pavlik 1987, Pavlik & Barbour 1988) and ecological restoration research is needed to identify mortality factors, disturbance regimes, ecological niches and appropriate management regimes for disturbance-dependent plant species.

Introduction of artificial disturbance processes may be required when former disturbance agents are unknown, or when rare plant species are confined to anthropogenic communities. Domestic cattle and horses are often used to maintain species diversity in Europe (van Wieren 1991, Berendse *et al.* 1992). Horses were introduced into Badgeworth fen, for example, to promote *Ranunculus ophioglossifolius* by reducing dominant vegetation cover through grazing and trampling (Frost 1981). It is critical, however, that the introduced artificial disturbance is instituted at an appropriate scale. On small reserves, reintroduction of bison as the disturbance agent for running buffalo clover may be problematic, because of their migratory habit and ability to devastate vegetation when confined. Here, controlled disturbance (i.e. rotations) by bison or alternative herbivores, or by humans, may be necessary for the persistence and restoration of running buffalo clover.

How important is community restoration for species that persist under anthropogenic disturbances in exotic communities? Should restoration of rare plants such as *Amsinckia grandiflora* require only maintenance of an appropriate disturbance (burning) regime in an otherwise highly modified habitat? If plant communities are dynamic and transient in time (*sensu* Davis 1984), and species are individualistic and respond to competition in a diffuse manner, then specific biotic communities may be irrelevant as long as general climatic, habitat, and disturbance characteristics are met. Attention to the community would be important for species having mutualistic interactions. For example, loss of pollinators in anthropogenic habitats could be significant in eroding genetic diversity of outcrossing plants (Karron 1991, Weller, Chapter 4 of this volume). Thus, for *Amsinckia grandiflora*, reintroduction of fire may be an appropriate short-term restoration goal, but restoration into a natural perennial bunchgrass community may be the most effective way of increasing habitat patchiness that promotes *Amsinckia* population growth (Pavlik *et al.* 1993) and may provide an evolutionary context for long-term survival. When habitat alteration makes historical sites inhospitable to rare species by shifting the disturbance regime, and restoration of the former disturbance regime is impossible or unlikely (e.g. disruption of watersheds occupied by *Plantago cordata*), introduction or translocation to new favorable sites that are inaccessible to the species by natural dispersal may be appropriate.

Finally, when a former or novel disturbance regime is introduced, catastrophic mortality may occur. Experimental manipulation of alternative disturbance regimes for management enhances understanding of mortality and density-dependent regeneration in response to disturbance so that such negative effects can be avoided or counterbalanced. For example, initial application of fire after long-term litter accumulation may result in extreme heat intensity and plant mortality. But if some plants or seed banks persist, episodic regeneration may follow, showing positive indirect effects of disturbance, such as those shown for fame flower. In contrast, disturbance-dependent plants that lack persistent seed banks (e.g. *Bromus pseudosecalinus*, Hodgson 1991) and depend on local dispersal for recolonization may not recover from large scale disturbance.

Summary

Many rare plant species are successional and require disturbances for their regeneration (Connell 1978, Petraitis *et al.* 1989, Hobbs & Huenneke 1992). Their persistence depends on concordance of their life histories with the temporal and spatial patterns, and intensity or severity, of disturbance regimes. These species are classified into three response categories: 1) species that persist only under natural disturbance regimes in natural habitats and decline under human impact, 2) species that occur under both natural and anthropogenic disturbance regimes and habitats, and 3) species that no longer occur under natural habitats, but persist in anthropogenically disturbed habitats. Managing or restoring disturbance-dependent rare plant species requires an understanding of the relationship between the scale of suitable patch disturbance regimes and population dynamics. When disturbance regimes eliminate populations and the species can disperse only in space, restoration of the landscape-scale disturbance regime will be necessary to maintain viable metapopulations. If disturbance patches are smaller than the population scale or occur at the microsite level, then population persistence requires only maintenance of the appropriate disturbance regime at the population level. Irrespective of the patch disturbance size, landscape-scale reserves may be required to allow disturbance agents or processes to spread.

Anthropogenic habitats may also act as refugia for disturbance-dependent plants, sometimes allowing higher densities (e.g. fame flower) than in natural habitats. Although high densities are tempting restoration goals, they may alter evolutionary directions, and their management may result in natural community degradation. Therefore, management should strive to maintain not only the species, but also its natural environmental context.

Disturbance regimes are one of the most important considerations for *in situ* conservation and restoration of endangered plants. Depending on the species rarity, isolation and breeding system (Weller, Chapter 4 of this volume), genetic considerations may also be important (Barrett & Kohn 1991, DeMauro, Chapter 12 of this volume); however, once genetic concerns are met, ecological considerations will be important in any *in situ* restoration. Successful ecological restoration of a rare species requires the identification and recreation of its dynamic environment, including the spatial and temporal components of the disturbance regime, and the identification and mitigation of those discordant environmental factors that could hinder short-term restoration efforts and long-term persistence. *In situ* restoration research of disturbance-dependent rare plants will continue to be a fertile ground for understanding the relationship among disturbance scale, species life history, and population viability and evolution.

Acknowledgements

Conversations with and critical reviews by Marlin Bowles, Joel Brown, Don Waller, Tom Poulson, Chris Whelan, Marcy DeMauro, Kathryn McEachern and Sarah Pavlovic greatly improved this manuscript. The assistance of John King, Ken Arzarian, and Sandy Whisler in the fame flower field work was greatly appreciated. The National Park Service provided logistic and financial support for the fame flower research.

Literature cited

Barrett, S. C. H. (1983) Crop mimicry in weeds. *Economic Botany*, **37**, 255–82.

Barrett, S. C. H. & Kohn, J. R. (1991) Genetic and evolutionary consequences of small population size in plants: Implications for conservation. In *Genetics and Conservation of Rare Plants*, ed. Falk, D. A. & Holsinger, K. E., pp. 3–30. New York: Oxford University Press.

Bartgis, R. L. (1985) Rediscovery of *Trifolium stoloniferum* Muhl. ex A. Eaton. *Rhodora*, **87**, 425–29.

Baskin, C. C. & Baskin, J. M. (1988) Germination ecophysiology of herbaceous plant species in a temperate region. *American Journal of Botany*, **75**, 286–305.

Baskin, J. M. & Baskin, C. C. (1990) Seed germination biology of the narrowly endemic species *Lesquerella stonensis* (Brassicaceae) *Plant Species Biology*, **5**, 205–213.

Baskin, J. M., Baskin, C. C. & Chester, E. W. (1992) Seed dormancy pattern and seed reserves as adaptations of the endemic winter annual *Lesquerella lescurii* (Brassicaceae) to its floodplain habitat. *Natural Areas Journal*, **12**, 184–90.

Batianoff, G. N., Reeves, R. D. & Specht, R. L. (1990) *Stackhousia tryonii* Bailey: A nickel-accumulating serpentinite-endemic species of Central Queensland. *Australian Journal of Botany*, **38**,121–130.

Berendse, F., Oomes, M. J. M., Altena, H. J. & Elberse, W. T. (1992) Experiments on the restoration of species-rich meadows in The Netherlands. *Biological Conservation*, **62**, 59–65.

Boucher, C. (1981) Autecological and population studies of *Orothamnus zeyheri* in the Cape of South Africa. In *The Biological Aspects of Rare Plant Conservation*, ed. Synge, H. pp. 343–54. New York: John Wiley and Sons.

Bowles, M. L. (1983) The tallgrass prairie orchids *Platanthera leucophaea* (Nutt.) Lindl. and *Cypripedium candidum* Muhl. ex Willd.: Some aspects of their status, biology, and ecology, and implications toward management. *Natural Areas Journal*, **3**, 14–37.

Bowles, M. L. (1994) *Recovery plan for the eastern prairie fringed orchid* (Platanthera leucophaea). Minneapolis/Saint Paul: US Fish and Wildlife Service.

Bowles, M. L. & Apfelbaum, S. I. (1989) Effects of land use and stochastic events on the heart-leaved plantain (*Plantago cordata* Lam.) in an Illinois stream system. *Natural Areas Journal*, **9**, 90–101.

Bowles, M. L., DeMauro, M. M., Pavlovic, N. & Hiebert, R. D. (1990) Effects of anthropogenic disturbances on endangered and threatened plants at the Indiana Dunes National Lakeshore. *Natural Areas Journal*, **10**, 187–200.

Bowles, M. L., Flakne, R., McEachern, A. K. & Pavlovic, N. B. (1993) Recovery planning and restoration of the federally threatened Pitcher's thistle (*Cirsium pitcheri*) in Illinois. *Natural Areas Journal*, **13**, 164–76.

Bradshaw, M. E. & Doody, J. P. (1978) Plant population studies and their relevance to nature conservation. *Biological Conservation*, **14**, 223–242.

Brooks, R. E. (1983) *Trifolium stoloniferum*, running buffalo clover: Description, distribution, and current status. *Rhodora*, **85**, 343–54.

Brown, J. S. & Pavlovic, N. B. (1992) Evolution in heterogeneous environments: Effects of migration on habitat specialization. *Evolutionary Ecology*, **6**, 360–82.

Brown, J. S. & Venable, D. L. (1986) Evolutionary ecology of seed bank annuals in temporally varying environments. *American Naturalist*, **127**, 31–47.

Brown, J. S. & Venable, D. L. (1991) Life-history evolution of seed-bank annuals in response to seed predation. *Evolutionary Ecology*, **5**, 12–29.

Calder, D. M., Cropper, S. C. & Tonkinson, D. (1989) The ecology of *Thelymitra epipactoides* F. Muell. (Orchidaceae) in Victoria, Australia, and the implications for management of the species. *Australian Journal of Botany*, **37**, 19–32.

Campbell, J. J. N., Evans, M., Medley, M. E. & Taylor, N. L. (1988) Buffalo clovers in Kentucky (*Trifolium stoloniferum* and *T. reflexum*): Historical records, presettlement environment, rediscovery, endangered status, cultivation, and chromosome number. *Rhodora*, **90**, 399–418.

Carlquist, S. (1976) *Alexgeorgea*, a bizarre new genus of Restionaceae from Western Australia. *Australian Journal of Botany*, **21**, 281–95.

Case, F. W. (1991) *Orchids of the Western Great Lakes Region*. Cranbrook Institute of Science Bulletin 48. Bloomfield Hills: Cranbrook Insitute of Science

Caswell, H. (1990) *Matrix Projection Models: Construction, Analysis and Interpretation*. Sunderland: Sinauer Associates.

Cochrane, T. S. (1993) Status and distribution of *Talinum rugospermum* Holz. (Portulacaceae). *Natural Areas Journal*, **13**, 33–41.

Connell, J. H. (1978) Diversity in tropical rain forests and coral reefs. *Science*, **199**, 1302–10.

Crow, G. E. (1982) *New England's rare, threatened, and endangered plants*. Washington: US Department of Interior Fish and Wildlife Service.

Cunningham, G. M. & Milthorpe, P. L. (1981) The vascular plants of five exclosure sites in Western New South Wales. *Cunninghamia*, **1**, 23–34.

Cusick, A. W. (1989) *Trifolium stoloniferum* (Fabaceae) in Ohio: History, habitats, decline, and rediscovery. *Sida*, **13**, 467–80.

Davis, M. B. (1984) Climatic instability, time lags, and community disequilibrium. In *Community Ecology*, ed. Diamond J. & Case, T., pp. 269–84. New York: Harper and Row.

Denslow, J. S. (1985) Disturbance-mediated coexistence of species. In *The Ecology of Natural Disturbance and Patch Dynamics*, ed. Pickett, S. T. A. & White, P. S., pp. 307–23. New York: Academic Press.

Dunn, P. V. (1987) Endangered species management in Southern California coastal salt marshes: A conflict or an opportunity? In *Conservation and Management of Rare and Endangered Plants*, ed. Elias, T. S., pp. 441–6. Sacramento: The California Native Plant Society.

Eastman, D. C. (1990) *Rare and endangered plants of Oregon*. Wilsonville, Oregon: Beautiful America Publishing Company.

Elkington, T. T. (1981) Effects of excluding grazing animals from grassland on sugar limestone in Teesdale, England. *Biological Conservation*, **20**, 25–35.

Farrell, L. (1985) Biological Flora of the British Isles No. 160. *Orchis militaris* L. *Journal of Ecology*, **1**, 1041–53.

Fernald, M. L. (1950) *Gray's Manual of Botany*. New York: Van Nostrand Reinhold Company.

Fiedler, P. L. (1987) Life history and population dynamics of rare and common mariposa lilies (*Calochortus* Pursh: Liliaceae). *Journal of Ecology*, **75**, 977–95.

Freas, K. E. & Murphy, D. D. (1988) Taxonomy and the conservation of the critically endangered Bakersfield saltbush, *Atriplex tularensis*. *Biological Conservation*, **46**, 317–24.

Frost, L. C. (1981) The study of *Ranunculus ophioglossifolius* and its successful conservation at the Badgeworth Nature Reserve, Gloucestershire. In *The Biological Aspects of Rare Plant Conservation*, ed. Synge, H., pp. 481–9. New York: John Wiley and Sons.

Gauch, H. G. Jr. & Whittaker, R. H. (1981) Hierarchical classification of community data. *Journal of Ecology*, **69**, 537–57.

Gehlbach, F. R. & Polley, H. W. (1982) Relict trout lilies *Erythronium mesochoreum* in central Texas: A multivariate analysis of habitat for conservation. *Biological Conservation*, **22**, 251–8.

Glenn-Lewin, D. C. & Ver Hoef, J. M. (1988) Prairies and grasslands of the St. Croix National Scenic Riverway, Wisconsin and Minnesota. *Prairie Naturalist*, **20**, 65–80.

Gomez-Campo, C. & Malato-Beliz, J. (1985) The Iberian Peninsula. In *Plant Conservation in the Mediterranean Area*, ed. Gomez-Campo, C., pp. 47–70. Dordrecht: Dr W. Junk Publishers.

Goodman, D. (1987) How do any species persist? Lessons for conservation biology. *Conservation Biology*, **1**, 59–62.

Grime, J. P. (1979) *Plant Strategies and Vegetation Processes*. Chichester: Wiley Interscience.

Grubb, P. J. (1977) The maintenance of species-richness in plant communities: the importance of the regeneration niche. *Biological Reviews*, **52**, 107–45.

Hamann, O. (1979) Regeneration of vegetation on Santa Fe and Pinta Islands, Galapagos, after the eradication of goats. *Biological Conservation*, **15**, 215–36.

Heady, H. F. (1987) Valley grasslands. In *Terrestrial Vegetation of California*, ed. Barbour, M. G. & Major, J., pp. 491–514. New York: John Wiley & Sons.

Hickey, R. J., Vincent, M. A. & Guttman, S. I. (1991) Genetic variation in running buffalo clover (*Trifolium stoloniferum*, Fabaceae). *Conservation Biology*, **5**, 309–16.

Hobbs, R. J. & Huenneke, L. F. (1992) Disturbance, diversity, and invasion: Implications for conservation. *Conservation Biology*, **6**, 324 37.

Hodgson, J. G. (1991) Management for the conservation of plants with particular reference to the British flora. In *The Scientific Management of Temperate Communities for Conservation: The 31st Symposium of the British Ecological Society, Southampton 1989*, ed. Spellerberg, I. F., Goldsmith F. B. & Morris, M. G., pp. 81–102. Oxford: Blackwell Scientific Publications.

Homoya, M. A., Aldrich, J. R. & Jacquart, E. M. (1989) The redisovery of the globally endangered clover, *Trifolium stoloniferum*, in Indiana. *Rhodora*, **91**, 207–12.

Howarth, F. G. (1985) Impacts of alien land arthropods and mollusks on native plants and animals in Hawai'i. In *Hawai'i's Terrestrial ecosystems: Preservation and management*, eds. Stone, C. P. & Scott, J. M., pp. 142–79. Honolulu: Cooperative National Park Resources Study Unit, University of Hawai'i.

Hughes, F., Vitousek, P. M. & Tunison, T. (1991) Alien grass invasion and fire in the seasonal submontane zone of Hawai'i. *Ecology*, **72**, 743–47.

Huntly, N. & Inouye, R. (1988) Pocket gophers in ecosystems: patterns and mechanisms. *Bioscience*, **38**, 786–93.

Karron, J. D. (1991) Patterns of genetic variation and breeding systems in rare plant species. In *Genetics and Conservation of Rare Plants*, ed. Falk, D. A. & Holsinger, K. E., pp. 45–62. Oxford University Press.

Klinkhamer, P. G. L. & De Jong, T. J. (1988) The importance of small-scale disturbance for seedling establishment in *Cirsium vulgare* and *Cynoglossum officinale*. *Journal of Ecology*, **76**, 383–92.

Lande, R. (1987) Extinction thresholds in demographic models of territorial populations. *American Naturalist*, **130**, 624–35.

Lesica, P. (1992) Autecology of the endangered plant *Howellia aquatilis*; Implications for management and reserve design. *Ecological Applications*, **2**, 411–21.

Lesica, P., Leary, R. F., Allendorf, F. W. & Bilderback, D. E. (1988). Lack of genetic diversity within and among populations of an endangered plant, *Howellia aquatilis*. *Conservation Biology*, **2**, 275–82.

Loope, L. L. & Scowcroft, P. G. (1985) Vegetation response within exclosures in Hawai'i: A review. In *Hawai'i's Terrestrial ecosystems: Preservation and management*, ed. Stone, C. P. & Scott, J. M. pp. 377–402. Honolulu: Cooperative National Park Resources Study Unit, University of Hawai'i.

Loveless, M. D. & Hamrick, J. L. (1988) Genetic organization and evolutionary history in two North American species of *Cirsium*. *Evolution* 42(2), 254–65.

MacDonald, I. A. W., Thebaud, C., Strahm, W. A. & Strasberg, D. (1991) Effects of alien plant invasions on native vegetation remnants on La Reunion (Mascarene Islands, Indian Ocean) *Environmental Conservation*, 18, 51–61.

Macior, L. W. (1980) Population ecology of the Furbish lousewort, *Pedicularis furbishiae* S. Wats. *Rhodora*, 82, 105–111.

Marks, P. L. (1983) On the origin of the field plants of the Northeastern United States. *American Naturalist*, 122, 210–28.

Martz, C. (1987) Endangered plants along California highways: Considerations for right-of-way management. In *Conservation and Management of Rare and Endangered Plants*, ed. Elias, T. S. pp. 79–84. Sacramento: The California Native Plant Society.

Mathez, J., Quezel, P. & Raynaud, C. (1985) The Maghreb countries. In *Plant Conservation in the Mediterranean Area*, ed. Gomez-Campo, C., pp. 141–57. Dordrecht: Dr W. Junk Publishers.

McClintock, E. (1987) The displacement of native plants by exotics. In *Conservation and Management of Rare and Endangered Plants*, ed. Elias, T. S., pp. 185–8. Sacramento: The California Native Plant Society.

McDonald, B., Butterworth, S. & Stihler, C. (1992) State Reports: West Virginia. *Natural Areas Journal*, 12, 115–17.

Meagher, T. R., Antonovics, J. & Primack, R. (1978) Experimental ecological genetics in *Plantago*. III. Genetic variation and demography in relation to survival of *Plantago cordata*, a rare species. *Biological Conservation*, 14, 243–57.

Mehrhoff, L. A. (1989) Reproductive vigor and environmental factors in populations of an endangered North American orchid, *Isotria medeoloides* (Pursh) Rafinesque. *Biological Conservation*, 47, 281–96.

Menges, E. S. (1986) Predicting the future of rare plant populations: Demographic monitoring and modeling. *Natural Areas Journal*, 6, 13–25.

Menges, E. S. (1988) Population biology of a rare prairie forb, *Silene regia*, 1985–1987. Holcomb Research Institute Report No. 101. Indianapolis: Butler University.

Menges, E. S. (1990) Population viability analysis for an endangered plant. *Conservation Biology*, 4, 52–62.

Menges, E. S. (1991a) The application of minimum viable population theory to plants. In *Genetics and Conservation of Rare Plants*, ed. Falk, D. A. & Holsinger, K. E., pp. 45–62. Oxford: Oxford University Press.

Menges, E. S. (1991b) Site-related variation in demography and reproductive biology in *Dicerandra frutescens*, an endemic mint of Florida's Lake Wales Ridge. In *Fifth annual meeting of the Society for Conservation Biology*, p. 42. Madison: University of Wisconsin.

Menges, E. S. (1992) Habitat preferences and response to disturbance for *Dicerandra frutescens*, a Lake Wales Ridge (Florida) endemic mint. *Bulletin of the Torrey Botanical Club*, 119, 308–13.

Menges, E. S. & Gawler, S. C. (1994) Conservation biology of an endemic plant. In *Managing for Viable Populations*, ed. Marcot, B. G. & Murphy, D. Cambridge University Press. (In press).

Morgan, S. W. (1984) *Select rare and endangered plants of Missouri*. Missouri Department of Conservation. Jefferson City: Conservation Commission of the State of Missouri.

Mymudes, M. S. & Les, D. H. (1993) Morphological and genetic variability in *Plantago cordata* (Plantaginaceae), a threatened aquatic plant. *American Journal of Botany*, **80**, 351–9.

New Mexico Native Plant Protection Advisory Committee. (1984) *A handbook of rare and endemic plants of New Mexico*. Albuquerque: University of New Mexico Press.

Olson, J. S. (1958) Rates of succession and soil changes on southern Lake Michigan sand dunes. *Botanical Gazette*, **119**, 125–70.

Palmer, R., Vanbianchi, R., Schofield, L. & Nugent, S. (1987) Ecology and distribution of *Poa marcida* Hitchc. in Northwestern Oregon. In *Conservation and Management of Rare and Endangered Plants*, ed. Elias, T. S., pp. 341–50. Sacramento: The California Native Plant Society.

Pavlik, B. M. (1987) Attributes of plant populations and their management implications. In *Conservation and Management of Rare and Endangered Plants*, ed. Elias, T. S. pp. 311–19. Sacramento: The California Native Plant Society.

Pavlik, B. M., Nickrent, D. L. & Howard, A. M. (1993) The recovery of an endangered plant. I. Creating a new population of *Amsinckia grandiflora*. *Conservation Biology*, **7**, 510–26.

Pavlik, B. M. & Barbour, M. G. (1988) Demographic monitoring of endemic sand dune plants, Eureka Valley, California. *Biological Conservation*, **46**, 217–42.

Pavlovic, N. B. & Bowles, M. L. (1994). Rare plant monitoring program at Indiana Dunes National Lakeshore. In *Applications of Long-Term Research in U. S. National Parks*, ed. Davis G. & Halverson, W. University of Arizona Press. (In Press.)

Pavlovic, N. B., Bowles, M. L., Crispin, S. R., Gibson, T. C., Herman, K. D., Kavetsky, R. T., McEachern, A. K. & Penskar, M. R. (1993) *Draft Pitcher's Thistle (Cirsium pitcheri) Recovery Plan*. Minneapolis/Saint Paul: US Fish and Wildlife Service.

Petraitis, P. S., Latham, R. E. & Niesenbaum, R. A. (1989) The maintenance of species diversity by disturbance. *The Quarterly Review of Biology*, **64**, 393–418.

Pickett, S. T. A. & Thompson, J. N. (1978) Patch dynamics and the design of nature reserves. *Biological Conservation*, **13**, 27–37.

Pickett, S. T. A. & White, P. S. eds. (1985) *The Ecology of Natural Disturbance and Patch Dynamics*. New York: Academic Press.

Platt, W. J. (1975) The colonization and formation of equilibrium plant species associations on badger disturbances in a tall-grass prairie. *Ecological Monographs*, **45**, 285 305.

Platt, W. J. (1976) The natural history of a fugitive prairie plant (*Mirabilis hirsuta* (Pursh) MacM.) *Oecologia*, **22**, 399–409.

Plumb, M. L. (1979) The dynamics of short-lived species in a sand prairie. Ph.D. dissertation, Madison: University of Wisconsin. 242 pp.

Preston, C. D. & Whitehouse, H. L. K. (1986) The habitat of *Lythrum hyssopifolia* L. in Cambridgeshire, its only surviving English locality. *Biological Conservation*, **35**, 41–62.

Rykiel, E. J. (1985) Towards a definition of ecological disturbance. *Australian Journal of Ecology*, **10**, 361–5.

Schoener, T. W. (1987) The geographic distribution of rarity. *Oecologia*, **74**, 161–73.

Schwegman, J. E. & Nyboer, R. W. (1985) The taxonomic and population status of *Boltonia decurrens* (Torr. & Gray) Wood. *Castanea*, **50**, 112–15.

Sheviak, C. J. (1974) *Introduction to the ecology of the Illinois Orchidaceae.* Illinois State Museum Scientific Papers XIV. Springfield: Illinois State Museum.

Silvertown, J. W. (1987) *Introduction to Plant Population Ecology.* Harlow, England: Longman Scientific & Technical.

Smith, C. W. (1985) Impact of alien plants on Hawai'i's native biota. In *Hawai'i's Terrestrial Ecosystems: Preservation and Management*, ed. Stone, C. P. & Scott, J. M., pp. 251–97. Honolulu: Cooperative National Park Resources Study Unit, University of Hawai'i.

Sousa, W. P. (1984) The role of disturbance in natural communities. *Annual Review of Ecology and Systematics*, **15**, 353–91.

Stacey, P. B. & Taber, M. (1992) Environmental variation and the persistence of small populations. *Ecological Applications*, **2**, 18–29.

Stone, C. P. & Scott, J. M. (1985) *Hawai'i's Terrestrial ecosystems: Preservation and management.* Honolulu: Cooperative National Park Resources Study Unit, University of Hawai'i.

Thomas, L. P. & Willson, G. D. (1992) Effect of experimental trampling on the federally endangered species, *Lesquerella filiformis* Rollins, at Wilson's Creek National Battlefield, Missouri. *Natural Areas Journal*, **12**, 101–5.

US Fish & Wildlife Service. (1991a) Listing proposals - December 1990: White irisette (*Sisyrinchium dichotomum*) *Endangered Species Technical Bulletin*, **16**(1), 7.

US Fish & Wildlife Service. (1991b) Final listing rules published for three species: Sentry Milk-vetch (*Astragalus cremnophylax* var. *cremnophylax*). *Endangered Species Technical Bulletin*, **16**(1), 8.

US Fish & Wildlife Service. (1991c) Listing proposals - December 1990: Telephus spurge (*Euphorbia telephioides*) *Endangered Species Technical Bulletin*, **16**(1), 6–7.

US Fish & Wildlife Service. (1991d) Final listing rules approved for four species: Schweinits's sunflower (*Helianthus schweinitzii*). *Endangered Species Technical Bulletin*, **16**(6), 8.

van Wieren, S. E. (1991) The management of populations of large mammals. In *The Scientific Management of Temperate Communities for Conservation*, ed. I. F. Spellerberg, Goldsmith, F. B. & Morris, M. G., pp. 103–27. Oxford: Blackwell Scientific Publications.

Waller, D. M., O'Malley, D. M. & Gawler, S. C. (1988) Genetic variation in the extreme endemic *Pedicularis furbishiae*. *Conservation Biology*, **1**, 335–40.

Warwick, S. I. (1990) Genetic variation in weeds - with particular reference to Canadian agricultural weeds. In *Biological Approaches and Evolutionary Trends in Plants*, ed. Kawano, S. pp. 3–18. London: Academic Press.

Weller, S. G. & Ornduff, R. (1977) Cryptic self-incompatibility in *Amsinckia grandiflora*. *Evolution*, **31**, 47–51.

White, P. S. (1979) Pattern, process, and natural disturbance in vegetation. *The Botanical Review*, **45**, 229–99.

White, P. S. (1984) Impacts of cultural and historical resources on natural diversity: lessons from Great Smoky Mountains National Park, Tennessee. In *Natural Diversity of Forest Ecosystems*, ed. Cooley, J. L. & Cooley, J. H., pp. 120–32. Athens, Georgia: US Forest Service, Institute of Ecology.

Wilczynski, C. J. (1989) Fellowship-funded research furthers understanding of roadside rarity. *Plant Conservation*, **4**, 6–7.

Willoughby, J. W. (1987) Effects of livestock grazing on two rare plant species in the Red Hills, Tuolumne County, California. In *Conservation and Management of*

Rare and Endangered Plants, ed. Elias, T. S., pp. 199–208. Sacramento: The California Native Plant Society.

Wisheu, I. C. & Keddy, P. A. (1989) The conservation and management of a threatened coastal plain plant community in Eastern North America (Nova Scotia, Canada). *Biological Conservation*, **48**, 229–238.

York, R. P. (1987) California's most endangered plants. In *Conservation and Management of Rare and Endangered Plants*, ed. Elias, T. S., pp. 109–20. Sacramento: The California Native Plant Society.

8

A metapopulation approach to Pitcher's thistle (*Cirsium pitcheri*) recovery in southern Lake Michigan dunes

A. KATHRYN McEACHERN, MARLIN L. BOWLES
AND NOEL B. PAVLOVIC

Introduction

Successful recovery planning for a rare species relies upon knowledge of its life history and ecology, as well as an understanding of its habitat requirements and disturbance regime (Gilpin & Soulé 1986, Lande 1988a). Species that depend upon early-successional or transient habitats in landscape mosaics present unique recovery challenges (Menges 1990). They require perpetuation of multiple populations within a shifting mosaic of local habitats. Recovery plans for these species must be formulated from an understanding of population demography within the context of community and landscape dynamics. Processes that maintain landscape mosaics must be given long-term protection if recovery is to succeed.

Pitcher's thistle, *Cirsium pitcheri* (Torr.) T. and G., is listed as threatened in the United States and Canada (Harrison 1988). This monocarpic plant is endemic to the western Great Lakes sand dunes. It is an early-successional species that colonizes open patches in dynamic dune landscapes (Pavlovic *et al.* 1993). Its recovery depends upon the perpetuation of interacting mosaics of populations, or metapopulations, in Great Lakes dune systems. The concept of metapopulation dynamics (Levins 1970, den Boer 1981, Gilpin 1987, Goodman 1987a, Gilpin & Hanski 1991) is useful for understanding *Cirsium pitcheri* ecology and management options. It describes species persistence in environments where the probability of local extinction is high, and has applications to species recovery and reserve design (e.g., Shaffer 1981, Gilpin & Soulé 1986, Goodman 1987b, Lande 1988b, Menges 1990, Murphy, Freas & Weiss 1990). In this chapter, we present a recovery model for Pitcher's thistle based upon metapopulation theory and apply it to recovery sites in Illinois and Indiana.

Metapopulation theory and recovery of rare plants

Metapopulation theory provides a framework linking landscape processes with population dynamics, which is essential to understanding mechanisms of species persistence in fluctuating environments. A metapopulation is a collection of interacting populations dispersed through a spatially and temporally variable landscape. The fate of each population is influenced by its genetic, demographic, and environmental history. Variability among populations contributes to metapopulation characteristics, which develop within the physical and biological constraints of the landscape. Landscape processes can influence metapopulation dynamics on at least two levels. At a coarse scale, landscape habitat dispersion and dynamics affect metapopulation patterning in space and time. At a fine scale, fates of individuals are influenced by their interactions with local biotic and abiotic factors, affecting extinction probabilities of locally distributed populations.

Shaffer (1981) identified four causes of population extinction, which can be applied to the components of a metapopulation. Two, widespread catastrophes and local environmental stochasticity, can affect all members of a population simultaneously and can drive both small and large populations to extinction. The other two, demographic and genetic stochasticity, produce variation in survival of individuals. They can drive very small populations to extinction, whereas the extinction probabilities of larger populations are determined to a greater extent by environmental events. Thus, these causes drive population dynamics differently because of the ways they affect overall variance in population growth rates over different population sizes (Goodman 1987a).

Metapopulations can persist even when the rate of component population extinction is high (Menges 1990, Murphy *et al.* 1990). Metapopulation persistence depends upon the balance between landscape and population dynamics (Goodman 1987b). First, population establishment rates must equal or exceed population extinction rates. Second, local environmental events causing population decline must act on populations independently. Third, spatial variation in demographic processes must occur, ensuring that not all populations will decline or be extirpated at the same time.

A metapopulation framework allows examination of species persistence with explicit reference to mechanisms interacting at different scales (Fig. 8.1). At a fine scale, variation in individual population demographic structure and dynamics can be correlated with local environmental processes. At a coarse scale, metapopulation structure can be correlated with demographic variation among populations, landscape patch dynamics and population dispersion, and

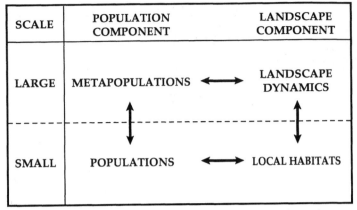

Fig. 8.1. Scalar considerations in applying metapopulation dynamics to species management.

fluctuations in the magnitudes and frequencies of landscape-scale environmental processes. Management or recovery prescriptions can then be focused at the appropriate population or habitat level.

Great Lakes dune environments and Pitcher's thistle

Landscape dynamics

The Great Lakes dunes are structurally variable, dynamic systems, ranging from linear beaches and foredunes to extensive dune complexes. Their vegetation is a series of early- to late-successional community stages (Cowles 1899) across beach, foredune, dune trough and secondary dune zones (Fig. 8.2) in response to gradients of increasing dune age and decreasing wind and wave disturbance (Olson 1958a). Early-successional vegetation can also be maintained on windward faces of secondary dunes, or it can be established in blowouts created by storms or human impacts. Blowouts undergo rapid succession if disturbance is not sustained, losing their colonizing species over several decades (Olson 1958b). Similar succession can occur on dunes that become sheltered or experience decreased winds due to climate fluctuation.

Great Lakes dune systems are built from sand supplied by longshore currents. They are shaped in response to prevailing wind direction and velocity, and in response to coastline configuration relative to storm tracks (Fig. 8.3) (Larsen 1985, Thompson 1989). There are at least two disturbance regimes that affect the availability of open habitats that can be colonized by *C. pitcheri* (Fig. 8.2). One is the stochastic occurrence of severe storms that erode beaches

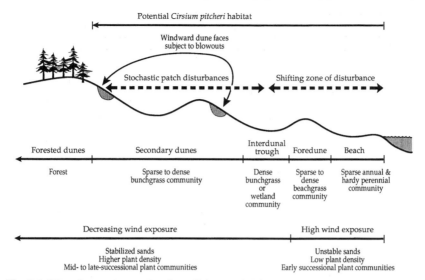

Fig. 8.2. Disturbance, successional gradients, and *Cirsium pitcheri* habitat distribution across Great Lakes dune systems (redrawn from Pavlovic *et al.* 1993).

and open inland blowouts. The other is a nested cycle of dune system responses to annual and longer term climate change. Shorelines characteristically recede during fall and early winter periods of storm erosion and rebuild during spring and summer. They also undergo more severe erosion and accretion cycles as lake levels fluctuate in response to climate shifts. Lake Michigan levels fluctuate on approximately 30-year cycles nested within 100-year and 300-year cycles (Olson 1958b, Larsen 1985, Thompson 1987). Lakes Superior and Huron undergo similar fluctuations, but have slightly different cycle periods and magnitudes of change (Farrand & Drexler 1985).

Lake level fluctuations cause dune habitats to shift differently in space over time, depending upon their locations. For example, during high lake levels, beaches and foredunes erode and shift inland, while more inland dunes may remain stable or lose sand on their windward faces. During low lake levels, new lakeward dunes are built and these further shelter the inland dunes. In contrast, dunes perched upon bluffs receive sand nourishment when high lake levels undercut and destabilize bluff faces (Marsh & Marsh 1987), but stabilize during low lake levels when bluff faces are stable. Therefore, dune system responses to climate change occur differently in different parts of dune fields and lake basins. Such cyclic and stochastic processes of dune building and erosion have been operating in the Great Lakes at least since the late Holocene (Farrand & Drexler 1985, Larsen 1985, Hansel & Mickelson 1988, Thompson 1989).

Fig. 8.3. *Cirsium pitcheri* species and habitat distribution and shoreline dynamics of western Great Lakes dune systems (redrawn from: Bird & Schwartz 1985, Dorr & Eschman 1971, Hands 1970, Saulesleja 1986, Pavlovic *et al.* 1993).

Metapopulation adaptations

Because individual populations may have high extinction probabilities, *Cirsium pitcheri* population dynamics must be considered at both the landscape (metapopulation) and local habitat (population) levels. Seed dispersal from existing populations allows thistles to become established in open habitat throughout the beach and grassland portion of the dune landscape (Pavlovic *et*

Table 8.1. *Characteristics of habitat patches inhabited by* Cirsium pitcheri *in Great Lakes dunes (modified from McEachern 1992).*

Data collected from northern Indiana and northeastern lower Michigan on Lake Michigan, and upper peninsula Michigan on Lake Superior; groups were identified by Ward's cluster analysis of plant communities.

Characteristic	Group 1	Group 2	Group 3
Successional rank	Early	Mid	Late
Topographic position	Foredunes and blowouts	Blowouts	Secondary dunes
Disturbance regime	Cyclically shifting nearshore zone and stochastically created inland patches	Stochastically created inland patches	Sustained moderate disturbance
Sand movement	High	Moderate	Low
Mean (sd) % sand cover	85.8 (9.4)	68.1 (14.4)	70.1 (8.2)
Mean (sd) % litter cover	4.5 (6.3)	14.6 (11.2)	13.1 (7.7)
Mean (sd) % vegetation	9.6 (4.9)	17.2 (3.6)	16.2 (0.4)
Mean species richness	7.9 (3.4)	17.0 (4.4)	8.5 (0.7)
Mean (sd) C. pitcheri density per square meter	2.6 (2.1)	2.1 (1.2)	0.9 (0.4)

al. 1993). These populations exist primarily in early- to mid-successional habitat with more than 70% open sand and moderate amounts of sand movement (McEachern 1992, Bowles *et al.* 1993). Such open sand conditions are maintained between erosion cycles by intermediate wind and wave disturbance of upper beaches and foredunes, and may be available on windward exposure of secondary dune slopes. In blowouts, these conditions persist for several decades through the mid-successional vegetation stage (Table 8.1, Olsen 1958b). Populations in each of these habitats have an extinction probability linked to either periodic catastrophic erosion or to the effects of succession (McEachern 1992). *C. pitcheri* thus persists as a collection of populations repeatedly colonizing the transient habitats of dynamic coastal dune landscapes. Its adaptation to both landscape and local processes fits a metapopulation model.

Pitcher's thistle metapopulation characteristics

Pitcher's thistle biology

Cirsium pitcheri has low genetic diversity throughout its range, although a significant negative correlation in genetic similarity occurs with increasing distance between widely separated populations (Loveless & Hamrick 1988). The *C. pitcheri* genome is a subset derived from *C. canescens* Nutt., a central Great Plains sandhill thistle (Loveless & Hamrick 1988). The *C. pitcheri* progenitor probably reached the Great Lakes sometime during the late-Wisconsin glaciation, likely through migration along sandy outwash habitats at glacial margins (Loveless & Hamrick 1988) or by a single long-distance dispersal event (Johnson & Iltis 1963). It became established during the period of rapid erosion, deposition and isostatic rebound that created the modern Great Lakes shorelines (Farrand & Drexler 1985, Hansel & Mickelson 1988). The Great Lakes dunes landscape apparently reinforced selection on a preadaptation to the shifting habitat mosaic of the continental interior dune ecosystem (Loveless 1984).

As with *C. canescens*, and *C. rhothophilum* Blake., a dune thistle of the southern Californian coast (Zedler *et al.* 1983), *C. pitcheri* appears adapted to the xeric conditions of open dunes. It has a deep taproot and a thick cuticle that gives a blue-green cast to its white-tomentose leaves. A monocarpic perennial, it requires five to eight years to reach maturity. Flowering is determinant, in inflorescences of up to 100 cream-colored flower heads. It has a mixed mating system that is predominantly outcrossing, although selfing is possible (Loveless 1984). It is pollinated by a variety of generalist bees, butterflies, and skippers over about a three-week midsummer flowering period. Seeds are large relative to other thistle species, and have a weakly attached pappus. They can disperse singly, blown by the wind, or as groups in inflorescences that fall from the parent plant. Primary seed dispersal is generally within four meters of parent plants (Keddy & Keddy 1984, Loveless 1984, Ziemer 1989), and field germination is highest among buried seeds (Loveless 1984).

C. pitcheri does not reproduce vegetatively and so depends upon seed production for population growth. New habitats are most likely colonized through wind dispersal of single seeds or, rarely, entire seed heads. The mixed mating system thus appears adaptive for population establishment from single or related founders. If rates of colonization exceed rates of local extinction, then *C. pitcheri* metapopulations are likely to persist. Indeed, thistle patch densities are highest in large, unfragmented dune systems (Pavlovic *et al.* 1993) where mechanisms of dispersal and establishment appear sufficient for colonization.

Life history traits and demography

Many *Cirsium pitcheri* life history traits are temporally and spatially variable (Table 8.2), correlating with community successional status, rates and amounts of sand movement, grazing and insect predation pressure, recreational impact, and widespread landscape factors such as drought and various land manage-

Table 8.2. Cirsium pitcheri *life-history and demographic characteristics*

Characteristic	Study Results
Flowering date	Late May to mid-September
Years to flowering	3 to 11+
Flowering size	10–63 cm tall, 1–12 branches, 5–40 cm longest leaf
No. heads per adult	4–31
No. seeds per plant	289–572
Average seed weight	0.009–0.013 g
Seed set date	June to September
Seed dispersal date	July to October
Seed dispersal distance	0–5.5 m, average <2 m
Head dispersal distance	0–4 m, average <1 m
Germination dates	June (peak) to August
% Seeds damaged by larvae	0–42
% Germination – buried	<2–73.3
% Germination – not buried	0–3.3
% Greenhouse germination	10.2

Source: From Keddy & Keddy 1984, Loveless 1984, Ziemer 1989, McEachern 1992

ment practices (Keddy & Keddy 1984, Loveless 1984, Dobberpuhl & Gibson 1987, Ziemer 1989). This variability produces a wide range of population structures across a dune system (McEachern 1992). Therefore, it is important to understand both local environmental effects on population demography and landscape-scale effects on metapopulations.

C. pitcheri habitat colonization and population persistence are aided by high phenotypic plasticity in such life history traits as relative growth rate, size at flowering, and seed production. For example, foredune plants mature more slowly and have higher seedling and juvenile mortality, but also have higher fecundity than plants in secondary dunes (Loveless 1984). Such plasticity could enhance growth of populations, while reducing variability in growth rates among populations. This would contribute to metapopulation persistence in a system where independent environmental events drive population dynamics (Goodman 1987a).

External abiotic and biotic factors can greatly influence *C. pitcheri* population demography. For example, large established plants can survive up to 20 cm of annual sand deposition but less than 4 cm of erosion, while seedlings cannot be established from seeds buried more than 8 cm (McEachern 1992); these responses influence population structure differently among habitats. Density-dependent predispersal seed predation of *C. pitcheri* by the plume moth, *Platyptilia carduidactyla*, was shown to reduce reproductive output by as much as 42% in a Canadian population (Keddy & Keddy 1984). Other biotic

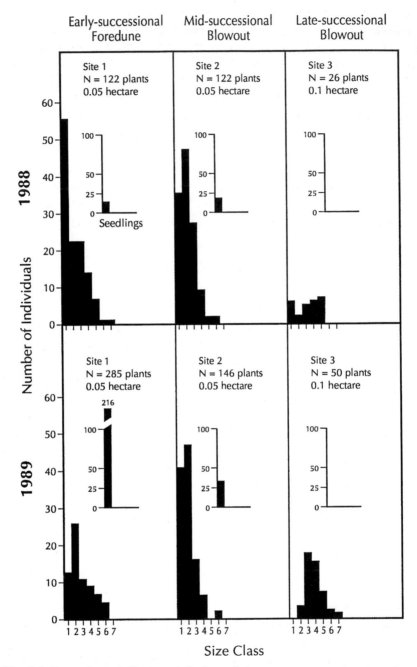

Fig. 8.4. Comparison of *Cirsium pitcheri* population structures over time in early- to late- successional Great Lakes dune communities, 1988 and 1989. See Fig. 8.2 for sources of population profiles.

impacts on individual reproductive success include seed predation by goldfinches and ground squirrels (Loveless 1984) and foliage grazing by rabbits (McEachern 1992). In addition, recreational trampling can selectively eliminate smaller plants, thus skewing populations toward larger size-classes and increasing their potential for extinction (Dobberpuhl & Gibson 1987).

In response to demographic variation, population size and structure can vary between years within and among populations (Fig. 8.4). Temporal variation in population structure buffers metapopulations against loss from widespread environmental catastrophes such as drought or outbreaks of seed-feeding insects. Similarly, population dispersion in space buffers metapopulations against catastrophes such as highly localized sand accretion. This illustrates why restoration and recovery management must consider both large-scale environmental heterogeneity and small-scale population demography.

Pitcher's thistle recovery planning

Status and recovery goals

Cirsium pitcheri historically inhabited intermittently stable beaches and open patches in grassland dunes of the Lake Michigan, Huron and Superior shorelines (Fig. 8.3, Cowles 1901, Gates 1912, Pepoon 1927, Peattie 1930, Guire & Voss 1963). Because of increasing coastal development and changing shoreline dynamics, *C. pitcheri* has declined throughout most of its range, resulting in its federal listing (Harrison 1988). The most severe impacts have occurred along the southern tip of Lake Michigan, where shorelines have experienced a long history of intensive land use (Moore 1959, Fraser & Hester 1974, Purdue University 1986). Few *C. pitcheri* populations remain in Indiana and Wisconsin, and it has been extirpated from Illinois.

Recovery and eventual delisting of endangered and threatened species is planned under provisions of the United States Endangered Species Act of 1973. Recovery for *C. pitcheri* is guided by '*Recovery 2000*', a US Fish and Wildlife Service (1990) planning document, and the Pitcher's thistle federal recovery plan (Pavlovic *et al.* 1993). Recovery goals include identification and protection of suitable habitat throughout the species' range, amelioration of conditions that led to metapopulation decline, and recovery or restoration of metapopulations that can persist through time and space in a dynamic landscape (Pavlovic *et al.* 1993).

Because of its severe decline in the southern Lake Michigan region, federal recovery objectives include reintroduction of an historic *C. pitcheri* population to Illinois, and restoration of existing Indiana populations to a viable metapopulation (Pavlovic *et al.* 1993). Planning for reintroduction to Illinois requires identification of dune systems with appropriate landscape characteristics for *C. pitcheri* persistence. Restoration planning in Indiana requires identification of factors causing local population decline and colonization limitation. A metapopulation framework can then be used at both sites to link landscape and population processes with specific recovery prescriptions and management goals. The dune systems must be of sufficient size so that environmental processes do not affect all populations at the same time. The systems must have long-term management and protection that allow processes of dune building, erosion, and plant succession to operate. Techniques will vary between the Illinois and Indiana sites according to their landscape area, local habitat quality and availability, and habitat turnover. These provide opportunities to test our understanding of metapopulation function by applying different experimental designs for reintroduction and restoration in contrasting environments.

Demographic and biological aspects of recovery

Because *Cirsium pitcheri* is monocarpic, establishment of successive cohorts in restorations is required to avoid potential population extinction correlated with reproductive failure of a single cohort. Although the mixed mating system and low genetic diversity of this species may accommodate reintroductions based on seed samples from few parents, use of propagules collected from multiple parents might increase genetic diversity within reintroduced populations and thereby decrease inbreeding among closely related genotypes (Barrett & Kohn 1991, Fenster & Dudash, Chapter 2 of this volume). However, because of range-wide genetic differences between metapopulations, propagules used for recovery should be derived from sources near the reintroduction sites.

Controlling external biotic impacts on reproduction also appears critical in *C. pitcheri* recovery. Predispersal insect predation on flowers or seeds of *C. canescens* (Louda *et al.* 1990), *C. rhothophilum* (Zedler *et al.* 1983) and *C. pitcheri* (Keddy & Keddy 1984, Loveless 1988, McEachern 1992) suggests that insects can limit population growth. Insect exclusion should have positive cumulative effects on seed production, seedling establishment, and population growth (Louda, Chapter 5 of this volume). Control of postdispersal seed predation and herbivory by birds and mammals (Loveless 1984) should also increase plant survival and population growth. Similarly, control of recreational impacts may be needed to enhance seedling establishment and cohort survival. Recovery experiments should produce 'win–win' situations in which knowledge is gained while reproduction is enhanced (Louda, Chapter 5 of this volume).

Physical aspects of recovery in Illinois and Indiana

Potential metapopulation recovery sites in Illinois and Indiana are restricted to Illinois Beach State Park and the Indiana Dunes National Lakeshore and State Park. Both areas are large fragments of historically more extensive dune systems that supported *Cirsium pitcheri*. They are affected by recreation and by offshore structures that alter longshore currents and sand supply. Nevertheless, they are the largest undeveloped dune systems left in the extreme southern Lake Michigan basin, and they have long-term habitat protection. These systems differ in their landscape area, habitat availability, and habitat turnover because they are located in different positions on the Lake Michigan shoreline and are exposed to different sediment sources, longshore currents, prevailing winds, and storm tracks (Fig. 8.3).

Illinois Beach State Park is located 70 km north of Chicago, on a 1.5- km wide ridge-and-swale sand deposit extending 22.6 kilometers along the Lake Michigan shoreline (Fig. 8.5). This sand deposit is transient in geologic time; it is undergoing progressive southward erosion and deposition by the longshore current and reaches a maximum age of 3600 years near the Illinois–Wisconsin state line (Larsen 1985). Its shoreline position also fluctuates in relation to cyclic lake level changes (Hester & Fraser 1973), and erosion by the longshore current has accelerated (Fraser & Hester 1974) owing to high lake levels and blockage of longshore current sand transport by shoreline structures. This erosion is ameliorated by periodic artificial sand replenishment.

The Indiana Dunes National Lakeshore and State Park is located at the extreme southern tip of Lake Michigan. The youngest dunes with open grassland habitat suitable for *C. pitcheri* formed during and after the Hypsithermal approximately 5000–3000 years ago. The shoreline has been adjusting to a new climatic equilibrium since then (Thompson 1989); the eastern Indiana Dunes shoreline is undergoing net erosion and landward displacement, while the western shoreline is accreting. This process has been altered locally in the Indiana Dunes by construction of revetments and offshore structures (Fig. 8.6). Deposition increased up-current from these structures from 1967 to 1984, and down-current erosion occurred over the same time period. Thus, the Indiana Dunes shoreline is now in human-induced disequilibrium, and will remain so as long as sediment-control structures are maintained (Purdue University 1986). This has important implications for ecosystem management.

A serious impediment to *C. pitcheri* recovery at both sites is that the upper beach, once typical thistle habitat (Cowles 1899, Gates 1912) and potential linkage between populations, may no longer be suitable habitat because disturbances from recreational use and accelerated shoreline erosion exceed thresh-

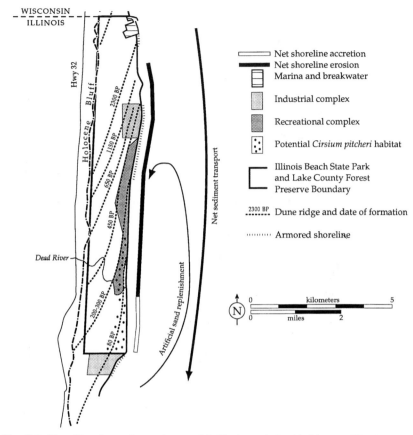

Fig. 8.5. Shoreline dynamics and potential *Cirsium pitcheri* habitat at Illinois Beach State Park, Lake County, Illinois.

olds for thistle persistence and completion of life cycles. Although beach replenishment might appear to benefit *C. pitcheri* recovery, it does not prevent erosion and thus may not protect thistles. Thus, restoration of natural shoreline dynamics may be required before beaches can resume their role as linkages in metapopulation dynamics.

The recovery strategy in Illinois

Thistle decline and modern habitat conditions

Cirsium pitcheri is now extirpated from Illinois. Former habitat descriptions are mostly vague notes (e.g. 'dunes,' 'sandy shoreline,' and 'dry sand beaches') in plant collection records made between 1862 and 1919 (Bowles *et al.*

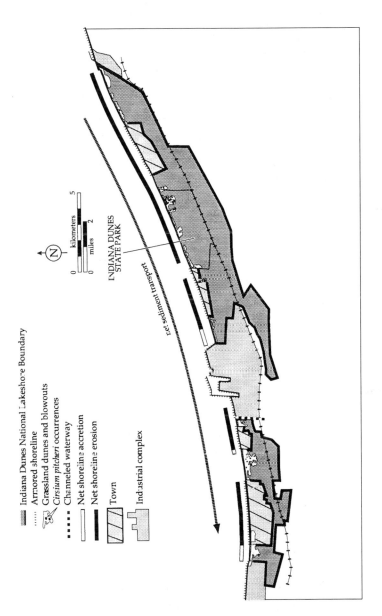

Indiana Dunes National Lakeshore Boundary
Armored shoreline
Grassland dunes and blowouts
Cirsium pitcheri occurrences
Channeled waterway
Net shoreline accretion
Net shoreline erosion
Town
Industrial complex

INDIANA DUNES
STATE PARK

net sediment transport

N

0   5
kilometers
0   2
miles

Fig. 8.5. *Cirsium pitcheri* population distribution, habitat fragmentation and shoreline dynamics at Indiana Dunes National Lakeshore and State Park.

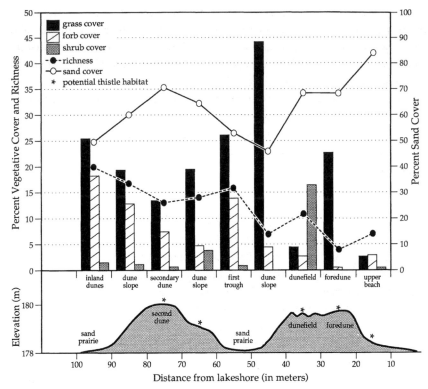

Fig. 8.7. Change in plant community structure and potential *Cirsium pitcheri* habitat across a dune and swale habitat gradient at Illinois Beach State Park, Lake County, Illinois.

1993). Only Gates (1912) provided a specific habitat description, from observations of plants in the upper beach association (*sensu* Cowles 1899) in an area now protected as part of Illinois Beach State Park. It is likely that by 1912, increasing shoreline use was already impacting a narrowly-distributed population highly susceptible to over-collecting, beach use, and the environmental, demographic, and genetic causes of extinction in small populations. Apparently the plants disappeared rapidly. Only one subsequent Illinois Beach collection was made (in 1919), and Pepoon (1927) did not mention *C. pitcheri* in his lengthy discussion of the same area studied by Gates.

The landscape in the southern part of Illinois Beach is of sufficient size and condition to support experimental reintroduction of a thistle metapopulation. It contains natural disturbance-mediated successional community gradients that extend inland from Lake Michigan across the upper beach, foredune, and older dune ridges and swales (Fig. 8.7), and southward along the accreting shoreline.

The beach ridges are compressed into a narrow dunefield north of the Dead River, but are more widely spaced as they accrete southward. Climatic lake level cycles and the southward shoreline migration provide shifting disturbance zones to which thistle metapopulations are adapted. Habitats south of the Dead River are in natural condition and free of recreational impact. The dunefield north of the Dead River was formerly conifer-forested (Gates 1912, Pepoon 1927), but is now open and used for recreation. This use may help maintain disturbance conditions suitable for Pitcher's thistle; however, trampling could limit the establishment and survival of seedlings (Dobberpuhl & Gibson 1987).

Thistle recovery in Illinois

A primary step in restoring *C. pitcheri* to Illinois Beach is the identification of microhabitats along the dune system successional gradients that provide necessary conditions to support thistle populations. Potential habitats that are within colonizing distance of one another, yet only weakly environmentally correlated, are needed to maintain metapopulation dynamics. This juxtaposition would allow thistles to colonize from established populations along a shifting successional gradient while being buffered against local stochastic environmental impacts.

In the absence of clear historic *C. pitcheri* habitat descriptions for Illinois Beach, ordination and cluster analysis of plant community characteristics were used to compare potential Illinois habitats with those currently supporting thistle populations in Indiana and Wisconsin (Bowles *et al.* 1993). These comparisons provided correlations at the landscape and microhabitat scale. At Illinois Beach, habitats with greater than 65% bare sand cover included the upper beach and foredune, the secondary dune top and dune slope, and the dunefield (Fig. 8.7). These sites clustered within groups that contained Indiana and Wisconsin habitats supporting *C. pitcheri* populations, indicating a strong similarity in community composition within clusters, and thus potential for the Illinois habitats to support *C. pitcheri* reintroduction.

The optimum habitats for population reintroduction appear to be the secondary dune top and dune slope, which are free from shoreline erosion, competition, and recreational impact. The dunefield is similar to thistle habitat in Wisconsin, and its high sand cover suggests that it may be suitable for population maintenance. However, its low grass cover apparently results from trampling, which could negatively impact thistle seedlings. The upper beach and foredune at Illinois Beach also appear to meet habitat criteria for thistle population maintenance, but erosion and periodic beach nourishment rates may be too great for thistle establishment and survival. Therefore, the secondary dune foreslope and ridge top were chosen for initial population reintroduction.

Cirsium pitcheri restoration began in the secondary dune habitat at Illinois Beach in 1991, with the experimental planting of 77 first-year juvenile plants grown from southeastern Wisconsin and northwestern Indiana seeds (Bowles *et al.* 1993). The planting strategy was based on known characteristics of thistle populations, and avoided factors associated with mortality (Loveless 1984, Louda, Potvin & Collinge 1990, McEachern 1992, Louda, Chapter 5 of this volume). Seeds were collected from multiple parents to accommodate the mixed mating system of this species, and to maximize genetic diversity. Seedlings were germinated and propagated in a greenhouse, and then transplanted in order to avoid postdispersal seed predation and the high mortality associated with small seedlings. Initial field experiments found Indiana seedlings to significantly outperform Wisconsin seedlings in growth and survivorship, and no significant impacts from grazing (Bowles *et al.* 1993).

Since planting of greenhouse stock avoids environmental selection that might occur during seedling establishment, experimental seed dispersal will supplement the plantings. Insecticide treatment of flowering plants will be used to deter seed predators, while seed collection and planting will enhance seedling establishment, thus developing a 'win–win' experimental approach to restoration (*sensu* Louda, Chapter 5 of this volume). Subsequent plantings will expand the population size and extent, and allow development of cohort structures that mimic natural populations. This will enhance potential for population persistence as the microhabitats shift along the successional gradient in time and space.

Although the secondary dune population may persist and shift spatially with shoreline position as lake levels fluctuate in the future, establishment of an environmentally independent second population is critical for recovery success. The dunefield is potential habitat for such a second population. If beach and foredune habitat can serve as a migratory corridor connecting the dunefield and secondary dune habitats, metapopulation scale recovery may be achieved at Illinois Beach. However, successful metapopulation maintenance will require further experimentation and management. This would include evaluating the impact of recreation on seedlings in dunefield habitat and monitoring impacts of beach erosion and replenishment rates on thistle colonization of upper beach and foredune habitats. Supplemental planting and experimentation to maximize population size and cohort diversity may be a key to overcoming extinction thresholds and allowing colonization of new habitats.

The recovery strategy in Indiana

Thistle decline and modern habitat conditions

Cirsium pitcheri is a former component of the Indiana upper beach and fore-dune flora (Cowles 1899, Pepoon 1927), and Olson (1951) found it along transects in nearshore secondary dune blowout locations in the 1940s. Populations now exist in only eight of the blowouts scattered throughout the western portion of the Indiana Dunes National Lakeshore and State Park, although apparently good thistle habitat exists in all blowouts (Fig. 8. 6). It is absent from the eastern one-third of the National Lakeshore, where natural erosion has been augmented by the effects of ditches, jetties, breakwaters and revetments. Its current absence from Indiana beaches and foredunes may result from natural disturbance exacerbated by human use.

Cyclic high lake levels almost completely erode beaches and foredunes in the Indiana Dunes area. The foredunes rebuild naturally within several years following lake recession in locations still supplied by sand through longshore sediment transport (Cowles, 1899, 1901; Peattie 1930; Olson 1958b; Purdue University 1986; Thompson 1989). If cyclic erosion has long been a component of the natural disturbance regime, then blowouts have served as habitat refugia for *C. pitcheri* during high lake levels. Beach and foredune recolonization could occur from blowout populations between erosional episodes, providing metapopulation linkage between blowouts. However, human use of the Chicago area beaches has been consistently intense since the late 1800s (Moore 1959). Given the apparent susceptibility of *C. pitcheri* to trampling (Dobberpuhl & Gibson 1987), it may be eliminated from beaches and foredunes by recreational use, and it is unlikely that it will reestablish there as long as beach use continues.

Thistle recovery in Indiana

The Indiana Dunes National Lakeshore and State Park can be viewed as a metapopulation landscape unit, with populations historically linked through intermittent beach corridors. Such a view allows specific hypotheses about metapopulation functioning to be generated within a management framework. *C. pitcheri* is declining at Indiana Dunes because of problems (Table 8.3) at both the population and metapopulation levels (McEachern & Pavlovic 1991). Some of these can be addressed by restoration treatments now, while others are beyond current economic and legislative management capacity and must be left as long-term restoration goals.

Table 8.3. Cirsium pitcheri *metapopulation persistence problems at Indiana Dunes National Lakeshore and State Park*

Problems at the population scale	Restoration at the population scale
Low reproductive output in isolated populations	Introduce seedlings to increase population size and genetic diversity
Deterministic elimination of individuals during plant succession	Reduce vegetation and litter cover to artificially retard succession
Low reproductive vigor or loss of plants due to vertebrate and insect herbivory	Exclude herbivores, fertilize or water adults to increase reproductive vigor
Catastrophic population loss due to recreational impact	Plan and implement visitor use control near populations through education, law enforcement, and boardwalk and trail development
Problems at the metapopulation scale	*Restoration at the metapopulation scale*
Colonization not occurring between distantly isolated suitable habitats	Establish new populations in suitable habitats between separated established populations
Barriers to dispersal in nearshore zone created by heavy recreational use of beach and foredune	Designate natural areas for species preservation in which visitor use is restricted
Barriers to seed dispersal created by housing and commercial developments	Purchase land and restore dune systems to suitable habitat
Sand delivery reduced by shoreline structures, causing shifts in landscape dynamics	Remove structures to restore sand flow
Shoreline erosion created by shoreline structures, eliminating habitats	Remove structures, initiate sand nourishment for shoreline restoration

At the local scale, extirpation of many small populations appears imminent. Most populations are small and structurally fragmented. Over the past four years at three demographic study sites (McEachern 1992), plants reproduced at small sizes, seed maturation was poor, insect and goldfinch seed predation appeared to be high, seedlings were not establishing, and rabbit grazing was reducing juvenile plant vigor. In addition, high mortality is occurring among smaller size classes in areas heavily used by the public. Consequently, most Indiana Dunes populations are dysfunctional because of low local recruitment and failure to colonize new habitats.

Local *C. pitcheri* population decline probably results from interactions of several of these factors. Decline in some National Lakeshore sites is accelerated by heavy foot traffic. Several thistle habitats in the State Park that were open sand blowouts heavily used by the public at the turn of the century have now reached late-successional conditions. Prior to their protection as natural areas in the 1920s, these sites appeared fragmented and degraded in historic photos, much like some in the National Lakeshore today. Thus their recovery potential for thistles was initially low, and the effects of plant succession now exacerbate the problem. As a result, most *C. pitcheri* found in these late-successional blowouts are scattered in open patches maintained on slopes exposed to northerly winter winds. In addition, insect predation, rabbit grazing, and drought-induced mortality are higher at Indiana Dunes than in comparable areas farther north (McEachern 1992). Hypotheses that these historic and current environmental effects contribute to population degradation can be tested in the process of restoration at the Indiana Dunes.

Experimental restorations are being conducted in declining local populations with the objectives of increasing population sizes, changing population growth rates from negative to positive, and dampening between-year variances in population growth. Treatments include watering and fertilizing to increase individual adult reproductive vigor, insecticide treatment of inflorescences to deter flower and seed predators, seed and seedling planting in areas protected from herbivores, and fencing of individual plants to exclude grazers. Plantings will be made in open microhabitats within late-successional blowouts, and in areas free from heavy foot traffic in recreational areas. In addition to these population manipulations, the National Lakeshore's management plan for the West Beach recreational area is being revised for the development of a trail system that guides visitors away from *C. pitcheri* locations. This should reduce habitat fragmentation from diffuse visitor use, and increase the chances for dune community recovery and *C. pitcheri* restoration success.

Unlike problems that affect individual plants at local scales, landscape-scale problems are related to population interactions. Two categories of landscape use interfere with potential pollen flow and habitat colonization by seed: 1) use that prevents interactions between populations and available habitats, and 2) use that alters landscape dynamics so that habitat does not exist. Blowouts within the Indiana Dunes that have no *C. pitcheri* (Fig. 8.6) have been isolated from colonization sources by commercial and residential developments for decades, exacerbated by the lack of incipient linkage through foredune and upper beach populations. Reestablishment of linkages appears unlikely in the face of current land use zoning and recreational beach use. Therefore, artificial reintroduction of genetically diverse populations to such isolated sites is essential to the maintenance of metapopulation structure. In addition, landscape fragmentation should decrease with continued planned acquisition of National Lakeshore land and dune community restoration, improving within-metapopulation linkage. Given the natural dynamics of shoreline erosion demonstrated by Thompson (1987), community restoration efforts may have a better chance of success in nearshore blowout sites to the west than in eastern portions of the National Lakeshore.

Landscape alteration that eliminates habitats requires longer-term planning for restoration of sand flow and shoreline dynamics along the southern tip of Lake Michigan. This restoration will require such costly actions as removal of jetties and other hard shoreline structures, or mechanical passage of sand around the structures. These problems transcend the National Lakeshore and State Park boundaries, and must involve legislative and market-driven incentives if they are to succeed. In the final analysis, *C. pitcheri* recovery at Indiana Dunes may be constrained by total landscape area and local habitat colonization opportunity. Therefore, realistic short-term goals for the area are the restoration of population vigor and landscape linkage to the extent possible under current legislative and economic conditions. Long-term goals are the restoration of shoreline dynamics to reestablish the landscape context within which the metapopulation functions.

Conclusions

Recovery strategies for *Cirsium pitcheri* must be viewed within the context of the highly dynamic environment to which this species is adapted. Within a dune system, discrete *C. pitcheri* populations may be viewed as components of a metapopulation in which they interact spatially and temporally through pollen flow and seed dispersal. Such metapopulations are dispersed across a range of habitats that differ by their topographic position and community successional status. Dune systems and habitat conditions change through time in response to storms and large-scale cyclic climate fluctuations, but local habitats may change independently, depending upon their positions relative to shoreline dynamics. As a result, component populations can vary in size, structure, and growth rates, and demographic patterns can be uncorrelated between populations.

Recovery and restoration of *Cirsium pitcheri* should be approached at both the local and landscape levels. Experimental testing of seedling and transplant survival is critical in reintroducing populations, such as in Illinois, and the establishment of successive cohorts appears essential in developing population structure. Experimental establishment across different habitats is also critical as an initial step in re-establishing metapopulation dynamics. Transplanting propagated plants can speed the establishment of population cohorts, but seed dispersal is needed to allow selection to operate at the dispersal stage, and to add all life-history stages to the experimental design. At the Indiana Dunes, intervention in declining populations will allow testing of the hypotheses that insect predation, grazing, trampling, sand movement and plant succession alter population structure. Monitoring will follow the effects of environmental amelioration on population demography, and will contribute to an understanding of the role of demographic variability among populations in metapopulation persistence.

The scale of spatial habitat dispersion differs between Indiana Dunes and Illinois Beach, and may allow different approaches to metapopulation recovery. However, linkage of populations at both sites requires management for natural shoreline processes. Long-term monitoring of *C. pitcheri* distribution is needed to determine how changing landscape patterns affect population persistence and contribute to metapopulation dynamics. The results of these observations and experiments should then be applicable to *C. pitcheri* populations in other areas.

Even without experimental results that clarify mechanisms of metapopulation function, it is clear that the fate of *Cirsium pitcheri* is closely tied to the fate of its landscape. Its decline parallels human alteration of dune systems and shoreline processes. In this case, preservation of the dune ecosystem is consistent with management for an individual species. Recovery management for *C. pitcheri*, therefore, must emphasize metapopulation and landscape protection, with the long-term maintenance of naturally functioning Great Lakes dune systems as an ultimate goal.

Acknowledgments

We thank the members of the federal *Cirsium pitcheri* recovery team (Pavlovic *et al.* 1993) for their insights into Pitcher's thistle ecology, distribution and recovery potential.

Literature cited

Barrett, C. H. & Kohn, J. R. (1991). Genetic and evolutionary consequences of small population size in plants, implications for conservation. In *Genetics and Conservation of Rare Plants*, ed. D. A. Falk & K. E. Holsinger, pp. 3–30. New York: Oxford University Press.

Bird, E. C. F. & Schwartz, M. L. (1985). *The World's Coastline*. New York: Van Nostrand Reinhold.

Bowles, M. L., Flakne, R., McEachern, A. K. & Pavlovic, N. B. (1993). Recovery planning and reintroduction of the Federally threatened Pitcher's thistle (*Cirsium pitcheri*) in Illinois. *Natural Areas Journal* **13**, 164–70.

Cowles, H. C. (1899). Ecological relations of the vegetation on sand dunes of Lake Michigan. *Botanical Gazette*, **27**, 95–117, 167–202, 281–308, 361–88.

Cowles, H. C. (1901) The physiographic ecology of Chicago and vicinity. *Botanical Gazette*, **31**, 73–108, 145–82.

den Boer, P. J. (1981) On the survival of populations in a heterogeneous and variable environment. *Oecologia* **50**, 39–53.

Dobberpuhl, J. M. & Gibson, T. J. (1987) Status surveys and habitat assessment of plant species. I. *Cirsium pitcheri* (Torr.) T. & G. Madison: Wisconsin Department of Natural Resources.

Dorr, J. A. & Eschman, D. F. (1971) *Geology of Michigan*. Ann Arbor: University of Michigan Press.

Farrand, W. R. & Drexler, C. W. (1985) Late Wisconsin and Holocene History of the Lake Superior basin. In *Quaternary Evolution of the Great Lakes*, Special Paper 30, ed. Carrow, P.F. & Calkins, P.E., pp. 17–32. Geological Association of Canada.

Fraser, G. S. & Hester, N. C. (1974) *Sediment distribution in a beach ridge complex and its application to artificial beach replenishment*. Environmental Geology Notes EGN 67. Urbana: Illinois State Geological Survey.

Gates, F. G. (1912) *The vegetation of the beach area in northeast Illinois and southeastern Wisconsin*. Bulletin Volume IX, Article V. Urbana, Illinois: Illinois State Laboratory of Natural History.

Gilpin, M. E. (1987) Spatial structure and population vulnerability. In *Viable Populations for Conservation*, ed. Soulé, M. E., pp. 125–39. Cambridge University Press.

Gilpin, M. E. & Hanski, I. eds. (1991) *Metapopulation Dynamics: Empirical and Theoretical Investigations*. New York: Academic Press.

Gilpin, M. E. & Soulé, M. E. (1986) Minimum viable populations: processes of species extinction. In *Conservation Biology: The Science of Scarcity and Diversity*, ed. Soulé, M.E., pp. 19–34. Sunderland, Massachusetts: Sinauer Associates.

Goodman, D. (1987a) The demography of chance extinction. In *Viable Populations for Conservation*, ed. Soulé, M.E., pp. 11–34. Cambridge University Press.

Goodman, D. (1987b) How do any species persist? Lessons for conservation biology. *Conservation Biology,* **1**, 59–62.

Guire, K. E. & Voss, E. G. (1963) Distributions of distinctive plants in the Great Lakes region. *Michigan Botanist* **2**, 99–114.

Hands, E. B. (1970). A geomorphic map of Lake Michigan shoreline. In *Proc. 13th Conference on Great Lakes Research*, ed. Anderson, D. V. & Seddon, J. S., pp. 250–65. International Association of Great Lakes Research. Detroit: Great Lakes Research Center, US Lake Survey.

Hansel, A. K. & Mickelson, D. M. (1988) A reevaluation of the timing and causes of high lake phases in the Lake Michigan basin. *Quaternary Research* **29**, 113–28.

Harrison, W. F. (1988) Endangered and Threatened Wildlife and Plants: determination of threatened status for *Cirsium pitcheri*. *Federal Register*, **53**, No. 137, 27137–141.

Hester, G. S. & Fraser, N. C. (1973) *Sedimentology of a beach ridge complex and its significance in land-use planning*. Environmental Geology Notes EGN 63. Urbana: Illinois State Geological Survey.

Johnson, M. F. & Iltis, H. H. (1963) Preliminary reports on the flora of Wisconsin. No. 48. Compositae I-Composite family. *Transactions of the Wisconsin Academy of Arts and Sciences*, **52**, 255–342.

Keddy, C. J. & Keddy, P. A. (1984) Reproductive biology and habitat of *Cirsium pitcheri*. *Michigan Botanist*, **23**, 57–67.

Lande, R. (1988a) Genetics and demography in biological conservation. *Science*, **241**, 1455–60.

Lande, R. (1988b) Demographic models of the Northern Spotted Owl (*Strix occidentalis caurina*). *Oecologia*, **75**, 601–7.

Larsen, C. E. (1985) *A stratigraphic study of beach features on the southwestern shore of Lake Michigan: new evidence of Holocene lake-level fluctuations.* Environmental Geology Notes EGN 112, Urbana: Illinois State Geological Survey.

Levins, R. (1970) Some mathematical questions in biology. In *Lectures on Mathematics in the Life Sciences*, Vol. 11, ed. Gerstenhaber, M., pp. 75–107. Providence, Rhode Island: American Mathematical Society

Louda, S. M., Potvin, M. A. & Collinge, S. K. (1990) Predispersal seed predation, postdispersal seed predation and competition in the recruitment of seedlings of a native thistle in sandhills prairie. *American Midland Naturalist*, **124**, 105–13.

Loveless, M. D. (1984) *Population biology and genetic organization in Cirsium pitcheri, an endemic thistle.* Ph.D. dissertation. Lawrence: University of Kansas.

Loveless, M. D. & Hamrick, J. M. (1988) Genetic organization and evolutionary history in two North American species of *Cirsium*. *Evolution, 42*, 254–65.

Marsh, W. M. & Marsh, B. D. (1987) Wind erosion and sand dune formation on high Lake Superior bluffs. *Geografiska Annaler, 69*, 379–91.

McEachern, A. K. (1992) Disturbance dynamics of Pitcher's thistle (*Cirsium pitcheri*) in Great Lakes sand dune landscapes. Ph.D. dissertation, Madison: University of Wisconsin.

McEachern, A. K. & Pavlovic, N. B. (1991) *Metapopulation dynamics in species recovery planning: Pitcher's thistle as an example*, poster abstract. 53rd Midwest Fish and Wildlife Conference Proceedings. DesMoines: Iowa Department of Natural Resources.

Menges, E. S. (1990) Population viability for an endangered plant. *Conservation Biology, 4*, 52–62.

Moore, P. A. (1959) *The Calumet Region: Indiana's Last Frontier.* Indiana Historic Collections, vol. 39. Indianapolis: Indiana Historic Bureau.

Murphy, D. D., Freas, K. E. & Weiss, S. B. (1990) An environment-metapopulation approach to population viability analysis for a threatened invertebrate. *Conservation Biology, 4*, 41–51.

Olson, J. (1951) Vegetation-substrate relations in Lake Michigan sand dune development, Ph.D. dissertation, Chicago: University of Chicago.

Olson, J. (1958a) Lake Michigan dune development. 3. Lake-level, beach and dune oscillations. *Journal of Geology, 66*:473–83.

Olson, J. (1958b) Rates of succession and soil changes on southern Lake Michigan sand dunes. *Botanical Gazette, 119*, 125–70.

Pavlovic, N. B, Bowles, M. L., Crispin, S., Gibson, T., Herman, K., Kavetsky, R., McEachern, A. K. & Penskar, M. (1993) Pitcher's Thistle (*Cirsium pitcheri*) Recovery Plan. Minneapolis: U.S. Department of the Interior, Fish and Wildlife Service.

Peattie, D. C. (1930) *Flora of the Indiana Dunes.* Chicago: Field Museum of Natural History.

Pepoon, H. S. (1927) *An Annotated Flora of the Chicago Area.* Chicago: Chicago Academy of Sciences.

Purdue University. (1986) *Indiana Dunes National Lakeshore shoreline situation report: executive summary.* West Lafayette: School of Civil Engineering, Great Lakes Coastal Research Laboratory.

Saulesleja, A. (1986) *Great Lakes Climatological Atlas.* Ottawa: Environment Canada.

Shaffer, M. L. (1981) Minimum population sizes, species and conservation. *BioScience, 31*, 131–4.

Thompson, T. A. (1987) Sedimentology, internal architecture, and depositional history of the Indiana Dunes National Lakeshore and State Park. Ph.D. dissertation, Bloomington: Indiana University.

Thompson, T. A. (1989) Anatomy of a transgression along the southern shore on Lake Michigan. *Journal of Coastal Research* **5**, 711–24.

U.S. Fish and Wildlife Service. (1990) *Recovery 2000*. Twin Cities, Minnesota: U.S. Fish and Wildlife Service Endangered Species Division.

Zedler, P. H., Fuehlstorff, K. G., Scheidlinger, C. & Gautier, C. R. (1983) The population ecology of a dune thistle *Cirsium rhothophilium* (Asteraceae). *American Journal of Botany,* **70**, 1516–27.

Ziemer, L. S. (1989) *A study of factors limiting the number and distribution of Cirsium pitcheri*. Lansing: Michigan Department of Natural Resources.

9

Restoration of woodland caribou to the Lake Superior region

PETER J. P. GOGAN AND
JEAN FITTS COCHRANE

Introduction

Woodland caribou (*Rangifer tarandus caribou*) historically occupied the boreal forest zone across the North American continent. The distribution and abundance of the species has declined in the past century. In particular, it has been extirpated from much of the southern limits of its historical range on both sides of the boundary between Canada and the United States (Bergerud 1974). Translocation of animals from extant populations may be used to reestablish populations in portions of the species' former range. Recently, wildlife biologists in Ontario have translocated woodland caribou to a number of sites in or adjacent to Lake Superior. While it is too soon to evaluate their long-term success, these restoration efforts do provide useful insights into factors likely to influence the outcome of woodland caribou translocations elsewhere. In this chapter, we examine the 1) historical changes in range distribution, 2) natural history characteristics and requirements, and 3) results of recent translocations of woodland caribou, and use them to evaluate several alternative sites for possible woodland caribou restoration in the Lake Superior region. We also apply minimum viable population analysis to evaluate several translocation scenarios.

Distribution of woodland caribou

The woodland caribou's distribution and abundance along the southern edge of its range declined dramatically in the late 1800s and early 1900s (Bergerud 1974). In the Lake Superior region, woodland caribou were extirpated from the mainland of Michigan in 1912 (Baker 1983) and from Isle Royale in 1928. They disappeared from Minnesota in the 1940s (Fashingbauer 1965), but there were sporadic sightings of at least two woodland caribou in extreme northeastern Minnesota during the winter of 1981–82 (Peterson 1981, Mech, Nelson & Drabik 1982).

219

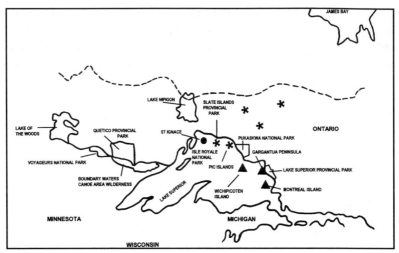

Fig. 9.1. Location of woodland caribou remnant herds (asterisks), successful reintro-ductions (triangles), and a failed reintroduction (circle), and sites being evaluated for restoration of the species in the Lake Superior region. Dashed line represents the southern limit of continuous distribution.

In Ontario, woodland caribou retracted gradually northward from Lake Superior between 1900 and 1950 (Cringan 1957), and disappeared from the western shore between 1905 and 1912 (Riis 1938a, b, c, d) (Fig. 9.1). In the Lake Nipigon area, where they were once the only cervid, they became uncom-mon soon after the Canadian National Railway was constructed across the north end of the lake around 1910 (Dymond, Snyder & Logier 1928). They were declining and scarce on the Sibley Peninsula by 1914 (Cringan 1957). Farther east, woodland caribou range was still continuous south to Lake Superior in 1950, and, possibly as late as the 1960s, to what is now Pukaskwa National Park (Bergerud 1989).

The decline in numbers and continued northward shift in distribution of woodland caribou in the Lake Superior region parallels a continent-wide trend that has prompted British Columbia (Stevenson & Hatler 1985), Alberta (Edmonds 1986, 1988, Edmonds & Bloomfield 1984), Manitoba (Shoesmith 1986) and Ontario (Darby *et al.* 1989) to review the species' status. Populations have been restored to portions of Quebec (Bonefant 1974) and Newfoundland (Bergerud & Mercer 1989), and a remnant population along the border between British Columbia and Idaho has been reinforced (Servheen 1988, 1989). A reintroduction to Maine in 1989 and 1990 failed (McCollough & Connery 1991), perhaps because of black bear predation.

Hypotheses proposed for the decline in the distribution and abundance of woodland caribou include 1) logging and catastrophic fire have destroyed habitat, 2) hunting has increased, 3) predation has increased, partly because gray wolf (*Canis lupus*) density has increased in response to an increase in other prey species, such as moose (*Alces alces*) and white-tailed deer (*Odocoileus virginianus*), 4) woodland caribou have contracted meningeal brainworm (*Parelaphostrongylus tenuis*) from white-tailed deer as the deer expanded their range north and colonized the early-successional forests resulting from catastrophic fires and logging, and 5) a combination of these factors (Bergerud 1974).

The current southern boundary of continuous woodland caribou distribution crosses Ontario at about 50 degrees latitude (Darby *et al.* 1989, Abraham *et al.* 1990). This line bisects the boreal coniferous forest, and moose and wolves decline to its north (Darby *et al.* 1989, Bergerud 1989). Darby *et al.* (1989) list only six native herds of woodland caribou remaining south of 50° latitude, in 1) Slate Islands Provincial Park, 2) Pic Island and Neys Provincial Park, and 3) Pukaskwa National Park, all on Lake Superior, and 4) three inland bands (Fig. 9.1). Gene flow between these herds is limited to the occasional wandering of young bulls (Bergerud 1989). In 1990, there were approximately 500 woodland caribou in the six herds. About 100 of them were on the Slate Islands (Abraham *et al.* 1990); this herd had declined from an estimated 600 to 100 during the winter of 1989–90 (A.T. Bergerud, personal communication). All of these relict populations are tenuous, because they are small and isolated, there are high wolf densities in adjacent areas, and predicted global warming trends would allow white-tailed deer to expand their range (Bergerud 1989).

Natural history characteristics and requirements

Habitat use

Woodland caribou may select habitat to avoid predators, by avoiding habitat preferred by predators (Bergerud & Page 1987, Jakimchuk, Ferguson & Sopuck 1987), avoiding habitat used by alternate prey and hence potentially having greater predator densities (Bergerud & Page 1987), and selecting good escape habitat regardless of predator densities (Bergerud 1989). These patterns apply especially in spring and summer, when woodland caribou are most vulnerable. Within the constraint of avoiding predators, they select sites with optimal forage resources or to escape deep snow or biting insects (Bergerud, Ferguson & Butter 1990). Schaefer & Pruitt (1991), however, conclude that woodland caribou select habitats *primarily* for optimal forage, and secondarily for suitable snow conditions in winter.

While woodland caribou are generally associated with mature, northern boreal forests, they will exploit young deciduous forests where predation risks are low. For example, woodland caribou on the Slate Islands and the islands in Lake Nipigon use early- to mid-successional mixed deciduous forests as much as or more than they use mature coniferous forest (Euler, Snyder & Timmermann 1976, Bergerud *et al* 1990). Woodland caribou in southeast Manitoba also use mixed deciduous forest, but less than they use mature coniferous forest (Darby & Pruitt 1984).

Woodland caribou in their typical boreal forest habitat migrate short distances or not at all, and remain widely dispersed from each other for most of the year (Fuller & Keith 1981, Shoesmith & Storey 1977, Cumming & Beange 1987, Edmonds 1988, Darby & Pruitt 1984, Bergerud 1989, Bergerud *et al*. 1990); this spacing minimizes contact with predators (Bergerud 1983, Bergerud *et al*. 1990). Bergerud (1980) calculated that in boreal forests woodland caribou typically need 2.6 km^2 per animal to minimize contacts with predators (to 'space out'), but only 0.25 km^2 per animal to find adequate food supplies (see also Bergerud *et al*. 1990).

Some observers consider lichens to be highly important to woodland caribou diet and range selection (Bergerud 1972, 1974, Euler *et al*. 1976). Caribou confined to the taiga biome of northern Canada in winter are restricted to a diet of lichens (Skoog 1968); however, remnant and translocated woodland caribou herds persist on Lake Superior islands where ground lichens are browsed out (Slate Islands, Pic Island) (Euler *et al*. 1976; Bergerud 1983; Ferguson, Bergerud & Ferguson 1988) or on which there is deciduous forest with few lichens (Michipicoten Island) (G. Eason, personal communication).

The relationship between woodland caribou, ground lichen abundance, and fire is poorly understood. *Cladina* lichen stands in jack pine (*Pinus banksiana*) and black spruce (*Picea mariana*) forests are fire-dependent, but fire temporarily reduces their abundance (Abraham *et al*. 1990). In one case, woodland caribou used burned taiga habitats in southern Manitoba less about five years after a forest fire, as deadfalls increased and remnant lichen stands decreased (Schaefer & Pruitt 1991). Ground lichen biomass peaks 40–100 years post-fire, when the tree canopy is relatively open (Bergerud 1978, Abraham *et al*. 1990), but snow conditions improve for woodland caribou as the forest canopy closes and reduces the depth of snow on the ground (Schaefer & Pruitt 1991).

Woodland caribou shift between seasonal ranges to avoid predators, deep snow, and biting insects, and to find food (Shoesmith & Storey 1977, Fuller & Keith 1981, Darby & Pruitt 1984, Edmonds & Bloomfield 1984, Cumming & Beange 1987, Bergerud *et al*. 1990). Typically, woodland caribou move from isolated calving and summering habitat on islands and adjacent shores, or in remote bogs, to gather in fall rutting habitat, also on islands or open bogs. They remain in the rutting habitat until snow depth exceeds 50 cm, then switch to more exposed ridges or jack pine habitat (Abraham *et al.* 1990). Bergerud (1989, A. T. Bergerud, personal communication) hypothesized that they select open habitats primarily because they can more easily detect or escape predators, and secondarily because they can survive on the plants of open habitats (bog shrubs and sedges, and ground lichens). Forested habitats provide relief from biting insects and coincide with prime escape habitat in open areas and along shorelines (Bergerud *et al.* 1990).

Home range and density

The home ranges of individual woodland caribou vary from 13 km^2 in summer, when the herds are most dispersed, to 335 km^2 in winter (Shoesmith & Storey 1977, Fuller & Keith 1981, Darby & Pruitt 1984). The ranges of entire herds have been calculated as 95–140 km^2 in winter and 175–190 km^2 in summer in southern Manitoba (Darby & Pruitt 1984), and 390 km^2 in winter near Lake Nipigon, Ontario (Cumming & Beange 1987).

Bergerud (1983, p. 48) calculated an average mainland woodland caribou herd's density to be 0.4 per km^2, using a 'synthesis of boreal populations, frequently in joint equilibrium with self-sustaining wolf populations (two to four wolves per 1000 km^2)'. Bergerud (personal communication) would now revise this woodland caribou density estimate to 0.3 per km^2. Where moose are also present and wolf densities are higher (7–15 per 1000 km^2), woodland caribou herd densities are typically lower (less than 0.2 per km^2) (Bergerud 1983). Densities of the remnant population at Pukaskwa National Park have varied from 0.05 to 0.12 per km^2 (Bergerud 1980). Densities across Ontario vary from 0.006 to 0.05 per km^2 in areas ranging from 4300 to 293 000 km^2, not all of which is occupied by woodland caribou (Ontario Ministry of Natural Resources 1986, Darby *et al.* 1989, Cumming & Beange 1987, Bergerud *et al.* 1990). Thus, much of the variation in density estimates reflects differences in the resolution of the censuses, which is affected by region, study area, occupied polygons, subsets of prime habitat, and seasonal ranges. For example, the density of the Lake Nipigon woodland caribou herd has been reported as 0.006 per km^2 for a 32 000 km^2 study area, 0.07 per km^2 for the area that the woodland caribou actually used, and 1.8 per km^2 for small islands in summer (Cumming & Beange 1987), and as 0.05 per km^2 for an area that included the waters of Lake Nipigon (Bergerud *et al.* 1990).

Woodland caribou densities on islands are generally higher than on the mainland (A.T. Bergerud, personal communication). On the predator-free Slate

Islands, woodland caribou densities have fluctuated between 4 and 17 per km^2 for many decades (Bergerud 1980, A.T. Bergerud, personal communication). Populations of woodland caribou on the Slate Islands and on Pic Island, at densities ranging between 2 and 5 per km^2, continue to be highly productive despite food shortages (Bergerud 1983; Ferguson *et al.* 1988; A.T. Bergerud, personal communication). In general, however, food resource depletion is apparent by the time woodland caribou densities reach 5 per km^2 (Bergerud 1980). Peak densities on the Slate Islands have been followed by die-offs and no reproductive success in following years (A.T. Bergerud, personal communication). Overgrazing is evident on islands in Lake Nipigon, at a current average summer density of 1.8 per km^2 (Cumming & Beange 1987, Bergerud *et al.* 1990).

Predators

Woodland caribou protect themselves from predators by avoiding detection ('hiding in space' or dispersing), running, or using escape features such as water and steep cliffs, and the cows do not defend their young against predators (Bergerud 1980, 1985; Bergerud, Butler & Miller 1984; Bergerud & Page 1987; Cumming & Beange 1987; Ferguson *et al.* 1988; Bergerud *et al.* 1990). Islands are frequented in summer, and the few that do not freeze in (e.g. Slate Islands and Pic Islands) provide year-round refugia (Simkin 1965, Bergerud 1974, Shoesmith & Storey 1977, Cumming & Beange 1987, Ferguson *et al.* 1988, Bergerud 1989, Bergerud *et al.* 1990) by separating woodland caribou from mainland predators and offering water escape.

Woodland caribou will continue to seek refuge on islands when forage is greatly depleted, even if abundant forage is available nearby on the mainland (Ferguson *et al.* 1988, Bergerud *et al.* 1990). Bergerud *et al.* (1990) found that at Lake Nipigon, migration is timed according to ice development and melt, not insect or vegetation cycles. Woodland caribou use the shoreline as escape habitat, and remain within 100 m of shore at Lake Nipigon, Pic Island, Pukaskwa National Park, and Reed Lake, Manitoba (Shoesmith & Storey 1977, Bergerud 1984, Cumming & Beange 1987, Ferguson *et al.* 1988, Bergerud 1988, Bergerud *et al.* 1990).

Predation has been proposed as the most consistent regulator of woodland caribou populations in the boreal forest (Bergerud 1983). Many mainland North American woodland caribou populations have declined in areas that have moose and high wolf densities (7–15 wolves per 1000 km^2) (Bergerud 1983). Bergerud & Elliot (1986, p. 1525) reviewed woodland caribou population dynamics in numerous North American herds and concluded that 'caribou cannot coexist (with wolves) away from refuge habitat when moose biomass allows wolf numbers to increase to high levels (more than 6.5 per 1000 km²)'.

Relict herds of woodland caribou persist in the face of high wolf densities only where excellent escape habitat is available for young calves (Bergerud 1980, 1984). For instance, woodland caribou presently survive at Lake Nipigon, where wolf densities are commonly 10–14 per 1000 km², by calving and summering on islands inaccessible to wolves in summer (Cumming & Beange 1987, Bergerud *et al.* 1990). The small band of woodland caribou at Pukaskwa National Park, where wolf densities average 13–14 per 1000 km², follows a similar strategy (Bergerud 1989).

Although a number of woodland caribou reintroductions to sites in Newfoundland where black bears (*Ursus americanus*) are potential predators have been successful (Bergerud & Mercer 1989), predation by black bears was an important cause of mortality in woodland caribou released in northern Maine in 1989 and 1990 (McCollough & Connery 1991).

Parasites and diseases

White-tailed deer are the normal definitive host and terrestrial gastropod snails are the intermediate host for the meningeal brainworm. Meningeal brainworm may become prevalent in white-tailed deer even where there is a low incidence of larvae in the intermediate host (Nudds 1990). Infection of woodland caribou with this parasite is generally fatal (Anderson & Strelive 1968, Anderson 1971). In areas occupied by white-tailed deer where woodland caribou reintroductions have failed, it has been confirmed or suspected that the woodland caribou were infected with meningeal brainworm (Bergerud & Mercer 1989). Although specific documentation of the mortality of woodland caribou translocated to white-tailed deer ranges is frequently lacking (see Nudds 1990), three of four sites in Minnesota that had appropriate habitat for the release of woodland caribou were rejected because they had a high risk of meningeal brainworm infection (Karns 1980).

In Newfoundland, where reindeer have been introduced, free-ranging woodland caribou have been infected with a Eurasian reindeer parasite, *Elaphostrongylus cervi rangiferi*. Moose experimentally infected with *E. cervi* developed pathological changes and paralysis (Lankester 1976). Moose in northeastern Minnesota may have been exposed to this parasite when European reindeer were stocked in Superior National Forest in the 1910s to 1930s (Aldous 1931, R.C. Anderson, personal communication). An *E. cervi*-like parasite was tentatively identified in woodland caribou in Ontario

(Lankester 1976, Lankester & Northcott 1979, Gray & Samuel 1986), but it has now been positively identified as a muscle worm (*Parelaphostrongylus andersoni*) (Lankester & Hauta 1989) common in white-tailed deer across North America (Anderson & Prestwood 1981, Pybus & Samuel 1984) and woodland caribou in Labrador and Ontario (Lankester & Hauta 1989). It apparently is not detrimental to either species, but its impact on moose is unknown. The impact of the transmission of *P. andersoni* to the isolated population of moose if woodland caribou are restored to Isle Royale is potentially serious, especially since the moose are already heavily infested with both hydatid tapeworms (*Echinococcus granulosus*) and winter ticks (*Dermacentor albipictus*) (R. O. Peterson, personal communication).

Population dynamics

Compared with other cervids, woodland caribou have a low reproductive rate, because they mature slowly and have single births. Typically, female caribou become sexually mature at 2.5 years, although a few breed as yearlings and some do not breed until 3.5 years or older (Bergerud 1974, 1978, 1980). Pregnancy rates average 84% for females 2.5 years or older (Bergerud 1980), and 96% for females 3.5 years or older (R. Page, personal communication). These rates are very consistent within herds from year to year; the proportion of non-parous two-year-olds accounts for annual variation in population productivity (Bergerud 1980, R. Page, personal communication).

Although sex ratios at birth typically favor males (Bergerud 1980, 1983), the adult ratio of males to females averages 39:61 (Bergerud 1980). Males suffer higher mortality from at least four years old, and in some populations from birth (Bergerud 1971, 1980, 1989, Thomas, Barry & Kiliaan 1989). Female woodland caribou may live to 17 years, and males may live to 13 years (Bergerud 1980). Because of the preponderance of females among adults, when the calves are newborn, they comprise 27–30% of the population (Bergerud 1980). In an average year, only 20% of mature bulls breed, each siring six to eight calves (R. Page, personal communication). However, dominance is associated with stress and high mortality rates, and the turnover of dominant males is high; they rarely live through the winter of their fifth or sixth year (R. Page, personal communication).

In the first year, woodland caribou calf mortality averages 50% and sometimes reaches 80 or 90% (Bergerud 1980, 1983, Bergerud & Page 1987). Without predation, annual adult mortality averages 5 or 6%. With predation, annual adult mortality averages 10% (7% for females, 13% for males) (Bergerud 1983); in declining populations it can be as high as 20 or 30%

(Bergerud 1989, A. T. Bergerud, personal communication). Thus, calf recruitment (to one year) averages 10–15% in stable populations (Bergerud 1980, 1983, R. Page, personal communication). Under ideal conditions (e.g. release onto predator-free islands) caribou populations grow at an intrinsic rate of 30–35% per year (Bergerud 1980). Observed population growth rates in mainland herds averaged 28% per year without wolf predation, and 2% per year with 'normal' wolf densities (four wolves per 1000 km^2) (Bergerud 1980).

Restorations and translocations in the Lake Superior region

Since 1982, the Ontario Ministry of Natural Resources has restored or introduced woodland caribou from the Slate Islands to a number of islands and the shoreline of eastern Lake Superior, with varying success (Table 9.1, Fig. 9.1) (G. Eason, personal communication). All island release sites are free of both white-tailed deer and large predators.

In 1982, eight woodland caribou were moved to Michipicoten Island (Table 9.1), a provincial park 15 km from the north shore of Lake Superior. A single adult male, presumably from the Pukaskwa herd, was already on the island.

In 1984, efforts to restore woodland caribou to the offshore islands of Lake Superior Provincial Park began. Of nine animals reintroduced to Montreal Island (Table 9.1), two adult females dispersed and were replaced with two additional adult females. In 1986, three woodland caribou were moved from the Slate Islands to Leach Island, joining one of the females that had dispersed from the 1984 Montreal Island reintroduction (Table 9.1).

To date, the most ambitious effort to establish woodland caribou along the Lake Superior shoreline was in October 1989, in the Gargantua Peninsula area of Lake Superior Provincial Park (G. Eason, personal communication). The mainland has high winter densities of moose (more than 1 per km^2), and white-tailed deer are occasionally sighted. Black bears are common, but their precise densities are unknown. Wolves are common, but they apparently avoid the Gargantua Peninsula area in most winters because of deep snow. Thirty-nine woodland caribou, 17 with radio collars, were translocated to the Gargantua Peninsula and two small islands, which are 0.5 km and 1 km off shore.

The fate of this translocation is still uncertain (G. Eason, personal communication), but another attempt to restore woodland caribou to the north shore of Lake Superior failed, possibly because of wolf predation. Of six woodland caribou translocated to a small island adjacent to St. Ignace Island in October

Table 9.1. *Fate of recent translocation of woodland caribou in the Lake Superior region*

Site	Size (km²)	Year of trans-location	Number of animals				Last census	
			male		female			
			adult	calf	adult	calf	year	number
Michipicoten Is.	183	1982	1	—	4	3	1988	26
Montreal Is.	7	1984	1	3	1	1	1989	14
Leach Is.	5	1986	1	—	1	1	1990	4[a]
Gargantua Peninsula	—	1989	10	1	26	2	—	—

Note: [a]Possibly all female.
Source: after G. Eason, personal communication.

1985, only one was thought to be alive by early April 1986 (Bergerud & Mercer 1989).

Planning for restorations

Administrative setting

Any translocation of woodland caribou in the Lake Superior region would likely involve United States and Canadian federal agencies, including the Canadian Park Service and the United States Departments of Agriculture (USDA) and Interior (USDI), as well as provincial and state agencies, including the Ontario Ministry of Natural Resources (OMNR) and the Michigan or Minnesota Department of Natural Resources (MDNR). All existing woodland caribou herds in Ontario are under the administrative authority of OMNR, except the herd at Pukaskwa National Park, which is under the Canadian Park Service.

The OMNR has not as yet developed a provincial policy on the woodland caribou (Darby *et al.* 1989), but it has identified the herd at the Slate Islands as the source stock for restorations in northwestern Ontario. The Manitoba Ministry of Natural Resources (MMNR) has agreed to provide a limited number of adult males to any restoration, to reduce the probability of inbreeding depression. Furthermore, the management plan for Quetico Provincial Park states that native species such as woodland caribou may be restored to the park (Ontario Ministry of Natural Resources 1988). OMNR has stipulated that it will only consider requests for woodland caribou for restorations outside the province from government (not private) organizations with an approved restoration plan.

If woodland caribou are translocated from Canada to the United States, the complexity and the number of administrative agencies involved will increase. First, all animals, regardless of their destination, would have to be approved by the Animal and Plant Health Inspection Service of the USDA and the Department of Agriculture of the state receiving the animals. Furthermore, the Minnesota DNR has stipulated that it be the agency initiating any request to any Canadian provincial or federal agency to transfer woodland caribou to Minnesota. Some of the potential restoration sites, like the Superior National Forest (which includes the Boundary Waters Canoe Area Wilderness [BWCAW]), would also be under the authority of the USDA Forest Service (FS). Similarly, woodland caribou restored to Voyageurs National Park would be under the concurrent authority of the MDNR and the USDI National Park Service (NPS). At both sites, federal policies and regulations take precedence over those of the state.

Once reestablished, woodland caribou translocated to the United States could be listed as threatened or endangered under the United States Endangered Species Act of 1973, as amended, in which case management authority would revert to the USDI Fish and Wildlife Service.

In addition to state, provincial, and federal governments, the North Central Caribou Corporation (NCCC), a private nonprofit organization established in 1988, would play a key role in restoring woodland caribou to the western Lake Superior region. The NCCC, dedicated to the restoration of woodland caribou to the border of the central United States and Canada, is composed of five members of the Duluth Safari Club (not affiliated in any way with Safari Club International) and six biologists, representing the NPS, the FS, the MDNR, the OMNR (2 members), and the MMNR. The NCCC has created a technical advisory committee with members from federal and state agencies, the academic community, the Minnesota Zoo, and Friends of the BWCAW, and funded studies of the feasibility of woodland caribou restorations in the Lake Superior region, often with matching funds from the federal agencies and the university. Although the NCCC has no administrative authority, it is an example of how state and federal agencies and private organizations can work cooperatively and effectively toward restoration.

Evaluating the feasibility of restoration

The North Central Caribou Corporation developed an assessment methodology to identify the factors necessary for successful restoration of woodland caribou (Fig. 9.2). These factors can be broken down into two broad categories.

First, woodland caribou demographics and genetics were used to develop guidelines for estimating the number of woodland caribou the potential restoration sites could possibly support at carrying capacity, the number and schedule of woodland caribou releases that would establish the populations, and the estimated probability of survival of the restored populations over particular time intervals. Population Vulnerability Analysis (Gilpin & Soulé 1986) and a Monte Carlo model were used to estimate population extinction probabilities (VORTEX, Lacy 1991).

Second, the potential restoration sites were evaluated according to woodland caribou natural history requirements, including 1) the extent and quality of year-round habitat, 2) the types and abundances of potential caribou predators, especially gray wolves and black bears, and 3) the potential for transmission of the meningeal brainworm parasite from white-tailed deer to woodland caribou, and of other parasites from woodland caribou to moose or white-tailed deer.

Population Vulnerability Analysis

Population Vulnerability Analysis is the process of estimating minimum viable population (MVP) sizes for specific populations (Gilpin & Soulé 1986). An MVP is the threshold number of organisms that ensures, at some defined level of risk, that a population will persist for a given time interval at a particular location. Conventional standards for MVP's include 1) greater than 90% certainty of long-term (usually centuries) persistence, 2) population maintenance in nature with no significant demographic or genetic manipulation, and 3) retention of replacement levels of immediate fitness (vigor, fertility, fecundity) and sufficient genetic variation to adapt by natural selection to changing environments (Soulé 1987). Based upon the last criterion, Lande & Barrowclough (1987) suggested that at least several hundred individuals are necessary for an MVP to be established.

Not all potential release sites will be large enough to support several hundred individuals at carrying capacity. For instance, based upon the range of woodland caribou densities reported in Ontario, Isle Royale National Park could support at most 54 animals. In such cases, it may be necessary to manage several small populations as a single metapopulation (see also Lacy, Chapter 3,

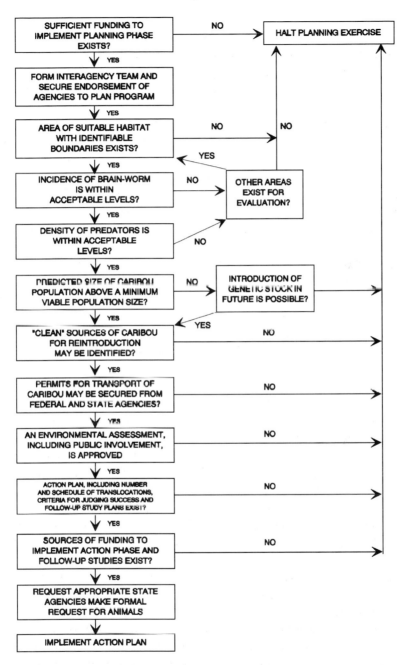

Fig. 9.2. Flow chart for assessing the feasibility of restoring woodland caribou to the Lake Superior region (Gogan *et al.* 1990).

Pavlovic, Chapter 7, McEachern *et al.*, Chapter 8, this volume). A metapopulation consists of a constellation of small populations that interact loosely, but experience environmental impacts independently, and have differential probabilities of dispersal, establishment, growth, and extinction. Managing several small populations as a metapopulation could involve providing corridors for the natural dispersal of individuals among populations, direct relocation, and including captive individuals at zoological parks as a population (Gogan 1990).

Because several small populations of woodland caribou have persisted along the north shore of Lake Superior, it might appear that small populations are viable. These herds, however, have been isolated for only 15–30 years, and in the last 15 years stray bulls have moved between some north shore herds (Bergerud 1985, 1989; Darby *et al.* 1989). The prognosis for most of the existing Lake Superior herds is actually bleak. Bergerud (1989), for example, predicted a high probability of extinction for the Pukaskwa National Park herd within 25 years. Food resources are greatly depleted on Pic Island (Ferguson *et al.* 1988) and the Slate Islands (A.T. Bergerud, personal communication). Fluctuations in the size of the Slate Islands herd, characterized by periodic widespread starvation, have been increasing in amplitude recently (A.T. Bergerud, personal communication), suggesting that total population collapse is likely despite a mean population size of 250–400 animals. It seems likely that historic Lake Superior populations (including Isle Royale) were part of a regional metapopulation, with regular gene flow and ready recolonization of islands from the mainland.

VORTEX population extinction modeling

Using the population extinction model VORTEX (Lacy 1991), various restoration scenarios were examined for Isle Royale National Park, Michigan. Focusing these simulations on Isle Royale highlights the isolation of woodland caribou at any of the release sites under consideration in the western Lake Superior region. The VORTEX model uses Monte Carlo simulations of demographic events, environmental variation, and catastrophes to calculate persistence times for numerous release scenarios, permitting predictions of how long populations established by different restoration schemes would survive. It is possible to estimate how many animals would have to be released over how many years, and with what frequency reinforcements would have to be released, to sustain a population for a given number of years. For the woodland caribou, the number of animals released, number of years of releases, mortality rates, and carrying capacities were varied between simulation runs.

Table 9.2. *Simulated population persistence times (in years) of selected release scenarios for woodland caribou released to Isle Royale by use of program VORTEX (Cochrane 1991).*

K	Mortality Rate	Percent of populations surviving			
		90	50	10	0
54	moderate	63	79	93	>100
54	high	31	44	55	70
27	high	21	31	39	50

In preliminary simulations, high carrying capacities were used (so that population size was not immediately truncated below the number of animals initially released). Persistence times were not improved by releasing more than about 75 animals or by extending the release time over more than one year (not accounting for logistical complications). Subsequent simulations with lower, more realistic carrying capacities were reduced to three basic variants (Table 9.2). The model found that a translocated caribou population with fewer than 54 animals and suffering high mortality would not survive for 50 years (mean time to extinction was 31 or 44 years). With less severe mortality and an average population size of 54 animals, mean persistence times would increase to 79 years. Unfortunately, the VORTEX program could not satisfactorily model two release options that might have been shown to overcome the initial effects of high wolf predation; 1) 'swamping' the release site with woodland caribou (in excess of long-term carrying capacity), and 2) releasing woodland caribou while wolves are absent and subsequently restoring wolves (i.e. allowing wolf predation rates to increase gradually).

Models of woodland caribou restoration strategies were developed previously as part of the Maine woodland caribou reintroduction plan (McCollough 1987). A stochastic model based on that of Grier (1980) was used to evaluate six release options for three projected levels of herd survival and fecundity. The Maine simulation predicted only short-term probabilities of achieving the approximately 100 animals believed necessary for long-term viability (M. McCollough, personal communication). The results revealed that only restorations that had initial high survivorship and intermediate or high fecundity exceeded 100 animals after 10 years. A total of 98 to 115 animals released over five years (with adult sex ratios heavily skewed towards females) performed better than fewer than 75 animals released over three years. Initial survival rate had a greater effect on success than did fecundity, especially when the animals released were yearlings.

In the actual two years of releases of woodland caribou to the Baxter State Park region in Maine, mortality far exceeded that of the models, principally because of black bear predation and diseases carried from captivity (McCollough & Connery 1991). Based on this experience, the advisory committee of the Maine project concluded that three releases of more than 100 animals would be necessary to overcome the initial high mortality rates and establish a core herd of animals acclimatized to the new habitat.

Evaluation of potential restoration sites

Since 1988, the North Central Caribou Corporation has been evaluating three sites for potential woodland caribou restoration. The 4450 km² Boundary Waters Canoe Area Wilderness (BWCAW), Superior National Forest, Minnesota, and the adjacent 4790 km² Quetico Provincial Park, Ontario, compose the largest potential area for restoration. Voyageurs National Park, Minnesota, has the next largest area available (880 km²). Both of these are mainland sites. The last site, the 545 km² Isle Royale National Park, Michigan, is an island 24 km south of the north shore of Lake Superior. A summary of site characteristics can be found in Table 9.3.

BWCAW/Quetico Provincial Park

A previous restoration plan (Karns 1980) identified a 520 km² area southwest of Little Saganagana Lake within the BWCAW as the most suitable habitat in Minnesota for woodland caribou. The Natural Resources Research Institute, University of Minnesota, Duluth, is determining the extent of year-round habitat for woodland caribou in this region by classifying a satellite image of the BWCAW according to important woodland caribou habitat attributes on a geographical information system (GIS), using US Forest Service stand compartment maps, aerial photography, and ground verification (M. Broschart & J. Pastor, personal communication). Preliminary analyses suggest that an area of suitable habitat extends across the international boundary into Quetico Provincial Park.

The summer distribution of white-tailed deer around the Little Saganagana Lake region is the outer boundary of the area that might be reasonably expected to support woodland caribou. The reported incidence of meningeal brainworm in white-tailed deer in this region ranges from less than 10% to greater than 90% (Lankester & Anderson 1968). Long-term studies of white-tailed deer in northern Minnesota show that the population concentrates at winter yards away from the proposed Little Saganagana Lake release site. The frequency of meningeal brainworm larvae in pellet groups of wintering white-

Table 9.3. *Evaluation of factors considered critical to success of woodland caribou restoration at three sites in the Western Lake Superior Region*

Site	Habitat quality	Predators		White-tailed deer	
		wolves per 1000 km^2	black bears	density	incidence of brainworm (%)
Little Saganagana Lake, BWCAW	Evaluation pending	15	Evaluation underway	Low	44–60
Voyageurs N.P.	Evaluation pending	30	Common	High	>90
Isle Royale N.P.	Evaluation pending	20	Absent	Absent	—

tailed deer in these yards in 1989 ranged between 44 and 60% (Jordan & Pitt 1989). In summer, most white-tailed deer range about 26 km from these winter yards (M.E. Nelson, personal communication). Thus, although the Little Saganagana Lake area is beyond the range of most white-tailed deer using the nearest wintering yards, low densities of white-tailed deer may be expected to be present in summer. These low densities of white-tailed deer are reflected in two surveys for the presence of meningeal brainworm. A survey around Little Saganagana Lake in 1977 found an incidence of 5% (Karns 1980). A summer 1989 survey of a 130 km^2 area around Little Saganagana Lake found none of the intermediate host gastropod snails, and only one of four deer pellet groups located contained meningeal brainworm larvae (Jordan & Pitt 1989).

Wolf densities in the BWCAW average 15 per 1000 km^2 (M.E. Nelson, personal communication), half again the maximum density that woodland caribou can tolerate without secure escape habitat (Bergerud & Mercer 1989).

A deer-free area of 6500 km^2 in the BWCAW and Quetico Provincial Park should support between 40 and 130 woodland caribou, providing adequate predator escape cover is available. Such a population may persist for many generations, but will not persist indefinitely in isolation from other populations.

Voyageurs National Park

Voyageurs National Park has contracted for Habitat Evaluation Procedures (HEP) (US Fish and Wildlife Service 1981) to be used to develop a Habitat Suitability Index (HSI) Model for woodland caribou, which will be applied to the Park and adjacent lands. The HSI model will summarize existing knowledge of woodland caribou habitat requirements and identify those components that are most likely to limit the growth of a restored woodland caribou population. Preliminary habitat analysis suggests that currently Voyageurs National Park would not provide year-round habitat for woodland caribou.

There are currently 30 wolves per 1000 km² at Voyageurs National Park (P. J. P. Gogan, unpublished data), more than three times the maximum density that woodland caribou can tolerate without secure escape habitat (Bergerud & Mercer 1989). Actual densities of black bears are unknown, but they are quite common, and are often seen swimming between islands in the park's larger lakes.

White-tailed deer densities at Voyageurs National Park may reach 19 per km², and the incidence of meningeal brainworm larvae in white-tailed deer fecal samples and mature parasites in the crania of white-tailed deer dying of natural causes exceeds 90% (P. J. P. Gogan, unpublished data).

According to the overall density estimate of 0.05 per km² for woodland caribou at the inland site at Lake Nipigon (Bergerud *et al.* 1990), the 880 km² of land and waters within Voyageurs should under favorable conditions support approximately 45 woodland caribou. However, because of the high densities of predators and white-tailed deer infected with meningeal brainworm, current conditions are far from favorable.

Isle Royale National Park

Plans call for habitat conditions at Isle Royale National Park to be assessed by modifying the HSI model being developed for Voyageurs National Park. The model will be adjusted for the absence of black bear, white-tailed deer and meningeal brainworm. The presence and configuration of offshore islets adjacent to Isle Royale will weigh heavily in the assessment of escape habitat suitability.

The wolf population on Isle Royale has declined to 12 from a high of 50 in 1980 (Peterson 1991). The population is expected to remain low in the foreseeable future, and has a high probability of declining to extirpation owing to inbreeding and reproductive failure (R. O. Peterson, personal communication). Hence, densities should remain below 20 per 1000 km² for several years. Still, this density is twice that identified as likely to allow restoration of woodland caribou without substantial escape habitat (Bergerud & Mercer 1989).

Although white-tailed deer were introduced to Isle Royale in 1910, they died out by no later than 1936 (Holte & Holte 1965). There is no evidence of meningeal brainworm in moose at Isle Royale. A report of meningeal brainworm larvae in Isle Royale moose feces (Karns & Jordan 1969) was based on a misidentification (Lankester & Hauta 1989). Whether or not reintroduced woodland caribou will infect the Isle Royale moose with parasites or pathogens must be determined.

In the short term, a small release (12–24 animals) of woodland caribou to Isle Royale might be sufficient to establish a nuclear herd, given adequate winter escape habitat. A. T. Bergerud (personal communication) predicts that 20–25 woodland caribou could survive on Isle Royale by using other islands to escape from wolf predation. Initially, population growth would be good. But as the herd grew, it would be subject to increasing mortality rates (10–20% or higher annual adult mortality) and, with six or more wolves, the population probably could not exceed an average density of 0.1 per km² (a carrying capacity of 54). Under these conditions, the VORTEX model predicts that, without supplementation, the woodland caribou population would not survive beyond a few years even if 75 animals were released over three years (VORTEX incorporates a density-dependent reduction in reproduction and survival when carrying capacity is exceeded).

Thus, in the long term, caribou could not persist at Isle Royale without management intervention, such as 'artificial immigration' of breeding males through periodic translocations. VORTEX modeling, and evidence from Pukaskwa National Park and elsewhere (Klein 1968), indicates that mature males disappear first from declining, small populations, owing to disproportionately high mortality and dispersal rates. The current Isle Royale wolf decline and restoration debate (wolf numbers on Isle Royale are unlikely to ever reach a long-term (more than 100-year) MVP and the population will probably need management intervention to persist) foreshadows this dilemma.

Conclusions

Small numbers of ungulates translocated into favorable habitats have frequently grown into large populations (Griffith *et al.* 1989). In discussing the potential of restoring woodland caribou to the Lake Superior region, numerous biologists pointed out that woodland caribou herds have prospered from initial transplants of fewer than 20 animals. Griffith *et al.* (1989) found that for native game species, 20–40 founding animals was sufficient for high translocation success. However, success was defined vaguely as a 'self-sustaining population,' and no time frame was provided. Soulé (1986) points out that 'viability' has traditionally been equated with short-term persistence in a constant environment, or 'resilience'. MVP estimates rise dramatically, and call for larger founding populations, when they take into account long-term threats such as epidemics, catastrophes, and genetic drift.

It is difficult to restore woodland caribou to mainland sites (Bergerud & Mercer 1989), and of the three restoration sites that the North Central Caribou

Corporation is currently evaluating, Isle Royale is the only island. However, it has a relatively high density of wolves and limited escape cover, and can support only a relatively small number of woodland caribou. Yet, in some ways, Isle Royale offers the best scenario for woodland caribou restoration in the Lake Superior region, because it is free of white-tailed deer and meningeal brainworm, it is free of black bears, and reintroduced woodland caribou are unlikely to disperse to the mainland.

Nevertheless, the release of a reasonably achievable number of woodland caribou (e.g. 100) on Isle Royale would not result in an independently viable population, or in any population at all, without follow-up releases within 10 years. Based on MVP theory assuming high mortality rates, high variance in mortality, and a carrying capacity of no more than 54 animals, this is not surprising.

Woodland caribou translocated to the BWCAW/Quetico Provincial Park area would be exposed to mortality agents, such as black bear predation and meningeal brainworm, not present at Isle Royale. However, the site has more land, and a correspondingly larger herd with a greater probability of long-term persistence could be established. The total area of potentially suitable habitat and barriers to dispersal into deer-free areas require further delineation.

The limited number of woodland caribou that Voyageurs National Park can support, plus its high densities of predators and of white-tailed deer with a high incidence of meningeal brainworm, render it the least favorable of the three restoration sites under consideration.

VORTEX modeling indicates that any herd reintroduced within the constraints imposed by the western Lake Superior region will not achieve long-term population viability. It is possible, however, that one or more herds could be restored to this region and, with management, developed into a part of a larger metapopulation.

Acknowledgements

Numerous people aided in our assessment of the potential of restoring woodland caribou by discussing and sharing information on caribou biology, translocation, and the region's natural resources. We are grateful to Gordon Eason, Wawa District, Ontario Ministry of Natural Resources, for providing information on recent translocations of woodland caribou to the eastern end of Lake Superior and reviewing earlier drafts of this manuscript. We are also grateful to Terry Kreeger and his students at the University of Minnesota for the numerous runs of program VORTEX. Financial support was provided to one of us (JFC) by the North Central Caribou Corporation and the Natural

Heritage Program of the Michigan Department of Natural Resources. We are grateful to NCCC president Jim Nelson, and other members of NCCC and its advisory committee, for their continued efforts to reestablish woodland caribou in the border region.

Literature cited

Abraham, K., Darby, B., Day, Q., Foster, B., McNicol, J., Racey, G. & Timmermann, T. (1990) *Timber management guidelines for the provision of woodland caribou habitat.* Report to Ontario Ministry of Natural Resources. Thunder Bay, Ontario Ministry of Natural Resources.

Aldous, C. M. (1931) *A report of the investigations of reindeer grazing in the Superior National Forest.* Washington, D.C.: Division of Investigations, US Biological Survey.

Anderson, R. C. (1971) Neurological disease in reindeer (*Rangifer tarandus tarandus*) introduced into Ontario. *Canadian Journal of Zoology*, **49**, 159–66.

Anderson, R. C. & Prestwood, A. K. (1981) Lungworms. In *Diseases and parasites of White-Tailed Deer*, ed. Davison, W. R., Hayes, F. A., Nettles, V. F., & Kellog, F. E., pp. 266–317. Miscellaneous Publication 7. Tall Timbers Research Station.

Anderson, R. C., & Strelive, U. R. (1968) The experimental transmission of *Pneumostrongylus tenuis* to caribou (*Rangifer tarandus terranovae*). *Canadian Journal of Zoology*, **46**, 503–10.

Baker, R. H. (1983) *Michigan Mammals.* East Lansing: Michigan State University Press.

Bergerud, A. T. (1971) The population dynamics of Newfoundland caribou. *Wildlife Monographs*, **25**, 1–55.

Bergerud, A. T. (1972) Food habits of Newfoundland caribou. *Journal of Wildlife Management*, **36**, 913–23.

Bergerud, A. T. (1974) Decline of caribou in North America following settlement. *Journal of Wildlife Management*, **38**, 757–70.

Bergerud, A. T. (1978) Caribou. In *Big Game of North America, Ecology and Management*, ed. Schmidt, J. L. & Gilbert, D. L., pp. 83–101. Harrisburg: Stackpole Books.

Bergerud, A. T. (1980) A review of the population dynamics of caribou and wild reindeer in North America. In *Proceedings of the Second International Reindeer/Caribou Symposium*, ed. Reimers, E., Gaare, E. & Skenneberg, S. pp. 556–81. Direktoratet for vilt og ferkvannsfisk. Trondheim, Norway.

Bergerud, A. T. (1983) The natural population control of caribou. In *Symposium on Natural Regulation of Wildlife Populations (1978)*, ed. Bunnell, F. L., Eastman, D. S. & Peek, J. M., pp. 14–61. Moscow: Forest, Wildlife and Range Experiment Station.

Bergerud, A. T. (1985) Antipredator strategies of caribou, dispersion along shorelines. *Canadian Journal of Zoology*, **63**, 1324–29.

Bergerud, A. T. (1988) Caribou, wolves and man. *Trends in Ecology and Evolution*, **3**, 68–72.

Bergerud, A. T. (1989) *The abundance, distribution and behaviour of caribou in Pukaskwa National Park, 1972–1988.* Bergerud and Associates Contract Report #88-CPS-PUK, Scientific Review of Caribou Management Activities in Pukaskwa National Park. Fulford Harbour.

Bergerud, A. T., Butler, H. E., & Miller, D. R. (1984) Anti-predator tactics of calving caribou, dispersion in mountains. *Canadian Journal of Zoology*, 62, 1566–75.

Bergerud, A. T. & Elliot, J. P. (1986) Dynamics of caribou and wolves in northern British Columbia. *Canadian Journal of Zoology*, **64**, 1515–29.

Bergerud, A. T., Ferguson, R. & Butler, H. E. (1990) Spring migration and dispersion of woodland caribou at calving. *Animal Behavior*, **39**, 360–8.

Bergerud, A. T. & Mercer, W. E. (1989) Caribou introductions in eastern North America. *Wildlife Society Bulletin*, **17**, 111–20.

Bergerud, A. T. & Page, R. E. (1987) Displacement and dispersion of parturient caribou at calving as antipredator tactics. *Canadian Journal of Zoology*, **65**, 1597–606.

Bonefant, C. (1974) Resurgence of the caribou in Quebec. *Canadian Geographic*, **92**, 48–56.

Cochrane, J. F. (1991) *Feasibility study for the restoration of woodland caribou at Isle Royale National Park*. Resources Management Report. Houghton: Isle Royale National Park.

Cringan, A. T. (1957) History, food habits and range requirements of the woodland caribou of continental North America. *Transactions of the North American Wildlife Conference*, **22**, 485–501.

Cumming, H. G. & Beange, D. B. (1987) Dispersion and movements of woodland caribou near Lake Nipigon, Ontario. *Journal of Wildlife Management*, **51**, 69–78.

Darby, W. R. & Pruitt, W. O. Jr. (1984) Habitat use, movements and grouping behavior of woodland caribou, *Rangifer tarandus caribou*, in southeastern Manitoba. *Canadian Field-Naturalist*, **98**, 184–90.

Darby, W. R., Timmermann, H. R., Snider, J. B., Abraham, K. F., Stefanski, R. A. & Johnson, C. A. (1989) *Woodland Caribou in Ontario, Background to Policy*. Toronto: Ontario Ministry of Natural Resources.

Dymond, J. R., Snyder, L. L. & Logier, E. B. S. (1928) A faunal survey of the Lake Nipigon region, Ontario. *Transactions of the Royal Canadian Institute*, **16**, 233–91. (Reprinted as Contribution no. 1, Royal Ontario Museum of Zoology.)

Edmonds, E. J. (1986) Woodland caribou, their status and distribution in Alberta. *Alberta Naturalist*, **16**, 73–8.

Edmonds, E. J. (1988) Population status, distribution, and movements of woodland caribou in west central Alberta. *Canadian Journal of Zoology*, **66**, 817–826.

Edmonds, E. J. & Bloomfield, M. (1984) *A study of woodland caribou* (Rangifer tarandus caribou) *in west central Alberta, 1979 to 1983*. Edmonton: Alberta Energy and Natural Resources, Fish and Wildlife Division. 203 pp.

Euler, D. L., Snyder, B. & Timmermann, H. R. (1976) Woodland caribou and plant communities on the Slate Islands, Lake Superior. *Canadian Field-Naturalist*, **90**, 17–21.

Fashingbauer, B. A. (1965) The caribou in Minnesota. In *Big Game in Minnesota*, ed. J.B. Moyle, pp. 136–166. Technical Bulletin 9. St. Paul: Minnesota Department of Conservation.

Ferguson, S. H., Bergerud, A. T. & Ferguson, R. (1988) Predation risk and habitat selection in the persistence of a remnant caribou population. *Oecologia*, **76**, 236–45.

Fuller, T. K. & Keith, L. B. (1981) Woodland caribou population dynamics in northeastern Alberta. *Journal of Wildlife Management*, **45**, 197–211.

Gilpin, M. E. & Soulé, M. E. (1986) Minimum viable populations, processes of species extinction. In *Conservation Biology, the Science of Scarcity and Diversity*, ed. Soulé, M.E., pp. 19–34. Sunderland: Sinauer Associates.

Gogan, P. J. P. (1990) Considerations in the reintroduction of native mammalian species to restore natural ecosystems. *Natural Areas Journal*, **10**, 210–7.

Gogan, P. J. P., Jordan, P. A. & Nelson J. L. (1990) Planning to reintroduce woodland caribou to Minnesota. *Transactions of the North American Wildlife and Natural Resources Conference*, **55**, 599–608.

Gray, J. B. & Samuel, W. M. (1986) *Parelaphostrongylus odocoilei* (Nematoda: Protostrongylidae) and a protostrongylid nematode in woodland caribou (*Rangifer tarandus caribou*) of Alberta, Canada. *Journal of Wildlife Diseases*, **22**, 48–50.

Grier, J. (1980) Ecology, A simulation model for small populations of animals. *Creative Computing*, **6**, 116–21.

Griffith, B., Scott, J. M., Carpenter, J. W. & Reed, C. (1989) Translocation as a species management tool: Status and strategy. *Science*, **245**, 477–80.

Holte, I. & Holte, E. (1965) *Interview with L. Rakeestraw 9/10/65, Wright Island, Isle Royale, Michigan*. Isle Royale National Park Oral History No. 2. Isle Royale National Park: Michigan Department of Natural Resources.

Jakimchuk, R. D., Ferguson, S. H. & Sopuck, L. G. (1987) Differential habitat use and sexual segregation in the central arctic caribou herd. *Canadian Journal of Zoology*, **65**, 534–41.

Jordan, P. A. & Pitt, W. C. (1989) *A survey for Parelaphostrongylus tenuis in the proposed caribou reintroduction site Little Saganagana area of the BWCAW, Minnesota*. Report by the North Central Caribou Corporation. Duluth: North Central Caribou Corporation.

Karns, P. D. (1980) *Environmental analysis report. Reintroduction of woodland caribou, Superior National Forest*. Report prepared for the United States Forest Service. Duluth: United States Department of Agriculture.

Karns, P. D. & Jordan, P. A. (1969) *Pneumostrongylus tenuis* in moose on a deer-free island. *Journal of Wildlife Management*, **33**, 431–3.

Klein, D. R. (1968) The introduction, increase, and crash of reindeer on St. Matthew Island. *Journal of Wildlife Management*, **32**, 350–67.

Lacy, R. (1991) *VORTEX, Simulation model of stochastic population change. Version 8.0*. Brookfield. Chicago Zoological Park.

Lande, R. & Barrowclough, G. F. (1987) Effective population size, genetic variation and their use in population management. In *Viable populations for conservation*, ed. Soulé, M. E., pp. 85–123. Cambridge: Cambridge University Press.

Lankester, M. W. (1976) A Protostrongylid nematode of woodland caribou and implications in moose management. *North American Moose Conference and Workshop*, **12**, 173–90.

Lankester, M. W. & Anderson, R. C. (1968) Gastropods as intermediate hosts of meningeal worm, *Pneumostrongylus tenuis* Dougherty. *Canadian Journal of Zoology*, 46, 373–383.

Lankester, M. W., Crichton, V. J. & Timmermann, H. R. (1976) A protostrongylid nematode (Strongylida, protostrongylidae) in woodland caribou (*Rangifer tarandus caribou*). *Canadian Journal of Zoology*, **57**, 1384–92.

Lankester, M. W. & Hauta, P. L. (1989) *Parelaphostrongylus andersoni* (Nematoda, Protostrongylidae) in caribou (*Rangifer tarandus*) of northern and central Canada. *Canadian Journal of Zoology*, **67**, 1966–75.

Lankester, M. W. & Northcott, T. H. (1979) *Elaphostrongylus cervi* Cameron 1931 (Nematoda, Metastrongyloidea) in caribou (*Rangifer tarandus caribou*) in Newfoundland. *Canadian Journal of Zoology*, **57**, 1384–92.

McCollough, M. (1987) *A management and research plan for the reintroduction of woodland caribou to Maine*. Maine Caribou Project. Orono: University of Maine.

McCollough, M. & Connery, B. (1991) *An attempt to reintroduce woodland caribou to Maine 1986–1990*. Final Report. Maine Caribou Project, 1986–1990. Orono: University of Maine.

Mech, L. D., Nelson, M. E. & Drabik, H. F. (1982) Reoccurrence of caribou in Minnesota. *American Midland Naturalist*, **108**, 206–8.

Nudds, T. D. (1990) Retroductive logic in retrospect: the ecological effects of meningeal worms. *Journal of Wildlife Management*, **54**, 396–402.

Ontario Ministry of Natural Resources. (1986) *Slate Islands Provincial Park Management Plan; Preliminary Draft*. Terrace Bay: Ontario Ministry of Natural Resources.

Ontario Ministry of Natural Resources. (1988) *Quetico Provincial Park Management Plan. 1988 Policy Review*. Toronto: The Queen's Printer.

Peterson, R. O. (1991) *Ecological studies of wolves on Isle Royale; Annual Report 1990–1991*. Houghton: Isle Royale Natural History Association.

Peterson, W. J. (1981) Coming of the caribou. *Minnesota Volunteer*, **44**, 17–23.

Pybus, M. J. & Samuel, W. M. (1984) *Parelaphostrongylus andersoni* (Nematoda: Protostrongylidae) and *P. odocolei* in two cervid definitive hosts. *Journal of Parasitology*, **70**, 507–15.

Riis, P. B. (1938a) Woodland caribou and time. *Parks and Recreation*, **21**, 529–35.

Riis, P. B. (1938b) Woodland caribou and time. *Parks and Recreation*, **21**, 594–600.

Riis, P. B. (1938c) Woodland caribou and time. *Parks and Recreation*, **21**, 639–45.

Riis, P. B. (1938d) Woodland caribou and time. *Parks and Recreation*, **22**, 23–30.

Schaefer, J. A. & Pruitt, W. O. (1991) Fire and woodland caribou in southeastern Manitoba. *Wildlife Monograph*, **116**, 1–39.

Servheen, G. (1988) *Selkirk Mountains caribou transplant: October 1987 – September 1988*. Boise: Idaho Department of Fish and Game.

Servheen, G. (1989) *Selkirk Mountains caribou transplant: October 1988 – September 1989*. Boise: Idaho Department of Fish and Game.

Shoesmith, M. (1986) Woodland caribou in Manitoba. *Provincial Museum of Alberta Natural History Occasional Paper*, **9**, 311–13.

Shoesmith, M. W. & Storey, D. R. (1977) Movements and associated behaviour of woodland caribou in central Manitoba. *Proceedings of the International Congress of Game Biologists*, **13**, 51–64.

Simkin, D. W. (1965) *A preliminary report of the woodland caribou study in Ontario*. Section Report (Wildlife) No. 59, Toronto: Ontario Department of Lands and Forests.

Skoog, R. O. (1968) Ecology of the caribou in Alaska. Ph. D. dissertation, Berkeley: University of California.

Soulé, M. E. (1986) Conservation biology and the real world. In *Conservation Biology: the Science of Scarcity and Diversity*, ed. Soulé, M. E., pp. 1–12. Sunderland: Sinauer Associates.

Soulé, M. E. (1987) Introduction. In *Viable Populations for Conservation*, ed. Soulé, M. E., pp. 1–10. Cambridge University Press.

Stevenson, S. K. & Hatler, D. F. (1985) *Woodland caribou and their habitat in southern and central British Columbia*. Report Number 23. Victoria: British Columbia Ministry of Forest Land Management.

Thomas, D. C., Barry, S. J. & Kiliaan, H. P. (1989) Fetal sex ratios in caribou: maternal age and condition effects. *Journal of Wildlife Management*, **53**, 885–90.

US Fish & Wildlife Service. (1981) *Standards for the development of habitat suitability index models*. 103 ESM. Washington, D. C.: US Fish and Wildlife Service, Division of Ecological Services.

III

Implemented restorations

This section describes four currently implemented restorations, although they vary widely in their progress. Factors such as persecution (e.g., collecting, hunting, trapping), habitat loss, small population size and associated problems such as inbreeding, susceptibility to disease, and incompatible mating types, contributed to the initial decline of the species in question. Translocations, captive propagation, population viability analysis, metapopulation theory, dedica tion, and long-term commitment are among the factors contributing to each restoration attempt. We read of both interagency cooperation, and interagency feuding and mistrust.

Carbyn *et al.* (Chapter 10), Clark (Chapter 11), and DeMauro (Chapter 12) provide historical sketches of the decline of the species in question, followed by a description of the restoration effort. In contrast, Pavlik (Chapter 13) first describes two powerful demographic monitoring techniques, and follows with a description of a preliminary restoration effort that demonstrates their utility.

Of these examples, the restoration of swift foxes described by Carbyn *et al.* has been in operation for the longest time, and this effort appears to have established self-maintaining populations. They show better survival of swift foxes when they are released in the fall, when natal dispersal normally takes place, and better survival of translocated rather than captive-reared foxes. Given this last finding, it is fortunate that healthy populations of swift fox exist in several states within its range in the United States, and that cooperation among state, provincial, and two federal governments has been possible. Predation caused most mortality (58%), which occurred within a month after release. An estimated 150–225 foxes are now restored in Canada and dispersal into new areas is occurring. This program appears to be well on the way to success.

In contrast, Clark describes the black-footed ferret, a creature so rare that only captive-reared animals are available for restoration. Further, because of severe reduction of their obligate prey, the prairie dog, only small populations

243

can be sustained at most potential restoration sites (prairie dog colonies). Hence, Clark concludes that restored ferret populations must be managed as parts of a metapopulation. On the brighter side, although derived from only five individuals, a fairly large and productive captive population now exists at a number of institutions. Unfortunately, judging from what has been found with the swift fox, the necessity of using captive-reared ferrets for release may decrease the initial chances for success. If the use of captive-reared individuals does 'stack the deck' against initial restoration success, then other factors that interact to affect postrelease survivorship may become critical. For example, we can see from the example of the swift fox that factors such as release technique and the time of year of the release can strongly influence the likelihood of post-release survival. Should the ferret program assume that these results will similarly apply to the ferret? Alternatively, there may be no guarantee that what works best for swift foxes will necessarily work best for ferrets. From this view, especially given a now healthy captive breeding population of ferrets, several release techniques should be used experimentally, as was done with the swift fox, to find the release technique that maximizes postrelease survival. Unfortunately, as Clark discusses briefly, interagency squabbling is currently hindering such an experimental approach. This is precisely the situation for which good organizational management and open communication, as discussed by Clark & Cragun (Chapter 1), are essential.

DeMauro, working with the Lakeside daisy, discovered that individuals in a remnant (now extinct) population fragment in Illinois all shared the same self-incompatibility allele and were thus incapable of sexual reproduction. Fortunately, as with the swift fox, reproductive populations existed in Ohio and Ontario, and by translocating individuals from these populations for crossing with the Illinois plants, she restored the ability for breeding and established populations in a greenhouse. Individual plants used in a subsequent field restoration were grown from seeds derived from three sources: F1 hybrids from crosses between Illinois and Ohio plants, open-pollinated F1 plants, and both the Ohio and Ontario populations. She used extensive sampling of extant communities to design the structure of the restored population, and she suggests continued monitoring of both extant and restored populations to determine whether further intervention is necessary in the future. Such intervention could be based on the core–satellite metapopulation model, with extant Ohio and Ontario populations serving as the core population for restored populations in Illinois and, in the future, perhaps elsewhere.

In Pavlik's chapter, more emphasis is placed on various monitoring techniques than on the restoration itself. Trend analysis, in which characteristics such as survivorship, reproduction, and establishment are monitored, allows prediction of population growth, stability, or decline in extant populations. Factor resolution examines critical variables likely to influence trends in population trajectory as suggested by trend analysis. Both of these monitoring techniques can help identify extant populations most in need of active management, and experimentally decide which key factors are responsible for downward trends in population size. Furthermore, both techniques can be extremely useful when restoring or creating new populations. Restorations can use factor analysis to determine experimentally which restoration strategies offer the best probability for success. Trend analysis can be used to predict the future trajectory of a restored population, and this prediction can be tested by continued monitoring. Pavlik illustrates each of these techniques with a restoration of an endangered California plant, *Amsinckia grandiflora*.

The four restorations described here demonstrate the uniqueness of each restoration attempt. For the swift fox, one of the first questions was whether the widespread habitat conversion from grassland to agriculture eliminated the animal's niche, rendering restoration impossible. In contrast, for the black-footed ferret, its habitat, though greatly reduced, still existed, but the ferret had been reduced in numbers so severely before action was taken, a question at one time was whether the species even existed! Questions concerning site-fidelity and local adaptation confronted both the swift fox and the lakeside daisy, while for the ferret and *Amsinckia*, remnant populations available for source organisms were so reduced that this simply was not an issue. Interagency cooperation was achieved with apparent ease in the cases of the fox and the daisy, while interagency problems have plagued recovery efforts for the ferret. This does not seem to have been an issue for *Amsinckia*. Disease almost wiped out the few remaining wild ferrets before they were taken into captivity, while population reduction (and subsequent loss of genetic variability via drift and/or inbreeding) led to sterility of a population of the daisy due to self-incompatibility.

These implemented restorations also suggest several generalizations. First, experimental approaches are useful for restorations of both animals and plants. But as is clear from these chapters, experiments are often easier with plants, at least initially. Animals disperse from the release site, radio collars fall off or cease functioning, etc. Plants grow or die where they are planted, they can often be planted in controlled, easily replicatable plots, and they are easily monitored for survival and reproduction. Subsequent seed dispersal, in contrast, may prove just as difficult to monitor as animals are following initial release. Regardless, despite logistic difficulties, experimental approaches in restoration efforts maximize efficiency of effort, money, and most important, biological material.

Second, as discussed in Section I, metapopulation management is critical for both animals and plants. For many reasons, sites available for restoration are often limited in size and in number, and thus restorations will often result in fragmented, small populations. These conditions can lead to problems such as inbreeding depression or loss of genetic variation, susceptibility to disease, extinction due to catastrophic storms, etc. Metapopulation management requires multiple restoration sites, a commitment to long-term monitoring of population viability, genetic characteristics, etc., and carefully planned movement of organisms among the different restoration sites. Movement could be more-or-less natural, for instance, when appropriate habitat corridors connect restoration sites and allow natural dispersal. In most cases, however, it is more likely that movements will be human-directed translocations. Such translocations could be from captive (zoo or greenhouse) populations to restored populations for augmentation, or from natural, 'healthy' populations to restored populations for augmentation, or between restored populations themselves, to manage for genetic variability, to bolster declining populations, etc.

Third, stumbling blocks for restorations often involve non-biological issues; thus, restorationists need to equip themselves with more than simply biological knowledge and skills. For instance, restorations frequently require cooperation among two or more government agencies, as well as involvement of private organizations and sometimes, even private citizens. Clearly, interagency cooperation is essential, and knowledge of organization and management theory, as discussed by Clark & Cragun (Chapter 1) should help prevent organizational problems, or help analyze and fix problems after they arise.

Finally, it is abundantly clear that any restoration of any animal or plant exists within a larger context, the biotic and abiotic conditions necessary for continued survival. This entails maintenance and possibly restoration of more than simply the target species. Viable ecosystems are absolutely vital for restoration to have any chance for success.

10

The swift fox reintroduction program in Canada from 1983 to 1992

LUDWIG N. CARBYN, HARRY J. ARMBRUSTER
AND CHARLES MAMO

Introduction

The swift fox (*Vulpes velox*), the smallest North American canid, disappeared from the Canadian prairies in the 1930s, about fifty years after the demise of the bison (*Bison bison*). These changes were symbolic of a much larger trend. In less than 100 years the northern prairie ecosystem, which had developed over 10 000 years, was transformed so dramatically that nine vertebrate species disappeared from it. Almost 80% of the mixed-grass biome disappeared (World Wildlife Fund Canada 1988). Modern agricultural practices were primarily responsible for these rapid changes, and transportation corridors, oil and gas exploration, and industrial activities put pressure on what little native prairie remained. Currently, global climatic trends could affect the remaining islands of natural prairies. Restoration of the swift fox to the Canadian prairie landscape has therefore become an important symbolic gesture, focusing attention on the need for protection and restoration, to the extent still possible, of a greatly threatened ecosystem. In this chapter, we describe the background and accomplishments of the Canadian swift fox reintroduction program.

Biological background

Taxonomy

The first records of swift foxes in North America are in a reference of fur shipments from the Pembina post of the Northwest Company's Red River District in 1801 (Fauna West 1991); however, the swift fox was not taxonomically described until 1823 (T. Say in James 1823).

Merriam described two subspecies of swift foxes; the northern (*Vulpes velox hebes*), and the southern (*Vulpes velox velox*) (Merriam 1902). The northern subspecies was listed as endangered in the United States, but was subsequently delisted (US Fish and Wildlife Service 1979, 1982). Stromberg & Boyce (1986) concluded that the northern subspecific status was not justified, but cautioned that there may be geographic variations that should be considered in reintroduction programs. It is possible that there are different geographic 'races' adapted to different latitudes.

The species status of kit foxes (*Vulpes macrotis*) and swift foxes has also been debated. Hall (1981) considered them to be one species. Dragoo *et al.* (1990) concluded that all arid-land foxes in North America are one species but two subspecies, *Vulpes velox velox* and *Vulpes velox macrotis*, should be recognized.

General biology

Swift foxes opportunistically prey on a variety of small mammals, birds, insects, reptiles, and carrion. They are primarily nocturnal, but individuals often sun themselves at their dens on cold, sunny, windless winter days.

Swift foxes generally breed in their second year. They appear to be monogamous (Kilgore 1969); however, as in other small canids (Egoscue 1962, 1975), polygamy has been recorded. The species is monestrous, and the timing of estrus appears to vary according to latitude (C. Schroeder, personal communication). Whelping occurs from March to April in Oklahoma (Kilgore 1969), and in late April to May in the captive breeding facilities at Cochrane, Alberta (R. Dyke, personal communication). Swift foxes released as part of the Canadian reintroduction program in southern Alberta and Saskatchewan produced pups mostly in late April to early May (C. Mamo, personal observation). The average date on which the pups first emerged from their dens was 28 May ($n = 10$ litters), when they were probably three to four weeks old. Litters in the wild range from one to eight and average four or five pups.

Captive male swift foxes have produced pups until they were eleven years old; females have produced pups until they were eight years old. Five-year-old females produced the largest litters (R. Dyke, personal communication). There were 149 males and 151 females born in captivity during this study; they were released into the wild as dispersers (when they were five months old).

Mortality of swift foxes in the wild is particularly high in the first year of life. In the north, predators of swift foxes include coyotes (*Canis latrans*), golden eagles (*Aquila chrysaetos*), and badgers (*Taxidea taxus*). Trapping, shooting, secondary poisoning, and vehicular traffic also kill swift foxes. Swift foxes harbor a variety of internal parasites, and have ectoparasites such as ticks (*Ixodes* spp.) and fleas (*Pulex* spp.), but not much is known about the prevalence of disease in swift foxes.

Unlike red foxes (*Vulpes vulpes*) and coyotes, swift foxes use dens year-round. Swift foxes may modify and use burrows prepared by other mammals, including prairie dogs (*Cynomys* spp.) (Kilgore 1969), or dig their own. Hines (1980) found den entrances to range from 100 to 430 cm. In some studies, den entrances were too small for coyotes and badgers, indicating that swift foxes avoid dens dug by larger species (Egoscue 1979), but our studies showed that swift foxes frequently use badger dens and may even take over old dens. Pairs with litters tend to have a number of dens.

Hines (1980) reported average swift fox home ranges in Nebraska to be 17.3 km^2 (6.7 mi^2) for adult males and 12.4 km^2 (4.8 mi^2) for adult females. A study in South Dakota suggested that a denning pair requires about 2 sections (3.2 km^2) of land (J. Sharps, personal communication), but ranges were larger during winter. Recent studies on kit foxes in the sparsely vegetated desert of western Arizona revealed that home ranges were 12 km^2 for males and 10 km^2 for females (Zoellick & Smith 1992).

Distributional background

Historical status of swift foxes

The swift fox is adapted to short-to-mid grasslands, and at one time ranged from southern Canada to northern Mexico, occupying most of the Great Plains of North America (Fig. 10.1). In Canada, its distribution paralleled the mixed prairie regions in the southern portion of Alberta, Saskatchewan, and possibly Manitoba (Anderson 1947, Merriam 1902, Rand 1948, Seton 1909, Soper 1961, Miller & Kellogg 1955, Pattimore 1985). In Alberta, its northern- and westernmost distribution in Canada, the swift fox ranged north to the 53rd parallel and west to the foothills along the eastern edge of the Rocky Mountains (Soper 1964). The largest portion of its historic range in Canada was in Saskatchewan, where it extended north to the Saskatchewan River. There are no good records of its having been in Manitoba (Pattimore 1985), but if it was, it would have been in the southwestern corner of the province, in the Souris River and Pembina Hills area.

The historic range in the United States extended south to northern Texas (Davis 1974), southeastern New Mexico (Best 1971), and the Oklahoma panhandle. The western range limits were east of the Rocky Mountains in Montana, Wyoming, and Colorado (Cahalane 1947). The eastern boundary included all of North and South Dakota and the western edges of Minnesota and Iowa (Allen 1870, Bowles 1975). Most of Nebraska and the western half of Kansas had swift foxes (Cahalane 1947).

Swift foxes apparently were abundant during the time of the first European settlers. Fur companies exported many swift fox pelts to meet European fashion demands (Bailey 1926, Carlington 1980). In Canada, the Hudson's Bay Company sold more than 100 000 swift fox pelts from 1853 to 1877 (MacFarlane 1905 as cited in Rand 1948). In the United States, the American Fur Company bought and sold 10 614 swift fox pelts from 1835 to 1838 (Johnson 1969). Although fur records do not provide reliable information about the regional abundance of furbearing animals because the trade in skins takes place over large areas (Carbyn & Killaby 1989), they do give a general indication of the prevalence of a species.

In both countries, swift fox numbers declined dramatically as Europeans settled the prairies. The last Canadian museum specimens were collected in Saskatchewan near Ravenscrag in 1927 and near Govenlock in 1928 (Rand 1948, Banfield 1974). The last possible record in Alberta is in a 1938 newspaper article (Soper 1964). There were no reported sightings of swift foxes in North Dakota from 1915 to 1970, in South Dakota from 1914 to 1966, in Nebraska from 1901 to 1953 (Jones 1964, Pfeifer & Hibbard 1970, Hillman & Sharps 1978), and in Wyoming between 1900 and 1958 (Long 1965; Lindberg 1986). One record of a swift fox trapped in Haakon County, South Dakota, may have been the first record for that state in the comeback of the species in the area.

Swift foxes appeared to survive only in parts of Texas, Oklahoma, New Mexico, Colorado, and Wyoming (H. Harju, personal communication). The causes of the species' decline throughout the western Great Plains are under review (Carbyn, Brechtel, Hjertaas & Mamo 1993); possibilities include fur trapping, habitat loss, disease, climate change (particularly drought and winter severity), and continuous predator control.

If predator control programs were intensive enough, they could have resulted in local extinctions in Montana, Wyoming, North Dakota, South Dakota, Nebraska, Oklahoma, and Kansas (Martin & Sternberg 1955, Glass 1959, Jones 1964, Long 1965, Van Ballenberghe 1975, Chambers 1978), and in Alberta, Saskatchewan, and Manitoba (Herrero *et al.* 1991). Widespread poisoning of predators began in the 1880s and 1890s in both countries, but poisoning may have been less of a factor in Canada, because control programs there never reached the intensity they reached in the United States. In Wyoming, aerial gunning for coyote control started in the 1940s and was most intense in open areas. Swift foxes survived in greater numbers where aerial gunning of predators was more common than poisoning (H. Harju, personal communication).

Current range and status

Around 1955, after an absence of nearly 50 years, swift foxes reappeared in parts of the United States. Since then, swift fox sightings have become more numerous. Specimens were taken near Bridgeport, Nebraska, in 1954, in the North Dakota and Wyoming region in 1958, and in southeastern Montana in 1978 (Chambers 1978). Swift foxes have been sighted more recently in North Dakota and Montana (Moore & Martin 1980, Pfeifer & Hibbard 1970). A swift fox was documented in southwestern North Dakota in 1976 (Seabloom, Crawford & McKenna 1978 in Fauna West 1991). More recently, a single male was trapped in Dawson County, eastern Montana (K. Walcheck, personal communication). These individuals likely dispersed from Wyoming and South Dakota (Hillman & Sharps 1978). The northernmost recent (1990) record of a swift fox is from the Missouri National Grasslands area of North Dakota, about 225 km from the Canadian border. The current population status of the swift fox in the United States varies from doubtful in North Dakota (extirpated); to maringal in South Dakota, Oklahoma, and Montana; to established but in low numbers in Nebraska; to well-established but in variable numbers in Texas, Colorado, Kansas, New Mexico, and Wyoming (Scott-Brown, Herrero & Reynolds 1987 and D. Eklund personal communication).

The rise of swift fox sightings in some areas of the United States may be due to 1) an end to indiscriminate strychnine poisoning programs, 2) restrictions, beginning in the early 1970's, on the use of Compound 1080 or 'coyote getters' on public land, and 3) increasing environmental awareness and federal legislation protecting endangered species, resulting in better funding and more manpower to monitor endangered species. Nevertheless, swift foxes are still hunted and trapped (generally by accident in traps set for more valuable fur species) in the United States. Hunting and trapping seasons vary from state to state, and some states have no bag limit. In large portions of the former ranges of swift foxes, the species appears to be in trouble.

Why is there not a more rapid movement northward? There are at least three possible answers. First, swift foxes may regularly move north, become established, but die out. This seems unlikely, because swift foxes are often inquisitive and unwary (Cutter 1958, Seton 1937), and even if they were not seen, they would likely be caught in traps set for more highly prized fur species, and an established population would soon be detected. Trapping for coyotes and red foxes is still common in the Canadian prairies, but until the recent reintroductions, there were no reports of swift foxes having been caught. Since the reintroductions, swift foxes have again been trapped. Second, swift foxes might simply be poor dispersers. Third, there may be barriers to moving north.

For example, the Big Horn basin, west of the Big Horn Mountains, is probably suitable terrain, but it is heavily farmed and irrigated (P. Achuff, personal communication). Other potential barriers are extensive breaks (eroded, rough terrain) along river systems such as those of the Missouri, Yellowstone and Souris rivers.

In 1978 the swift fox was officially designated as extirpated in Canada. Alberta has listed the swift fox as endangered, and the species' status in the United States is constantly under review. In 1992, a petition was filed with the US Fish and Wildlife Service to have the species declared officially endangered in parts of its northern and central range.

The Canadian release program

Beginnings

The desire to return the swift fox to Canada evolved over ten years, stimulated by the private sector. Miles & Beryl Smeeton established a wildlife reserve in which they raised an assemblage of wildlife, including two pairs of swift foxes that they imported in 1973. These became the focus of a popular book (Smeeton 1984). From such beginnings, the project developed into a major program involving four federal and provincial groups, at least six major private organizations, and numerous smaller contributors including government, oil companies, an adopt-a-fox project, and private donations. Much of the funding was organized by the non-profit organizations.

In 1976, the project received governmental support and was placed into a broader endangered species program. By 1983, suitable release sites had been chosen and enough swift foxes were available to begin the releases. Since 1986, the Swift Fox Conservation Society, based largely in Calgary, has actively promoted the reintroduction program and until 1990 actively promoted an adopt-a-fox program. Subsequently, interests of the Society diverged from that of the Smeeton family, and the Society refocused its activities to other areas of the project.

Environmental influences on the choice of release sites

Because swift foxes have only very limited distribution in some cultivated areas (Lindberg 1986) and only about 24% of the estimated 24 million hectares of mixed-grass prairie in Canada is still uncultivated (World Wildlife Fund Canada 1988), it is unlikely that swift foxes will ever regain their original abundance. Nevertheless, it is possible that, with protection and restoration of their habitat and judicious selection of reintroduction sites, a viable population of swift foxes can be established.

Human activities, such as the intentional or inadvertent taking of swift foxes through trapping and rodent and predator control programs, might limit swift fox populations (Hillman & Sharps 1978, Hines 1980, Scott-Brown *et al.* 1987). To a lesser extent, swift foxes are killed on highways and roads, run over by farm implements (Kilgore 1969), and indiscriminately shot.

In the reintroduction program, these hazards can be minimized by carefully choosing release sites. Areas having intense coyote, rodent, and skunk control programs should be avoided. Areas having a high density of granaries, sheds, or other farm buildings are also undesirable, as swift foxes occasionally take up residence under these buildings, and are then subject to the malicious destruction of their dens or to harassment by farm dogs. Areas that are heavily hunted should be avoided because newly released swift foxes are vulnerable to hunting.

Pesticides and rodenticides used in cultivated fields are potentially significant. These chemicals may alter the prey base by locally affecting insects and the mammals that feed on them. Swift foxes' tolerance of these chemicals is unknown, but because they consume large quantities of insects that could have high pesticide contents, there is cause for concern. So far the swift foxes reintroduced to Alberta and Saskatchewan have not made much use of cultivated fields. Some have been located in cultivated areas, but none has remained, and there have been no documented cases of pups raised in these areas.

Petroleum exploration, with its field developments and increased vehicular traffic, alters local habitats and can affect adjacent swift fox populations. Once built, however, petroleum exploration structures are not expected to significantly affect swift fox populations or their prey base. Roads may be beneficial to swift foxes where microenvironments along ditches create special conditions that favor the survival of potential prey, and where road kills are available.

Release sites should have adequate prey diversity and density. As opportunistic carnivores, swift foxes take a variety of prey and carrion. At certain times of the year grasshoppers and beetles are important prey. Winter snow conditions and temperatures affect prey availability.

The present swift fox release sites in Alberta and Saskatchewan are on private and community pasture lands. The effects of livestock grazing on habitat quality for swift foxes are poorly understood. If ranges are not overgrazed, grazing could benefit swift foxes by reducing cover, yet providing seeds, for small mammal prey. Heavy grazing, however, especially by both cattle and sheep, could adversely affect swift foxes and their prey. For kit foxes, overgrazing diminished prey diversity and, therefore, kit fox densities (O'Farrell 1983).

The ultimate threat to swift foxes reintroduced to Canada is the loss of suitable habitat. Cultivation, industry, mineral exploration, and intensive range management will influence swift fox habitat. The expansion of irrigated farming and associated irrigation canal and dam development will convert rangelands to cultivation. Fragmentation of habitat, particularly because Canada is on the fringe of the species' former distribution, could hamper long-term reestablishment, especially if stochastic events impact all of the swift foxes within an area.

Description of release sites

1. Alberta–Saskatchewan border area

The Alberta–Saskatchewan border area has a continental climate, characterized by cold harsh winters, warm summers, and low precipitation. The terrain of the area is generally flat to rolling, except where bisected by numerous coulees. The predominant vegetative association is the spear grass/blue gramma association. The area was chosen because it represents part of the largest single block of native prairie in Canada. It is also very flat and therefore resembles ecosystems similar to those in regions further south. Annual precipitation is about 340 mm.

2. Milk River Ridge (Knight/McIntyre ranch area) in southern Alberta

This area is located in Southwestern Alberta. The climate is inland continental, characterized by cold winters and warm summers. Precipitation is almost twice (500–550 mm) that along the Alberta–Saskatchewan border area. The Milk River Ridge area is along the transition between mixed-grass prairie and fescue prairie.

3. Wood Mountain area in Saskatchewan

The Wood Mountain upland area is an undulating region that ranges from 700 to 1000 m above sea level. Spear grass dominates the vegetation. Annual precipitation is about 350 mm.

Methods

The Canadian swift fox reintroduction program required captive breeding, which has been widely used for other species (Kleiman 1989). Because of the possibility that there are different geographical races adapted to different latitudes, the northernmost available breeding stock (from Wyoming, Colorado, and South Dakota) was used. Swift foxes were raised in Moose Jaw Wild Animal Park (Saskatchewan), Cochrane Wildlife Reserve, Calgary Zoo, and

Table 10.1. *Summary of the locations, total number, and number of radio-collared swift foxes released during hard release programs in southern Alberta and Saskatchewan*

Total hard releases, 433; total soft releases, 136; grand total, 569.

Year/ season of release	Albta/Sask Border		Wood Mountain		Milk River Ridge	
	No. released	No. collared	No. released	No. collared	No. released	No. collared
Fall 1987	57	18	—	—	—	—
Fall 1988	53	12	—	—	—	—
Spring 1989	—	—	—	—	28	14
Fall 1989	35	13	—	—	33	13
Spring 1990	28	27	—	—	—	—
Fall 1990	38	0	51	20	—	—
Spring 1991	—	—	29	28	—	—
Fall 1991	35	0	46	10	—	—
Site total	246	70	126	58	61	27

Edmonton Valley Zoo (Alberta). From 1983 to 1991, they and wild swift foxes captured in the same source states were released in the areas shown in Fig. 10.1, and in the numbers summarized in Table 10.1.

One hundred and thirty-six captive-raised or wild-caught swift foxes were soft-released, and 433 were hard-released. In soft releases, used from 1983 to 1987, paired swift foxes were held in field release pens (3.7 m × 7.3 m) constructed in natural prairie habitats (Fig. 10.2A) and fenced for protection from disturbance by free-ranging cattle. The swift foxes were placed in the pens in October or November and held during the mating season (January or February). If they had not produced young, they were generally released the following spring. If they had produced young, they and their young were released in summer to early fall. Soft-released swift foxes were given supplemental feedings for one to eight months.

In hard releases, swift foxes were transported from the captive facilities and released into the wild without prior conditioning in release pens (Fig. 10.2B). Because this method was successful and cost-effective, after 1987 all swift foxes were hard-released. Fall releases were in September or October, when the young would normally have dispersed. Wild pups have been observed dispersing earlier, and appear to be independent when they are five months old. Hard-released swift foxes were not given supplemental feedings, except for a few individuals during the severe winter of 1988–89.

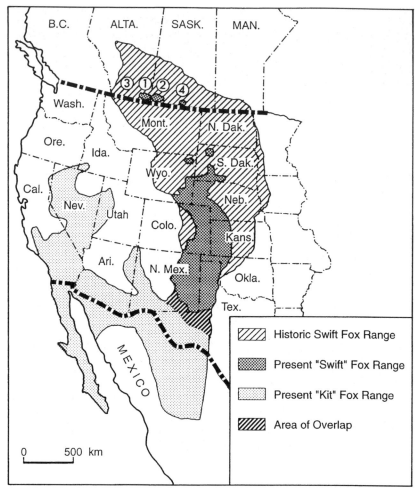

Fig. 10.1. North American distribution of the swift–kit fox complex. Numbers refer to Canadian release sites. Site 1: Alberta/Saskatchewan border area-Lost River Ranch. Site 2: Border area. Site 3: Knight/McIntyre Ranch complex. Site 4: Wood Mountain area.

Wild swift foxes were caught and released to compare their survival with that of captive-raised animals. They were captured in October or in January, just prior to the main mating period, and quarantined for a minimum of 30 days. Twice, equal numbers of wild-caught and captive-raised swift foxes were experimentally released at the same time and area.

Some swift foxes were radio-collared and monitored from the ground and from the air. At flight altitudes of 10 000 feet (about 3000 m), signals could be picked up for a distance of 20 km or less, while ground signals were picked up from distances of 1–3 km if the swift foxes were above ground. In the early

Fig. 10.2. Examples of two methods used to reintroduce swift foxes to the wild in the Canadian swift fox restoration. A. Soft release method. B. Hard release method. See text for details.

years, telemetry consisted almost entirely of ground searches, which by itself was inefficient. Later, aerial searches provided significantly more information. To determine survival in the main release area (Area 1), swift foxes were extensively live-trapped from 3 November to 7 December, 1990.

The population was also monitored through night lighting and scent station surveys. Searching for tracks, which requires favorable weather, and sign (scat) was useful for determining distribution, and gave some indication of abundance. Landowner and public sightings also provided useful information.

Live-trapping allowed field workers to replace expired radio collars, mark the young of the year to obtain recapture and productivity data, determine swift fox density, and identify male to female, wild born to released, and marked to unmarked ratios. A township (6 miles × 6 miles, or 9.6 km × 9.6 km) of prairie habitat, assumed to represent general conditions in the release area, was selected and spanned with Tomahawk live traps, constructed of wire mesh and approximately 38 cm wide × 38 cm high × 107 cm long. The traps were set in pairs every mile along six 9.6 km (6 mi) transects that were 9.6 km (6 mi) long and spaced 1.6 km (1 mi) apart. They were baited with road kills (usually jackrabbit) or meat scraps and 'sweetened' with sardines or bacon, set in late afternoon or evening along fence lines, trails, and cattle paths that swift foxes were likely to frequent, and checked early the next morning. To capture pups, however, four or five traps were set around the natal den.

Captured swift foxes were checked for body condition, tooth condition and wear, sex, markings, wounds, and external parasites. In some cases, ivermectin (which kills internal and external parasites) and vaccines against rabies, distemper, and other diseases were administered. Radio collars were replaced, removed, or put on as required, and unmarked foxes were marked in an ear; in early years the ears were notched, in later years they were tattooed.

Results and discussion

Survival of released swift foxes

A total of 569 swift foxes (Table 10.1) were released at three locations (Fig. 10.1). One hundred and thirty-six swift foxes were released on soft releases and 433 on hard releases. Here we define survival as 'minimal survival', that is, the total number of radio-collared swift foxes proven alive divided by the total number of radio-collared swift foxes. Some animals actually surviving may not have been detected for such reasons as failure of the radio-collar, or attenuation of the signal while the animal was in a burrow during critical survey intervals. Table 10.2 summarizes the survival of 200 soft- and hard-released radio-collared swift foxes for 6, 12 and 24 months after release. A breakdown of survival of hard-released foxes only is shown in Table 10.3 and Fig. 10.3. Fig. 10.4 shows survival if data are restricted to foxes with known status only.

Table 10.2. *Summary of survival of 200 radio-collared swift foxes for 6, 12 and 24 months*

Descending sample sizes reflect losses of radios to dispersal or radio failure. Survival is 'minimum survival'; the total number of collared swift foxes proven alive/total number of collared swift foxes.

Release method	Number radio collared	Survival		
		to 6 mo.	to 12 mo.	to 24 mo.
Soft	45	25/45 = 55%	14/45 = 31%	6/45 = 13%
Hard	155	52/155 = 34%	20/117 = 17%	5/43 = 12%

Table 10.3. *Survival of 155 hard-released radio-collared swift foxes*

Descending sample sizes reflect losses of radios to dispersal or radio failure. Survival is 'minimum survival'; the total number of collared swift foxes proven alive/total number of collared swift foxes.

Category	Live at 3 mo.	Live at 6 mo.	Live at 9 mo.	Live at 12 mo.
Wild-captured: spring & fall release	20/33 = 61%	17/33 = 52%	15/33 = 46%	9/19 = 47%
Captive-raised: spring & fall release	50/122 = 41%	35/122 = 29%	28/112 = 25%	11/98 = 11%
Captive-raised: spring release	7/41 = 17%	5/41 = 12%	3/41 = 7%	1/27 = 4%
Captive-raised: fall release	43/81 = 53%	30/81 = 37%	20/71 = 28%	10/71 = 14%

Wild-captured foxes were most successful with 47% surviving for one year. The next most successful foxes were those born in the release area with 33% surviving from age three months to twelve months. Captive-raised foxes released in the fall were more successful (14% survival) than captive raised spring releases (4% survival). This is surprising, as it was expected that swift foxes released in fall and facing winter would have a lower survival rate than would swift foxes first exposed to the wild in spring. It is possible that, since the fall-released swift foxes were younger and entered the wild at their natural dispersal time, they were better able to adapt to new situations. The spring-released swift foxes were held in captivity longer, and may therefore have had more trouble adjusting to the wild.

Trapping in a core area from 3 November to 7 December 1990 resulted in the capture of 41 swift foxes (19% trapping success in 215 trap nights). This compares favorably with 11% trapping success (205 trap nights) in an established population in Wyoming. Fourteen of the 41 swift foxes caught in the Alberta experimental program were marked, hence of released origin, and 27 swift foxes were unmarked. Eleven of the 27 unmarked swift foxes were young of the year. Most revealing was that three of the marked swift foxes had sur-

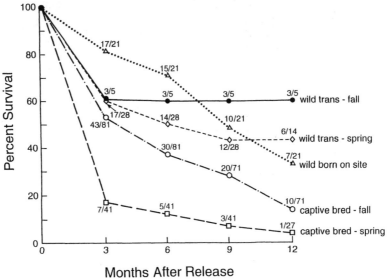

Fig 10.3. Survival of radio-collared foxes (total alive/total collared). Sample size decreases as time progresses, because some collared foxes were not in the program long enough to have reached this 12 month period.

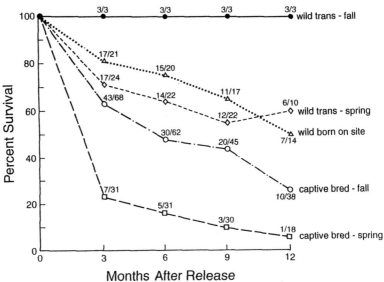

Fig. 10.4. Survival of radio-collared swift foxes that were released on "hard-"release programs from 1987 to 1991. Includes only animals of known status (live/live and dead); all collars of unknown status were deleted.

Table 10.4. *Survival of hard-released radio-collared swift foxes monitored in the Alberta–Saskatchewan border area and Wood Mountain area.*

Unk, status unknown.

Origin	Release Area	Date	Status 3 months post-release				Status 6 months post-release				Status 9 months post-release				Status 12 month post-release		
			Unk	Dead	Live	Total	Unk	Dead	Live	Total	Unk	Dead	Live	Total	Unk	Dead	Live
Wild Wyoming Transplants	Border area	Spring 1990	2	3	9	14	4	3	7	14	4	3	7	14	4	4	6
	Wood Mtn/Sk	Spring 1991	2	4	8	14	2	5	7	14	2	7	5	14	—	—	—
Total			4	7	17	28	6	8	14	28	6	10	12	28	4	4	6
Captive-raised	Border Area	Spring 1990	2	8	3	13	2	9	2	13	2	9	2	13	3	9	1
	Wood Mtn/Sk	Spring 1991	2	10	2	14	2	10	2	14	3	11	0	14	—	—	—
Total			4	18	5	27	4	19	4	27	5	20	2	27	3	9	1

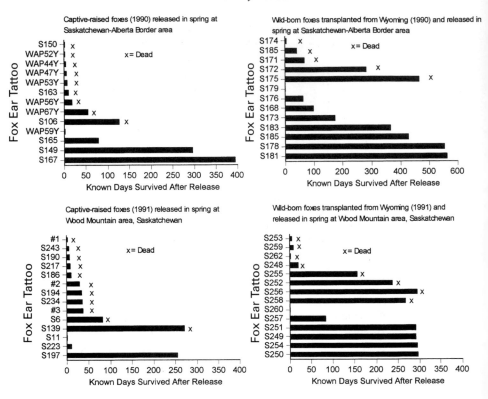

Fig. 10.5. Results from experimental releases on the survival of captive-raised versus wild swift foxes.

vived for 3.5 years, two for 2.5 years, one for 1.5 years, and two for half a year, indicating that current habitat conditions are still suitable.

Survival of wild-caught versus captive-raised swift foxes

In May 1990, fourteen wild-caught (captured in Wyoming in January 1990 and quarantined) and thirteen captive-raised swift foxes were simultaneously released near the Alberta and Saskatchewan border. In May 1991, fourteen wild-caught (captured in Wyoming in January 1991 and quarantined) and fourteen captive-raised swift foxes were simultaneously released in the Wood Mountain area, Saskatchewan. Their different survival rates (combining both years) are revealing (Fig. 10.5).

Five out of 27 (19%) captive-raised swift foxes were known to be alive three months after their release, compared to seventeen out of 28 (61%) for wild-caught Wyoming swift foxes (Table 10.4). Six months after their release, four out of 27

Table 10.5. *Summary of cause of death of 89*
hard-released swift foxes found during field
studies from 1987 to 1991.

Cause	Number	Percentage
Known coyote predation	28	32%
Suspected coyote predation	6	7%
Known badger predation	3	3%
Suspected badger predation	3	3%
Known avian predation	5	6%
Suspected avian predation	2	2%
Unknown predation	5	6%
Road kills	5	6%
Other - accidental death	2	2%
Unknown cause of death	30	34%
Total kills	89	101%

(15%) captive-raised swift foxes were known to be alive, compared with fourteen of the 28 (50%) wild-caught swift foxes. Nine months after their release, two out of 27 (7%) captive-raised swift foxes were known to be alive, compared with twelve out of 28 (43%) wild-caught swift foxes. Wild-caught swift foxes were clearly superior to captive-raised swift foxes in surviving the releases.

Causes of Mortality

Among the 89 animals found dead during hard-released swift fox monitoring from 1987 to 1991, predation, particularly by coyotes, clearly was the greatest cause of mortality (Table 10.5). Predation by any species accounted for 58% of mortality in the cases in which the carcasses were found. Road kills accounted for 6% of the deaths. The greatest proportion of deaths occurred within the first month after release (L. Mamo, unpublished data).

Dispersal

The mean dispersal distance of 162 radio-collared swift foxes (31 wild-caught from Wyoming, 110 captive-raised in Canada, and 21 wild-born in Canada) in both spring and fall in three release areas from 1987 to 1991 was 12.8 km (Table 10.6). Examples of unusually long distance dispersals (movements) were 70, 80, 165, and 190 km. Overall, the wild-caught swift foxes dispersed farther (mean of 19.2 km, $n = 31$) than the captive-raised swift foxes (mean of 12.6 km, $n = 110$). The high mortality of the spring-released captive-raised

Table 10.6. *Comparison of mean dispersal distances (km) of wild-caught (USA), wild-born (Canada), and captive-raised foxes.*

	Fall	Spring	Total
Wild (USA)	4.7 (N = 3)	20.8 (N = 28)	19.2 (N = 31)
Captive	11.4 (N = 76)	15.0 (N = 34)	12.6 (N = 111)
Wild (Canada)	—	—	4.3 (N = 21)
All foxes			12.8 (N = 162)

swift foxes within the first three months could explain this difference; some captive-raised swift foxes simply did not live long enough to move very far.

Considering only fall releases, the captive-raised swift foxes dispersed farther (11.4 km, *n* = 76) than the wild-caught swift foxes (4.7 km, *n* = 3). Given that only three wild-caught fall-released swift foxes were studied, the significance of this difference is questionable, but it does suggest that in fall, the wild-caught foxes were better able to obtain prey, find escape terrain, and avoid predation in the release area.

Both the wild-caught and the captive-raised swift foxes dispersed farther in spring than in fall. It is possible that food shortages in spring caused them to search farther afield. Insects, such as grasshoppers, are less available in the spring than in the fall. Captive-raised swift foxes also had their highest mortality when they were released in spring, but mortality did not similarly increase for wild-caught swift foxes. Evidently, compared to the captive-raised swift foxes, the wild-caught swift foxes could travel farther to a site of their own choosing with less risk of mortality. Experimental work may be required in the future to enhance survival of captive-raised foxes.

Intraspecific interactions could also have influenced the released swift foxes' dispersal. The wild-caught swift foxes dispersed farther in the border area between Alberta and Saskatchewan (24.6 km, *n* = 14), where there was already a small population of reintroduced swift foxes when they were released, than they did at Wood Mountain (16.8 km, *n* = 14), where there was no known swift fox population (Table 10.7). Captive-raised swift foxes, on the other hand, consistently dispersed farther at Wood Mountain than they did in the border area.

It is difficult to determine why swift foxes establish in particular areas. Wild-caught swift foxes consistently established in habitat that strongly resembled the open, flat or slightly rolling short grass prairie from which they originated. Captive-raised swift foxes had less consistent establishment patterns; some were found under buildings, some were found close to brushy areas, and some were found close to cultivated fields, roads, or human habitation.

Table 10.7. *A comparison of mean distance (km) moved by swift foxes in each release area*

	Fall Captive-raised	Spring Captive-raised	Spring Wild-caught
Alta/Sask. Border	10.9 ($N = 33$)	14.6 ($N = 12$)	24.6 ($N = 14$)
Wood Mtn. Sask.	13.5 ($N = 30$)	19.8 ($N = 12$)	16.8 ($N = 13$)
MRR (Knight/McInt.)	7.1 ($N = 13$)	9.6 ($N = 10$)	—

Reintroduced swift fox distribution

During the program, swift foxes reoccupied a minimum of 278 sections of land. To be considered reoccupied, an area had to have a proven swift fox record, such as a visual sighting, radio location, or an animal that had been trapped, shot, or killed on a highway.

The core area of occupation was within 32 km of the release sites, and the greatest known dispersal distance was 195 km. Some swift foxes moved south into northern Montana.

Population density

Extensive trapping throughout about 1196 km² in roughly thirteen townships from September to December 1991 resulted in the estimate that the area had 150–225 swift foxes. Although these figures are not precise, from this we estimated a density of about 1 swift fox per 5–8 km². With more precise saturation trapping, eleven swift foxes were caught in one township (92.16 km²), giving a density of 1 swift fox per 8.4 km².

Denning and social structure

From 1984 to 1991, observed litters ranged from one to seven pups. During this time, at least eleven pairs of swift foxes produced two or more litters. From 1987 to 1990, 108 radio-collared captive-raised and 19 radio-collared wild-caught swift foxes were released (approximately a 5:1 ratio). During 1991, seven of the eight surviving radio-collared wild-caught swift foxes produced a litter. Even though five times as many radio-collared captive-raised swift foxes had been released, only five of them bred in 1991.

The most natal dens ($n = 18$) were found in the spring of 1991. Locating natal

Table 10.8. *Origins of known 1991 breeding pairs*

The origin of at least one swift fox in a pair was known

	Soft-release	Hard release	Wild-caught	Wild-born
1991	1*	7 (5 radio-collared)	7	10

*Born in a soft release pen of adults that were soft-released.

dens was greatly assisted by live-trapping and radio-collaring 34 swift foxes during the winter of 1990–91, and following them back to their natal dens during the summer of 1991. That year had a particularly wet spring, limiting the accessibility of the denning sites, and it is believed that, in the Saskatchewan and Alberta border area, there were at least twice as many natal dens as could be found. Litters in which the young were seen above ground in August averaged 4.2 pups (for twelve pairs having a total of fifty pups). Of the 25 parent swift foxes of known origin, seven were wild-caught, seven were captive-raised hard releases (five of which had radio collars), one was a captive-raised soft release, and ten were the offspring of swift foxes born in the release area (Table 10.8).

Although determining the details of social structure will require further research, preliminary observations indicate that swift foxes are not territorial yet cluster in areas of prime habitat. In thousands of hours of ground tracking, no evidence indicated that other individuals used mated pairs' natal dens (C. Mamo, personal observation). Swift foxes in a newly released, newly established population were essentially monogamous. In winter, individuals tended to move over larger areas, presumably because food was less available than in summer or because of mating activities. There was some evidence that neighboring swift foxes used each other's satellite dens. Males were not observed at the natal dens during whelping, but were there sometime after whelping.

In 54 dens observed, there was no evidence of supernumerary or 'helping' females associated with the raising of young, although this is quite common among smaller canids (Moehlman 1989). A matrilineal 'helping' society is possible, particularly in established populations. Such appears to have been the case, for example, in a study of radio-collared swift foxes in southeastern Colorado (D. Covell, personal communication).

In this study, there was evidence that a swift fox may associate with more than one other swift fox at a time, indicating a flexible mating system. For example, along the Saskatchewan–Alberta border area during the winter of 1990–91, there were three occasions in which three swift foxes were live-trapped at the same location:

1) Three females were captured at the same location two days apart. The first, caught on 5 November 1990, was unmarked, and believed to have been wild-born the previous year. Two others were caught on 7 November 1990 within 300 m of each other. One had been born in captivity in May 1989 and released in September 1989, and the other was unmarked and believed to have been wild-born in 1990.

2) On 6 November 1990, two females were captured approximately 400 m from each other. One was an adult (born May 1987 in captivity) that had been released in September 1987 about 10 km from where she was trapped. The other had been born in May 1990 and released in September 1990 approximately 26 km from where she was trapped. On 7 November 1990, a male was captured in the same trap as the younger female. He had been captured in Wyoming in February 1988 and released in September 1988.

3) Two unmarked males (presumed wild-born in the study area) were caught within about 0.5 km of each other on 6 December 1990. On 7 December 1990, an adult marked female (born and released in 1987) was caught in the same trap as one of the males from the previous night. All three were radio-collared. The movements of one male were followed for 223 days; he remained within 2–3 km of the area where he was caught. His collar failed, but on 6 March 1991, he was found with an uncollared female.

Conclusions

To reintroduce the swift fox to the Canadian prairies, it was necessary to determine if its ecological niche was still present and if a minimum viable population, in which reproduction is high enough to match or exceed mortality over a reasonable period of time and through stochastic risks, could be established.

After an approximately 50-year absence, the species can still survive in what is left of the once expansive Canadian prairie ecosystem. That the Canadian reintroduction program has established a core population of an estimated 150–225 swift foxes, in which some have survived for up to four years and some have reproduced, indicates that the habitat is still suitable. That some are spreading into new areas indicates that natural repopulation has likely been prevented by some type of barrier, rather than by poor dispersal ability or by repeated failure of established populations. The degree to which new populations become established will be a measure of the species' ability to cope at the extreme edge of its range.

Whether or not a minimum viable population has been established, however, is open to question, because the impact of stochastic events is unknown. In a drought year, for example, scarce winter food resources may be limiting.

The summer of 1988 was particularly dry and was followed by a moderate to severe winter; swift fox survival and reproduction were lower in this than in other years. The effects of drought are especially important in the light of potential long-term climate change. Additionally, it is not certain that the factors that originally caused the demise of this species in its northern range have been eliminated and will not recur.

The Canadian reintroduction program experimented with various reintroduction and monitoring techniques, and the results could be instructive for other reintroduction projects. For example, Foose (1991) writes of captive breeding and reintroduction programs, 'it is often difficult to be numerate because so little quantitative data on population sizes and distribution exists'. We found that radio collaring and trapping gave us reasonable confidence in determining the lower population limits of the reintroduced swift foxes. Some swift foxes may have dispersed out of the range of our field operations, in which case they are more numerous than our data indicate.

We also found that the captive breeding portion of the project was vital in gaining political and institutional support for the project, but that the wild-born and wild-caught swift foxes had better survival and reproduction than the captive-raised swift foxes. Of the captive-raised swift foxes, those released around the time that they would naturally disperse, in fall, survived better than those released in spring.

Another benefit of the Canadian reintroduction program has been the opportunity to study swift fox social structure. Although a great deal remains to be learned, we conclude that the species is not strictly monogamous, but can be found in groups of several animals, as can red foxes and other smaller canids (MacDonald 1981, Moehlman 1989). Because the population has just recently been established, its members might interact differently from those of saturated populations.

The Canadian reintroduction program's objective is to reintroduce a species to an area where it once existed, and its legal status is irrelevant within this context. The restoration of this appealing species to the Canadian prairies from which it has been extirpated has broad public impetus and support. It can symbolize the importance of protecting and managing whole ecosystems, on behalf of all their components.

Acknowledgments

Reintroduction programs are often high-publicity, high-risk ventures producing extra organizational stress. The human factor becomes paramount, and we would like to thank the literally hundreds of volunteers, participants, and cooperators. Although there is not enough space to recognize them all, we would be remiss if we did not acknowledge the very crucial involvement of the Recovery Team. Steve Brechtel was instrumental in supervising the Alberta portion of the program, and Dale Hjertaas supervised the Saskatchewan portion. Roger Edwards, Chief, Endangered Species, Canadian Wildlife Service, Western and Northern Region, provided much needed support throughout the study. Ranchers, particularly Mary Jane and Leonard Pietrowski, were most helpful.

Kelly Sturgess was an effective field worker. D. S. Fitzgerald, John Sharps, and the Wyoming Game and Fish Department helped to acquire wild swift foxes. The Calgary Zoo staff was supportive in a number of ways, and we are particularly grateful to Pam McDougall for keeping records of the captive animals and to veterinarians Sandy Black and Sue Mainka. Roy Dyke analyzed reproduction in captive swift foxes and allowed us to use unpublished data. The staff of the various captive breeding facilities, particularly P. Rhodes and C. Smeeton, were enthusiastic participants and important to the program. Mona Regnier typed the manuscript. The program was funded by the Canadian Wildlife Service, Alberta Fish and Wildlife, World Wildlife Fund Canada, Petro Canada, Esso Resources, Swift Fox Conservation Society, Alberta Recreation Parks and Wildlife, Canadian National Sportsman's Show, Elsa Foundation, Grant McEwan Native Foundation, and Canadian Automobile Association, through the auspices of the Swift Fox Conservation Society, a non-profit organization; and from thousands of schoolchildren and other participants in an 'adopt-a-fox' program.

Literature cited

Allen, J. A. (1870) Notes on the mammals of Iowa. *Proceedings of the Boston Society of Natural History*, **13**, 178–94.

Anderson, R. M. (1947) Catalogue of Canadian recent mammals. *Bulletin of the Natural Museum of Canada*, **102**, 1–238.

Bailey, V. (1926) A biological survey of North Dakota. *North American Fauna*, **49**, 1–226. USDA Biological Survey, Washington, D.C.

Banfield, A. W. F. (1974) *The Mammals of Canada*. Toronto, Ontario: University of Toronto Press.

Best, T. L. (1971) Notes on the distribution and ecology of five eastern New Mexico mammals. *Southeast Naturalist*, **16**, 210–11.

Bowles, J. B. (1975) Distribution and biogeography of mammals of Iowa. *Special Publication, Museum, Texas Tech. University*, **9**, 1–84.

Cahalane, V. H. (1947) *Mammals of North America*. New York: Macmillan.

Carbyn, L. N. & Killaby, M. (1989) Status of the Swift Fox in Saskatchewan. *Blue Jay*, **47**, 41–52.

Carbyn, L. N., Brechtel, S., Hjertaas, D. & Mamo, C. (1993) An update on the swift fox reintroduction program in Canada. In *Proceedings of the Third Prairie Conservation and Endangered Species Workshop*, ed. Holroyd, G. L. & Dickson, H. L., pp. 366–72. *Natural History Occasional Papers* (**19**). Edmonton: Provincial Museum of Alberta.

Carlington, B. (1980) Reintroduction of the swift fox (*Vulpes velox*) to the Canadian prairies. Master's Thesis, Calgary: University of Calgary.

Chambers, G. D. (1978) Little fox on the prairie. *Audubon,* **80**(4), 62–71.

Cutter, W. L. (1958) Denning of the swift fox in northern Texas. *Journal of Mammalogy*, **39**, 70–4.

Davis, W. B. (1974) The Mammals of Texas. *Bulletin of the Texas Parks and Wildlife Department*, **41**, 1–294.

Dragoo, J. W., Choate, R., Yates, L. & O'Farell, T. P. (1990) Evolutionary and taxonomic relationships among North American arid-land foxes. *Journal of Mammalogy,* **71**, 318–32.

Egoscue, H. J. (1962) Ecology and life history of the kit fox in Toole County, Utah. *Ecology,* **43**, 481–97.

Egoscue, H. J. (1975) Population dynamics of the kit fox in western Utah. *Bulletin of the Southern California Academy of Sciences*, **74**, 122–7.

Egoscue, H. J. (1979) Vulpes velox. *Mammalian Species*, **122**, 1–5.

FaunaWest Wildlife Consultants. (1991) *An Ecological and Taxonomic Review of the Swift Fox (Vulpes velox) with a Special Reference to Montana.* Summary prepared for Montana Department Fish, Wildlife and Parks. Bozeman: Montana Department for Fish, Wildlife and Parks.

Foose, T. (1991) Captive breeding specialist group action plans. *Captive Breeding Specialist Group Newsletter*, **2**, 5–7.

Glass, B. P. (1959) Status of the kit fox (Vulpes velox) in the high plains. *Proceedings of the Oklahoma Academy of Science*, **37**, 162–3.

Hall, E. R. (1981) *The Mammals of North America.* Volume 2. pp. 601–1181. New York: John Wiley and Sons.

Herrero, S., Mamo, C., Carbyn, L. & Scott-Brown, M. (1991) Swift fox reintroduction into Canada. In *Proceedings of the 2nd Endangered Species & Prairie Conservation Workshop*, ed. Holroyd, G. & Smith, H., *Provincial Museum of Alberta Natural History Occasional Paper*, **15**, 246–52.

Hillman, C. N. & Sharps, J. C. (1978) Return of swift fox to northern great plains. *Proceedings of the South Dakota Academy of Science*, **57**, 154–62.

Hines, T. (1980) An ecological study of *Vulpes velox* in Nebraska. Master's thesis, Lincoln: University of Nebraska.

James, E. (1823) *Account of an expedition from Pittsburg to the Rocky Mountains performed in the years 1819 and 1820 under the command of Major S.H. Long.* 2 vols. Philadephia: Carey & Lea.

Johnson, D. R. (1969) Returns of the American Fur Company, 1835–1839. *Journal of Mammalogy*, **50**, 836–9.

Jones, J. K., Jr. (1964) Distribution and taxonomy of mammals of Nebraska. *University of Kansas Museum of Natural History Publication*, **16**, 252–4.

Kilgore, D. L. (1969) An ecological study of the swift fox (Vulpes velox) in the Oklahoma panhandle. *American Midland Naturalist*, **81**, 512–34.

Kleiman, D. (1989) Reintroduction of captive mammals for conservation. *BioScience*, **39**, 152–61.

Lindberg, M. (1986) *Swift fox distribution in Wyoming: A biogeographical study.* Master's thesis, Laramie: University of Wyoming.

Long, C. A. (1965) The mammals of Wyoming. *University of Kansas Museum of Natural History Publication*, **14**, 493–758.

MacDonald, D. W. (1981) Resource dispersion and the social organization of the red fox, *Vulpes vulpes*. In *Proceedings of the Worldwide Furbearer Conference*, ed. Chapman, J. A. & Ursley, D., pp. 918–49. Frostburg: Worldwide Furbearer Conference.

MacFarlane, R. (1905) Notes on mammals collected and observed in the northern Mackenzie River District, Northwest Territories of Canada, with remarks on explorers and explorations of the far north. *Proceedings of the U.S. National Museum*, **28**, 704.

Martin, E. P. & Sternberg, G. F. (1955) A swift fox, Vulpes velox velox (Say) from western Kansas. *Transactions of the Kansas Academy of Science*, **58**, 345–6.

Merriam, C. H. (1902) Three new foxes of the kit and desert fox groups. *Proceedings of the Biological Society of Washington*, **15**, 73–4.

Miller, G. S. Jr. & Kellogg, R. (1955) List of North American recent mammals. *Bulletin of the United States National Museum*, **205**, 1–954.

Moehlman, P. (1989) Intraspecific variations in canid social systems. In *Carnivore Behaviour, Ecology and Evolution*, ed. Gittleman, J., pp. 143–63. Ithaca: Cornell University Press.

Moore, R. E. & Martin, N. S. (1980) A recent record of the swift fox (*Vulpes velox*) in Montana. *Journal of Mammalogy*, **61**, 161.

O'Farrell, T. P. (1983) *The San Joaquin Kit Fox Recovery Plan*. Portland: United States Fish and Wildlife Service.

Pattimore, G. (1985) The feasibility of reintroducing the swift fox to southern Manitoba. Master's thesis. Winnipeg: University of Manitoba.

Pfeifer, W. K. & Hibbard, E. A. (1970) A recent record of the swift fox (*Vulpes velox*) in North Dakota. *Journal of Mammalogy*, **51**, 835.

Rand, A. L. (1948) Mammals of the eastern Rockies and western plains of Canada. *National Museum of Canada Bulletin*, **108**, 1–237.

Scott-Brown, J. M., Herrero, S. & Reynolds, J. (1987) Swift fox. In *Wild Furbearer Conservation and Management in North America*, ed. Novak, M., Baker, J. A., Obbard, M. E. & Malloch, B., pp. 432–41. Toronto: Ontario Ministry of Natural Resources.

Seabloom, R. W., Crawford, R. D. & McKenna, M. G. (1978) *Vertebrates of southwestern North Dakota: Amphibians, Reptiles, Birds, Mammals*. Institute of Ecology Studies, University of North Dakota. Research Report 24. North Dakota: University of North Dakota.

Seton, E. T. (1909) Kit fox or swift. *Life Histories of Northern Animals; an Account of the Mammals of Manitoba*, Vol. 2, pp. 700–705. New York: Charles Scribner's & Sons.

Seton, E. T. (1937) *Lives of Game Animals*. New York: Literary Guild of America.

Smeeton, M. (1984) *Completely Foxed*. Toronto: Key Porter Press.

Soper, J. D. (1961) The mammals of Manitoba. *Canadian Field Naturalist*, **75**, 171–219.

Soper, J. D. (1964) *The Mammals of Alberta*. Edmonton: The Hamley Press Ltd.

Stromberg, M. R. & Boyce, M. S. (1986) Systematics and conservation of the swift fox *Vulpes velox* in North America. *Biological Conservation*, **35**, 97–110.

US Fish and Wildlife Service. (1979) *Federal Register*, 17 June, 1979, p. 3638. Washington, D.C.: National Archives and Record Service.

US Fish and Wildlife Service. (1982) *Federal Register*, 30 December, 1982, pp. 58454–60. Washington, D.C.: National Archives and Record Service.

Van Ballenberghe, V. (1975) Recent records of the swift fox (*Vulpes velox*) in South Dakota. *Journal of Mammalogy*, **56**, 525.

World Wildlife Fund Canada. (1988) *Prairie Conservation Action Plan: 1989–1994*. Toronto: World Wildlife Fund.

Zoellick, B. & Smith, N. S. (1992) Size and spatial organization of home ranges of kit foxes in Arizona. *Journal of Mammalogy*, **73**, 83–8.

11

Restoration of the endangered black-footed ferret: a 20-year overview

TIM W. CLARK

Introduction

The black-footed ferret (*Mustela nigripes*) is one of the world's most critically endangered mammals. Until about 1920, the carnivorous ferret occupied nearly 40 million ha over 12 Great Plains and Rocky Mountain states and two Canadian provinces. Agricultural interests and federal and state rodent control programs drastically eliminated ferret habitat–prairie dog (*Cynomys* spp.) colonies (the 'prairie dog ecosystem', Clark, Hinckley & Rich 1989b)–and fragmented the remainder into small patches, thus rendering isolated ferret populations highly vulnerable to extinction from various causes, including local catastrophes. Extensive searches in the late 1970s yielded no ferrets, and they were feared extinct, but in 1981 a small population was found near Meeteetse in northwestern Wyoming. By early 1986, only about ten individual ferrets were known, four in the wild and six in a single captive breeding facility. Fortunately, as of January, 1992, there were 175 ferrets in six captive breeding facilities, and 49 ferrets had been introduced to the wild. There is every reason to believe that the ferret will eventually be restored to the wild in viable numbers and distributions. Overviews of the ferret and prairie dog conservation and management effort are given by Casey, DuWaldt & Clark (1986), Clark (1986a), and Reading & Clark (1990).

The ferret's conservation history has been complex and unpromising. Both the ferret and determination of its critical habitat ranked very high in the first US Redbook of Endangered Wildlife in 1964, and again in a US Fish and Wildlife Service list of endangered species priorities in 1976. By 1980, the ferret was presumed gone from much, if not all, of its former range and was generally considered 'unrecoverable', a euphemism for extinct or nearly so, by the US Fish and Wildlife Service (FWS). In late 1981, a ferret population was found near Meeteetse, Wyoming. Conservationists viewed the Meeteetse ferrets as the hoped-for opportunity to recover the species. In this chapter, I give an account of the background and history of the species, and briefly review ferret restoration efforts based on the Meeteetse population. The review is generally chronological and summarizes work over 20 years. This history of the Meeteetse ferrets is based on numerous research papers, and on plans written by my colleagues and me beginning in 1981, the FWS ferret recovery plan (Forrest & Biggins 1987), the Wyoming Department of Game and Fish (WGF) and National Zoo ferret captive breeding plan (Ballou & Oakleaf 1987), and the WGF (1991) reintroduction plan.

Historical background

Species account

The black-footed ferret (Mustelidae) is the only ferret native to North America (Linder & Hillman 1973, Hillman & Clark 1980) and is one of about 14 living species of *Mustela*. No subspecies of *M. nigripes* has been recognized. The steppe or Siberian ferret or polecat (*M. eversmanni*) of Eurasia is its nearest living relative (Anderson *et al.* 1986). The historic range of the ferret is similar to that of prairie dogs, its main prey. The ferret was widespread and at least locally abundant, if not common, throughout much of its former range.

Large-scale, government-sponsored programs to eradicate prairie dogs, which began about 1915, are considered the major cause of the ferret's demise. These programs continue today, though on a smaller scale. Although prairie dogs still occupy much of their former range, their numbers are but a minute fraction of those that existed about 1920.

Black-footed ferret litters average about 3.3 (range 1 to 5), and gestation is about 45 days (Hillman & Carpenter 1980). Young first appear above ground in July. All observations suggest a high rate of either emigration or mortality from habitat loss, disease, human-related causes, and predation.

History of study

Ferrets showed up in fur-bearer traps in the 1830s (Johnson 1969), but the species was not described until 1851 (Audubon & Bachman 1851), and the first full account of the species was published in 1877 (Coues 1877). The first ferret population to be studied scientifically was in Mellette County, South Dakota; this population died out by 1974. About 90 individuals, including 11 litters, were observed over 11 years, and nine ferrets were taken into captivity (Hillman & Linder 1973). The first efforts to breed ferrets in the late 1960s and early 1970s were unsuccessful, although much was learned about ferret biology. Searches for ferrets elsewhere were unsuccessful. Nevertheless, the FWS established a recovery team in hopes of locating additional ferrets. Ferret history is given by Clark (1989).

The Meeteetse, Wyoming, ferrets

The Wyoming ferrets were discovered on 26 September 1981, near the town of Meeteetse, Park County, in the Big Horn Basin (Clark & Campbell 1981). Study of and recovery efforts for the Meeteetse ferrets began almost immediately (USFWS 1983, Clark 1983). Several federal, state, and non-governmental organizations were involved in ferret restoration efforts. State officials quickly bureaucratized the overall effort under their direct control. As a result, the program was conflict-laden and many problems ensued (see Clark & Westrum 1987; Clark & Harvey 1988; Clark, Crete & Cada 1989a, Thorne & Oakleaf 1991). It is therefore unlikely that a single comprehensive history of the Meeteetse ferret studies acceptable to all interests will be written, but it is hoped that all major interests will write a ferret history from their perspectives for comparison.

Two major program goals were identified (Clark 1981, 1984) (Table 11.1): a conservation goal and a recovery goal. This recovery scenario called for: 1) maximizing the number of Meeteetse-derived ferrets, 2) maintaining ferrets at Meeteetse as a 'nursery' (an outdoor captive breeding site), 3) maximizing the number of prairie dogs at Meeteetse, 4) maximizing the captive rearing opportunities at indoor sites at the earliest possible date, and 5) minimizing costs and time at Meeteetse and of captive rearing and reintroductions (Maguire & Clark 1985).

Initial field work included acquiring key information about the health of the Meeteetse ferret population and widening searches for other ferrets near Meeteetse, in other areas, and in other states. If a 'surplus' of young appeared each fall after only 2 or 3 years' study, they would be captured, used in captive rearing programs, and their offspring reintroduced to the wild to establish additional protected wild populations (Clark 1989). In this scenario, ferrets could have been well on the road to full recovery in five or so years from the date they were first located. If more ferrets were found elsewhere, they would accelerate the species' recovery. Simultaneously, the necessary management protection of the wild Meeteetse ferret population and any other ferret populations would be forthcoming (Clark 1987).

A well-planned but flexible data acquisition program (planning via feedback or 'adaptive management', Holling 1978) was planned (Clark 1981, 1984); it aimed to avoid disturbing the ferrets, maximize data, and provide the basis for

Table 11.1. *Conservation and recovery goals for the Meeteetse, Wyoming,*
black-footed ferrets (after Clark 1981, 1984, 1989)

1. **Conservation Goal.** To assure the long-term persistence of the Wyoming ferret population and the natural communities it requires under conditions providing for potential adaptation.
A. Where are the ferrets?
B. How well are they doing?
C. What are the immediate threats to the ferrets and their habitat?
D. What management guidelines are needed?

2. **Recovery Goal.** To restore ferret numbers to at least 500 genetically effective individuals in the wild and captive populations over a broad geographic area. A genetically effective population of 500 may be adequate to accommodate continuing evolution (Frankel & Soulé 1981).
A. Do additional populations exist?
B. Are surplus ferrets produced annually in the known population?
C. Are transplant or captive breeding sites or options available for relocation of surplus ferrets?
D. What are long-term management needs?

cooperative studies. But this approach came into conflict with Wyoming state officials, who wanted the program under their control via bureaucratic and political oversight. It is beyond the scope of this chapter, which emphasizes the biological dimension of ferret restoration, to detail these kinds of problems, but they permeated the entire program and reduced its overall effectiveness and efficiency. This will be addressed in detail in subsequent publications by various authors.

Ultimately, data on the Meeteetse ferrets were obtained, conservation and recovery plans were devised, and the appropriate, timely use of information and plans was encouraged. Field methods included snow-tracking, spotlighting, capture–recapture, direct observation, radio-tagging, and environmental, habitat, and prey studies (Clark *et al.* 1984a, Biggins *et al.* 1986, Forrest *et al.* 1988).

Ferret population viability assessment

Prior to the study, the Meeteetse ferrets were expected to occur in low numbers and limited habitat as a result of past and perhaps ongoing systematic extinction pressures. In addition, they were considered to be highly susceptible to extinction from demographic, genetic, and environmental stochastic events. Given these considerations and the initially limited information about ferret demographics, behavior, and habitat requirements, selective, careful, timely conservation research, focused on understanding those key aspects of ferret biology needed to recover the species, was necessary (Clark 1989). This included estimating the population's viability based on the ferrets' paleobiology, biogeography, and systematics; population characteristics; genetics; behavior and activity patterns; and habitat and environmental relationships.

Ferret paleobiology, biogeography, and systematics

A first component in the overall effort was determining ferret history and systematics. Ferrets crossed the Bering Land Bridge, entered North America, and spread southward through ice-free corridors into the Great Plains about 100 000 years Before Present (BP) (Anderson *et al.* 1986). The colonization rate is estimated to have been 7.5 km per year, or 750 km per century. Pleistocene and Holocene North American faunas show ferret remains (N=21). Eight Native American tribes are known to have used ferrets in modern times (Henderson, Springer & Adrian 1969, Clark 1975).

Of 412 specimens in museums, at least 103 were killed by federal predator and rodent control personnel, and at least 41 were taken alive and held in captivity. About 1920, prairie dogs occupied about 41 900 000 ha (Nelson 1919). If ferrets then occurred at densities of 1 per 40–60 ha, as seen at Meeteetse (Forrest *et al.* 1985a), or at 1 per 37 ha, as seen in South Dakota in 1964–74 (Hillman, Linder & Dahlgren 1979), then a minimum of 500,000 to 1 million ferrets lived at that time.

Ferret systematics were investigated by Anderson *et al.* (1986), who examined 68 mammal collections and measured 120 recent skulls (72 of known sex) and 17 skeletons. Fifty-five Pleistocene and Holocene fossils and one skeleton of the Siberian ferret were also examined. Meeteetse ferret remains were compared to ferret specimens from other locations and shown to be similar, with no basis for subspecific designations. More recently, C. Mullen *et al.* (unpublished data) were unable to find any evidence of fluctuating skeletal asymmetry in ferrets as an indication of development stress brought about by inbreeding.

Ferret population characteristics

A second component in ferret recovery was estimating ferret population characteristics. Important considerations included distribution, numbers, density, age and sex structure, natality, emigration and immigration, and mortality (Forrest *et al.* 1985a, b, 1988, Clark 1984, 1989). These attributes are summarized in this section.

Upon the discovery of a single ferret in September 1981, researchers immediately sought the wild population from which it originated. Prairie dog colonies in the region were systematically surveyed seasonally and yearly for sight and sign of ferrets. Techniques included repeated snow-tracking, spotlighting, and searches for skeletal remains, scats, and ferret diggings. Ferrets were found to live in an area containing 37 white-tailed prairie dog (*C. leucurus*) colonies. These colonies were dynamic, reflecting yearly changes in prairie dog populations. The prairie dog–ferret complex covered 126 km², or about 11% of the surface area of the region. In 1982, the region contained 3000 ha of live prairie dog colonies and 5400 ha of identifiable inactive colonies (Clark 1986a). Other evidence suggests there may have been over 30 000 ha of prairie dogs in the 1930s, when large-scale prairie dog poisoning programs began.

From 1981 through 1985, at least 282 different ferrets were observed. Minimum ferret numbers, based on spotlighting, were 61 in 1982, 88 in 1983, 129 in 1984, and 58 in 1985. In 1986, 14 or 15 ferrets were seen (B. Miller, personal communication). The 1982 total is not comparable to other years because of the limited search effort; not all of the 37 colonies had been located and mapped. Forrest *et al.* (1988) estimated the 1982 numbers at between 79 and 99, median 89. The 1982, 1983, and 1984 population counts contrasted markedly with the early August 1985 spotlight count of 58, which declined over the fall of 1985 (Forrest *et al.* 1988). By early 1987, the Meeteetse wild population was extinct.

The mark–recapture population estimate each fall in 1983, 1984, and 1985 was similar to the count from each summer's spotlighting (Forrest *et al.* 1988). In 1985, repeated mark–recapture estimates showed a dramatic and consistent decline in ferret numbers: in early August, spotlighting revealed 58 ferrets, and on 1 November, about 6 ferrets. Data showed that the low 1985 ferret numbers could not be attributed to successful dispersal. There were no large unoccupied prairie dog colonies nearby for ferrets to colonize; therefore, if any ferrets had dispersed, they were at great risk of dying. In addition to these population estimates, 12 ferrets were taken into captivity (in two groups of six each) between early October and 1 November 1985. As will be discussed, the first group all later died of canine distemper (*Morbilivirus*). The second group composed the captive breeding nucleus in 1986.

The 10 colonies that supported only one ferret averaged 49.1 ha (Forrest *et al.* 1985a). The smallest prairie dog colonies at Meeteetse supporting ferret litters were 49.0 ha and 51.1 ha. Of the 11 litters found in South Dakota, six were on colonies 40 ha or larger (Hillman *et al.* 1979). The two sites contained white-tailed and black-tailed prairie dogs, respectively, with black-tails usually showing greater densities.

Each August, the population was composed of about 67% juveniles and 33% adults. Sex ratios were 1.0 males : 1.0 females for juveniles about four months postpartum based on live trapping (n=83), and 0.4 males : 1.0 females for adults based on spotlighting surveys (n=112) (Forrest *et al.* 1988). Litter sizes were estimated by counting numbers of young in each litter that came above ground during July and August. Litter sizes at birth in the wild are unknown. From 1982 through 1985, 68 litters were found, and litter sizes ranged from one to five, with a mean of 3.3 (SD=0.89). Mean litter sizes were similar each year, with a slight drop in 1985. In 1986, only two litters, of five apiece, were found (B. Miller, personal communication).

The largest class of annual movements occurred in juveniles from September to late October (Forrest *et al.* 1985a, 1988, Biggins *et al.* 1988). Intercolony movements were documented for 10 juveniles (7 males and 3 females); movements of 2 to 3 km were common. Large numbers of ferrets disappeared each year from mortality and emigration (Forrest *et al.* 1988), but between fall 1984 and fall 1985 about 150 ferrets disappeared – a catastrophic event! For one colony, the disappearance rate of all ferrets in 1982–83 was 69%; in 1983–84 it was 53%; in 1984–85 it was 86% (Forrest *et al.* 1988). The longest-lived ferret was a male more than three years old; several ferrets lived past two years.

The large population decline in 1985 was attributed to canine distemper, probably introduced into the ferret population by native carnivores: raccoons (*Procyon lotor*), skunks (*Mephitis mephitis*), red foxes (*Vulpes vulpes*), coyotes (*Canis latrans*) or one of the other common native carnivores. This disease is 100% fatal to ferrets (Carpenter *et al.* 1976, Carpenter & Hillman 1978, Thorne & Williams 1988). Sylvatic plague in the prairie dog population may have contributed to the ferrets' demise.

The population characteristics discussed above were used to assess ferret population viability in demographic, environmental, and genetic simulation models. These viability models estimated persistence of the Meeteetse ferrets and provided a basis for estimating population sizes needed as recovery targets. Harris, Clark & Shaffer (1989) constructed a demographic and environmental stochastic simulation model for ferrets based largely on the Meeteetse population data. The computer simulations considered most realistic demonstrated that about 120 animals were required for a greater than 95% probability of ferret populations persisting 100 years. These results indicated that, because of its small size, the Meeteetse ferret population was at considerable risk of extinction.

Ferret population genetic considerations

A third component important in ferret recovery was estimating the Meeteetse ferrets' genetic status. Kilpatrick, Forrest & Clark (1986) tried to estimate their genetic diversity by analyzing saliva samples from 22 ferrets. Absence of genetic variation may be the result of a recent genetic 'bottleneck', or may be typical for carnivores. O'Brien *et al.* (1989) examined tissues from both black-footed and Siberian ferrets and concluded that the Meeteetse ferrets showed a low level of genetic diversity, that *Mustela nigripes* is distinct from *M. eversmanni*, and that the two species separated genetically about 0.5 to 2 million years ago.

Using Lehmkuhl's (1984) equations, Groves & Clark (1986) calculated that the N_e/N ratio (ratio of genetically effective population to census population) for a ferret population is 0.23. Brussard & Gilpin (1989) estimated the N_e/N ratio to be 0.25. Thus the Meeteetse ferrets, with a breeding population of about 30 from 1982 to 1985, were subject to inbreeding and genetic drift. Lacy & Clark (1989) examined the genetic consequences of rarity in general, and in the Meeteetse ferret population in particular, and concluded that because of random genetic drift, ferrets probably lost 37–84% of the heterozygosity that was present in the population prior to 1935. Evidence suggests that the Meeteetse ferrets had initially low genetic diversity. Thus, the few remaining ferrets are probably highly inbred, and may display a very low adaptability to changing environments and have low resistance to disease. If true, how this loss will ultimately affect species recovery and persistence remains to be tested.

Ferret behavior and activity patterns

A fourth component in ferret recovery was understanding ferret behavior and activities. At least 282 individual ferrets were observed for 243 hours from 1981 through 1985 (Clark *et al.* 1986b). Maintenance behaviors (locomotion, alert, grooming, sunning, defecation, urination, digging, and predation) and social behavior (population, ontogeny, maternal, play, agonistic) were described, as well as some ferret–human interactions. Ferret predatory behavior observed in summer suggested that killing behavior was stereotyped and followed a typical mustelid neck-biting (e.g., throat) pattern. In winter, ferrets spent a high percentage of foraging time searching for prey. Prey were probably consumed in the burrows where kills were made, although snow marks indicated that ferrets dragged at least some prairie dog carcasses to other burrows (Richardson *et al.* 1987). Play, seen both day and night and common in July, was the most observed social behavior. Object play, autoplay, and social play (approach/withdrawal and rough-and-tumble) were common.

When spotlighted, ferrets generally oriented toward the light and stayed in or near burrows. When approached on foot, they retreated to burrows. Juveniles were more shy than adults. Ferrets were readily located during most months, especially in summer. In July, above-ground activity peaked at 0330 to 0400, while activity of litters peaked at 2200 and 0330. Although largely nocturnal, ferrets were observed above ground until 1200. Weather did not appear to limit ferret activities; ferrets were active at -39 °C, and in snow, rain, and winds to 50 kph (Clark et al. 1986b, Biggins et al. 1986).

Ferrets were snow tracked from 1981 through 1984. Richardson et al. (1987) reported that 170 complete ferret track routes averaged 1406 m (SE=109.2, range 2 to 6908) and that mean track length differed by month, increasing from December through March. Ferrets changed their direction of travel frequently. Ferrets tracked for 3–10 consecutive days were inactive an average of 34% of all track nights. Richardson et al. (1987) reported nightly ferret activity areas ranging from 0.4 to 136.6 ha. A sample of 149 nightly ferret track routes demonstrated that ferrets encountered an average of 68 burrow openings (SE=6.1) per night (Clark et al. 1984b).

Stromberg, Rayburn & Clark (1983) constructed a ferret–prairie dog predator–prey model prior to the discovery of ferrets at Meeteetse. At the time, little was known of ferret-prairie dog population interactions, and no ferrets were available for direct study. The model estimated that 167–355 ha of white-tailed prairie dog colonies would be required to sustain annual predation by a female ferret and young, but in fact, the Meeteetse ferrets occurred at about one per 50 ha of prairie dog colonies.

Powell et al. (1985) estimated ferret winter energy expenditure and prey requirements at Meeteetse by constructing an additive model that indicated that each ferret at Meeteetse required 20 prairie dogs during December through March. During summer months, lactating females might require several times this number of prairie dogs.

Miller extensively studied captive ferrets, including their ethology and reproductive behavior (Miller 1988; Miller et al. 1988a, b, 1989, Miller & Anderson 1989a, b, 1992). These studies significantly extend knowledge of ferret reproductive physiology that can be useful in the captive breeding of ferrets, and of ferret behavior. For example, Miller & Anderson (1992) studied and filmed wild and captive ferrets, presented detailed descriptions of their activities, and grouped the activities into 13 categories. These behaviors are used in a model of ferret life history evolution.

Although the Meeteetse and South Dakota ferrets were associated with different prairie dog species, different biogeographic areas, and different climatic regimes, their gross behavior and activity patterns were apparently similar, although studies in South Dakota were limited. Comparisons with related species from the literature suggest that black-footed ferret behavior is similar to that described for similar mustelids (Forrest et al. 1985a).

Ferret habitat and preserve characteristics

The fifth component in ferret recovery was determination of their habitat requirements (Forrest *et al.* 1985b, Clark *et al.* 1986a). Understanding ferret habitat was necessary to locate areas that possibly contained undiscovered ferrets and areas suitable for reintroducing ferrets. Redistribution of ferrets from the Meeteetse site via captive breeding and translocation to several new secure sites was essential for recovery and to guard against species loss.

Habitat at Meeteetse was measured and described. The vegetation at Meeteetse was characterized as wheatgrass–needlegrass/shrubsteppe (*Agropyron/Artemisia*) type. It was dominated by the grasses *Koeleria cristata, Agropyron spicatum*, and *A. smithii*, and mixed shrubs (largely *Artemisia tridentata*), as described by Collins & Lichvar (1986), and had been heavily grazed by cattle, horses, and sheep for about 100 years.

The 37 active prairie dog colonies totaled 2995 ha, contained about 125 000 burrow entrances, and showed considerable annual fluctuation in prairie dog population size. Ferret habitat was dynamic: some prairie dog colonies died out, others shrank, others grew, some new areas were colonized, and a few areas that were originally dead were repopulated.

The overall climate, geology, soil, vegetation, and land use history of the Meeteetse area is similar to much of Wyoming and other areas throughout the West where prairie dogs are found today. Ferrets have probably always inhabited the Meeteetse region. Their persistence there into the 1980s was probably due to the lack of prairie dog eradication programs, which left active colonies or parts of colonies unpoisoned (although prairie dogs have apparently been kept at low levels since the 1930s), and very good luck. Beginning in the 1940s and continuing through the 1960s, limited poisoning was carried out. Since 1970, only a few small areas in the overall prairie dog–ferret complex have been poisoned.

The population status of the Meeteetse prairie dogs was a major variable of ferret habitat. The following discussion relies on several studies of the prairie dogs, including Clark *et al.* (1985), K. Fagerstone (unpublished data), Menkens (1987), and Biggins *et al.* (unpubl. data). Prairie dogs were periodically surveyed in the Meeteetse region from October 1981 to July 1983 by Clark *et al.* (1985) and later by Menkens (1987). They were active until late November, when they hibernate, and emerged in late January. Prairie dog density and age structure were sampled in an area characterized by some of the highest burrow opening densities and possibly greatest ferret densities (Clark *et al.* 1985). A maximum density of 9.3 dogs ha^{-1} was recorded in late June 1983. The maximum mean density for four (1.5 ha) plots was 7.5 dogs ha^{-1} on

23 June (1983) The mean density for all plots was 3.8 dogs ha⁻¹. Age classification of 969 prairie dogs in the Meeteetse plots showed 3.4 young per adult.

B. Gould, a veterinarian in Meeteetse, reported that the prairie dog population in one ferret-occupied area had 'crashed' at least three times in the previous 21 years. The cause of these crashes remains undocumented, but sylvatic plague (*Yersinia pestis*) had been reported for Park County, Wyoming, on several occasions. Plague was diagnosed in May–June 1985 in several of the Meeteetse colonies by the Center for Disease Control in Fort Collins, Colorado (S. Ubico & G. Maupin personal communication). *Yersinia pestis* is a bacterial disease that often decimates prairie dogs (Raynor 1985). Fleas are the main vectors of the disease, and mammals are the hosts. From infected rodent pockets, the enzoötic infective plague may spread rapidly and aperiodically through susceptible populations in epizoötic proportions. D. Biggins (personal communication) gave the most complete account of the effects of plague in summer 1985 by counting 'active' vs. 'inactive' burrows and numbers of prairie dogs. The survey (26 July and 4 August) required 14.5 person-days and sampled 2404.5 ha (77%) of the prairie dog complex, including most major prairie dog colonies. About 22% (698.5 ha) of the sampled area was inactive. Additional surveys in 1986 and 1987 showed that plague had significantly reduced the Meeteetse prairie dog complex; it remained reduced through 1991.

The Meeteetse prairie dog complex before the plague die-off (pre-1985) was compared with seven other large white-tailed prairie dog areas in Wyoming and Utah (Clark *et al.* 1986a). The Meeteetse complex fell within the range of values examined and, except for the high density of burrow openings, did not appear unique. It showed a very different configuration of prairie dog colonies from the Mellette County, South Dakota, complex where ferrets were studied in the 1960s and 1970s. Mellette County had many small colonies (*n*=86 in the ferret complex, mean colony size=8.5 ha), whereas Meeteetse showed fewer but larger colonies (*n*=37, mean size=80.9 ha).

Based on viable population size considerations presented by Groves & Clark (1986), Harris *et al.* (1989), Lacy & Clark (1989), and others, prairie dog colony complexes that can support large viable populations should be chosen for initial ferret translocations. This requires that areas with white-tailed prairie dogs be larger than Meeteetse (ca. 3000 ha). Smaller complexes (<3000 ha) could likely maintain ferret populations if genetic and population manipulations (artificial migration and possibly predator control) are conducted. Smaller areas could also be feasible for ferret reintroduction into black-tailed prairie dog habitat, because the size of suitable reintroduction areas ultimately depends on the density of prey. Until prairie dogs return to at least pre-plague numbers and distributions, the Meeteetse area should not be considered a suitable translocation site.

The Meeteetse habitat decriptions served as bases for various methods for locating ferret preserves. These methods are described later.

Conservation management and species recovery

The USFWS's Black-Footed Ferret Recovery Plan (1978), as rewritten by Forrest & Biggins (1987, p. 21), lists as its goal 'to insure immediate survival of the black-footed ferret by: 1) increasing the number of captive black-footed ferrets to an effective population size of 200 breeding adults by 1991, and 2) establishing a prebreeding census population of 1500 free-ranging black-footed ferret breeding adults in 10 or more populations with no fewer than 30 breeding adults in any population by the year 2010' (a metapopulation). To establish such a metapopulation and meet recovery targets, suitable translocation sites must be identified and protected, and all ferret populations, both captive and wild, must be managed. This requires that a complex, interactive set of biological, socioeconomic, programmatic, and policy concerns be addressed (Clark 1989, Reading *et al.* 1991). Many of these elements are discussed by Forrest & Biggins (1987), Ballou & Oakleaf (1987), a Wyoming Game and Fish Department plan (WGF 1991), and the Montana Department of Fish, Wildlife, and Parks (North Central Montana Black Footed Ferret Working Group 1991).

Recovery options and considerations

The three original options for ferret recovery, presented by Richardson *et al.* (1986) shortly after the Meeteetse ferrets were found, were to: 1) increase available habitat at Meeteetse so the ferret population could increase to an N_e of 50; 2) find more wild ferrets at other sites; and 3) manipulate ferret numbers directly to restore populations to a viable and secure status. These options, and the recent restoration effort, are briefly discussed below.

Increase ferret habitat at Meeteetse

The Meeteetse area could support a viable ferret population if adequate habitat were available. Theoretically, inactive prairie dog colonies near the currently active ones could have been reconstituted by encouraging prairie dog expansion. Increasing prairie dog numbers and distribution five-fold would require 5–10 years or longer. However, regardless of the size of the Meeteetse ferret population, it would still be vulnerable to catastrophic stochasticity (e.g. diseases), because all individuals of the species would still be in a single population. Thus, this option was not recommended by Richardson *et al.* (1986), for reasons well-illustrated in the 1985 and 1986 plague and canine distemper outbreaks.

Find new ferret populations

Searches for ferrets have been conducted over the last two decades, but have not located any new populations. For several years, the New York Zoological Society's Wildlife Conservation International offered a US $5000 and later a US $10 000 reward for a valid ferret sighting, but no more ferrets were located. It is possible that small remnant populations exist. If so, however, they might be highly inbred, and might not contribute significantly to species recovery. Updated survey methods may enhance finding ferrets.

Direct manipulation of ferret numbers

Direct manipulation can increase ferret numbers. Translocation would have involved the removal of some ferrets from Meeteetse. Richardson *et al.* (1986) reviewed the pros and cons of translocations, including mustelid translocations and reintrodutions over the last two decades. They concluded that feasibility studies and at least 30 animals were needed in each release to the wild, sex ratios should favor females, short handling and transportation times were needed, and an acclimatization period prior to release would favor successful translocations.

Captive propagation uses animals in captivity to increase numbers rapidly so that the young or the original stock can be released into the wild (see Lacy, chapter 3 of this volume). This technique provides control of a reservoir of animals to protect against extinction in the wild, to produce stock for release to the wild, for the study of life history and behavior critical for future conservation and reintroduction efforts, and to inform the public and enlist their support of recovery programs. Richardson *et al.* (1986), whose paper was originally distributed in 1983, proposed a scenario for captive breeding and concluded that it was highly likely that Meeteetse ferrets could be successfully maintained and propagated in captivity. In 1984, several captive propagation facilities were available and offered to breed ferrets: the FWS's Patuxent Wildlife Research Center, the National Zoo, and Washington State University. Several other facilities, including the Brookfield Zoo and the Denver Zoo, also expressed an interest in helping. Indeed, as early as 1983, Richardson *et al.* (1986) strongly recommended that captive-rearing and reintroduction be undertaken soon, as did Clark *et al.* (1985) in 1984. Unfortunately, despite these recommendations, government officials made no effort to either hold or breed ferrets in captivity until after the catastrophic decline of the wild ferrets in mid-1985.

An extensive checklist for planning and carrying out a captive ferret propagation and reintroduction program was provided by Richardson *et al.* (1986), covering the initial selection of animals from the wild and the assessment of rearing and release sites, captive facilities, animal care, costs, release considerations, and biological data needed. The current ferret captive breeding and reintroduction efforts based on the work of Forrest *et al.* (1985a), Richardson *et al.* (1986), and others are described below.

Ferret recovery

The actual ferret recovery effort has used the foundation described above to successfully breed ferrets in captivity, locate reintroduction sites, and develop procedures for managing wild ferrets.

Captive breeding ferrets

Captive breeding of endangered species to build up numbers for later release to the wild is a widely recognized recovery technique. Prior to the 1985 capture of 12 Meeteetse ferrets, only one previous attempt to propagate ferrets in captivity had been undertaken, using South Dakota ferrets. Although the experiment was ultimately unsuccessful, several dozen ferrets were held in captivity, some for several years (Carpenter & Hillman 1978, Richardson *et al.* 1986), and much was learned. Carpenter & Hillman (1978) describe the husbandry, reproduction, and veterinary care of captive black-footed ferrets. Carpenter (1985) describes their breeding biology and behavior, including vaginal cytology, photoperiod, surrogate females, artificial insemination, hormonal therapy, and various health problems and medical considerations: vaccination, medications, surgical procedures, parasites and diseases, pneumonia, diabetes mellitus, hydroephrosis, and neoplasia.

The first ferret propagation program was initiated in 1971 at the Patuxent Wildlife Research Center, Laurel, Maryland. Four females and two males were brought in from western South Dakota. All four females died from canine distemper induced by a modified-live virus vaccine (Carpenter *et al.* 1976). One male died in 1976 from diabetes mellitus and associated complications (Carpenter & Novilla 1977). Another male was caught in 1973, two females were caught in 1972 and 1973, and another ferret of unknown sex was caught in 1974. The last animal died in 1979. During the eight years that surrogate species (Siberian and European ferrets) and black-footed ferrets were held at Patuxent, two black-footed ferret litters were produced: eight young were stillborn and two live kits died within two days. Breeding difficulties and a variety of pathological complications suggested that the wild South Dakota population was highly inbred. J. Carpenter (personal communication) was optimistic that, in the future, ferrets could be bred in the laboratory provided that genetically heterozygous breeding stock could be located. Since then, many new techniques have been developed that could aid captive propagation of ferrets, such as artificial insemination, embryo manipulation, and genetic engineering (Polge 1985), gamete and embryo storage (Moore 1985), endocrine control of reproduction (Hodges 1985), and encouragement of successful lactation and neonatal survival (Hearn 1985, Loudon 1985). This background of experience on ferret propagation served as the foundation for the Meeteetse ferret captive breeding program.

The 18 Meeteetse ferrets captured from 1985 to 1987 were the nucleus of the captive population. Many, if not all 18, are closely related (e.g. brothers and sisters, and parents and offspring). An additional two adult males, one juvenile male, one adult female, and two juvenile females were trapped in fall 1985, but all later died of canine distemper in a Wyoming Game and Fish Department facility, partly because of alleged management deficiencies. Data from T. Thorne (personal communication), Wyoming Game and Fish Department, summarize the capture of the first six ferrets from 12 September to 11 October, the first death on 20 October, and the final death on 6 January 1986. Housing all six in close proximity no doubt spread the disease. The second group of six ferrets was taken between 25 and 31 October 1985 and housed individually. These were two juvenile males, two adult females, and two juvenile females; four or five of these six may be closely related.

In late 1985, the Captive Breeding Specialists Group (CBSG) of the International Union of the Conservation of Nature and Natural Resources (IUCN) became involved in advising, formulating, and finally directing the Wyoming Game and Fish Department and the FWS in captive breeding ferrets (reviews of the IUCN role and captive breeding can be found in Clark 1989, Seal et al. 1989, Thorne & Oakleaf 1991, and Williams et al. 1991). By the end of 1985, CBSG had reviewed the state's limited facilities, resources, personnel, support, and plans, and made numerous recommendations necessary for upgrading efforts for a successful program. CBSG concluded that it would be desirable to have at least 20 breeders as founders of the captive population for maximum retention of genetic diversity. On this basis, and because the two males in captivity were immature and unlikely to breed in 1986, CBSG strongly recommended immediately bringing in at least three additional animals, especially adult males. About six ferrets were thought to remain in the wild at Meeteetse at this time. Action on CBSG's recommendation was deferred by government officials until summer 1986. The six captive ferrets did not breed in 1986.

CBSG also recommended that if fewer than 10 ferrets were found at Meeteetse in summer 1986, all animals should be brought in for the captive propagation program. Otherwise, prospects of successful captive rearing were remote (estimated at less than 10% success). Fortunately, four or five adults persisted in the wild after the catastrophic canine distemper outbreak, and in the summer of 1986 they produced two litters (five kits each, D. Biggins personal communication). By early 1987, 12 of these wild ferrets were added to the captive population (18 total in captivity). The other three wild ferrets were not captured and presumably died. No additional wild ferrets have been found since early 1987, and the species is presumed extinct in the wild at Meeteetse. A litter of six and a litter of two were produced in captivity in the summer of 1987. One kit in the litter of two died soon after birth.

For 1988, the CBSG recommended using a wide variety of techniques to encourage successful reproduction in the captive population of 25 individuals. Numerous genetic and demographic management recommendations for the captive population were given by Ballou & Oakleaf (1987), Don Carlos & Doherty (1987), and Lacy & Clark (1989). Much of the captive breeding effort and reproductive biology of the ferret is described in Seal *et al.* (1989). In 1988, 13 litters with 34 surviving young were produced, and the captive ferret population grew to 58.

In 1989, the 58 ferrets in captivity produced 24 litters (67 surviving young). Three facilities were in use: Wyoming Game and Fish Department, the US National Zoo at Front Royal, Virginia, and the Henry Doorley Zoo in Omaha, Nebraska. As of early 1990, 118 ferrets survived.

At the end of 1990, the population was about 180. Ferrets were distributed to two new facilities: the Cheyenne Mountain Zoo in Colorado Springs, Colorado, and the Louisville Zoo in Louisville, Kentucky.

In 1991, reproduction was high; the 139 kits added brought the overall captive population to about 320. The Phoenix Zoo in Arizona is constructing a captive breeding facility and it will be stocked shortly, as will the Toronto Zoo in Canada. Thus, the captive breeding effort reached the goal outlined in the FWS Recovery Plan of having at least 200 breeding adults in captivity before starting releases to the wild; the first reintroductions began in 1991 (see below).

The population increases in captivity, however, can ultimately be traced back to only five ferrets that successfully bred. Of the original 18 ferrets taken into captivity, 13 left no surviving offspring.

Locating ferret populations

Locating additional wild ferret populations would greatly enhance the chances of species recovery. Current methods (described earlier) are based on ferret signs and the possibility of direct sightings (Clark *et al.* 1984a, b). However, new techniques need to be developed, and innovation is encouraged wherever possible. Surveys for additional ferrets should be continued.

Establishing reintroduction sites

If the species is to be recovered, reintroduction sites are needed to support several ferret populations. The necessary size, location, and distribution for reintroduction sites as described below rely largely on the Habitat Suitability Index (HSI) model developed by Houston, Clark & Minta (1986) and modified by Minta & Clark (1989), and on descriptions of the Meeteetse and Mellette County ferret–prairie dog areas by Henderson et al. (1969), Hillman et al. (1979), Forrest et al. (1985a), and Clark et al. (1986a). The HSI model was modified slightly by Miller, Menkens & Anderson (1988b) and simplified by the USFWS (Biggins et al. 1989).

First, Houston et al. (1986) applied the HSI model format to the Meeteetse ferret environment. This model was used to compare other prairie dog areas to ferret habitat at Meeteetse, to use those comparisons to select areas to be searched for ferrets, and to identify suitable areas for transplant sites. The HSI model assumes a ferret can meet its year-round habitat requirements within prairie dog colonies providing that prairie dog colonies are large enough, burrows are numerous enough, and adequate numbers of prairie dogs and alternate prey are available. The specific equations in this model were chosen to mimic those perceived biological relationships as closely as possible. This model was applied to several sites in Montana and compared to Meeteetse in Minta & Clark (1989).

Second, Minta & Clark (1989) modified the Houston et al. (1986) model and applied it to the north central Montana prairie dog complex. The revised model included pure spatial variables (reserve design), biological spatial variables (ferret ecology), and ferret food, cover, and reproduction variables. Discussion included other habitat variables (e.g. disease).

Third, Miller et al. (1988b) and FWS (Biggins et al. 1989) used simplified models that included some of the important variables identified by Houston et al. (1986) and Minta & Clark (1989). The FWS adopted the Biggins et al. (1989) model to compare potential reintroduction sites over several states. The goal in deriving their model was to produce an easily understood and practical system for evaluating the potential ability of prairie dog complexes to support ferrets. Their system is based on a numeric rating derived from ferret energetics and integration of the numeric rating with qualitative attributes into a comprehensive evaluation system. However, they noted that subjectivity cannot be removed from the process, and so expert opinions must be heavily relied on in final site selections.

Fig. 11.1. Black-footed ferret (photo by T. Clark).

Several states are seeking reintroduction sites. The Montana Department of Fish, Wildlife and Parks, in close cooperation with FWS-Montana Office, the Bureau of Land Management, and the conservation community, has led the national effort in many important ways. The Department has been active in finding reintroduction sites and developing habitat management plans (Clark *et al.* 1987, 1989b, Minta & Clark 1989, North Central Montana Black Footed Ferret Working Group 1991).

Montana is within the original range of the ferret, and 44 confirmed specimens are known from the state (Anderson *et al.* 1986). Much of Montana formerly contained extensive areas of prairie dogs (Flath & Clark 1986). For example, north central Montana had about 600 prairie dog colonies in 1985; they totalled about 15 390 ha scattered through 2 million ha of rangelands. Four major prairie dog complexes (clusters of colonies) within this area totalled 7800 ha, made up of 104 colonies ranging from 2 to 435 ha (mean 75 ha). An HSI comparison was made between the north central Montana areas and Meeteetse and Mellette County. Overall, HSI values compared favorably, and the four complexes are capable of supporting ferrets individually or collectively. By 1991, this site had grown substantially to over 20 000 ha.

Besides several potential Montana reintroduction sites, at least two are available in Wyoming, and others are possible in Utah, Colorado, South Dakota, Arizona, North Dakota, New Mexico, Mexico, and Canada. The availability of reintroduction sites, if they can be identified and prepared, should not limit ferret recovery. Currently, though, sites are not being located and developed as rapidly as needed.

The ferret population viability assessment by Harris *et al.* (1989) and the minimum viable ferret population size estimates by Groves & Clark (1986) and Lacy & Clark (1989) serve to set target ferret population sizes for recovery. For example, Figure 3 from Harris *et al.* (1989) describes the probability that ferret populations of various sizes (n=20, 40, 60, 80, 100, or 120) will persist for 100 years. The largest Montana reintroduction area may support about 450 breeding female ferrets and would likely persist indefinitely, according to these estimates.

These biological studies were supplemented by R. P. Reading & S. R. Kellert (unpublished data), who studied the knowledge and attitudes of Montanans about the ferret restoration effort there. Additionally, Reading, Clark & Kellert (1991) described a reintroduction paradigm that was, in part, developed as a result of the Montana ferret reintroduction planning process. Some components of the paradigm have influenced the Montana program. In many respects, Wyoming has followed the lead of Montana in its cooperative management plan for ferret reintroductions (Wyoming Game and Fish Department 1991).

Conservation and management of wild ferrets

A framework for monitoring and protecting wild ferrets and their habitat and for meeting special management considerations was provided by Clark (1986b). Three monitoring activities were proposed: spotlight counts in summer, capture–mark–recapture in fall, and snow tracking and sign searches in winter. Techniques for each monitoring activity, expected data products, and sources of existing baseline data for comparative purposes were provided. Plans to protect ferrets from harassment, diseases, and predators and competition were also discussed. In addition, several special management considerations were described: multiple land use management, oil and gas development, hunting and trapping, livestock grazing, road and fence construction, catastrophes (e.g. diseases), cooperation with local public and ranchers, and private–state–federal interorganizational arrangements needed to monitor and protect the ferrets and their habitat. Collectively, all these management actions offer considerable protection for wild ferret populations and their habitat once reintroduced populations are established.

Ferret reintroduction in 1991

In September through November 1991, the first ferret reintroduction to the wild took place. The site chosen by the Wyoming Game and Fish Department was in the Shirley Basin/Medicine Bow area of southcentral Wyoming (Wyoming Game and Fish Department 1991). The area of the management plan includes abut 295 000 ha with about 61 000 ha of prairie dogs. This area is estimated to be capable of supporting about 142 ferret families or about 213 adults. The ferrets were reintroduced with an 'experimental, nonessential' designation under the Endangered Species Act as sought by Wyoming. Legal challenges to the experimental nonessential status have been threatened as this status does not provide maximum protection to the only known wild population of ferrets. Meeteetse, Wyoming, was not chosen as a release site because prairie dog habitat there is still drastically degraded below its status in the early 1980s.

Trial releases of polecats (*Mustela eversmanni*, ferrets from Siberia) to prairie dog colonies by the US Fish and Wildlife Service preceeded the black-footed ferret releases to the Shirley Basin/Medicine Bow area. The trial releases were designed to test reintroduction strategies and assess the effects of supplemental feeding on relased animals. In 1989, 13 radio-tagged polecats were released into a black-tailed prairie dog colony near Wheatland, Wyoming (Biggins *et al.* 1990). All 13 died, mostly from predation by coyotes, badgers, and raptors. In 1990, 44 polecats were released to prairie dog colonies in Colorado and Wyoming (Biggins *et al.* 1991). All died, from similar causes and from starvation. These studies indicated potentially important factors influencing reintroduction success and compared different reintroduction protocols.

Over a 6 week period in 1991, 49 (32 male : 17 female) young black-footed ferrets were released at Shirley Basin/Medicine Bow. Most animals were radio-collared for at least some time. The US Fish and Wildlife Service carried out nearly all the radio telemetry studies. Several animals dispersed over 10 km. As of mid-November, nine ferrets were confirmed to be alive (B. Miller, personal communication). Biggins *et al.* (1991) discuss the results of the ferret reintroduction through mid-November. Of 49 ferrets released, there were nine official known mortalities. Five were killed by coyotes, one was killed by a badger, and three were removed from the experiment and rehabilitated because of malnutrition or injury. Of 37 radio-collared ferrets, regardless of the length of time, 17 dispersed beyond the 'core' area. Straight-line distances from release point to the last known telemetric fix of dispering ferrets ranged from 4.1 to 17.1 km. However, radio contact was lost for 14 ferrets. Details of the release protocols and subsequent behavior of the animals, as well as the monitoring effort, should be available within the next few months. Reading (1991) provides the only overview assessment of this part of the program to date. He notes that only some released animals had radio collars, and several more had their collars removed, thus making assessment of the status of released animals difficult. He discusses that collar removal from some of the ferrets, along with a number of other aspects of the release protocol, was very controversial. Interagency relations were often strained and conflict-laden. General mistrust and suspicion prevailed among key participants and agencies. State and federal officials have been unable to productively manage their interagency relations after more than 10 years of involvement in the ferret program.

Conclusions

Black-footed ferrets must be managed as a metapopulation. Many prairie dog complexes, each representing a patch of habitat, are needed to support ferret populations of various sizes (most below 200 ferrets), because there are few large prairie dog complexes remaining. Recovery will entail maintaining many small ferret populations over many habitat patches. These considerations are reflected in the FWS Black-Footed Ferret Recovery Plan and various reintroduction plans and efforts. Captive breeding has been successful to date and the first reintroduction is now underway in Wyoming. However, ultimate species restoration depends on successfully restoring at least 10 ferret populations and an extended management commitment over many years by a host of state and federal government agencies. Full protection of the prairie dog ecosystem is required (Clark *et al.* 1989b, Miller *et al.* 1990). If species recovery is achieved over the next decade or two, the black-footed ferret will emerge as an example of successful endangered species restoration.

Acknowledgments

Denise Casey of Northern Rockies Conservation Cooperative, Jackson, Wyoming, and Richard Reading of Yale University, New Haven, Connecticut, reviewed the manuscript. This chapter was completed with support from The World Wildlife Fund-U.S., Newman's Own, Fanwood Foundation, Lost Arrow, Nu Lambda Trust, and The Eppley Foundation for Research. The work reviewed in this chapter reflects the commitment and hard work of many individuals and organizations over more than 20 years.

Literature cited

Anderson, E., Forrest, S. C., Clark, T. W. & Richardson, L. (1986) Paleobiology, biogeography, and systematics of the black-footed ferret, *Mustela nigripes* (Audubon and Bachman), 1851. *Great Basin Naturalist Memoir*, **8**, 11–62.
Audubon, J. J. & Bachman, J. (1851–1854) *Quadrupeds of North America. 3V.* New York: V.G., Audubon.

Ballou, J. D. & Oakleaf, B. (1987) *Demographic and genetic breeding recommendations for the captive population of black-footed ferrets.* Minneapolis: Captive Breeding Specialist Group, SSC/IUCN.

Biggins, D., Hanebury, L. R. & Miller, B. J. (1991) *Trial release of Siberian polecats (Mustella eversmanni).* Progress Report, National Ecology Research Center, Fort Collins: United States Fish and Wildlife Service.

Biggins, D., Hanebury, L. R., Miller, B. J. & Powell, R. A. (1990) *Trial release of Siberian polecats (Mustella eversmanni).* Progress Rept., National Ecology Research Center, Fort Collins, Colorado: United States Fish and Wildlife Service.

Biggins, D., Miller, B. J., Hanebury, L., Oakleaf, B., Farmer, A., Crete, R. & Dood, A. (1989) *A system for evaluating black-footed ferret habitat.* Denver: United States Fish and Wildlife Service.

Biggins, D., Schroeder, M. H., Forrest, S. C. & Richardson, L. (1986) Activity of radio-tagged black-footed ferrets. *Great Basin Naturalist Memoir*, **8**, 135–40.

Brussard, P., F. & Gilpin, M. E. (1989) Demograhic and genetic problems of small populations. In *Conservation Biology and the Black-Footed Ferret*, ed. Seal, U. S., Thorne, E. T., Bogan, M. A, & Anderson, S. H., pp. 37–48. New Haven: Yale University Press.

Carpenter, J. W. (1985) Captive breeding and management of black-footed ferrets. In *Black-Footed Ferret Workshop Proceedings, September 18–19, 1984*, ed. Anderson, S. H. & Inkley, D. B., pp. 12.1–12.13. Laramie, Wyoming: Wyoming Game and Fish Dept.

Carpenter, J. W., Appel, M. J. G., Erickson, R. C. & Novilla, M. N. (1976) Fatal vaccine-induced canine distemper virus infection in black-footed ferrets. *Journal of the American Veterinary Medical Association*, **169**, 961–4.

Carpenter, J. W. & Hillman, C. N. (1978) Husbandry, reproduction, and veterinary care of captive ferrets., *American Association Zoo Annual Proceedings*, Knoxville, Tennessee, **171**, 36–47.

Carpenter, J. W. & Novilla, M. N. (1977) *Diabetes mellitus* in a black-footed ferret. *Journal of the American Veterinary Medical Association*, **171**, 890–3.

Casey, D. E., DuWaldt, J. & Clark, T. W. (1986) Annotated bibliography of the black-footed ferret. *Great Basin Naturalists Memoir*, **8**, 185–208.

Clark, T. W. (1975) Some relationships between prairie dogs, black-footed ferrets, Paleo-Indians and ethnographically known tribes. *Plains Anthropologist*, **20–67**, 71–4.

Clark, T. W. (1981) *The Meeteetse black-footed ferret conservation studies: A proposal.* Box 2705, Jackson, Wyoming.

Clark, T. W. (1983) Last of the black-footed ferrets? *National Geographic*, **163**, 828–38.

Clark, T. W. (1984) Strategies in endangered species conservation: A research view of the ongoing black-footed ferret conservation studies. In *Symposium on Issues in Technology and Management of Impacted Western Wildlife, Steamboat Springs, Colorado, November, 1982*, ed. Corner, R. D., Merino, J. M., Monarch, J. W., Pustmueller, C., Stallmaster, M., Stocker, R., Todd, J. & Right, W., pp. 145–54. Boulder: Montana Bureau of Land Management.

Clark, T. W. (1986a) *Annotated prairie dog bibliography 1973 to 1985.* Montana BLM Wildlife Technical Bulletin No. 1. Billings: United States Bureau of Land Management and Montana Department of Fish, Wildlife and Parks.

Clark, T. W. (1986b) Some guidelines for management of the black-footed ferret. *Great Basin Naturalist Memoirs*, 8, 160–168.

Clark, T. W. (1987) Restoring balance between the endangered black-footed ferret

(*Mustela nigripes*) and human use of the Great Plains and intermountain west. *Journal of the Washington Academy of Sciences, 77,* 168–73.

Clark, T. W. (1989) *Conservation biology of the black-footed ferret.* Special Scientific Report No. 3. Wildlife Preservation Trust.

Clark, T. W. & Campbell, T. M. III (1981) Additional black-footed ferret (*Mustela nigripes*) reports from Wyoming. *Great Basin Naturalist, 41,* 360–1.

Clark, T. W., Campbell, T. M. III, Schroeder, M. H. & Richardson, L. (1984a) *Handbook of methods for locating black-footed ferrets.* Wyoming BLM Wildlife Technical Bulletin, No. 1. Cheyenne: United States Bureau of Land Management and Wyoming Game and Fish Department.

Clark, T. W., Crete, R. & Cada J. (1989a) Innovative organizational responses to endangered species recovery. *Environmental Management, 13,* 159–70.

Clark, T. W., Forrest, S. C., Richardson, L., Casey, D. & Campbell, T. M. III. (1986a) Description and history of the Meeteetse black-footed ferret environment. *Great Basin Naturalist Memoir, 8,* 72–84.

Clark, T. W., Grensten, J., Gorges, M., Crete, R. & Gill, J. (1987) Analysis of black-footed ferret translocation sites in Montana. *Prairie Naturalist, 19,* 43–56.

Clark, T. W. & Harvey, A. H. (1988) Implementing endangered species recovery policy: Learning as we go? *Endangered Species UPDATE, 5,* 35–42.

Clark, T. W., Hinckley, D. & Rich, T. eds. (1989b) *The prairie dog ecosytem: managing for biological diversity.* Montana BLM Wildlife Technical Bulletin No. 2. Billings: United States Bureau of Land Management and Montana Department of Fish, Wildlife and Parks.

Clark, T. W., Richardson, L., Casey, D., Campbell, T. M. III, & Forrest, S. C. (1984b) Seasonality of black-footed ferret diggings and prairie dog hole plugging. *Journal of Wildlife Management, 48,* 1441–4.

Clark, T. W., Richardson, L., Forrest, S. C., Campbell, T. M. III, Casey, D. E. & Fagerstone, K. A. (1985) Black-footed ferret prey base. In *Black-Footed Ferret Workshop Proceedings, September 18–19, 1984,* ed. Anderson, S. H. & Inkley, D. B., pp. 7.1–7.14. Laramie: Wyoming Game and Fish Department.

Clark, T. W., Richardson, L., Forrest, S. C., Casey, D. & Campbell, T. M. III. (1986b) Descriptive ethology and activity patterns of black-footed ferrets. *Great Basin Naturalist Memoir, 8,* 115–34.

Clark, T. W. & Westrum, R. (1987) Paradigms and ferrets. *Journal of Sociological Studies in Science, 17,* 3–34.

Collins, E. I. & Lichvar, R. W. (1986) Vegetation inventory of current and historic black-footed ferret habitat in Wyoming. *Great Basin Naturalist Memoir, 8,* 85–93.

Coues, E. (1877) *Fur-Bearing Animals: A Monograph of North American Mustelidae.* US Geological Survey of the Territories, Miscellaneous Publication No. 8. Washington, D.C.: United States Government Printing Office.

Don Carlos, M. W. & Doherty, J. (1987) *1988 Black-footed Ferret Captive Breeding Management Plan.* Report to the International Union for the Conservation of Nature/Captive Breeding Specialists' Group. Minneapolis: International Union for the Conservation of Nature.

Flath, D. L. & Clark, T. W. (1986) Historic status of black-footed ferret habitat in Montana. *Great Basin Naturalist Memoir, 8,* 63–71.

Forrest, S. C. & Biggins, D. E. (1987) *Black-footed Ferret Recovery Plan.* Denver: United States Fish and Wildlife Service.

Forrest, S. C., Biggins, D. E., Richardson, L., Clark, T. W., Campbell, T. M. III & Fagerstone, K. A. (1988) Black-footed ferret (*Mustela nigripes)* population attributes, Meeteetse, Wyoming, 1981–1985. *Journal of Mammalogy, 69,* 261–73.

Forrest, S. C., Clark, T. W., Richardson, L., Biggins, D., Fagerstone, K. A. & Campbell, T. M. III. (1985a) *Black-footed ferret habitat: some management and reintroduction considerations.* Wyoming BLM Wildlife Technical Bulletin, No. 2. Cheyenne: United States Bureau of Land Management and Wyoming Fish and Game Department.

Forrest, S. C., Clark, T. W., Richardson, L., Biggins, D., Fagerstone, K. A. & Campbell, T. M., III. (1985b) Life history characteristics of the genus *Mustela*, with special reference to the black-footed ferret, *Mustela nigripes.* In *Black-Footed Ferret Workshop Proceedings, September 18–19, 1984.* ed. Anderson, S. H. & Inkley, D. B., pp. 23.1–23.14. Laramie: Wyoming Game and Fish Department.

Groves, C. R. & Clark, T. W. (1986) Determining minimum population size for recovery of the black-footed ferret. *Great Basin Naturalist Memoir*, **8**, 150–9.

Harris, R., Clark, T. W. & Shaffer, M. (1989) Estimating extinction probabilities for black-footed ferrets. In *Conservation Biology and the Black-Footed Ferret*, ed. Seal, U. S., Thorne, E. T., Bogan, M. A. & Anderson, S. H. pp. 69–82. New Haven: Yale University Press.

Hearn, J. P. (1985) Early embryonic development and the conservation of mammals. In *Advances in Animal Conservation*, ed. Hearn, J. P. & Hodges, J. K., pp. 169–82. Oxford: Clarendon Press.

Henderson, F. R., Springer, R. F. & Adrian, R. (1969) *The black-footed ferret in South Dakota.* South Dakota Deptartment of Game, Fish and Parks Technical Bulletin No. 4. Pierre: South Dakota Department of Game, Fish and Parks.

Hillman, C. N. & Carpenter, J. W. (1980) Masked mustelid. *Nature Conservancy News*, March-April, 20–23.

Hillman, C. N. & Clark, T. W. (1980) *Mustela nigripes. Mammalian Species* No. 126. 3 pp.

Hillman, C. N. & Linder, R. L. (1973) The black-footed ferret. In *Proceedings Black-Footed Ferret and Prairie Dog Workshop, Sep., 4–6, 1973*, ed. Linder, R. L. & Hillman, C. N. pp. 10–20. Brookings: South Dakota State University.

Hillman, C. N., Linder, R. L. & Dahlgren, R. B. (1979) Prairie dog distributions in areas inhabited by black-footed ferrets. *American Midland Naturalist*, **102**, 185–7.

Hodges, J. K. (1985) The endocrine control of reproduction. In *Advances in Animal Conservation*, ed. Hearn, J. P. & Hodges, J. K., pp. 149–68. Oxford: Clarendon Press.

Holling, C. S. (1978) *Adaptive Environmental Assessment & Management.* New York: John Wiley and Sons.

Houston, B., Clark, T. W. & Minta, S. (1986) Habitat suitability index model for the black-footed ferret: A method to locate transplant sites. *Great Basin Naturalist Memoir*, **8**, 99–114.

Johnson, D. (1969) Returns of the American Fur Company, 1835–1839. *Journal of Mammalogy*, **50**, 836–9.

Kilpatrick, C. W., Forrest, S. C. & Clark, T. W. (1986) Estimating genetic variation in the black-footed ferret: A first attempt. *Great Basin Naturalist Memoir*, **8**, 145–9.

Lacy, R. & Clark, T. W. (1989) Genetic variability in black-footed ferret populations: Past, present, and future. In *Conservation Biology and the Black-Footed Ferret*, ed. Seal, U. S., Thorne, E. T., Bogan, M. A. & Anderson, S. H., pp. 83–106. New Haven: Yale University Press.

Lehmkuhl, J. F. (1984) Determining size and dispersion of minimum viable populations for land management planning and species conservation. *Environmental Management*, **8**, 167–76.

Linder, R. L. & Hillman, C. N. eds. (1973) *Proceedings Black-Footed Ferret and Prairie Dog Workshop, Sep. 4–6, 1973.* Brookings: South Dakota State University.

Loudon, A. S. I. (1985) Lactation and neonatal survival of mammals. In *Advances in Animal Conservation*, ed. Hearn, J. P. & Hodges, J. K., pp. 183–210. Oxford: Clarendon Press.

Maguire, L. A. & Clark, T. W. (1985) *A decision analysis of management options concerning plague in the Meeteetse black-footed ferret habitat.* Report to United States Fish and Wildlife Service. Denver: United States Fish and Wildlife Service.

Menkens, G. E. (1987) Temporal and spatial variation in white-tailed prairie dogs (*Cynomys leucurus*) populations and life histories in Wyoming. Ph.D. dissertation, Laramie: University of Wyoming.

Miller, B. J. (1988) Conservation and behavior of the endangered black-footed ferret (*Mustela nigripes*) with a comparative analysis of reproductive behavior between black-footed ferrets and the congeneric domestic ferret (*Mustela [Putorius] furo*). Ph.D. dissertation, Laramie: University of Wyoming.

Miller, B. J. & Anderson, S. H. (1989a) Courtship patterns in induced oestrous and natural oestrous domestic ferrets (*Mustela putorius furo*). *Journal of Ethology*, **7**, 65–73.

Miller, B. J. & Anderson, S. H. (1989b) Failure of fertilization following abbreviated copulation in the ferret (*Mustela putorius furo*). *Journal of Experimental Zoology*, **249**, 85–9.

Miller, B. J. & Anderson, S. H. (1992) Ethology of the endangered black-footed ferret (*Mustela nigripes*). *Advances in Ethology*, **31**, 1–48.

Miller, B. J., Anderson, S. H., Don Carlos, M. W. & Thorne, E. T. (1988a) Biology of the endangered black-footed ferret and the role of captive breeding in its conservation. *Canadian Journal of Zoology*, **66**, 765–73.

Miller, B. J., Biggins, D., Wemmer, C., Powell, R. & Calvo, L. (1989) Predator avoidance behaviors in captive raised ferrets (*Mustela eversmanni*). Northeast Regional Animal Behavior Meeting, November 10–12, 1989, Brown University, Providence, Rhode Island.

Miller, B. J., Menkens, G. E. & Anderson, S. H. (1988b) A field habitat model of black-footed ferrets. In *Eighth Great Plains Wildlife Damage Control Workshop Proceedings. April 28–30, 1987. Rapid City SD., Gen., Tech., Rept RM-154, USDA Forest Service*, ed. Uresk, D. W., Schenbeck, G. L. & Cefkin, R., pp. 98–102. Fort Collins: Rocky Mountain Forest and Range Experiment Station.

Miller, B. J., Wemmer, C., Biggins, D. & Reading, R. (1990) A proposal to conserve black-footed ferrets and the prairie dog ecosystem. *Environmental Management*, **14**, 763–9.

Minta, S. C. & Clark, T. W. (1989) Habitat suitability analysis of potential translocation sites for black-footed ferrets in northcentral Montana. In *The prairie dog ecosystem: managing for biological diversity*, ed. Clark, T. W., Hinckley, D. & Rich,T., pp. 29–46. Montana BLM Wildlife Technical Bulletin No. 2. Billings: United States Bureau of Land Management and Montana Department of Fish, Wildlife and Parks.

Moore, H. D. M. (1985) Storage of gametes & embryos. In *Advances in Animal Conservation*, ed. Hearn, J. P. & Hodges, J. K., pp. 137–48. Oxford: Clarendon Press.

Nelson, G. W. (1919) Annual report of Chief of Bureau of Biological Survey. In *Annual Report of the Department of Agriculture for Year Ended June, 1919*, pp. 275–298. Washington, D.C.: U.S. GPO.

North Central Montana Black-Footed Ferret Working Group. (1991) *A cooperative black-footed ferret reintroduction & management plan for the northcentral*

Montana complex. September, 1991. Helena: Montana Department of Fish, Wildlife, and Parks.

O'Brien, S. J., Martenson, J. S., Eichelberger, M. A., Thorne, E. T. & Wright., F., (1989) Genetic variation and molecular systematics of the black-footed ferret. In *Conservation Biology and the Black-Footed Ferret,* ed. Seal, U. S., Thorne, E. T., Bogan, M. A. & Anderson, S. H., pp. 21–36. New Haven: Yale University Press.

Polge, C. (1985) Embryo manipulation and genetic engineering. In *Advances in Animal Conservation,* ed. Hearn, J. P. & Hodges, J. K., pp. 123–36. Oxford: Clarendon Press.

Powell, R. A., Clark, T. W., Richardson, L. & Forrest, S. C. (1985) Black-footed ferret (*Mustela nigripes*) energy expenditure and prey requirements. *Biological Conservation,* **33,** 1–15.

Raynor, L. S. (1985) Dynamics of a plague outbreak in Gunnison's prairie dog. *Journal of Mammalogy,* **66,** 194–6.

Reading, R. P. (1991) *Experimental black-footed ferret reintroduction program in Wyoming and its implications for Montana.* Report prepared for Montana Bureau of Land Management and Montana Black-footed Ferret Working Group, Nov. 27, 1991. Billings: United States Bureau of Land Management and Montana Department of Fish, Wildlife and Parks.

Reading, R. P. & Clark, T. W. (1990) *An annotated bibliography of the black-footed ferret: 1986-1990.* Montana BLM Wildlife Technical Bulletin. No. 3. Billings: United States Bureau of Land Management and Montana Department of Fish, Wildlife and Parks.

Reading, R. P., Clark, T. W. & Kellert, S. R. (1991) Toward an endangered species reintroduction paradigm. *Endangered Species UPDATE* **8,** (11), 1–4.

Richardson, L., Clark, T. W., Forrest, S. C. & Campbell, T.M. III. (1986) Black-footed ferret recovery: A discussion of some options and considerations. *Great Basin Naturalist Memoir,* **8,** 169–84.

Richardson, L., Clark, T. W., Forrest, S. C. & Campbell, T. M. III. (1987) Winter ecology of black-footed ferrets (*Mustela nigripes*) at Meeteetse, Wyoming. *American Midland Naturalist,* **117,** 225–39.

Seal, U. S., Thorne, E. T., Bogan, M. A. & Anderson, S. H. eds. (1989) *Conservation Biology and the Black-footed Ferret.* New Haven: Yale University Press.

Stromberg, M. R., Rayburn, R. L. & Clark, T. W. (1983) Black-footed ferret prey requirements: An energy balance estimate. *Journal of Wildlife Management,* **47,** 67–73.

Thorne, E. T. & Oakleaf, B. (1991) Species rescue for captive breeding: black-footed ferret as an example. *Symposium of the Zoological Society of London,* **62,** 241–61.

Thorne, E. T. & Williams, E. (1988) Diseases and endangered species: The black-footed ferret as a recent example. *Conservation Biology,* **2,** 66–73.

United States Fish & Wildlife Service. (1978) *Black-Footed Ferret Recovery Plan.* Denver: United States Fish and Wildlife Service.

United States Fish & Wildlife Service. (1983) Only known ferret population receives careful attention. *Endangered Species Technical Bulletin,* VIII, 5–8.

Williams, E. S., Thorne, E. T., Kwiatkowski, D. R., Anders, S. L. & Lutz, K. (1991) Reproductive biology and management of captive black-footed ferrets (*Mustela nigripes*). *Zoo Biology,* **10,** 383–98.

Wyoming Department of Game and Fish. (1991) *A cooperative management plan for black-footed ferrets, Shirley Basin/Medicine Bow, Wyoming.* Cheyenne: Wyoming Game and Fish Department.

12

Development and implementation of a recovery program for the federal threatened Lakeside daisy (*Hymenoxys acaulis* var. *glabra*)

MARCELLA M. DEMAURO

Introduction

The successful reintroduction of rare plants to the wild will depend upon knowledge of a species' life history and habitat requirements, the consideration of key genetic, demographic and ecological traits that affect vulnerability to stochastic extinction processes (Lande 1988, Menges 1991), and the identification of suitable restoration sites. Unfortunately for many rare plants, much of this information is lacking when recovery plans are written. As a result, the plans are often standardized, and the recommended research and management actions are too broad or are unrelated to immediate population survival (Cook & Dixon 1986).

Here I present a comprehensive approach to developing and implementing an Illinois recovery program for a federal threatened Great Lakes endemic, *Hymenoxys acaulis* var. *glabra* (Asteraceae), commonly known as the Lakeside daisy. After first providing distribution and life history information, I review the relevant aspects of breeding system studies and plant community and population structure data collected from naturally occurring populations. Second, I describe how these results were used in recovery strategies, specifically in planning the genetic composition and size of restored populations, the transplant design, and in the selection of suitable recovery sites. Finally, I describe the restoration process and provide preliminary results of the Lakeside daisy recovery program.

The Lakeside daisy

Distribution and status

Hymenoxys acaulis is distributed from western Canada southward to California, east through the western Great Plains and southeast into Texas

Fig. 12.1. Distribution of Lakeside daisy (*Hymenoxys acaulis* var. *glabra*) (De Mauro 1993).

(Harrington 1964). Five varieties have been described (Parker 1950), but only var. *glabra* is disjunct in the western Great Lakes region (Fig. 12.1) (Fernald 1950), where it is considered a rare endemic (Morton & Venn 1984). Either *H. acaulis* or var. *glabra* migrated east during the postglacial Xerothermic Interval between 4000 and 6000 years ago, and survived in favorable habitats as the climate became increasingly moist and humid (Cowles 1926, Voss 1935). Many western grassland species expanded east into the prairie peninsula during this period (Gleason 1923, Transeau 1935, Webb, Cushing & Wright 1983).

Lakeside daisy is restricted to dolomite prairies or alvars associated with postglacial exposures of dolomite and limestone, or to dry gravel prairies on sand and gravel terraces formed by erosion of glacial valley train deposits (Wunderlin 1971, Swink & Wilhelm 1979, Morton & Venn 1984). The dolomite prairies and alvars have shallow soils, are relatively flat and open, and are moderately wet in spring and fall, but become droughty in summer (Morton & Venn 1984). The dry gravel prairies occupy excessively well-drained crests and steep south- and southwest-facing slopes of stream valleys (White 1978).

Historically, Lakeside daisy is known from two Illinois counties (Wunderlin 1971) and one Ohio county (Cooperrider 1982); it is endangered in each state (Sheviak 1981, Cusick & Burns 1984). In Canada, Lakeside daisy is somewhat continuous near the south shores of Manitoulin Island (Morton & Venn 1984), but it was not observed on the Bruce Peninsula until the 1960s, and was possibly introduced there (US Fish and Wildlife Service 1990).

While Canadian populations have remained intact, only one native US population, on the eastern half of the Marblehead Peninsula, Ottawa County, Ohio, is extant. At this location, Lakeside daisy was infrequent in the original limestone prairie (Moseley 1899), but declined with limestone quarrying. Because of the piecemeal quarrying pattern, undisturbed patches of Lakeside daisy were left to recolonize and exploit the apparently suitable abandoned quarry habitat. Eventually nearly all of the original prairie was eliminated, but the Lakeside daisy had become established across three square miles of abandoned quarry lands, undoubtedly in greater number and density than presettlement levels. The population is conservatively estimated at over 1 000 000 adults, but only 2% (ca. 19 acres) of the quarry is publicly owned. The federal recovery plan calls for protection of the population core, approximately 475 acres adjacent to the active section of the quarry, prior to delisting (US Fish and Wildlife Service 1990).

Illinois had the only known inland Lakeside daisy sites. The central Illinois (Tazewell County) population was in dry gravel prairie in the Illinois River valley. Although 'many' plants were observed (Voss 1935), the population went extinct by the late 1940s. Northeastern Illinois populations (Will County) were in dolomite and dry gravel prairie along a three to five mile segment of the lower DesPlaines River valley near Joliet (DeMauro 1988a). Intense industrial development of this river corridor reduced these populations to approximately thirty plants on a privately owned, one acre site (Illinois Natural Areas Inventory 1976) which was destroyed in 1981 (Illinois Nature Preserves Commission 1983). Three plants were collected from the population in 1979 and maintained in a private garden.

Life history

Lakeside daisy is an herbaceous polycarpic perennial with multiple basal rosettes that persist through winter. By late fall, a single inflorescence bud will form at the center of a single rosette that has 33.0 ± 5.68 s.d. leaves (DeMauro 1993). Flowering is from late April to early June. The solitary, bright yellow inflorescences have two floret types, both of which are fertile. Ray florets are pistillate and disc florets are hermaphroditic and protandrous. Total floret number ranges from 50 to over 200. Pollination is by bumble bees (Apidae), carpenter bees (Xylocopidae) and halictid bees (Halictidae), or wind.

In natural populations the mean seed:ovule ratio was 46.9% ± 15.1% s.d. (DeMauro 1993). This is approximately 49 achenes per inflorescence. Partial herbivory on the peduncle, florets or inflorescence disc (primarily by insects), or total consumption of the inflorescence (primarily by white-tailed deer and eastern cottontail rabbit) greatly reduces or entirely prevents seed production (DeMauro 1988b, unpublished data).

In early summer, achenes are gravity- or wind-dispersed approximately four to six weeks after fertilization. Dispersal distance is unknown, but it may be limited because the pappus scales are small relative to the 3–4 mm long achene body. Most seedlings have been observed within one meter of adult plants (DeMauro, unpublished data). Apparently there is no enforced dormancy, as achenes germinate whenever the soil is moist and warm (DeMauro 1993). In natural populations, germination would typically occur in the following spring, but could also occur in the first summer or fall after dispersal if the soil conditions are suitable.

Lakeside daisy genets spread vegetatively by rhizomes and by branching of the decumbent woody caudex (stem). Typically, rosettes live at least one year, then die back near the plant center as new peripheral rosettes form. When stressed (e.g. by drought or rarely, by leaf herbivory), extensive rosette mortality can occur. This results in adjacent and distinct patches of physiologically independent but genetically identical rosettes that are the functional equivalent of juvenile plants (DeMauro 1990).

Relationship of breeding system to rarity in Lakeside daisy

Breeding system

By the early 1970s, the only Illinois Lakeside daisy population was reduced to approximately thirty plants equally divided into three patches on a one acre dolomite prairie remnant along the DesPlaines River in Will County. Although insects were observed visiting plants at this site from 1970 to 1979, no viable seeds were ever produced (R. Betz, personal communication). In 1979, three plants, one from each patch, were collected from this population and were vegetatively propagated in a private garden. All hand cross-pollination attempts over a six-year period, however, failed (J. Kolar, personal communication).

Table 12.1. *Assigned mating groups in Lakeside daisy[a]*

Plant ID	Collection Site	Mating Group	Plant ID	Collection Site	Mating Group
1IL	Will Co.	1	9OH	3	8
2IL	Will Co.	1	10OH	2	9
3IL	Will Co.	1	17OH	2	9
4IL	Will Co.	1	11OH	2	10
3OH	1[b]	2	12OH	2	11
4OH	1	3	15OH	2	11, 12[c]
5OH	1	4	16OH	2	12
6OH	1	5	13OH	2	13
7OH	3	6	14OH	2	14
8OH	3	7	18OH	2	15

Notes: [a]DeMauro (1993). IL=Illinois, OH=Ohio.
[b]Ohio plants collected from three different sites within the Marblehead Quarry.
[c]15OH was cross-incompatible with 12OH and 16OH. Because the cross 12OH×16OH was not completed, it could not be assumed these plants were in the same mating group as 15OH. Thus two mating groups are indicated.

In 1985, studies were initiated at the University of Illinois at Chicago to determine the cause of reproductive failure and to examine the relationship between this species' breeding system and its population persistence. Sixteen of the twenty Lakeside daisies used in these investigations were collected from three sites within the Marblehead Quarry, Ohio, and four were from the private garden collection derived from the last Will County, Illinois, population (DeMauro 1993).

By comparing seed:ovule ratios and observing where pollen was inhibited in the different hand-pollination treatments, Lakeside daisy was found to have a strong, functional sporophytic self-incompatibility system (DeMauro 1988b). Self-incompatibility is the inability of a fertile hermaphrodite seed-plant to produce zygotes following self-pollination (de Nettancourt 1977) owing to the shared genetic identity between the pistil and pollen (Mulcahy & Mulcahy 1985). The incompatibility reaction also occurs if two plants of the same mating type, i.e. possessing the same self-incompatibility or S alleles, are crossed. In sporophytic self-incompatibility systems fertilization is prevented when growth of incompatible pollen is inhibited on the stigma (de Nettancourt 1977). For a more detailed review of self-incompatibility systems refer to Weller (Chapter 4 of this volume).

Among the twenty Lakeside daisies tested, there were fifteen mating groups (plants within a mating group are of the same mating type). All Illinois plants were in the same mating group (Table 12.1) and produced seed only when out-crossed to Ohio plants. Approximately 33.3% of the other within-site crosses were incompatible; all of these cross-incompatible plants were collected from one site at the Marblehead Quarry (Table 12.1). All other intra- and interpopulation crosses produced seed in amounts comparable to those observed in natural populations (DeMauro 1993).

Self-incompatibility, population size and persistence

Generally, there are a large number of S alleles segregating in populations of self-incompatible species, thus providing many compatible mating types (Emerson 1939, Bateman 1954, Sampson 1967, Imrie & Knowles 1971, Ockendon 1974, de Nettancourt 1977). Small populations, however, would likely maintain a lower number of S alleles and have less compatible mating types (Imrie, Kirkman & Ross 1972). Since a minimum number of S alleles must be segregating in a population for the incompatibility system to function (de Nettancourt 1977), small populations of self-incompatible species may be vulnerable to extinction if enough S alleles are lost as a result of a bottleneck or genetic drift.

No known empirical data address the relationship between population size, persistence, and the number of S alleles maintained in a population. For species with sporophytic incompatibility systems, this analysis is complicated because S-allele dominance can vary in the pistil and the pollen. Imrie *et al.* (1972), however, used computer simulations to study the effects of population size (where $n=8$, 16, 32 and 64), genetic drift, migration and seed bank on the maintenance of six S alleles in *Carthamus flavescens*, an annual with sporophytic self-incompatibility. Within a few generations, genetic drift caused the rapid loss of S alleles in small populations. When migration and seed bank recruitment were excluded, an effective population size of 32 plants could maintain four S alleles, but populations of 16 plants or fewer always went extinct because they could not maintain the three S alleles necessary for the breeding system to function. When population size was allowed to increase through migration or, to a much lesser extent, through seed bank recruitment, population extinction was delayed. Here, migration reintroduced S alleles that had been lost to genetic drift. Thus, in the absence of such an ameliorating process, genetic drift could result in the extinction of small self-incompatible populations. Although other theoretical models (based on species with gametophytic self-incompatibility) have shown that low mutation rates at the S locus could buffer against the slow loss of S alleles to genetic drift (Wright 1939, Fisher 1958, Ewens 1964, Wright 1964), it is less likely that mutation rates could balance the effects of genetic drift in small populations.

Self-incompatible species are probably not at any greater risk of extinction than self-compatible species when large populations are compared. Even large populations, however, can have clusters of related individuals or neighborhoods as a result of limited seed and pollen dispersal (Levin & Kerster 1974, Levin 1981), or of extensive clonal growth producing genetically identical patches (Harper 1977, Weller, Chapter 4 of this volume). Because Lakeside daisy has both limited seed dispersal and clonal growth, it is not surprising that plants collected from one of the sites in the Marblehead Quarry were cross-incompatible.

Given the potentially non-random distribution of mating types within populations, self-incompatibility is of critical concern in small populations that have endured a bottleneck. If a population bottleneck is selective with respect to space such that only one patch survives or with respect to genotypic properties such as drought tolerance, the chances that the surviving individuals are related and share S alleles are also increased (K. Karoly, personal communication). Under this scenario, the number of compatible mating types and the opportunities for successful reproduction and population rebound would be reduced. Consistently small populations would be vulnerable to the further loss of genetic variation through inbreeding and genetic drift (Soulé 1980, Franklin 1980, Frankel & Soulé 1981, Gilpin and Soulé 1986, Lande & Barrowclough 1987).

The available evidence suggests that this is what happened to the last Will County, Illinois, population of Lakeside daisy. Historically, these plants were part of a larger and more widely distributed metapopulation that was fragmented and isolated as habitat within the DesPlaines River valley was destroyed. It is likely that plants in this remnant population belonged to a single mating group given the: 1) lack of seed production over a ten year period despite the presence of pollinators; 2) plant's capacity for clonal growth and small patch size occupied by the population, increasing the chances the plants were related; and 3) evidence of cross-incompatibility among the last three plants, which were collected from the three patches of the remnant population. If this was the case, then the effective population size was $N_e=1$. Although the population may have persisted through clonal growth, it was essentially extinct well before the site was destroyed.

The Lakeside daisy provides strong evidence for the extinction vulnerability of small, self-incompatible plant populations, and it is not an isolated case. Breeding system and electrophoretic studies in 23 populations of the rare perennial composite *Aster furcatus* indicated that the species was self-incompatible and genetically depauperate, and that genetic drift and inbreeding likely resulted in the loss or fixation of alleles during early recovery phases following population bottlenecks (Les, Reinhartz & Esselman 1991). Apparently the populations were recently derived from a homogeneous gene pool, and local extinctions were delayed by vegetative growth (Les *et al.* 1991).

Self-incompatibility and inbreeding depression

Self-incompatibility likely evolved in response to selection against inbreeding depression, and consistently high levels of inbreeding depression would be necessary to maintain this mating system in populations (Charlesworth & Charlesworth 1987). Thus, self-incompatible species are likely to carry a high genetic load, and inbreeding depression would be expected when these plants are inbred.

Seed:ovule ratios can be a sensitive measure of inbreeding depression (Franklin 1970); however, it has rarely been documented using controlled pollination within family lines of a self-incompatible species (but see Doloi & Rai 1981). In Lakeside daisy, inbreeding depression, expressed as a significantly lower seed/ovule ratio in inbred vs. outcrossed hand-pollination, occurred after just one generation of full-sib crosses (between F1 progeny) and backcrosses (between F1 progeny and their maternal parents) in several family lines (DeMauro 1988b).

Inbreeding has several conservation consequences (see Frankel & Soulé 1981 and Barrett & Kohn 1991 for thorough reviews). In the short term, inbreeding decreases genetic variation (heterozygosity) in populations (Franklin 1980). If inbreeding depression is expressed, individual fitness will decline and result in lower rates of survivorship, growth and reproduction. In the long-term, this loss of genetic variation may reduce the species' ability to respond to environmental changes or to maintain evolutionary potential (Soulé 1980, Frankel & Soulé 1981). These effects are intensified in small populations because they are more rapidly inbred (Barrett & Kohn 1991).

Community and population structure

To obtain data on suitable recovery habitat, plant communities were sampled at Lakeside daisy sites in the Marblehead Quarry, Manitoulin Island, and the Bruce Peninsula (DeMauro 1987). Importance values, based on relative frequency and percent cover, were generated for all plant species and microhabitats along randomly located transects. In addition, permanent transects for demographic monitoring were established on a 4.4 ha site at the Marblehead Quarry (DeMauro 1987). All Lakeside daisies encountered were mapped and categorized by size class: seedling, i.e. a single rosette having fewer than 10 leaves and less than 10 cm in height; juvenile, i.e. a non-flowering plant having more than 10 leaves and greater than 10 cm in height; and adult, i.e. a flowering or non-flowering plant, the latter having previously flowered as evidenced by last year's flower stalks. From these data, the descriptions of plant community and population structure were derived.

Table 12.2. *Site comparison of the relative contribution of vegetation and substrate to community structure*[a]

	SITE[b]					
Description	MB	BI	MSL	PB	DR	OHIO
Woody						
Gymnosperms	0.0850	0.1195	0.0507	0.0204	0.1214	0.0032
Angiosperms	0.1540	0.1274	0.0365	0.0605	0.0255	0.0451
Subtotal:	**0.2390**	**0.2469**	**0.0872**	**0.0809**	**0.1469**	**0.0483**
Bryophtes and						
lichens	0.0064	0.0480	0.0385	0.1093	0.1406	0.1303
Sedges and						
rushes	0.0834	0.1631	0.0365	0.1124	0.1104	0.0103
Grasses	0.1132	0.0585	0.2157	0.1504	0.0721	0.1241
Forbs	0.3823	0.3611	0.3334	0.2926	0.3608	0.3878
Lakeside						
daisy	0.0335	0.0576	0.0656	0.0564	0.0751	0.0273
Subtotal:	**0.4158**	**0.4187**	**0.3990**	**0.3490**	**0.4359**	**0.4151**
Substrate microhabitat						
Bedrock	0.0612	0.0576	0.0837	0.1491	0.0941	0.0323
≥100 mm	0.0523	—	0.1053	0.0278	—	0.0223
≥10 mm–	0.0039	0.0079	0.0338	—	—	—
<100 mm						
<10 mm	0.0184	—	—	0.0053	—	0.2159
Sand	0.0064	—	—	0.0150	—	—
Subtotal:	**0.1422**	**0.0655**	**0.2228**	**0.1972**	**0.0941**	**0.2705**
TOTAL:	**1.000**	**1.001**	**0.9997**	**0.9992**	**1.000**	**0.9986**

Notes: [a]A total of 138 plant species were found in 151 one meter square quadrats. Importance values for all plants species and microhabitats were categorized and summed by vegetation type and by rock size, respectively.
[b]Populations sampled on Manitoulin Island: MB = Misery Bay, BI = Burnt Island, MSL = Mississagi Strait Lighthouse, and PB = Portage Bay. DR = Dyers Road Population on the Bruce Peninsula. OHIO = 4.4 ha study site at the Marblehead Quarry.

Plant community structure

Lakeside daisy sites in Ontario and Ohio are superficially similar because of limestone bedrock outcrops, a rocky ground surface, an open aspect, the presence of prairie floral elements, and a low vegetation density (DeMauro 1987, 1988b). The sites differ, however, in the relative contributions of vegetation and substrate types to plant community structure (Table 12.2) that are due in part to different disturbance histories and regional floras.

Table 12.3. *Some descriptive demographic parameters for Lakeside daisy at the Marblehead Quarry, Ohio*[a]

	Variable			
Size class	Number observed	Percent frequency	Mean density ± s.d.	% Contribution to pop. struc.
Cotyledons	297	11.5	4.13 ± 7.04	22.7
Seedlings	542	22.8	3.82 ± 6.16	41.4
Juveniles	202	18.6	1.74 ± 1.48	15.4
Adults	269	18.4	1.88 ± 1.53	20.5
Total:	1310	37.8	5.55 ± 8.28	100.0

Note: [a]Data sampled from 624 one square meter quadrats (DeMauro 1987).

The most prevalent surface substrate in the relatively undisturbed Ontario sites is limestone bedrock pavement, while mosses, lichens and small rock substrate each contribute nearly twice as much to community structure in the Ohio habitat. Grasses are somewhat equally prevalent, but the dominant species at Ontario sites is the native prairie grass, *Andropogon scoparius*, whereas the dominant species at the Marblehead Quarry is the Eurasian grass *Poa compressa*. These structural characteristics indicate that the plant community at the Marblehead Quarry is in an early-successional stage. Low-growing shrubs and conifers are more prevalent at Ontario sites along the edges of the dolomite pavement. These woody species, together with several herbaceous species, are associated with the boreal forest flora, and are completely absent from the Marblehead Quarry.

Despite these differences, Lakeside daisy ranked among the dominant species at each site, and was most consistently associated with *Arenaria stricta, Solidago nemoralis, Houstonia* spp. and *Brium* spp. (DeMauro 1987). Although Lakeside daisy was equally frequent in all sites, plants at the Marblehead Quarry were generally smaller, which is reflected in the species' lower importance value there.

Population structure

Approximately 20% of the 1310 Lakeside daisies within the demographic quadrats at the Marblehead Quarry were adults (Table 12.3). Of these, 210 (78%) were flowering plants with 3.862 ± 4.280 s.d. inflorescences per plant and 10.10 ± 10.45 s.d. rosettes per plant (DeMauro 1987). The size distribution of adult Lakeside daisies was strongly skewed to the smaller size classes

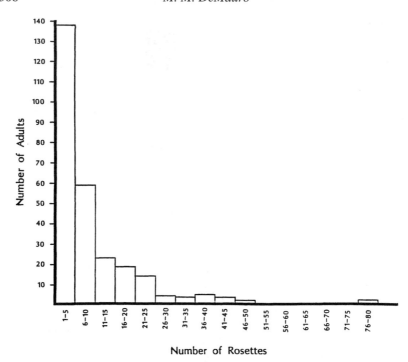

Number of Rosettes

Fig. 12.2. Size class distribution of the Lakeside daisy at the Marblehead Quarry, Ottawa County, Ohio.

(Fig. 12.2). Over half (51%) of the adults encountered had five or fewer rosettes, and only 6.3% had greater than 25 rosettes. The high variability in density estimates (Table 12.3) results from Lakeside daisy's highly aggregated distribution pattern (DeMauro 1987).

In approximately 60% of the demographic plots, the surface microhabitat in which Lakeside daisies occurred was recorded and included: bedrock; rocks >100 mm; rocks between > 5 mm – ≤ 10 mm; rocks ≤ 5 mm; mosaic, consisting of rocks of all sizes, including > 10 mm – ≤ 100 mm; and a vegetation matrix. These microhabitats were relatively homogeneous and not encountered with equal frequency.

The distribution of Lakeside daisy was not independent of microhabitat (G=525.6, P<0.001) (Fig. 12.3). As rock size decreased, the number of Lakeside daisies increased, peaking where rocks were between > 5 mm – ≤ 10 mm. Lakeside daisy was less frequent where rocks were ≤ 5 mm (this microhabitat may favor other plants), or where vegetation was relatively dense. Several microhabitats were favorable for juveniles and adults, but the > 5 mm – ≤ 10 mm microhabitat appeared optimal for initial establishment; 68% of all seedlings occurred here.

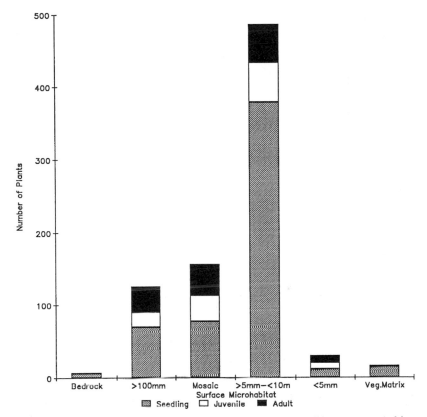

Fig. 12.3. Distribution of Lakeside daisy by growth stage in different microhabitats. Microhabitats are discrete classes of surface rock particle sizes (in mm). The mosaic microhabitat includes two or more of these classes. The vegetation matrix is a microhabitat dominated by moss, grasses, or sedges at the surface.

Recovery strategy

The goal of the Illinois Lakeside daisy recovery program is to delist the species by establishing reproducing, self-sustaining populations in protected sites having enough suitable habitat within the species' historical range in Illinois (DeMauro 1988a). A successful restored population was defined as one which resembled a natural population with respect to distribution, density, population structure (e.g. Table 12.3), and a stable size class distribution (e.g. Fig. 12.2) (DeMauro 1990, US Fish & Wildlife Service 1990). Using an extant population as the model for site and population recovery criteria, however, may not be the best strategy if the surviving populations are peripheral to the species' range or if the remaining habitat is marginal or unrepresentative for the species (L. Huenneke, personal communication).

Genetic, demographic and ecological considerations

Based on its breeding system and habitat requirements, six genetic, demographic and ecological protocols were developed for the Lakeside daisy in Illinois (DeMauro 1987). These addressed: 1) outcrossing potential, 2) population size, 3) transplant density, 4) spatial arrangement of transplants, 5) migration, and 6) self-sustainability.

1) Increase outcrossing potential within restored populations by maximizing the probability of sampling different S alleles from multiple population sources.

Because the only remaining Illinois Lakeside daisies were of the same incompatible mating type, they could not be the sole genetic stock for recovery. Therefore, propagules were derived from three sources: F1 hybrid seeds from interpopulation crosses between Illinois and Ohio plants; seeds from open-pollinated F1 plants; and field-collected seeds from Ohio and Ontario populations.

There were concerns about the potential negative effects of different geographic sources on propagule fitness, specifically with respect to ecotype differences and outbreeding depression in the hybrids (see Fenster & Dudash, Chapter 2 of this volume). In the Lakeside daisy, however, using propagules from different geographic sources was necessary in order to obtain seeds from the original Illinois material, to ensure that the Illinois gene pool would be represented in restored populations, and to enhance the long-term population viability of restored populations by increasing the number of compatible mating types. In addition, use of different source material could increase genetic variation in the restored populations. It is unclear if higher genetic variation has any adaptive value to transplants exposed to new conditions, but it could be useful, especially if the habitat conditions are unlike their site of origin (Huenneke 1991).

2) The initial size of a restored population should be large enough to buffer against immediate losses, e.g. from transplant mortality, the erosion of genetic variation or the loss of alleles from other stochastic processes (demographic, environmental or natural catastrophes, *sensu* Shaffer 1981).

For small, self-incompatible populations, the effective population size may be best approximated by the number of compatible mating types or groups. While this was feasible for a small test group of Lakeside daisies in which the N_e (15) was 25% lower than the census number (20), it would be difficult to estimate this for a larger population.

The initial, minimal size of restored populations was targeted at 1000 plants, based on the mean effective population sizes for the long-term persistence of other species populations (e.g. Frankel & Soulé 1981, Lande & Barrowclough 1987). This also conforms to predictions from minimum viable population analyses on other perennial plants for buffering environmental stochasticity and natural catastrophes (Menges 1991). Population sizes large enough to buffer against these losses likely would also be sufficient to conserve the population's genetic diversity and demographic properties (Menges 1991, Barrett & Kohn 1991).

Approximately five thousand seeds representing 25 maternal families were randomly chosen from the three propagule sources. Seeds were germinated and grown in flats at the University of Illinois at Chicago greenhouse. When seedlings became large enough, they were transferred to individual pots and labeled to indicate their genetic identity.

The use of transplants for *in situ* restoration has some disadvantages. For example, selection occurs in the greenhouse and critical demographic barriers associated with dispersal, germination and seedling establishment are circumvented (see Pavlik, Chapter 13 of this volume). In the Lakeside daisy, single rosette plants were used as transplant material for several reasons. Composite achenes have no endosperm (Lawrence 1951), and at least one-third of the Lakeside daisy seeds had been stored for three years. Thus, if the introduced seeds had failed, it would not have been known if low seed viability, losses from seed predation, or unsuitable microhabitat conditions were responsible. Using plants would accelerate population establishment because the chances for seed production were maximized (see below) and would likely occur within one year of transplanting, assuming favorable environmental conditions and presence of pollinators. This was based on the minimum size for flowering in Lakeside daisy (see above). Lastly, because the genetic origin of each transplant was known, their differential success could be monitored over time.

3) The density of transplants should be within the range observed in natural populations.

Although highly variable, plant densities in natural Lakeside daisy populations typically range from one to six adults per square meter (Table 12.3; see also DeMauro 1990, US Fish & Wildlife Service 1990), and this was replicated in restored populations. Transplant densities did not exceed natural population densities in order to minimize any density-dependent effects on growth and survivorship.

4) Maximize the probability of seed production and minimize the chances of inbreeding by manipulating the spatial arrangement of transplants.

Since the genetic origins of the transplants were known, unrelated plants or plants from families in different mating groups could be transplanted adjacent to one another. This would maximize chances for seed production among compatible neighbors. Because the initial population size may be relatively small, inbreeding could be more intense in the early stages of a restoration program. In addition, the deleterious effects of inbreeding tend to manifest more strongly later in a plant's life cycle (Barrett & Kohn 1991); this would be extremely detrimental to initial population expansion, or recovery from a population bottleneck. The initial planting was designed to minimize inbreeding, at least in the first transplant cohorts.

5) Over time, provide for periodic migration from other Lakeside daisy populations.

Population size and migration were the most important factors contributing to the maintenance of self-incompatibility in *Carthamus flavescens*, and migration (or to a much lesser extent, the seed bank) was the only way previously lost S alleles could be reintroduced (Imrie *et al.* 1972). Thus, a diverse pool of S alleles could be maintained in restored populations by introducing seeds or plants from different populations. Even migration rates as low as 1% per generation can significantly delay S allele loss in populations (Imrie *et al.* 1972).

6) Determine the potential for self-sustainability of the restored populations.

Ultimately, the success of the Lakeside daisy recovery program will depend on whether or not the restored populations are self-sustaining (Pavlik, Chapter 13, of this volume). This will be objectively evaluated through a demographic monitoring program in which transplant survivorship, seed production and establishment of seedling cohorts are tracked over time.

Site selection

Since transplants generally are less fit than the indigenous residents, potential recovery sites should, as closely as possible, match the habitat conditions found where the source populations occur (Huenneke 1991). A hierarchial screening process was used to assess the suitability of potential Lakeside daisy recovery sites in Illinois (DeMauro 1988a).

Potential recovery sites were initially identified by using geologic maps to locate exposures of dolomite bedrock and gravelly valley train deposits within and adjacent to the species' historic range. Recent black and white aerial photographs (1:400) were then examined to eliminate areas that had been heavily disturbed (e.g. pastured or in row crops) or developed. The remaining areas were field surveyed in 1987 and evaluated by comparing specific habitat conditions to those of known Lakeside daisy sites. These 'first order' habitat conditions were location with respect to historic range, geology, soils, topography, aspect, hydrology, plant community type, and range of microhabitats. Habitat descriptions were based on community and population sampling at extant Ontario and Ohio populations and a literature review for descriptions of former Illinois Lakeside daisy sites, including state natural heritage databases and herbarium records. Plant species lists were compiled for proposed recovery sites and compared with plant associates from former and existing Lakeside daisy sites (DeMauro 1988a). Using coefficients to compare the similarity of plant communities in extant and former Lakeside daisy sites with potential recovery sites was of limited use in site assessment because of inherent factors affecting species number and composition, such as site size (differences ranged over two orders of magnitude) and degree of post-settlement disturbance.

Six sites were identified and further evaluated by the 'second order' habitat conditions, which were size, amount of suitable habitat, habitat quality (i.e. degree of post-settlement disturbance), and protection status. Only three sites met all habitat conditions to be considered suitable for recovery. Manito Prairie (8 ha), Lockport Prairie (103 ha) and Romeoville Prairie (85 ha), are all managed state nature preserves in public ownership. Manito Prairie is the historic Tazewell County location for Lakeside daisy. Lockport Prairie and Romeoville Prairie are in Will County along the DesPlaines River approximately six and ten miles, respectively, upstream of the last historic site. Although the Will County sites had been more disturbed by past grazing and have had exotic weed and brush encroachment, prescribed burning and brush removal since 1983 have been improving habitat quality and diversity. Generally, the Illinois sites more closely resemble the Marblehead Quarry, except that the former have intact soils with less surface coverage by rocks.

Based on Lakeside daisy density estimates from the Marblehead Quarry, each of the recovery sites contained enough dry to dry mesic gravel or dolomite prairie to theoretically accommodate large numbers of Lakeside daisy: on the order of 10^4 and 10^6 adults at Manito Prairie and the Will County sites, respectively. If all size classes are included, the total numbers would be at least one order of magnitude higher (US Fish & Wildlife Service 1990). The actual number of plants that the recovery sites can expected to support, however, is likely lower given that the density estimates are derived from highly disturbed quarried sites in which microhabitats are more continuously distributed and vegetative cover is less dense.

Implementation and preliminary assessment of recovery actions

With the approval of all appropriate state agencies, the Illinois Lakeside daisy recovery program was initiated in the spring of 1988 at Lockport Prairie and Romeoville Prairie nature preserves utilizing Will County Forest Preserve District staff and volunteers. Approximately two months prior to the transplanting date, the greenhouse-raised plants (all initially single rosette) were started on a 'hardening-off' process. Specific transplanting areas within each preserve were identified by the community type (dry and dry mesic dolomite prairie), the occurrence of known plant associates, and presence of surface rocks representing all sizes but optimally between 5 and 10 mm to enhance seedling establishment. A grid system was established in each area to facilitate mapping.

On the day of transplanting, pots were first arranged at a density no greater than 4 plants m^{-2} within suitable habitat (dry and dry mesic dolomite prairie). Number- and color-coded tags identified which plants could be neighbors. The rosettes were transplanted at the proper height above ground to reduce the potential for root rot and frost heaving, and were watered and mapped within the grid system. A total of 1215 Lakeside daisies were transplanted (605 at Lockport and 610 at Romeoville), requiring 20 people for one day per site. Supplemental watering continued on every third day for two weeks.

Only 5% (60) of the spring transplants (cohort 1) survived the summer of 1988, which had record high temperatures and the worst recorded drought in Illinois history (Illinois State Water Survey 1989) (Fig. 12.4). Continuing the supplemental watering was impractical and would not have counteracted the drought effects. Because of the availability of a large greenhouse 'source' population, a second cohort of 1031 Lakeside daisies was transplanted in the fall of 1988, 520 at Lockport Prairie and 511 at Romeoville Prairie. Three hundred plants were also transplanted into Manito Prairie Nature Preserve.

Survivorship and reproduction in transplant cohorts

Of the 5% cohort 1 transplants surviving the 1988 drought, 90% of these were still present by 1991. Overall survivorship among the cohort 2 transplants fared better: 84% at Lockport and 59% at Romeoville (Fig. 12.4). Since 1989, the total number of transplants has either remained steady (Lockport) or

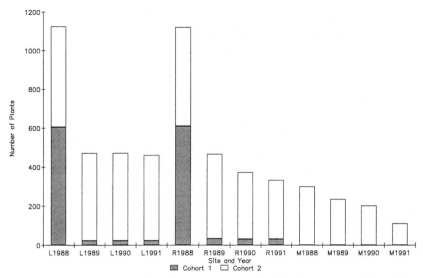

Fig. 12.4. Survivorship of restored Illinois Lakeside daisy populations from 1988–1991. L = Lockport Prairie Nature Preserve, R = Romeoville Prairie Nature Preserve, M = Manito Prairie Nature Preserve. Cohorts 1 and 2 were transplanted in spring and fall of 1988, respectively.

declined by approximately one-third (Romeoville). Manito Prairie had the lowest transplant survivorship (37%), partly because small mammals uprooted Lakeside daisies and the lack of fire allowed the surrounding vegetation to increase (J. Schwegman, personal communication).

Although flowering rates have varied from site to site and year to year, the Will County sites have consistently had a lower proportion of flowering plants (Fig. 12.5). In at least one year (1991), two-thirds of all inflorescences at the Will County sites were either partly herbivorized by insects or totally consumed by white-tailed deer and eastern cottontail rabbits (M.M. DeMauro, unpublished data). Nevertheless, the total number of flowering plants was greater, and seed production is likely to be higher at the Will County sites than at Manito Prairie. This may be one of the reasons why recruitment rates are different between recovery sites (Fig. 12.5). Seedlings were observed as early as summer 1989 at the Will County sites while none were observed at Manito Prairie until spring 1991 (J. Schwegman, personal communication).

Recruitment at the Will County sites was much higher in 1990 than 1991 (Table 12.4), which is likely related to a severe drought during the summer of 1991. Over half (57%) of the juveniles recorded in 1991 were not observed as seedlings the previous spring. This suggests opportunistic seed germination whenever soil moisture is favorable during the growing season. Recruitment

Table 12.4. *Preliminary recruitment data for restored populations of*
Lakeside daisy in Illinois

	Year/size class[a]							
	1989	1990			1991			
Description	S	S	J	TOT	S	J	A	TOT
Lockport prairie								
New from Seed	+[b]	264	59	323	168	152	1	321
Died between 90–91		(171)	(14)	(185)				
Recruited from								
Sdlgs. or Juvs.[c]		—	—	—	—	56	2	58
Carryover[d]		—	—	—	35	45	—	80
TOTAL:		264	59	323	203	253	3	459
Romeoville prairie								
New from Seed	+[b]	118	7	125	34	9	0	43
Died between 90–91		(98)	(2)	(100)				
Recruited from								
Sdlgs. or Juvs.[c]		—	—	—	—	15	0	15
Carryover[d]		—	—	—	5	5	0	10
TOTAL:		118	7	125	39	29	0	68

Notes: [a] Numbers of plants observed. S=seedling, J=juvenile, A=adult.
[b] + = seedlings observed late in 1989 but not quantified.
[c] Plants recruited from seedling or juvenile size class as opposed to new plants from seed.
[d] Carryover represents the number of plants that remained in the same size class between sample years.

has been most successful at Lockport Prairie, where the Lakeside daisy population has doubled in number (Figure 12.5). Three of the flowering adults in 1991 at this site were recruited from seed produced by transplants in spring 1989.

In the short term, recovery actions have been moderately successful, especially at the Will County sites. The initial number of transplants has continued to decline, but the surviving individuals have continued to increase in size and flower. More importantly, there has been recruitment, establishment, and growth of new individuals, some of which have already flowered. Herbivores are one potentially serious short-term threat to population survival and growth because their actions result in the loss of individuals (uprooting) or lowering of reproductive success (loss of inflorescences). The long-term viability and success of the Illinois Lakeside daisy recovery program will continue to be evaluated by monitoring and comparing restored and natural populations to

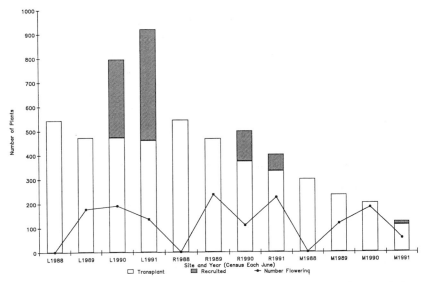

Fig. 12.5. Population size and flowering in restored Illinois Lakeside daisy populations from 1988 to 1991. Annual censusing was conducted in June of each year. L = Lockport Prairie Nature Preserve, R = Romeoville Prairie Nature Preserve, M = Manito Prairie Nature Preserve.

determine if restored populations fall within targeted ranges for site, population, and demographic variables (DeMauro 1990, US Fish & Wildlife Service 1990).

Summary

In small populations, genetic and breeding system considerations are critical to the success of any initial recovery actions; however, to insure long-term success, demographic and ecological factors must be incorporated in recovery planning. In the case of Lakeside daisy, a self-incompatible perennial composite, habitat destruction caused a population bottleneck in which self-incompatibility alleles were lost, and the last Illinois population was rendered effectively extinct because no compatible individuals remained. These results illustrate how extinction mechanisms can operate in small populations of self-incompatible plants. To circumvent this, the genetic composition and spatial arrangement of transplants in restored populations were manipulated to maximize random sampling of different S alleles, and increase the likelihood of successful seed production between compatible neighbors.

Because plants are sessile, recovery sites with appropriate habitat for the establishment and growth of all age and size classes must be selected. To develop recovery site selection criteria, it was necessary to identify Lakeside daisy's narrow habitat requirements. It was also necessary to sample the remaining natural populations to develop criteria for transplant size, and density and distribution patterns. In the site selection and implementation stages of the recovery program, these criteria were considered solid ecological guidelines rather than absolutes because they were derived from extant populations in which the different successional stage and structure of the plant communities were due in part to different site disturbance histories. Long-term demographic monitoring in natural and restored populations will allow comparison of population parameters over time to objectively assess the status of restored populations and determine if additional intervention is needed.

After reviewing population viability analyses and assessing their implications for plant conservation, Menges (1991) concluded that environmental stochasticity and natural catastrophes were the primary threats to *in situ* populations. The initial results from newly established Lakeside daisy populations confirm these predictions. A severe drought eliminated 95% of the first transplants within two months. This necessitated a second transplant attempt, which has been moderately successful. At each site, the number of transplants was approximately 600 or fewer, values which are near the low end of the suggested range for population maintenance when no detailed population viability analysis exists (Menges 1991). When feasible, future restoration attempts should start with a larger population size, at least on the order of 10^3. If habitat and climatic conditions are favorable, populations should increase and become self-sustaining.

Restoration can be a viable conservation strategy if a comprehensive and experimental approach to recovery planning and actions, such as with the Lakeside daisy, is undertaken. As with any experiment, there will be successes and failures, but if there is any chance of successfully restoring a population to the wild, conservationists must take some risks. Through the experimentation process, enough knowledge will be gained to benefit other *in situ* recovery programs and advance rare plant conservation.

Literature cited

Barrett, S. C. H. & Kohn, J. R. (1991) Genetic and evolutionary consequences of small population size in plants: implications for conservation. In *Genetics and Conservation of Rare Plants*, ed. Falk, D. A. & Holsinger, K. E., pp. 3–30. New York: Oxford University Press.

Bateman, A. J. (1954) Self-incompatibility systems in Angiosperms II. *Iberis amara*. *Heredity,* **8**, 305–22.

Charlesworth, D. & Charlesworth, B. (1987) Inbreeding depression and its evolutionary consequences. *Annual Review of Ecology and Systematics,* **18**, 237–68.

Cook, R. E. & Dixon, P. (1986) *A review of recovery plans for threatened and endangered plant species: a report for the World Wildlife Fund*. Ithaca: Cornell University.

Cooperrider, T. S., ed. (1982) *Endangered and threatened plants of Ohio*. Ohio Biological Survey, Biological Notes No. 16. College of Biological Sciences. Columbus: Ohio State University.

Cowles, H. C. (1926) The succession point of view in floristics. *Proceedings International Congress Plant Science, Ithaca*, **1**, 687–91.

Cusick, A. W. & Burns, J. F. (1984) *Hymenoxys acaulis* (Pursh) Parker var. *glabra* (Gray) Parker. In *Ohio Endangered and Threatened Vascular Plants*, ed. McCance, R. M. Jr. & Burns, J. F., p. A-357. Columbus: Department of Natural Resources.

DeMauro, M. M. (1987) *A permanent monitoring program for the lakeside daisy (Hymenoxys acaulis var. glabra) at the Marblehead Quarry, Marblehead, Ottawa County, Ohio*. Report to the Ohio Department of Natural Resources, Columbus: Ohio Department of Natural Resources.

DeMauro, M. M. (1988a) A proposal for the Conservation of the Lakeside Daisy, *Hymenoxys acaulis* var. *glabra*, in Illinois. Report to the Illinois Endangered Species Protection Board, March, 1988 and the Illinois Natures Preserve Commission, May (1988) Joliet: Forest Preserve District of Will County.

DeMauro, M. M. (1988b) *Aspects of the reproductive biology of the endangered Hymenoxys acaulis var. glabra; implications for conservation*. Masters thesis, Chicago: University of Illinois at Chicago.

DeMauro, M. M. (1990) *Baseline population monitoring for the Lakeside daisy (Hymenoxys acaulis var. glabra) at the Rt. 163 Site and Lakeside Daisy State Nature Preserve, Ottawa County, Ohio*. Report to the Ohio Department of Natural Resources, Columbus: Ohio Department of Natural Resources.

DeMauro, M. M. (1993) Relationship of breeding system to rarity in the Lakeside daisy (*Hymenoxys acaulis* var. *glabra*). *Conservation Biology*, **7**, 542–50.

Doloi, P. C. & Rai, B. (1981) Inbreeding depression in rapeseed. *Indian Journal of Genetics and Plant Breeding*, **41**, 368–73.

Emerson, S. (1939) A preliminary survey of the *Oenothera organensis* population. *Genetics*, **24**, 524–37.

Ewens, W. J. (1964) On the problem of self-sterility alleles. *Genetics*, **50**, 1433–38.

Fernald, M. L. (1950) *Gray's Manual of Botany*. 8th edn. Portland: Dioscorides Press.

Fisher, R. A. (1958) *The Genetical Theory of Natural Selection*. New York: Dover Publications.

Frankel, O. H. & Soulé, M. E. (1981) *Conservation and Evolution*. New York: Cambridge University Press.

Franklin, E. C. (1970) *Survey of mutant forms and inbreeding depression in species of the family Pinaceae*. USDA Forest Service Research Paper SE-61. Asheville: USDA Forest Service.

Franklin, I. R. (1980) Evolutionary changes in small populations. In *Conservation Biology: An Evolutionary-Ecological Perspective*, ed. Soulé, M. E. & Wilcox, B.A., pp. 135–49. Sunderland: Sinauer Associates.

Gilpin, M. E. & Soulé, M. E. (1986) Minimum viable populations: processes of species extinctions. In *Conservation Biology: The Science of Scarcity and Diversity*, ed. M. E. Soulé, pp. 19–34. Sunderland: Sinauer Associates.

Gleason, H. A. (1923) A vegetational history of the midwest. *Annals of the Association of American Geographers*, **12**, 39–45.

Harper, J. L. (1977) *Population Biology of Plants*. New York: Academic Press.

Harrington, H. D. (1964) *Manual of the Plants of Colorado*. 2nd edn. Chicago: Sage Books, Swallow Press.

Huenneke, L. F. (1991) Ecological implications of genetic variation in plant populations. In *Genetics and Conservation of Rare Plants*, ed. Falk, D. A. & Holsinger, K. E., pp. 31–44. New York: Oxford University Press.

Illinois Natural Areas Inventory. (1976) *Main Data Form for the Lakeside Daisy Site, Area No. 885, Reference No. 27*. Springfield: Department of Conservation.

Illinois Nature Preserves Commission. (1983) *Illinois Nature Preserves System: 1981–1982 Report*. Springfield: Department of Conservation.

Illinois State Water Survey. (1989) Spring/Summer drought dominates 1988 weather. *Currents*, 4, 6. Champaign: Illinois State Water Survey.

Imrie, B. C. & Knowles, P. F. (1971) Genetic studies of self-incompatibility in *Carthamus flavescens* Spreng. *Crop Science,* 11, 6–9.

Imrie, B. C., Kirkman, C. J. & Ross, D. R. (1972) Computer simulation of a sporophytic self-incompatible breeding system. *Australian Journal–Biological Sciences*, 25, 343–9.

Lande, R. (1988) Genetics and demography in biological conservation. *Science*, 241, 1455–1460.

Lande, R. & Barrowclough, G. F. (1987) Effective population size, genetic variation, and their use in population management. In *Viable Populations for Conservation*, ed. M. E. Soulé. Sunderland: Sinauer Associates.

Lawrence, G. H. M. (1951) *Taxonomy of Vascular Plants*. New York: MacMillan Publishing Co.

Les, D. H., Reinhartz, J. A. & Esselman, E. J. (1991) Genetic consequences of rarity in *Aster furcatus* (Asteraceae), a threatened, self-incompatible plant. *Evolution*, 45, 1641–50.

Levin, D. A. (1981) Dispersal versus gene flow in plants. *Annals of the Missouri Botanic Garden*, 68, 233–53.

Levin, D. A. & Kerster, H. W. (1974) Gene flow in seed plants. *Evolutionary Biology*, 7, 139–220.

Menges, E. S. (1991) The application of minimum population viable population theory to plants. In *Genetics and Conservation of Rare Plants*, ed. Falk, D. A. & Holsinger, K. E., pp. 45–61. New York: Oxford University Press.

Morton, J. K. & Venn, J. M. (1984) The Flora of Manitoulin Island. *University of Waterloo Biology Series No. 28*. Waterloo: University of Waterloo.

Moseley, E. (1899) Sandusky Flora. A catalogue of the flowering plants and ferns growing without cultivation, in Erie County, Ohio, and the peninsula and islands of Ottawa County. *Ohio State Academy of Sciences Special Papers No. 1*. Columbus: Ohio State Academy of Sciences.

Mulcahy, G. B. & Mulcahy, D. L. (1985) Pollen-pistil interactions. In *Biotechnology and ecology of pollen: proceedings of the International Conference on the Biotechnology and Ecology of Pollen*, ed. Mulcahy, G. B., Mulcahy, D. L. & Ottaviano, E., pp. 173–178. New York: Springer-Verlag.

Nettancourt, N de. (1977) *Incompatibility in Angiosperms: Monographs on Theoretical and Applied Genetics*. New York: Springer-Verlag.

Ockendon, D. J. (1974) Distribution of self-incompatibility alleles and breeding structure of open-pollinated cultivars of brussel sprouts. *Heredity,* 33, 159–71.

Parker, K. F. (1950) New combinations in *Hymenoxys*. *Madroño*, 10, 159.

Sampson, D. R. (1967) Frequency and distribution self-incompatibility alleles in *Raphanus raphanistrum*. *Genetics*, 56, 241–51.

Shaffer, M. L. (1981) Minimum population sizes for species conservation. *BioScience*, 31, 131–4.

Sheviak, C.J. (1981) Endangered and threatened plants. In *Endangered and Threatened Species of Illinois: Status and Distribution*, ed. Bowles, M. L.,

Diersing, V. E., Ebinger, J. E. & Schultz, H. C., pp. 70–1. Springfield: Department of Conservation.

Soulé, M. E. (1980) Thresholds for survival: maintaining fitness and evolutionary potential. In *Conservation Biology: An Evolutionary-Ecological Perspective*, ed. Soulé, M. E. and Wilcox, B.A., pp. 151–69. Sunderland: Sinauer Associates.

Swink, F. & Wilhelm, G. (1979) *Plants of the Chicago Region.* 2nd edn. Lisle: The Morton Arboretum.

Transeau, E. N. (1935) The prairie peninsula. *Ecology*, **16**, 423–37.

US Fish and Wildlife Service. (1990) *Recovery plan for the Lakeside daisy (Hymenoxys acaulis* var. *glabra)*. Minneapolis/Saint Paul: US Fish and Wildlife Service.

Voss, J. (1935) *Actinea herbacea. Torreya*, **62**, 61–2.

Webb, T. III, Cushing, E. J. & Wright, H. E. Jr. (1983) Holocene changes in the vegetation of the Midwest. In *Late Quaternary Environments of the United States*, ed. Wright, H. E. Jr., pp. 142–65. Minneapolis: University of Minnesota Press.

White, J. (1978) *Illinois Natural Areas Inventory Technical Report*. Springfield: Illinois Department of Conservation.

Wright, S. (1939) The distribution of self-sterility alleles in populations. *Genetics*, **24**, 538–52.

Wright, S. (1964) The distribution of self-incompatibility alleles in populations. *Evolution*, **18**, 609–19.

Wunderlin, R. P. (1971) Contributions to an Illinois flora. No. 4. *Transactions of the Illinois Academy of Sciences,* **64**, 317–27.

13

Demographic monitoring and the recovery of endangered plants

BRUCE M. PAVLIK

Introduction

The recovery of endangered plants requires that natural populations be within protected, appropriate habitat and able to maintain themselves over long periods of time. Protected natural populations contain the subtle genetic and ecological characteristics that reflect the evolutionary history of a species. In extreme cases, recovery may also require the creation of new self-maintaining populations within the species' historic range and the enhancement of small natural populations *in situ*. Created populations reduce the probability that the species will become extinct, and restore it to a greater ecological potential. Enhanced natural populations are larger, less likely to lose their genetic variability, and less susceptible to small-scale perturbation. No plant taxa have, in fact, been recovered and consequently regarded as conserved *in situ*, despite numerous attempts to protect (e.g. Elias 1987), create (e.g. Brookes 1981, Morgan & Wilson 1981, Griggs & Jain 1983, Havlik 1987, Falk 1988, Simonich & Morgan 1990, Reichenbacher 1990, Olwell *et al.* 1987, Olwell, Cully & Knight 1990, Pavlik *et al.* 1993b, DeMauro, chapter 12 of this volume) or enhance (Given 1983, Ferreira & Smith 1987, Pavlik & Manning 1993) populations. Under the United States' Endangered Species Act, recovery would lead to downlisting (changing from endangered to threatened status) or delisting (removing protected status) if the minimum number of viable populations were acheived (Bartel 1987, Knudsen 1987, Rohlf 1991). Recovery projects have fallen short for a variety of reasons. Some have not established whether the natural, new, or enhanced populations can maintain themselves in the wild. This is particularly true for long-lived perennial plants, or when transplanting has been used to circumvent critical life history phases (Fahselt 1988). Other projects are limited because they create only one or two small populations when five or six large ones, for example, are required by recovery plans. This is often the case when critical habitat is in short supply or few propagules of the target species are available.

Perhaps the greatest and most common deficiency, however, is the lack of detailed demographic data that would allow researchers to predict short-term trends and analyze factors that limit population establishment and growth. When demographic monitoring is incorporated into a field experiment, existing habitat conditions or management techniques can be evaluated, and alternative techniques can be designed to hasten recovery (Harvey 1985, Menges 1986).

In this chapter, I examine the essential role of demographic monitoring in recovering the most endangered plant taxa: those with only a few, highly localized populations. I wish to specifically address agency personnel, reserve managers, and restoration biologists, emphasizing that: demographic monitoring should consist of two principal activities, trend analysis and factor resolution; management decisions can be based on the results of trend analysis and factor resolution; and trend analysis and factor resolution provide the framework for creating new populations and enhancing existing natural populations of endangered plants.

Relationship of monitoring and recovery to plant conservation

The *in situ* conservation of endangered plants can be viewed as a five-part process: inventory, survey, habitat protection, monitoring, and recovery (Bratton & White 1981). Inventory is a geographically based assessment of rare taxa that documents their occurrence within mapped political units (e.g. Ayensu & DeFilipps 1978, Skinner & Pavlik 1994). Survey is an ecologically based assessment of populations in the field with respect to habitat and endangerment factors (e.g. Nelson 1984, Taylor & Palmer 1987). Habitat protection includes land-use restrictions that can be applied to or negotiated for the most imperiled populations (ideally) or those that generate minimal political resistance (realistically). Land-use restrictions include zoning changes, conservation easements, property acquisition, and others (Meyer 1984, Lozier 1987, Knudsen 1987). Inventory, survey, and habitat protection techniques have been refined, somewhat standardized, and widely applied by public resource agencies and private conservation groups over the past 15–20 years (e.g. Elias 1987).

Endangered plant monitoring and recovery are less well-developed. Despite a recent series of papers emphasizing the importance of demographic monitoring (Bradshaw 1981, Davy & Jefferies 1981, Given 1983, Sutter 1986, Menges 1986, Travis & Sutter 1986, Pavlik 1987, Pavlik & Barbour 1988, Given 1989), agency personnel and reserve managers have been slow to incorporate it into management plans for rare species (Palmer 1986, 1987). Because demographic

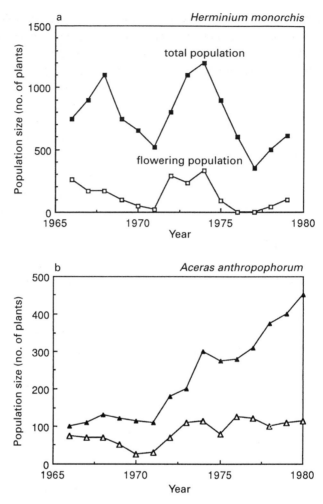

Fig. 13.1. Fluctuations in the total (closed symbol) and flowering (open symbol) population sizes of two British orchids as revealed by census over a 14 year period. a) *Herminium monorchis* and b) *Aceras anthropophorum*. Data from Wells (1981).

studies are more time- and resource-intensive than surveys, many managers substitute yearly population censusing for detailed monitoring. In a census, the number of individuals in a rare plant population at flowering is counted and compared with tallies from previous years. A summary of changes in the population, which may or may not indicate the need for management intervention, is obtained. This concept of monitoring, emphasizing the detection and documentation of change, was advocated for many years as a tool for conserving rare plants (Jenkins & Bedford 1973, White & Bratton 1981).

There are at least five reasons why census data alone are insufficent, and sometimes misleading, for monitoring rare plants, designing recovery projects, and evaluating recovery methods (Bradshaw 1981, Bratton & White 1981, Davy & Jefferies 1981, Sutter 1986). First, the number of plants counted per year is not necessarily significant to population biology or conservation. Change in the size of a population is not always a matter of concern; in fact, great fluctuations in observed population sizes (Fig. 13.1) are the norm for some plant life forms (annuals, some herbaceous perennials, see Harper 1981). Second, significant change can be slow, and therefore difficult to detect over the relatively short time periods associated with typical bureaucratic or fiscal constraints. Five to fifteen years, or more, may be required to obtain a genuine trend, and in that time employees can leave, survey methods can change, budgets can be cut, and interest in the project can fade. Third, many rare plant taxa lack replicate populations, which are needed to determine the significance of detectible change. Fourth, change detected from census data for reproductive individuals has an obscure relationship to the population and to the species as a whole: seeds, seedlings, and juveniles might better indicate demographic change. Fifth, the biological processes that affect population stability (e.g. survivorship, fecundity, duration in the seed bank) must be known if meaningful management of the population is to be designed, implemented, or evaluated.

The last point is particularly crucial for recovery. Regardless of whether existing natural populations are to be enhanced or new populations are to be created within historic range, the recovery of rare plant populations is a demographic and experimental venture. Habitat manipulation, transplanting potted plants, sowing seeds, and other restoration techniques have population-level effects that should be quantified and evaluated. In this way, the prospects for species recovery (as defined in recovery plans) can be determined and used to make policy and economic decisions. Therefore, the key to implementing a successful recovery program for a rare plant is effective demographic monitoring.

Demographic monitoring

Demographic monitoring follows the fates of individual plants in a population and makes repetitive *in situ* measurements (Davy & Jefferies 1981, Travis & Sutter 1986, Pavlik & Barbour 1988). It is an aid for identifying the timing and causes of poor performance and, therefore, providing management recommendations. It can help identify which populations require management, provide an experimental framework for creating or enhancing populations, and evaluate the project's effectiveness and efficiency (Given 1984, Harvey 1985,

Baskin & Baskin 1986, Pavlik 1987). The manager who understands distinct but integrated demographic processes has a fulcrum with which to lever the fate of the endangered species. This is why demographic monitoring of existing natural populations should be used to design and implement recovery actions.

How can demographic measurements be used to recover endangered plant populations? To answer, I will divide demographic monitoring into trend analysis and factor resolution. Trend analysis asks, 'which populations of a species require management intervention?' Factor resolution asks, 'what kinds of intervention would result in a growing or stabilized population?' To my knowledge, no previous studies have separated their monitoring activities according to this scheme. Yet, all studies that I have reviewed contain components of trend analysis, factor resolution, or both (see also Huenneke, Holsinger & Palmer 1986). By erecting these two categories, I hope to help regulators, managers, and biologists select the kinds of measurements that should be made in demographic monitoring and clarify how different measurements can be used to make decisions and meet management objectives.

Trend analysis

Demographic trend analysis is used to determine whether a population has the potential for growth or stability in the near future. It can, but does not necessarily, predict rates of growth or decline. Primarily, trend analysis searches for indicators of stability among a few important characteristics, such as survivorship, reproduction *sensu lato*, and frequency of establishment. Trend analysis should provide the information of census data, but in a fraction of the time (2–4 years instead of 5–15 years). This is because the significant changes in a population take place over many years, but result from smaller, cumulative changes in short-term demographic processes. Because we have virtually no historical census data for endangered plant populations, changes in the number of individuals must be measured against the current population size. It will often be the case, especially with long-lived taxa, that trend analysis will indicate the ability of a population to maintain its current size (its potential for stability), rather than net increase or decrease *per se*. Potential for stability is the minimum determination of trend analysis.

How is potential for stability assessed? Basically, all techniques for predicting the fate of a population are either integrated or nonintegrated. Integrated approaches incorporate two or more related variables into a single model of population dynamics. That model generates an index, the value of which indicates stability, growth, or decline. Life table analysis, for example, allows for the calculation of R_o, the net reproductive rate of the population (Begon & Mortimer 1981), based on mortality and fecundity schedules. Although widely applied to animals, life tables are rarely constructed for plants. As Harper (1977) has pointed out, the difficulty lies in following the age-specific fates of ovules during reproduction and the fates of seeds after they disperse from the parent plant but before they emerge as germinules. The possibility of using life table analysis for rare plant conservation is remote because it would require sampling ovaries prior to seed set and sampling the seed bank before, during, and after germination (Pavlik 1987). These procedures could result in unacceptable, not-easily-mitigated perturbations of the life cycle.

Another integrated approach to trend analysis, based on the matrix projection models of Leslie (1945) and Lefkovitch (1965), is population viability analysis (PVA, Gilpin & Soulé 1986). PVA has been used on several plant species, including the endangered *Pedicularis furbishiae* (Menges 1990) and two endangered species of *Calochortus* (Fiedler 1987). Instead of age-specific schedules, size-class (or life cycle stage class) categories are used, thus avoiding some of the problems imposed by life table analyses (Menges 1986 and 1992 review this technique). The measured parameters are mortality, survivorship (between each size class), and fecundity (e.g. seed or fruit production within each size class); these are arranged in algebraic matrix. Solving the matrix yields several useful parameters, including lambda (λ), the equilibrium finite growth rate of the population. If $\lambda > 1.0$, the population will be growing, if $\lambda < 1.0$, it will be declining, and if $\lambda = 1.0$, it will be stable. This kind of deterministic modeling of population behavior simplistically assumes that the measured demographic characteristics in the same population or between different populations of the same species will not change. This can be circumvented by sampling several populations during several years, or by using stochastic simulation models to predict population trends under non-equilibrium conditions (Menges 1992).

Regardless of whether deterministic or stochastic approaches are used for PVA, the technique cannot be readily applied to all plant species. Cryptic clonal growth (e.g. bulbils), long-distance seed dispersal, and extreme longevity in some size or stage classes (so that some transition probabilities during the study period cannot be measured) impose difficulties for predicting population viability. Species that have long-lived seeds are especially problematic, because survivorship within the seed bank must be thoroughly assessed and incorporated into the projection matrices. This may exclude most annuals and many short-lived perennials and further limit PVA as a trend analysis method for endangered plants. Menges (1986), however, has suggested that the relevant seed bank data can be obtained from empirical studies

Table 13.1. *Example of integrated trend analysis using PVA*

Values of λ (finite rate of increase) from 15 populations of *Pedicularis furbishiae* during 2 or 3 growing seasons. Data from Menges (1990).

Population	λ values during			predicted trend
	1983–84	1984–85	1985–86	
Ferry Landing	—	1.81	1.67	growing
Fox Brook South	—	1.71	1.00	growing
Negro Brook	—	1.64	1.02	growing
St. Paul	—	1.39	1.10	growing
Jandreau	—	1.36	1.00	growing
Fox Brook Ledges	—	1.16	1.18	growing
Hamlin	—	1.05	1.12	growing
Cone Burner	—	1.24	0.96	potentially stable
Wesley Veratrum	—	1.05	0.88	potentially stable
Gardner's New	—	1.04	0.95	potentially stable
Wiggins	—	1.00	0.94	potentially stable
Fort Kent	0.68	1.27	0.94	probably declining
Gardner's Old	0.76	1.03	0.90	probably declining
St. Francis	0.64	0.98	0.58	declining
Wesley Ledges	—	0.92	0.92	declining

in the field. Standard procedures that circumvent the technical problems currently associated with PVA should be developed, so that PVA can be applied to a wider variety of plant populations.

When PVA has been employed, it has proven powerful. Menges (1990) used PVA to analyze trends in 15 populations of *Pedicularis furbishiae* along the St. John's River in northern Maine and adjacent New Brunswick. This distinctive species is particularly amenable to PVA because there is no seed dormancy or long-lived seed bank, there is no clonal growth, reproductive output (seed production) is high and can be readily estimated from measurements of plant size (in this case, inflorescence length), individuals are relatively short-lived, and an extensive autecological database had been generated during the previous 10 years. Seven of the fifteen *P. furbishiae* populations had $\lambda > 1.0$ during two of the study years, indicating that they were viable and would require no management intervention (Table 13.1). Four populations had λ values < 1.0 in two study years, and were, therefore, headed for extinction in the absence of management. The remaining populations exhibited $\lambda > 1.0$ in one year but not another; these could be regarded as stable but requiring further analysis and, possibly, eventual management.

Non-integrated approaches to trend analysis do not mathematically incorpo-

Table 13.2. *Some general indicators of population stability*

Non-integrated trend analysis would collect data on several demographic parameters in order to reach a conclusion regarding trends in endangered populations. Based on principles of plant population biology (Harper 1977).

Parameter	Life form	Population is stable if:
survivorship	annual	mortality inflection point on survivorship curve (Deevey Type I) follows onset of seed production.
	perennial	the number of individuals in a new cohort equals or exceeds the number of established individuals after slope of survivorship curve (Deevey Type III) $\rightarrow$ 0.
age structure	perennial	number of established, reproductive individuals is less than the number of established juveniles and/or the number of recruited seedlings.
seed production	all	seed production per individual of an endangered taxon equals or exceeds that of a non-endangered relative with similar life form.
seed bank	all	density of viable seeds in soil prior to season of germination far exceeds the average density of established individuals.
	annuals + herbaceous perennials	year to year changes in density of viable seed are not correlated with changes in the density of established, reproductive individuals.
frequency of establishment	annual	frequency of establishment is less than the half-life of seeds in the seed bank.
	perennial	frequency of establishment is less than the half life of established, reproductive plants.

rate different variables into a single predictive model. Instead, they rely on parallel interpretation of data on survivorship, reproduction, and frequency of establishment. In some cases, it is necessary to include measurements of seed bank size and dynamics. The non-integrated approach is used when demographic variables cannot be numerically related to one another (e.g. when seeds are long-lived and there is an appreciable seed bank) and, therefore, integrated approaches cannot be used.

Various general indicators of population stability can be used in non-integrated trend analysis (Table 13.2). These examples are not universal or comprehensive: they are simply *a priori* statements based on general demographic principles for different life histories (Harper 1977). It must also be emphasized that none of these indicators could by itself predict the stability of a population. Plants have complex life histories that are greatly influenced by variations in the environment. For example, a pyramidal age structure, indicating frequent

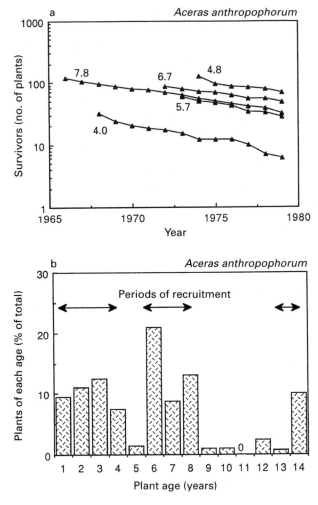

Fig. 13.2. Trend analysis on the orchid *Aceras anthropophorum*. a) Survivorship of five cohorts and their calculated half-lives. b) Age structure and periods of recruitment in the population. Data from Wells (1981).

establishment and constant regeneration, may not be observed in populations of long-lived shrubs, trees, and clonal herbs. This could not be interpreted as a sign of decline unless adult survivorship and seed or ramet production (for example) also indicated the possibility of decline. Every time a relevant indicator is added, confidence in the results of trend analysis rises. The importance of using multiple relevant indicators cannot be overemphasized.

Zero-sum compensations between demographic characteristics within a population can help in drawing conclusions about population trends. Does frequent or abundant seed production by adult plants compensate for infrequent seedling establishment? Does frequent production of new cohorts compensate for short cohort half-life? Obviously, there are a number of uncertainties associated with this type of interpretation, and it relies heavily on the validity of *r–K* selection theory (Grime 1979, Watkinson 1981, Griggs & Jain 1983). However, it is likely to detect disturbance of the habitat or the population (a primary cause of endangerment) by determining that one or more of the compensating mechanisms within a population is impaired.

For example, for 14 years Wells (1981) analyzed the population dynamics of several species of uncommon orchids in Britain, including *Aceras anthropophorum* (Fig. 13.2). Estimates of cohort half-life (from survivorship curves) ranged between 4.0 and 7.8 years, and significant establishment periods (from age structure data) occurred at least three times during the study. Flowering took place to some extent every year; above-average events occurred in two-to-three-year intervals. Since cohort half-life was longer than the intervals between establishment and reproduction, it appears that this species' population is capable of growing under current environmental and management conditions. This was confirmed by trends in long-term census data (Fig. 13.1). The study found other species' populations to be unstable, either because of high mortality (*Herminium monorchis*) or decreasing frequency of reproduction (*Spiranthes spiralis*). Changes in management policy, guided by a detailed study of the factors that affect mortality and reproduction, would therefore be warranted (see *Factor resolution*, below).

Although the orchid data were gathered over 6–14 years, it is possible to make reasonable decisions regarding population trends from short-term studies (Sarukhan & Harper 1973, Harper 1977, Meagher, Antonovics & Primack 1978, Smith 1987; Borchert 1989). After two years of monitoring marked plants on a desert sand dune, Pavlik & Barbour (1988) determined that populations of three highly endangered herbaceous species were either stable or growing. Established adults of the coarse hummock grass *Swallenia alexandrae* (Poaceae) had a half-life of 15.9 years, which compared well to the half-lives of other arid land grasses and to the estimated frequency of establishment. The other two species had much shorter half-lives (less than 3 years), but compensated with copious seed production and yearly establishment. Additional monitoring will be necessary to verify conclusions from such a short-term study, but management attention can now be turned to other, more critically threatened taxa.

Conclusions can also be reached by comparing important demographic variables among populations of the same species or among populations of species with similar life histories and general ecological characteristics. For example,

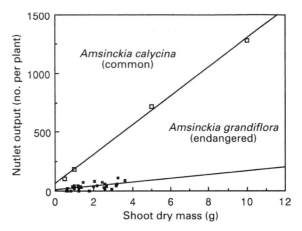

Fig. 13.3. Comparison of nutlet output as a function of plant size between an endangered annual (*Amsinckia grandiflora,* closed symbols) and its widspread, weedy relative (*A. calycina,* open symbols). Data from Pavlik (1988).

Pavlik (1988) compared nutlet production in the endangered *Amsinckia grandiflora* (Boraginaceae) with that in a widespread, weedy congeneric, *A. calycina.* Total nutlet output as a function of plant size (shoot dry mass or inflorescence length) was consistently lower in the endangered than in the common species (Fig. 13.3). A primitive form of heterostyly in *A. grandiflora* may be partly responsible (Ornduff 1976), but competition from annual grasses was also shown to be significant (see below). Such measurements indicate that endangered populations of *A. grandiflora* are unlikely to grow and maintain themselves at the rate of *A. calycina* because of factors affecting reproductive output. A comparative approach to reproductive output was also taken by Meagher *et al.* (1978) in studies of rare and common *Plantago* species, by Griggs & Jain (1983) with *Orcuttia* species, and by Rabinowitz *et al.* (1989) in studies of rare prairie grasses.

A plant's efficiency in converting ovules into viable seeds (the seed/ovule ratio, or S/O) can also be used to assess seed production in relation to population stability. In an extensive survey of relatively common species, Wiens (1984) has found that regardless of breeding system, S/O is approximately 0.85 in annuals and 0.50 in perennials. If, in endangered species, S/O approached these values or was similar to that of common relatives, it would be unlikely that low seed production was leading to instability or decline (Table 13.3). Significant depressions in S/O, perhaps caused by deleterious genetic load and inbreeding or low resource availability (Wiens *et al.* 1987, Harper & Wallace 1987, Ackerman 1989), could restrict population growth. Populations of the rare desert shrub *Dedeckera eurekensis* consistently have S/O ratios below

Table 13.3. *Variation in seed/ovule ratios between related endangered and common taxa, Antioch Dunes, California.*

In trend analysis these data indicate that growth of the endangered populations would not be limited by the effects of genetic load or inbreeding depression on seed production. Factor resolution would determine the reasons behind year-to-year fluctuations. Values (mean ± SD) followed by different letters are significantly different at $P< 0.01$ (ANOVA, arcsine transformed). Data from Pavlik *et al.* (1993a).

	Erysimum capitatum		Oenothera	
	angustatum (endangered)	capitatum (common)	deltoides howellii (endangered)	hookeri (common)
1987	0.495 ± 0.061[a]	0.499 ± 0.103[a]	0.195 ± 0.139[b]	$0.628 \pm .071$[c]
1988	0.125 ± 0.068[b]	—	0.413 ± 0.111[a]	—

0.05 despite large fluctuations in environmental conditions (Wiens *et al.* 1989). In this case, genetic factors reduce viable seed production. Unfortunately, if genetic factors are responsible for low reproductive output (or lowered fitness in other life cycle stages, such as germination (Menges 1991), there may be very few management options. If S/O is depressed because critical resources (e.g. pollinators, water, etc.) are in short supply, successful manipulation may be possible. The S/O ratios of *Erysimum capitatum* var. *angustatum* and *Oenothera deltoides* ssp. *howellii*, two endangered endemic perennials at Antioch Dunes, California (Pavlik & Manning 1993, Pavlik *et al.* 1993a), were shown to vary widely from year to year (Table 13.3), but because S/O did average 0.50 in at least one year for each species, it was concluded that resource availability, rather than genetic factors, was responsible and that there was little overall effect on population stability. The populations were sufficiently small, however, to warrant remedial action. As will be discussed below, factor resolution was subsequently used to identify the most critical resource(s) and prescribe management options for the populations.

Factor resolution

Once trend analysis has been used to determine that one or more populations of an endangered species are potentially declining or unstable, the responsible factors must be identified and prioritized for management. These factors can be intrinsic (e.g. demographic characteristics, breeding system, levels of genetic variability) or extrinsic (the biotic and abiotic components of environment, including human disturbance).

In most cases, a subset of potentially important factors will be apparent from the results of trend analysis. For example, if S/O ratios were extremely low, then factor resolution could experimentally manipulate water, nutrient, and pollen resources to determine the effect on reproductive output. A transition matrix with high seedling mortality might suggest experimental studies on microherbivory, habitat availability, and interspecific competition. A juvenile-poor age structure despite high seed production calls for descriptive studies of seed dispersal, germination, and predation as well as experimental studies of seedling survivorship under alternative management regimes. The point is that factor resolution should first examine the critical variables suggested by trend analysis, before attempting to describe or evaluate an array of general ecological characteristics. This approach introduces the risk that not all of the factors that limit population growth will be identified, but this risk is outweighed by the benefits of finding one or two critical factors that can be manipulated to produce a positive and significant demographic response. Such sharp focus is essential for meeting the narrow, immediate objectives of a recovery effort: stabilizing, enlarging, or creating populations. In addition to the examples given below, work by Macior (1980), Menges, Waller & Gawler (1986), and Gawler, Waller & Menges (1987) on *Pedicularis furbishiae,* and Karron (1987, 1989) on *Astragalus* species illustrate a focused, factorial approach.

Data from PVA have been used to examine limiting factors. Menges (1990) collected environmental data for each of the monitored populations of *P. furbishiae* and found that high canopy cover by woody plants was correlated with low values of λ. Sites with low soil moisture also appeared to be less favorable, but the effect was not as strong or consistent as that of canopy cover. He concluded that conditions that kept sites open (in early seral stages) were of paramount importance to the species. Therefore, maintaining the natural flood regime along the St. John's River, which periodically removes overstory shrubs, would be a major management objective for recovering this species. Fiedler (1987) used projection matrices for rare and common species of *Calochortus* to examine the relative importance of factors affecting seed production (e.g. defoliation by herbivores) on population viability. This 'sensitivity analysis' revealed that the population growth rates of the rare species were less likely than those of common species to respond favorably to factors that increased seed output. In other words, sexual reproduction in the rare species was less opportunistic and, therefore, less likely to benefit from herbivore control measures.

Harvey & Meredith (1981) used factor resolution to make management suggestions for populations of *Peucedanum palustre*, a peat fen species becoming rare in Britain. They examined an array of demographic characteristics, including those needed for trend analysis (survivorship by stage class, seed produc-

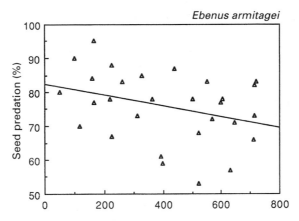

Fig. 13.4. Effect of flower density on the predation of *Ebenus armitagei* seeds by buprestid beetles. Regression is significant (P<0.05) with a negative slope. Data from Hegazy & Eesa (1991).

tion) and others required for factor resolution in this particular case (germination, seed predation and longevity, herbivory). They concluded that grazing by terrestrial slugs and snails was the principal factor responsible for the low seedling survivorship and limited growth of *Peucedanum* populations. They were then able to make specific management recommendations, including the return of a more natural flooding regime to the fen to control grazer populations. Subsequently, Harvey (1985) compared and summarized the important factors that constrained population growth for eight species of conservation interest.

In a recent study of the rare shrub *Ebenus armitagei* (Leguminosae), Hegazy & Eesa (1991) found that the study population did not increase despite abundant flowering and fruit formation. Age structure and survivorship data indicated that seedlings and established juveniles (0–4 years old) suffered moderate levels of mortality, but more importantly, up to 94% of the yearly seed production was destroyed by a native beetle (*Callosobruchus maculatus*, Buprestidae). The intensity of seed predation declined significantly as the density of flowers in the habitat increased (Fig. 13.4), allowing some seeds to escape during dispersal. High winds pushed many of these into unsuitable habitat. The authors suggested erecting shelter belts within the population boundary to enhance the probability of establishment within high-quality habitat. If successful, the artificial inhibition of dispersal could increase plant and flowering density, thereby minimizing the need to use insecticides to control seed predation.

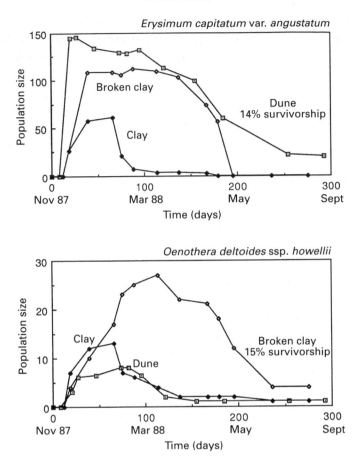

Fig. 13.5. Limitations imposed by soil type (clay, mechanically broken clay, and dune sand) on germination and survivorship in experimental populations of two endangered, riverine dune plants, Antioch, California. Data from Pavlik & Manning (1993).

Experimental manipulations of natural or artificial populations of endangered plants are another form of factor resolution (see Travis & Sutter 1986 for a discussion of experimental design and statistical methods). Returning to the Antioch Dunes example (Pavlik & Manning 1993, Pavlik *et al.* 1993a), populations of the two endemics *Erysimum capitatum* var. *angustatum* and *Oenothera deltoides* ssp. *howellii* had become severely depleted as the result of 50 years of sand mining, which removed dunes, created an extensive clay hardpan, and helped to promote the growth of sand-stabilizing weeds. In initial attempts to create better soil conditions, areas of clay adjacent to the endangered populations were disked. Replicate plots on clay, disked clay, and dune sand soils were sown with seeds of the two species so that the fate of each seed could be determined over the next 300 days (precision sowing). For *E. c.* var. *angustatum*, emergence and survivorship were significantly higher on the dune sand than on the other substrates (Fig. 13.5). The survivors grew vigorously, flowered, and set much seed at the end of their second year. For *Oe. d.* ssp. *howellii*, however, emergence and survivorship were higher on the broken clay, but the only individual that reproduced was on the dune sand. Thus, disking did not create suitable habitat for either species. The US Fish and Wildlife Service is now attempting to create dune habitat by importing large amounts of dredged riverine sand, and that effort can also be evaluated using an experimental approach, perhaps with competition from colonizing weeds as a variable.

Demographic monitoring in recovery

The ultimate goal of recovery programs is to ensure that species with limited distribution and abundance have the highest possible probability of long-term persistence and evolutionary viability (Schonewald-Cox *et al.* 1983). This can be accomplished in the short term if target species have multiple populations in appropriate and protected habitat throughout their historic ranges. The minimum size and number of those populations depend on the taxon's life history, genetic system, breeding system, demographic responses to changes in the habitat, and other ecological characteristics. Therefore, no one formulation of population structure can be tailored to fit all plant taxa (Gilpin & Soulé 1986, Fiedler 1987). Estimates of minimum viable population size have ranged between 50 and 2500 individuals (see Mace & Lande 1991), but Given (1994) has suggested 500 as a first approximation for most plant species. Presumably, the number of viable populations of a recovered species should be proportional to the former area of distribution; taxa that were wide-ranging should have more populations than geographically restricted taxa. The distribution of populations should also correspond to the distribution of genetic variation within a species. Since widespread taxa tend to be more genetically variable than restricted taxa (Hamrick, Linhart & Mitton 1979, Soltis & Soltis 1991), conserved populations of widespread endangered taxa must include more genetic variation than those that are ecologically or geographically confined. This acts to preserve the evolutionary viability of a species by exposing the largest possible array of genes and gene combinations to the fullest palette of ecogeographic variation.

A recovery effort begins by determining via trend analysis which natural populations of the target species are stable or growing and which are declining. To minimize disturbance of viable natural populations and to increase efficiency in the use of money, time, and effort, only the latter should be actively managed. Although 70–80% of all rare plant species in the United States are known from five or fewer populations (Brown & Briggs 1992, Guerrant 1992), some endangered taxa will have too many populations for intensive study at all sites, and a subset of populations will have to be selected for trend analysis. The number and nature of the subset cannot be prescribed, because each taxon will be unique. But, because population size and the degree of past disturbance have been shown to be most relevant with respect to persistence (Shaffer 1981, 1987, Bowles *et al.* 1990, Menges 1992), it seems prudent to include relatively large (more than 500 individuals) and small (fewer than 100 individuals) populations (Mace & Lande 1991, Given 1994) and those that have experienced different levels of perturbation. Trend analysis would then be performed on a minimum of four representative populations (large and undisturbed, small and undisturbed, large and disturbed, small and disturbed). Declining species that have only one or two populations might benefit from a trend analysis that includes widespread relatives or ecologically equivalent species with viable populations.

Whether integrated or non-integrated trend analysis is employed depends on many conditions. The principal advantages of integrated approaches are the objective, straightforward interpretation of the table or matrix sum (R_o or λ, respectively), the focus on fitness components for measurement (survivorship and fecundity), and the potential for additional modeling to incorporate stochasticity or determine limiting factors (e.g. sensitivity analysis). The principal disadvantages include that many plant species have life history characteristics that do not fit the design of current models, and that integrated trend analysis requires a good deal of time, money, and expertise. Nonintegrated approaches may not yield such final, completely quantitative conclusions, and if preliminary evidence for zero-sum compensation was ambivalent, they could require that a larger number of demographic variables be measured. They can, however, be applied to nearly all plant species (although short-lived species are easiest), and they provide useful demographic information with less time and money. There is also a great deal of literature on the general demography of common plants, which can be compared with non-integrated data from endangered species.

The best management regime for recovering declining or unstable populations is suggested by factor resolution: comparing demographic characteristics between viable and non-viable populations or experimentally testing relevant hypotheses can reveal limits to population growth. Some of these limits will be readily ameliorated by restoring natural processes or key species to the habitat (e.g. fire or flooding regimes, host or nurse plants, pollinators). Others might require that population size be increased artificially through transplanting or intensive care of natural seedlings and juvenile plants. In any case, demographic monitoring should be used to document the effects of management.

How do we know if we have successfully managed a species back from the brink of extinction? There are no simple criteria for determining when a species is 'recovered'. Models that generate extinction probabilities under a variety of demographic and environmental scenarios are providing valuable insights, but relatively few species have been analyzed in this way. Minimum viable population sizes have been derived for a few animals, and more universal numbers have been suggested (Mace & Lande 1991). However, these may be inappropriate for plants with unusual life histories or habitat requirements. For some long-lived species, viable populations might not require large numbers of individuals. Furthermore, localized extinction and recolonization are features of many species with complicated metapopulation dynamics (such as *P. furbishiae*). In such cases, it makes no sense to manage every declining population. Species persistence at the landscape scale, rather than population persistence at specific sites, should be the management goal (Griggs & Jain 1983, Shaffer 1990, Menges 1990, McEachern *et al.*, Chapter 8 of this volume).

Rather than using a specific, minimum population size as a goal, perhaps recovery should be based on the *in situ* restoration of critical demographic processes in a majority of a species' populations (see Whitson & Massey 1981, Soulé 1987). For most species, these processes include seed or ramet production, dispersal into high-quality habitat, germination, and seedling survival. All of these can be manipulated to some degree, and all such manipulations can be evaluated for success (whether or not the population has grown or stabilized) and cost-effectiveness (population increase per unit of time, money, and effort expended). Such an approach has recently been proposed for a large number of Britain's most endangered vascular plants (Whitten 1990). Additionally, it will often be necessary to create new viable populations to spread the risk of extinction.

Using demographic monitoring to create new populations

In contrast to monitoring natural populations, creating new populations begins with factor resolution and ends with trend analysis. Experiments are used to determine the most important factors limiting the growth of the founding population, allowing prescription of appropriate management. The predicted fate of the newly created population can be tested in future years. Created populations not only spread the risk of extinction, they also amplify our understanding of the target species and increase our ability to successfully manipulate its natural populations. As Guerrant (1992) has pointed out, however, there have only been a few attempts to create new populations of endangered plants that incorporate demographic monitoring and population genetics into the empirical framework. These include work on *Stephanomeria malheurensis* (Brauner

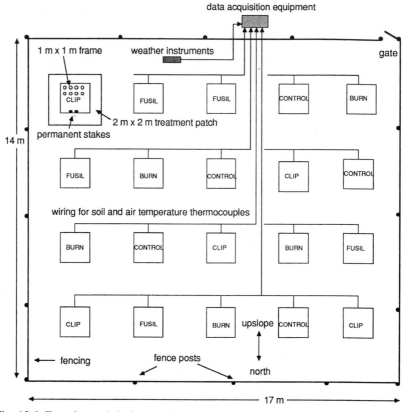

Fig. 13.6. Experimental design used to create a new population of *Amsinckia grandi-flora* within its historic range. Each of the 20 plots was either a treatment (burned, hand clipped, grass-specific herbicide Fusilade®) or a control in order to measure the effects of competition from non-native grasses. Air, soil, and precipitation data were taken in each plot by a data acquisition system. From Pavlik *et al.* (1993b).

1988, Parenti & Guerrant 1990), *Pediocactus knowltonii* (Olwell *et al.* 1987, 1990), *Iris lacustris* (Simonich & Morgan 1990), *Hymenoxys acaulis* var. *glabra* (DeMauro, Chapter 12 of this volume), and *Amsinckia grandiflora* (Pavlik 1988, 1990, 1991a, b, Pavlik *et al.* 1993b). Creating new populations is central to the recovery of *A. grandiflora* and many similar endangered species in the California flora. The role of demographic monitoring in structuring and evaluating such efforts is demonstrated below.

Amsinckia grandiflora (Boraginaceae) is an annual known from only three natural populations in the dry grasslands east of Livermore, California. One population is large (approximately 3200 individuals in 1991) and apparently stable. The second is much smaller (23–355 individuals), but in the mid-1960s had thousands of individuals. The third has only 16–29 individuals. Current

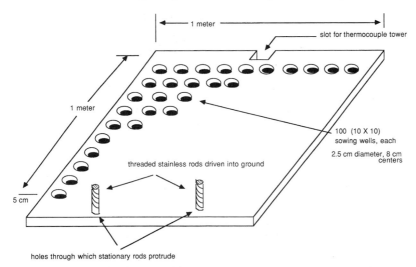

1 meter

slot for thermocouple tower

1 meter

100 (10 X 10)
sowing wells, each

2.5 cm diameter, 8 cm
centers

threaded stainless rods driven into ground

5 cm

holes through which stationary rods protrude

Fig. 13.7. 100 hole plot frame used for sowing and monitoring the nutlets of *Amsinckia grandiflora*. The frame can be removed and installed precisely, allowing the fates of seeds, seedlings, and juvenile plants to be determined. A data sheet resembling the frame layout facilitates field work and computation. From Pavlik (1990,1991a).

thrcats to the populations are both intrinsic (low genetic variability, low seed production *in situ*, specific habitat requirements) and extrinsic (exotic grasses, livestock grazing, intensive land use). Consequently, *A. grandiflora* can be considered one of the most endangered plants in California, and perhaps in the nation. The US Fish and Wildlife Service recovery plan called for the estab lishment of four new *A. grandiflora* populations within historic range.

Using existing data on the distribution and ecology of the species, Pavlik & Heisler (1988) characterized and evaluated the habitat of natural *A. grandiflora* populations and searched for similar habitat within historic range. Twelve finalist sites, all of which supported mesic annual grassland on loamy-clay soils, were identified, and one was chosen for the first experimental reintroduction (Lougher Ridge near Stewartville). Preliminary monitoring of the natural populations had suggested that declining populations were associated with high cover of introduced grasses, and this was confirmed by growth and seed output studies in weed-free experimental gardens (Pavlik 1988). Therefore, the first attempt to create a new population of *A. grandiflora* examined the effects of annual grass competitors and the efficacy of three treatments to con trol the grasses (burning, hand clipping, and a grass-specific herbicide).

A total of 3460 nutlets were sown into 20 plots at Lougher Ridge (Fig. 13.6) using removable wooden frames (Fig. 13.7). The frames allowed the fate of every nutlet, seedling or established plant to be followed during the growing season. As a result, treatment effects and the success of the reintroduction could be rigorously assessed by measuring germination, stress (desiccation, etiolation, microherbivore grazing), survivorship, nutlet production, and other demographic characteristics. Individuals from different nutlet populations (natural vs. cultivated), which were shown to have electrophoretically detectable genetic differences, were also monitored as subsets of the founding propagules.

Overall, the new population of *A. grandiflora* was successful, at least in its first year. Of the 3460 nutlets, 1774 produced germinules during the 1989–90 growing season (November to April), and 1101 of these survived to reproduce. From these plants, an estimated 35 800 resident nutlets were produced, indicating that the population had the potential to grow in its second year. Genetic differences between nutlet source populations produced minor differences in phenology and response to burning, but these had no significant or immediate demographic effects. Demographic data for the different nutlet sources were used, however, to predict resultant levels of genetic variation in the new population for future comparisons with natural populations.

Annual grass cover was found to have no effect on *in situ* germination, but it had a significant negative effect on survivorship to reproduction, plant size, and nutlet production (Table 13.4). Therefore, to promote population growth and stability in *A. grandiflora*, annual grass cover would have to be controlled. Different methods for controlling grasses, however, had different demographic consequences. Burning increased *A. grandiflora* survivorship but had little or no effect on nutlet output because grasses reinvaded the plots and became competitive by early spring. Herbiciding grasses had no effect on *A. grandiflora* survivorship, but plant size and, therefore, nutlet output per plant and per plot were significantly increased. Thus, a combined treatment of burning and herbiciding during the first few years of population management could increase both survivorship and nutlet production. In clipped plots, however, *A. grandiflora* plants were small and tended to produce fewer nutlets than control plants; clipping would not be recommended for controlling grass cover and enhancing population growth of *A. grandiflora* (Pavlik 1990, Pavlik *et al.* 1993b).

Prior to its second growing season, the new population was divided into two treatment blocks. One block was burned in the fall and sprayed with grass herbicide in the late winter; the other block was only herbicided. Although unusual weather patterns during the second growing season altered some responses to these treatments, the new population grew by 18% and had a total of 1301 reproductive plants in April 1991. Nutlet production grew by 44%, indicating that this population would continue to contribute to the recovery of

Table 13.4. *Use of demographic monitoring during the creation of a new population of an endangered plant within its historic range*

Experimental treatment effects on germination, population size, survivorship to reproduction, maximum plant size and nutlet output of *Amsinckia grandiflora*. Values (mean ± SD) in a column followed by the same letter are not statistically different (P<0.05, ANOVA, arcsine transformed %) unless otherwise indicated. Data from Pavlik *et al.* (1993b).

	Total germination (% of sown)	Repro. plants (mean #/ plot)	Survivorship to reproduction (% of germ.)	Mean max. plant size (cm)	Nutlet output (mean no. per plant)
Control	55.4 ± 5.2[a]	38.6 ± 15.8[a]	42.7 ± 16.5[a]	26.0 ± 3.1[a]	15.1 ± 10.1[a]
Burn	55.4 ± 9.9[a]	67.2 ± 19.8[b]	75.3 ± 11.6[b*]	33.7 ± 5.3[b]	29.1 ± 14.4[a]
Clip	54.1 ± 4.8[a]	57.8 ± 16.5[a]	63.1 ± 12.0[a]	23.1 ± 3.7[a]	6.6 ± 5.6[a]
Herbicide	54.0 ± 8.1[a]	56.4 ± 15.6[a]	64.4 ± 10.8[a]	40.5 ± 4.1[b*]	53.6 ± 16.5[b*]

* Different at $P < 0.01$.

A. grandiflora (Pavlik 1991b). During the spring of 1992, with no site management, there were 1640 reproductive plants in the population. Despite the precarious status of *Amsinckia grandiflora* in the wild, this project has demonstrated that sites for new populations can be located, evaluated, and successfully 'innoculated'; data on genetic variability can be used to determine the composition of the founding propagules; and detailed demographic monitoring can provide data for evaluating the new population, predicting its short-term fate, and suggesting effective management techniques to ensure future population growth. Such an approach is now being used to recover the serpentine endemic *Acanthomintha duttonii* (known from only one population), and can be modified to accommodate a wider variety of plant life forms.

Conclusions

The framework presented in this chapter allows managers to understand how demographic monitoring fits into the practical realm of plant conservation and recovery *in situ*. A framework is necessary because not all concepts and techniques are equally insightful or useful for managing endangered populations. When demographic monitoring is broken into trend analysis and factor resolution, the selection of population attributes for monitoring at specific stages in the recovery process is simplified. We will never have the luxury of knowing the many intricacies of a species' existence before having to make crucial decisions for purposes of conservation. Therefore, sharp focus on a few critical factors can provide data on which to base decisions that are both biologically effective and economically feasible.

First, trend analysis, applied to all or a representative portion of a species' populations, identifies those populations that are declining or unstable and require demographic manipulation. Here, survivorship, seed (or ramet) production, and frequency of establishment are most important. These data can be integrated into a predictive model or subjected to nonintegrated analysis. Next, factor resolution, through comparison or experiment, indicates the specific manipulations that could lead to population recovery. The choice of population attributes is wider, but rigorously guided by the results of trend analysis. If a species has fewer than five populations, it may be important to create new populations using a factorial approach to the founding propagules. Under no circumstances should seeds or ramets be released into suitable habitat without the controlled, statistically empowered design of a good experiment. How else can the expenditure of rare biological material be justified? How else can the effort be evaluated, modified, or extended to other taxa?

Still, a plethora of detailed demographic data cannot effect recovery without clear management objectives. In a few special cases, objectives can be drawn from models of minimum population size and probabilities of extinction in stochastic environments. For most plants, the models are not yet applicable and the 'magic numbers' for population viability are unavailable. Recovery objectives should then be tailored to peculiarities of life history and to the circumstances that put such species at risk. In general, if we act to restore critical demographic processes rather than specific numbers of individuals, we will avoid debates that forestall reasonable action, and we are more likely to achieve self-maintaining populations. This approach complements the objectives of endangered species legislation and the genetic and ecological principles that guide contemporary conservation biology. With so many species, so much threat, and so little money, self-maintenance will be a membership requirement for all wild species in the world of tomorrow. Once the short-term objective of self-maintenance is met, we can turn to the long-term questions of species persistence and evolutionary potential.

Acknowledgments

This manuscript was much improved by comments from Drs. David Given (Department of Scientific and Industrial Research, Land Resources Division, New Zealand), Eric Menges (Archbold Biological Station, Florida, USA), David Norton (Department of Forestry, University of Canterbury, New

Zealand), and Michael Morgan (University of Wisconsin, USA). It was completed while I was on sabbatical from Mills College and hosted by the Department of Scientific and Industrial Research, Land Resources Division in New Zealand. I also thank Ken Berg, Susan Cochrane, and Ann Howald (Endangered Plant Program, California Department of Fish and Game, Sacramento) for their ongoing support of my research on endangered plants.

Literature cited

Ackerman, J. D. (1989) Limitations to sexual reproduction in *Encyclia krugii* (Orchidaceae). *Systematic Botany,* **14**, 101–109.

Ayensu, E. S. & DeFilipps, R. A. 1978. *Endangered and Threatened Plants of the United States.* Washington, D.C.: Smithsonian Institution Press.

Bartel, J. A. (1987) The federal listing of rare and endangered plants: What is involved & what does it mean? In *Conservation and Management of Rare and Endangered Plants,* ed. Elias, T., pp. 15–22. Sacramento: California Native Plant Society.

Baskin, J. M. & Baskin, C. C. (1986) Some considerations in evaluating and monitoring populations of rare plants in successional environments. *Natural Areas Journal,* **6**, 26-30.

Begon, M. & Mortimer, M. (1981) *Population Ecology: A Unified Study of Animals and Plants.* Oxford: Blackwell Scientific Publications.

Borchert, M. (1989) Postfire demography of *Thermopsis macrophylla* H.A. var. *agnina* J. T. Howell (Fabaceae), a rare perennial herb in chaparral. *American Midland Naturalist,* **122**, 120-32.

Bowles, M. L., DeMauro, M. M., Pavlovic, N. & Hiebert, R. D. (1990) Effects of anthropogenic disturbances on endangered plants at Indiana Dunes National Lakeshore. *Natural Areas Journal,* **10**, 187-99.

Bradshaw, M. E. (1981) Monitoring grassland plants in Upper Teesdale, England. In *The Biological Aspects of Rare Plant Conservation,* ed. Synge, H., pp. 241–51. London: John Wiley & Sons.

Bratton, S. P. & White, P. S. (1981) Rare and endangered plant species management: Potential threats and practical problems in US national parks and preserves. In *The Biological Aspects of Rare Plant Conservation,* ed. Synge, H., pp. 459–474. London: John Wiley & Sons.

Brauner, S. (1988) Malheur wirelettuce (*Stephanomeria malheurensis*) biology and interactions with cheatgrass: 1987 study results and recommendations for a recovery plan. Burns: US Bureau of Land Management.

Brookes, B. S. (1981) The discovery, extermination, translocation and eventual survival of *Schoenus ferrugineus* in Britain. In *The Biological Aspects of Rare Plant Conservation,* ed. Synge, H., pp. 421-8. London: John Wiley & Sons.

Brown, A. H. D. & Briggs, J. D. (1992) Sampling strategies for genetic variation in *ex situ* collections of endangered plant species. In *Genetics and Conservation of Rare Plants,* ed. Falk, D. A. , pp. 99–119. Oxford University Press.

Davy, A. J. & Jefferies, R. L. (1981) Approaches to the monitoring of rare plant populations. In *The Biological Aspects of Rare Plant Conservation,* ed. Synge, H., pp. 219–32. London: John Wiley & Sons.

Elias, T. ed. (1987) *Conservation & Management of Rare and Endangered Plants.* Sacramento: California Native Plant Society.

Fahselt, D. (1988) The dangers of transplantation as a conservation technique. *Natural Areas Journal*, **8** (4), 238-44.

Falk, D. A. 1988. Helping to ensure a future in the wild. *Plant Conservation*, **3**, 3.

Ferreira, J. & Smith, S. (1987) Methods of increasing native populations of *Erysimum menziesii*. In *Conservation and Management of Rare and Endangered Plants*, ed. Elias, T., pp. 507–11. Sacramento: California Native Plant Society.

Fiedler, P. L. (1987) Life history and population dynamics of rare and common mariposa lilies (*Calochortus* Pursh: Liliaceae). *Journal of Ecology*, **75**, 977-95.

Gawler, S. C., Waller, D. M. & Menges, E. S. (1987) Environmental factors affecting establishment and growth of *Pedicularis furbishiae*, a rare endemic of the St. John River Valley, Maine. *Bulletin of the Torrey Botanical Club*, **114**, 280–92.

Gilpin, M. E. & Soulé, M. E. (1986) Minimum viable populations and processes of species extinctions. In *Conservation Biology: The Science of Scarcity and Diversity,* ed. Soulé, M. E. , pp. 19–34. Sunderland: Sinauer Associates.

Given, D. R. (1984) Monitoring and science - the next stage in threatened plant conservation in New Zealand. In *Conservation of Plant Species and Habitats*, ed. Given, D. R., pp. 83–101. Wellington, New Zealand: IUCN Nature Conservation Council.

Given, D. R. (1989) Monitoring of threatened plants. In *Proceedings of a Symposium on Environmental Monitoring in New Zealand with Emphasis on Protected Natural Areas*, ed. Craig, B., pp. 192–8. Wellington: Department of Conservation.

Given, D. R. (1994) *Principles and Practice of Plant Conservation*. Portland: Timber Press.

Griggs, F. T. & Jain, S. K. (1983) Conservation of vernal pool plants in California, II. Population biology of a rare and unique grass genus *Orcuttia*. *Biological Conservation*, **27**, 171-93.

Grime, J. P. (1979) *Plant Strategies and Vegetation Processes*. Chichester: John Wiley & Sons.

Guerrant, E. O. (1992) Genetic and demographic considerations in rare plant conservation. In *Conservation Biology: The Theory and Practice of Nature Conservation, Preservation and Management*, ed. Fiedler, P. L. & Jain, S., pp. 321–344. NY: Chapman & Hall.

Hamrick, J. L., Linhart, Y. B. & Mitton, J. B. (1979) Relationships between life history characteristics and electrophoretically-detectable genetic variation in plants. *Annual Review of Ecology. & Systematics*, **10**, 173-200.

Harper, J. L. (1977) *The Population Biology of Plants*. London: Academic Press.

Harper, J. L. (1981) The meanings of rarity. In *The Biological Aspects of Rare Plant Conservation*, ed. Synge, H., pp. 189–204. London: John Wiley & Sons.

Harper, J. L. & Wallace, H. L. (1987) Control of fecundity through abortion in *Epilobium montanum* L. *Oecologia*, **74**, 31-8.

Harvey, H. J. (1985) Population biology and the conservation of rare species. In *Studies on Plant Demography. A Festschrift for John L. Harper*, ed. White, J., pp. 111–23. London: Academic Press.

Harvey, H. J. & Meredith, T. C. (1981) Ecological studies of *Peucedanum palustre* and their implications for conservation management at Wicken Fen, Cambridgeshire. In *The Biological Aspects of Rare Plant Conservation*, ed. Synge, H., pp. 365–78. London: John Wiley & Sons.

Havlik, N. A. (1987) The 1986 Santa Cruz Tarweed relocation project. In *Conservation and Management of Rare and Endangered Plants*, ed. Elias, T., pp. 421–3. Sacramento: California Native Plant Society.

Hegazy, A. K. & Eesa, N. M. (1991) On the ecology, insect seed-predation and conservation of a rare and endemic plant species: *Ebenus armitagei* (Leguminosae). *Conservation Biology*, **5**, 317-24.

Huenneke, L. F., Holsinger, K. & Palmer, M. E. (1986) Plant population biology and the management of viable plant populations. In *Management of Viable Populations: Theory, Applications and Case Studies*, ed. Wilcox, B. A., Brussard, P. F. & Marlot, B. G., pp. 169–183. Stanford University: Center for Conservation Biology.

Jenkins, R. E. & Bedford, W. B. (1973) The use of natural areas to establish environmental baselines. *Biological Conservation*, **5**, 168-74.

Karron, J. D. (1987) The pollination ecology of co-occurring geographically restricted and widespread species of *Astragalus* (Fabaceae). *Biological Conservation*, **39**, 179-93.

Karron, J. D. (1989) Breeding systems and levels of inbreeding depression in geographically restricted and widespread species of *Astragalus* (Fabaceae). *American Journal of Botany*, **76**, 331-40.

Knudsen, M. D. (1987) Recovery of endangered and threatened plants in California: The federal role. In *Conservation and Management of Rare and Endangered Plants*, ed. Elias, T., pp. 461–9. Sacramento: California Native Plant Society.

Lefkovitch, L. P. (1965) The study of population growth in organisms grouped by stages. *Biometrics*, **21**, 1-18.

Leslie, P. H. (1945) On the use of matrices in certain population mathematics. *Biometrica*, **33**, 183-212.

Lozier, L. (1987) The California Nature Conservancy's landowner contact and registry program: Voluntary protection for rare plant sites. In *Conservation and Management of Rare and Endangered Plants*, ed. Elias, T., pp. 567–71. Sacramento: California Native Plant Society.

Mace, G. M. & Lande, R. (1991) Assessing extinction threats: Toward a reevaluation of IUCN threatened species categories. *Conservation Biology*, **5**, 148-57.

Macior, L. W. (1980) The population biology of Furbish's lousewort (*Pedicularis furbishiae* S. Wats.). *Rhodora*, **82**, 105-11.

Meagher, T. R , Antonovics, J. & Primack, R. (1978) Experimental ecological genetics in *Plantago*. III. Genetic variation and demography in relation to survival of *Plantago cordata*, a rare species. *Biological Conservation*, **14**, 243-57.

Menges, E. S. (1986) Predicting the future of rare plant populations: demographic monitoring and modeling. *Natural Areas Journal*, **6**, 13-25.

Menges, E. S. (1990) Population viability analysis for an endangered plant. *Conservation Biology*, **4**, 52-62.

Menges, E. S. (1991) Seed germination percentage increases with population size in a fragmented prairie species. *Conservation Biology*, **5**, 158-64.

Menges, E. S. (1992) Stochastic modeling of extinction in plant populations. In *Conservation Biology: The Theory and Practice of Nature Conservation, Preservation, and Management*, ed. Fiedler, P. L. & Jain, S., pp. 253–75. New York: Chapman & Hall.

Menges, E. S., Waller, D. M. & Gawler, S. C. (1986) Seed set and seed predation in *Pedicularis furbishiae*, a rare endemic of the St. John River, Maine. *American Journal of Botany*, **73**, 1168-77.

Meyer, L. S. (1984) Landowner contact - a new profession for natural area preservation. *Natural Areas Journal*, **4**, 6-12.

Morgan, S. & Wilson, J. H. (1981) Plant recovery activities at the state level. *Natural Areas Journal*, **1**, 7-10.

Nelson, J. R. (1984) Rare plant surveys: Techniques for impact assessment. *Fremontia*, **12**, 19-23.

Olwell, P., Cully,. A., & Knight, P. (1990) The establishment of a new population of *Pediocactus knowltonii:* third year assessment. In *Ecosystem Management: Rare Species and Significant Habitats*, ed. Mitchell, R. S., Sheviak, C. J. & Leopold, D. J., pp. 189-193. Albany: New York State Museum Bulletin 471.

Olwell, P., Cully, A., Knight, P. & Brack, S. (1987) *Pediocactus knowltonii* recovery efforts. In *Conservation and Management of Rare and Endangered Plants*, ed. Elias, T., pp. 519–22. Sacramento: California Native Plant Society.

Ornduff, R. (1976) The reproductive system of *Amsinckia grandiflora*, a distylous species. *Systematic Botany*, **1**, 57-66.

Palmer, M. E. (1986) A survey of rare plant monitoring: Programs, regions and species priority. *Natural Areas Journal*, **6**, 27-9.

Palmer, M. E. (1987) A critical look at rare plant monitoring in the United States. *Biological Conservation*, **39**, 113-27.

Parenti, R. L. & Guerrant, E. O. Jr. (1990) Down but not out: Reintroduction of the extirpated Malheur wirelettuce, *Stephanomeria malheurensis*. *Endangered Species Update*, **8**, 62-3.

Pavlik, B. M. (1987) Autecological monitoring of endangered plants. In *Conservation and Management of Rare and Endangered Plants*, ed. Elias, T., pp. 385–90. Sacramento: California Native Plant Society.

Pavlik, B. M. (1988) Nutlet production and germination of *Amsinckia grandiflora*. I. Measurements from cultivated populations. Sacramento: California Department of Fish and Game, Endangered Plant Program.

Pavlik, B. M. (1990) Reintroduction of *Amsinckia grandiflora* to Stewartville. Sacramento: California Department of Fish and Game, Endangered Plant Program.

Pavlik, B. M. (1991a) Reintroduction of *Amsinckia grandiflora* to three sites across its historic range. Sacramento: California Department of Fish and Game, Endangered Plant Program.

Pavlik, B. M. (1991b) Management of reintroduced and natural populations of *Amsinckia grandiflora*. Sacramento: California Department of Fish and Game, Endangered Plant Program.

Pavlik, B. M. & Barbour, M. G. (1988) Demographic monitoring of endemic sand dune plants, Eureka Valley, California. *Biological Conservation*, **46**, 217-42.

Pavlik, B. M. & Heisler, K. (1988) Habitat characterization and selection of potential sites for establishment of new populations of *Amsinckia grandiflora*. Sacramento: California Department of Fish and Game, Endangered Plant Program.

Pavlik, B. M. & Manning, E. (1993) Assessing limitations on the growth of endangered plant populations. I. Experimental demography of *Erysimum canpitatum* var. *angustatum* and *Oenothera deltoides* ssp. *howellii*. *Biological Conservation*, **65**, 257–650.

Pavlik, B., Ferguson, M., Nelson, N. & Nelson, M. (1993a) Assessing limitations on the growth of endangered plant populations. II. Seed production and seed bank dynamics of *Erysimum capitatum* var. *angustatum* and *Oenothera deltoides* ssp. *howellii*. *Biological Conservation*, **65**, 267–78.

Pavlik, B. M., Nickrent, D. L. & Howald, A. M. (1993b) The recovery of an endangered plant. I. Creating a new population of *Amsinckia grandiflora*. *Conservation Biology*, **7**, 510–26.

Rabinowitz, D., Rapp, J. K., Cairns, S. & Mayer, M. (1989) The persistence of rare prairie grasses in Missouri: Environmental variation buffered by reproductive output of sparse species. *American Naturalist*, **134**, 525-44.

Reichenbacher, F. W. (1990) Reintroduction brings Kearney's Blue Star from extinction's edge. *Plant Conservation*, **5**, 3.

Rohlf, D. J. (1991) Six biological reasons why the Endangered Species Act doesn't work - and what to do about it. *Conservation Biology*, **5**, 273-82.

Sarukhan, J. & Harper, J. L. (1973) Studies on plant demography: *Ranunculus repens* L., *R. bulbosus* L. & *R. acris* L. I. Population flux and survivorship. *Journal of Ecology*, **61**, 675-716.

Schonewald-Cox, C. M., Chambers, S. M., MacBryde, B. & Thomas, W. L. (1983) *Genetics and Conservation*. Menlo Park: Benjamin/Cummings.

Shaffer, M. L. (1981) Minimum populations sizes for species conservation. *BioScience*, **31**, 131-4.

Shaffer, M. L. (1987) Minimum viable populations: coping with uncertainty. In *Viable Populations for Conservation*, ed. Soulé, M. E., pp. 69–86. Cambridge University Press.

Shaffer, M. L. (1990) Population viability analysis. *Conservation Biology*, **4**, 39-40.

Simonich, M. T. & Morgan, M. D. (1990) Researchers successful in transplanting dwarf lake iris ramets (Wisconsin). *Restoration and Management Notes*, **8**, 131-2.

Skinner, M. W. & Pavlik, B. M. (1994). *California Native Plant Society's Inventory of Rare and Endangered Vascular Plants of California*, 5th edition. Sacramento: California Native Plant Society.

Smith, W. R. (1987) Studies of the population biology of prairie bush-clover (*Lespedeza leptostachya*). In *Conservation and Management of Rare and Endangered Plants*, ed. Elias, T., pp. 359–66. Sacramento: California Native Plant Society.

Soltis, P. S. & Soltis, D. E. (1991) Genetic variation in endemic and widespread plant species: Examples from Saxifragaceae and *Polystichum* (Dryopteridaceae). *Aliso*, **13**, 215-23.

Soulé, M. E. (1987) Introduction. In *Viable Populations for Conservation*, ed. Soulé, M. E., pp. 1–10. Cambridge University Press.

Sutter, R. D. (1986) Monitoring rare plant species and natural areas - ensuring the protection of our investment. *Natural Areas Journal*, **6**, 3-5.

Taylor, D. W. & Palmer, R. E. (1987) Ecology and endangered status of *Silene invisa* populations in the central Sierra Nevada, California. In *Conservation and Management of Rare and Endangered Plants*, ed. Elias, T., pp. 321–8. Sacramento: California Native Plant Society.

Travis, J. & Sutter, R. (1986) Experimental designs and statistical methods for demographic studies of rare plants. *Natural Areas Journal*, **6**, 3-12.

Watkinson, A. R. (1981) The population ecology of winter annuals. In *The Biological Aspects of Rare Plant Conservation*, ed. Synge, H., pp. 253–64. London: John Wiley & Sons.

Wells, T. C. E. (1981) Population ecology of terrestrial orchids. In *The Biological Aspects of Rare Plant Conservation*, ed. Synge, H., pp. 281–96. London: John Wiley & Sons.

White, P. S. & Bratton, S. P. (1981) Monitoring vegetation and rare plant populations in US national parks and preserves. In *The Biological Aspects of Rare Plant Conservation*, ed. Synge, H., pp. 265–80. London: John Wiley & Sons.

Whitson, P. D. & Massey, J. R. (1981) Information systems for use in studying population status of threatened and endangered plants. In *Rare Plant Conservation: Geographical Data Organization*, ed. Morse, L. E. & Henifin, M. S., pp. 217–36. Bronx: New York Botanical Garden.

Whitten, A. J. (1990) Recovery: A proposed programme for Britain's protected species. Nature Conservancy Council, CSD Report No. 1089. Peterborough: Nature Conservancy.

Wiens, D. (1984) Ovule survivorship, brood size, life history, breeding systems, and reproductive success in plants. *Oecologia*, **64**, 47-53.

Wiens, D., Calvin, C. L., Wilson, C. A., Davern, C. I., Frank, D. & Seavey, S. R. (1987) Reproductive success, spontaneous embryo abortion, and genetic load in flowering plants. *Oecologia*, **71**, 501-9.

Wiens, D., Nickrent, D. L., Davern, C. I., Calvin, C. L. & Vivrette, N. J. (1989) Developmental failure and loss of reproductive capacity in the rare paleoendemic shrub *Dedeckera eurekensis*. *Nature*, **338**, 65-7.

IV

Synthesis and future directions: biology, politics and reality

In the forward, we posed two related questions. First, do biological differences between animals and plants imply different restoration strategies and regulations for these two major groups of organisms? Second, how should political boundaries, which are clearly 'extra-biological', play a role in restorations? Upon reflection of the contributions in this volume, we here briefly offer our views.

Perhaps the most obvious, potentially important difference between animals and plants in restoration is the mobile lifestyles of animals versus the sedentary lifestyles of plants. This difference, we have found, appears to have led to a general belief that animal and plant restorations often pose different sorts of problems, particularly with respect to 'ecotypes', or genetic adaptation to biotic and abiotic environmental components, ranging from soils and climate, to competitors and mutualists. Put another way, this view assumes implicitly that animals and plants tend to differ in profound ways with respect to genetic population structure, which should dictate different restoration strategies and/or guidelines. But the rather obvious difference of mobility masks a perhaps lesser difference in vagility. We now recognize that many plants are capable of impressive pollen and/or seed dispersal, while some animals disperse very little among separated populations. Differences with respect to genetic population structure are likely to vary widely among taxa, irrespective of animal or plant (Hamrick 1992). Further, the genetic structures of animal and plant populations are becoming better understood only recently, with the application of powerful, but recently developed, molecular techniques. In truth, today we simply do not know much about the genetic structure of populations in nature. Generalization, therefore, seems premature.

In this volume we read of many facets regarding endangered species restoration that apply equally, or at least similarly, to animals and plants. Recovery teams will face similar sorts of organizational problems and challenges irre-

351

spective of taxa (Chapter 1). Many genetic problems result from habitat loss and fragmentation and consequent reduction in population size, rather than taxonomic affinity (Chapters 2, 3, 4), and strategies devised to manage genetic viability of captive animals (Chapter 3) may work equally well with greenhouse plants (Chapter 4). Plants exhibit a bewildering array of breeding systems (Chapters 4, 12), but animals similarly employ a myriad of social systems and reproductive strategies (Wilson 1975, Emlen & Oring 1977). Trophic interactions can potentially limit restoration success, whether the interaction is between herbivore and producer (Chapter 5), carnivore and herbivore (Chapter 9), carnivore and carnivore (Chapters 10, 11), or even parasite and host (Chapter 9). Use of surrogate species to experimentally test restoration strategies or identify limiting factors can work well with both animals and plants (Chapters 2, 5, 11, 13). Finally, careful experimentation, whenever possible, together with adequate monitoring, will unquestionably aid restoration success, as well as advance the theoretical bases upon which restoration decisions are made (Chapters 2, 5, 7, 10, 11, 12, 13). Clearly, with respect to biology, restorations of animals and plants share many problems and solutions.

When restoring endangered species, however, biology is often the least of the problems. Restorations occur within a societal context, and therefore, economic and political issues often equal if not surpass the biological issues in determining the course of a restoration (see also Chapter 1, Rohlf 1991, 1992, Falk & Olwell 1992, O'Connell 1992). In some cases, societal demands may make biological issues moot. For instance, how would restoring wolves to Yellowstone affect neighboring ranchers, and should their concerns for successful ranching outweigh the goal of restoring a top carnivore to a system it once occupied (see Naess & Mysterud 1987 for consideration of a similar situation in Scandinavia)? As restorationists, we need to remind ourselves that our vocation may frequently be frustratingly embroiled in such issues, and success ultimately will depend upon greater societal approval. In the end, if society does not view restoration ecology as a benefit, or at least a worthwhile pursuit, the field will likely be restricted to a movement of zealots operating on the fringes of society. We urge restoration ecology, as a field, to develop and mature within this greater perspective, incorporating knowledge from fields such as business, economics, law, and sociology, into its theoretical and empirical arsenals (see also Soulé 1987, Orr 1991, Rohlf 1991).

On the other hand, restorationists need to acquaint society with knowledge gained through our professional experience and development of the field, with the aim of achieving a better political climate in which to effect restorations (see Ehrlich 1992, for a related discussion). For example, the public should be aware that state-by-state differences in regulating restorations (e.g. McMahan

1991) ignore the biological reality that organisms do not recognize political boundaries! We need to develop restoration guidelines at the federal, if not the international, level that facilitate restoration success and minimize 'turf' battles and conceptual differences between political agencies. Moreover, these restoration guidelines need to be founded on sound biological knowledge. Further, governments and voters need to understand that as biological knowledge relevant to restoration ecology grows in the near future, guidelines that seem reasonable or prudent today may become obsolete tomorrow. Guidelines or regulations or policies regarding restoration should be viewed not as cast in stone but as needing periodic reevaluation and revision.

Literature cited

Ehrlich, P. R. (1992) One ecologist's opinion on the so-called Stanford scandals and social responsibility. *BioScience*, **42**, 702–5.

Emlen, S. T. & Oring, L. W. (1977) Ecology, sexual selection, and the evolution of mating systems. *Science*, **197**, 215–23.

Falk, D. A. & Olwell, P. (1992) Scientific and policy considerations in restoration and reintroduction of endangered species. *Rhodora*, **94**, 287–315.

Hamrick, J. L. (1992) Patterns and levels of gene flow in plant populations. Abstract. *Experimental and Molecular Approaches to Plant Biosystematics. V. International Symposium, June 11–15, 1992*. St Louis: International Organization of Plant Biosystematists.

McMahan, L. R. (1991) Advice for the modern plant explorer: pack your permits. *The Public Garden*, **6**, 12–16.

Naess, A. & Mysterud, I. (1987) Philosophies of wolf policies I: general principles and preliminary exploration of selected norms. *Conservation Biology*, **1**, 22–34.

O'Connell, M. (1992) Response to: "six biological reasons why the endangered species act doesn't work and what to do about it." *Conservation Biology*, **6**, 140–3.

Orr, D. (1991) Biological diversity, agriculture, and the liberal arts. *Conservation Biology*, **5**, 268–70.

Rohlf, D. J. (1991) Six biological reasons why the endangered species act doesn't work – and what to do about it. *Conservation Biology*, **5**, 273–82.

Rohlf, D. J. (1992) Response to O'Connell. *Conservation Biology*, **6**, 144–5.

Soulé, M. E. (1987) History of the Society for Conservation Biology: how and why we got here. *Conservation Biology*, **1**, 4–5.

Wilson, E. O. (1975) *Sociobiology: The New Synthesis.* Cambridge: Belknap Press of Harvard University Press.

14

Restoration ecology: living with the Prime Directive

JOEL S. BROWN

Introduction

In the television series *Star Trek*, the starship *Enterprise* warps around galaxies exploring new worlds and seeking out new intelligent life forms. The Prime Directive provides a guiding principle, dictating that the starship's crew must not interfere with the machinations, politics, cultures, or lifestyles of the various aliens found on distant planets. This 'look but don't touch' philosophy embedded in the Prime Directive provides moral backbone and ample opportunities for ethical dilemmas as the crew of the *Enterprise* find themselves crossing the line from observer to meddler in the affairs of other galactic organisms. This same dilemma characterizes our present relationship with nature. At once, we perceive ourselves as product, beneficiary, caretaker, trespasser, and vandal of the earth's evolutionary ecology.

On the one hand, we feel obliged to compete with, prey upon, and make war on the villainous, yet vibrant, components of our ecology. Few speak of preserves or restoration projects for mosquitoes, human parasites, Norway rats, or numerous species of household commensals. In times past, we celebrated the eradication of wolves, much as today we celebrate successful extirpations of tsetse flies or smallpox. On the other hand, we sanctify other species whose niches we have swept away, or those species posing little threat to our livelihoods. As each population of rhinoceros, honeycreeper, or Monarch butterfly disappears, we perceive a vanishing Garden of Eden. While we strive for the extermination of that biodiversity labeled as pests, we generally view as calamitous the present rates and trends of species extinction. We seek a diverse yet kinder, gentler nature.

Whether loss of biodiversity represents a symptom or cause of human environmental problems and challenges, whether this loss is viewed as an unethical crime against nature or as simply aesthetically displeasing, or whether lost diversity has trifling or profound implications for human ecology, we presently

355

desire to preserve and restore certain species, habitats, and ecological communities that have disappeared or are quickly disappearing. This, then, is the domain of restoration ecology; that applied branch of evolutionary ecology that attempts to understand and implement the reintroduction of species, the recreation of habitats and species assemblages, and the revitalization of threatened organisms and communities.

It is not my intention merely to belabor the human foibles and contradictions associated with nature, or to take sides in the animated debates over development versus preservation. Rather, my goal is to elucidate restoration ecology's fascinating position on the boundary between the science of evolutionary ecology and the evolving aspirations of humans to change, manage and secure a place within nature. For in this region, emotion often transcends fact, and decisions are as likely to be made on political as on scientific grounds. While this may evoke despair and cynicism, it should not. Restoration ecology presents an extremely exciting field for all those interested in the environment. Such persons should and can take an active interest in all aspects of restoration ecology including the political and economic decisions of committing resources and land to ecological preservation, and the scientific decisions of how best to identify and implement restoration projects. In short, restoration ecology provides the forum for a person, a group, or a culture to conceive and implement their own Prime Directive regarding our relationship with other organisms.

As this prospective on restoration ecology unfolds, I intend to follow a roadmap that roughly runs from the political (Slobodkin 1988, Wilson 1988, Chapter 1) and philosophical (Naess 1986, Fox 1990), to the development of restoration ecology as a science. As a science, important developments have and will come from conservation genetics (Lande 1988, Chapters 2 & 3), population and community ecology (Chapters 4, 5, 7, & 12), landscape ecology (Saunders, Hobbs & Margules 1991), and evolutionary ecology. Rather than filibuster on all aspects of these topics, I will limit myself to those that seem sufficiently contentious or propitious. Regarding politics and organization, I will argue that restoration ecology should be far more aggressive in advocating and attempting restorations. As a science, I will advocate the development of a closer coupling between theory and empiricism built around rigorous experimentation.

Living with and developing a prime directive

I begin with the philosophy of restoration ecology because any successful endeavor requires coordination of the often disparate goals of the participants. We often have hidden and contradictory agendas pertaining to our own personal Prime Directives. Developing a practical Prime Directive for a single project, for an entire country, or for the world presents serious problems. Most human populations perceive diffuse or distant benefits from the preservation of nature, while perceiving more tangible and immediate benefits from other land use practices. Fortunately, various types of Prime Directives are emerging and should be encouraged. In the United States these include the Endangered Species Act and the Wetland Protection Act, and internationally these include the World Conservation Strategy.

The US Environmental Protection Agency (USEPA 1990) lists benefits of protecting and restoring endangered species, including ecological stability, medical research, agricultural research, and economic benefits (e.g. recreation). While these benefits are compelling, they often crumple in the face of a large missed opportunity cost (=the benefits from using the land for something else), such as the benefits a group could derive from developing a habitat or exploiting the natural resources of an area. Hence, restoration ecology cannot ignore and, in fact, should embrace the economic issues pertaining to tradeoffs involved when deciding to shift resources, labor, and land to restoration. The viability of a restoration project must include consideration of the perceived costs and benefits of the restoration. As already mentioned, the biggest cost may be the missed opportunity of not using the land or species under consideration for something else. Education, stewardship, and recreation may be the field's best means for increasing the perceived benefits; and finding means to reduce the missed opportunity cost may best reduce the perceived costs of restoration. All else equal (which rarely happens!), land that has fewer and/or less valuable alternative uses should be preferable for a restoration project.

Restoration ecologists need to increase their awareness and involvement with the political and economic (Stanley-Price 1989, Culbert & Blair 1989, Chapter 1) issues surrounding any restoration project. In fact, in the face of continued human population growth, all of restoration ecology may be akin to 'rearranging deck chairs on the *Titanic*'. Overpopulation insures an ever-increasing missed opportunity cost of using land for preservation and restoration. Restoration ecology cannot divorce iteself from issues of population growth and changing land use practices.

Clark & Cragun (Chapter 1) emphasize the need for defining attainable goals within a restoration project. For the field as a whole this requires a statement of goals (e.g. those of the Species Survival Committee) and the determination of metrics that permit evaluation of progress towards these goals. Drawing from nursing ethics, we need to ask 'Who is the patient?' To whom or what is the restorationist representing or beholden? Goals of restoration ecology fall in a hierarchy. At one level, restoration ecology may be no more than stamp-collecting viable populations of certain taxa. To one person, viable populations may include the sum of zoo populations, while to another, viable necessarily means self sustaining in the absence of continued human intervention. At a second level, restoration ecology may attempt to save and recreate species interactions, and concomitantly, species assemblages. By restoring habitats and communities the restorationist may be less successful at preserving any constituent species but more successful at attaining a self-sustaining and functioning ecosystem. Thirdly, restoration ecology may be concerned with continued maintenance of the evolutionary context of a species. This restoration goal may be most appealing in that it promotes both ecological and evolutionary sustainability (see below), but it may be least practical in terms of the cost in land and habitats. Moving along the hierarchy represents the transition from more modest and easily measurable goals to increasingly desirable but less quantifiable goals. Unfortunately, in the absence of the third goal, we may be trying to hold a moonbeam in our hands when restoring species outside of their evolutionary context (see the section on **Essentialism versus evolution**).

Motives aside, restorations are a subset of species introductions or reintroductions. The level of politicizing or aggressiveness associated with different forms of species introductions are instructive. At one extreme, introductions include the accidental, careless, or casual establishment of exotic species into new habitats. Using quarantines or fumigations, some countries (e.g. Australia) have become quite aggressive in policing inadvertent transportation of exotic species. There are also numerous planned introductions of exotic species. At the level of the household, these include the release of exotic pets and readily available seed mixes and nursery-reared plants. These 'Meadow in a Can' type of introductions occur frequently and with little regulation. Other releases include intentional seedings of exotic plants onto rangelands, forests, and roadsides. Under the aegis of local, state, or national government agencies, hundreds of introductions of exotic game animals occur annually within the United States and elsewhere. While receiving increasing scrutiny, these introductions occur aggressively with often little thought for the ecological consequences.

Now consider species introductions that represent some form of restoration. On the boundary of restoration ecology might sit reforestation programs, rangeland restoration, and fish stocking (when native rather than exotic?). These are fairly standard practices within the repertoire of applied ecologists. They often receive little scrutiny or politicizing, probably because of their regularity and involvement with common and abundant species.

A dramatic rise in timidity occurs when the restoration involves rare, threatened, or extirpated species (e.g. black-footed ferrets, Chapter 11; Lakeside daisy, Chapter 12). This decline in aggressively tackling introductions generally has less to do with heightened ecological risks and much more to do with the higher levels of regulation and politicizing. In the United States, restoration projects involving black-footed ferrets, wolves, or California condor occur in a political glasshouse.

The contrast can be striking between 'standard' species introductions and restorations of endangered species and ecosystems. In the former, less consideration goes to the probability of success (many introductions of game animals fail outright and then are simply repeated on a trial and error basis), to the consequences of gene flow, and to site fidelity with respect to the species' former and present distributions. In the latter case, much concern may be raised over the probability of success. While commendable when the species breeds poorly or slowly in captivity (e.g. Javan rhinoceros or California condors), much opportunity for trial and error exists when the species breeds well (e.g. Lakeside daisy, black-footed ferret). Elevated concerns often get raised regarding the restoration of the wrong gene-types or ecotypes (e.g. Florida panther). Finally, there may be an obsession with restoring the species to former or nostalgic sites rather than taking advantage of alternative sites that may be more propitious given present land use practices.

In conclusion, we may want to swap practices associated with introductions of exotic plants and game animals with those associated with restorations of threatened habitats and species. In this way we would be more timid and scrupulous regarding reforestation, fish stocking, and range management, and more aggressive and bold in our attempts at restorations of rare species. Much of this will come about only through education of the public and lobbying efforts by professional organizations. But, we have come full circle, such efforts will require: clear identifications of goals, metrics to measure the attainment of goals, and shared guiding principles.

Art versus science in restoration ecology

Howe (1994) has implemented small-scale controlled experiments to test for the effects of fire season on the dominance and establishment of ten or so prairie plants within the midwestern United States. These experiments, when presented at a recent seminar, inspired a fairly typical discussion between practitioners of restoration ecology and ecologists involved with basic research. To argue against burn season as a particularly relevant issue, the restorationists harped on the scale of the experiments, the small number of species, the successional status of the species, the notable successes of current practices, the impracticality of shifting burn seasons, and the complexity and uniqueness of ecological communities. Howe's riposte included emphasizing the consistency between the hypotheses and the experimental results, and a query regarding whether any of these issues can be resolved in the absence of experimentation.

The previous paragraph highlights a burning issue in restoration ecology: Are species and ecological communities so idiosyncratic that the professional judgment of expert naturalists must supersede any science of restoration ecology? While somewhat rhetorical (obviously, one wants to utilize as much useful information as possible, scientific or otherwise, when conducting a restoration project), this question challenges restoration ecologists to develop and validate relevant paradigms and theories; and challenges basic researchers to include issues in restoration ecology as a motivation for theory and experimentation. Creating this lockstep between theory and application should be a central concern of restoration ecology.

The subdisciplines of ecology from which restoration can draw its theories probably already exist. As in the case of most applied ecology, these theories reside within conservation genetics, population and community ecology, the emerging field of landscape ecology, and evolutionary ecology. Applications of restoration ecology are growing in number as local and international organizations attempt to preserve and recreate natural habitats, and as an increasing number of national governments attempt to rescue vanishing natural heritages. A missing ingredient often seems to be controlled experiments in restoration ecology to identify and validate useful theories and practices. Until such experiments become an integral part of restoration projects, it will be difficult to separate ecologically sound practices from those motivated by force of habit and conventional wisdom.

Experiments can be useful at two levels. Firstly, experiments can be used to identify and validate important theories that have common applicability to restoration ecology (Chapters 2 & 5). These experiments have the additional advantage that appropriate species need not be threatened or already subject to restoration projects. This kind of experimental work can provide the lockstep between theory and empiricism in restoration ecology. In this way restoration ecology not only benefits from but also directs theoretical developments. Secondly, experiments may be valuable for identifying the particulars regarding lifehistory, breeding ecology (Chapter 4), and restoration protocols of a target species (Chapters 10, 13). Here, the focus is on answering questions regarding the peculiarities of a particular restoration project. More likely than not, the species under restoration or a closely related species must be the experimental subject (Chapters 5, 8, 13). This second class of experiments may be essential to understanding the idiosyncrasies of a given project.

Conservation genetics

Population genetics provides theory that predicts the genetic structure of a population in response to evolutionary forces (genetic drift, mutation, migration, and natural selection) and in response to life history, breeding systems, and population structure. Molecular biology provides a growing number of techniques for directly or indirectly measuring the genetic compositions of individuals, families, subpopulations, subspecies, and species. This ability to model and empirically measure the recipe of inheritance has influenced conservation biology in three important ways. First, conventional wisdom holds that preserving genetic variability is desirable. Second, genetic differentiation among populations can be used to define the units of conservation. Third, genes can be used as characters in analyses of species' phylogenies. These three utilities of conservation genetics have and should influence and be influenced by restoration ecology. However, in what follows, I argue that some applications of conservation genetics are probably overplayed while others deserve more attention. Lest we be caught re-arranging genetical deck-chairs on an ecological *Titanic*, genetical considerations should provide a tool and not a goal of restoration ecology (Joseph 1991).

Genetic variability is thought to influence the viability of populations. Loss of genetic variance may cause inbreeding depression, loss of heterozygote superiority, and loss of adaptability (Chapters 2 & 3; Lacy 1987). 'Inbreeding depression and loss of heterozygosity probably undermine most components of the population phenotype, including metabolic efficiency, growth rate, reproductive physiology, and disease resistance' (Gilpin & Soulé 1986). With such dire consequences, no wonder maintaining genetic variability has become a major or sole priority of many species survival plans, restoration projects, and captive breeding programs. Minimal viable population sizes may be determined primarily or entirely on genetical considerations based on population genetics models of effective population sizes (Harris & Allendorf 1989). While cases of inbreeding depression have been documented (cf. Allendorf & Leary 1986), the longer-term conservation implications of low genetic variance are equivocal. The issues of inbreeding depression and loss of genetic variance, while related in population genetics models, are conceptually and operationally somewhat different issues. Inbreeding, while speeding the loss of genetic variance, can have the more immediate consequence of lowering the viability of all or some of the offspring. This inbreeding depression may result from either the bringing together of deleterious recessive alleles or from the loss of heterozygote superiority at homozygous loci. When caused by the former, inbreeding depression can be bred out of a population (cf. Chapter 2).

Hughes (1991) argues that the loss of genetic variability at most loci is of little consequence. Rather, for vertebrate species, variability at loci of major histocompatibility complexes may be essential in conferring resistance to diseases and pathogens (Hughes & Nei 1989). In some plants (Chapters 2, 4 & 12), loss of genetic variability at incompatibility loci effectively results in population sterility and extinction. Population genetics theory tells us that we have tradeoffs in any breeding program. A program that minimizes the loss of heterozygosity at all loci will actually hasten the loss at particular loci, while a program that minimizes the loss of heterozygosity at preselected loci will hasten the loss of heterozygosity at other loci (Lacy 1987, Chapter 3).

There is little evidence that lack of genetic variability has hindered restoration projects (see Lande 1988 and references therein) or caused the failure of a reintroduced population. DeMauro (Chapter 12) provides a notable exception wherein the lack of mating type diversity doomed the Illinois Lakeside daisy to extirpation. In fact, numerous small founder populations of introduced exotics have thrived in new habitats with few documented cases of failure due to high inbreeding, low heterozygosity, or other genetic bottleneck effects. Unfortunately, these 'experimental restorations' lack controls and little knowledge exists regarding the innumerable failures of most casual species introductions. There is much room for additional experimentation and model validation.

Certain shifts in emphasis regarding the preservation of genetic variability may be merited. In the face of habitat destruction, and environmental and demographic stochasticity, loss of genetic variability should be only a secondary concern (Lande 1988) and such loss is probably not a major component of the extinction "vortices" described by Gilpin & Soulé (1986). Similarly, in restoration projects, genetic variability may arise as a concern in situations where variability at particular loci confer breeding and fitness advantages (Hughes 1991). In captive breeding programs maintaining genetic variability may be a laudable goal, but when it becomes time-consuming and expensive (as when large mammals are transported at great expense among zoos) other conservation considerations like habitat preservation, applied ecological research, and education might take priority. In fact, when sufficient numbers of animals exist in a captive breeding program, it may be useful to subject portions of this population to inbreeding to discern the severity of inbreeding depression and to ascertain whether this inbreeding depression can be bred from the population. An early lead on inbreeding depression may prove useful in restorations where inbreeding inevitably results from the release of small numbers of captively cultivated animals or plants.

Another important application of conservation genetics concerns identifying the units of conservation. Here the goal is to maintain, preserve, or restore the genetic distinctiveness of subpopulations, subspecies, or species. This application is driven more by the variety and resolution of molecular techniques than by theories of population genetics. Several important issues regarding genetic distinctiveness deserve additional attention: When are subpopulations (or subspecies) sufficiently genetically distinct to warrant separate management and restoration programs? What are the consequences of introducing genetically distinct individuals from one population into another as part of a restoration project? These two issues – what does genetic distinctiveness mean and when is it important? – await additional empirical and theoretical considerations (O'Brien & Mayr 1991, Vane-Wright, Melnick & Western 1991).

At the positive end, measuring genetic distinctiveness provides a finer scale of resolution for inventorying and cataloging the earth's biotic resources (Cohn, 1990). Such information can help direct and prioritize restoration projects. Ashley *et al.* (1990) concluded that the various remnant populations of black rhinoceros showed little to no genetic differentiation. Treating all black rhinoceros as taxonomically identical members of a metapopulation simplifies their management in zoos and increases the number of restoration options for translocating individuals among subpopulations or into new areas (see Maguire & Lacy (1990) for a contrasting treatment with tigers). The red wolf provides a fascinating example of how molecular techniques can offer surprising and controversial data. The absence of distinct red wolf mitochondrial DNA (only wolf or coyote mtDNA has been recorded) suggests either recent genetic extinction through introgression or worse, red wolves may simply be a recent hybrid of gray wolves and coyotes (Wayne & Jenks 1991; but see Dowling *et al.* 1992). Resolution of this question awaits theory to determine the probability of losing mtDNA while retaining species-level distinctiveness of the nuclear genome, and empirical information from the nuclear genome and from more individuals.

At the negative end, the fine resolution made possible by genetic sequencing techniques encourages genetic 'stamp collecting' where the identifiable distinctiveness of subpopulations increases the number (and rarity) of the units of conservation and restoration. Beyond the temptation to split hairs, we need to understand the significance of genetic differentiation in restoration projects. To what extent is genetic differentiation indicative of adaptive ecotypic variation? This is perhaps the most compelling reason for preserving ecotypes in restoration projects. Transplanting individuals among distinct subpopulations may not only endanger the success of the introduced individuals but may compromise the viability of the entire population as maladaptive genes are introduced into the new population (Chapter 2).

A less compelling but none the less important consideration for restoration concerns our personal or cultural desire to maintain genuine populations. North American beavers, *Castor canadensis*, introduced into Europe may satisfactorily fill the niche and ecosystem role of native European beavers, *C. castor*. However, for many the knowledge that a beaver seen in Europe is not authentic may detract from the aesthetic value of beavers.

Independent of adaptive ecotypes or the essentialistic desire to maintain genuine articles, genetic differentiation may provide a political expediency and tool for mandating conservation and restoration projects. Useful measurements of genetic differentiation should play an increasingly important role in the identification of restoration and conservation units under legal mandates such as the Endangered Species Act. But even here a caveat should be added. As in the case of the Florida panther (*Felis concolor coryi*), genetic distinctiveness may not be a primary or even desirable goal. The introduction of pumas from elsewhere (*F. c. araucanus* or *F. c. patagonica*) may add vitality to the indigenous panthers by providing some hybrid relief from the negative consequences of inbreeding (O'Brien *et al.* 1990).

Finally, independent of genetic differentiation, national, state, or provincial boundaries may dictate the differentiation of conservation units. Independent of genetic or ecotypic differentiation, subpopulations become ascribed with a nationality for purposes of restoration (see Chapter 9 on the woodland caribou). For instance, restoration of the Lakeside daisy probably would not have been an issue if Ohio (abundant populations) formed part of Illinois (state endangered). And if a restoration had been attempted, there may have been little concern regarding the genetic dilution of Illinois daisies with kin from Ohio (Chapter 12). The 'nationality' of a subpopulation may hamper restoration in other ways. Generally speaking it is far easier to translocate individuals within boundaries rather than across boundaries (Chapters 9 & 10). For the purposes of restoration projects, conservation genetics should add welcome insights into real and artificial boundaries.

While conservation genetics may provide a better inventory of the diversity of life that may be threatened with extinction, it can also provide valuable insights into the relatedness of different conservation units at scales of taxonomic resolution ranging from subpopulations within subspecies to higher taxa such as Families and Orders. In the future, using conservation genetics to infer genealogy should pay handsome rewards in situations where restorations require the reintroduction of individuals from related subpopulations or in situations in which there is no more room on the ark and triage becomes necessary or inevitable. In the former situation, it has been suggested that, all else equal, it may be advisable to reintroduce individuals from subpopulations with nearest kin (e.g. dusky seaside sparrow, Avise & Nelson 1989). In the latter situation, it may be advisable to preserve or restore taxa that are more distantly related. In this way, a taxon that has close kin might receive a lower restoration priority than one that has only more distant kin (Vane-Wright *et al.* 1991). Such an approach to weighing the value of taxa insures that species such as the tuatara (see Daugherty *et al.* 1990) or kiwi receive high priority.

A potentially powerful application of conservation genetics is still a chimera but, in conclusion, deserves mention. Genetic engineering looms on the horizon of restoration ecology. Applications of genetic engineering may include correcting genetic defects, inserting beneficial genes, and perhaps rearranging portions of genomes to shift individuals from a common taxon to an endangered one. While mere science fiction today, *Jurassic Park* (the fictional adventure of genetically engineered dinosaurs) may have elements of prophesy for restoration ecology of the future where DNA from extinct organisms may provide the blueprints for recreating species. At present, the Environmental Protection Agency of the USA reviews, regulates and classifies genetically engineered organisms as new chemicals (e.g. genetically engineered bacteria, *Rhizobium* spp., for increased nitrogen fixation). The release of such organisms is occurring and will probably become commonplace. While it may be a long time before woolly mammoths are presented to the EPA as a 'new chemical', applications of genetic engineering to restoration ecology are probably near at hand.

Population, community, and landscape ecology

The success or failure of most restoration projects depends heavily on such ecological processes as demographic stochasticity, environmental stochasticity, intra- and interspecific interactions, habitat scale, and habitat destruction. Hence, restoration ecology should draw heavily from and contribute to these ecological principles. The question becomes one of identifying those areas of ecology that offer promise and deserve scrutiny within restoration ecology. Here I discuss the issues of small population size, population interactions, small numbers of populations, reduced habitat scales, and species–area relationships.

When restorations involve relatively small numbers of individuals, ecological theories pertaining to Allee effects, and extinction probabilities through demographic or environmental stochasticity, should be relevant and deserve attention (Lande 1987, Quinn & Hastings 1987, Dennis, Munholland & Scott 1991, Mace & Lande 1991). Many of these theories are sufficiently mature to provide assistance in developing a conceptual model for a particular restoration project (e.g. population viability analysis: Murphy, Freas & Weiss 1990, Chapter 9). However, these theories tend to lack an important ingredient unique to restorations. The dynamics and consequences of introducing ten individuals into a novel environment are quite different from following the fate of a small extant population of ten individuals. In this regard, restoration has more in common with the ecology of biological invasions or colonizations (Drake , Mooney & di Castri 1989).

The biotic environment will generally be less hospitable to new intruders than to established individuals. Introduced individuals may be more suscepti- ble to predators, inept at seeking resources and shelter, and preempted from ecological opportunities by existing biota. Introduced individuals must not only hurdle the handicap of small population size and inexperience but must also overcome the 'home-team' advantage of the existing biota. Models and experimental studies of priority effects (Alford & Wilbur 1985, Sredl & Collins 1991) deserve attention when considering the home-team advantage in restoration ecology. Priority effects can occur when communities possess mul- tiple stable states in which one persistent state may include the species in ques- tion while other community states may be uninvadable by small numbers of the species. While not precluding the reintroduction of wolves into parts of their former range, the increase and spread of coyotes might decrease the chances of a successful reintroduction. Evidence for this comes from following successive introductions of bird species into Hawaii and Tahiti; as the commu- nity becomes more diverse the probability of a successful introduction declines (Lockwood, Moulton & Anderson 1993 and reference therein).

Another issue especially relevant to restoration ecology concerns the sources of the individuals for the reintroduction. Some of this concern arises from possible ecotypic variation among populations, but, concern can arise from the ways organisms developmentally, physiologically, and behaviorally respond and acclimate to their environment. Captive-reared offspring of cap- tive parents may have greater difficulties than wild-reared individuals translo- cated among similar habitats and communities (Chapter 10). There is much room for research on the acclimation process of organisms to new circum- stances and experimental work on the relative success rates of restored popula- tions as influenced by propagule source.

'Nature abhors a vacuum'; this saying suggests that the net effect of species interactions within a community works against restoration projects. Because most ecological opportunities (or niches) are more or less effectively exploited, a rare or introduced species may find its recovery and growth impaired by competitors and predators alike. The negative consequences of population interactions on restorations motivates a number of standard practices in plant restoration ecology. Prior to reestablishing a prairie, common practice involves removing the existing vegetation by plowing or herbicides. Selective weeding of exotic plants from a natural area is common practice for promoting the growth of native species.

Beyond the obvious cases for removing potential competitors, what ecological principles of population interactions should be incorporated into the conceptual models of restoration ecologists? Population interactions include direct effects, indirect effects, nonlinear effects, and higher-order interactions (see Abrams 1993 and references therein). Direct effects recognize that individuals from the same or different species may influence a population's growth rate; eagle owls killing gerbils represents a direct effect of owls on gerbils. Direct effects have signs (competition, mutualism, predation) and magnitudes. The presence of competitors, predators, and mutualists will directly influence the success of a restoration.

Indirect effects represent the product of two or more effects; eagle owls killing sand vipers that kill gerbils represents a positive indirect effect of owls on gerbils. Indirect effects have signs and magnitudes that may differ greatly from the direct effects involved. Several important indirect effects include apparent competition (Holt 1977), indirect mutualisms, cascading trophic effects, and resource competition. Most notions of keystone species (Paine 1966) emerge from indirect effects. For instance, a keystone predator promotes the success of predator-resistant species by reducing the population size of a dominant competitor.

Nonlinear effects occur when the presence of individuals of the same or different species alter the sign and/or magnitude of the direct effect between the species in question (see Abrams 1993); if eagle owls make it harder for other eagle owls to kill gerbils, they reduce the magnitude of the direct effect of owls on gerbils. These nonlinear effects are sometimes referred to as behavioral indirect effects, in which the behavioral responses of organisms to conspecifics, competitors and predators influence the signs and magnitudes of population interactions (e.g. the ghost of competition past and density-dependent habitat selection, Rosenzweig 1981). Inducible chemical defenses in plants and anti-predatory behaviors in animals attest to the importance of these nonlinear effects (Lima & Dill 1990).

Higher-order interactions occur when the presence of one species alters the sign or magnitude of the direct effect of another species on itself, or the direct effect between two other species; eagle owls making (by scaring gerbils into shrubs) it easier for sand vipers to kill gerbils represents a higher-order interaction of owls on gerbils (Kotler, Blaustein & Brown 1993). In this way a species can also be keystone through the way it alters the interactions among other species (Werner 1992). Incorporating and/or testing explicit hypotheses regarding these types of population interactions into the conceptual model of a restoration project should add rigor and clarity (e.g. herbivory and granivory by insects, Chapter 5).

The viability of populations threatened by Allee effects, demographic stochasticity, or genetic stochasticity can be increased simply by increasing the population density or size. However, buffering a population from the negative effects of environmental stochasticity (Iwasa & Mochizuki 1988) involves spreading the risk across a number of weakly coupled subpopulations (Goodman 1987). Just as population viability can be modeled and analyzed as a minimum viable population size, population viability may be viewed as a minimum viable number of subpopulations (Quinn & Hastings 1987). Theories pertaining to the dynamics of metapopulations (see DeAngelis & Waterhouse 1987) should prove particularly fruitful (e.g. Murphy *et al.* 1990). Each subpopulation may not be viable, but the exchange of individuals among subpopulations may promote the viability of the metapopulation through rescue effects (Brown & Kodric-Brown 1977), risk spreading, and active habitat selection (Chapters 7, & 8, Morris & Brown 1993 and references therein).

Habitat destruction and habitat fragmentation often create the need for restorations. Consequently, many restorations occur under circumstances of reduced habitat scales. Reduced habitat scales means that processes occurring within a habitat or restoration site may be influenced strongly by biotic and abiotic processes in adjacent habitats or areas. Under these circumstances, models and concepts of source–sink processes deserve attention (Pulliam 1988). Areas adjacent to a restoration project may represent a more or less severe sink in the sense that individuals that find themselves within sink habitats have negative per capita growth rates. The severity of the sink habitat can have profound effects on the viability of the restored population within the source habitat. Moderate sinks may actually enhance population sizes and viability while increasing the severity of the sink habitat may greatly reduce the source population's viability. The decision to protect or kill wolves that stray from Yellowstone National Park may be crucial to the success of any wolf reintroduction program.

Recent and continuing developments in understanding species–area relationships should continue to figure prominently in restoration projects involving the preservation of biodiversity (e.g. prairie restoration projects). Our understanding of these relationships continues to grow. Hypotheses for small areas having fewer species than large include: sampling error, higher extinction rates and faunal relaxation, lower habitat heterogeneity, smaller scale of habitat heterogeneity that favors generalist over specialist species, short food chains from loss of top predators or consumers, less opportunity for metapopulation structure to balance negative consequences of environmental stochasticity. Two metrics that have been used to measure these patterns include the slope of the relationship (log species number versus log area), and the degree of nestedness of species compositions on successively smaller areas (Patterson & Atmar 1986). Steep slopes and high degrees of nestedness argue for single, large restoration sites; shallow slopes and low nestedness argue for several smaller restoration sites.

Essentialism and ecology

We know that ecological communities are temporally and spatially dynamic and we know that species are evolutionarily dynamic. Yet, we often apply a static and essentialist philosophy to restoration ecology. Perhaps this is defensible. After all, while we know that Newtonian physics is wrong, it works quite well in our world of slow speeds and short distances. Similarly, at the time scales of human memories and human history, ecosystems may be kept static and species may be evolutionarily stable. This, however, is probably not true.

Prairie restorations in the areas around Chicago illustrate some of this essentialism. The goal is generally to achieve the 'pre-settlement' community of plants where presettlement refers to the advent of Europeans. Several motivations are given for desiring this snapshot in time; it can be seen as representing the clearest image of Western culture's nostalgic and collective memory (Hoen 1993), or it may be seen as the transition between the 'natural' behavior of Native Americans and the 'unnatural' depredations of European settlers. But, there is considerable debate regarding the 'presettlement' communities of the area. Sites under restoration may not even have been prairie; they may have been oak savanna or oak–maple forest. Several lines of evidence almost guarantee that past communities of this area were constantly in flux, even on scales of hundreds of years. Pollen core samples indicate numerous transitions in plant communities; the region lies at the fluid interface between prairie and forest, and its location inside the tip of the last glaciation insures several thousand years of very dynamic (and swampy) soil hydrology. Even as the first urban humans built Jericho, areas near Chicago were under a kilometer of ice.

Public and scientific reactions to the 1988 fires in Yellowstone National Park further illustrate a sometimes essentialist view towards communities. Were the fires going to destroy or revitalize Yellowstone? Were the fires altering the way Yellowstone should look? Was Yellowstone sent back into the Stone Age regarding successional processes? Without a doubt the fires altered somewhat the community composition of Yellowstone, but it certainly was not being destroyed as a functioning ecosystem. How Yellowstone should look is an open question subject to much bias (Chase 1986, Rolston 1990). At the scale of fires, Yellowstone represents only several subpopulations within what would have been a much vaster metapopulation in the region. In the face of certain scales of environmental stochasticity, it is unrealistic to expect the various communities to reach a state of dynamic equilibrium within the Park boundaries. Most of the ecological communities and species within Yellowstone can probably persist within the boundaries, but their relative frequencies and distributions will always be subject to change. Percolation theory (Nicolis & Prigogine 1977), catastrophe theory (Zeeman 1977), models of chaotic population dynamics (e.g. Schaffer 1984), and network approaches to ecosystems (Higashi & Burns 1991) should provide useful tools for conceptualizing and modeling such non-equilibrium dynamics.

The prairies and Yellowstone illustrate a dilemma regarding restoration projects. The maintenance of a formally natural and static community may often require costly human intervention; in this way many prairie restoration projects become gardens rather than preserves of prairie plants. The maintenance of a functioning ecosystem free of direct human meddling may require accepting a degraded and ever-changing ecosystem. A system may be natural in terms of its species composition or it may be natural because ecosystem functions and population interactions occur in the absence of humans. At any given spatial scale, naturalness of composition probably trades off with naturalness of function. The only way to simultaneously increase both structural and functional naturalness is to increase the area of the restoration or conservation project.

Three promising areas of research exist for evaluating the essential nature of communities. The first, as already discussed concerns the temporal and spatial permanence of a community. The second concerns communities as units of conservation or restoration. One school of thought views communities as legitimate units of restoration comprised of rather specific sets of co-occurring species that tend to succeed or fail together. Another school questions this super-organismic view of communities. Instead communities are viewed as the somewhat haphazard and unique assemblage of those species in an area that can persist together (e.g. Brown & Kurzius 1987). Individual species succeed or fail idiosyncratically. The third concerns the niche diversity of communities. Ideas pertaining to species-packing rules in communities continue to provide an attractive way of looking at species assemblages (Fox & Kirkland 1992). In this way the arrangements of niches within a community may be much more fixed than the identities of the community's species.

To stay out of the trap of imposing an essentialist viewpoint on the ecology of a restoration project, it becomes necessary to clearly delineate the project's goals. These goals will generally fall into three categories of restoring either a target species, the diversity of species within an ecological community, or ecosystem functions of a community. In addition to preserving appropriate habitats, restoring a target species may involve captive breeding programs, control of competitors and predators, and human intervention to maintain habitat suitability. In addition to preserving appropriate habitat diversity, restoring species diversity will often require human intervention to mimic disturbance regimes such as fire, or control the success of a keystone competitor or predator. Restoring ecosystem functions often becomes the priority in reclamation projects of watersheds, wetlands, or abandoned mining and quarrying activities. Here, there may be little emphasis on restoring target species or particular diversities of species. Rather, the goal is to revegetate or repopulate an area with species that prevent erosion, restore water quality, or provide recreational benefits.

Essentialism versus evolution

Despite the observation that many species appear to have remained unchanged for millions of years, all species can be evolutionarily dynamic. Mutation, genetic drift, and natural selection provide avenues for evolutionary change. In fact, such change becomes even more likely under circumstances of habitat alterations in which species find themselves experiencing novel and different selection regimes. With species restoration, are we trying to hold a moonbeam in our hands?

Changing the selection regime of a population will generally result in evolutionary change. Selection experiments with *Drosophila* have amply demonstrated evolutionary changes in behavioral, morphological, and physiological characters (see Joshi & Mueller 1993, Partridge & Fowler 1993 and references therein). Seventy-six generations of various directional selection experiments with corn (*Zea mays*) have resulted in dramatic changes in plant height and in the oil and protein contents of kernels (Dudley 1977). In addition to the characters under direct selection, there have been several unexpected and correlated changes among the different corn lines including changes in flowering dates, seed size and shape, and ear morphology.

By changing selection regimes, human activities cause evolution. Pesticide-resistant insects, antibiotic-resistant strains of bacteria, and chloroquine-resistant malaria attest to an evolutionary arms race between pests and human technology. Heavy metal tolerance has evolved a number of times among plants that have successfully colonized mine tailings (Antonovics 1971).

Barrett (1983) documents weeds that have evolved 'agro-ecotypes': hand-weeding selects for seedling mimicry, seed cleaning procedures select for flowering-time and seed mimicry, and mowing and reaping select for dwarfism. Harvesting by humans may be selecting for 'jacks' (one-year old spawning males) in salmon and for reduced size at maturity in Atlantic cod (Garrod 1988, Law & Grey 1989). Such species as dingos (*Canis dingo*), house mice (*Mus musculus*) and flour beetles (*Tribolium* spp.) may be products of evolution in response to human-altered environments.

A simple message emerges from these examples. Species stripped of their original evolutionary context can be expected to acclimate first and then evolve to their novel circumstances. The need to protect a species' evolutionary context may provide the strongest plea for maintaining pristine environments.

Evolutionary considerations become particularly important for species maintained by captive breeding. In mammals, captive breeding may select for docility, stupidity, lethargy, and loss of antipredator behaviors (Chapters 3 & 11). To prevent zoo animals from evolving domestication, zoos must receive a continual input of animals from the wild. Similarly, maintaining plant restorations from cultivated stocks will select for species adapted to the cultivation regime and not to the restoration site.

Evolutionary game theory (Maynard Smith & Price 1973; see Vincent & Brown 1988 and references therein) and the Optimization Research Programme (Mitchell & Valone 1990) offer promising frameworks for modeling the evolutionary consequences of changed environmental circumstances. Without direct recourse to the genetic basis of a character, the Optimization Research Programme explains character evolution as the consequence of evolution by natural selection. Within this framework, one considers the set of evolutionarily feasible strategies available to a species or population, and one considers the fitness consequences of these strategies. Evolution by natural selection is expected to promote the success of those strategies that maximize per capita growth rates given the circumstances. The circumstances can include evolved responses to abiotic factors (sometimes density-independent selection), population densities (density-dependent selection), the strategies of others (frequency-dependent selection), and the structure of subpopulations (certain forms of 'group selection'). Density-independent selection promotes those strategies that maximize population growth rates (this has some similarities to the notion of 'r-selection'). In variable environments, fitness is sensitive to both the mean and the temporal variance in reproductive success (Cohen 1966). As a result, environmental stochasticity may promote a variety of bet-hedging adaptations that mitigate the effects of unfavorable periods (e.g. Brown & Venable 1986). In plants, these include seed dormancy, seed-dispersal mechanisms, or adult phenologies that are highly resistant to adverse conditions (e.g. deciduous leaves, physiological responses to drought or cold). The combined effects of ecological opportunities and the variability of these opportunities promote suites of characters that simultaneously allow organisms to exploit the opportunities and tolerate the stresses. Restoration projects often involve creating and maintaining a favorable abiotic environment for the species. If the conditions under restoration do not mimic the normal variability of stresses and opportunities then evolved changes in the organism's bet-hedging strategies should occur. Restorations made under temporally more favorable conditions should select for strategies that increase population growth rates and reduce tolerance to temporally unfavorable periods.

Density-dependent selection promotes strategies that maximize population sizes, enhance competitive abilities, and result in the efficient utilization of limiting resources (similar to 'K-selection'). Adaptations arise to mitigate the effects of overcrowding (Levin, Cohen & Hastings 1984). For instance, in annual plants seed dispersal and seed dormancy can serve as a hedge against environmental stochasticity, as a means for avoiding over-crowding, and as a means for reducing competition among siblings (Venable & Brown 1993). Restoring species to favorable environments may unwittingly alter the balance of limiting resources (Chapter 8). Such a shift in limiting resources may not only alter competitive relationships (Tilman 1982) but may also select for evolutionary changes in characters that influence patterns of resource utilization (Abrams 1990).

One of the most important balances of resources involves food and safety (Werner 1992). Islands provide a number of natural experiments into the evolutionary consequences of providing increased safety through the absence of predators. These include flightlessness in birds, reduction in secondary compounds in plants, and loss of predator avoidance behaviors in many vertebrates. The extreme docility of many island species of vertebrate may represent increased selection to utilize food resources more efficiently in the absence of counterbalancing selection from predators. The prey that startles easily may avoid predators but it pays a price in terms of energy expended or reduced feeding rates.

Frequency-dependent selection may occur intraspecifically when the fitness of an individual is simultaneously influenced by the evolutionary strategies of conspecifics (see Maynard Smith 1982), or it may be interspecific when fitness is influenced by the strategies employed by individuals of other species (for some of the modeling consequences see Brown & Vincent 1987, Taper & Case 1992). An important consequence of frequency-dependent selection concerns the maintenance of polymorphisms and species diversity through natural selection. At the level of alleles at a locus, frequency-dependent selection promotes diversity through mechanisms such as overdominance and heterozygote superiority. At the level of behaviors or morphs within a species, frequency-dependent selection may result in a mixed strategy Evolutionarily Stable Strategy (ESS) that maintains several different strategies within the population. At the level of different species, frequency-dependent selection may promote disruptive selection and result in competitive speciation (Rosenzweig 1979).

Theories of predator–prey coevolution provide examples of the potential significance of frequency-dependent selection among species. Such evolution is generally frequency-dependent in that the strategy of the predators often has profound consequences for their prey and vice versa. An extreme case of this is embodied within the notion of Red Queen evolution where each selective advantage in one species consequently disadvantages the other species: 'The deer flees, and the wolf pursues' (Bakker 1986).

Removing a predator may have further consequences than simply changing the selective regime experienced by its prey. The predator may be ecologically keystone in that its removal results in the extinction of one or more of the prey species. The predator may also be evolutionarily keystone in that the predator may promote the disruptive selection that actually caused or maintains the evolutionary divergence of two or more prey species (Brown & Vincent 1992). Under the ghost of predation past, a predator may be evolutionarily keystone without presently being ecologically keystone. Removing the predator may have little or no effect in ecological time. Following the loss of the predator, the two prey species may continue to coexist. However, the removal of the predator may change their selective regimes in a way that results in convergent evolution and the eventual extinction of one of the prey. This theoretical result (Brown & Vincent 1992) awaits empirical investigation. But likely systems for its occurrence are insect–plant associations, or other predator–prey systems where the prey are likely to have evolved in response to strongly conflicting demands for resources and safety.

With some understanding of the different kinds of selection, it is possible to speculate on some of the evolutionary changes that might occur in species' restoration projects. Habitat fragmentation generally insures that the species experiences reduced habitat scales. As a result of density-independent selection this should result in the evolutionary enhancement of adaptations to mitigate the effects of environmental stochasticity.

As a result of reduced scales of habitat heterogeneity, density-dependent and frequency-dependent selection will favor generalists over specialists (Brown & Pavlovic 1992). Interestingly, the species under restoration into a natural area may be under strong selection to survive and thrive within human-altered habitats. While solid documentation remains rare, there is growing anecdotal evidence that some herbivorous insects have evolved to broaden their specificity by including exotic and weedy plant species within their diet (e.g. apple maggot fly, Feder, Chilcote & Bush 1988). In this way, an insect species that may have been rare by virtue of its specificity to a rare plant species may rebound in population size and expand its range by evolving a more generalist strategy (R. Panzer, personal communication).

Another feature of many restorations involves maintaining island populations within a sea of unsuitable habitat. In the case of mammals (and some birds) several ecological and evolutionary trends emerge from insular populations. Pimm, Jones & Diamond (1988) showed that birds of intermediate size had lower extinction rates on offshore islands than either small or large bird species. Pimm invokes environmental and demographic stochasticity to explain this observation. Smaller bird species are extinction-prone because of heightened sensitivity to the negative effects of environmental stochasticity. While large species are buffered from environmental stochasticity, they can only maintain small population sizes and suffer from the negative effects of demographic stochasticity. In this way, body size represents a tradeoff between susceptibilities to demographic and environmental stochasticities.

The ecological processes that may selectively preserve island bird species of intermediate size may also explain a pattern in the evolution of body size among island mammals. Small mammals (<100 g) tend to evolve gigantism on islands (e.g. *Peromyscus maniculatus* on the Channel Islands, California, Ashley & Wills 1987), and large mammals tend to evolve dwarfism (e.g. island forms of elephants, hippopotamus, and deer). This evolution can be quite rapid. By examining fossils, Lister (1989) found that male red deer on Jersey, Channel Islands, had evolved from a body size of 200 kg to a size of 36 kg within less than 6000 years.

The insularity of many preserves and restoration projects for large mammals suggests that humans may be selecting for dwarfism and that small but tangible evolutionary changes may occur within the 100 year planning horizons suggested for many projects. In response to a single and severe El Niño event (1982–83), Grant & Grant (1993) found that bill depth in *Geospiza fortis* evolved to be smaller in response to a decline in seed size. Such rapid evolutionary changes demonstrate that evolutionary changes can and probably will occur in response to persistent habitat or climate changes.

A number of questions arise from evolutionary considerations. A wrong question is to ask whether species under restoration will evolve; rather the question should be how much evolutionary change might occur and how quickly will this change happen (Brown & Parman 1994). Another question concerns how we view and deal with species that evolutionarily jump from the endangered list to the pest list. Do these represent conservation nightmares or success stories? A third question concerns the extent to which we need or want to preserve the evolutionary context of species. Do we care whether species evolve gigantism, dwarfism, novel bet-hedging adaptations, or more generalist strategies? As in preserving ecological processes, there is probably a management tradeoff. Preservation of species, in their present form will probably require increasing amounts of intervention into the species evolutionary context. Maintaining the naturalness of processes by minimizing human intervention will probably result in novel and sometimes surprising evolutionary changes. Documenting and modeling the validity of such evolutionary possibilities should provide an exciting and increasingly important subdiscipline of restoration ecology.

Conclusion

As a final thought on future developments in restoration ecology, there should and certainly will be a continued emphasis on natural history. Understanding the particulars of a species' ecology and life history is essential to a successful restoration. But, an understanding of ecological and evolutionary processes will become increasingly important. As increased knowledge accrues around these concepts, the artistry of restorations will give way to an applied science that has broader applicability, that learns quickly from the analysis of mistakes, and that rapidly evaluates, verifies, disseminates, and revises concepts and ideas.

This plea for a process- and concept-based science of restoration ecology may sound like an evolutionary ecologist striving to justify his existence, but there is more to this plea. We may be too preoccupied with the actors, those products of ecological and evolutionary processes; to the exclusion of these processes. For the species and organisms themselves come and go, and humans have certainly hastened their exits, but the processes that produce and mold the diversity of life still go on.

But, a science of restoration ecology is of little applied use unless it helps to bring about a person's, group's or society's hopes for maintaining, restoring, and conserving biodiversity. This requires a set of goals and a well-defined environmental ethic. This places the discipline at an exciting juncture of science, philosophy, politics, and economics. Carefully or carelessly, restoration ecology conceives and implements a Prime Directive.

Acknowledgments

Many thanks to Marlin Bowles, Marcy DeMauro, Noel Pavlovic, and Christopher Whelan for organizing the symposium on the Restoration of Endangered Species, Society for Ecological Restoration, 1990. Discussions with many people have formed and influenced my thoughts on restoration ecology. I am particularly grateful to Mary Ashley, M. Bowles, M. DeMauro, Cathy Geraghty, Henry Howe, Robert Morgan, N. Pavlovic, and C. Whelan for valuable comments and many hours of stimulating and enjoyable conversation.

Literature cited

Abrams, P. A. (1990) Mixed responses to resource densities and their implications for character displacement. *Evolutionary Ecology,* **4**, 93-102.

Abrams, P. A. (1993) Why predation rate should not be proportional to predator density. *Ecology,* **74**, 726-33.

Alford, R. A. & Wilbur, H. M. (1985) Priority effects in experimental pond communities: competition between *Bufo* and *Rana. Ecology,* **64**, 1097-105.

Allendorf, F. W. & Leary, R. F. (1986) Heterozygosity and fitness in natural populations of animals. In *Conservation Biology: The Science of Scarcity and Diversity,* ed. Soulé, M. E., pp. 57–76. Sunderland, Massachusetts: Sinauer.

Antonovics, J. (1971) The effects of a heterogeneous environment on the genetics of natural populations. *American Scientist,* **59**, 593-9.

Ashley, M. V., Melnick, D. J. & Western, D. (1990) Conservation genetics of the black rhinocerus (*Diceros bicornis*), I.: Evidence from mitochondrial DNA of three populations. *Conservation Biology,* **4**, 71-7.

Ashley, M. & Wills, C. (1987) Analysis of mitochondrial DNA polymorphisms among Channel Island deer mice. *Evolution,* **41**, 854-63.

Avise, J. C. & Nelson, W. S. (1989) Molecular genetic relationships of the extinct dusky seaside sparrow. *Science,* **243**, 646-8.

Bakker, R. T. (1986) The deer flees, the wolf pursues: incongruencies in predator-prey coevolution. In *Coevolution,* ed. Futuyma, D. J. & Slatkin, M., pp. 350–82. Sunderland: Sinauer Associates.

Barrett, S. C. H. (1983) Crop mimicry in weeds. *Economic Botany,* **37**, 255-82.

Brown, J. H. & Kodric-Brown, A. (1977) Turnover rates in insular biogeography: effect of immigration on extinction. *Ecology,* **58**, 445-9.

Brown, J. H. & Kurzius, M. (1987) Composition of desert rodent faunas: combinations of coexisting species. *Annales Zoologici Fennici,* **24**, 227-37.

Brown, J. S. & Parman, A. O. (1994) Consequences of size selective harvesting as an evolutionary game. In *The Exploitation of Evolving Resources,* ed. Stokes, T. K., McGlade, J. & Law, R., pp. 248–61. Lecture Notes in Biomathematics, Volume 99. Berlin: Springer-Verlag.

Brown, J. S. & Pavlovic, N. B. (1992) Evolution in heterogeneous environments: Effects of migration on habitat specialization. *Evolutionary Ecology,* **6**, 360-82.

Brown, J. S. & Venable, D. L. (1986) Evolutionary ecology of seed bank annuals in temporally varying environments. *American Naturalist,* **127**, 31-47.

Brown, J. S. & Vincent, T. L. (1987) Coevolution as an evolutionary game. *Evolution,* **41**, 66-79.

Brown, J. S. & Vincent, T. L. (1992) Organization of predator-prey communities as an evolutionary game. *Evolution,* **46,** 1269-83.

Chase, A. (1986) *Playing God in Yellowstone: The Destruction of America's First National Park.* New York: Harcourt Brace Jovanovich.

Cohen, D. (1966) Optimizing reproduction in a randomly varying environment. *Journal of Theoretical Biology,* **12,** 119-29.

Cohn, J. P. (1990) Genetics for wildlife conservation. *BioScience,* **40,** 167-71.

Culbert, R. & Blair, R. (1989) Recovery planning and endangered species. *Endangered Species UPDATE,* **8,**64-5.

Daugherty, C. H., Cree, A., Hay, J. M. & Thompson, M. B. (1990) Neglected taxonomy and continuing extinctions of tuatara (*Sphenodon*). *Nature,* **347,** 177-9.

DeAngelis, D. L. & Waterhouse, J. C. (1987) Equilibrium and nonequilibrium concepts in ecological models. *Ecological Monographs,* **57,** 1-21.

Dennis, D., Munholland, P. L. & Scott, M. J. (1991) Estimation of growth and extinction parameters for endangered species. *Ecological Monographs,* **61,** 115-43.

Dowling, T. E., DeMarais, B. D., Minckley, W. L., Douglas, M. E. & Marsh, P. C. (1992) Use of genetic characters in conservation biology. *Conservation Biology,* **6,** 7-8.

Drake, J. A., Mooney, H. A., di Castri, F., *et al.* eds. (1989) *Biological Invasions: A Global Perspective, SCOPE 37.* Chichester: J. Wiley & Sons.

Dudley, J. W. (1977) 76 generations of selection for oil and protein percentage in maize. In *The Proceedings of the International Conference of Quantitative Genetics,* ed. Pollack, E., Kempthorne, O. & Bailey, T. B., pp. 259–73. Ames: Iowa University Press.

Feder, J. L., Chilcote, C. A. & Bush, G. L. (1988) Genetic differentiation and sympatric host races of the apple maggot fly, *Rhagoletis pomonella. Nature,* **336,** 61-4.

Fox, W. (1990) *Toward a Transpersonal Ecology.* Boston: Shambhala.

Fox, D. J. & Kirkland, G. L. (1992) An assembly rule for functional groups applied to North American soricid communities. *Journal of Mammalogy,* **73,** 491-503.

Garrod, G. J. (1988) North atlantic cod: fisheries and management to 1986. In *Fish Population Dynamics,* 2nd edition, ed. Gulland, J. A., pp. 185–218. London: J. Wiley and Sons.

Gilpin, M. E. & Soulé, M. E. (1986) Minimum viable populations: processes of species extinction. In *Conservation Biology: The Science of Scarcity and Diversity,* ed. Soulé, M. E., pp. 19–34. Sunderland: Sinauer Associates.

Goodman, D. (1987) How do any species exist? Lessons for conservation biology. *Conservation Biology,* **1,** 59-62.

Grant, B. R. & Grant, P. R. (1993) Evolution of Darwin's finches caused by a rare climatic event. *Proceedings of the Royal Society, London,* B**251,** 111-17.

Harris, R. B. & Allendorf, F. W. (1989) Genetically effective population size of large mammals: an assessment of estimators. *Conservation Biology,* **3,** 181-91.

Higashi, M. & Burns, T. P., eds. (1991) *Theoretical Studies of Ecosystems: The Network Perspective.* Cambridge University Press.

Hoerr, W. (1993) The concept of naturalness in environmental discourse. *Natural Areas Journal,* **13,** 29-32.

Holt, R. D. (1977) Predation, apparent competition, and the structure of prey communities. *Theoretical Population Biology,* **12,** 197-229.

Howe, H. F. (1994) Response of early- and late-flowering plants to fire season in experimental prairies. *Ecological Applications,* **4,** 121–33.

Hughes, A. L. (1991) MHC polymorphism and the design of captive breeding programs. *Conservation Biology,* **5,** 249-51.

Hughes, A. L. & Nei, M. (1989) Nucleotide substitution at major histocompatibility complex class II loci: evidence for overdominant selection. *Proceedings of the National Academy of Sciences, USA*, **86**, 958-62.

Iwasa, Y. & Mochizuki, H. (1988) Probability of population extinction accompanying a temporary decrease in population size. *Researches in Population Ecology*, **30**, 154-64.

Kotler, B. P., Blaustein, L. & Brown, J. S. (1993) Predator facilitation: the combined effect of snakes and owls on the foraging behavior of gerbils. *Annales Zoologici Fennici*, **29**, 199-206.

Joseph, L. (1991) Genetics and conservation. *Australian Natural History*, **23**, 706-13.

Joshi, A. & Mueller, D. (1993) Directional and stabilizing density-dependent natural selection for pupation height in *Drosophila melanogaster. Evolution*, **47**, 176-84.

Lacy, R. C. (1987) Loss of genetic diversity from managed populations: interacting effects of drift, mutation, immigration, selection, and population subdivision. *Conservation Biology*, **1**, 143-58.

Lande, R. (1987) Extinction thresholds in demographic models of territorial populations. *American Naturalist*, **130**, 624-35.

Lande, R. (1988) Genetics and demography in biological conservation. *Science*, **241**, 1455-60.

Law, R. & Grey, D. R. (1989) Evolution of yields from populations with age-specific cropping. *Evolutionary Ecology*, **3**, 343-59.

Levin, S., Cohen, D. & Hastings, A. (1984) Dispersal strategies in patchy environments. *Theoretical Population Biology*, **26**, 165-91.

Lima, S. L. & Dill, L. M. (1990) Behavioral decisions made under the risk of predation: a review and prospectus. *Canadian Journal of Zoology*, **68**, 619-40.

Lister, A. M. (1989) Rapid dwarfing of red deer on Jersey in the last interglacial. *Nature*, **342**, 539-42.

Lockwood, J. L., Moulton, M. P. & Anderson, S. K. (1993) Morphological assortment and the assembly of communities of introduced passeriformes on oceanic islands: Tahiti versus Oahu. *American Naturalist*, **141**, 398-408.

Mace, G. M. & Lande, R. (1991) Assessing extinction threats: Toward a reevaluation of IUCN threatened species categories. *Conservation Biology*, **5**, 148-57.

Maguire, L. A. & Lacy, R. C. (1990) Allocating scarce resources for conservation of endangered subspecies: partitioning zoo space for tigers. *Conservation Biology*, **4**, 157-65.

Maynard Smith, J. & Price, G. R. (1973) The logic of animal conflict. *Nature*, **246**, 15-18.

Maynard Smith, J. (1982) *Evolution and the Theory of Games*. Cambridge University Press.

Mitchell, W. A. & Valone, T. J. (1990) The optimization research program: studying adaptations by their function. *Quarterly Review of Biology*, **65**, 43-52.

Morris, D. W. & Brown, J. S. (1993) The role of habitat selection in landscape ecology. *Evolutionary Ecology*, **6**, 357-9.

Murphy, D. D., Freas, K. E. & Weiss, S. B. (1990) An environment-metapopulation approach to population viability analysis for a threatened invertebrate. *Conservation Biology*, **4**, 41-53.

Naess, A. (1986) Intrinsic value: will defenders of wildlife please rise? In *Conservation Biology: The Science of Scarcity and Diversity*, ed. Soulé, M. E., pp. 504–515. Sunderland: Sinauer Associates.

Nicolis, G. & Prigogine, I. (1977) *Self Organization in Non-equilibrium Systems*. New York: J. Wiley & Sons.

O'Brien, S. J. & Mayr, E. (1991) Bureaucratic mischief: recognizing endangered species and subspecies. *Science*, **251**, 1187-8.

O'Brien, S. J., Roelke, M. E., Yuhki, N., Richards, K. W., Johnson, W. E., Franklin,
    W. L., Anderson, A. E., Bass, O. L., Jr, Belden, R. C. & Martenson, J. S. (1990)
    Genetic introgression within the Florida panther *Felis concolor coryi*. *National
    Geographic Research*, **6**, 485-94.
Paine, R. T. (1966) Food web complexity and species diversity. *American Naturalist*,
    100, 65-7
Partridge, L. & Fowler, K. (1993) Responses and correlated responses to artificial
    selection on thorax length in *Drosophila melanogaster*. *Evolution*, **47**, 213-26.
Patterson, B. D. & Atmar, W. (1986) Nested subsets and the structure of insular
    mammalian faunas and archipelagos. In *Island Biogeography of Mammals*, ed.
    Heaney, L. R. & Patterson, B. D., pp. 65–82. London: Academic Press.
Pimm, S. L., Jones, H. L. & Diamond, J. (1988) On the risk of extinction. *American
    Naturalist*, **132**, 757-85.
Pulliam, H. R. (1988) Sources, sinks, and population regulation. *American Naturalist*,
    132, 652-61.
Quinn, J. F. & Hastings, A. (1987) Extinction in subdivided habitats. *Conservation
    Biology*, **1**, 198-208.
Rolston, H. (1990) Biology and philosophy in Yellowstone. *Biology and Philosophy*,
    5, 241-58.
Rosenzweig, M. L. (1979) Competitive speciation. *Biological Journal of the Linnean
    Society*, **10**, 275-89.
Rosenzweig, M. L. (1981) A theory of habitat selection. *Ecology*, **62**, 327-35.
Saunders, D. A., Hobbs, R. J. & Margules, C. R. (1991) Biological consequences of
    ecosystem fragmentation: A review. *Conservation Biology*, **5**, 18-32.
Schaffer, W. M. (1984) Stretching and folding in lynx fur returns: evidence for a
    strange attractor. *American Naturalist*, **124**, 798-820.
Slobodkin, L. B. (1988) Intellectual problems of applied ecology. *Bioscience*, **38**, 337-42.
Sredl, M. J. & Collins, J. P. (1991) The effect of ontogeny on interspecific interactions
    in larval amphibians. *Ecology*, **72**, 2232-9.
Stanley-Price, M. R. (1989) *Animal Re-introductions: the Arabian Oryx in Oman*.
    New York: Cambridge University Press.
Taper, M. L. & Case, T. J. (1992) Models of character displacement and the
    robustness of the taxon cycle. *Evolution*, **46**, 317-33.
Tilman, D. (1982) *Resource Competition and Community Structure*. Princeton
    University Press.
USEPA (1990) Environmental fact sheet: Endangered species. Office of Pesticides
    and Toxic Substances, Office of Pesticide Programs, H7501C, United States
    Environmental Protection Agency.
Vane-Wright, R. I., Humphries, C. J. & Williams, P. H. (1991) What to protect? –
    Systematics and the agony of choice. *Biological Conservation*, **55**, 235-54.
Venable, D. L. & Brown, J. S. (1993) The population-dynamic functions of seed
    dispersal. In *Frugivory and Seed Dispersal: Ecological and Evolutionary
    Aspects*, ed. Fleming, T. H. & Estrada, A., pp. 31–55. Dordrecht: Kluwer
    Academic Publishers.
Vincent, T. L. & Brown, J. S. (1988) The evolution of ESS theory. *Annual Review of
    Ecology and Systematics*, **19**, 423-43.
Wayne, R. K. & Jenks, S. M. (1991) Mitochondrial DNA analysis implying extensive
    hybridization of the endangered red wolf (*Canis rufus*). *Nature*, 351, 565-8.
Werner, E. E. (1992) Individual behavior and higher-order species interactions.
    American Naturalist, **140**, S5-32.
Wilson, E. O., ed. (1988) *Biodiversity*. Washington, D. C.: National Academy Press.
Zeeman, E. C. (1977) *Catastrophe Theory*. New York: Addison-Wesley.

Taxonomic index

aalii 148
Acacia koa 148
Acanthomintha duttonii 343
Aceras anthropophorum 330, 331
Actaea
  pachypoda 107
  rubra 107, 108
Agalinis acuta 177
Agropyron
  smithii 281
  spicatum 281
Alces alces 221
Alexgeorgea subterranea 175
Alsinidendron spp. 101, 108
amakihi 106
Ammodramus maritimus nigrescens 50
Amsinckia
  calycina 332
  douglasiana 104
  grandiflora 104, 170, 179, 180, 184–5,
    332, 340–3
  spectabilis 104
  spp. 110
  vernicosa var. *furcata* 104
Andropogon scoparius 307
antelope 65–6
ant
  Argentine 140, 147, 153
  introduced 106
Apidae 301
Aquila chrysaetos 248
Arctostaphylos densiflora 176
Arecaceae 146
Arenaria stricta 307
Argemone pleiacantha subsp. *pinnatisecta*
  177
Argyroxiphium 140
  grayanum 146, 151, 155
  sandwicense 106, 109, 140

  subsp. *macrocephalum* 149, 152–6
  virescens 140, 146, 147, 149, 153–5
Aristida tuberculosa 175
Artemisia
  caudata 162
  mauiensis 146
  tridentata 281
Aspidiaceae 146
Aspleniaceae 147
Asplenium
  kaulfussii 147
  leucostegioides 147
Aster furcatus 102–3, 109, 304
Asteraceae 108, 109, 146, 147, 175
Astragalus
  altus 176
  cremnophylax var. *cremnophylax* 181
  kentrophytus 176
  linifolius 99, 107, 109
  lonchocarpus 107
  osterhouti 99, 109
  pectinatus 99
  spp. 334
  tyghensis 176
Avena
  barbata 44
  maroccana 175

badger 248, 249, 263, 291
banana poka 148
barley 45
bear, black 220, 225, 227, 230, 234, 236,
  238
beaver
  European 364
  North American 364
bee 99
  bumble 301
  carpenter 301

bee (*cont.*)
  halictid 301
  native 106
beetle
  buprestid 335
  flour 372
Bidens micrantha 139, 156
  subsp. *kalealaha* 149, 150
bison 247
Bison bison 247
blackberry 148
bladderpod, Missouri 181
Boltonia decurrens 175
Boraginaceae 110
Brassicaceae 175
Brium spp. 307
Bromus pseudosecalinus 185
Buprestidae 335

Cakile edentula 181
Calamagrostis expansa 146
Callosobruchus maculatus 335
Calochortus
  albus 174
  longebarbatus 174
  spp. 327, 334
Campanula aparinoides 176
Campanulaceae 108, 176
Canis
  dingo 372
  latrans 248, 278
  lupus 10, 221
Capidosoma bakeri 147
Capra hircus 145
Carex
  macloviana 152
  pensylvanica 162
  thunbergii 151
  wahuensis 152
caribou, woodland 219–42, 364
carpet weed 162
Carthamus flavescens 303
Caryophyllaceae 107, 108, 109, 110, 146,
  147, 176
Castor
  canadensis 364
  castor 364
cattle 152, 154
Centaurea lainzii 175
Chamaecrista fasciculata 42–3
Cirsium
  canescens 98, 123–8, 200, 204
  peckii 175
  pitcheri 98, 108, 124, 170, 171, 172, 184,
    194–218
  rhothophilum 200, 204
Cistaceae 175

Cladina 222
Clermontia
  arborescens 106, 108
  lindseyana 147
  peleana 147
  samuelii 146
  tuberculata 146
clidemia 148
Clidemia hirta 148
clover, running buffalo 179–80, 182, 184
cod, Atlantic 372
condor, California 10, 16, 64, 69, 359
copepod 43
Coprosma montana 152
corn 371
Cortaderia jubata 148
coyote 248, 249, 250, 251, 253, 263, 278, 291,
  363, 366
crabgrass 162
Crassulaceae 108
Cyanea
  aculeatiflora 146
  aff. *glabra* 146
  horrida 146
  kunthiana 146
  longissima 146, 147
  pohaku 146, 147
Cyathea cooperi 148
Cynomys
  leucurus 277
  spp. 249, 272
Cyperaceae 174
Cyperus filiculmis 162
Cypripedium candidum 97, 108
Cyrtandra hashimotoi 146

daisy, Lakeside 55, 298–321, 358–9, 362, 364
Dalea scariosa 176
Dedeckera eurekensis 332
deer
  red 375
  white-tailed 221, 225, 227, 230, 234, 235,
    236, 238, 301
Dendroseris
  litoralis 100, 108
  micrantha 100, 109
Dermacentor albipictus 226
Dicerandra frutescens 170, 173, 178
Dichelostemma ida-maia 174
Digitaria sanguinalis 162
dingo 372
Dodonaea viscosa 148
Draba incana 175
Drosophila spp. 43, 46, 371
Dryopteris sp. 146
Dubautia
  dolosa 146

Dubautia (*cont.*)
 menziesii 146
 platyphylla 146
 reticulata 146

eagle, golden 248
earwig, European 147
Ebenus armitagei 335
Echinococcus granulosus 226
Eichhornia
 crassipes 105
 paniculata 38, 105
 spp. 110
Elaphostrongylus cervi rangiferi 225
Encyrtidae 147
Equus przewalskii 78
Eragrostis spectabilis 162
Ericaceae 176
Erysimum capitatum var. *angustatum* 333,
 336, 337
Erythronium
 albidum 103
 grandiflorum var. *candidum* 99
 grandiflorum var. *grandiflorum* 99, 109
 propullans 103, 109
Eucalyptus
 caesia 107, 109
 globulus 148
Euglandina rosea 147
Euphorbia telephioides 176
Euphorbiaceae 176

Fabaceae 109, 176
fame flower 140, 160–169, 180, 181, 184,
 185, 186
Felis
 concolor araucanus 364
 concolor coryi 63, 364
 concolor patagonica 364
fern, Australian tree 148
ferret
 black-footed 10–11, 16–17, 20, 63, 69,
 272–97, 358
 European 285
 Siberian 64, 273, 276, 279, 285
fiddleneck, large-flowered 179, 180
flea 248
flies
 apple maggot 375
 picture-winged 124
Forficula auricularia 147
fox
 kit 248, 256
 red 278
 swift 247–71
Fritillaria
 pluriflora 174

 roderickii 174

Gardenia remyi 147
Gazella spekei 80
gazelle, Speke's 38, 80
Geospiza fortis 375
Geraniaceae 146
Geranium
 arboreum 146
 hanaense 146, 151
 multiflorum 146
gerbil 367
Gesneriaceae 108, 146
ginger, kahili 148
Gnaphalium sandwicensium subsp.
 hawaiiense 152
goat (feral) 139, 145, 148, 149, 150, 152, 154
goldenbush
 coastal 121–2
 scaly 122–3
gorse 148
grass
 fountain 148
 molasses 148, 150
 Pampas 148
guava, strawberry 148
guinea pig 46
gum, blue 148
Gymnogyps californianus 10

Halictidae 301
Haplopappus
 squarrosa var. *grindelioides* 122–3
 venetus subsp. *vernonioides* 121–3
hawkmoths 106
Hazardia squarrosa 122
Hedychium gardnerianum 148
Helianthemum
 bicknellii 175
 dumosum 175
Helianthus schweinitzii 175
Herminium monorchis 331
Holcus lanatus 152
Homeosoma stypticellum 124
Hordeum spontaneum 45
horse, Asian wild 78, 79
Houstonia spp. 307
Howellia aquatilis 170, 171, 172, 181, 182
Hudsonia tomentosa 176, 178
Huperzia haleakalae 147
Hymenophyllaceae 147
Hymenoxys acaulis var. *glabra* 102–3, 109,
 112, 298–321, 340

i'iwi 106
Illiciaceae 103, 109
Illicium floridanum 103, 109

Ipomopsis aggregata 43
Iridaceae 174
Iridomyrmex humilis 147, 153
Iris
    lacustris 340
    tenuis 174
Isocoma veneta 121–2
Isotria
    medeoloides 97, 108, 174
    verticillata 97
Ixodes 248

Jankaea heldreichii 98, 108
Juncaceae 174
Juncus scirpoides 174, 178

kiwi 365
koa 148
Koeleria cristata 281

Labordia venosa 146
Labiatae 97
Lamiaceae 108, 109, 146
Leguminosae 335
Leitneria floridana 176
Leitneriaceae 176
Leontopithecus
    rosalia chrysomelas 66
    rosalia rosalia 64
Lesquerella
    aurea 175
    filiformis 175, 181
    gooddingii 175
    lescurii 170, 175, 179, 180, 183
    stonensis 170, 175, 179, 180, 182, 183
Leucospar rothschildi 64
Liliaceae 109, 174
Lindsaea repens var. *macraeana* 147
Lindsaeaceae 147
Lobelia
    grayana 146
    hillebrandii 146
Lobeliaceae 146, 147
Loganiaceae 146
lousewort, Furbish's 140, 171, 184
lovegrass 162
Loxops virens 106
Lupinus
    duranii 176
    milo-bakeri 176
    monoensis 176
    spectabilis 176
Luzula hawaiiensis 152
Lythrum
    hyssopifolia 179
    salicaria 104

Mabrya spp. 98, 108
maize 41, 43, 46
Malvaceae 177
mamani 148
mammoth, woolly 365
Manduca sp. 106
Mariscus hillebrandii 139, 149–150, 156
Melinis minutiflora 148
meningeal brain worm 221, 225, 230, 234–5, 236, 238
Miconia calvescens 148
Milium effusum 175
milk vetch, sentry 181
Mimulus guttatus 50–1
molasses grass 148, 150
Mollugo verticillata 162
moose 221, 223, 224, 225, 227, 230, 236
monarch butterfly 355
Morbilivirus 277
moth, sunflower 124
mouse 147
    beach 64
    house 372
Mus
    domesticus 147
    musculus 372
Mustela
    eversmanni 64, 273, 279, 291
    nigripes 10, 63, 272–97
myna, Bali 64
Myrtaceae 109

oak, black 161–2, 164
Odocoileus virginianus 221
Oenothera
    brandegeei 100, 108
    caespitosa 100
    cavernae 100, 108
    deltoides subsp. *howellii* 333, 336
    grandis 100, 109
    hookeri 333
    laciniata 100
    organensis 102
ohelo 148
Onagraceae 108, 109
orchid
    Australian metallic sun 173
    eastern prairie fringed 173, 178
    western prairie fringed 106
Orchidaceae 108, 147, 174
Orchis
    militaris 174
    spectabilis 97, 108
Orcuttia 332
Orellia occidentalis 124
Oreobolus furcatus 151

Orothamnus zeyheri 177
oryx, Arabian 64
Oryx leucoryx 64
Osteomeles anthyllidifolia 148
Oxalidaceae 110
Oxalis
    section *Corniculatae* spp. 105, 110
    section *Ionoxalis* 105, 110
    sukdorfii 105
Oxychilus alliarius 147

Panicum
    implicatum 162
    tenuifolium 147
    virgatum 127
panther, Florida 63–4, 69, 359, 364
Papaveraceae 177
Paracantha culta 124
Parelaphostrongylus
    andersoni 226
    tenuis 221
parrot, orange-bellied 11
Partula 64
Passiflora mollissima 148
Pedicularis furbishiae 98–9, 109, 170, 171,
    173, 181, 182, 327, 328, 334, 339
Pediocactus knowltonii 340
Pelea
    balloui 146
    orbicularis 146
    ovalis 146
Pennisetum setaceum 148
Peperomia kipahuluensis 146
Peromyscus 38
    maniculatus 375
    polionotus trissyllepsis 64
Peucedanum palustre 334–5
Phyllostegia bracteata 146, 147
Picea mariana 222
Picoides borealis 10
pig, feral 139, 145, 149, 151, 154
pine 148
pine, jack 222
Pinus banksiana 222
    spp. 148
Piperaceae 146
Pipturus forbesii 146
Plantago 332
    cordata 170, 171, 172, 173, 181, 185
    pachyphylla 139, 149, 151, 156
Plantain, heart-leaved 140, 171–2, 184
Platanthera
    holochila 147
    leucophaea 170, 173, 175, 178, 179
    peramoena 175
    praeclara 106, 108
Platyptilia carduidactyla 201

Poa 98
    alsodes 175
    compressa 307
    marcida 175
Poaceae 108, 110, 146, 147, 175, 331
Polygonaceae 177
Polygonella articulata 177, 178
Polystichum sp. 146
Pontederiaceae 105, 110
Portulacaceae 177
poultry 46
prairie dog 63, 249, 272, 273, 274, 276, 277,
    278, 279, 280, 281, 282, 283, 288, 289,
    291, 292
    black-tailed 277, 282, 291
    white-tailed 277, 282
Primula
    eximia 104
    tschuktschorum 104, 110
Primulaceae 110
Pritchardia arecina 146
Procyon lotor 278
Proteaceae 177
Psidium cattleianum 148
pukiawe 148
Pulex spp. 248

Quercus velutina 161

rabbit, eastern cottontail 301
raccoon 278
Rangifer tarandus caribou 219
Ranunculaceae 108, 147, 177
Ranunculus
    hawaiensis 147
    mauiensis 147
    ophioglossifolius 177, 184
raptor 291
rat, alien 147
Rattus spp. 147
Restionaceae 175
rhino
    black 363
    Javan 359
Rhododendron bakeri 176
Rubiaceae 147
rue, goat's 161
Rubus argutus 148
Rutaceae 146
Rytidosperma tenue 98, 108

Santalaceae 146
Santalum haleakalae 146
Schiedea
    haleakalensis 139, 146, 149, 150–1, 156
    implexa 146, 147
    spp. 101, 108, 110

Scirpus hallii 174, 178
Scrophulariaceae 108, 177
scrub balm, Florida endemic 173, 178
sea rocket 181
Sedum section *Gormania* spp. 100, 108
Selaginella
    deflexa 151
    rupestris 174
Selaginellaceae 174
Sidalcea campestris 177
Silene
    cryptopetala 146, 147
    degeneri 146, 147
    regia 107, 109, 176
silversword
    flowering 153
    Haleakala 154
    Hawaiian 106
Sisysrinchium 139
    acre 149, 152, 156
    angustifolium 174
    dichotomum 174
skunk 278
slug 335
snail 64, 147, 335
Solanaceae 147
Solanum incompletum 147
Solidago nemoralis 307
Sophora chrysophylla 148, 152
sparrow, dusky seaside 50, 365
Spiranthes
    lucida 175
    spiralis 331
spruce, black 222
Stackhousia tryonii 177
Stackhousiaceae 177
Stenogyne
    haliakalae 146, 147
    kanehoana 106, 109
    rotundifolia 146
Stephanomeria
    exigua subsp. *coronaria* 100
    malheurensis 100, 108, 339
Styphelia tameiameiae 148
Sus scrofa 145
Swallenia alexandrae 331
Synandra hispidula 97, 108

Talinum rugospermum 160–9, 170, 177,
    181–2
tamarin
    golden lion 64
    golden-headed lion 66
tapeworm, hydatid 226

Taxidae taxus 248
Tephritidae 124
Tephrosia virginiana 162
Tetramolopium lepidotum subsp. *arbusculum*
    147
Thalictrum cooleyi 177
Thelymitra epipactoides 170, 173, 175, 179
thistle, Pitcher's 124, 130–2, 140, 141, 142,
    171, 172, 194–218
thistle, Platte 123–8, 130–2
Thymelaeaceae 146
tick 248
    winter 226
Tigriopus californicus 43
Topminnow 47–8
Tribolium sp. 372
Trifolium stoloniferum 170, 179–80
Trisetum glomeratum 151
tuatara 365

ulei 148
Ulex europaeus 148
Ursus americanus 225
Urticaceae 146

Vaccinium reticulatum 148, 152
Vandenboschia draytoniana 147
Vestiaria coccinea 106
Vespula pensylvanica 147
Viola mauiensis 151
Vulpes
    macrotis 248
    velox 247
    velox hebes 247
    velox macrotis 248
    velox velox 247, 248
    vulpes 278

wasp 147
white-eye, Japanese 106
Wikstroemia monticola 146
wolf 359, 363
    gray 221, 223, 227, 230, 233, 235–6, 237
    northern Rocky Mountain (gray) 10
    red 64, 363
woodpecker, red-cockaded 10
wormwood 162

Xylocopidae 301

yellow jacket, western 147

Zosterops japonica 106

Subject index

agencies, government
  Animal and Plant Health Inspection Service
    229
  Bureau of Land Management 289
  Canadian Park Service 228
  Manitoba Ministry of Natural Resources
    (MMNR) 228
  Minnesota Department of Natural
    Resources (MDNR) 228
  Montana Department of Fish, Wildlife &
    Parks 283, 289
  Ontario Ministry of Natural Resources
    (OMNR) 227, 228
  US Department of Agriculture (USDA) 228
  US Department of Agriculture Forest
    Service (FS) 229
  US Department of Interior (USDI) 228, 229
  USDI National Park Service (NPS) 229
  US Environmental Protection Agency
    (USEPA) 357, 365
  US Fish & Wildlife Service (FWS) 10, 11,
    143, 149, 252, 272, 274, 284, 286, 288,
    289, 291, 337, 341, 343
  Wyoming Game & Fish Department 272,
    283, 286, 290
agencies, private
  Captive Breeding Specialist Group (CBSG)
    286, 287
  International Union for Conservation of
    Nature & Natural Resources (IUCN) 69,
    71, 286
  Montana Black Footed Ferret Working
    Group 16, 283, 289
  National Audubon Society 3
  Nature Conservancy 145
  New York Zoological Society -
    Conservation International 284
  North Central Caribou Corporation
    (NCCC) 142, 229, 234, 237

  Swift Fox Conservation Society 252
  World Wide Fund for Nature (WWF) 3
Allee effect 365, 368
Amsinckia grandiflora
  recovery and demographic monitoring
    337–43
anthropogenic impacts
  direct vs. indirect effects 159–60
  disturbance regimes
    concordance and discordance with plant
      life history 140, 160, 167, 168, 180–2
  fire suppression 169
  fragmentation 3, 83, 111, 247, 272, 304,
    368
  habitat alteration
    livestock grazing 139, 152, 154, 290, 341
    logging and catastrophic fire 220
  pest/predator control
    compound 1080 251
    effects on black-footed ferret 273
    effects on prairie dog 273
    effects on swift fox 251
  on *Cirsium pitcheri* habitat 205–6, 211–14
  on disruption of pollinator activity 107, 111
  on fame flower abundance 164–5, 167, 169
  on Lakeside daisy 300
  on persistence of disturbance-dependent
    plants 140, 169–80
  on rarity 91, 94
  on soils 162–3
  on vegetation 161–2
  selection in human altered environments
    371–6

biological invasions and rare plants in Hawaii
    143–58
  effects on Haleakala National Park 145–8
  Haleakala National Park 144–5
  management of biological invasions 148–9

biological invasions (*cont.*)
  invading species
    blackberry 148
    blue gum 148
  rare plant species and restoration case
    studies 149–55
    Argyroxiphium sandwicense 152–3
    Argyroxiphium virescens 153–5
    Bidens micrantha 150
    Mariscus hillebrandii 149–50
    Plantago pachyphylla 151–2
    Schiedea haleakalensis 150–1
breeding systems, plant
  application to conservation of rare species
    111–13
  rarity and, relationship to genetic variability
    94–7
  suggestions for evaluating in rare plant
    species 107, 111
  that influence rarity 100–7, 108–10
    dimorphic 110
    heteromorphic self-incompatibility
      103–5, 110
    homomorphic self-incompatibility 102–3
    monomorphic, presence/absence of self-
      incompatibility unknown 109
    pollinator rarity 105–7
  with no detectable relationship to rarity
    96–101
    gynodioecy, subdioecy, and dioecy 101
    monomorphic, homomorphic self-
      incompatibility 98–100, 109
    monomorphic self-compatibility 97–8,
      108

captive breeding of animals
  genetic consequences 65–8, 372
  genetic improvement 78–81
captive breeding of plants
  purging of inbreeding depression 37–9
  selection by cultivation 112, 372
caribou, woodland (*Rangifer tarandus
  caribou*) 219–42, 364
  distribution 219–21
  natural history characteristics and
    requirements 221–7
    habitat use 221–3
    home range and density 223–4
    parasites and diseases 225–226
    population dynamics 226–7
    predators 224–5
  restoration planning 228–37
    administrative setting 228–9
    feasibility evaluation 230
    population vulnerability analysis 230–4
    restoration site evaluation 234–7
      Boundary Water Canoe Area

      Wilderness/Quetico Provincial Park
      234–5
      Isle Royale National Park 236–7
      Voyageurs National Park 235–6
    VORTEX modeling 232–4
    restorations/translocations in Lake
      Superior region 227–8
chloroplast (cp) DNA 48, 50–3, 55
clonal propagation 91
coadapted gene complexes 3, 40–4, 46, 47
compensation, or lack of, for herbivory 119
competition from grasses 124, 127, 128
compound 1080 251
cryptorchid 64

daisy, Lakeside (*Hymenoxys acaulis* var.
  glabra) 55, 102, 112, 298–321, 340,
  358–9, 362, 364
  community and population structure 305–8
    community 306–7
    population 307–8
  distribution and status 298–300
  implementation and preliminary assessment
    of recovery actions 314–17
  survivorship and reproduction 314–17
  life history 300–1
  recovery strategy 309–14
    genetic, demographic and ecological
      considerations 310–12
    site selection for restoration 312–14
  relationship of breeding system to rarity
    301–5
    breeding system 301–3
    self-incompatibility and inbreeding
      depression 305
    self-incompatibility, population size and
      persistence 303–04
demographic monitoring and recovery of
  endangered plants 322–50
  demographic monitoring 325–37
    factor resolution 245, 323, 326, 333–7,
      338, 339, 343, 344
    trend analysis 244–5, 323, 326–33,
      334, 337, 338, 339, 343, 344
    demographic monitoring in recovery
      337–9
    demographic monitoring of newly
      created populations 339–43
    plant conservation, monitoring and
      recovery 323–5
disease 112
  alien birds as vectors 147
  affecting black-footed ferret
    canine distemper 63, 278, 282
    diabetes mellitus 285
    sylvatic plague epidemics of prairie dogs
      63, 277, 278, 282

disease (*cont.*)
    of swift fox 248
    of woodland caribou
        meningeal brainworm 141, 225–6, 236,
            238
        Eurasian reindeer parasite 225
        potential for transfer of muscle worm to
            moose 225
disturbance-dependent rare plants 159–93
    anthropogenic impacts on persistence
        169–80
    confined to anthropogenic habitats 179–80
    found in both anthropogenic and natural
        disturbance regimes 173–9
    that persist only in natural habitats 169–73
disturbance processes 140
disturbance regimes
    anthropogenic 140, 159–193
    concordance and discordance of 140, 160,
        167, 168, 180–2
    rare plants and 160, 179
    restoration of 182–5
distyly 103, 104

ecological considerations
    Allee effect 365, 368
    ecotypic variation
        differentiation 40, 45, 53, 364
        preserving 55, 363
    essentialism and ecology 369–71
    herbivory 118–30, 204, 315, 316
    insular populations 375
    nested species assemblages 369
    niche diversity 370
    niche space, realized 159
    non-equilibrium dynamics, modeling 370
    population, community, and landscape
        ecology 365–9
        population interactions
            direct effects 367
            indirect effects 367
                apparent competition 367
                indirect mutualism 367
                resource competition 367
                trophic cascade 367
            higher-order interactions 367
            keystone species 367
            nonlinear effects 367
    priority effects 366
    rescue effects 368
    scale
        of disturbance 182
        of habitats 195–6, 368
        of landscape 195–6
    source–sink population processes 368
    species–area relationships 368–9
    trophic interactions 118–32

implications for restoration 128–9
    insect herbivory in plant performance
effective population size (N_e) 66–7, 75, 283,
    304, 310
    inbreeding effective number 67
    variance effective number 67
El Niño 375
electrophoresis 36, 48, 94, 95, 96, 98, 103
Endangered Species Act 229, 291, 322, 357,
    364
    experimental, nonessential status 291
evolutionary context of species 358
evolutionary lineages 49–55
    detection 50–5
    role in conservation biology 52–4
evolutionary potential of species
    maintenance 48–55
Evolutionarily Stable Strategy 374
experiments
    artificial seed augmentation 121
    consumer exclusion 120, 121
        cage 125–7
        insecticide 125, 126, 127
    effect of burn season in management 359
    enforced inbreeding 38
    factor resolution 334
    restoration ecology 245, 339, 341–3, 356,
        360
    transplant 45, 127
    'win–win' 6, 129, 131, 204, 210
    with ecological analogs (surrogate species)
        5–6, 35, 39, 47, 48, 49, 55, 129–31, 204,
        285, 291
exotic species (*see also* feral animals)
    animal impacts or threats 139, 145, 147–8
        Argentine ant threat to *Argyroxiphium
            sandwicense* pollinators 106, 140,
            147, 153
        Eurasian reindeer and parasite threat to
            woodland caribou 225
    interaction with pollinators
        birds as pollinators 105–6
        insect pollinators 91
        insect predation on pollinators 147, 153
    management control 148–9, 152, 156,
        341–3
    plant impacts 139, 148
        competition with *Amsinckia grandiflora*
            341–3
        competition with *Plantago pachyphylla*
            151
        competition with *Sisyrinchium acre*
            152
extinction vortices 362

factor resolution 245, 323, 326, 333–7, 338,
    339, 343, 344

fame flower (*Talinum rugospermum*) 140,
160–9, 181, 186
 disturbance effects on habitats and
  populations 161–9
  effects of human disturbance on soils
   162–3
  habitat characteristics 161–2
  spatial patterns 163–9
feral animals
 control 140, 148–9, 150, 151, 156
 impacts 145, 147–8, 150, 151, 152, 153,
  154
ferret, black-footed (*Mustela nigripes*) 10, 11,
 20, 272–97, 358
 conservation management and species
  recovery 283–5
  recovery options and considerations
   283–5
   direct manipulation of ferret numbers
    284–5
   increase ferret habitat at Meeteetse
    283–4
 historical background 273–4
  history of study 273–4
  species account 273
 Meeteetse, Wyoming population 274–5
 population viability assessment 275–83
  behavior and activity patterns 279–80
  habitat and preserve characteristics
   281–3
  paleobiology, biogeography and
   systematics 276
  population characteristics 276–8
  population genetic considerations 278–9
 recovery 285–90
  captive breeding 285–7
  conservation and management of wild
   ferrets 290
  establishing reintroduction sites 288–90
  locating populations 287–8
 reintroduction 290–2
fire
 and Hawaiian Islands 143
  threat of fire-adapted alien grasses to
   native vegetation 148
 as disturbance regime 173, 178, 179
 as management tool 359–60
 effect on *Amsinckia grandiflora* 179, 185,
  341–3
 effect on *Dicerandra frutescens* 178
 effect on fame flower
  community structure 164–5, 169, 181–2
  population structure 164–5, 181–2
 effect on *Thelymitra epipactoides* 173
 effect on woodland caribou 220
 Yellowstone 369
fox, swift (*Vulpes velox*) 247–71

biological background 247–9
 general biology 248–9
 taxonomy 247–8
Canadian release program 252–267
 beginnings 252
 description of release sites 254
  Alberta–Saskatchewan border 254
  Milk River Ridge 254
  Wood Mountain 254
 environmental influences on choice of
  release sites 252–4
 methods of release 254–8
 results of the Canadian program 258–67
  causes of mortality in released swift
   foxes 263
  denning and social structure 265–7
  dispersal 263–4
  distribution 265
  population density 265
  survival 258–62
 distributional background 249–50
  current range and status 251–2
  historical status 249–50
  wild-caught versus captive-raised swift
   foxes 262–3
Franklin's 50/500 rule 66–7

game theory, evolutionary 372
 Evolutionarily Stable Strategy 374
genetics
 allele
  founder, probility of loss 73
  probability of sampling 70
 allelic diversity
  conflict with preserving heterozygosity
   77, 362
  retaining 77, 82
 coadapted gene complexes 3, 40–4, 46, 47
 conservation genetics 361–5
 cytoplasmic inheritance 46–7
 DNA
  chloroplast (cp) 48, 50–3, 55
  mitochondrial (mt) 50, 363
 dominance 36
 epistasis 36, 37, 40, 41, 42, 44–7, 82
  diminishing 47–8
  reinforcing 47–8
 founder genome equivalent 72
 G_{ST} statistic 94–5
 gene drop simulations 72
 gene flow 37, 43, 47, 55, 91, 112
 genetic (population) bottlenecks 34, 38, 54,
  98, 99, 279, 304, 312, 317, 318, 362
 genetic consequences of captive
  propagation 65–78, 372
 genetic considerations for plant restoration
  34–62

genetics (*cont.*)
  genetic diversity of source populations
    47–8
  genetic manipulation to restore
    population vigor 35–9
    inbreeding depression 35–9
      genetic basis 37
      mating system, and 39
      selective purging 37–9
      outbreeding depression 39–47
        causes 40–1
        cautionary note 47
        mating system, and 44–5
        measuring 45–7
        scale for detection 41–3
  maintenance of evolutionary potential
    48–9
    evolutionary lineage 49–54
      detection 50–2
      role in conservation 52–4
genetic distinctiveness 363
genetic drift 34, 51, 53, 55, 65–7, 73, 82,
  91, 102, 245, 303, 371
genetic heterozygosity
  expected 68, 82
  H_f (founder heterozygosity) 70–1, 73, 74
  H_w (wild population heterozygosity)
    70–1, 72, 73
  observed 68
genetic management 79–83
  population subdivision 81–3
  selection 78–81
  to restore population vigor 35–47
genetic variability
  relationship of breeding systems and
    rarity 94–6
genetic variance–covariance matrix 53–4
  correlation with phenotypic
    variance–covariance matrix 54
genetic variation, strategies for retention
  75–8
H_{es} statistic 94–5
Hardy–Weinberg 68, 74
heterosis 36, 39, 40, 43
heterozygosity 37, 38, 47, 66, 67, 68, 73,
  75–8, 279, 305, 361
  expected (gene diversity) 68, 73, 74
  mean expected in founder stock 70–1, 74
  observed 68
inbreeding
  coefficient 67, 75
  depression 34, 35–9, 76, 99, 100, 103,
    107, 112, 285, 305, 361
    overdominance model 37
    partial dominance model 37, 38
    genetic basis 37
    genetic management and 76

mating system and 39
  selective purging 37–9
isozyme 48, 50–2, 54, 94
linkage 37, 42, 44, 81
MHC locus, and captive breeding 80,
outbreeding depression 35, 39–47
  causes 40–1
  cautionary note 47
  mating systems and 44–5
  measuring 45–7
  scale for detecting 41–3
overdominance 36, 37
panmictic populations 82, 83
polymorphic loci 94–5
selection 40, 43, 45, 51, 53, 54, 55, 65, 361,
  371
  artificial 38, 43, 78–81
  density-dependent 373, 374
  density-independent 372, 374
  direct and indirect 53
  directional 81–2, 371
  diversifying 81–2
  epistatic 44
  frequency dependent 91, 102, 373–4
  in human-altered environments 371–6
  K-selection 331, 372
  multivariate 52–3
  r-selection 331, 373
  single trait 52
  to captivity 65–8
geographic information service (GIS) 234
grasslands, Great Plains 123
grazing, browsing
  cattle/livestock 139, 152, 154, 290, 341
  effects on swift foxes 253
  goats 139, 145, 148, 149, 152
  rabbits 203, 212, 213
  pigs 145, 149, 151
  slugs and snails 335
Great Lakes dune environments and Pitcher's
  thistle
  landscape dynamics 196–7
  shoreline dunes 172
  thistle metapopulation adaptations 198–9
gynodioecy 101

Habitat Evaluation Procedures (HEP) 235
Habitat Suitability Index (HSI) 235, 288
Haleakala National Park 139, 144–50, 153–6
  effects of biological invasions 145–8
Hawaiian plant species and restoration case
  studies 149–55
  Argyroxiphium sandwicense 152–3
  Argyroxiphium virescens 153–5
  Bidens micrantha 150
  Mariscus hillebrandii 149–50
  Plantago pachyphylla 151–2

Hawaiian plant species (*cont.*)
  Schiedea haleakalensis 150–1
herbivory 118–30, 204, 315, 316
heterostyly 103–5, 107, 332
  distyly 103–4
  tristyly 103–5
homostyly 103

insect impacts on plant populations 118–38
  implications for restoration ecology 128–9
    general methodology 129–30
    prediction for Pitcher's thistle 130–1
  insect herbivory in plant performance
    119–28
    case 1: goldenbushes 121–3
    case 2: Platte thistle 123–8
insular populations 375
  and body size 375

K-selection 331, 374
keystone species 367
kinship (consanguinity) 72, 75–8, 80
  and conservation priority 365
  coefficient 75
  mean 72, 75, 76, 78

lambda (λ); finite rate of population increase
  327, 328, 334, 338
landscape considerations
  dynamics 139–40, 196–7,
  landscape ecology 3, 365–9
  metapopulation level processes 198–9, 368,
    369
  scale of habitat, 195–6, 368

managing and organizing endangered species
  recovery programs 9–33
  culture of the organization, project, or team
    22–4
    functions of culture 23
  managerial processes 17–22
    controlling teams 21–2
    leading teams 20–1
    organizing teams 17–19
    planning in teams 19–20
  organizational dimension 10–13
  organizational problems and action plans
    24–6
  task environments and information
    processing 13–15
  task forces and project teams 15–17
managing genetic diversity in captive animals
  63–89
  captive propagation, genetic consequences
    65–8
  captive propagation, phases 68–78
    capacity phase 75–8

captive phase 68–9
  founder phase 69–73
  growth phase 73–5
  genetic mangement, additional options
    population subdivision 78–83
    selection 78–81
  restoration of wild population from captive
    stock 83
maximal reproduction strategy 74
metapopulation 2, 3,4,81, 82, 140, 141, 171,
  172, 181, 194–215, 283, 304, 368, 369
  management 81–82, 142, 183, 231–2, 238,
    246, 283, 339
  recovery planning 203–6, 214–5
  theory and recovery of rare plants 195–96
migration among populations 82–3
minimum viable population (MVP) 231, 237,
  267, 290, 337, 339, 368
mitochondrial (mt) DNA 50, 363

nested species assemblages 369
niche diversity 370
niche space, realized 159
non-equilibrium dynamics, modeling 370

organization and management of recovery
  programs
  decision analysis 20
  goal displacement 11
  intelligence failure 11
  managerial processes 17–22
    controlling teams 21–2
    leading teams 20–1
    organizing teams 17–19
    planning in teams 19–20
  program evaluation and review technique
    (PERT) 20
  task environment 13

parasites
  of swift fox 248
  of woodland caribou 225–6
phenotypic variance–covariance matrix 54
phenotypic variation 68
plant rarity and reproductive biology 90–117
  breeding system influences on rarity 101–7
    homomorphic self-incompatibility 102–3
    heteromorphic self-incompatibility 103–5
    pollinator rarity 105–7
  breeding system unrelated to rarity 96–101
    gynodioecy, subdioecy, and dioecy
      100–1
    homomorphic self-incompatibility
      98–100
    self-compatibility 97–8
  breeding systems, rarity and genetic
    variability 94–6

plant rarity and reproductive biology (*cont.*)
  evaluating breeding sytems of rare plants
    107, 111
  natural and anthropogenic 91–4
  breeding systems and rare plant species
    conservation 111–3
pollinator
  amakihi 106
  bee
    halictid 301
    native 106
  hawkmoths 106
  Hawaiian honeycreeper 106
  i'iwi 106
  honeyeaters 107
  introduced birds 105–6
  nectar thieves 106
  rarity 105–7, 111
  specialized 106
  white-eye, Japanese 106
population
  bottlenecks 34, 38, 54, 98, 99, 279, 304,
    312, 317, 318
  effective size (N_e) 3, 66–7, 75, 283, 304,
    310
  extinction modeling 232–4
  fragmentation 82
  interactions 367–8
    direct effects 367
    indirect effects 367
      apparent competition 367
      indirect mutualism 367
      resource competition 367
      trophic cascade 367
    higher-order interactions 367–8
    keystone species 367
    nonlinear effects 367
  subdivision for genetic management 81–3
  viability analysis (PVA) 2, 275–83, 290,
    318, 327–8, 334
  vulnerability analysis 230–2
prairie dog ecosystem 272, 292
prairie, Sandhills 123–4
predator exclusion tests 129
pre-dispersal insect damage 119–28
Principal Components Analysis (PCA) 162–3
priority effects 366
propagation phases 68–78
  capacity phase 75–8
  captive phase 68–9
  founder phase 69–73
  growth phase 73–5

R_o (net reproductive rate) 327, 338
r-selection 331, 372
rarity, plant
  natural and anthropogenic 91, 94

unrelated to breeding system 96–101
  gynodioecy, subdioecy and dioecy 100–1
  homomorphic self-compatibility 98–100
  self-compatibility 97–8
related to reproductive systems 101–7
  heteromorphic self-incompatibility 103–5
  homomorphic self-incompatibility 102–3
  pollinator rarity 105–7
relationship to genetic variability 94–6
recovery plans or teams
  Amsinckia grandiflora 341
  Argyroxiphium virescens 154–5
  black-footed ferret 16, 17, 283, 289
  California condor 16
  Lakeside daisy 309–12
  orange-bellied parrot 11
  Pitcher's thistle 203–10
reforestation 358
restoration ecology and prime directive
  353–80
  art versus science 359–60
  conservation genetics 361–5
  developing a prime directive 356–9
  essentialism and ecology 369–71
  essentialism versus evolution 371–6
  population, community, and landscape
    ecology 365–9
restoration ecology, as science 356
restoration of wild population from captive
  stock 83

scale
  of disturbance 182
  of habitats 195–6, 368
  of landscape 195–6
seed predation
  by goldfinches 203
  by ground squirrels 203
  by insects 121–4, 126, 130, 132, 204, 213,
    335
  post-dispersal 124, 125–6, 128, 204
  pre-dispersal 120–8, 204
  prevention by insecticide treatment of
    flowering plants 125, 126, 127, 210, 213
  vertebrate exclosure to prevent 125–6, 127
seed-to-seedling linkage 121
self-compatibility 90–1, 97–8, 112
self-incompatibility
  gametophytic 90, 112
  heteromorphic 91, 103–5
  homomorphic 98–100, 102–3
  inbreeding depression, and 305
  population size and persistence 303–4
  S-alleles 90, 102, 111, 302, 303, 312, 317
  sporophytic 90, 112, 302
soils, effects of human disturbance on 162–3
species–area relationships 368–9

Species Survival Committee (SSC) 357
stocking
    fish 358, 359
    rangeland 358
synapomorphy 51

theory
    catastrophe 370
    conservation genetics 360, 361–5
    evolutionary ecology 360, 371–6
    evolutionary game 372
    network 370
    Optimization Research Programme 372
    percolation 370
    population, community and landscape
        ecology 360, 365–9
thistle, Pitcher's (*Cirsium pitcheri*) 124,
        130–2, 140–1, 142, 171, 172, 194–218
    Great Lakes dune environment, and 196–9
        landscape dynamics 196–7
        metapopulation adaptations 198–9
    metapopulation characteristics 199–203
        biology 199–200
        life history traits and demography 200–3
    predictions for restoration 130–2
    recovery planning 203–6
        demographic and biological aspects 204

physical aspects in Illinois and Indiana
            205–6
        status and recovery goals 203–4
    recovery strategy in Illinois 206–10
        decline and modern habitat 206–9
        recovery 209–210
    recovery strategy in Indiana 211–14
        decline and modern habitat 211
        recovery 211–14
trend analysis 323, 326–33, 334, 337, 338,
        339, 343, 344
tristyly 38, 103, 104
trophic interactions 118–32
    implications for restoration 128–31
    insect herbivory in plant performance
        119–28
TWINSPAN 161, 163–9

VORTEX population extinction modeling
        230, 232–4, 237, 238

Wetland Protection Act 357
worksheet for endangered species
    problems and action plans 31–3
World Conservation Strategy 357

Xerothermic Interval 299